TRANSATLANTIC REGULATORY COOPERATION

Transatlantic Regulatory Cooperation

Legal Problems and Political Prospects

Edited by

GEORGE A. BERMANN, MATTHIAS HERDEGEN,
and PETER L. LINDSETH

OXFORD
UNIVERSITY PRESS

OXFORD
UNIVERSITY PRESS

Great Clarendon Street, Oxford OX2 6DP

Oxford University Press is a department of the University of Oxford.
It furthers the University's objective of excellence in research, scholarship,
and education by publishing worldwide in

Oxford New York

Athens Auckland Bangkok Bogotá Buenos Aires Cape Town
Chennai Dar es Salaam Delhi Florence Hong Kong Istanbul Karachi
Kolkata Kuala Lumpur Madrid Melbourne Mexico City Mumbai Nairobi
Paris São Paulo Shanghai Singapore Taipei Tokyo Toronto Warsaw

and associated companies in Berlin Ibadan

Oxford is a registered trade mark of Oxford University Press
in the UK and in certain other countries

Published in the United States
by Oxford University Press Inc., New York

British Library Cataloguing in Publication Data

Data available

Library of Congress Cataloging in Publication Data
Data available

ISBN 0–19–829892–7

1 3 5 7 9 10 8 6 4 2

Typeset by Hope Services (Abingdon) Ltd.
Printed in Great Britain
on acid-free paper by
T. J. International Ltd., Padstow, Cornwall

This book is dedicated to the memory and example of Professor Walter Gellhorn: eminent legal scholar at Columbia University School of Law, champion of international and comparative legal research and study, inspiring mentor and teacher, and dedicated public servant.

Foreword

Ambassador Richard N. Gardner

This is an important book on an increasingly important subject. The economic relationship between the United States and the fifteen countries of the European Union is by far the most significant economic relationship in the world. It is a two-trillion-dollar relationship, if one adds to the two-way flow of annual trade the annual production in the United States and Europe by local subsidiaries of one another's corporations. Thanks to our postwar success in reducing external barriers to trade and investment, such as tariffs and quotas, the principal area of potential economic conflict and the principal area of opportunity for improving the US–European economic relationship now lies in eliminating domestic regulatory obstacles. In other words, as Sir Leon Brittan puts it so well in his contribution to this book: 'Regulatory cooperation . . . lies at the very heart of contemporary EU–US economic relations.'

During my recent service as US Ambassador to Spain, I observed, and had the privilege of playing a small part in, the movement of transatlantic regulatory cooperation to the centre stage it now occupies. Early in 1995 a far-sighted Foreign Minister of Spain, Javier Solana, reported that his government wished to make the European Union's relations with the United States a central priority of Spain's six-month EU Presidency during the second half of that year. A visionary US Ambassador to the European Union, Stuart Eizenstat, and a dynamic EU Commissioner, Sir Leon Brittan, shared that objective. Consequently, negotiations were launched on the historic New Transatlantic Agenda (NTA) which was signed in Madrid in December 1995.

The NTA initiated a process by which US–EU relations might progress from consultation to common action in four main areas:

1. Promoting peace and stability, democracy, and development around the world.
2. Responding to global challenges such as international crime, drug-trafficking, terrorism, environmental destruction, and infectious diseases.
3. Contributing to the expansion of world trade and closer economic relations.
4. Building bridges across the Atlantic through educational and cultural cooperation.

The section dealing with the third of these priorities contained the following language whose full significance we are only now beginning to appreciate:

We will strengthen regulatory cooperation, in particular by encouraging regulatory agencies to give a high priority to cooperation with their respective transatlantic counterparts, so as to address technical and non-tariff barriers to trade resulting from divergent regulatory processes. We aim to conclude an agreement on mutual recognition of conformity assessment (which includes certification and testing procedures) for certain sectors as soon as possible. We will continue the ongoing work in several sectors and identify others for further work.

Significantly, the main impetus for this paragraph came from the business community in the United States and the European Union, which understood that creating the 'new transatlantic marketplace' called for in part three of the NTA would require an unprecedented measure of regulatory cooperation. This was a key recommendation of the first session of the Transatlantic Business Dialogue which took place in Seville in November 1995, and it influenced the final text of the NTA signed a month later in Madrid.

Two direct results that followed the Seville and Madrid meetings have been the Mutual Recognition Agreement (MRA), covering such sectors as telecommunications equipment, pharmaceuticals, and medical devices, and the Action Plan of the more recently established 'Transatlantic Economic Partnership' which has become the vehicle for extending the MRA to additional sectors and for pursuing a more general alignment of regulatory standards between the United States and the European Union.

The controversies that have recently arisen over hormone-treated beef, genetically modified foods, aircraft noise, and data privacy all testify to the growing importance of transatlantic regulatory cooperation and to the costs of transatlantic regulatory conflict. The EU's engagement in accession negotiations with twelve candidate countries in Central, Eastern, and Southern Europe means that regulatory cooperation will have to be extended to new countries at the same time that it is extended to new product and service sectors. Some of these countries have weak regulatory institutions and little regulatory experience. As the United States and the European Union confront the variegated and increasingly complex challenges of transatlantic regulatory cooperation, their government officials, business leaders, scholars, and students will find this volume to be the best possible introduction to the subject.

Acknowledgements

The editors acknowledge with gratitude the financial support of the Transcoop Program of the Deutsche-Amerikanische Akademische Konzil (DAAK), the European Commission (through its grant to the European Union Center of New York), Columbia University School of Law, and the Parker School of Foreign and Comparative Law. The authors likewise thank both Columbia University School of Law and the University of Bonn (Germany) for their administrative support. Such support made possible the preparation of this volume and the organization of the conference out of which it grew.

The editors also express their sincere appreciation to Robert Diklich and Dan Henson for their painstaking and steady editorial assistance in the preparation of the volume.

Contents

PART VI: THE INTERFACE BETWEEN INTERNATIONAL REGULATORY INITIATIVES
AND THE DOMESTIC LEGAL ENVIRONMENT

PART VII: TRANSATLANTIC REGULATORY COOPERATION, DEMOCRACY, AND
ACCOUNTABILITY

PART VIII: THE FUTURE OF REGULATORY COOPERATION: STRATEGIC
DIRECTIONS AND INSTITUTIONAL IMPLICATIONS

Notes on Contributors

David L. Aaron is Senior International Ambassador at the law firm of Dorsey & Whitney in Washington DC. He was formerly the Under Secretary of Commerce for International Trade at the US Department of Commerce.

David R. Andrews is Partner at the San Francisco office of McCutchen, Doyle, Brown & Inersen. He is also special negotiator for the Iran–US Claims Tribunal in the Hague, in which capacity he retains the title of Ambassador. He was formerly the Legal Adviser to the US Department of State.

George A. Bermann is the Charles Keller Beekman Professor of Law and Director of the European Legal Studies Center at Columbia Law School.

The Rt. Hon. Lord Brittan of Spennithorne QC is currently Vice Chairman of UBS Warburg. He is a former Vice President of the European Commission and was responsible for External Economic Affairs and Trade Policy.

Paul Demaret is Professor of Law at the University of Liège, where he holds the Jean Monnet Chair in European Economic Law, and is also the Director of European legal studies at the College of Europe, Bruges.

Jean-Louis Dewost is Director-General of the Legal Service of the European Commission and a member of the French Conseil d'État, where he holds the rank of conseiller d'État.

Josef Drexl is a law professor at the University of Munich (Germany), Institute for International Law (European and International Economic Law). He is also affiliated with the Max Planck Institute for Foreign and International Patent, Copyright and Competition Law at Munich.

Hans-Ulrich Engel is CFO of BASF Corporation and was active in the Transatlantic Business Dialogue (TABD).

Eleanor M. Fox is the Walter J. Derenberg Professor of Trade Regulation at New York University School of Law.

Richard N. Gardner is Professor of Law and International Organization at Columbia Law School, to which he recently returned from a leave of absence as US Ambassador to Spain (1993–7). He is also Of Counsel to Morgan Lewis, a global law firm.

Klaus W. Grewlich is Professor at the College of Europe, Bruges, and a member of the law faculties at both the Universities of Freiburg and Bonn. He holds an LL M from the University of California at Berkeley and is formerly Director General, International Business, and Board Representative at Deutsche Telekom in Bonn.

Matthias Herdegen is a Professor of Law at the University of Bonn, where he holds the Chair for Public Law, European and International Law, and is also the Director of the Institute of International Law and the Institute for Public Law.

Robert Howse is Professor of Law at the University of Michigan School of Law and a member of the faculty, World Trade Institute, Berne, Switzerland. He has also taught at the University of Toronto, as a Visiting Professor at Harvard Law School, and in the Academy of European Law, European University Institute, Florence.

Merit E. Janow is Professor in the Practice of International Trade at Columbia University's School of International and Public Affairs (SIPA), where she is also the Director of the International Economic Policy and Co-Director of Columbia's APEC Study Center.

Ludger Kühnhardt is Director of the Center for European Integration Studies at the University of Bonn, where he is also Professor of Political Science.

Peter L. Lindseth is Associate Professor of Law at the University of Connecticut School of Law, and formerly the Associate Director of the European Legal Studies Center at Columbia Law School.

Gerhard Lohan is a Head of Division in Directorate-General III of the European Commission, responsible for coordination of DG III positions on major international matters such as the WTO, the EU–US Transatlantic Business Dialogue (TABD) and the Transatlantic Economic Partnership.

Jonathan R. Macey is the J. DuPratt White Professor of Law and Director of the John M. Olin Program in Law and Economics at Cornell Law School. He is a member of the Legal Advisory Committee to the Board of Directors of the New York Stock Exchange.

Giandomenico Majone is Visiting Distinguished Professor of International Affairs at the Graduate School of Public and International

Affairs and at the European Union Center, University of Pittsburgh. Until 1995 he was Professor of Public Policy at the European University Institute in Florence, Italy, where he remains an External Professor.

Walter Mattli is an Assistant Professor in the Department of Political Science at Columbia University, where he is a member of both the Institute of War and Peace Studies and the Institute on Western Europe.

Petros C. Mavroidis is Professor of Law at the University of Neuchâtel, Switzerland, where he teaches Public International, EC, and WTO Law, and is a Visiting Professor of Law at Columbia Law School. He is also a member of the Center for Economic Policy Research (CEPR).

Kalypso Nicolaïdis is University Lecturer at Oxford University and Fellow at St Antony's College. She is currently on leave from her position as Associate Professor, Kennedy School of Government, Harvard University.

Joel R. Paul is Professor of Law at the University of California Hastings College of the Law.

Ernst-Ulrich Petersmann is Professor of International and European Law at the University of Geneva and at its Graduate Institute of International Studies.

Mauro Petriccione is Head of Unit Trade / F / 2 (Investment, standards and certification, TBT) at the European Commission.

Sol Picciotto is a Professor of Law at Lancaster University, England, where he is also Director of the Programs in European and International Legal Studies, and in International Law and International Relations.

Wulf-Henning Roth is Professor of Law at the University of Bonn, where he is also the Director of both the Institute of International Private Law and Comparative Law and the Center for European Economic Law.

Saskia Sassen is Professor of Sociology at the University of Chicago and Centennial Visiting Professor at the London School of Economics.

Anne-Marie Slaughter is the J. Sinclair Armstrong Professor of International Foreign and Comparative Law, and Director, Graduate and International Legal Studies, at Harvard Law School.

Francis Snyder is currently Fellow at the Wissenschaftskolleg (Institute for Advanced Study) in Berlin. He is Professor of Law at the Université d'Aix-Marseille III and Centennial Professor at the London School of Economics. He is also Co-Director of the Academy of European Law in Florence, where from 1992 to 2000 he was Professor of European Community Law at the European University Institute.

Paul B. Stephan is the Percy Brown Jr. Professor and the Barron F. Black Research Professor at the University of Virginia School of Law.

Peter L. Strauss is Betts Professor of Law at Columbia Law School.

Joel P. Trachtman is interim Academic Dean and Professor of International Law at the Fletcher School of Law and Diplomacy, Tufts University.

Reimer von Borries is Ministerial Counsellor (*Ministerialrat*) and Head of Division (*Referatsleiter*) in the Division for European Law, European Department, Federal Ministry of Finance, Berlin, Germany. He holds an LL M from Columbia Law School.

Introduction

George A. Bermann, Matthias Herdegen, and
Peter L. Lindseth

While national authorities are still the principal actors in the regulatory arena, regulation is increasingly an international affair. In some cases, regulatory norms are established in truly international fora. Far more often, they are enacted nationally, but only after numerous formal and informal processes entailing a wide variety of cross-border exchanges and deliberations, many of which involve such non-governmental actors as the private sector, policy communities, and standardization bodies. International regulatory cooperation comprises a highly differentiated bundle of techniques for reconciling the needs of international trade with the diversity of national regulatory environments and public demands.

Considering the profound importance of these processes in the shaping of regulatory policy, it is no longer adequate to examine international regulatory relations exclusively through the prism of formal international organizations, on the one hand, or formal channels for the resolution of international trade disputes, on the other. To be sure, both of these represent important dimensions of international regulation, but neither offers an adequate means of understanding the ways in which international regulatory relations are managed or may be managed more effectively. An emphasis on international organizations as such risks overstating the readiness of states to cede regulatory authority to international institutions, while an emphasis on formal dispute resolution risks ignoring the reality of, and prospects for, cooperative international regulatory behaviour.

In no geographic area has the challenge of devising appropriate techniques for reconciling the needs of international trade with the diversity of national regulatory environments been more directly and imaginatively confronted than the transatlantic. In this area in particular, cooperative initiatives abound. The fact remains, however, that the processes of transatlantic regulatory cooperation are still poorly understood, due in part to the fact that they have been very largely improvisational and remain very much a work in progress. A better understanding of these processes was the goal of an international conference organized at Columbia University School of Law in April 1999, in cooperation with the faculty of law of the University of Bonn, Germany. Supported by both universities, as well as by a grant from the Transcoop Program of the Deutsche-Amerikanische

Akademische Konzil (DAAK) and the European Commission (via the European Union Center of New York), the conference brought together some thirty-five speakers drawn from law, the social sciences, and the public sector to deal as systematically as current knowledge and experience permit with the transatlantic regulatory cooperation phenomenon.

This book, which comprises the various contributions to that conference, seeks to present an account of the transatlantic regulatory cooperation phenomenon that, while comprehensive, also reflects the less than fully coherent and systematic fashion in which it has evolved. To begin with, these processes were not launched as an abstract exercise in global governance. They emerged from an awareness that EU–US interdependence, coupled with a strong sense of common values, justified introducing important cooperative elements into the basically competitive regulatory relationship. Part I of the book depicts the political framework within which cooperative and competitive impulses play themselves out, and does so largely in the words of persons who have had a direct hand in shaping that framework.

Sir Leon Brittan and *Ambassador David Aaron* separately present the larger political considerations that have guided policymakers in devising structures and processes for channelling the cooperative and competitive impulses to which we refer, while at the same time defusing the highly particularized conflicts that from time to time erupt. Sir Leon Brittan makes the case for 'building regulatory bridges', and for doing so in both bilateral and multilateral fora. He further predicts that the most useful bridges will be those designed to prevent regulatory disputes from arising in the first place, for example, by identifying and defining them before they crystallize into hardened policy positions, while at the same time giving definitional content to notions like the 'precautionary principle' in light of which the justification for trade barriers can be assessed. He argues specifically for a skilful mix of regulatory harmonization and mutual recognition of standards. As the observations of Ambassador David Aaron remind us, however, it may be easier for governments to commit in general terms to bilateral and multilateral cooperation than to defuse actual regulatory conflicts or prevent them from coming into being. This is so not only because governments have different regulatory 'habits' (for example, different conceptions of the role and scope of such fora), but also because they still remain answerable to their political constituencies and the policy preferences that those constituencies voice.

While recognizing that the origins of transatlantic regulatory cooperation are indisputably political in the broadest sense of the term, this book—like the conference from which it emerges—looks to the place that law might occupy in ensuring that its processes operate with regularity, proceed effectively and, not least of all, enjoy an important measure of political legitimacy. We recognize that law generally plays only a supporting role in cooperative processes that are driven chiefly by political and economic considerations, yet we insist that law's role is nonetheless fundamental.

For the European Union and United States, respectively, *Jean-Louis Dewost* and *David Andrews* have accordingly set in motion a crucial consultative process which, while shoring up the regularity and efficacy of the cooperative initiatives undertaken, ensure that neither legality nor legitimacy as understood in their respective communities is compromised. Yet even they, as legal interlocutors, do not occupy entirely matching positions. For Dewost, Director-General of the Commission Legal Service, among the most challenging aspects of the enterprise is identifying the differences in context between, on the one hand, the European Union, whose integration has been the concern of his Service, and, on the other hand, the transatlantic regulatory arena. Due to various asymmetries between the United States and the European Union, it is not a matter of simply 'transposing' the EU method, but rather of capitalizing on those specific techniques—mutual recognition, positive comity, joint risk assessment—that accommodate, even while bridging, the differences in regulatory regimes and domestic legal and political environments. Andrews, on the other hand, faces a situation in which regulatory authority at the federal level, unlike in the European Union, is highly fragmented among agencies. The fact that these agencies bear primary substantive responsibility for regulatory affairs leaves his office—Legal Adviser of the State Department—with a coordinative or, as Andrews puts it, a 'facilitative' role at best. Given this situation, it is perhaps not surprising that the State Department acts where it has a comparative advantage, namely in interpreting all relevant sources of international law and in ensuring the compatibility of international cooperative arrangements with domestic constitutional and administrative law precepts, not only in the United States but also among its 'partners'.

At the same time, we know that transatlantic regulatory cooperation is not purely the product of governmentally willed partnerships. Much of the political impetus for cooperation has been private sector-driven. *Ambassador Richard Gardner*'s foreword to this volume has already called attention to the Transatlantic Business Dialogue as a major stimulant of EU–US cooperation. This private sector 'conversation', joined in later years by companion transatlantic consumer, labour, and environmental dialogues, has lent a cooperative dimension to what might otherwise have evolved as a chiefly adversarial relationship. The contribution of *Hans-Ulrich Engel*, emphasizing experience in the chemical industry, provides more precise insight into how the Transatlantic Business Dialogue in particular has acted as a crucial catalyst for regulatory convergence.

The involvement of private-sector interests shows that transatlantic regulatory cooperation, while channelled by politics and law, remains indisputably driven by economics and, more specifically, by the economics of interdependence and globalism. Part II deals directly with this economic landscape. *Saskia Sassen*'s contribution on 'The locational and institutional embeddedness of the global economy' gives a rich and deeply informed account of the economy of the North Atlantic area, an area consisting of a network of financial centres constituting the veritable 'centre of gravity' of the global economy. The various institutions that populate this economic area are the actors that figure in all the transatlantic regulatory initiatives referred to in this book, and their role must be taken account of by those who would design appropriate transatlantic regulatory regimes and international standards. According to Sassen, we are witnessing de-nationalized zones for economic transactions and consequently a need for de-nationalized zones of governance.

While the transatlantic is indisputably today's densest arena of regulatory interdependence, it is nevertheless part of a larger and still evolving regulatory network. One of the challenges facing transatlantic leaders is that of strengthening the transatlantic network without deepening the conditions leading to the exclusion from global governance of other regions of the world. This is the challenge depicted by *Francis Snyder*. It is, of course, an immense one, given the diversity of institutions, norms, and dispute resolution processes in the various 'sites' that a truly global governance network must accommodate. The structures of governance within this network are necessarily themselves diverse, and it is Snyder's objective to identify the variables that determine what those structures look like and the categories of legal foundations on which they may be based.

Having traced the political and economic forces driving transatlantic regulatory cooperation, and having at least broached the contribution of law to the necessary institution- and process-building, the volume turns in Part III to several theoretical overviews in which two questions predominate: By reference to what models may the transatlantic regulatory framework best be understood? Perhaps more important, by reference to what models may it be made more effective, more productive, and more consonant with accepted measures of legality and legitimacy? Without meaning to exhaust the possibilities, each of the three chapters that follows addresses these questions in distinctive terms.

Advancing a 'neo-institutionalist' approach, *Giandomenico Majone* places institutions rather than pursuit of national and private interests at the heart of the analysis of transnational regulatory regimes. Such regimes, under this view, are to be analysed and evaluated in terms of opportunities for political control, the functioning of delegations, and the capacity to formulate sound and credible regulatory policy. Majone thus classifies regimes according to the structures, processes, and mechanisms of governance that they entail, accounting for a gamut of regimes ranging from the purely 'spontaneous' (e.g. parametric adjustment, exchange of information, self-regulation) to the highly 'formal' (e.g. mandatory harmonization, independent regulatory agencies, transnational regulatory networks with degrees of decisional authority). With respect to each major category, Majone discerns both the underlying logic and the inevitable problems and limitations of cooperative activity (e.g. policy externalities, enforcement). While institutions are not the only things that count, they do tend to make governance systems better or worse in terms of effectiveness, legitimacy, and accountability.

By contrast, *Jonathan Macey* decisively adopts a 'public-choice' perspective, according to which what matters most in determining which international regulatory processes will emerge and prove effective is not some neutral institutional assessment, but rather the political motivations of regulators, bureaucrats, and other public officials. According to this view, regulators enter into international arrangements if and to the extent they determine that it is in their interest to do so. Under some circumstances, regulators may eschew commitments because the latter entail sacrifices in autonomy; increasingly, under contemporary technological and globalized conditions, regulators find that international arrangements enhance rather than weaken their authority within a national regulatory environment in which they may otherwise find their authority sharply challenged. Macey cites, for example, the Basle Accords, establishing minimum capital requirements among the world's banks, as the product of an awareness among regulators of the mobility of capital and the vulnerability of their domestic markets and their own regulatory autonomy and influence.

A third theoretical approach, taken by *Paul Stephan*, neither implicitly favours building effective cooperative institutions nor explains international regulatory behaviour by reference to 'rent-seeking' among regulators. Rather, it posits regulatory competition as an alternative paradigm for pursuing international regulatory relations. Like Majone, and unlike Macey, Stephan adopts a normative stance. But, unlike Majone, Stephan presses the advantages of competition among national regulatory regimes, and accordingly warns against the naturally anticompetitive risks of harmonization and other forms of regulatory convergence. Canvassing a range of regulatory fields, Stephan explores the circumstances in which regulatory competition holds out promise or, as he puts it, in which the costs of government failure resulting from regulatory cooperation outweigh the costs of market failure.

Part III of this volume places transatlantic regulatory cooperation in the larger context of international trade and competition law. *Mauro Pettricione* chiefly addresses the fundamental challenge of reconciling domestic regulation with the development of bilateral trade. For him, a common commitment to higher standards of health and safety, as well as protection of workers, consumers, and the environment, does not exclude the possibility of clashes in approaches between regulators on both sides of the Atlantic. The development of the internal market within the European Union illustrates a forging of tools which are necessary for weeding out the harmful effects of divergent domestic regulation. Pettricione positively assigns to the European Union and the United States a kind of joint leadership in achieving a sound balance between the protection of essential public interests and the enhancement of international trade through regulatory cooperation in the form of international harmonization, mutual recognition of conformity assessments, mutual recognition of technical regulation and functional equivalences, and a general quest for appropriate deregulation.

Joel Trachtman analyses more specifically the inhibiting effect that regulatory diversity in accounting standards has had on international trade. He discerns in the contemporary state of the WTO, and in particular the inadequacy of the GATS rules as normative guidance to conduct, a posture of excessive deference to rule-making by specialist international agencies. Such deference conceals a problem that is inherent in situations in which specialized agencies lack the ability to conduct cross-sectoral negotiations and to respond to trade effects in a sufficiently sensitive way. Trachtman subjects the various conceptual approaches (harmonization, mutual recognition, and maintenance of regulatory diversity) to a cost–benefit analysis which can guide the exercise of options by political actors.

Transatlantic regulatory cooperation holds evident potential for the field of competition law. An argument can be made that a simpler and more coherent international regulatory environment will generally enable enterprises to compete more effectively in economic terms, with resulting economic and consumer benefit. At the same time, competition policy as a regulatory field is itself a serious candidate for cooperative initiatives. In her contribution, *Eleanor Fox* emphasizes how experience with the extraterritorial application of US antitrust law reveals the inherent limitations of 'negative' comity as a vehicle for resolving bilateral clashes of interest. More promising is recourse to 'positive' measures, e.g. cooperation in investigation and enforcement. This approach is reflected in the cooperation agreement between the European Union and United States on the application of competition laws, an agreement followed in 1998 by a further agreement on enforcement cooperation between competition authorities. The path to still further cooperation is not yet clear. US endeavours to obtain evidence located abroad on the basis of mutual assistance agreements has so far been met with little enthusiasm from its partner, but so too has the largely European campaign in support of the installation of a truly internationalized competition law regime. In the United States, the fear still prevails that multilateral or plurilateral approaches could erode cherished antitrust values, causing US authorities to favour a 'soft' convergence of law, for example along lines worked out in recommendations by the OECD. Fox forcefully states her case for a 'cosmopolitanism' coupled with subsidiarity within a flexible framework providing for some form of adjudicatory or mediatory dispute resolution.

Merit Janow strikes a somewhat different note. She pleads for 'soft harmonization' through greater sensitivity to foreign regulatory interests and enhanced mutual assistance between competition authorities (including intensified coordination in the gathering of relevant facts and in intergovernmental exchange of confidential information). On the other hand, she squarely rejects the idea of creating new bilateral institutions as a forum for cooperation in competition policy. More promising, and in any event more workable, are improvements such as the streamlining of information requirements in merger cases that would reduce transaction costs for the undertakings concerned. Janow does not view the European plea for negotiating horizontal competition rules on the WTO level as very realistic, though she welcomes greater sensitivity within the WTO towards competition issues. Not surprisingly, then, Janow finds the OECD the far more appropriate forum for reaching agreement on most competition policy issues.

The import of *Petros Mavroidis*'s contribution ('exclusive club' or 'open regionalism') is that, while transatlantically orchestrated competition rules present great promise, they also present problems, and specifically from a WTO perspective. He sees the institutional flexibility of the transatlantic partnership as a distinct advantage in terms of the exchange of knowledge and experience. At the same time, however, Mavroidis finds exclusive mutual recognition agreements within the transatlantic partnership to be problematic under WTO law, and more specifically under the most-favoured-nation principle. By contrast, he considers it safe to assume that transatlantic agreements on common standards and technical regulations do not justify claims by third states for inclusion in similar agreements.

Part V turns in a more focused vein to specific 'key sectors' that have been the subject of experiments in transatlantic regulatory cooperation: telecommunications, 'cyberspace', biotechnology, and industrial and intellectual property protection. All are fields of vital importance for new technologies and investment decisions in the transatlantic context.

Klaus Grewlich describes the revolutionary impact of digitalization both on fields having a long history of traditional regulation (telecommunications) and on much less regulated fields of communication and information, such as the Internet. The potential linkage of previously closed data networks (and layers of networks) has generated a rapid technical convergence of different communication services. The result is that regulatory authorities are considering new and comprehensive regimes having either a more liberal or a more heavily regulated flavour. These regulatory challenges relate both to the opening of markets by 'access regulation' and to the safeguarding of various public interests, like human dignity, security, and privacy. Grewlich calls upon the pertinent transatlantic regulatory fora to cooperate intensively to determine the appropriate scope of patents and patent protection, particularly in light of the prolific grant of exclusive rights on both sides of the Atlantic. Similarly important is the theme of protection of personal data. Given the wide and deep stakes, Grewlich foresees the necessity of 'constitutionalizing' the regulatory regime for telecommunications so as to safeguard adequately both competition and the public interest and the possibility that such a regime would entrust an important regulatory role both to sub-national institutions and to non-governmental groups and entities.

Biotechnology is possibly *the* key sector in which divergent regulatory philosophies, as well as their economic impact, are most conspicuous. As *Matthias Herdegen* describes it, the divergences are fuelled by different perceptions of risk, notably with respect to genetic engineering. The European Community follows a 'process approach' which assumes that genetic engineering is intrinsically risky, while the United States has for some time adopted a 'product approach' which focuses on the risks presented by specific products or organisms, even when produced from processes of genetic modifications. The emphasis in European regulation on risk-prevention (including phantom risk-prevention) has manifested itself economically in the momentous advantage that US enterprises have gained in research, development, and industrial production. The differences in approaches to risk management also raise delicate issues under WTO law. In the 'hormones' dispute between the European Union and the United States, for example, the WTO appeals ruling came down heavily in favour of a requirement of sound empirical justification in support of controversial health standards.

Josef Drexl assesses the prospects for harmonization and other forms of international regulation in intellectual property protection. Echoing the predictions of Paul Stephan, Drexl reports a situation of sound and healthy competition (as distinct from cooperation) between the regulatory systems of the United States and the European Union in the field of patent law. In his estimation, the patent protection directive demonstrates the effectiveness of transatlantic regulatory competition, resulting in a victory for the patentability of biological material containing genetic information over fundamentalist opposition. At the same time, he advocates a plainly cooperative approach, in the form of a bilateral trade agreement, with respect to the principle of international exhaustion of intellectual property rights in the field of trademark law.

Each of these sectors—and others—raises prospects for governance through the adoption of standards by international standards organizations. Standardization will have a place under virtually any transatlantic regulatory regime, and to that end consideration needs to be given to the ways in which standards bodies can be made more representative of national regulatory attitudes, while at the same time more transparent and accessible to affected parties. The contribution by *Walter Mattli* traces the evolution of the role that standards bodies have assumed in contemporary regulation, as well as strategies for enabling standardization to play a more effective and widely approved role in transatlantic regulation.

Section VI considers the problem of integrating transatlantic regulatory cooperation, however constructed, into domestic legal and political systems, and more particularly those prevalent in the United States and the European Union. This section poses the question: What will be the 'interface' between the emergent processes of transatlantic cooperation, on the one hand, and domestic institutional structures and rule-making processes, on the other? This question in turn raises a host of further questions going to the heart of constitutional and administrative law systems on both sides, questions that implicate such values, for example, as the separation of powers, federalism, and subsidiarity. Appropriately, the perspectives brought to bear here come from a group of three American and three European contributors.

Among the Americans, *Jonathan Macey* opens with an overview of the potential impediments that structures of governance in both Europe and the United States may pose to the realization of an ambitious programme of regulatory cooperation. While dealing with various structural aspects, Macey calls special attention to the disaggregation of regulatory power in the area of American banking law, his area of particular expertise. The unique 'dual banking system' in the United States—in which the federal government and the states both charter and regulate the same financial institutions—provides an excellent concrete example of the American phenomenon of disaggregated regulatory power.

The contribution of *George Bermann* focuses squarely on federalism as a uniquely American complication for transatlantic regulatory cooperation. Bermann notes that, as exemplified by a spate of recent decisions by the US Supreme Court, the values of federalism are as deeply embedded as ever in American law. For him, federalism may be viewed in the same light as other normative concerns that arise in the transatlantic regulatory context—transparency, participation, diversity, representativeness, accountability, and the rule of law. Because federalism values are so central to the American system of governance, and because transatlantic regulatory cooperation has significant potential for disturbing them, Bermann asserts that the question of US federalism must be incorporated into transatlantic regulatory negotiations at the earliest possible stage.

Joel Paul considers a second major structural feature of the American system potentially affected by transatlantic regulatory cooperation, namely the separation of powers. Paul focuses on the central role that the

US President has historically played in advancing forms of international cooperation via the use of executive agreements, i.e. international compacts signed by the President without the advice and consent of two-thirds of the Senate, as is constitutionally required for treaties. Nearly all trade-related agreements entered into by the United States in fact take the form of executive agreements. Although many such agreements involve congressional approval ('congressional-executive agreements'), others are concluded on the sole authority of the President. Paul questions the 'discourse of executive expediency' that has been used to justify deviation from constitutionally mandated treaty procedures, and concludes that executive agreements, in light of serious questions as to their legal effect, are in fact a poor instrument for implementing regulatory cooperation.

Gerhard Lohan of the European Commission offers a first European contribution to the 'interface' question. Lohan depicts the general complexity of the EU regulatory system, illustrating it through an analysis of European product regulation—production methods, performance and design requirements, testing and conformity assessment, labelling, and recycling and waste management. After surveying the initiatives in transatlantic regulatory cooperation that have been launched in the product field, he concludes that integration of these initiatives do not pose significant legal or institutional problems for the European Union, although he does note the many unanswered questions.

Vertical relations within the European Union are the focus of *Paul Demaret*, who offers a comprehensive overview of the respective powers of the Community and the Member States in their external relations. Demaret pays special attention to the impact of this allocation of powers on the launch and conduct of transatlantic regulatory initiatives, stressing how much the EU's external relations outside the commercial field (strictly defined) are characterized by joint action on the part of the Community and the Member States. While this does not always make for 'external coherence' of the internal market, as he describes it, it nevertheless reflects the current stage of European political integration.

Reimer von Borries continues the vertical analysis, but with special emphasis on the implementation of transatlantic regulatory arrangements. Based on his experience within a major ministry of the German federal government, von Borries concludes that the significance of the distribution of competences between the European Union and the Member States does not end with the conclusion of international agreements to which the Community is a party, but rather also extends to their implementation. Having addressed the factors which determine the competence question, he considers the various mechanisms—consultation procedures, mutual recognition agreements, agreements on common standards or the harmonization of laws—that are at the disposal of national and

Community regulators to implement such agreements. Each of these mechanisms raises its own distinctive issues concerning the division of power between the national and supranational levels.

The contributors to Part VII of the book confront the difficult problems of democratic legitimacy associated with transatlantic regulatory cooperation. *Robert Howse* sketches several models of democracy by which programmes of regulatory cooperation may be domestically legitimized. Of these he finds two to be especially promising. First, transatlantic regulatory cooperation may be legitimized in terms of 'competitive federalism' to the extent that it promotes regulatory information flows across borders, thus allowing persons in different jurisdictions to test the quality of domestic decision-making against alternative regimes elsewhere. Second, a complementary 'deliberative' model of democracy may impel governments to undertake explicit and rigorous analysis of risks, to consider closely alternative instruments for addressing those risks, and to incorporate non-governmental organizations into the processes of regulatory cooperation as deliberative intermediaries.

By contrast to Howse, *Ludger Kühnhardt* offers a perspective drawn in important respects from traditional conceptions of representative democracy. Kühnhardt recognizes that regulatory cooperation entails a series of trade-offs between transparency and participation, on the one hand, and regulatory efficiency and technocratic autonomy, on the other. For those pursuing novel means of legitimizing efficiency and autonomy in the international context, however, he queries whether one can de-emphasize the importance of traditional majoritarian voting in any particular polity as a basis of 'democracy'. Because democratization in this traditional, essentially state-confined, sense is not possible in the international context, Kühnhardt suggests that international regulatory processes should focus on legal rather than political institution-building. Accordingly, the development of democratic mechanisms outside the confines of the nation-state will, as the EU experience demonstrates, likely be an evolutionary process.

Like Howse and Kühnhardt, *Sol Picciotto* finds that global socio-economic integration (of which transatlantic regulatory cooperation is one manifestation) carries major implications for political structures and processes of accountability and legitimation, both within and between states. He too identifies the challenge as nothing less than finding new democratic forms to match the new global realities. Contemplating the emergence of a new global public sphere, Picciotto foresees fundamental changes in the form and functions of both states and international structures. For him, the core issue is whether and how this emergent public sphere, which to date has been primarily the creature of international elites, may be genuinely democratized. Recognizing the centrality of regulatory networks in the new global governance, he opts for a 'directly deliberative' model of democracy based upon new forms of active citizenship and political action and conscious pursuit of such 'constitutive' principles as transparency, accountability, responsibility, and empowerment.

Accountability is the preoccupation of the contribution by *Anne-Marie Slaughter*. In a world marked by what she calls 'transgovernmentalism', how do we ensure that the government networks that practise regulatory cooperation will not become international agencies 'on the loose'? In a tightly argued presentation, Slaughter argues that the concern is largely misplaced because the nature of governmental regulatory networks has itself been largely misunderstood. For her, salvation lies chiefly in the fact that transgovernmental networks are primarily 'talking shops' whose vocation is not to produce hard law through a denationalized rule-making process, but rather to promote the exchange of information among national regulators who retain the power of regulatory decision. That transgovernmental networks do not pose intractable accountability problems is fortunate, because in her opinion they offer important governance advantages: speed, flexibility, and decentralization. Slaughter concludes with some suggestions for rendering networks more democratically accountable, but without undermining these advantages.

A proposal that Slaughter and others specifically embrace for achieving new forms of transparency and participation in the regulatory cooperation process is strategic use of the Internet. This is a theme advanced with particular sharpness by *Peter Strauss*, whose presentation at the conference out of which this volume emerged was itself, in his words, 'as much a visual as an auditory performance'. Using a computer and an Internet connection, Strauss explored 'the challenges of globally accessible process' through the use of new information technologies. His particular message is that the incorporation of these technologies in agency processes at the US federal level has created possibilities for the most transparent, participatory, and broadly deliberative regulatory system in the world to become still more so. As demonstrated by recent American experience, the Internet promises not merely to expand access to information about the substance and process of regulation, but also, in Strauss' words, to 'move government closer to the citizen, by providing a framework that facilitates the active participation of citizen groups'. US agency experience suggests that both the body of information efficiently made available to the public and the opportunity for on-line public participation are vast. The transposition of such technologies to international regulatory processes would be all the more transformative of those processes.

What, then, of the future of transatlantic regulatory cooperation? Contributors throughout the volume have treated this question, if only implicitly, but the three authors in Part VIII make it the centrepiece of their analysis. *Kalypso Nicolaïdis* argues that the key strategy will be to develop modes of regulatory cooperation that do not involve radically new doses of centralization of the sort that characterized nineteenth-century state-formation. To this end, she develops a strategic model that differentiates among the various aims of regulatory cooperation. She finds that 'not all regulatory strategies are created equal' and that, as regulatory cooperation yields to trade imperatives, a strategy denominated 'managed mutual recognition' of regulatory standards will become the dominant mode of cooperation. Managed mutual recognition has the advantage of enabling forms of delegation required for efficient rule-making, without having recourse to supranationalist notions, be they institutional or normative.

Wolf-Henning Roth, too, questions both the utility and the practicability of creating new supranational institutions of a legislative or adjudicatory character to undergird programmes of transatlantic regulatory cooperation. Analysing in detail the institutional structure of the current Transatlantic European Partnership (TEP), Roth finds it to be predominantly intergovernmental in nature, and with good reason. There is not yet, in his judgement, sufficient support on either side of the Atlantic for movement towards a more ambitious 'TAFTA', or Transatlantic Free-Trade Area. Indeed, even if a proposal for a TAFTA were on the table, Roth believes that the demonstrated attitudes to such a regime on the part of both the United States (consider NAFTA) and the European Union (consider EEA) clearly reveal a reluctance to relinquish either legislative or adjudicative power to a supranational body. He finds the internal EU experience itself unique, in that European supranationalism is supported by a widespread European 'ideology', requiring for its achievement something on the order of a genuine federal-type constitutionalism.

Although *Ernst-Ulrich Petersmann* would no doubt agree that the task of constitutionalizing international relations is a monumental one, he nevertheless invites us to think ambitiously in this regard. Rejecting the notion that socio-economic globalization alone can be allowed to determine the future shape of international regulatory cooperation, and international relations generally, Petersmann calls for the development of explicitly constitutional rules reflecting deeper values of human rights. The United States and Europe should use their economic and political weight to promote new constitutional rules that do not stop at building global economic markets, but, in a more Kantian sense, entrench the international rule of law, international human rights, and an international 'democratic peace'. Thus, for example, competition policies need to promote freedom, non-discrimination and consumer welfare. Human (including moral, civil, political, economic, and social) rights must receive pervasive recognition and protection from the dynamically evolving global system of government constraints.

This volume thus assembles a broad range of legal, economic, and political perspectives on what we have come to think of as transatlantic regulatory cooperation. The emergence of cooperative arrangements stems from identifiable political and economic trends involving networks whose centre of gravity is located in the transatlantic arena, but whose reach is truly global. The contributions to this volume show that international regulatory cooperation is a large notion, encompassing an array of more or less well-defined processes and techniques—bilateral harmonization of various sorts, mutual recognition, information exchange, concerted study and rule-making, positive comity, multilateral standard-setting, to name only the most salient—each with its own peculiar characteristics. Transatlantic regulatory cooperation in particular may be unsystematic in its manifestations, but it is pervasive and widespread. It interfaces in complex ways with international trade and competition law, while operating quite differently in the various economic sectors where it has been practised. Transatlantic regulatory cooperation also has several distinctive theoretical underpinnings, including both institutional and public choice theory, and at the same time must contend with the challenge of an alternative 'regulatory competition' model.

Processes of transatlantic regulatory cooperation have still other critical interfaces. One such interface is with the more or less well-established domestic environments with which they must be integrated. Squaring transatlantic cooperation with constitutional and administrative law imperatives—of which the horizontal separation of powers and the vertical division of powers are simply the most obvious examples—is a serious challenge. Still more daunting is the ever clearer necessity of reconciling these processes with enduring political values of democracy, legitimacy, transparency, participation, and accountability. Charting the future course of transatlantic regulatory cooperation requires the embrace of strategies that will permit cooperation to produce its regulatory rewards while keeping faith with these values and at the same time respecting commitments to other parts of the world. Finally, there linger questions over the scale of solutions to be launched, and the speed and deliberateness with which to launch them. Are we to content ourselves with procedural improvements ('fine-tuning'), coupled with a permanent general commitment to consider 'mutual' interests, in the hope of producing a good deal of subcutaneous, 'soft' convergence? Or are more formal, more explicitly normative, and more comprehensive solutions to be favoured? It is clear that whatever preferences are shown, they will have to withstand scrutiny from a global perspective.

Part I

*Transatlantic regulatory cooperation:
the political and legal framework*

Transatlantic economic partnership: breaking down the hidden barriers

The Right Honourable Lord Brittan of Spennithorne, QC

I. INTRODUCTION

The subject of transatlantic regulatory cooperation might seem to the uninitiated to be about very technical and dry issues. While I suppose the uninitiated would be right to feel that way about it, that does not make the subject any less important. In fact, what we are discussing under this rubric goes to the very heart of the contemporary EU–US economic relationship and, more specifically, to our efforts further to promote trade and investment, and to avoid economically and politically destructive disputes.

It has become apparent in the last few years that the most significant barriers to trade between Europe and the United States are now the hidden technical barriers which add costs and frustrations to the conduct of business. This is to some extent a testament to our success in removing the other more visible barriers like tariffs and subsidies, and certain other non-tariff barriers. The Transatlantic Business Dialogue has performed an important service in identifying regulatory obstacles as the central priority to be addressed in promoting further transatlantic trade and thereby jobs and well-being for our peoples.

Regulatory obstacles also constitute the main actual and potential causes of dispute. Tomorrow's EU–US trade wars—if they have to happen—will not be about tariffs and subsidies. The banana problem is an old-style trade dispute with its roots in particular historical circumstances. Rather than a paradigm for the future, it is a blast from the past.

II. NEW PROBLEMS AND HOW TO AVOID THEM

Future difficulties between the European Union and the United States are likely to arise from the more intangible, complex, and politically sensitive issues such as genetic modification, food safety, data privacy, and consumer and environmental protection. The emergence of such issues is a sign of our having entered a new era of trade policy resulting from the acceleration of technological innovation and the much greater openness of markets. In these fields of public policy, political authorities on each side feel obliged to introduce regulations in order to protect health and safety. In doing so, both the European Union and the United States must, as democratic governments, be responsive to the political demands and sensitivities of their electorates, which are by no means always identical. There are, quite clearly, genuine differences between public attitudes about food safety issues such as genetically modified organisms and hormone treatment of beef, and about the ways of dealing with them, such as labelling. These political facts cannot simply be ignored; they must be dealt with within the multilateral-trade framework. Because regulatory differences having an adverse impact on trade result from perfectly legitimate political differences, we need to adopt a cautious yet constructive approach in addressing them. Since governments in both Europe and the United States are committed to maximizing trade between them, this necessity must be faced.

The best approach to dealing with the problem is to find ways of preventing disputes from arising in the first place. Early preventive dialogue—between scientists, between consumer groups, between politicians, between businessmen, between regulators—is fundamental. Timely dialogue allows us to foresee problems, to reach agreement on their nature and scope, and either to develop common approaches to dealing with them or, failing that, to settle on approaches that are as compatible with one another as possible. Disputatious litigation is not the solution.

What I have identified amounts to the single most important challenge for trade policy-makers and the trading communities on both sides of the Atlantic. Fortunately, this philosophy animates the recently launched Transatlantic Economic Partnership (TEP). Within that framework, the European Union and the United States are establishing both official and non-governmental fora for pursuing dialogues with precisely this purpose in areas such as biotechnology, the environment, and consumer safety. Identifying the disputes of the future and preventing them from happening is good for everyone, except perhaps inveterate trade warriors.

Building regulatory bridges is crucial in multilateral fora as well as bilateral relations, and the challenge there is no less great. While the Uruguay Round provided the WTO with a clear methodology and mechanisms for many other subjects, their applicability to the new issues is less clear cut. Consumer groups, environmentalists, and animal welfare activists are often dissatisfied with the thrust of the WTO-rules (and the multilateral system more generally), which they perceive as an obstacle to achieving their highly laudable objectives. The agricultural sector in Europe is likewise concerned about the effect of high European environmental, health, or animal welfare standards on their competitiveness, and demand the imposition of equivalent standards on imported products. Witness recent discussions in Europe on battery hens, on the protection of animals kept for farming purposes, and on the ban on certain antibiotics in animal foodstuffs. The WTO will have to find ways of addressing such concerns in future trade rounds, especially as these issues matter more to the general public than the old-style disputes over import duties and subsidies.

Doing as I suggest will require closer attention than we have paid to the meaning of the 'precautionary principle'. Multilateral and regional conventions increasingly employ precautionary language, without clarifying whether that principle has evolved from a term of art into a norm of general or customary international law in areas such as food safety. While I accept the legitimacy of the concept of precaution in the field of environment and health, I see dangers in deploying a general, open-ended precautionary principle without defining what it means and in what circumstances it might be used. We need to develop a methodology which allows us to apply the principle in a consistent and workable manner, and ultimately to achieve a balance. Using the precautionary principle to justify measures that reduce risks to zero would be excessive. Aiming for zero risk across the board could bring us to a scientific standstill, since there are risks involved in any new venture. On the other hand, we need to be able to protect people, animals, and plants from life-threatening risk, even where only provisional scientific data is available. The European Union is itself grappling with the distinction between the precautionary principle and a zero-risk approach in the case of hormone-treated beef. The international community too needs to produce a clear statement on the precautionary principle and incorporate it into the WTO.

III. REMOVING TECHNICAL BARRIERS

Not all barriers to trade are highly political or contentious. Some are simply the result of unnecessary and duplicative routine procedures. Because these also impose hidden costs, they too must be got rid of wherever possible. Herein lies the impetus for using the TEP to advance mutual recognition of existing technical standards so as to minimize incompatibility and improve our regulatory cooperation across the board.

While all technical barriers to trade arise directly from domestic regulatory requirements (or from the difference between the regulatory requirements of two trading partners), the origin and motivation behind them is not always the same. In some cases, a technical barrier has been deliberately erected to have an impact on trade. Hoping and believing that this is not the case between the European Union and the United States, I do not dwell on this type of barrier here. In other cases (and typically between the

European Union and the United States), perfectly legitimate policy goals may lie behind a regulation, which nonetheless has an unnecessarily trade-restrictive effect. Technical barriers of this sort are not fundamentally different from other forms of non-tariff barriers, such as quantitative restrictions or subsidies, and they can be dealt with in a broadly similar way, by establishing effective and enforceable multilateral disciplines to prevent their use. Basically, this is the approach enshrined in the EC Treaty, in the Tokyo Round GATT Agreements, and eventually in the Uruguay Round WTO Agreements.

The European experience with the Internal Market demonstrates, however, that multilateral trade liberalization of this sort is not a full answer. This is so because even quite legitimate, non-discriminatory, and proportionate domestic regulations can still hamper trade, simply by virtue of the fact that they exist and are different from one another. As trade relations intensify and are liberalized between two economies, this problem becomes ever more prominent. It has accordingly become most glaringly obvious in trade between the highly developed economies of Europe and North America, where trade flows freely without governmental intervention, and often within multinational companies or between closely linked enterprises.

This awareness led in the European Union to broad harmonization of standards and technical regulations, coupled with a broad principle of mutual acceptance of products regardless of applicable standards. Harmonization and mutual recognition have become the cornerstone of the Internal Market, giving very real substance to the EC Treaty's principle of free circulation of goods. Admittedly, these European notions cannot automatically be extended to international trade outside the special institutional and legal environment of the European Union. On the other hand, they can serve as the philosophical lodestar for our wider efforts at eliminating technical trade barriers.

As I have just suggested, the mechanisms that we have available to address the problem fall into two broad categories: either we achieve common standards and regulatory requirements with our trading partners by adapting both our standards and theirs, or we accept differences between our standards and regulatory requirements while containing their trade effects.

IV. ACHIEVING COMMON STANDARDS

A first approach consists of achieving common standards with trading partners by harmonizing the standards already in place. This can be done bilaterally or multilaterally, and it can be done informally or through international institutions. Because harmonization is generally a slow and laborious process, the Community has tended to prefer multilateral harmonization. The prize of broader application of harmonized standards better rewards the effort.

The role of international standards bodies in multilateral harmonization is crucial. For this reason, standards bodies like ISO/IEC and ITU need to be revitalized in the sense of being made more effective, more open, and more responsive to the often conflicting demands that arise in the field of standards-setting. At present, standards bodies are sometimes too technical, and sometimes too political. Beyond that, the international standardization process, as seen from Europe, also suffers from the apparent reluctance of the United States to give its full support. Whether because of the way voting rights are organized or because of close links with European standards bodies, the US tends to perceive international standardization bodies as being European-dominated. In any event, the United States is sometimes perceived by others as unable to deliver an effective application of international standards in the domestic regulatory system.

Common standards can of course also be arrived at bilaterally, that is through cooperation between domestic regulatory authorities, leading to the development of similar, or at least compatible, regulatory requirements. Pooling knowledge about product hazards and about the sensitivity of the public to them should improve both the effectiveness of regulators and their ability to avoid conflicting requirements. However, success in regulatory cooperation such as has been achieved between the European Union and United States presupposes first a broadly comparable state of development of domestic economic activity and regulatory structures. It then presupposes basic agreement on the need to regulate. Even under these circumstances, regulatory cooperation, if it is to work, must be initiated at a very early stage in the process between the identification of a potential problem and the adoption of preventive or remedial regulation. The later in time a dialogue takes place, the greater the obstacles that may already have been erected and the greater the sensitivity of the regulators to interference.

We have seen that regulatory agencies are sometimes reluctant to enter fully into the spirit of regulatory negotiations because of a felt need to protect their turf. In the MRA negotiations, for example, governments proved to be more eager than their agencies to cooperate. The fact remains that regulatory cooperation has to be pursued with respect for the legitimate responsibilities and prerogatives of domestic regulators. Regulatory agencies are entrusted with the safeguard of highly important public policy interests and bear responsibility to the public for their performance. But they have, for their part, a duty not to allow that responsibility to prevent legitimate cooperation with other regulators whose standards and integrity are as great as their own.

V. DEALING WITH DIFFERENT STANDARDS AND REGULATORY REQUIREMENTS

The major alternative to devising common regulatory standards is to accept existing differences between our regulatory requirements and find means of reducing their trade effects. Transparency of domestic requirements is of course essential. Quite apart from the cost of complying with additional or different requirements, lack of knowledge about standards and regulatory requirements can deter trade, especially when compounded by distance and language problems. But there are ways to bring us further along this road, among them the development of new instruments based on the concepts of equivalence and mutual recognition. Actually, the idea of recognizing other nations' test data, test results, and certificates has been around for a while, and there are even some multilateral examples of this, such as the OECD's 'Mutual Acceptance of Data' (or 'MAD') Decision on good laboratory practices for testing chemical products. Obviously, this strategy has been employed most extensively within the European Union, with its expanding network of mutual recognition agreements and protocols on European conformity assessment.

Historically, mutual recognition has chiefly concerned certification and testing. It has been based upon, but also in turn promoted, confidence that testing laboratories in an exporting country are competent to certify products for conformity with the standards of the importing country, thus avoiding double testing. The TEP is taking the notion of mutual recognition well beyond testing, to the underlying standards themselves. In other words, it is exploring whether, at least in certain sectors, we can establish confidence in one another's standards for protecting health, consumer safety, the environment, etc. 'Mutual recognition of technical regulations' means recognizing that our standards themselves are directly equivalent. For example, both the European Union and the United States have standards to ensure that life-saving equipment on ships actually works. Their standards are different, but they are both based on those set by the International Maritime Organization and they both give ships a comparable level of safety. Appyling mutual recognition to these standards would enable manufacturers of life jackets to export them transatlantically, without having to adapt them to different standards.

VI. CONCLUSIONS

Regulatory cooperation, like the issues associated with it, lies at the very heart of contemporary EU–US economic relations. It is capable of unlocking new trade and investment, while at the same time preventing and preempting possible trade disputes. For this reason, it figures importantly in the TEP programme and in the work of the TABD.

The European Union and the United States share very similar objectives in establishing levels of protection in areas of essential public interest, such as health, safety, and the environment. The European Union and the United States also share a desire to achieve a balance between these objectives and the need to stimulate economic activity. Translating these opportunities into regulatory cooperation entails overcoming differences in regulatory approaches and culture that lead to hidden barriers that are not always easy to overcome. Nevertheless, the European Union and the United States have a strong interest in tackling the problem, due both to the economic gain they stand to make and to the benefits of avoiding disputes. The alternative is to continue to burden our industries and consumers in the European Union and the United States with unnecessary costs and to deprive them of the benefits of more open, but nevertheless safeguarded, trade. The multilateral trade negotiations in coming trade rounds will provide an opportunity to introduce these advantageous principles of regulatory cooperation into an even broader context.

The United States and Europe: seeking common ground

Ambassador David L. Aaron

The timing of a conference on the prospects of strengthening regulatory cooperation between the United States and Europe could hardly be better. As the media has copiously documented, economic and trade relations between the United States and Europe have not been at their most harmonious lately. We are at odds over a number of issues, from bananas to beef to aircraft engines to privacy. While our two perspectives need reconciling, that is not always easily accomplished.

Early in this century French Prime Minister Georges Clemenceau said, 'America is the only nation in history which miraculously has gone directly from barbarism to degeneration without the usual interval of civilization'. A few years later, the great American humorist Will Rogers was uncharacteristically acerbic in his assessment of Europe. 'That's one good thing about European nations,' he said, 'they can't hate you so bad they wouldn't use you.' Rogers later offered another, more balanced comment on the relationship, writing, 'Headlines in papers say: "Europe criticizes U.S." If memory serves, we haven't complimented them lately ourselves.' That was in 1924!

For many decades, security cooperation has been seen as the bedrock of US relations with Europe. Recently we stood shoulder to shoulder in Kosovo, as we did during forty years of Cold War. NATO's intervention in particular underscores the commonality of our interests, and the critical importance of our continued bonds. But the economic ties between the United States and Europe are no less fundamental. The major multilateral institutions built since World War II—the World Bank, the IMF, and GATT, and now the WTO—are overwhelmingly US and European creations. Tariffs between the United States and Europe have fallen by 90 per cent over the past half-century. Together, we have set standards of market access, intellectual property rights and dispute resolution that have spread around the world and form the basis for today's bounty of international commerce. The United States and Europe represent the twin pillars of a post-war prosperity that has seen average per capita income around the globe double, production quadruple, and world trade grow fifteenfold.

Today, the US–EU commercial relationship is the largest in the world, by far, reaching about one-and-a-quarter trillion dollars. Europe is twice as large a market for US companies as Canada and Japan combined. If they were all put together, American companies in Europe would represent the fourth largest economy on the continent. Nine million Europeans work for US firms. The scale of European investment in America is just as great—US$145 billion, connected to US$900 billion in annual sales. One out of every twelve US factory workers is now employed by a European-owned firm.

The US and European economies have grown so close together that I sometimes visualize them as finely meshed gears. Even small issues, like grains of sand in a gearbox, can cause terrible noise and threaten to wreck the machinery. They must be purged or they can do serious damage. Increasingly the sand in the gears is regulatory. There are two reasons for this. First, tariffs and quotas between the United States and Europe have declined dramatically. As a result, trade barriers are more likely to take the form of standards and regulations. Second, as the nations of Europe try to build a single market, they are increasingly taking unilateral regulatory actions that—deliberately or not—can adversely affect other countries and undermine international bodies such as the WTO, ICAO, and ITU.

The fact that Europe is not yet a country makes dealing with Europe somewhat more difficult—particularly in regulatory matters. Henry Kissinger famously asked, 'When you want to talk to Europe, whom do you call?' In regulatory matters, it can be very unclear. Europe lacks an FDA, an FAA, an SEC and other institutions essential for a unified market to function efficiently. Moreover, there are shared competencies. Individual country interests are still crucial, as are their economic and political circumstances. Overall, however, the European Union is an increasingly unified economic force, and a critical economic partner for the United States.

Recent high-profile trade disputes between the United States and Europe have given the transatlantic relationship its most conspicuous challenge. Let me expand on two disputes that have a particularly high priority: aircraft noise and data privacy.

On aircraft noise, the EU Council is considering a regulation that would ban the use in Europe of replacement engines and of so-called 'hushkits'—essentially jet engine mufflers—to achieve aircraft noise reduction.[1] Interestingly, this rule would affect only US products to the tune of roughly a billion dollars, while allowing the amount of European-made equipment that is equally noisy to increase. It would also undermine 40 years of multilateral cooperation on aircraft noise regulation in the International Civil Aviation Organization (ICAO). The US Government

---

[1] Common Position (EC) No. 66/98 on a Council regulation on the registration and operation within the Community of certain types of civil subsonic jet aeroplanes, OJ C 404 (23 Dec. 1998).

strongly opposes this initiative as unilateral and discriminatory and strongly urges a multilateral solution.

Air transport is the quintessentially global industry, and it would be extremely damaging to balkanize international aviation rules. In fact, this is not an isolated instance. The European Commission is readying several more proposals that would impose unilateral standards on aircraft. As shown by the President of ICAO's call for postponement of this EU action, the international community cannot accept such an approach. Instead, the European Union should work through ICAO to develop new and tougher worldwide standards. If it is willing to do so, it will find us willing partners in an accelerated effort to devise an ICAO proposal for more stringent noise rules.

Data privacy is another major issue that reveals a profound difference in regulatory approach. The European Union has adopted a privacy directive that creates a comprehensive regulatory umbrella, including data privacy 'czars' in each country.[2] The United States has evaluated and rejected this approach. Basically, the European system assumes a mainframe world and did not anticipate the Internet. At the same time, we have different traditions and distinct historical concerns about privacy. The United States prefers legislation that targets individual privacy problems, supplemented by industry self-regulatory codes and backed up by the Federal Trade Commission and state fair trade laws. Indeed, we are concerned that the EU approach could actually lead to invasions of privacy. More specifically, the EU directive requires the blocking of data flows to countries deemed not to provide adequate privacy protection. At present, the European Union is deciding whether the US regime meets this adequacy standard. What is at stake is at least a portion of the hundreds of billions of dollars in trade and investment between the United States and Europe, not to mention the nearly unlimited potential of electronic commerce.

We have been discussing this matter for a year, which is not surprising considering that the issues are technically complex and culturally profound. The bottom line, however, is that we are both committed to protecting privacy. Accordingly we have tried to bridge the gap by means of a set of safe-harbour principles, which would govern such major issues as notice to an individual that information is being given out, choice to the individual of whether or not to allow it, access to information that has been gathered, third-party transfer, enforcement, and so on. A US firm subscribing to the safe-harbour principles would be deemed to be providing adequate privacy protection, and would be allowed to continue receiving data from European sources. (I hasten to add that these principles would cover only data exchange with Europe. They are emphatically not a template for

---

[2] Directive 97/66/EC of 15 Dec. 1997, concerning the processing of personal data and the protection of privacy in the telecommunications sector, OJ L 24 (30 Jan. 1998).

government action to change the domestic US privacy regime.) Discussions over the safe-harbour principles are ongoing and give some promise of a resolution that will protect both privacy and the flow of information necessary to growing commerce between our continents.

Two other well-known quarrels are also worthy of mention: bananas and beef. In both cases, European regulations contravene global trade rules. In the banana dispute, the WTO has ruled against Europe several times and Europe now seems to be prepared to accept its ruling. The difficulty is compounded in the beef hormone case by the fact that European regulations have no scientific basis; basically they are driven by the mad cow scare. The European Union claims to be unable to meet the deadline for complying with the WTO ruling. In the absence of a negotiated settlement, US retaliation has become inevitable.

These experiences tell us that waiting to negotiate until regulatory issues have become crises is not the best approach. We need to work on such issues in advance. As a vehicle for such an expanded dialogue, both sides have committed to a Transatlantic Economic Partnership (TEP) initiative. The TEP is meant to help us tackle regulatory issues in a more timely and systematic way. Under the TEP, we will first review technical standards to remove barriers and avoid conflicts, while at the same time protecting health and safety. Second, we will seek to guarantee that, whatever the regulatory policy pursued, the process is transparent, predictable and scientific.

An additional channel for dealing with common regulatory problems in a timely and effective way is the Transatlantic Business Dialogue (TABD). The TABD, composed of corporate heads from both sides of the Atlantic who come together to make recommendations to senior US and EU officials, has provided the impetus for several important international regulatory agreements. Among the best known is the US–EU Mutual Recognition Agreement, which should produce savings for US companies of a billion dollars a year in six sectors ranging from telecommunications to pharmaceuticals.

By way of conclusion, let me acknowledge that the United States has differences with Europe, and probably always will. But since the continued relationship is vital to both, keeping the relationship healthy should be, and from all appearances is, a mutual priority. Sharing similar standards for protecting health, consumers, and the environment, the United States and the European Union are well-positioned to achieve regulatory harmonization. A cooperative relationship between them is vital to the rest of the world, and thus to global progress. Together, we must do what only we two can. If both the United States and Europe exercise the right kind of unselfish economic leadership, even while attending to the full plate of domestic issues at hand, they can secure a brighter economic future for the entire world.

Globalization and the rule of law

Jean-Louis Dewost

On the occasion of a conference on the legal aspects of the transatlantic regulatory relationship, it seems appropriate that the Legal Adviser of the US State Department and the Director General of the European Commission Legal Service should reflect on the direct dialogue that they have initiated within the framework of the New Transatlantic Agenda. It is no accident that regulatory relations figure so prominently on that Agenda, or that they have commanded the attention of high legal offices on both sides.

I would like to divide my personal reflections into three parts. First, I would like to suggest that globalization is a common challenge. Second, I find that the European Union's own experience shows the necessity of developing methods for meeting this kind of challenge. Third, transferring such methods to the specific context of EU–US relations requires adjustments on which I hope to shed some light.

I. GLOBALIZATION IS A COMMON CHALLENGE

Discussions of the transatlantic regulatory relationship demonstrate that we are facing challenges that stem from a globalization that has become a fact of international life. As the presentations at this conference have shown, globalization has its economic dimension (e.g. the role of international financial markets), its technological dimension (e.g. the impact of the digital revolution on telecommunications and the Internet), and its political dimension (e.g. the existence of 'competing sites' for decision-making on global issues and related problems of legitimacy and democratic deficit).

The impact of globalization is not, however, merely visible in changing economic, technological, and political structures. Increasingly, it also has striking social repercussions. By way of example, the processes of globalization are fueling environmental preoccupations and, indirectly, misgivings over certain of the consequences of industrial development. Globalization is generating widespread doubts about the safety of distantly produced foodstuffs and causing people, quite frankly, to wonder what precisely they are eating. There is even a social dimension to the political arena, as persons everywhere feel the necessity to bring decision-making closer to them. Both the new EU constitutional principle of 'subsidiarity' (establishing the parameters of EU legislative activity) and recent trends in US Supreme Court case law in favour of 'states rights' (whether concerning freedom of religion, assisted suicide, or gun control) illustrate this phenomenon.

II.   THE METHOD NEEDED TO CONFRONT THE NEW GLOBAL CHALLENGE

The presence of these economic, technological, political, and social dimensions to the global challenge implies the need to develop a sophisticated 'method' capable of meeting this challenge. The EU's experience in facing a similar spectrum of challenges yields a number of important methodological lessons.

First, the EU experience suggests that globalization does not necessarily imply the recognition of vast new fields of 'non-law' or dictate the conclusion that some regulatory areas lie 'beyond the pale'. On the contrary, the aim of establishing a 'level playing field' requires the development of common legal principles on a vast range of matters such as the applicable law, competent jurisdiction and authorities, free and fair competition, consumer protection, civil liability, execution of judgments, and recognition of legal relationships constituted abroad.

Second, the globalization of markets is too often proceeding at present on the basis of international regulatory provisions that reflect the 'lowest common denominator'. If we perpetuate this approach, we may be led to sacrifice our wider social values—such as the protection of social rights, health, or the environment—simply in order to make global rules work, or work better. It is likewise possible that the rule of law will be replaced by soft law or even by mere 'behavioural commitments', resulting in prejudice to citizens' right of access to justice. The challenge now confronting the rule of law at the international level is to ensure that the drive towards globalization remains in harmony with higher societal values.

This is not to say that we should not vigorously pursue harmonization, but rather that in doing so we should carefully evaluate the risk of impoverishment to our heritage of legal and social discourse. In this regard, I invoke the words of Commission President Prodi to the European Parliament on 13 April 1999: 'The search for a European "soul" is increasingly proving to be the major problem facing our continent as it looks to the future.'

In this respect, the regional experience of the European Union deserves to be studied carefully. Within Europe, the aim of economic liberalization—basically the free movement of goods, persons, services, and capital—has been grounded on an ongoing search for political balance between pluralism and solidarity, between regulation and freedom, and between trade interests and social values. This balance has been pursued within a legislative and judicial framework that has had to evolve in order to adapt to new objectives.

The EU experience suggests that there is no inherent contradiction between a regulatory and a market-driven approach. By drawing upon both, the European Union has been able effectively to identify common values in areas as diverse as health and trade (e.g. genetically modified organisms and product liability directives) and electronic commerce (e.g. consumer protection and data protection).

These achievements were not, however, realized in a legal and institutional vacuum. On the contrary, policy progress in the European Union has depended on the existence of a legal and institutional framework exhibiting four main features. First, the balance between competing goals is ultimately struck through the taking of majority vote decisions by political institutions, rather than through the purely informal 'government networks' frequently alluded to in these proceedings. Second, the participants have acknowledged the necessity of guaranteeing a minimum of legal certainty and consistency, and thereby predictability and trust. Third, and closely related, the entire process has been anchored from the beginning in a commitment to the rule of law. Finally, it was agreed that the final arbitration of conflicts would be performed by an independent judicial body, a court composed of professionally-trained judges and lawyers.

III. TRANSPOSITION OF THE EU METHOD TO EU–US RELATIONS

There would be no point in even considering the transposition of the EU method to EU–US relations were it not for the fact that the two entities share many common values and that their economies are increasingly intertwined. The political and legal systems of Europe and the United States, and their societies more generally, share basic values such as the rule of law, independence, individual freedom, and a balance of powers between the executive and legislative branches of government. The 1999 resignation of the European Commission under pressure from the European Parliament is only the most recent and striking illustration of the growing democratic accountability of the EU institutions, very largely aligning the EU's practice with the Member States' advanced democratic traditions.

As for the economic intertwining of the United States and the European Union, this is largely a matter of common sense. Despite regulatory obstacles (e.g. recent OECD discussions of the Multilateral Agreement on Investment), trade flows are expanding, investments are growing, and the number of US trademarks registered as European trademarks in Alicante, Spain, is burgeoning.

On the other hand, we should not underestimate the difficulties flowing from our cultural differences, from differences in our political and legal structures, and more specifically from differences in our approach to regulation. For example, it is fair to say that responsibility for protecting the public interest (e.g. safety, public health, public order) is entrusted more substantially in the European Union to public institutions (notably, the Commission, Council, and Parliament), than it is in the United States, where private initiative—supported and shaped by the judiciary—plays a more energetic role. Within Europe, matters such as product liability, data protection, and electronic commerce are very clearly the 'stuff' of legislation.

Similarly, differences in the political and legal structures of the European Union and the United States inevitably create asymmetries in the agreements reached between the two. For example, the European Union can fully commit both the Community and its Member States to the agreements reached, so that all its component entities agree to be, and are effectively, bound. Generally speaking, however, the US may be more limited by the scope of federal power and, even within that scope, by the difficulties entailed in compelling sub-federal entities within the United States to respect the agreed upon rules. Although the result in such cases as the Massachusetts 'Burma' law was ultimately favourable, it followed a period of some uncertainty, and failed to put all doubts to rest. Another example of institutional difference concerns regulatory structures themselves, as evidenced by the contrast between a unitary European Commission (albeit under close Council and Parliamentary control), on the one hand, and the looser configuration of independent federal agencies in the United States (albeit under looser presidential and congressional control), on the other.

There are process differences as well. Compare the growing demand of the European Parliament to be more closely involved in Commission delegated decision-making under the supervision of Council committees (the so-called 'comitology' procedures) with the quite distinctive tendency towards 'privatization' of the regulatory power that we are now observing in the US.

Still, while these differences subsist, I detect a growing readiness to address public policy issues in an international arena—often within the framework of discrete international organizations such as UNCITRAL, the OECD, WIPO, and the WTO—and with this comes a greater chance of actually arriving at common, or more common, solutions. Even in the absence of international initiatives, some degree of convergence is afoot. For example, the European Union has moved in the direction of the United States by giving management and labour a privileged role in the innovative legislative procedures for social policy first introduced by the Maastricht Treaty and now embodied in the Amsterdam Social Chapter and by introducing the new anti-discrimination clause of Article 13 (formerly Article 6a) introduced by the Amsterdam Treaty.

This leads me then to consider what would be the most effective way to transpose the EU experience to EU–US relations.

Given the basic commonality of interests between the United States and the European Union, and the 'imperatives' of globalization, I submit that considerable progress stands to be made even in the absence of any new bilateral institutions. Notwithstanding their cultural and institutional differences, the prevailing pragmatic approach has yielded impressive results, whether we look at the recent mutual recognition agreements, positive 'comity' arrangements (as in the competition field), or the development of common risk assessment methods in biotechnology. One cooperative initiative which the Commission Legal Service has particularly pursued is Internet domain names and addresses. Fueled by efforts made throughout the international community—but particularly on the part of the United States and the European Union—a new Internet body, the ICANN, has emerged, combining the features of (a) private, non-profit status, with (b) an international governmental function, and (c) new (WIPO-developed) rules on domain names and trademarks, along with new procedures for resolving disputes. While this initiative had the unique advantage of support from both government and the private sector, and solid promotion by the worldwide Internet community itself, it nevertheless showcases the more general prospects for successfully integrating diverse governance systems into a common regulatory regime.

IV. CONCLUSIONS

The challenge is to steer a sound middle course between Utopian (and therefore unattainable 'single world') visions, at one extreme, and destructive 'unilateralism' at the other. I believe that economic realities and our commonality of values will sustain that effort. But I also believe that this process requires a conscious willingness to appreciate each other's cultures, and more particularly each other's starting points. The exchange of experiences and views will not only help us to construct appropriate cooperative regimes based upon a 'meeting of minds',[1] but also equip us with an 'early prevention' mechanism for the conflicts that, sooner or later, in one domain or another, are bound to surface. The bi-annual meetings, in Brussels and Washington, between the State Department Legal Adviser and the Director General of the Commission Legal Service are an important cross-sectoral element of this process.

---

[1] William Wallace, 'Meeting of Minds', *Financial Times*, 15 Apr. 1999, 30.

Listening in on the US–EU legal dialogue

David R. Andrews

Transatlantic regulatory cooperation between the United States and European Union is a matter of enormous importance. The combined annual trade and investment between the two areas, totalling a trillion dollars, exceeds US trade and investment with both Canada and Japan. The US–EU relationship has also resulted in substantial and wide-ranging accomplishments in combating crime, terrorism, pollution, drugs, and disease. For example, the partnership entails efforts to limit terrorists' access to funds, to halt the spread of child pornography over the Internet, and to break up prostitution rings that entrap women from Eastern Europe. Regulatory cooperation is an important element in sustaining and expanding our economic relationship, while at the same time addressing critical social problems.

In his account of the legal dialogue between the US State Department and the Commission Legal Service, Jean-Louis Dewost addressed in broad terms the relationship between globalization and the rule of law. My approach is a somewhat narrower one, namely the specific role that a legal office such as mine in the Department of State plays and can play in the context of US–EU regulatory cooperation.

Realistically speaking, the State Department has a very limited role to play on substantive aspects of transatlantic regulatory cooperation. Since the political responsibility and technical expertise naturally reside in the specialized agencies of the US Government, the Department of State typically does not take the lead on such matters. By contrast, the United States Office of Trade Representative (USTR) and the Departments of Commerce, Agriculture, and Transportation, for example, all play much the more central and active role. The issue of electronic commerce, with which I deal separately below, represents an important exception to this pattern.

The role typically played by the State Department in promoting international regulatory cooperation can best be described as one of facilitation. Facilitation occurs in two ways. The first way is by establishing lines of communication. The New Transatlantic Agenda (NTA) rightly places a premium on the creation of parallel dialogues involving government, business, labour, and consumer and environmental non-governmental organizations. The ongoing conversation initiated between the Office of Legal Adviser and the Commission Legal Service represents a kind of 'legal' dialogue meant to support all the others.

A second facilitative function played by the Department of State, and more particularly by its Office of Legal Adviser, consists of taking responsibility for interpreting and applying all relevant treaty law. Part of this function is assessing the legal sufficiency of the agreements into which the United States and the European Union have entered in the interest of promoting or performing regulatory cooperation.

Questions of legal sufficiency are especially likely to arise in dealing with the European Union due to the fact that it is both composed of national member states and represented by a supranational European Commission. In this regard, the European Union is a salient example of what treaty lawyers like to call a 'regional economic integration organization' or 'REIO'. Not surprisingly, the traditional international law of treaties and institutions, premised on the notion of a nation state, has been stretched by new and ever-changing concepts and institutions such as those now taking shape in Europe. The treaty practices and institutional arrangements that we adopt with respect to the European Union are important not only in their own right, but also because of the precedents they set for dealings with future REIOs that emerge in other regions.

A recurring question of legal sufficiency in dealings with the European Union is 'competence'. The Office of Legal Adviser has to consider, with respect to any particular agreement, whether the European Union, the Member States, or both will sign, and what the implications for the agreement's efficacy will then be. We know from experience that over some subject areas the Member States have exclusive competence, over others the Community has exclusive competence, and over still others competence is shared. Moreover, the allocation of competence within the European Union is constantly evolving. As one would expect in any such institution, even the Member States and the European Commission themselves do not always have identical perspectives on the allocation of competence with respect to a particular issue. The point is not to criticize these uncertainties, which are inevitable in an ambitious and rapidly changing institution like the European Union, but rather to underscore the particular challenges that they present to EU treaty partners, like the United States, seeking to improve regulatory cooperation.

In the case of 'mixed agreements' in particular, uncertainties can also arise at the implementation stage. If a treaty partner is concerned that there may have been a breach of an agreement by a REIO (such as the European Union) and/or the Member States, to whom does the treaty partner turn for redress? What if the REIO and some or all Member States are in substantive disagreement as to the resolution of the problem? Worse still, what if the REIO claims that the Member State is responsible for that particular aspect of the agreement and the Member State claims that the REIO is responsible? The answers to these questions, as well as our ability to find comfort within a legal environment of uncertain and shifting competence, may be vital to the future of transatlantic regulatory cooperation.

The complexities of entering into international agreements with an entity whose constituent parts may themselves have authority to enter the same treaty surfaced recently in negotiations over the Mutual Recognition Agreement or MRA. (The MRA, on product testing and certification, has reduced the costs of exporting in six industrial sectors covering in total $50 billion in two-way trade. It is itself a major milestone in transatlantic regulatory cooperation.) Bringing the MRA into force turned out to be extremely difficult both because of developments in US law and because of the way in which the European Union obtains negotiating authority from its Member States. After negotiations on the MRA had concluded, the State Department learned of a change in domestic US law which necessitated a minor revision to one of the MRA's six annexes. As a logistical matter, this change, though minor, would ordinarily have required the European Union to seek reapproval from each Member State, potentially reopening the entire negotiation and occasioning a lengthy delay. Fortunately, this scenario was able to be averted.

Although, as mentioned, the Department of State (and thus the Office of Legal Adviser) does not typically deal directly with the European Union on the substance of issues related to regulatory cooperation, one exception is electronic commerce. This is an area in which the Office of Private International Law within the Legal Adviser's Office plays a major role and has drawn important insights into the US–EU relationship. As we are all increasingly aware in our private and professional lives, the Internet is growing at a breathtaking rate. Computer-based technology changes and new applications of that technology in commerce spring up almost daily, with no sign of slowing. For example, Internet purchasing and contract arranging between remote parties with no previous business relationship, and with no actual certainty as to where the other's commercial operations may be, are becoming commonplace.

Internet commerce is not only very new; by the nature of the medium, it is often inherently transnational. Indeed, due to the speed with which electronic commerce is emerging, we are engaged for perhaps the first time in the concurrent development of national and international rules. The world's new information systems demand the adaptation of existing legal standards and traditional legal approaches to contracts, data rights, and telecommunications. This is an example of the deterritorialization of law, that is to say, of legal regimes divorced from national boundaries.

The dynamic intersection between new technology and trade, with immediate transnational effects, highlights the difference between US-led efforts to let market forces shape new rules, on the one hand, and the preference of the European Commission and some EU Member States for a more centralized regulatory approach, on the other. The European Union's readiness to fill the gap with new laws, and to pursue harmonization across the Atlantic and the world, has the merit of giving commercial actors a significant measure of certainty and predictability. But this approach runs the risk of stifling innovation and competitive ideas. While some new technological developments and applications will still grow out of this environment, as a practical matter regulatory approaches at this stage inevitably focus on the chosen regulatory framework and limit the ability to develop new technologies and applications.

By contrast, US policy tends to avoid committing to a particular regulatory framework or to the resolution of issues on the basis of any given technology. It takes the view that electronic commerce is still at an early stage in its development, and that we are better served by a minimal regulatory environment, one which will support the use of all technologies and applications. The US thus inclines to give industry sectors more freedom, not less, to develop their own commercial practices and regimes.

The comparison reflects a broader difference in culture between the European Union and the United States even on matters of commerce and regulation. But while these differences inject tension into the processes of regulatory cooperation in electronic commerce, fundamental shared values on political, economic, and legal issues point the way forward. The way forward, whether in the area of electronic commerce or other areas of future cooperation, is through close coordination and dialogue. The legal dialogue initiated between the Commission Legal Service and the US Department of State, Office of Legal Adviser, is part of this process. In my relatively short time as Legal Adviser—under two years—I have seen interactions between our offices on the Mutual Recognition Agreement, on treaty issues relating to issues of competence, and many other issues. But given the importance of the US–EU trade relationship, the need for a vibrant legal dialogue will only increase in importance. The United States and the European Union alike are mindful both of the need to break down regulatory barriers and enhance regulatory cooperation and of the challenges to doing so. The fact that we sometimes have different perspectives on the problems at hand, as well as different inclinations as to their solution, does not diminish our willingness to engage in meaningful regulatory dialogue, legal or otherwise.

The Transatlantic Business Dialogue: the perspective of the European chemical industry

Hans-Ulrich Engel

The foregoing contributions have already outlined why closer cooperation between the United States and the European Union will be mutually advantageous. One way to advance today's cooperation, however, is through the Transatlantic Business Dialogue (TABD). My observations shall comment on the notion of the TABD, its progress and its prospects from the point of view of the European chemical industry, a perspective shared, by the way, by the American chemical industry.

I. THE TABD IN GENERAL

Let me start with a look at a trade dispute the first chancellor of the Federal Republic of Germany, Konrad Adenauer, had to deal with almost 40 years ago. In the early sixties the chemical industry in Germany initiated an anti-dumping complaint against the United States relating to polyethylene. The case was well prepared, with clear evidence of a substantial dumping margin, and thus a request was made to Adenauer to apply an anti-dumping duty to imports from the United States. Adenauer's knowledge of anti-dumping matters was presumably not extensive, but looking at the application and the measure proposed, he exclaimed—so it has been reported—'I will not sign a measure which is directed against my American friends.' (Later on in the late sixties an anti-dumping duty of 42 per cent on polyethylene imports from the United States was imposed by the European Commission.)

What does this story tell us?

Perhaps it is that solidarity could be one way to avoid conflicts. But there might be other and even better tools nowadays to develop a real transatlantic partnership and marketplace in political and economic terms. The decision of Chancellor Adenauer regarding polyethylene was based on a strong North Atlantic foreign (or security) policy concept at a time when the Iron Curtain divided Europe. But the climate has changed, and European integration has moved forward, to the point that the European Union will have at least five new members in central and eastern Europe by the year 2005. Moreover, NATO was expanded by the admission of the Czech Republic, Hungary, and Poland.

The Transatlantic Agenda signed in December 1995 at the EU–US Summit in Madrid seems to be a better way to stabilize and enhance the relationship between the United States and the European Union over time. Common goals were identified, such as sustaining growth and creating and preserving peace worldwide. The TABD is part of that process and I would like to repeat what Juergen Strube, CEO of BASF and the first European co-chairman of the TABD, said in Seville in November 1995: 'Transatlantic economic partnership without political partnership will not survive for long, but economic cooperation and integration is one of the best foundations for political partnership between the European Union and the United States of America.'

This Transatlantic Business Dialogue originated from a proposal of the late US Secretary of Commerce, Ron Brown. Secretary Brown concluded that business leaders needed to get actively involved in the trade policy-making process. The TABD has developed significantly over the last three and a half years, for four major reasons.

First, the TABD is a unique form of government–business relationship. There is direct involvement of CEOs in the United States and the European Union who share the goal to reduce and, eventually, to remove the remaining barriers to trade and investment between the United States and the European Union.

Second, the TABD does not deal with specific business opportunities or investment plans. It is a macro- and not a micro-economic exercise on which business people embark.

Third, TABD is not a negotiating forum. It is a process involving four parties: US business, EU business, and the two administrations on both sides of the Atlantic. The business side discusses and agrees on common positions on certain issues. The tedious preparation work is done by five issue groups, one on Standards and Regulatory Policy, one on Business Facilitation, one on Global Issues, one on Small and Medium-Sized Enterprises, and one on Electronic Commerce. The TABD presents its recommendations to the administrations. The negotiations then take place between the two governments. I can assure you that the joint recommendations of the two business communities put some pressure on the governments to proceed.

Fourth, there is the commitment of all people involved in the process, even though the TABD does not have either a formal structure or an official secretariat, strengthened by a clear focus on results. Just to give you an example: the TABD developed a 'scorecard', a tool for analysis whereby each sector and issue group measures the progress and the expected date of the implementation of its various recommendations.

Meanwhile, the creation of a US-government interagency group on the implementation of TABD recommendations and a similar procedure in the European Commission give support to their efficient implementation. About one-third of the TABD recommendations have already led to concrete action of the governments. Additionally, a substantial amount is currently under active discussion. The most visible achievement in the framework of US–EU regulatory cooperation influenced by the TABD is the series of Mutual Recognition Agreements, which entered into force on 1 December 1998. The MRAs cover goods with a value of approximately US$50 billion in two-way-trade in the areas of telecommunication and information technology equipment, electrical and electronic products, pharmaceutical products and medical devices, and recreational marine craft.

II. THE SPECIFIC INTEREST OF THE CHEMICAL INDUSTRY

Why is transatlantic partnership a key issue for the chemical industry? Let me give you some figures—most of them for 1997—which explain the specific interest of the chemical industry in the TABD:

1. The transatlantic chemical markets (by sales) are huge.
   USA: US$400 billion (27 per cent of global sales);
   Western Europe: US$470 billion (33 per cent of global sales).
2. On both sides of the Atlantic chemicals represent 2 per cent of GDP and 10 per cent of the industrial sector.
3. Trade volumes between the United States and Europe are substantial. Total exports (1997):
   European Union to United States and vice versa: US$160 billion;
   and chemicals (1997) represent 10 to 15 per cent of bilateral exports (both ways).
4. Transatlantic foreign direct investment (FDI) is a key element of partnership all industries (1996):
   FDI of European companies in the United States: US$350 billion;
   FDI of American companies in the European Union: US$330 billion.
   European chemical FDI in the United States: US$60 billion equivalent to 390,000 jobs.
   US chemical FDI in Europe: US$40 billion equivalent to 300,000 jobs.

The chemical industry strives for global efficiency and therefore strongly supports all initiatives that promise to cut cost, reduce red tape, remove non-tariff trade barriers, and shorten innovation times. What does the chemical industry expect from the TABD process?

Above all, the removal of non-tariff barriers to chemicals trade.

Chemicals are among the most regulated products, and non-tariff barriers have become a significant impediment to trade. Take the registration for a new crop-protection active ingredient in Europe as an example. The information required by the authorities equals 2 tons of paper work. Every European country insists on separate sets of registration forms.

The list of unnecessary and inefficient testing measures for new product introduction is long on both sides of the Atlantic. Therefore we need:

- increased and faster introduction of product innovations;
- cost reduction by cutting red tape;
- avoidance of duplicate testing (e.g. animal tests);
- setting standards (EU–US) to avoid or reduce third countries non-tariff barriers to trade and to establish global standards.

Our vision is: 'approved once, accepted everywhere'. For industrial chemicals the aforementioned objectives can only be achieved through a number of regulatory modifications on both sides of the Atlantic. The necessary regulatory modifications involve Mutual Recognition Agreements on the acceptance of health and environmental data, some regulatory convergence and ultimately an equivalence agreement on new chemical-notification requirements.

Allow me to give you a simple example. When you compare the environmental, health, and safety protection laws of the European Union and the United States, you will find that the level of protection is comparable. Nevertheless, when you break down this comparison to individual regulations you will see remarkable differences, which create heterogeneous standards and duplicative regulatory requirements on both sides of the Atlantic. This places a heavy burden on trade, in particular with chemicals. Such differences provide no value-added protection to workers, consumers, and the environment, but increase the cost to the producer and, ultimately, to the consumer. From the business perspective, we consider it therefore legitimate to pursue administrative and legislative convergence, in particular in those areas where the purpose of the law, namely to achieve a high level of protection, is the same.

In view of the vast differences in the regulatory schemes in Europe and the United States, a step-by-step process has been suggested, starting with regulatory modifications for R & D and low risk chemicals, i.e. catalysts, process intermediates, and polymers. A long-term objective is to enhance understanding and acceptance of methods used for hazard and risk-assessment which hopefully will reduce differing conclusions which now lead to trade barriers.

As you can imagine, the regulatory authorities are less keen than industry to follow-up these proposals. Nevertheless, a joint industry/agency working group has been established and is meeting regularly—and the situation so far looks promising.

It is needless to say that a prerequisite for success is joint EU–US industry proposals which need to be forwarded with one voice. Furthermore, it is very important to note that having developed the agreements between the European Union and the United States, the underlying concept is expected to be the driving force towards achieving a global standard. This would enhance the ability to market chemical products worldwide with minimal disruption yet also with sufficient protection of man and the environment.

During the TABD Meeting held in Charlotte at the end of 1998, the chemical industry reviewed the status of its 1997 TABD recommendations and outlined a work-plan to advance its recommendations. The primary focus is on the modification of the current systems of new chemicals introduction which include R & D chemicals, low-risk chemicals, and polymers.

The following example of R & D work on new chemical substances will illustrate why this issue has to be tackled first: in the United States, under the Toxic Organic Substances Control Act, R & D can be conducted on new substances without notification, as long as specified provisions are followed. In the European Union, however, when collaborating with third parties, R & D is constrained by both volume and time limits. Thus, assume a chemical company in the United States plans a research project with its European subsidiary and wants to ship a little more than one ton of a new chemical to Europe for scientific-oriented R & D. The stipulations of the European Dangerous Substances Directive would not allow that without a notification prior to introducing the substance to the European Union. Such a notification would take about a year for testing and paperwork, and it would cost about US$200,000. It goes without saying that such regulatory framework does not encourage transatlantic R & D cooperation at all.

In a global society where information becomes available everywhere simultaneously the customer does not understand and tolerate slower introduction of products in different countries. Take Viagra as an example. It has been approved once—and accepted (almost) everywhere, even though the drug does not have official registration in all the countries in which it is used. Nevertheless, the market pull is strong enough to overcome legal as well as price barriers. We can smile about this success story but how would we react if it was a drug against Aids or cancer? It would be difficult to communicate to the public why so much time has to elapse over approval issues such as synthesis methods, good manufacturing practices at production facilities, or packaging information. Viagra pills are reported to be sold one by one without packaging.

III. OUTLOOK

Although all these hurdles caused by non-tariff barriers to chemicals trade seem to be high, so too are the rewards from knocking them down, the sooner the better. We would all gain from this success: the patient, in receiving innovative medicines earlier; the health authorities, in saving resources by avoiding duplication; and—last but not least—the industry, in gaining rapid access to attractive markets and return on investment without unnecessary delay.

The TABD can provide a helpful platform also in resolving upcoming trade conflicts. Examples are the discussion about the Fastener Quality Act, cyberspace transactions, or specified risk materials related to the mad-cow-disease case. Moreover, the failure of OECD negotiators to conclude a multilateral agreement on foreign direct investment (MAI) shows that economic partnership needs constant support, like that given through the TABD, and takes a lot of time.

We are sure that the TABD can help to foster transatlantic partnership for mutual benefit. Not only the industry on both sides of the Atlantic but also customers, employees, and the societies in general will share the fruits of the economic success and growth that this partnership will stimulate.

Part II

Globalization and transatlantic regulatory cooperation

The locational and institutional embeddedness of the global economy

Saskia Sassen*

The geography of economic globalization is strategic rather than all-encompassing and this is especially so when it comes to the managing, coordinating, servicing, and financing of global economic operations. The fact that it is strategic is significant for a discussion about the possibilities of its regulation and governance. There are sites in this strategic geography where the density of economic transactions and the intensity of regulatory efforts come together in complex, often novel, configurations. Two of these sites are the focus of this contribution. They are foreign direct investment, which mostly consists of cross-border mergers and acquisitions, and the global capital market, undoubtedly the dominant force in the global economy today. Along with trade, they are at the heart of the structural changes constitutive of globalization and the efforts to regulate it. These two processes also make evident the enormous weight of the North Atlantic region in the global economy.

Both foreign direct investment and the global capital market raise specific organizational and regulatory issues. There has been an enormous increase in the complexity of management, coordination, servicing, and financing for firms operating worldwide networks of factories, service outlets, and/or offices, and for firms operating in cross-border financial markets. For reasons that I discuss in Part One (I) of this contribution, this has brought about a sharp growth in command and control functions, and their concentration in a cross-border network of major financial and business centres. This in turn contributes to the formation of a strategic geography for the management of globalization. Nowhere is this as evident as in the structure of the global capital market and the network of financial centres within which it is located and governed.

Each of these also is at the heart of a variety of regulatory initiatives discussed in Part Two (II) of the paper. The growth of foreign direct investment has generated a renewed concern over questions of extraterritoriality and competition policy, including the regulation of cross-border mergers. The growth of the global capital market in turn has brought with

* This contribution is based on the author's multi-year project on Governance and Accountability in the Global Economy. The author thanks the various funders who have supported the research.

it specific efforts to develop the elements of an architecture for its international governance: international securities regulation, new international standards for accounting and financial reporting, and various EU interventions. Overall, each has tended to be ensconced in fairly distinct regulatory frameworks: foreign direct investment in antitrust law and competition policy, and global finance in national regulatory frameworks for banking and finance. It is quite possible that globalization may have the effect of blurring the boundaries between these two regulatory worlds.

Further, while this strategic geography of globalization[1] is partly embedded in national territories, this does not necessarily mean that existing national regulatory frameworks can regulate those functions.[2] In my current research project, I am finding that the types and locations of regulatory functions have shifted increasingly from national frameworks towards a set of emerging or newly invigorated cross-border regulatory networks, new or newly invigorated forms of private authority, and an array of standards to organize world trade and global finance.[3] Specialized, often semi-autonomous regulatory agencies and the specialized cross-border networks they are forming are taking over functions once enclosed in legal frameworks. Private institutions, such as international commercial arbitration, are taking over from national public institutions, such as courts of justice. And standards are replacing the rules of international law.

Finally, the empirical patterns of foreign direct investment and global finance show the great extent to which their centres of gravity lie in the North Atlantic region.[4] The northern transatlantic economic system (particularly the links among the European Union, the United States, and Canada) represents the major concentration of processes of economic globalization in the world today. This holds whether one looks at foreign direct investment flows generally, at cross-border mergers and acquisitions in particular, at overall financial flows, or at the new strategic alliances among financial centres. This region accounts for two-thirds of worldwide stock market capitalization, 60 per cent of inward foreign

---

[1] I develop this in *The Global City: New York, London, Tokyo* (new updated edition, Princeton, NJ: Princeton University Press, 2000).

[2] See, e.g. Kris Olds, Peter Dicken, Philip F. Kelly, Lilly Kong, Henry Wai-Chung Yeung (eds), *Globalization and the Asian Pacific: Contested Territories* (London: Routledge, 1999); David Smith, D. Solinger, and S. Topik (eds), *States and Sovereignty in the Global Economy* (London: Routledge, 1999); Alfred C. Aman, Jr., 'The Globalizing State: A Future-Oriented Perspective on the Public/Private Distinction, Federalism, and Democracy', *Vanderbilt Journal of Transnational Law*, vol. 31, no. 4 (1998), 769–870; Geoffrey Garrett, 'Global Markets and National Politics: Collision Course or Virtuous Circle', *International Organization*, vol. 52, no. 4 (1998), 787–824.

[3] Saskia Sassen, 'Denationalized State Agendas and Privatized Norm-Making', Inaugural Lecture, Division of Social Sciences, University of Chicago (28 Apr. 1999). (On file with author.)

[4] See OECD, various years; UN Conference on Trade and Development 1998; various years.

investment stock and 76 per cent of outward stock, 60 per cent of world-wide sales in cross-border mergers and acquisitions (M & As), and 80 per cent of purchases in such M & As. There are other major regions in the global economy: Japan, South-East Asia, Latin America. But except for some of the absolute levels of capital resources in Japan, they are dwarfed by the weight of the northern transatlantic system.

This heavy concentration in the volume and value of cross-border trans-actions raises a number of questions. One concerns its features, and more specifically the extent to which there is interdependence and in that sense the elements of a cross-border economic system. The weight of these transatlantic links needs to be considered against the weight of established zones of influence for each of the major powers—particularly the Western Hemisphere in the case of the United States, and Africa, Central Europe and East Europe for the European Union.

If there is considerable interdependence in the northern transatlantic system then the question of regulation and governance is likely to be of a different sort than it would be if globalization for each of these major regions meant in practice strengthening its ties and presence in its respec-tive zones of influence. The US and individual EU members have long had often intense economic transactions with their zones of influence. Some of these have been reinvigorated in the new economic policy context of open-ing to foreign investment, privatization, and trade and financial deregula-tion.

In my reading of the evidence, both the relations with their respective zones of influence and the relations within the northern transatlantic sys-tem have changed. We are seeing the consolidation of a transnational eco-nomic system that has its centre of gravity in the North Atlantic system both in terms of the intensity and value of transactions and in terms of the emerging system of rules and standards. This system is articulated with a growing network of sites for investment, trade, and financial transactions in the rest of the world. It is through this incorporation in a hierarchical global network that has its centre in the North Atlantic that a region's rela-tions with its zones of influence are now constituted. Thus, while the United States is still a dominant force in Latin America, several European countries have become major investors in Latin America, on a scale far sur-passing past trends. And while several EU countries have become leaders in investment in Central and Eastern Europe, US firms are playing a role they never played before.

What we are seeing today is a new grid of economic transactions super-imposed on the old geo-economic patterns. The latter persist to variable extents, but they are increasingly submerged under this new cross-border grid, amounting to a new, though partial, geo-economics. In my own research I have found that these new configurations are particularly evi-dent in the organization of global finance and, though to a lesser extent, in direct foreign investment, especially cross-border mergers and acquisitions. I return to this in later sections.

In my view, also, the fact of systemic conditions in the new geo-economics is a significant factor for the question of regulation. The orders of magnitude and the intensity of transactions in the North Atlantic system facilitate the formation of standards even in the context of what are, relatively speaking, strong differences between the United States and Continental Europe in their legal, accounting, antitrust, and other rules. It is clear that even though these two regions have more in common with each other than with much of the rest of the world, these differences matter when it comes to the creation of cross-border standards. However, the fact of (broadly speaking) shared western standards and norms, in combination with enormous economic weight, has facilitated the circulation and imposition of US and European standards and rules on transactions involving firms from other parts of the world. There is a sort of globalization of western standards. Much has been said about the dominance of US standards and rules, but European Union standards are also evident, for instance in the new antitrust rules being developed in Central and Eastern Europe. I also return to these issues later.

In the ensuing sections, I develop various matters I have touched on in this introduction. The organizing effort is to map the locational and institutional embeddedness of foreign direct investment and of the global capital market. In so doing, the paper also seeks to signal that there might be greater potential for governmental participation in the governance of the global economy than much current commentary on globalization allows for, given its emphasis on hypermobility and telecommunications. But the manner of this participation may well be quite different from long-established forms. Indeed, we may be seeing instances where the gap between these older established conceptions and actual global dynamics—particularly in the financial markets—is making possible the emergence of a distinct zone for transactions and governance mechanisms, possibly quite autonomously from existing governmental frameworks. One of the challenges then would be to determine to what extent this is a zone which really exists beyond the boundaries of state authority or is simply a default option in view of the absence of adequate governmental frameworks or the difficulty of harmonizing government standards and rules. This contribution does not answer all these questions. It is in this regard more of a mapping of a broader conceptual landscape within which to understand economic globalization and regulation, particularly in the context of the North Atlantic region.

A. Worldwide networks and central command functions

There are, clearly, strong dispersal trends contained in the patterns of foreign investment and capital flows generally: the off-shoring of factories, the expansion of global networks of affiliates and subsidiaries, and the formation of global financial markets with a growing number of participating countries. What is left out of this picture is the other half of the story. This worldwide geographic dispersal of factories and service outlets takes place as part of highly integrated corporate structures with strong tendencies towards concentration in control and profit appropriation. Elsewhere, I have shown that when the geographic dispersal of factories, offices, and service outlets through cross-border investment takes place as part of integrated corporate systems, there is also a growth in central functions; we can see a parallel trend with financial firms and markets.[5] One way of saying this is that the more globalized firms and markets become, the more their central functions grow—in importance, in complexity, in number of transactions.[6] The North Atlantic system is the site for most of the strategic management and coordination functions of the new global economic system.

We can make this more concrete by considering some of the staggering figures involved in this worldwide dispersal, and imagining what this might entail in terms of coordination and management for parent headquarters. For instance, consider the fact that by 2000 firms had over half a million foreign affiliates worldwide; most of these belong to firms from North America and Western Europe.[7] There has been a greater growth in foreign sales through affiliates than through direct exports: the foreign sales through affiliates were over US$11 trillion in 1999, and through worldwide exports of goods and services US$8 trillion. This has of course also fed the intra-firm share of so-called free cross-border trade. The transnationality index of the largest transnational firms in the world shows that many of the major firms from the United States and Western

[5] Saskia Sassen, 'Global Financial Centers', *Foreign Affairs*, vol. 78, no. I (1999), 76–87.

[6] This process of corporate integration should not be confused with vertical integration as conventionally defined. See also Gary Gereffi on commodity chains ('Global Production Systems and Third World Development', in Barbara Stallings (ed.), *Global Change, Regional Response: The New International Context of Development* (Cambridge: Cambridge University Press, 1995), 100–42) and Porter's value-added chains (*The Competitive Advantage of Nations* (New York: Free Press, 1995)), two constructs that further illustrate the difference between corporate integration at a world scale and vertical integration as conventionally defined.

[7] I should note here that affiliates are but one form of operating overseas, and hence their number under-represents the dispersal of a firm's operations. There are today multiple forms, ranging from new temporary partnerships to older types of subcontracting and contracting (see e.g. John Dunning, *Alliance Capitalism and Global Business* (London and New York: Routledge, 1997)).

Europe have over half of their assets, sales, and workforces outside their home countries. Together these types of evidence provide a picture of this combination of dispersal and the growth of central functions. (In a later section, I discuss the global network of financial centres, which is yet another instance of this dynamic.) All of this represents a massive task of coordination and management for the firms involved. Let me clarify at the outset that much of this has been going on for a long time but has accelerated over the last two decades. Secondly, this dispersal does not proceed under a single organizational form; rather, behind these general figures lie many different organizational forms, hierarchies of control and degrees of autonomy.

Of importance to the analysis here is the dynamic that connects the dispersal of economic activities with the ongoing weight and often the growth of central functions. In terms of sovereignty and globalization, this means that an interpretation of the impact of globalization as creating a space economy that extends beyond the regulatory capacity of a single state is only half the story; the other half is that these central functions are disproportionately concentrated in the national territories of the highly developed countries.

I should perhaps clarify that by central functions I do not mean only top-level headquarters; I am referring to all the top-level financial, legal, accounting, managerial, executive, and planning functions necessary to run a corporate organization operating in more than one country, and increasingly in several countries. These central functions are partly embedded in headquarters, but also in good part in what has been called the corporate services complex, that is, in the network of financial, legal, accounting, and advertising firms that handle the complexities of operating in more than one national legal system, national accounting system, advertising culture, etc., and do so under conditions of rapid innovation in all these fields. Such services have become so specialized and complex that headquarters increasingly buy them from specialized firms rather than producing them in-house. These agglomerations of firms producing central functions for the management and coordination of global economic systems are disproportionately concentrated in the highly developed countries—particularly, though not exclusively, in the kinds of cities I call global cities, for example, New York, Paris, and Amsterdam. Such concentrations of functions represent a strategic factor in the organization of the global economy.

One argument I am making here is that it is important to unbundle analytically the fact of strategic functions for the global economy or for global operation, and the overall corporate economy of a country. These global command and control functions are partly embedded in national corporate structures but also constitute a distinct corporate subsector. This subsector can be conceived of as part of a network that connects global cities across the globe.[8] For the purposes of certain kinds of enquiry this distinction may not matter; for the purposes of understanding the global economy, however, it does. And, it seems to me, this distinction also matters for questions of regulation, notably regulation of cross-border activities. If the strategic central functions—both those produced in corporate headquarters and those produced in the specialized corporate services sector—are located in a network of major financial and business centres, the question of regulating what amounts to a key part of the global economy is different from what it would be if the strategic management and coordination functions were as distributed geographically as are factories, service outlets, and affiliates. However, the type of regulation involved is evolving towards multiple specialized and cross-border governance systems rather than overarching state-centric national frameworks.[9]

Another current instance of this negotiation between a transnational process or dynamic and a national territory is that of the global financial markets. The orders of magnitude of these transactions have risen sharply, as illustrated by the US$65 trillion in traded derivatives in 1999 in the global capital market, a major component of the global economy. These transactions are partly embedded in telecommunications systems that make possible the instantaneous transmission of money and information around the globe, a feature that has received much attention. But the other half of the story is the extent to which the global financial markets are located in particular cities in the highly developed countries; indeed, the degrees of concentration are unexpectedly high, a subject I discuss empirically in a later section.

Stock markets worldwide have become globally integrated. Besides deregulation during the 1980s in all the major European and North American markets, the late 1980s and early 1990s saw the addition of such markets as Buenos Aires, São Paulo, Bangkok, and Taipei. The integration of a growing number of stock markets has contributed to raising the capital that can be mobilized through stock markets. Worldwide market value reached US$22 trillion dollars in 1999. This globally integrated stock market, which makes possible the circulation of publicly listed shares

---

[8] In this sense, global cities are different from the old capitals of erstwhile empires, in that they are a function of cross-border networks rather than simply the most powerful city of an empire. There is, in my conceptualization, no such entity as a single global city as there could be a single capital of an empire; the category global city only makes sense as a component of a global network of strategic sites. The corporate subsector which contains the global command and control functions is partly embedded in this network.

[9] We are seeing the formation of an economic complex with a valorization dynamic that has properties clearly distinguishing it from other economic complexes whose valorization dynamic is far more articulated with the public economic functions of the state, the quintessential example being Fordist manufacturing. Global markets in finance and advanced services partly operate through a 'regulatory' umbrella that is not state-centred but market-centred. This in turn raises a question of control linked to the currently inadequate capacities to govern transactions in electronic space.

around the globe in seconds, is embedded in a grid of very material, physical, strategic places—that is, cities belonging to national territories.

In brief, the specific forms assumed by globalization over the last decade have created particular organizational requirements. The emergence of global markets for finance and specialized services, as well as the growth of investment as a major type of international transaction, have contributed to the expansion in command functions and in the demand for specialized services for firms.[10]

The next section situates the North Atlantic region in terms of the empirical evidence on foreign direct investment, with particular attention to cross-border mergers and acquisitions.

B. Inward and outward FDI stock and flows in the North Atlantic

The evidence on foreign direct investment (henceforth FDI) shows us rather clearly that Western Europe and the United States account for a large proportion of global flows. The orders of magnitude, though subject to fluctuations and country-specific patterns, are overall high and have grown over the last decade. Global FDI has continued to grow, including to the countries of the Asian financial crisis.[11] Deregulation, demonopolization, privatization, and the reform of trade and foreign investment have been central to the high levels of international direct investment in the 1990s.[12] In many smaller OECD countries and in less-developed coun-

---

[10] A central proposition here, developed at length in my work, is that we cannot take the existence of a global economic system as a given, but rather need to examine the particular ways in which the conditions for economic globalization are produced. This requires examining not only communication capacities and the power of multinationals, but also the infrastructure of facilities and work processes necessary for the implementation of global economic systems, including the production of those inputs that constitute the capability for global control and the infrastructure of jobs involved in this production. The emphasis shifts to the *practice* of global control: the work of producing and reproducing the organization and management of a global production system and a global marketplace for finance, both under conditions of economic concentration. Such an emphasis also brings with it a strong focus on regulatory questions. The recovery of place and work shows us that global processes can be studied in great empirical detail.

[11] As I will argue in the section on financial centres, this may well be a type of investment that is related to the crisis—not just because lower prices may make these investments more attractive, but also because of a loss of control by national elites over their economies, control that these elites had maintained even as foreign capital poured in during the period of high growth in the 1970s and 1980s. (Cf. my notion of denationalization as one mechanism we are seeing today in the formation of a global economic system. Saskia Sassen, *Losing Control? Sovereignty in an Age of Globalization*, The 1995 Columbia University Leonard Hastings Schoff Memorial Lectures (New York: Columbia University Press, 1996), chs. 1 and 2.

[12] Global FDI trends are to some extent self-perpetuating. When TNCs expand operations, other service firms follow to service them. Also, when one major firm invests abroad, competitors often follow. The global expansion of telecommunications and financial firms also reduces the risks and costs of operating abroad for industrial and commercial firms; these firms in turn create business for financial and telecommunications firms.

tries, it is privatization of public sector firms which has been the main reason and target for inward FDI in recent years.[13]

Inward and outward FDI in OECD countries reached unprecedented levels in 1997 and continued to grow in 1998. (See Table 1.) Firms from OECD countries invested US$355 billion abroad in 1997, or 19 per cent more than in 1996; they received over US$255 billion, for a 16 per cent increase over 1996. The weight of the North Atlantic system in worldwide stock and flows is quite clear. In 1997, the latest year for which comprehensive figures are available at the time of writing, Western Europe and the United States together accounted for over 60 per cent of worldwide inward FDI stock and almost 76 per cent of outward FDI stock. They account, then, for an enormous share of worldwide FDI stock.[14] The United States and the UK are the leading home and host countries in the world, representing more than half of all inflows and outflows of OECD countries. And both had record flows in 1997.

As is well known, most outward FDI flows in the European Union are among countries of the Union. European countries are, to a large extent, globalizing through FDI within the European Union and, secondly, within the North Atlantic system. Strategic positioning is more focused on the intra-European situation. Further, we see a predominant orientation to other developed countries in EU outward investment. In 1995 almost two-thirds of outward EU FDI stock was held by five countries: the United States, Switzerland, Australia, Canada, and Japan.

The 1997 performance of the European Union as a whole in attracting FDI obscures sharp differences among countries. For instance, inflows fell in some countries: most sharply in France by US$3.7 billion, in Austria by US$2.1 billion, and in Belgium and Luxembourg by US$1.6 billion. On the other hand, the United Kingdom received a sharply increased level of FDI inflows; its share in overall EU FDI inflows rose from 28 per cent in 1996 to 34 per cent in 1997.[15]

The United States was the second largest recipient of FDI after the EU. If intra-European FDI is netted out, then the United States is the single most important recipient during most of the years from 1986 to 1996. Like the EU countries, the United States still invests more in developed countries, even though we can see a growing and complex use of less-developed countries in the international organization of production of its

---

[13] Growing FDI by US firms in South Africa, Brazil, and Mexico is related to large-scale privatizations in those countries.

[14] Japan had record inflow and outflow increases for the fifth year. Germany had high outflows but negative inflows; foreign firms withdrew a share of their capital, as they had done in 1996. But, interestingly, US investment in Germany grew more than threefold in 1997.

[15] There is much support for UK economic policies in the investment community; for instance, according to the World Economic Forum (1997 meeting), the United Kingdom ranked at the top as a desirable investment location.

Table 1: Foreign direct investment flows by host region (millions USD and percentage) 1986–1987

| Region | FDI inflows | | | FDI outflows | |
	1986–1991 (Annual avg.)	1997	% of world totals in 1997	1986–1991 (Annual avg.)	1997	% of world totals in 1997
North Atlantic[1]	121144	213852	53.4	131646	323111	89.9
Latin America and the Caribbean[2]	9460	56138	14.0	1305	9097	2.5
South, East and South-East Asia[3]	15135	82411	20.6	8315	50157	14.0
World	159331	400486		180510	359236	

Notes: [1] North Atlantic region includes all countries in the European Union, Iceland, Norway, Switzerland, Gibraltar, Canada, and the United States. [2] and [3], please refer to source for detailed listing of all countries included.

Source: UNCTAD, World Investment Report 1998, Annex B, pp. 361–71.

companies. The United States and the EU countries use the differences between developed and less-developed countries in their strategies.

One significant difference from most other developed countries is that US outward FDI stock is a considerably smaller share of GDP (10 per cent); similarly with FDI flows as a percentage of gross fixed capital formation. This large-country bias, shared also by Japan, signals that the United States is unlikely ever to reach the ratios of countries such as the Netherlands and the UK. In 1995 outward EU FDI stocks were respectively 50 and 64 per cent of the total outward FDI stocks of the Netherlands and the United Kingdom, far higher than for the United States. The increase in the outward FDI stock/GDP ratio since 1980 has been relatively small for the United States compared to the world as a whole.

1. Cross-border mergers and acquisitions

Cross-border M & As dominate global FDI flows. OECD countries account for 89 per cent of purchases and 72 per cent of sales. A growing number of firms opt for mergers as a mode of overseas expansion or consolidation. In 1997 total cross-border acquisitions reached $341 billion, or 20 per cent more than in 1996 in terms of transaction value—though not in the numbers of such transactions—suggesting that the size of mergers is growing. Acquisitions represented 90 per cent of total FDI in the United States in 1996. In 1998 M & As in the North Atlantic reached US$256.5 billion, up from US$69.4 billion in 1995.

Western Europe has seen a sharp growth in such transactions. Cross-border M & As reached US$118 billion, 30 per cent higher than in 1996. British firms were the main target for foreign buyers, in spite of the strong pound. Almost half of the sales in Western Europe involved UK firms. Switzerland was the most active buyer in Europe, and second only to the United States at the global level.

In 1997 Western Europe saw 2,350 cases of sales, for a value of US$118 billion, representing 35 per cent of the worldwide value of such sales. At the same time it saw 2,620 purchases, for a value of US$168 billion or 49 per cent of worldwide purchases. Worldwide cases numbered 5,726, for a value of US$341 billion. North America (United States, Canada, and Mexico) had 25 per cent of sales and 31 per cent of purchases in value. The North Atlantic region then accounts for a majority of cross-border M & As worldwide. (See Tables 2 and 3.)

2. Transnationality index of largest transnational corporations (TNCs)

The transnationality index is an average based on ratios of the share that *foreign* sales, assets, and employment represent in a firm's total of each. If we consider the world's top 100 transnational corporations (TNCs) in 1997, the European Union has forty-eight of these firms and the United States twenty-eight; many of the remaining are from Japan. (See Table 4.)

Table 2: Cross-border mergers and acquisitions by region, 1997 (billions USD, percent)

Region	Sales			Purchases		
	Cases	Value	Share	Cases	Value	Share
Western Europe	2350	118	35	2620	168	49
North America[1]	1305	86	25	2111	107	31
Asia	830	34	11	821	46	13
Japan, Australia, NZL	77	2	1	390	18	5
ASEAN	264	13	4	174	10	3
Other Asia[2]	489	19	6	257	18	5
South America	330	32	9	38	4	1
Central, Eastern Europe	154	5	1	6	3	0
Total	5726	341	100	5726	341	100

Notes: [1] USA, Canada, Mexico; [2] Chinese Taipei, Hong Kong (China), Republic of Korea, China

Source: OECD, Financial Market Trends, no. 70, 1998, p. 101. Based on KMPG Corporate Finance, 1997.

Table 3: Top 15 buyer and seller countries in global mergers and acquisitions, 1997 (billions, USD)

Country	Buyers		Country	Sellers	
	Deals	Value		Deals	Value
United States	1655	81.8	United States	937	65.1
Switzerland	170	38.7	United Kingdom	551	55.4
United Kingdom	642	32.4	Germany	333	19.3
Canada	444	24.3	France	387	13.9
France	388	21.1	Australia	139	12.7
Netherlands	316	20.7	Brazil	131	12.6
Germany	324	16.0	Canada	298	11.0
Spain	85	13.0	China	379	9.1
Japan	313	11.7	Italy	179	8.8
Australia	80	9.9	Netherlands	131	8.0
Republic of Korea	77	6.7	Mexico	70	6.7
Sweden	133	6.2	Venezuela	21	6.4
Hong Kong (China)	127	5.5	Belgium	58	6.2
			Spain	142	6.2
Singapore	71	4.8	Hong Kong (China)	71	5.9
China	28	4.6			

Source: OECD, Financial Market Trends, no. 70, 1998, p. 101. Based on KMPG Corporate Finance, 1997.

Table 4: The world's top 25 TNCs ranked by transnationality (percentage and rank) 1997

Trans. index rank	Trans. Index (%)	Foreign assets rank	Corporation	Country	Industry
1	97.3	34	Seagram Company	Canada	Beverages
2	96.1	12	Asea Brown Boveri (ABB)	Switzerland/Sweden	Electrical equipment
3	95.3	11	Nestlé SA	Switzerland	Food
4	94.9	50	Thomson Corporation	Canada	Printing and publishing
5	92.2	83	Solvay SA	Belgium	Chemicals/pharm.
6	89.8	56	Holderbank Financière	Switzerland	Construction materials
7	88.7	62	Electrolux AB	Sweden	Electrical appliances
8	87.1	18	Unilever	Netherlands/United Kingdom	Food
9	87.0	21	Roche Holding AG	Switzerland	Pharmaceuticals
10	84.9	52	Michelin	France	Rubber & plastics
11	84.9	20	Philips Electronics N.V.	Netherlands	Electronics
12	81.7	92	Kvaerner ASA	Norway	Shipbuilding/engineering
13	80.6	85	Northern Telecom	Canada	Telecommunications
14	79.9	14	Bayer AG	Germany	Chemicals
15	78.1	49	Cable and Wireless Plc	United Kingdom	Telecommunications
16	77.9	70	Glaxo Wellcome Plc	United Kingdom	Pharmaceuticals
17	76.4	99	Eridania Beghin-Say SA	France	Food
18	76.2	69	Grand Metropolitan	United Kingdom	Food/beverages
19	75.8	25	Total SA	France	Petroleum expl./ref./dist.
20	75.2	26	Novartis	Switzerland	Pharmaceuticals/chem.
21	73.2	79	Akzo Nobel N.V.	Netherlands	Chemicals
22	72.7	4	Exxon Corporation	United States	Petroleum expl./ref./dist.
23	72.5	55	Ericsson LM	Sweden	Electronics
24	71.8	86	Petrofina SA	Belgium	Petroleum expl./ref./dist.
25	71.6	75	Hanson Plc	United Kingdom	Building material

Source: UNCTAD, *World Investment Report 1998: Trends and Determinants*, pp. 36–8.

Table 5: Regional distribution of the world's top 100 TNCs—1997

	Number of Companies
North Atlantic	80
Specific countries:	
Australia	2
Belgium	2
Canada	4
France	11
Germany	9
Italy	3
Netherlands	2
Netherlands/UK	1
Norway	1
Sweden	3
Switzerland	4
Switzerland/Sweden	1
United Kingdom	7
UK/Australia	1
UK/Netherlands	1
United States	28
Japan	18
Other[1]	2
Total	100

Note: [1] Includes the Republic of Korea and Venezuela
Source: UNCTAD, *World Investment Report 1998: Trends and Determinants*, pp. 36–8.

Thus together, the European Union and the United States account for over two-thirds of the world's 100 largest TNCs. The United States, the UK, France, Germany, and Japan together account for three-quarters of these 100 firms in 1997; this has been roughly the case since 1990. The largest single concentrations in the EU are in France with fourteen and in the UK with twelve.

Most of the US and EU TNCs in this top 100 list have very high levels of foreign assets as a percentage of total assets: for instance, 51 per cent for IBM, 55 per cent for Volkswagen Group, 91 per cent for Nestlé, 96 per cent for Asea Brown Boveri, 62 per cent for Elf Aquitaine, 91 per cent for Bayer, 79 per cent for Hoechst, 77 per cent for Philips Electronics, 43 per cent for Siemens, 45 per cent for Renault, 98 per cent for Seagram, 67 per cent for Rhone-Poulenc, 59 per cent for BMW, 69 per cent for Ferruzi/Montedison,

97 per cent for Thomson, 85 per cent for Michelin, 71 per cent for Ericsson, 58 per cent for Exxon, 85 per cent for Unilever, 55 per cent for McDonalds, 68 per cent for CocaCola, and so on. The foreign element in a firm's total employment is often even higher.[16]

The average transnationality index for the European Union is 56.7 per cent compared to 38.5 per cent for the US (but 79.2 for Canada). Within the European Union, the index ranges from about 40 per cent for Italy and Germany, to 68 per cent for the Netherlands and the United Kingdom, and over 70 per cent for Sweden. The index has grown for the 100 largest TNCs in the world since it was first used in 1990.

C. The locational and institutional embeddedness of global finance

Foreign direct investment is one of the central dynamics by which firms become global. But the orders of magnitude involved are dwarfed by those of the global capital market. This is illustrated by the size of net assets of investment companies shown in Table 6. The global capital market is increasingly a necessary component of the larger mergers and acquisitions, but its role involves a far broader domain of operation. It has become more important in government debt of all sorts and in the financing of national and global market-oriented firms. Indeed, kinds of debt that were thought to be basically local, such as municipal debt, are now entering the global capital market. Similarly, types of capital thought to be basically national, such as pension funds, are now being invested in the global capital market. In many ways, the expansion and diversification of the global capital market represents a key aspect of the organizational structure of economic globalization. Given my concern in this contribution with the locational and institutional embeddedness of the global economy, one way of examining this market is in terms of the network of financial centres within which and through which it operates.

Since 1980 the total stock of financial assets has increased two and a half times faster than the aggregate GDP of all the rich industrial economies. And the volume of trading in currencies, bonds, and equities has increased about five times faster. The global capital market makes it possible for money to flow to almost anywhere in this integrated network of national markets, regardless of national origin and boundaries. There are countries that are of course not integrated. Iraq and Libya are two prominent examples. There is no comprehensive measure of cross-border capital flows. One partial measure is the total value of derivatives traded (including exchange-based trades and over-the-counter trades); it stood at US$64,525.2 billion for 1998.[17] It is very difficult to establish what the

[16] See OECD, 'Recent Trends in Foreign Direct Investment', *Financial Market Trends*, vol. 70 (June 1998), 109–26, for the full listing.

[17] Page 132 in Bank for International Settlements 1999. *Annual Report*. 69th Annual Report (Basel: Bank for International Settlements).

Table 6: Growth of investment companies (billions USD and percentage)[1] 1987 and 1996

Country	Total net assets		By type of fund, in 1996 as a % of assets				In 1996 as a % of:	
	1987	1996	Money market	Bond	Equity	Balanced	GDP	Market capitalization
United States	770	3539	25	22	49	3	46	15
Japan	305	420	29	45	24	2	9	4
Germany	42	134	16	56	25	3	6	4
France	204	529	45	29	11	14	34	18
Italy	51	129	36	39	17	7	11	5
United Kingdom	68	188	0	5	88	6	16	8
Canada	16	155	15	9	52	14	26	14
Spain	4	136	51	41	3	6	23	14
Netherlands	16	67	10	30	54	6	17	8
Luxembourg	74	352	25	52	18	5	1840	337

Notes: [1] Open-end funds invested in transferable securities and money market instruments.
[2] Excluding money market funds.
[3] 1989.

Source: Bank for International Settlements, *Annual Report for 1997–1998*, p. 30. Based on Fédération Européenne des Fonds et Sociétés d'Investissement, Investment Company Institute, Investment Funds Institute of Canada, International.

actual meaning of this value of the global capital market is; all we know is that it signals that the orders of magnitude involved are on a much higher level than those mobilized in direct foreign investment or in world trade.

Can it grow bigger? Yes, it can. According to some estimates, we have reached only the mid-point of a 50-year process in terms of the full integration of these markets. For instance, figures show that countries with high savings have high domestic investment. Most savings are still invested in the domestic economy. About 15 per cent of the assets of the world's 500 largest institutional portfolios are invested in foreign assets. Some argue that a more integrated capital market would raise this level significantly and hence raise the vulnerability to and dependence on the capital markets. It should be noted that extrapolating the potential for growth from the current level may be somewhat dubious; it may not reflect the potential for capital mobility across borders of a variety of other factors which may be keeping managers from using the option of cross-border investments. The latter may well be an under-used option and it may remain that way no matter what the actual cross-border capacities in the system.

The financial markets are expected to expand even further in relation to the size of the real economy. It is estimated that the total stock of financial assets traded in the global capital markets is equivalent to well over twice the GDP of all OECD countries. The forecast is that this value will rise even more to 80 trillion dollars by the year 2000 to represent three times the aggregate OECD's GDP.

In my view, a crucial issue for understanding the question of regulation and the role of the state in the global capital market is the ongoing embeddedness of the global capital market in a network of financial centres operating not off-shore, but within national states. The North Atlantic system contains an enormous share of the global capital market through its sharp concentration of leading financial centres which manage and control capital originating both in the North Atlantic and in the rest of the world.[18] Two major developments may alter the present configuration: the growth of electronic trading and the growth of the Eurozone. As the system expands through the incorporation of additional centres into this network, the question of regulation also pivots on the existence of dominant standards and rules, i.e. those produced by the economies of the North Atlantic. This section examines some of these issues as they relate to the embeddedness of the global capital market.

---

[18] The role of new regional centres in the global network of financial centres is unclear. Shanghai, Dubai, and a reconstructed Beirut are located in regions that have significant concentrations of capital. To what extent they will concentrate some of the functions that now are executed in the larger centres remains to be seen. See Sassen, *The Global City* (2000), above, n. 1.

The creation of an enormous consolidated capital market in the Eurozone raises serious questions about the feasibility of maintaining the current pattern with as many international financial centres as there are member countries. A second question is whether London's lying outside the Eurozone puts it at a disadvantage, and will cause its decline as a financial centre, with the possible ascendance of Frankfurt as the leading European centre.[19] Further, the Asian financial crisis along with Japan's difficulties, besides spelling trouble for the global financial system as a whole, raises questions about the future of Tokyo and Hong Kong as key centres and hence the possible shift of some of their strategic functions to the North Atlantic. Finally, the rapid growth of electronic trading makes many wonder whether there will be a need for financial centres at all.[20]

The global financial system has reached levels of complexity that require the creation of a cross-border network of financial centres to service the operations of global capital. But this network of financial centres will increasingly differ from earlier versions of the 'international financial system'. In a world of largely closed national financial systems, each country duplicated most of the functions necessary for its economy; collaboration among different national financial markets was often no more than the execution of a given set of operations in each of the countries involved, as in clearing and settlement. With few exceptions, such as the off-shore markets and some of the large banks, the international system consisted of a string of closed domestic systems.

The global integration of markets pushes towards the elimination of various redundant systems and makes collaboration a far more complex matter, one which has the perhaps ironic effect of heightening the importance of leading financial centres. Rather than each country having its own centre for global operations, we are likely to see a leaner system, with fewer strategic centres and more hierarchy. In this context, London and New York with their enormous concentrations of resources and talent will continue to be powerhouses in the global network for the most strategic and complex operations for the system as a whole. They are the leading exporters of financial services and typically part of any major international public offering, whether it is the privatization of British Telecom or of France Telecom. But the Eurozone will spell the end of an era where each member country had a full-fledged financial centre. Very likely is a steep

---

[19] Some of these larger issues have taken on concrete form in the headlines announcing the growing competition between Frankfurt and London. This sense of competition is framed by two events. In May 1997 London's future exchange (LIFFE) had a 70% market share in Europe's most heavily traded contract, which as it happened is the German government bond future. A year later, the German DTB had captured most of the market. Further, this competition is set in a broader battle: electronic vs. floor trading, and London vs. the Eurozone. LIFFE has a trading floor; the DTB (now Deutsche Eurex) is all electronic.

[20] See Sassen, 'Global Financial Centers' (above, n. 5); The Global City (above, n. 1) for a fuller discussion.

hierarchy with Frankfurt at the top and a criss-cross of alliances between Frankfurt and the other major centres, and among the other centres without Frankfurt—the latter a vision initially advanced by the head of the Paris Bourse after the announcement of the London–Frankfurt alliance.

Outside the Eurozone, the 'international financial centres' of many countries around the world will increasingly fulfil gateway functions for the circulation, in and out, of national and foreign capital. The incorporation of a growing number of these financial centres is one form through which the global financial system expands: each of these centres is the nexus between that country's wealth and the global market, and between foreign investors and that country's investment opportunities. The overall sources and destinations of investment thereby grow in number. Gateway functions will become the main mechanism for integration into the global financial market, rather than, say, the production of innovations to package the capital flowing in and out. The complex operation will be executed by the top investment, accounting, and legal services firms, through affiliates or branches located in those cities, direct imports of those services, or some other form of transfer.

These gateways for the global market are also gateways for the dynamics of financial crises: capital can flow out as easily and quickly as it flows in. And what was once thought of as 'national' capital can now as easily join the exodus: for instance, during the Mexico crisis of December 1994, we now know that the first capital to flee the Mexican markets was national, not foreign; and in the flight out of Brazil of an estimated US$1 billion a day by early September 1998, amounting to over US$40 billion for that brief period, not all of it was foreign.

In my view, the globally integrated financial system is not only about competition among countries. We will see an increase in specialized collaborative efforts among these centres. Nobody would really gain from crushing Tokyo or Hong Kong. The ongoing growth of London, New York, or Frankfurt is in part a function of a global network of financial centres. Since its inception, Hong Kong has been a crucial intersection of different worlds, forever a strategic exchange node for firms from China to the rest of the world and from the rest of the world to China, as well as among all the overseas Chinese communties. In a way, only if all investor interest in China would cease could Hong Kong lose this historic role.[21] Today it still has the most sophisticated concentration of advanced services after London, New York, and Frankfurt. As for Tokyo, it will continue to be a crucial cog in the system, given its enormous concentration of

---

[21] Its historic advantage as a nexus between the world and China, and its concentration of state of the art specialized services secure a strategic role for Hong Kong. David Meyer's impressive *Hong Kong as a Global Metropolis: Social Networks of Capital* (Cambridge: Cambridge University Press, 2000) is one of the best explanations of this peculiar Hong Kong advantage as an intermediary for global networks of capital.

financial resources—i.e. US$1 trillion in assets under institutional management and US$10 trillion in savings and similar accounts which are about to be deregulated. But with a difference, and one brought about in good part by the crisis. The 'Wimbledon-effect', as one hears it described in Tokyo, may well take over: the court is ours but the main players and winners are foreigners.[22]

Finally, while electronic networks will grow in number and in scope, in my analysis they will not eliminate the need for financial centres, a subject to which I return below. Rather, they will intensify the networks connecting such centres in strategic or functional alliances, most dramatically illustrated by the link-up, announced in July 1998, but not yet completed by 2000, between the stock exchanges of Frankfurt and London.[23] Such alliances may well evolve into the equivalent of the cross-border mergers and acquisitions of firms. Electronic trading will also give rise to a radically new pattern whereby one market, for instance Frankfurt's Deutsche Eurex, can operate on screens in many other markets around the world, or whereby one brokerage firm, for instance Cantor Fitzgerald, can (as of September 1998) have its prices of Treasury futures listed on screens used by traders all around the US.

But electronic trading will not eliminate the need for financial centres because these combine multiple resources and talents necessary for executing complex operations and servicing global firms and markets. Frankfurt's electronic futures network is actually embedded in a network of financial centres. And the broker Cantor Fitzgerald has an alliance with the Board of Trade of New York to handle its computerized sale of US Treasury futures. Financial centres cannot be reduced to their exchanges. They are part of a far more complex architecture and they constitute far more complex structures within that architecture. I think of this feature of financial centres as important for exploring the question of regulation, particularly in the North Atlantic economy because of its enormous concentration of leading centres and its standard-setting powers for the rest of the world. The next section examines the function of centres.

---

[22] This paper does not focus on Tokyo and Hong Kong. I do this in Sassen, 'Global Financial Centers' (above, n. 5) and *The Global City* (above, n. 1).

[23] The driving force behind the memorandum of understanding came from the big investment banks, squeezed between powerful customers, on the one hand, and the high costs of share dealing, on the other. At present, they must channel share orders to Europe's various national stock exchanges and comply with all their separate rules, which adds to their costs. The London and Frankfurt exchanges hope to cut costs in many ways. They will develop software so that traders can deal on both exchanges from a single computer screen. They plan to harmonize rules on opening hours, the minimum and maximum size of dealing lots and so on, as well as procedures for offering and disclosing trades. Eventually, they want to build a new electronic trading system together rather than running separate ones.

1. *In the digital era: more concentration than dispersal?*

What really stands out in the evidence for the global financial industry is the extent to which there is a sharp concentration of the shares of many financial markets in a few financial centres.[24] London, New York, and Tokyo (notwithstanding a national economic recession) regularly appear at the top *and* represent a large share of global transactions. London, followed by Tokyo, New York, Hong Kong, and Frankfurt, account for a major share of all international banking. London, Frankfurt, and New York account for an enormous world share in the export of financial services. London, New York, Boston, and Tokyo account for over one-third of global institutional equity holdings, this even after a sharp decline in Tokyo's value since 1996. London, New York, and Tokyo account for 58 per cent of the foreign-exchange market; together with Singapore, Hong Kong, Zurich, Geneva, Frankfurt, and Paris, they account for 85 per cent in this, the most global of markets.

This trend towards consolidation in a few centres also is evident within countries. In the United States for instance, New York concentrates all the leading investment banks with only one other major international financial centre in this enormous country, Chicago, which is now seen by many (though not by me) as threatened by the rise of electronic markets. Sydney and Toronto have equally gained power in continental-sized countries and have taken over functions and market share from what were once the major commercial centres, respectively Melbourne and Montreal. So have São Paulo and Bombay, which have gained share and functions from respectively Rio de Janeiro in Brazil and New Delhi and Calcutta in India. These are all enormous countries and one might have thought that they could sustain multiple financial major centres. In France, Paris today concentrates larger shares of most financial sectors than it did ten years ago and once important stock markets like Lyon have become 'provincial', even though Lyon is today the hub of a thriving economic region. Milano privatized its exchange in September 1997 and electronically merged Italy's ten regional markets. Frankfurt now concentrates a larger share of the financial market in Germany than it did in the early 1980s, and so does Zurich, which once had Basle and Geneva as very significant competitors of sorts. By 1997, Frankfurt's market capitalization was five times greater than all other regional markets in Germany combined; in 1992 it had been

---

[24] Among the main sources of data for the figures cited in this section are the International Bank for Settlements (Basle); IMF national accounts data; specialized trade publications such as Wall Street Journal's WorldScope, MorganStanley Capital International; *The Banker;* data listings in the *Financial Times* and in *The Economist;* and, especially for a focus on cities, the data produced by Technimetrics, Inc. (Thomson Financial, as of 1999). Additional names of standard, continuously updated sources are listed in the two books referred to earlier: Sassen, *Losing Control?* (above, n. 11) and Sassen, *The Global City* (above, n. 1).

only twice as large. This story can be repeated for many countries. What stands out is that this pattern of consolidation in one leading financial centre is a function of rapid growth in the sector, not of decay in the losing cities.

We are seeing, then, both consolidation in fewer major centres across and within countries *and* a sharp growth in the numbers of centres that become part of the global network as countries deregulate their economies. São Paulo and Bombay, for instance, joined the global financial network so to speak after Brazil and India deregulated their financial systems, at least partly. This mode of incorporation into the global network often comes at the cost of losing functions which cities had when they were largely national centres; with incorporation, the leading—typically foreign—financial, accounting, and legal services firms enter their markets to handle the more complex aspects of the new cross-border operations. The incorporation of these centres typically happens without a gain in the share of the global market that they can command, even though they add to the total volume in the global market and even though capitalization in their national market can rise sharply.

Why is it that at a time of rapid growth in the network of financial centres, in overall volumes, and in electronic networks, we have such high concentration of market shares in the leading centres? Both globalization and electronic trading are about expansion and dispersal beyond what had been the confined realm of national economies and floor trading, so to speak. Indeed, given globalization and electronic trading, one might well ask why financial centres matter at all.

2. Why do we need centres in the global digital era?

The continuing weight of major centres is, in a way, countersensical, as is, for that matter, the existence of an expanding network of financial centres. The rapid development of electronic exchanges, the growing digitalization of much financial activity, the fact that finance has become one of the leading sectors in a growing number of countries, and that it is a sector that produces a dematerialized, hypermobile product, all suggest that location should not matter. In fact geographic dispersal would seem to be a good option, given the high cost of operating in major financial centres. Further, the last ten years have seen an increased geographic mobility of financial experts and financial services firms through the establishment of affiliates, branches, and other organizational options.

There has been geographic decentralization of certain types of financial activities, aimed at securing business in the growing number of countries becoming integrated into the global economy. Many of the leading investment banks have operations in more countries than they had 20 years ago. The same can be said for the leading accounting and legal services and other specialized corporate services. And it can be said for some markets:

for example, in the 1980s all basic wholesale foreign-exchange operations were in London. Today these are distributed among London and several other centres (even though their number is far smaller than the number of countries whose currency is being traded). Further, beyond concentration in terms of market share, there is operational concentration: for example, Reuters 2000 and EBS, an electronic broker owned by fourteen big foreign-exchange banks, probably handled about 60 per cent of London's 'spot' market in the mid-1990s.

There are, in my view, at least three reasons which explain the trend towards consolidation in a few centres rather than massive dispersal. I developed this analysis in *The Global City*, focusing on New York, London, and Tokyo, and since then events have made this even clearer and more pronounced.

a. The importance of social connectivity and central functions

First, while the new telecommunications technologies do indeed facilitate geographic dispersal of economic activities without losing system integration, they have also had the effect of strengthening the importance of central coordination and control functions for firms and, even, markets. Let us remember that many financial markets have 'owners' now, are run by firms so to speak, and thus also contain central management functions of sorts. Indeed, for firms in any sector, operating a widely dispersed network of branches and affiliates in multiple markets has made central functions far more complicated. Their execution requires access to top talent, not only inside headquarters but more generally in other milieux—in technology, accounting, legal services, economic forecasting, and all sorts of other, sometimes innovative, specialized corporate services.[25] Major centres have massive concentrations of state of the art resources that allow them to maximize the benefits of telecommunications and to govern the new conditions for operating globally. Even electronic markets such as NASDAQ and E*Trade rely on traders and banks which are located somewhere, with at least some in a major financial centre.

One fact that has become increasingly evident is that to maximize the benefits of the new information technologies you need not only the

---

[25] Risk management, for example, which has become increasingly important with globalization, due to the growing complexity and uncertainty that comes with operating in multiple countries and markets, requires enormous fine-tuning of central operations. We now know that many, if not most, major trading losses over the last decade have involved human error or fraud. The quality of risk management will depend heavily on the top people in a firm rather than simply on technical conditions, such as electronic surveillance. Consolidating risk-management operations in one site, usually a central one for the firm, is now seen generally as more effective. We have seen this in the case of several major banks: Chase and Morgan Stanley Dean Witter in the United States, Deutsche Bank and Credit Suisse in Europe.

infrastructure but a complex mix of other resources. Most of the value added that these technologies can produce for advanced service firms lies in the externalities. And this means the material and human resources: state of the art office buildings, top talent, and the social networking infrastructure that maximizes connectivity. Any town can have the fibre optic cables. But does it have the rest?

A second fact that is emerging with greater clarity concerns the meaning of 'information'. There are, one could say, two types of information. One is the datum: at what level did Wall Street close?, did Argentina complete the public sector sale of its water utility?, has Japan declared such and such bank insolvent? But there is a far more difficult type of 'information', akin to an interpretation/evaluation/judgement. It entails negotiating a series of data and a series of interpretations of a mix of data in the hope of producing a higher-order datum. Access to the first kind of information is now global and immediate, thanks to the digital revolution. You can be a broker in the Colorado mountains and have access to this type of information. But it is the second type of information that requires a complicated mixture of elements—the social infrastructure for global connectivity—which gives major financial centres a leading edge.

You can, in principle, reproduce the technical infrastructure anywhere. Singapore, for example, has technical connectivity matching Hong Kong's. But does it have Hong Kong's social connectivity? We could probably say the same for Frankfurt and London. When the more complex forms of information needed to execute major international deals cannot be obtained from existing databases, no matter what one can pay, then one needs the social information loop and the associated de facto interpretations and inferences that come with bouncing off information among talented, informed people. It is the importance of this input that has given a whole new weight to credit-rating agencies, for instance. Part of the rating has to do with interpreting and inferring. When this interpreting becomes 'authoritative', it becomes 'information' available to all. The process of making inferences/interpretations into 'information' takes quite a mix of talents and resources.

In brief, financial centres provide the social connectivity which allows a firm or market to maximize the benefits of its technological connectivity.

b. Cross-border mergers and alliances

Global players in the financial industry need enormous resources, a trend which is leading to rapid mergers and acquisitions of firms and strategic alliances among markets in different countries. These are happening on a scale and in combinations few would have foreseen just three or four years ago. In 1998 and 1999 alone we have seen a whole new wave of mergers, notably Citibank with Travellers Group (which few would have predicted just two years earlier), Salomon Brothers with Smith Barney, Bankers

Trust with Alex Brown, and so on.[26] This wave has been so sharp in the late 1990s that when firms such as Deutsche Bank and Dresdner Bank wanted to purchase a US security firm in 1998, they complained of having difficulty finding suitable candidates—they had all been bought up. Many analysts now think that mid-sized financial services firms will find it hard to survive in the global market, when there are global megafirms such as Merrill Lynch, Morgan Stanley Dean Witter, and Goldman, Sachs. We are also seeing mergers between accounting firms, law firms, insurance brokers, in brief, firms that need to provide a global service. Industry analysts foresee a system dominated by a few global investment banks and about twenty-five big fund managers.[27] A similar scenario is also predicted for the global telecommunications industry which will have to consolidate in order to offer a state-of-the-art, globe-spanning service to its global clients, among which are the financial firms.

I would argue that yet another kind of 'merger' is the consolidation of electronic networks that connect a very select number of markets. The Chicago BOT was until recently loosely linked to Frankfurt's futures exchange DTB, and the Chicago MEC to Paris' MATIF. The NYSE is considering linking up with exchanges in Canada and Latin America and has opened talks with the Paris Bourse. The National Association of Securities Dealers acquired the American Stock Exchange in June 1998. This has set off other combinations, notably the attempted merger of the Chicago Board Options Exchange and the Pacific Exchange. NASDAQ's parent is having similar talks with Frankfurt and London. Perhaps most spectacular is the link-up between the London Stock Exchange and Frankfurt's Deutsche Börse; the goal is to attract the top 300 shares from all over Europe—a blue-chip European exchange.[28] Paris reacted by proposing

[26] In October 1997, only four months after Swiss Bank and Union Bank of Switzerland merged to form the world's biggest financial institution with assets at the end of 1997 of US$638 billion, they were overtaken by the merger of Citicorp and Travelers group at US$698 billion. Then NationsBank and BankAmerica merged and now account for one-twelfth of US bank deposits. The Deutsche Bank and Banker's Trust merger creates the world's third-biggest bank by assets.

[27] Industry analysts also see problems for very large firms. For instance, UBS reported losses of US$1.2 billion from misjudging risks of derivatives trading and hedge-fund lending in 1997. It might be that, given the complexity of these markets, a more effective format would be smaller specialized firms intensely networked to other firms in similar lines and complementary lines of specialized servicing. Size does matter in finance, but perhaps not in the way that these big bankers seem to think. The market for financial products is becoming more disintegrated even as banks are becoming more integrated. Big corporations choose the best provider of specific services, rather than relying on one house banker as used to be the case. Specialized financial services firms have been growing fast; they focus on one particular slice of the financial market and hire outside specialists to handle specific highly specialized tasks. For these firms it makes more sense to sell first-rate financial products made by others than not-so-good ones made in-house.

[28] The workability of the alliance is not guaranteed. European competition authorities could veto the deal. There are technical issues: how to develop a single set of stock indices and to merge trade-processing systems. And there are regulatory differences. In Britain, for

that some of the other major European exchanges create an alternative alliance, which has now become the three-member Euronext (Paris, Amsterdam, and Brussels exchanges).

This may well mean the consolidation of a stratum of select financial centres at the top of the worldwide network of thirty to forty cities through which the global financial industry operates. We now also know that a major financial centre needs to have a significant share of global operations to be such. If Tokyo does not succeed in getting more of such operations, it is going to lose standing in the global hierarchy, notwithstanding its importance as a capital exporter. It is this same capacity for global operations that will keep New York at the top level of the hierarchy even though it is largely fed by the resources and the demand of domestic (albeit state-of-the-art) investors. And it will keep Chicago as a key player notwithstanding the loss of some of its futures contracts.

Does the fact of fewer global players affect the spread of such operations? In my view, not necessarily, but it will strengthen the hierarchy in the global network. For instance, by early 1999, before the mid-summer crisis, institutional money managers around the world controlled approximately US$15 trillion. The worldwide distribution of these equities under institutional management shows considerable spread among a large number of cities which have become integrated in the global equity market with deregulation of their economies and the whole notion of 'emerging markets' as an attractive investment destination over the last few years. Thomson Financial Investor Relations (1999), for instance, has estimated that at the end of 1998, twenty-five cities accounted for over 80 per cent of the world's valuation. These twenty-five cities also accounted for roughly 48 per cent of the total market capitalization of the world, which stood at US$20.9 trillion by early 1998. At the same time, there was a disproportionate concentration in the top six or seven cities.

These developments make clear a second important trend that in many ways specifies the current global era. These various centres do not just compete with each other: there is collaboration and division of labour. In the international system of the post-war decades, each country's financial centre, in principle, covered the universe of necessary functions to service its national companies and markets. The world of finance was, of course, much simpler than it is today. In the initial stages of deregulation in the 1980s there was a strong tendency to see the relation among the major centres as one of straight competition, especially among New York, London, and Tokyo, the heavyweights in the system. But in my research on these three centres I found clear evidence of a division of labour already in the

instance, deals struck over the telephone rather than the exchange's computer must still be reported to the exchange and published, with an allowable delay for big trades. In Germany, banks have no obligation to disclose trades, no matter what their size, if they have been struck over the telephone.

late 1980s. What we are seeing now is yet a third pattern, where this coop-eration or division of functions is somewhat institutionalized: strategic alliances not only between firms across borders but also among markets. There is competition, strategic collaboration, and hierarchy.

The trend towards hierarchy in the global network will be further reinforced by the formation of Europe's monetary union: elimination of various financial functions, notably the foreign-exchange trade, that have fed the existence of an 'international' financial centre in each Member Country; consolidation of the government bond market; a single currency market with a single short-term interest rate; and, eventually, a strong trend towards a basically single equity market. (This will happen slowly because stock markets will be subject to different local taxes, accounting rules, and local stock indices.) In the bond market it will be the creditwor-thiness of the borrower that will matter, rather than the national currency. According to some analysts the Euro bond market will begin to resemble the municipal bond market in the United States.

In brief, the need for enormous resources to handle increasingly global operations in combination with the growth of central functions I described earlier produces strong tendencies towards concentration, and hence hier-archy, in an expanding network.

c. De-nationalized elites and agendas

National attachments and identities are becoming weaker for these global players and their customers. Thus the major US and European investment banks have set up specialized offices in London to handle various aspects of their global business because they see it as the best location for certain functions. Even French banks have set up some of their global specialized operations in London, inconceivable even a few years ago and still not avowed in national rhetoric.

Deregulation and privatization have further weakened the need for *national* financial centres. The nationality question simply plays differently in these sectors than it did even a decade ago. Global financial products are accessible in national markets and national investors can operate in global markets. It is interesting to see that investment banks used to split up their analysts team by country to cover a national market; now they are more likely to do it by industrial sector.[29]

In my *Losing Control?*, I described this process as the incipient de-nation-alization of certain institutional arenas. I think such denationalization is a necessary condition for economic globalization as we know it today. The sophistication of this system lies in the fact that it only needs to involve strategic institutional areas—most national systems can be left basically unaltered. China is a good example. It adopted international accounting

---

[29] See, for example, *Latin American Finance,* various issues.

rules in 1993, a step necessary for engaging in international transactions. How much of its domestic economy did it have to change? Not much. Japanese firms operating overseas adopted such standards long before Japan's government considered requiring them. In this regard the wholesale side of globalization is quite different from the global consumer markets, in which success necessitates altering national tastes at a mass level.

This process of denationalization will be facilitated by the current acquisitions of firms and property in all the Asian countries in crisis.[30] In some ways one might say that the Asian financial crisis has functioned as a mechanism to denationalize, at least partly, control over key sectors of economies which, while allowing the massive entry of foreign investment, never relinquished that control.

Major international business centres produce what we could think of as a new subculture. In a witty insight, *The Economist* entitled one of its stories on the annual World Economic Forum meetings held in Davos 'From Chatham House Man to Davos Man' alluding, respectively, to the 'national' and the 'global' version of international relations. The long-standing resistance in Europe to M & As, especially hostile takeovers, or to foreign ownership and control in East Asia, signal national business cultures that are somewhat incompatible with the new global economic ethos. I would posit that major cities, as well as Davos meetings and similar occasions, contribute to denationalize corporate elites. Whether this is good or bad is a separate issue; but it is, I believe, one of the conditions for setting in place the systems and subcultures necessary for a global economic system.

3. A strengthened hierarchy?

London is, today, the leading platform for global finance. This position is in good part the consequence of US, continental European, and Japanese firms locating key operations and resources in London. In that sense London is the strongest instance of a denationalized business centre.

---

[30] For instance, Lehman Brothers bought Thai residential mortgages worth half a billion dollars for a 53% discount. This was the first auction conducted by the Thai government's Financial Restructuring Authority which is conducting the sale of US$21 billion of financial companies' assets. It also acquired the Thai operations of Peregrine, the HK investment bank that failed. The fall in prices and in the value of the yen has made Japanese firms and real estate attractive targets for foreign investors. Merrill Lynch has bought thirty branches of Yamaichi Securities, Société Générale Group is buying 80% of Yamaichi International Capital Management, Travelers Group is now the biggest shareholder of Nikko (the third largest brokerage), and Toho Mutual Insurance Co. announced a joint venture with GE Capital. These are but some of the best-known examples. Much valuable property in the Ginza—Tokyo's high-priced shopping and business district—is now being considered for acquisition by foreign investors, in a twist on Mitsubishi's acquisition of the Rockefeller Center a decade earlier.

London is now the leading centre for institutional equity management in the world, with over US$2.1 trillion in assets as of the end of 1998. This represented a sharp increase from its 1996 total of US$1.2 trillion. New York is a close second at US$2.0 trillion, reflecting a 25 per cent growth over 1997. London's stock market capitalization at July 1998 stood at over US$2 trillion, double Frankfurt's at US$1 trillion (though by the end of 1998 Frankfurt stood at US$1.3 trillion) and Paris under US$1 trillion. As of the late 1990s, London is the world's biggest net exporter of financial services, with an annual surplus of US$8.1 billion; it leads in international bank lending, in advice on cross-border mergers and acquisitions, and in the trading of international bonds where it accounts for three out of five new international bond issues over the last few years and handles three-quarters of international bond trading. London's foreign firms are significant contributors to its top place. London is the leading foreign-exchange market in the world with a 40 per cent share, far ahead of New York. For a long time it had the second biggest futures market, behind Chicago's BOT, and ahead of Chicago's MEC, Frankfurt's DTB (today the leader), and Paris' MATIF. London's stock market capitalization is equivalent to 160 per cent of UK GDP, compared to well under 100 per cent for most European countries (which does incidentally signal the possibility of considerable growth in these stock markets).

What London does not have is Wall Street's brilliant financial engineering or Frankfurt's Eurozone. It does not have Japan's enormous piles of what one can best describe as old-fashioned money—the real thing so to speak—in all those postal savings accounts of hard-working and hard-saving Japanese people. Nor does it have Hong Kong's strategic advantage as a nexus between global capital and China. And, much of its prominence depends on the leading US investment firms and a growing number of European firms locating key operations in London and hence feeding its top rank in several sectors.

It is precisely this unique role as a denationalized platform for global operations that is London's competitive advantage. Central to this function is its flexible regulation—most importantly the fact that it basically leaves wholesale financial traders alone, and concentrates its regulatory effort on retail finance to protect consumers. Its legal and accounting system have been one of the de facto international standards, a condition that will change little with the implementation of the new IASC international standards, which are basically Anglo-American. It is far more flexible in its regulatory framework for wholesale finance than the codified systems of continental Europe. Its history as an off-shore market has contributed to its internationalization, something that the newly announced electronic network between London's Stock Exchange and Frankfurt's will only strengthen. And its long tradition of empire has left it with a global network of contacts and bridges with just about any place in the world.

It is, in my view, these features that will make London the ultimate deregulated international centre for finance and business, and not, as many commentators assert, a loser in the new Eurozone. It will lose some business to the Eurozone. But if the Euro becomes a leading currency, London may become its key international trading centre for non-Europeans.

The large US commercial and investment banks are building up their operations in Europe, and particularly in London, looking forward to the Eurozone. So while they are cutting staff in many places they are typically adding staff in Europe.[31] They expect enormous growth in European financial services in the next decade. Analysts at Morgan Stanley have made some of the highest forecasts: they expect US$13 trillion will flow in EU equity markets between 1999 and 2010, for a tripling of their current size. If we consider that current worldwide stock market capitalization is a bit over US$20 trillion, we can see that this is an enormous growth. For others it will be more likely a doubling rather than a tripling. But there is a general expectation of a boom in all areas: share and bond issues, mergers and acquisitions, fund management, and securities trading. The expectation is that, replicating what happened in the United States, capital markets will grow at the expense of commercial banking as Europeans invest more in stocks and shares. The expected lower interest rates will raise the attractiveness of equity investments. Securitization of assets will grow, which will feed the growth of mutual funds and growth in private pension funds. US firms expect to take a good share of this business.

New York is doubtless still the Silicon Valley of finance. This has made the US investment firms leaders in the complex operations for the global market. For instance, when M & As in Europe began to take off in 1997, the top five firms in terms of value handling them were from the United States. In 1999 five of the top seven were from the United States. New York's top investment banks often operate through branches abroad—hence feeding the strength of, for instance, London. New York is by far the biggest domestic capital market. Some of Tokyo's markets are among the few that can match New York's. The NYSE is the largest in the world, listing about 3,000 companies and with a market capitalization of US$12

---

[31] Merrill Lynch has invested heavily in London. In 1995 it bought a British stockbroker, Smith New Court, and in 1997 it acquired Mercury Asset Management, Britain's third largest fund manager. So while it announced that it would cut 3,400 jobs worldwide, including 400 in London, it has strengthened its Europe-oriented divisions. Donaldson Lufkin & Jenrette also announced job cuts, but not for its European operations. Morgan Stanley has almost doubled its London staff over the past years to 3,000. US commercial banks are also entering the European market by strengthening their operations in London: Bankers Trust bought the investment-banking arm of the British bank National Westminster in April 1998 and is now building a team to develop the emerging European market in high-yield bonds. Mellon Bank recently acquired Newton, a British fund manager, and State Street has set up a European subsidiary in London. Citigroup has just announced 1,300 new back-office jobs in Ireland to service its European business.

trillion in early 1999. But it is an overwhelmingly domestic market. It has about 400 foreign firms listed, a number that reflects rapid growth in the last few years. In contrast, the Tokyo stock exchange is losing foreign firms, even after the government eased listing requirements and costs. To make itself more global the NYSE will be trading in decimals rather than fractions within the next few years; the SEC has lowered some of the barriers to foreigners, and has approved (after being among the last holdouts along with Japan) the new IASCA international accounting standards that will apply to all issuers regardless of national origin.

It is interesting to note that much of the innovative financial leadership of US firms has been a consequence of having an enormous and sophisticated domestic market. The United States as a whole accounts for one-fifth of world gross product, but almost half of the total value of the world's equity markets. This suggests one possible trajectory for Europe and its Eurozone, in so far as it will create a market almost comparable to that of the United States and may thereby push its markets towards greater sophistication.

The globalization of investment banking and fund management, two areas where New York firms are major players, may well have been more important in strengthening London's position as a financial centre than UK national growth per se. In *The Global City* I posited that the globalization of markets reduces the importance of national economic health for major cities to thrive as international business centres—not necessarily a desirable feature of the global economic system. This seems to be happening in several European countries where thriving stock markets commonly go along with slow economic growth and high unemployment.

Given the difficult and delicate issues facing the Eurozone in terms of deregulation and harmonization of standards, London, rather than losing out, may well emerge as the ultimate deregulated market. There are many routinized activities that will thrive in the Eurozone, but the strategic and complex operations now required in the global financial markets are likely to continue to find in New York the place for innovations and new products, and in London their main platforms for global operations. Frankfurt, which will certainly be the financial capital of the Eurozone, ranked twelfth in institutional equity holdings in 1998. This may well change, of course.[32]

---

[32] While this is not the paper to discuss Japan's place in this configuration, it is important to recognize that Japan remains a powerhouse in terms of the resources it concentrates and is part of the global financial equation. It accounts for an enormous share of worldwide equities under institutional management: at the end of 1998, this figure stood at US$1.1 trillion; this was after a loss of over 32%, or over half a trillion dollars in 1997, over its 1996 value. This enormous loss had *still* left Tokyo in the number four position worldwide for 1997, at a time when most of the other top centres had made enormous gains from 1996 to 1997, especially due to stock market value increases: London increased its holdings by 48%, the New York metropolitan area by 38%, Frankfurt by 48%, Milano by 60%, and so on. Indeed, Tokyo had

In brief, we are seeing a growing network and a sharpened hierarchy in the global financial system. There is a simultaneous expansion of the network through the addition of new centres and increases in overall volumes (partly due to this incorporation of new centres), but little change in overall market shares. And there is a shift upwards of top-level functions towards centres that are global rather than only national leaders, thus, one could say, producing a strengthening rather than a weakening in the hierarchy of centres, notwithstanding the globalization and expansion of the financial system.

II. PART TWO

A. The state and the global capital market[33]

The formation of a global capital market represents a concentration of power that is capable of influencing national government economic policy, and by extension other policies. These markets can now exercise accountability functions: they can vote governments' economic policies down or in; they can force governments to take certain measures and not others. Investors can move their money in and out of countries, often in quick and massive transactions.

Governments do have, or have traditionally had, a whole array of policies to govern their national economies: policies on taxes, on public spending, on interest rates, on credit controls, on exchange rates, on capital controls, and on income. These have generally been weakened or even neutralized by the deregulation of domestic financial markets, the liberalization of international capital flows, computers and telecommunications. In turn, these conditions have all contributed to an explosive growth in financial markets, further strengthening their capacity to influence government policy.

a firm hold on the number one position for several years, even after its economic troubles exploded in 1990. Further, Japanese investments in foreign securities represent a very significant share of such investment, especially in the US. In 1997 Japan's net purchases of foreign equity were US$13.1 billion, up by over 76% over 1996. Of these, US$10.5 billion were net purchases of US equity, a 322% increase over 1996. Most of the investments in foreign securities have been from pension funds. Japan has the largest foreign reserves in the world and is one of the largest holders of other governments' bonds. It holds over US$300 billion of US bonds. If Japan were suddenly to call in its debt, the US would feel it. Finally, Japan is the second largest international lender. To this we might add that direct investment abroad by Japanese grew from about US$110 billion in 1988 to about US$259 billion by early June 1998, and that Japan's GDP still is 70% of total Asian gross product, six times China's, and larger than Germany's. These are all big amounts even for the enormous global capital market that has evolved over the last decade. They signal Japan's weight in the global capital market, both in terms of the assets it owns and in terms of the exposure it has to bad loans in the Asian crisis.

[33] This section is based on Sassen, *Losing Control? Sovereignty in an Age of Globalization* (above, n. 11), ch. 2.

How does this massive growth of financial flows and assets and the fact of an integrated global capital market affect states in their economic policy-making? After all, conceivably a global capital market could just be a vast pool of money for investors to shop in without conferring power over governments. The fact that it can discipline governments' economic policy-making is a distinct power, one that is not *ipso facto* inherent in the existence of a large global capital market.

At least three characteristics of the global capital market as it has developed over the last decade have contributed to a massive concentration of power in this market. One is the orders of magnitude involved, made possible by the new information technologies, globalization, securitization of assets, deregulation, and the interaction of all of these. This has dwarfed the financial resources that most governments can mobilize on their own. Crucial here are the properties that the new information technologies bring to the financial markets: instantaneous transmission, interconnectivity, and speed. The speed of transactions has brought its own consequences. Thanks to vast computer networks, trading in currencies and securities is instant, and the high degree of interconnectivity in combination with instantaneous transmission signals the potential for exponential growth.

A second issue is the growing concentration of market power in institutions such as pension funds and insurance companies, and the diminishing role of individual investors, many of whom now channel their investments via institutions. For instance, institutional investors now manage two-fifths of US households' financial assets, up from one-fifth in 1980. US institutional investors' assets rose from 59 per cent of GDP in 1980 to well over 100 per cent by the mid 1990s. The growing control by institutional investors relative to individual investors can be seen as representing a growth in the concentration of power in the global capital market.

A third major factor is the explosion in financial innovations. Innovations have raised the supply of financial instruments that are tradeable, i.e. sold on the open market. There are significant differences by country. Securitization is well advanced in the United States, but just beginning in most of Europe, where it is estimated that over US$10 trillion in newly securitized assets will enter the financial markets over the next few years in the Eurozone.

Does this concentration of capital in variously deregulated markets affect national economies and government policies? Does it alter the functioning of democratic governments? Does this kind of concentration of capital reshape the accountability relation between governments and their people which have operated through electoral politics? Yes, it does.

There are several mechanisms through which the global capital market actually exercises its disciplining function on national governments and pressures them to become accountable to the logic of these markets. The power of governments over their economies in market-centred systems has traditionally been based on the ability to tax, to print money, and to borrow. The global financial markets have affected all three sharply.

Before deregulation, governments could, at least to some extent, directly control the amount of bank lending through credit controls and impose ceilings on interest rates, thus helping to make monetary policy more effective than it is today. With deregulation of interest rates in more and more highly developed countries, central banks now have to rely simply on changes in interest-rate levels to influence the level of demand in the economy. They can no longer use interest-rate ceilings. But the impact of interest rates on the economy, in turn, has been blunted by the widespread invention and use of derivatives.

Derivatives (futures, swaps, options) were invented precisely to reduce the impact of interest-rate changes and thereby can be seen as reducing the effectiveness of interest-rate policy by governments on the economy.[34] Indeed, an estimated 85 per cent of US Fortune 500 firms make some use of derivatives to insulate themselves from swings in interest rates and currency values; so do public sector entities, as in the notorious case of Orange County in California. Actually, most of these derivatives are on interest rates, which means that as their use expands, the power of central banks to influence the economy via interest rates will decline further, no matter how much the media makes of it each time central bankers change rates.[35] It is true that in so far as many firms and sectors now operate with levels of capital that are far larger than in the past, interest-rate changes can represent massive amounts of money in absolute terms.

One way of interpreting this combination of conditions is to say that with deregulation and the opening of economies, the impact of central banks through interest-rate policy has changed. In my view,[36] the role of central banks has partly shifted towards the implementation (in national economies) of monetary policies that serve the development of a global capital market. Further, while the US Central Bank has trend-setting powers in this regard, this is not quite the case for most other countries' central

---

[34] Since these derivatives entail a redistribution of interest sensitivities from one firm or sector to another in the economy, one could argue that the overall sensitivity to interest rates in the economy remains constant. But the fact is that different firms may have different sensitivities to changes in interest rates, so we can assume that what is happening is that the risk is being shifted from highly sensitive firms on to less sensitive firms, thereby reducing the overall impact of interest rates on the economy. Through the use of derivatives, interest-rate sensitivity is switched to less-sensitive sectors. But see also Bary Eichengreen and Albert Fishlow, *Contending with Capital Flows* (New York: Council of Foreign Relations, 1996).

[35] Media coverage of heads of central banks, notably Greenspan in the United States, portrays them as extremely powerful. The suggestion is that the whole country is hanging on each utterance. It is certainly the case that the stock market is sensitive to their decisions on interest rates. But a careful reading of the evidence indicates that frequently the decisions by the US Federal Reserve Bank strengthen what is in fact a market trend.

[36] Sassen, 'Denationalized State Agendas' (above, n. 3).

banks. A somewhat open question here is the future of the European Central Bank.

In addition to the changed impact that central banks can have through interest-rate policy, the power of governments to influence interest and foreign-exchange rates and fiscal policy can be severely reduced, if not neutralized, by the foreign-exchange markets and bond markets. For example, the markets can respond to a cut by the US Government in interest rates by raising the cost of loans to the US Government through an increased yield in long-term bonds. This has emerged as a standard procedure. Then there is the famous case of George Soros and his Quantum Fund which made 1 billion dollars in profits on Black Wednesday in 1992, by helping to push the British pound out of the European Exchange Rate Mechanism. Perhaps the most dramatic instance is the attack by currency speculators on the Thai currency in 1997 as its peg to the dollar became increasingly unsustainable.

There is more. The channel through which central banks have traditionally carried out their monetary policies is the banking sector. But in the United States, for instance, the banking sector is shrinking because of the new financial institutions and instruments developed over the last decade through deregulation. Thirty years ago banks provided three-quarters of all short- and medium-term business credit; today that figure is down to under 50 per cent. The share of commercial banks in total financial assets is down from over half to 25 per cent over the past 70 years.[37] The rise of electronic cash further reduces the control capacity of central bankers over the money supply. Electronic money moves through computer networks, bypassing the information-gathering system of central banks.

All of these conditions have reduced the control that central banks have over the money supply. It is certainly a matter of thresholds, since this control was never complete. But now it is seriously incomplete, so to say, given the rules of the game under which central banks operate. Clearly these outcomes vary in severity depending on the country's banking structure. Overall the impact of financial deregulation and innovation has been to make the effect of a change in interest rates on a national economy more uncertain, to put it kindly, and to increase the opportunities for mistakes.[38]

---

[37] Another issue is the currency markets. Governments with large debts are in fact partly in the hands of investors—whether foreign or national—who can switch their investments to other currencies. Governments and their central banks have been losing control over long-term interest rates. This is no minor matter if you consider that 60% or more of private-sector debt in the United States, Japan, Germany, and France is linked to long-term interest rates.

[38] There is a whole separate discussion to be had about who benefited from the earlier period, for example in the United States when its central bank, the Federal Reserve, had greater control. But one thing is certain: even though many were excluded, the beneficiaries represented a far wider spectrum of workers, communities, and firms than those who benefit from today's policy orientation.

A perhaps important countervailing tendency is the increasing convergence among central bankers in terms of policy which we have seen over the last decade, along with the increasing acceptance of central bank autonomy.[39] Central banks have become the national institutional home for monetary policies that support the existence of global capital markets.[40] Central banks and governments appear to be increasingly concerned about pleasing the financial markets rather than using monetary policy to set goals for social and economic well-being. One is reminded of the Argentinian and Brazilian Governments after the Mexican crisis promising not to devalue their currencies, indeed doing whatever it would take to avoid this—including plunging the lower middle-classes into poverty. Governments try to accommodate inflation-obsessed bond holders, and hence perhaps guard excessively against inflation, imposing excessive deflation on economies in a trade-off with job growth. This is certainly one of the critiques levelled against Tietmeyer while he was head of the German Central Bank. It is also a critique raised against the European Central Bank for excluding employment policy from its mandate.[41]

It could be argued that there may be some positive effects as well: if national debts become too large, bondholders will demand higher yields (i.e. raise the cost of a loan to governments) and lower the value of a national currency, as was clearly the case with the dollar in the United States from the mid-1980s to early 1990s.[42] But then we need to ask whether we want the global capital market to exercise this discipline over our governments? And to do so at all costs—jobs, wages, safety, health—and without a public debate?[43]

[39] In such gatherings as the World Economic Forum, held annually in Davos (Switzerland), which offers an opportunity for the CEOs of the 1,000 largest corporations in the world to mix with central bankers (and presidents and prime ministers), one central banker after the other, from Governor Trichet of France to Frenkel of Israel, will hold forth at length about their autonomy from their governments and from the financial markets. But it is not at all certain that just because they find themselves today in this increasingly strategic position, their autonomy from the financial markets is the same as having power to contest the logic of the latter. See Sassen, *Losing Control? Sovereignty in an Age of Globalization* (above, n. 11), ch. 2, for a further discussion.

[40] Sassen, 'Denationalized State Agendas' (above, n. 3).

[41] The rationale given is not unreasonable, one might argue. Member countries have such diverse employment policies (broadly defined) that it is simply unfeasible to replicate employment conditions through a single monetary policy.

[42] However, this only happened after more than a decade of Reagan–Bush excessive spending on defence in the 1980s. Indeed, the costs to pay for the added debt have been extracted from the social fund, reduced investment in infrastructure, public housing construction, school buildings, parks, etc. The dollar's plunge by 60% against the yen and German mark beginning in the mid-1980s and up to the early 1990s can be seen as a negative response to US economic policies on borrowing. In the past, inflation was a way of coping with growing debt (more money reduces the value of debt). But today the bond markets will raise the yields (and hence the cost of loans to governments), thereby sometimes terrorizing governments into keeping inflation under control.

[43] Further, the global financial markets discipline governments in a somewhat erratic way, even under the premises of market operation: they fail to react to an obvious imbalance for a

The issue here is not so much that these markets have emerged as a powerful mechanism where those with capital can influence government policy; this is in many ways an old story.[44] It is rather that the overall operation of these markets has an embedded logic that calls for certain types of economic policy objectives. Given the properties of the systems through which these markets operate—speed, simultaneity, and interconnectivity—the orders of magnitude they can produce signal a politico-economic situation where the outcome is much more than the sum of the parts. And this weight can be exercised on a rapidly growing number of countries that are integrated into the financial markets.

An examination of the global capital market makes it clear that, in so far as transnationalization and deregulation have been key to its growth and its distinct contemporary character, there has been a reduced regulatory role on the part of national states compared with the decades after World War II, which had seen an increase in regulation. This is illustrated by the worldwide pressure experienced by national states to deregulate their financial markets in order to allow integration into the global markets.[45] Thus London saw its 'big bang' of 1986, and Paris its 'petit bang' two years later, under governments as diverse as the Tories in England and the Socialists in France. Gill sees this development as a strategy he calls 'the

long time and then suddenly punish with a vengeance, as was the case with the Mexican, South-East Asian, and Russian crises, for example. The speculative character of so many markets means that they will stretch the profit-making opportunities for as long as possible, no matter what the underlying damage to the national economy might be. The Mexican case, by now much analysed, is a good example here. Investors threw money into Mexico even though its current account deficit was growing fast and reached an enormous 8% of GDP in 1994. Notwithstanding recognition by critical sectors in both the United States and Mexico that the peso needed a gradual devaluation, nothing was done. The rest is history. A sudden sharp devaluation with the subsequent sharp departure of investors threw the economy into disarray. The nationality of the investors is quite secondary; an IMF report says it was Mexican investors who first dumped the peso. Gradual action could probably have avoided some of the costs and reversals. Even in late 1994, many Wall Street analysts and traders were still urging investment in Mexico. It was not until February 1995 that foreign investors began getting out in hordes (that is, selling their Mexican equities). It all started with an excessive inflow, and concluded with an excessive outflow. For an examination of the role of credit-rating agencies in the various recent financial crises, see Saskia Sassen, 'Credit Rating Agencies', *Bloomberg Personal Finance* (August 1999) (the longer background report is on file with author). See also Stuart Corbridge, Ron Martin, and Nigel Thrift (eds), *Money Power and Space* (Oxford: Blackwell, 1994).

[44] See, for instance, Giovanni Arrighi, *The Long Twentieth Century: Money, Power, and the Origins of Our Times* (London: Verso, 1994). For a contemporary twist on this story of influence on governments, see 'Special Issue: The Internet and Sovereignty', *Indiana Journal of Global Legal Studies* (Spring 1999).

[45] It is important to note, and key to my argument, that the governments voluntarily implemented the legislative and administrative rules necessary for deregulation. There was no military occupation, so to speak. Yet the pressures from the 'outside' were real. For the United States, for instance, loss of capital to the Euro-markets and to a growing number of other off-shore markets which proliferated in the 1970s made deregulation a key strategy to recover much of that capital. For Argentina or Brazil, ten years later, deregulation and privatization were necessary mechanisms to bring in foreign capital.

new constitutionalism' which places constraints on the democratic control of public and private economic organization and institutions.[46] It is a strategy premised on the efficiency of market forces. Yet some states, such as the United States, are likely to be less accountable to international market forces than others, depending on their power in the global economy.

1. The elements of an architecture for global financial regulation

At the heart of global finance today lies the international regulation of securities, the latter being one of the key forms, and a growing one, for financial instruments covering a very broad range of sectors. In my understanding—as a political economist—of the internationalization of current securities regulation regimes, there are at least four regulatory levels to be considered. Though distinct, they all seek to facilitate or increase cross-border listing. But they differ in their scope, in the parties involved, and in their implementation procedures. From the perspective of my research and theorizing effort, such a formulation helps answer some of the questions about state sovereignty in the context of regulating a sector that is increasingly at the heart of global finance. These levels are EU initiatives, IASC efforts to set up international standards, bilateral agreements (exemplified by the Multi-Jurisdiction Disclosure System Agreement between the US and Canada), and national-level measures aimed at attracting foreign issuers. I would also point out the prospect of jurisdictional conflicts within sovereign states.

(a) To my knowledge, the EU efforts in securities law constitute the most comprehensive body of internationally harmonized securities law. Fourteen directives have been implemented, and several Council recommendations have been issued.[47] Because of the supranational nature of EU efforts and the comprehensiveness of the harmonization project, they are an important research site in an evaluation of internationalization of regulation and possible changes in the capacities associated with sovereignty.

(b) IASC is currently working on creating a comprehensive set of accounting standards that can be used internationally. These international standards take on greater importance because they have been supported and urged by IOSCO. Their impact on the securities industry and the

---

[46] See Stephen Gill, 'The Emerging World Order and European Change' in Ralph Milliband and Leo Panitch (eds), *New World Order? The Socialist Register 1992* (London: Merlin, 1992), 157–96. See also Andrew Calabrese and Jean-Claude Burgelman, *Communication, Citizenship, and Social Policy: Rethinking the Limits of the Welfare State* (Lanham, Md.: Rowman & Littlefield, 1999); Phillip Cerny, 'Paradoxes of the Competition State: The Dynamics of Political Globalization', *Government and Opposition*, vol. 32, no. 2 (1997), 251–74.

[47] The most important directives are the Listing Conditions Directive (1979), Listing Particulars Directive (1980), Regular Reports Directive (1982), Unit Trust Directive (1987), Mutual Recognition Directive (1987), Major Holdings Directive (1988), Public Offer Prospectus Directive (1989), Insider Dealing Directive (1988), and Investment Company Directive (1985).

internationalization of equity securities trading will, if the work succeeds, be substantial. It has become quite clear that differences in national accounting and auditing principles are one of the primary burdens for cross-border listing. If an international standard can be agreed upon, issuers will be able to use the same documents to fulfil the major part of their disclosure obligations. This will reduce compliance costs, but it can also reduce problems of distrust on the part of the issuer and the financial reporting system caused by disclosure of different net results in different jurisdictions.[48] But even if IASC does succeed, issuers will still have to deal with different disclosure obligations, different liability provisions, different insider-trading regulations, etc.

(c) Unlike comprehensive harmonization efforts, bilateral agreements are partial and, to the extent that they have been made, they too must be taken into account. One example of such an agreement is the Multi-Jurisdictional Disclosure Systems referred to above. Under MJDS, Canadian issuers can satisfy certain US registration and reporting requirements by providing disclosure documents prepared in accordance with the requirements of Canadian securities regulatory authorities, just as US issuers can use their SEC filings to satisfy Canadian requirements.[49] Although this looks like an agreement on mutual recognition, it should be noted that Canadian issuers that offer securities in the United States under MJDS must comply with US GAAP, much as they are subject to the US liability duties.

(d) National changes to accommodate the demand for the internationalization of regulatory regimes have partly been driven by states and private sector actors trying to attract foreign issuers. Although the special provisions implemented by various governments to that end are based on a country's regulatory system, they often offer important exemptions from the obligations that cover domestic issuers. There are two matters here that I find worth examining. One is to what extent under these conditions the state can be said to have lost or transferred sovereignty through lessening the burden on foreign issuers. The second concerns the possibility of cross-border convergence in this effort to accommodate the demands of foreign actors in a national system. These are clearly not necessarily mutually exclusive.

(e) As a political economist, I would also tentatively consider jurisdictional conflicts within sovereign states. In the United States there have been several cases where the overlap between corporate law (state jurisdiction) and securities regulation (federal jurisdiction) has been the cause of litigation in so far as it affects interstate commerce. Understanding this federal dimension might illuminate some of the challenges and problems

[48] Several foreign issuers have experienced problems reconciling their national standards to US GAAP when complying with US disclosure requirements.

[49] SEC Release 33-6902.

facing the European Union as a multi-jurisdictional system. For instance, the new principle of subsidiarity in Article 5, formerly 3b, of the EC Treaty holds that in areas which do not fall within its exclusive competence, the Community shall take action only if and in so far as the objectives of the proposed action cannot be sufficiently achieved by the Member States and can therefore be better achieved by the Community.[50]

In brief, the global capital market requires standards, transparency, and, preferably, convergence. Yet as the analysis of financial centres in section C of Part One of this contribution suggested, there has been enormous growth in the industry and expansion in the number of financial centres incorporated worldwide even as governments are still striving towards, or resisting, implementation of new standards and harmonization. There is an operational aspect that contributes to a de facto convergence in practices as more and more countries deregulate their economies and become integrated into the global capital market. As the latter grows, so does its disciplining power over governments.

B. Competition policy: from extraterritoriality to a cross-border system?

When it comes to foreign direct investment, firms need to be able to rely on governments to produce and enforce clear policies on competition. As is the case with the regulation of finance, we have seen a proliferation of efforts. Competition policy is emerging as a strategic arena, for it is key to the changing relation between the private and the public in the context of globalization and the existence of different models of competition policy, notably those of the United States and of Europe.

While many countries have had one version or another of competition policy, there has been a sharp jump in the numbers that have adopted such policies or reinvigorated inactive ones. The increase began in the 1980s and accelerated rapidly in the 1990s. Today more than seventy countries have something resembling Western antitrust rules, compared to forty in 1970.[51] Important also is the reactivation of existing antitrust laws.

---

[50] One scholar, Amir Licht, discusses the possibility that securities law and corporate law are interconnected and that the connection can cause roadblocks on the way to convergence. See Amir Licht, *International diversity in securities regulation: some roadblocks on the way to convergence* (Cambridge, MA: Harvard Law School, 1998); also listed as Discussion Paper No. 233 from the John M. Olin Center for Law, Economics, and Business, published in book form (82 pp.) by Harvard Law School, ISSN: 1045-6333.

[51] Brian Portnoy, 'Constructing Competition: The Political Foundations of Alliance Capitalism' (Ph.D. diss., Department of Political Science, University of Chicago, 1999), chs. 3 and 4. Much of the growth in the 1990s came from developing countries and transitional economies in Central and Eastern Europe. Including those now in the process of implementing such rules, Portnoy estimates that over 100 countries would have such rules by the year 2000. Among developed countries there were fewer than ten in 1950, twenty in 1975, and all twenty-nine by 1998 (including the developed countries from Central Europe). See also Edward O. Graham and J. D. Richardson, *Global Competition Policy* (Washington, DC: Institute for International Economics, 1997).

Overhauling is probably the best way of describing what is being done in the Netherlands, Great Britain, Denmark, Portugal, and Greece, especially in relation to the European Community and the development of a European competition regime. The leadership of the EC Commission has played a crucial role here, notably under recent Competition Policy Commissioners Sir Leon Brittan and Karel van Miert.

The enormous change in the international organization of business makes it difficult to apply the old norms of what a desirable competition policy might be. We see new forms of cross-border cooperation among firms, including the growth of business alliances and complex patterns of subcontracting and short-term partnerships.[52] In addition we are seeing the emergence of new industries that do not fit existing patterns and a new importance of intellectual property rights. Add to this the deregulation of markets and industries and the new technologies and it becomes clear that designing competition policy is a difficult task because it is not even clear what the new competitive structure should be in dynamic industries operating in cross-border markets and with cross-border organizational entities. The relation between competition policy and trade policy, i.e. antidumping provisions, is a central issue here. More theoretically, perhaps, the shifting boundary between private and public authority, and between regulation and various self-regulatory efforts taking place in some industries, further complicates matters.

To this one can add the efforts within the European Union to achieve agreement on specific EU company types—legal entities not based on or created through national legislation. These efforts also signal the difficulties of convergence. As far as I am aware, the proposed regulations for the European Company have not been agreed upon, thus illustrating the difficulties in the efforts towards convergence.[53] Among the reasons for the difficulty is the fact that not all Member States have the legal forms entailed by the proposals, or if they do, their features differ significantly from state to state. If this is a difficulty within the European Union, it is easy to imagine the difficulties present in broader cross-border configurations.

One can see a degree of convergence in regulatory responses to global economic pressures, particularly market liberalization and the growth of

---

[52] John Dunning, *Alliance Capitalism and Global Business* (London and New York: Routledge, 1997).

[53] Regulations were also proposed for the European Mutual Company, European Cooperative Company, and others. There was some notion that European company regulation would not be too difficult to reach agreement on since it followed the provisions of the company law harmonization directives. But the disagreement was substantial at the level of the directives. In the autumn of 1996, the Council established an expert panel to consider possible solutions. However, in May 1997, the panel concluded that the differences among countries foreclosed the possibility of harmonization as originally envisaged. (Regulations are more ambitious than directives in that they attempt to create unity concerning specific EU company types—legal entities not based on or created through national legislation.)

cross-border business activity. According to one line of analysis, this convergence is basically a form of Americanization of competition policy.[54] Countries have adopted different versions of American antitrust, but an even bigger effort is underway in many countries towards harmonizing their legal systems with EU policy, in a sort of Europeanization of antitrust law.[55] According to Waller, US antitrust law is not very exportable to other countries as it was developed under very specific historical, political, and industrial conditions not found elsewhere; further, in view of the many different interpretations of the Sherman Act, Waller argues that it is not clear what aspect of the Sherman Act might be exported.[56]

In fact, the internationalization of antitrust may have reinvigorated US antitrust law. In his research, Portnoy finds that the better explanation for the spread and convergence of antitrust law lies in the formation of transnational networks of regulators who increasingly interact and collaborate. He identifies the growing number of organizations and occasions where interaction and cooperation take place. The International Competition Policy Advisory Committee (ICPAC) is one key site for these processes. Some of these are public sector entities, others are private sector entities, and yet others are hybrids.[57]

In terms of the role of the state, we are seeing a shift from supporting strategic or basic industries to establishing conditions for competitiveness in a global economy. This shift is also a shift from macro- to microeco-

---

[54] Portnoy disagrees with this interpretation and notes that it was only with the general acceptance of extraterritoriality and the emergence of international antitrust cooperation that antitrust regimes proliferated in the late 1980s and 1990s. American power was high for many decades before this and yet did not impose antitrust on countries where it had undue influence (except for the cases of Japan and Germany in the immediate post-war period where it was subsequently not much enforced). In the 1980s, when it took off in other countries, antitrust had become a fairly lame regime in the United States: Portnoy, 'Constructing Competition' (above, n. 51), ch. 3.

[55] Portnoy, 'Constructing Competition' (above, n. 51), ch. 4. For instance, the countries of Central and Eastern Europe have been more likely to adopt the administrative form of European competition policy. This is understandable since they are countries where state bureaucracies are used to dealing with the economy and court litigation is underdeveloped.

[56] Spencer W. Waller, 'Neo-Realism and the International Harmonization of Law: Lessons from Antitrust', *University of Kansas Law Review*, vol. 42, no. 3 (1994), 557–604. See also Graham and Richardson (above, n. 51).

[57] Portnoy, 'Constructing Competition' (above, n. 51), ch. 4. Among the public entities that serve to constitute such cross-border networks for dealing with competition policy among developed countries are the OECD Competition Law and Policy Committee, operating since 1994; the US–Japan Structural Impediments Initiative Talks (1989–91); and the bi-annual US–EU Dialogue, operating since 1997. Among the private entities are the International Chamber of Commerce (ICC), the International Antitrust Section of the American Bar Association, the Business Industry Advisory Committee of the OECD; various industry associations; transnational law firms such as Skadden Arps and Covington Burling; and the Transatlantic Business Dialogue. Among the hybrid entities: US International Policy Advisory Committee 1997–9; the US Federal Trade Commission Global Competition hearings, operative since 1995; the EC Group of Experts, 1993–5; the Global Forum for Competition and Trade Policy (World Bank/IBA); and private consultants such as antitrust experts.

nomic issues. And it is a shift from Keynsian policies of general national welfare to the promotion of enterprise, innovation, and profitability in both private and public sectors.[58] In these shifts we can again detect a change in the boundaries between the private and the public domains.[59]

The issues of convergence and diversity in antitrust rules come to the fore in merger policy. Most countries have not had merger regulations. It is only in recent years that this has changed: over fifty countries now have merger rules, with most of this increase due to developing countries instituting such rules. When it comes to substance and procedure, much effort has gone into rationalizing merger control systems in the European Union. The Union has developed a two-tiered system since 1989: large mergers go to the EU merger control regime, while smaller ones are regulated by the national agencies. The result has been to unify a significant and growing portion of all European merger regulation.[60]

The most important inter-regional merger market is the North Atlantic. M & As between North America and Europe totalled US$256.5 billion in 1998, up from US$69.4 billion in 1995 (see section B of Part One above). There have long been significant differences between the United States and Western European merger control models. The latter is likely to define relevant markets more narrowly, to find competition threatened at lower market-share threshholds, to take much greater account of the well-being of individual competitors rather than generalized effects, and to adopt a more expansive definition of unlawful dominant firm behaviour.[61] These differences are beginning to weaken and there is growing convergence

[58] Phillip Cerny, 'Paradoxes of the Competition State: The Dynamics of Political Globalization', *Government and Opposition,* vol. 32, no. 2 (1997), 260. See also Robert Jessop, 'Reflections on Globalization and its Illogics' in Kris Olds *et al.* (ed) (see above, n. 2); Rodney Bruce Hall, 'Private Authority in the Changing Structure of Global Governance', presented at the workshop on Private Authority and International Order, Thomas J. Watson Institute for International Studies, Brown University, 12–13 Feb. 1999.

[59] For example, see Claire A. Cutler, Virginia Haufler, and Tony Porter (eds), *Private Authority in International Affairs* (Sarasota Springs, NY: SUNY Press); Thomas J. Biersteker, Rodney Bruce Hall, and Craig N. Murphy (eds), *Private Authority and Global Governance,* forthcoming.

[60] One of the regulations that has been agreed upon is the Merger Control Regulation; it provides for prior control of cross-border mergers that may restrict competition because a proposed merger may create or amplify a dominant market position. The directive on cross-border mergers is still only a draft proposal. As far as I know, the main reason for the difficulty in reaching agreement concerns the provisions on employee representation on the board. The directive on takeovers has not been agreed upon for various reasons. Germany, the Netherlands, and Belgium oppose the mandatory bid procedure in the proposal and, at the very least, the current limits that trigger this obligation. The United Kingdom is opposed to supervision and control coming from governmental authorities because in the UK takeovers are regulated by the Panel on Takeovers and Mergers and governed by the City of London Code on Takeovers and Mergers.

[61] William Kovacic, 'Merger Enforcement in Transition: Antitrust Controls on Acquisitions in Emerging Economies', *University of Cincinnati Law Review,* vol. 66, no. 4 (1998), 1086.

between the European Union and the United States, especially, perhaps, in the area of single firm and oligopolistic dominance.[62]

Disagreements remain on the question of efficiency as a reason for clearing a proposed merger; the European Union continues to show more concern with broader conditions such as the unemployment effects of a merger. It is important to emphasize that areas of convergence continue to exist in national contexts which are enormously diverse, including differences in the institutionalizing and implementing of antitrust rules, i.e. judicial vs. administrative institutionalization.

C. The growth of private authority

Globalization has also been accompanied by the creation and renovation of some older forms of governance that bypass national legal systems. Among the most important ones today are international commercial arbitration and the variety of institutions which fulfil rating and advisory functions that have become essential for the operation of the global economy. Also notable is the proliferation of self-regulatory regimes, especially in sectors dominated by a limited number of very large firms, a subject I will not address here.

Over the past 20 years, international commercial arbitration has been transformed and institutionalized as the leading contractual method for the resolution of transnational commercial disputes.[63] There has been

---

[62] Simply put, it could be said that in addition to their old concerns with oligopolistic coordination, US agencies are now focusing on single-firm dominance, long the central focus of EC merger review. Conversely, the European Union has moved towards the US approach to market definition, going beyond the measure of market share.

[63] International commercial arbitration represents one mechanism for resolving business disputes. The larger system includes arbitration controlled by courts, arbitration that is parallel to courts, and various court and out-of-court mechanisms such as mediation. See Yves Dezalay and Bryant Garth, 'Merchants of Law as Moral Entrepreneurs: Constructing International Justice from the Competition for Transnational Business Disputes', *Law and Society Review*, vol. 29, no. I, (1995), 27–64; Yves Dezalay and Bryant Garth, *Dealing in Virtue: International Commercial Arbitration and the Construction of a Transnational Legal Order* (Chicago: University of Chicago Press, 1996). For these authors, international commercial arbitration today carries a different meaning from what it did 20 years ago. It has become increasingly formal and more like US style litigation as it has become more successful and institutionalized. Today international business contracts, e.g. the sale of goods, joint ventures, construction projects, or distributorships, typically call for arbitration in the event of a dispute arising from the contractual arrangement. The main reason given today for this choice is that it allows each party to avoid being forced to submit to the courts of the other. Also important is the secrecy of the process. Such arbitration can be 'institutional' and follow the rules of institutions such as the International Chamber of Commerce in Paris, the American Arbitration Association, the London Court of International Commercial Arbitration, the World Bank's International Center for the Settlement of Investment Disputes, and others. It can also be 'ad hoc', typically adopting the rules of the UN Commission on International Trade Law (UNCITRAL). The arbitrators are private individuals selected by the parties: usually three arbitrators, acting as private judges, holding hearings and issuing judgments. There are few grounds for appeal to courts, and the final decision of the arbitrators is more easily enforced among signatory countries than would be a court judgment (under the terms of a widely adopted 1958 New York Convention).

enormous growth of arbitration centres. Excluding those concerned with maritime and commodity disputes—an older tradition—there were 120 centres by 1991, with another seven created by 1993; among the more recent centres created are those of Bahrain, Singapore, Sydney, and Vietnam. There were about 1,000 arbitrators by 1990, a number that had doubled by 1992, and seems to have stayed at that level.[64]

There has been a sharp growth in arbitration cases and a sharpening competition among arbitration centres to get the business. The development of the multinational legal market has further sharpened the competition as the large legal firms can choose the centres that work best for their clients. In Europe there has been a reinvigoration of arbitration laws beginning in the 1980s, mostly oriented towards the interests of firms seeking international arbitration activity. In the United States such a revision was brought about through the Supreme Court in 1985.[65] The overall trend has been towards strengthening international arbitration and further freeing it from the regulation of national court systems. One open-ended question is whether the formation of new structures, notably WTO, NAFTA, and the European Union, will require some new legal elements in the international arbitration world.

In their major study of international commercial arbitration, Dezalay and Garth conclude that there is a delocalized and decentralized market for the adjudication of international commercial disputes, connected by

[64] Yves Dezalay and Bryant Garth, *Dealing in Virtue* (above, n. 63); Gerald Aksen, 'Arbitration and other means of dispute settlement', in David Goldsweig and Roger Cummings (eds), *International Joint Ventures: A Practical Approach to Working with Foreign Investors in the US and Abroad* (Chicago: American Bar Association, 1990). Yet it is a tight community, with relatively few important institutions and limited numbers of individuals in each country who are the key players both as counsel and arbitrators. There is a kind of 'international arbitration community', a 'club'. The enormous growth of arbitration over the last decade arising out of the globalization of economic activity has produced sharp competition for arbitration business. Indeed, it has become big legal business. Jeswald Salacuse, *Making Global Deals: Negotiating in the International Marketplace* (Boston: Houghton Mifflin, 1991). Dezalay and Garth found that multinational legal firms further sharpen the competition since they have the capacity to forum-shop among institutions, sets of rules, laws, and arbitrators. The large English and American law firms have used their power in the international business world to impose their conception of arbitration and more largely of the practice of law. Dezalay and Garth 1996 (see above). This is well illustrated by the case of France. While French firms rank among the top providers of information services and industrial engineering services in Europe and have a strong though not outstanding position in financial and insurance services, they are at an increasing disadvantage in legal and accounting services. French law firms are at a particular disadvantage given the difference between their legal system (based on the Napoleonic Code) and Anglo-American law in a context where the latter dominates in international transactions. Anglo-American firms with offices in Paris dominate the servicing of the legal needs of French firms operating internationally out of France and of foreign firms operating in France. Jean-Francois Carrez, *Le developpement des fonctions tertiares internationales a Paris et dans les metropoles regionales*, Rapport au Premier Ministre (Paris: La Documentation Francaise, 1991). See also on legal services generally in France, Joel Bonamy and Nicole May (eds), *Services et mutations urbaines* (Paris: Anthropos, 1994).

[65] Thomas Carbonneau (ed.), *Lex Mercatoria and Arbitration* (Dobbs Ferry, NY: Transnational Juris Publications, 1990).

more or less powerful institutions and individuals who are both competitive and complementary. It is not a unitary system of justice and it is not organized around one great *lex mercatoria* 'that might have been envisioned by some of the pioneering idealists of law'.[66]

Another instance of a private regulatory system is represented by debt security or bond rating agencies which have come to play an increasingly important role in the global economy.[67] In the early 1980s, Moody's and Standard and Poor had no analysts outside the United States; ten years later each had about 100 in Europe, Japan, and Australia, and by the end of 1998, Standard and Poor alone had 250 in Europe and 100 in Asia. In his study of credit-rating processes, Sinclair found that these agencies have leverage because of their distinct gatekeeping functions with regard to investment funds sought by corporations and governments.[68] In this respect, they can be seen as a significant force in the operation and expansion of the global economy.[69] And as with business law, the US agencies have expanded their influence overseas; to some extent, their growing influence can be seen as both a function of, and a promoter of, US financial

---

[66] Dezalay and Garth, *Dealing in Virtue* (above, n. 63). See also Carbonneau, *Lex Mercatoria* (above, n. 65). Anglo-American practitioners tend not to support the highly academic continental notion of a *lex mercatoria* (see Carbonneau, above, n. 65). The so-called *lex mercatoria* was conceived by many as a return to an international law of business independent of national laws (Carbonneau, above, n. 65; Filip de Ly, *International Business Law and Lex Mercatoria* (North Holland, Neth.: Elsevier, 1992)). In so far as they are 'Americanizing' the field, they are moving it further away from academic law and *lex mercatoria*.

[67] Saskia Sassen, 'Credit Rating Agencies' (above, n. 43). There are two US agencies that dominate the market in ratings. Moody's Investors Service, usually referred to as Moody's, and Standard & Poor's Ratings Group, usually referred to as Standard & Poor. While there are several rating agencies in other countries, these are oriented to the domestic markets. The two major European agencies are London-based IBCA Fitch and French Euronotation.

[68] Timothy J. Sinclair, 'Passing Judgement: Credit Rating Processes as Regulatory Mechanisms of Governance in the Emerging World Order', *Review of International Political Economy*, vol. 1: 1 (Spring 1994), 133–59. The growing demand for ratings has given the notion of ratings a growing authoritativeness, which for Sinclair is not well founded, given the processes of judgement which are central to it. These processes are tied to certain assumptions, which are in turn tied to dominant interests, notably narrow assumptions about market efficiency. The aim is undistorted price signals and little if any government intervention. Sinclair notes that transition costs such as unemployment are usually not factored into evaluations and considered to be outweighed by the new environment created. Sinclair, 'Passing Judgement' (above), 143.

[69] The power of rating agencies has grown in good part because of the disintermediation and globalization of the capital market. The functions fulfilled by banks in the capital markets (i.e. intermediation) have lost considerable weight in the running of these markets. In so far as banks are subject to considerable government regulation, and what has replaced banks is not, the lesser role of banks inevitably brings with it a decline in government regulation over the capital markets. Rating agencies, which are private entities, have taken over some of the functions of banks in organizing information for suppliers and borrowers of capital. An important question here is whether these agencies, and the larger complex of entities represented by 'Wall Street', have indeed formed a new intermediary sector (cf. Thrift, 1987), only one largely not regulated the way the banking sector is. Nigel Thrift, 'The Fixers: The Urban Geography of International Commercial Capital', in Jeffrey Henderson and Manuel Castells (eds), *Global Restructuring and Territorial Development* (London: Sage, 1987).

orthodoxy, particularly its short-term perspective. The two large European rating agencies, Euronotation and IBCA Fitch, have also grown in importance.

These and other such transnational institutions and regimes do signal a shift in authority from the public to the private when it comes to governing the global economy. They also contain a shift in the capacity for norm-making, and in that regard raise questions about changes in the relation between state sovereignty and the governance of global economic processes. International commercial arbitration is basically a private justice system and credit-rating agencies are private gatekeeping systems. Along with other such institutions they have emerged as important governance mechanisms whose authority is not centred in the state.

Dezalay and Garth note that the 'international' is itself constituted largely from a competition among national approaches.[70] There is no global law.[71] Thus the international emerges as a site for regulatory competition among essentially national approaches, whatever the issue— environmental protection, constitutionalism, human rights.[72] From this perspective, 'international' or 'transnational' has become in the most recent period a form of 'Americanization'.[73] The most widely recognized

[70] Dezalay and Garth, 'Merchants of Law' (above, n. 63).

[71] Shapiro notes that there is not much of a regime of international law, whether through the establishment of a single global law-giver and law-enforcer or through a nation-state consensus. He also posits that if there was, we would be dealing with international rather than global law. Nor is it certain that law has become universal—i.e. that human relations anywhere in the world will be governed by some law, even if not by a law that is the same everywhere. Globalization of law refers to a very limited, specialized set of legal phenomena, and Shapiro argues that it will almost always refer to North America and Europe and only sometimes to Japan and certain other Asian countries. Martin Shapiro, 'The Globalization of Law', *Indiana Journal of Global Legal Studies*, vol. 1 (Autumn 1993), 37–64. There have been a few particular common developments and many particular parallel developments in law across the world. Thus, as a concomitant of the globalization of markets and the organization of transnational corporations, there has been a move towards a relatively uniform global contract and commercial law. This can be seen as a private law-making system in which two or more parties create a set of rules to govern their future relations. Such a system of private law-making can exist transnationally even when there is no transnational court or trans national sovereign to resolve disputes and secure enforcement. The case of international commercial arbitration discussed earlier illustrates this well.

[72] David Charny, 'Competition among Jurisdictions in Formulating Corporate Law Rules: An American Perspective on the "Race to the Bottom" in the European Communities', *Harvard International Law Journal*, vol. 32, no. 2 (1991), 423–56; Joel Trachtman, 'International Regulatory Competition, Externalization, and Jurisdiction', ibid., vol. 34, no. 1 (1993), 47–104. There are two other categories that may partly overlap with internationalization as Americanization, but are important to distinguish, at least analytically. One is multilateralism, and the other is what Ruggie has called multiperspectival institutions. See Sassen, 'Denationalized State Agendas' (above, n. 3).

[73] None of this is a smooth lineal progression. There is contestation everywhere, some of it highly visible and formalized, some of it not. In some countries, especially in Europe, we see resistance to what is perceived as the Americanization of the global capital market's standards for the regulation of their financial systems and standards for reporting financial information. Sinclair notes that the internationalization of ratings by the two leading US agencies could be seen either as another step towards global financial integration or as an American

instance of this is of course the notion of a global culture that is profoundly influenced by US popular culture.[74] But, though less widely recognized and more difficult to specify, this has also become very clear in the legal forms that are ascendant in international business transactions.[75] Through the IMF and the World Bank as well as GATT/WTO, this vision has spread to—some would say been imposed on—the developing world.[76]

agenda. See also Hall, 'Private Authority' (above, n. 58); Garrett (above, n. 2). Sinclair, 'Passing Judgement' (above, n. 68), 133–59. There is clearly growing resentment against US agencies in Europe, as became evident on the occasion of the 1991 downgrading of Credit Suisse and, in early 1992, the downgrading of Swiss Bank Corporation. It is also evident in the difficulty that foreign agencies have had in getting SEC recognition in the United States as Nationally Recognized Statistical Rating Organizations. There have been reports in the media, for example in the *Financial Times*, regarding private discussions in London, Paris, and Frankfurt about the possibility of setting up a Europe-wide agency to compete with the major US-based agencies.

[74] For a discussion of the concept of globalization see Anthony King, *Urbanism, Colonialism, and the World Economy: Culture and Spatial Foundations of the World Urban System*, The International Library of Sociology (London and New York: Routledge, 1990); Roland Robertson, 'Social Theory, Cultural Relativity and the Problem of Globality', in A. D. King (ed.), *Culture, Globalization and the World-System: Current Debates in Art History* 3 (Binghamton, NY: Department of Art & Art History, State University of New York at Binghamton, 1991), 69–90. Cf. Robertson's notion of the world as a single place, or the 'global human condition'. I would say that globalization is also a process that produces differentiation, except that the alignment of differences is of a very different kind from that associated with such differentiating notions as national character, national culture, national society. For example, the corporate world today has a global geography, but it is not found everywhere in the world: in fact it has highly defined and structured spaces; secondly, it also is increasingly sharply differentiated from non-corporate segments in the economies of the particular locations (e.g. a city such as New York) or countries where it operates. See also Max Castro (ed.), *Free Markets, Open Societies, Closed Borders?* (Berkeley: University of California Press, 2000); Peter J. Taylor, 'World cities and territorial states under conditions of contemporary globalization', *Political Geography*, vol. 19, no. 5 (2000), 5–32.

[75] Shapiro finds that law and the political structures that produce and sustain it are far more national and far less international than are trade and politics as such. He argues that the US domestic legal regime may have to respond to global changes in markets and in politics far more often than to global changes in law; for the most part, national regimes of law and lawyering will remain self-generating, though he adds that they will do so in response to globally perceived needs. Shapiro, 'The Globalization of Law' (above, n. 71), 63. In my view, it is this last point that may well be emerging as a growing factor in shaping legal form and legal practice.

[76] The best-known instance of this is probably the austerity policy imposed on many developing countries. This process also illustrates the participation of states in furthering the goals of globalization, since these austerity policies have to be run through national governments and reprocessed as national policies (Sassen, 'Denationalized State Agendas' (above, n. 3); Aman, 'The Globalizing State' (above, n. 2)). In this case, it is clearer than in others that the global is not simply the non-national and that global processes materialize in national territories and institutions. There is a distinction here to be made, and to be specified theoretically and empirically, between international law (whether public or private law), which always is implemented through national governments, and those policies which are part of the aim to further globalization. See e.g. 'Special Issue: Sovereignty and the Globalization of Intellectual Property', *Indiana Journal of Global Legal Studies*, vol. 6 (Autumn 1998), 1. See also for the particular issues raised by the Internet when it comes to national state authority Henry H. Perritt, Jr., 'International Administrative Law for the Internet: Mechanisms of Accountability', *Administrative Law Review*, vol. 51, no. 3 (1999), 871–900.

Competition among national legal systems or approaches is particularly evident in business law where the Anglo-American model of the business enterprise and competition is beginning to replace the continental model of legal artisans and corporatist control over the profession.[77] This holds true even for international commercial arbitration. Notwithstanding its deep roots in the continental tradition, especially the French and Swiss traditions, this system of private justice is becoming increasingly 'Americanized'.[78]

III. CONCLUSION

The evidence presented in this paper shows considerable patterning in many of the crucial cross-border flows at the heart of the global economy. Much of foreign direct investment consists of cross-border mergers and acquisitions. And much of the global capital market consists of a set of specific markets located in a network of financial centres which contain the key operational and institutional structures for that market. While there is a growing number of financial centres that are part of this network, there is a sharp hierarchy in the extent to which the leading centres concentrate a disproportionate share of all major financial markets.

Second, this patterning makes it clear that the centre of gravity of much of what we call the global economy is in the North Atlantic. There is a

[77] US dominance in the global economy over the last few decades has meant that the globalization of law through private corporate law-making assumes the form of the Americanization of commercial law. Shapiro, 'The Globalization of Law' (above, n. 71). Certain US legal practices are being diffused throughout the world, e.g. the legal device of franchising. Shapiro notes that this may be due not only to US dominance, but also to the receptivity of the common law to contract and other commercial law innovations. He posits that it is common in Europe to think that EC legal business goes to London because its lawyers are better at legal innovations to facilitate new and evolving transnational business relations than the civil law of the Continent. 'For whatever reasons, it is now possible to argue that American business law has become a kind of global *jus commune* incorporated explicitly or implicitly into transnational contracts and beginning to be incorporated into the case law and even the statutes of many other nations.' Shapiro, 'The Globalization of Law' (above, n. 71), 39.

[78] There are several reasons for this, all somewhat interrelated: the rationalization of arbitration know-how, the ascendance of large Anglo-American transnational legal services firms, and the emergence of a new specialty in conflict resolution. The large Anglo-American law firms which dominate the international market for business law include arbitration as one of the array of services they offer—a kind of litigation that uses a forum other than national courts. Specialists in conflict are practitioners formed from the two great groups that have dominated legal practice in the United States: corporate lawyers, known for their competence as negotiators in the creation of contracts, and trial lawyers whose talent lies in jury trials. The growing importance in the 1980s of such transactions as mergers and acquisitions, antitrust and other litigation contributed to a new specialization: knowing how to combine judicial attacks and behind-the-scenes negotiations to reach the optimum outcome for the client. Dezalay and Garth note that under these conditions judicial recourse becomes a weapon to be used in a situation which will almost certainly end before trial. Dezalay and Garth, 'Merchants of Law' (above, n. 63).

growing, though selective, incorporation of more and more locations (i.e. financial centres) and institutional orders (e.g. pension funds) into this global economic system. And there is a growing interdependence in this worldwide system. Yet the latter is clearly dominated by the financial centres and major firms from the North Atlantic region.

Third, the sharp growth in cross-border mergers and acquisitions and in the financial markets has proceeded in part at least in spite of the difficulties encountered by governments in harmonizing standards and rules and establishing appropriate regimes for these operations and markets. Long before governments approved some of these standards and regimes, the international business community had gone ahead with the globalization of economic activity. Firms adopted Anglo-American accounting and financial reporting standards as the de facto international standards, expanded the use and refined the features of international commercial arbitration to handle cross-border disputes which in the past might have been adjudicated in less flexible and slower national courts, and proceeded with cross-border mergers and acquisitions in the European Union even as the European Commission struggled unsuccessfully to create a European firm and a European directive on M & As.

Fourth, an enormous amount of government work has gone into the development of standards and regimes to handle the new conditions entailed by economic globalization. Much work has been done on competition policy and on the development of financial regulations, and there has been considerable willingness to innovate and to accept whole new policy concepts by governments around the world. The content and specifications of much of this work is clearly shaped by the frameworks and traditions evident in the North Atlantic region. This is not to deny the significant differences between the United States and the European Union, for instance, or among various individual countries, but rather to emphasize that there is a clear Western style that is dominant in the handling of these issues and, secondly, that we cannot simply speak of 'Americanization' since in some cases Western European standards emerge as the ruling ones.

At this stage, it is not clear to me as a political economist how this policy work interacts with the actual economic dynamics I have described. It is difficult to establish to what extent the obstacles to reaching convergence or harmonization in a range of policy domains have actually significantly altered the evolution of these economic dynamics. It is clear that the latter have been enabled by some of the major regulatory changes that have succeeded—deregulation and privatization—and which have shown themselves to be crucial to the process of globalization by creating an 'enabling environment'. It is also difficult to understand whether the growth of various forms of private authority is in part a response to the absence of new or innovative governmental regulation or is aiming at preventing the latter, or when it is one or the other.

Overall, it would seem to me that we are confronting a de facto formation of cross-border economic systems and that we need to understand to what extent this produces its own distinct zone for transactions and governance mechanisms. Governments play an important role here, but up until now it has been largely confined to enabling these economic processes. In capturing the extent to which these de facto economic systems are characterized by locational and institutional embeddedness, the paper sought to signal that governments could play a role that goes beyond enabling existing economic dynamics and address larger normative questions as well.[79] Given the strategic role played by the North Atlantic region it would mean that governments in this region would be particularly well situated to play such a role vis-à-vis the firms and markets of this region, firms and markets that in fact dominate much of the global economy.

---

[79] See Sassen, *Towards New Architectures for Global Governance* (The 2000 Theodore Hesburgh Lectures on Politics and Ethics) (South Bend, Indiana: University of Notre Dame Press, forthcoming 2001).

Global economic networks and global legal pluralism

Francis Snyder

I. INTRODUCTION

How are global economic networks—including transatlantic economic networks—governed?[1] I suggest that they are governed by the totality of strategically determined, situationally specific, and often episodic conjunctions of a multiplicity of sites throughout the world. These sites have institutional, normative, and processual characteristics. The totality of these sites represents a new global form of legal pluralism. This contribution aims to explore and, within limits, to substantiate this claim. It invites us to think systematically about how global economic networks are governed by global legal pluralism.

This chapter forms part of a broader research project on the governance of globalization. That project, which analyses the resolution of trade disputes between the European Union and China,[2] focuses on a series of case studies. Here I draw on one of these studies—concerning the international

[1] I wish to thank Chen Yong Quan, Cao Ge Feng, Candido Garcia Molyneux, Tom Heller, Emir Lawless, Cosimo Monda, Song Ying, Anne-Lise Strahtmann, Yang Zugong, and several government and industry representatives in the Shenzhen, China, Special Economic Zone, for their contributions to this chapter. I am also grateful for comments at the Columbia conference; a seminar on 2 April 1999 at the Institute of International Studies, Stanford University, while I was Visiting Senior Fellow at the Stanford Program in International Legal Studies; the Conference on 'The Regional and Global Regulation of International Trade', Institute of European Studies of Macau, 10–11 May 1999; and the Guangdong International Research Institute for Technology and Economy, 13 May 1999. A longer version of this contribution is being published as Francis Snyder, 'Governing Economic Globalization: Global Legal Pluralism and European Law', *European Law Journal*, vol. 5, no. 4 (1999), Special Issue on 'Globalization and Law'.

[2] For other publications from the project, see: Francis Snyder, 'Legal Aspects of Trade between the European Union and China: Preliminary Reflections', in Nicholas Emiliou and David O'Keeffe (eds), *The European Union and World Trade Law after the GATT Uruguay Round* (Chichester: John Wiley & Sons, 1996), 363–77; Francis Snyder, *International Trade and Customs Law of the European Union* (London: Butterworths, 1998), 594–600 and *passim*; Francis Snyder, 'Europeanisation and Globalization as Friends and Rivals: European Union Law and Global Economic Networks', in Francis Snyder (ed.), *The Europeanisation of Law* (Oxford: Hart Publishing, in press); Snyder, 'Governing Economic Globalization' (above, n. 1); Francis Snyder, 'Legal Issues in EU–China Trade Relations', *Wuhan University Law Review*, forthcoming (in Chinese); and Francis Snyder and Song Ying, *Introduction to European Union Law*, 2nd edition (Peking University Press, Beijing, forthcoming 2000 [in Chinese]).

trade in toys between the European Union and China—for the purpose of illustrating my theoretical argument. Though based on a specific example, this theoretical argument applies equally to transatlantic regulatory cooperation between the United States and the European Union.

This contribution aims to increase our understanding of how global economic networks are governed and to improve our capacity to analyse these new forms of governance, rather than to promote law reform or advance a specific political or institutional agenda. Consequently, its perspective is more sociological than normative. It adopts, for the most part, the standpoint of strategic actors. Relations among strategic actors can be envisaged as involving different types of organizations, whether firms, states, or regional or international organizations. Alternatively, we can see them as implicating different structures of governance, whether market-based, polity-based, or based on conventions in the form of international agreements. From a third perspective, these relationships put into play global economic networks and various sites of global legal pluralism. This contribution is intended to highlight all of these perspectives.

The remainder of this contribution is divided into four main parts. The next part (Part II) discusses the meaning of globalization. Part III introduces, by way of an empirical anchor for the theoretical argument, the case of the global commodity chain in toys. In Part IV, I summarize my basic theoretical argument regarding global legal pluralism. Part V identifies some of the sites of global legal pluralism which are the most significant for this global economic network. Based on this discussion, I set forth in the conclusion a series of hypotheses for future research.

II. THE MEANING OF GLOBALIZATION

Thinking about how global economic networks are governed requires a concept of globalization. By globalization, I refer to an aggregate of multi-faceted, uneven, often contradictory economic, political, social, and cultural processes which are characteristic of our time. This contribution concentrates primarily on the economic aspects, but these need to be set within a more general framework.

In economic terms, the most salient features of globalization, driven by multinational firms, are for the present purposes the development of international production networks (IPNs), dispersion of production facilities among different countries, a technical and functional fragmentation of production, a fragmentation of ownership, flexibility in the production process, worldwide sourcing, an increase in intra-firm trade, an interpenetration of international financial markets, the possibility of virtually instantaneous worldwide flows of information, changes in the nature of employment, and the emergence of new forms of work.

Viewed from a political standpoint, globalization has witnessed the rise of new political actors such as multinational firms, non-governmental organizations and social movements. At the same time, it has tended to weaken, fragment, and sometimes even restructure the state, but without by any means destroying or replacing it. Globalization has also altered radically the relationship between governance and territory to which we have become accustomed in recent history. It thus has blurred and splintered the boundaries between the domestic and external spheres of nation-states and of regional integration organizations; it has fostered an articulation of systems of multi-level governance, interlocking politics, and policy networks; and it has helped to render universal the discourse of, and claims for, human rights. In many political and legal settings, such as the European Union, globalization has raised serious questions about the nature and appropriate form of contemporary governance.

Among the manifold social processes involved in globalization are the spread of certain models of production and patterns of consumption from specific geographic/political/national contexts to others. Contradictory tendencies have developed towards internationalization and localization within as well as among different regions and countries. We have also witnessed the uneven development of new social movements based on different, if not alternative, forms of community.

Seen as a cultural phenomenon, globalization has implied the emergence of a new global culture, which is shared to some extent by virtually all elite groups. This in turn has enhanced the globalization of the imagination and of the imaginable.[3] At the same time, however, it has contributed to the marginalization of many local cultures. Consequently, it has sometimes increased the range and depth of international and infranational cultural conflicts, as well as resistance to new forms of cultural imperialism.

III. A GLOBAL ECONOMIC NETWORK: THE GLOBAL COMMODITY CHAIN IN TOYS

Global economic networks take various forms. I focus here by way of example on the international toy industry. The Barbie doll[4] illustrates the toy industry's domestic impact and global reach. In European countries, imports of toys from Asia have sometimes provoked reactions bordering on xenophobia. In the United States, they have triggered outrage against

---

[3] For this expression, I am indebted to Professor Pietro Barcellona, oral intervention at the Conference on 'Quelle culture pour l'Europe? Ordres juridiques et cultures dans le processus de globalisation', Réseau Européen de Droit et Société (REDS) and Istituto di Ricerca sui Problemi dello Stato e delle Istitutionzi (IRSI), Rome, 2–3 Nov. 1998.

[4] © Mattel Inc.

cheap Chinese labour and trade deficits with China, which in the case of the toy trade between China and the United States has been estimated by the United States to amount to US$5.4 billion.[5] This has not, however, been true by and large of the Barbie doll, which is usually viewed instead as a US or even global product.

The Barbie doll's label 'Made in China' suggests, correctly, that in the production of Barbie, China provides the factory space, labour, and electricity, as well as cotton cloth for the dress. However, it conceals the facts that Japan supplies the nylon hair, that Saudia Arabia provides oil, that Taiwan refines oil into ethylene for plastic pellets for the body, and that Japan, the United States, and Europe supply almost all the machinery and tools. Most of the moulds (the most expensive item) come from the United States, Japan, or Hong Kong. The United States supplies cardboard packaging, paint pigments, and moulds, and Hong Kong supplies the banking and insurance and carries out the delivery of the raw materials to factories in south China together with the collection of the finished products and shipping. Two Barbie dolls are marketed every second in 140 countries around the world by Mattel Inc. of El Segundo, California.

Of course, there is a Barbie doll museum in Palo Alto, California, and shortly after Barbie celebrated her fortieth birthday on 9 March 1999, the US Postal Service released a commemorative postage stamp in her honour.[6] The Barbie doll is quintessentially American in origin, style, and culture, and the result of a commodity chain powered by a US buyer. But Barbie is for all practical purposes a global product, if by 'global' we refer to the fragmentation of the production process, the dispersion of production facilities among different countries, and the organization of production within international production networks. We can understand this industry most easily by conceiving of it as a global commodity chain. By 'commodity chain', I mean 'a network of labor and production processes whose end result is a finished commodity'.[7] Global commodity chains, as Gereffi has shown,[8] tend to be strongly connected to specific systems of production and to involve particular patterns of coordinated trade. If we follow Gereffi's widely accepted schema, each global commodity chain has three main dimensions. The first relates to the structure of inputs and outputs: that is, products and services are linked together in a sequence in which each activity adds value to its predecessor. The second concerns territoriality: networks of enterprises may be spatially dispersed or concen-

  [5] Rone Tempest, 'Barbie and the World Economy', *Los Angeles Times World Report* (a Special Section Produced in Cooperation with *The Korea Times*) 13 Oct. 1996, 3.

  [6] Elizabeth Rapoport, 'Barbie at 40', *Sky* (Delta Air Lines), Mar. 1999, 54–7.

  [7] Terence K. Hopkins and Immanuel Wallerstein, 'Commodity Chains in the World-Economy Prior to 1800', *Review*, vol. 10 (1986), 159.

  [8] Gary Gereffi, 'The Organization of Buyer-Driven Global Commodity Chains: How US Retailers Shape Overseas Production Networks', in Gary Gereffi and Miguel Korzeniewicz (eds), *Commodity Chains and Global Capitalism* (Westport, Conn.: Greenwood Press, 1994), 96.

trated. The third dimension is the structure of governance: relationships of power and authority determine the flow and allocation of resources (financial, material, human) within the chain.[9]

Here we are interested especially in the third dimension, the structure of governance. Gereffi distinguishes two distinct types of governance structures in global commodity chains. On the one hand, we find producer-driven commodity chains, in which the system of production is controlled by large integrated industrial enterprises. On the other hand, we find buyer-driven commodity chains, in which production networks are typically decentralized and power rests with large retailers, brand-name merchandisers and trading companies.[10] This distinction provides a useful point of departure for analysing the global commodity chain in the EU–China toy trade.

The international toy industry is a prime example of an international commodity chain dominated by the buyers. It is hierarchically organized. At the top of the hierarchy are large buyers as well as large retailers. The buyers include several US manufacturers, two Japanese manufacturers, and one European company. The most important buyers are two American companies, Mattel and Hasbro. The key elements in the power of buyers are designs and brands. The large buyers are the node in various networks of inventors and creators of toys. Through contract, they control the access of inventors, intermediaries, and factories to the market. The most important retailers include large specialty stores such as Toys 'Я' Us, discount houses such as Wal-Mart in the United States, and hypermarkets or catalogue stores in the European Union. Taking buyers and retailers together, the power of this group lies in its control of design, brands, and marketing.

Buyers and retailers compete, however, with regard to access to retail markets. The powerful buyers are dependent to some degree on large retailers, such as Toys 'Я' Us. With regard to the retail market, as economic downturns reveal, the two groups have conflicting interests. To maintain market share, and to enhance their dominant position in the global commodity chain, buyers have tried recently to lessen their dependence on retailers. Their strategies for doing so include increased direct-to-consumer sales, including catalogue and Internet sales, whether from their own website or from online retailers.[11]

The US firms have regional headquarters and a significant share of the toy market in Europe. The EU toy market is supplied mainly through importer-wholesalers. As of 1995, the EU toy industry comprised about 2,600 firms, producing a great variety of toys, and employing just under 100,000 workers, with only fifteen firms having more than 500

---

[9] Gereffi, 'The Organization' (above, n. 8), 96–7.   [10] Ibid. 97.
[11] See George Anders and Lisa Bannon, 'E-toys to join web-retailer parade with IPO', *The Wall Street Journal* (6 April 1999), B1.

employees.[12] Each country has its own distinctive retail sector, ranging from catalogue stores to hypermarkets to independent retailers.[13] Except for Lego, established in Denmark in 1932 and now one of the world's ten largest toy manufacturers, there are no large manufacturers or specialist retailers based in Europe similar to those based in the US. Together with Lego and the Japanese firm Bandai, the US firms dominated the first main peak trade association, Toy Manufacturers of Europe, formed in the early 1990s, and are now the principal players in the current EU peak association, Toy Industries of Europe (TIE).

Further down the hierarchy come the Hong Kong companies which act as intermediaries between these multinationals and the toy factories. Within East Asia, Hong Kong has been of signal importance in the development of the toy industry. It began in the 1940s as an export platform, then developed in the 1980s as the base of original equipment manufacturers (OEMs) for overseas importers or of intermediaries between local manufacturers and overseas buyers, until, starting in the 1990s, it became a re-exporter of toys made in China. In 1998 licensing and contract manufacturing for overseas manufacturers, usually to production specifications and product designs provided by the buyers, accounted for an estimated 70 per cent of total domestic toy exports.[14] US buyers accounted for 51 per cent of Hong Kong's toy exports in the first ten months of 1995.[15] Today Hong Kong is the location of management, design, R & D, marketing, quality control, finance, and usually shipping.[16]

At the bottom of the hierarchy are the factories, most of which are located in China. By 1995 toy production in China involved about 3,000 factories employing more than 1.3 million people.[17] Such factories usually occupy the structural position of OEM, producing to other companies' specifications with machinery provided by the buyer. However, some now operate on the basis of original design manufacturer (ODM), producing to provided designs but sharing the cost of machinery and investment as well as sharing markets according to an agreement with the

[12] Commission of the European Communities, 'Report from the Commission to the Council on the surveillance measures and quantitative quotas applicable to certain non-textile products originating in the People's Republic of China', COM(95) 614 final at 41.

[13] See Hong Kong Trade Development Council, *Practical Guide to Exporting Toys for Hong Kong Traders* (Hong Kong Trade Development Council, Research Department, Mar. 1999), 34–58.

[14] 'Hong Kong's Toy Industry', *Hong Kong & China Economics*, on the Internet homepage of the Hong Kong Trade Development Council at http://www.tdc.org.hk/main/industries/t2_2_39.htm, last updated 2 July 1998.

[15] *Journal of Commerce*, 13 Jan. 1995, n.p.

[16] See the statement by Dennis Ting, who as of Jan. 1995 was chairman of Kader Industrial Co. Ltd., a leading Hong Kong toy firm, as well as of the Hong Kong trading agency's toy advisory committee and of the Hong Kong Toy Council: *Journal of Commerce*, 13 Jan. 1995, n.p.

[17] Jim Newton and Lai-hing Tse, '"Kids" Stuff: The Organisation and Politics of the China–EU Trade in Toys', in Roger Strange, Jim Slater, and Liming Wang (eds), *Trade and Investment in China: The European Experience* (London and New York: Routledge, 1998), 154.

buyer.[18] These contracts are often arranged and managed by Hong Kong-based entrepreneurs, who in addition to their role as intermediaries sometimes run their own toy manufacturing companies in China and play key roles in the main Hong Kong sectoral trade association, Hong Kong Toys Council. More than half of China's toy production is re-exported through Hong Kong.[19] For this reason, as well as to preserve maximum flexibility in a highly innovative and rapidly changing market, the production of toys for the export market usually takes place in wholly owned subsidiaries rather than joint ventures.[20] Today China and Hong Kong account for nearly 60 per cent of the world's toy trade.[21]

IV. THE SHAPE OF GLOBAL LEGAL PLURALISM

We usually view the legal arrangements which underpin such global economic networks in one of two ways. Often we see them essentially in terms of contracts between nominally equal parties, whose agreement is consecrated either in bilateral or multilateral form. Alternatively, we conceive of them in hierarchical terms, for example as constituting various regional or international forms of multilevel governance. I wish to suggest, however, that both of these conceptions, regardless of their force in normative terms, are descriptively inaccurate and analytically incomplete. There is a fundamental and growing disjunction between our traditional normative conceptions of the law governing international trade and the shape of the economic networks which are an integral part of economic globalization. Global economic networks are the product of, and a form of, strategic behaviour, even though such networks usually have a particular locus of power and a specific hierarchy. In order to understand how they are governed in practice, we need to revise our basic ideas about the shape of the global legal order, without necessarily expecting economic relations and the law to be isomorphic.

I suggest that the most adequate concept for understanding the global legal order is global legal pluralism. Global legal pluralism, as I use the term,[22] comprises two different aspects. The first is structural, the second relational.

---

[18] Interviews in Hong Kong, Guangzhou, and the Shenzhen Special Economic Zone, China.

[19] BBC Monitoring Service: Asia Pacific, 14 June 1995, cited in Newton and Tse, '"Kids" Stuff' (above, n. 17), 154.

[20] See Newton and Tse, '"Kids" Stuff' (above, n. 17), 153.

[21] 'Chinese Toy Making: Where the Furbies Come From', *The Economist*, 19 Dec. 1998, 95.

[22] My use of the term is broader than that of Gunther Teubner, '"Global Bukowina": Legal Pluralism in World Society', in Gunther Teubner (ed.), *Global Law without a State* (Dartmouth Publishers: Aldershot, England, 1997). For further discussion of Teubner's stimulating ideas, see Snyder, 'Governing Economic Globalization' (above, n. 1).

First, global legal pluralism involves a variety of institutions, norms, and dispute resolution processes located, and produced, at different structured sites around the world. Legal scholarship has traditionally paid most attention to understanding state, regional, and international (trade) legal institutions, legally binding norms, and dispute resolution processes involving law. The main exceptions in the legal world are international lawyers, who have also devoted much energy to the study of international negotiations and to norms that at least in principle are not legally binding. The analysis of international regimes, multilevel governance, and other types of institutional arrangements has largely been the province of political scientists and specialists in international relations. Examples in the field of EU legal scholarship include the work on multilevel governance, committees, and more generally on different types of settings, whether highly institutionalized with specified norms, rules and procedures or non-hierarchical and decentralized. While it is possible to generalize to some extent from this previous work, no one has tried to unite these different elements. Some basic questions therefore remain to be answered. What is a site? States and regional and international organizations are included, but so are a variety of other institutional, normative, and processual sites, such as commercial arbitration, trade associations, and so on. How are sites created, and how do they grow, survive, or die? How are they structured? What does it mean to say that different structured sites are the anchors of contemporary legal pluralism?

Second, the relations among these sites are of many different types, in terms of both structure and process. For example, in terms of structural relationships, sites may be autonomous and even independent, part of the same or different regimes, part of a single system of multilevel governance, or otherwise interconnected. In terms of process, they may be distinct and discrete, competing, overlapping, or they may feed into each other, for example in the sense of comprising a 'structural set', 'formed through the mutual convertibility of rules and resources in one domain of action into those pertaining to another'.[23] These relations of structure and process constitute the global legal playing field. They determine the basic characteristics of global legal pluralism, such as equality or hierarchy, dominance or submission, creativity or imitation, convergence or divergence, and so on. They influence profoundly the growth, development, and survival of the different sites.

Global legal pluralism is not merely an important part of the context in which global economic networks are constructed, in the sense that it is a factor to be taken into account by strategic actors. It is integral to these global economic networks themselves. In other words, global economic

---

[23] Anthony Giddens, 'A Reply to My Critics', in David Held and John B. Thompson (eds), *Social Theory of Modern Societies: Anthony Giddens and His Critics* (Cambridge: Cambridge University Press, 1989), 259.

networks are constructed on a global playing field, which is organized or structured partly by global legal pluralism. Global legal pluralism does more, however, than simply provide the rules of the game. It also constitutes the game itself, including the players.

V. GLOBAL LEGAL PLURALISM AND
THE GLOBAL COMMODITY CHAIN IN TOYS

A. The theory of commodity chains

We are now in a position to consider in greater detail the interconnection between global legal pluralism and the global commodity chain in toys. Following Hopkins and Wallerstein, let us use the term 'boxes' to refer to the separable processes involved in the international toy industry.[24] The boundaries of each box are socially defined, and so may be redefined.[25] Technological and social organizational changes play a role in these processes. So, too, does law. Conceived broadly to encompass the sites of global legal pluralism, with each site comprising its specific institutions, norms, and processes, law helps to construct and to define the boxes which make up the global commodity chain in toys.

Hopkins and Wallerstein propose a series of questions concerning the social organization of the constituent units of any single box in the chain.[26] Here I rephrase, elaborate, and add to their questions, giving special emphasis to the institutional, normative, and processual components of the sites of global legal pluralism. I give selected examples of the interconnections between these sites and the international commodity chain. The discussion is meant to be illustrative, not exhaustive.

B. Number of component units

There is, first, the number of component units in the box. To what degree is a box monopolized by a small number of production units? What are the main factors determining this structure? What incentives for a particular structure are provided by legal and other institutions, norms, and processes? Do different sites of global legal pluralism provide conflicting incentives, and, if so, how are these conflicts managed, if not neutralized? If demonopolization of any highly profitable box is an important process in the contemporary world economy, as Hopkins and Wallerstein

---

[24] Terence K. Hopkins and Immanuel Wallerstein, 'Commodity Chains: Construct and Research', in 'Commodity Chains in the Capitalist World-Economy Prior to 1800', in Gary Gereffi and Miguel Korzeniewicz (eds), *Commodity Chains and Global Capitalism* (Westport, Conn.: Greenwood Process, 1994), 18.

[25] Hopkins and Wallerstein, 'Commodity Chains' (above, n. 24), 18.

[26] Ibid. 18–19.

suggest,[27] what role do the sites of global legal pluralism play with regard to this process—for example by encouraging it, by countering it by redefining the boundaries of the box or by other means, or by creating incentives for shifting capital investment to other boxes, or even other chains?

Several sites of global legal pluralism play a role in shaping or determining the number of component units in any given box in the international commodity chain in toys. Consider three examples. First, US intellectual property law is of crucial significance in determining the number of buyers and in maintaining their market power. Antitrust law is crucial in defining the number of key buyers or manufacturers in the international toy industry. Secondly, US competition law affects the possibility of mergers among buyers. When in 1996 market leader Mattel Inc. acquired the third largest toy manufacturer, Tyco Toys Inc., Mattel was quoted in the US media as expressing confidence that the deal would not be blocked by US antitrust law, even though the companies' combined sales represented 19 per cent of the American toy market.[28] Thirdly, the lack of binding legal regulation of Internet retailing lowers barriers to entry into the retail market in toys. Consequently, when buyers are squeezed by traditional retailers, they turn without great difficulty to the Internet in order to enter the retail sector themselves, either through specialist Internet retailers or by means of the buyers' own websites.

C. Geographic concentration or dispersal

Consider, second, the question of geographic concentration or dispersal. What is the degree of geographic spread among the units in a specific box? In other words, are the units in a particular box geographically concentrated, or are they dispersed? For example, are the provision of finance, marketing, and retailing geographically concentrated, while production is dispersed? Is the prevailing geographic pattern influenced by the sites of global legal pluralism, and if so, how? For example, what incentives do different institutions, norms, and processes provide for either concentration or dispersal of the different sites? Do these institutions, norms, and processes play a role in the extent to which boxes shift from the core to the periphery of the world economy, assuming that, as Hopkins and Wallerstein argue, a box is likely to be relatively geographically concentrated in the core but dispersed on the periphery?

We have already seen that finance, marketing, and retailing in the international toy industry are concentrated, the former in the United States and Hong Kong, and the latter in the United States and, to a much lesser extent,

---

[27] Hopkins and Wallerstein, 'Commodity Chains' (above, n. 24), 18.
[28] James Madore, 'Mattel Confident Tyco Deal Will Pass Antitrust Scrutiny', *Buffalo News*, 19 Nov. 1996, n.p.

Europe and Japan. However, production is potentially much more dispersed, even though until recently it has tended to be concentrated in Asia. The geographical separation of production from finance, marketing, and retailing is encouraged by international norms concerning the customs operations known in the European Union as inward processing and outward processing.[29] It is no exaggeration to describe the existence and increased use of these customs rules as the legal basis for what has been called 'the new international division of labour'.[30] The overarching international legal framework is provided by the International Convention on the Simplification and Harmonization of Customs Procedures, which was signed at Kyoto on 18 May 1973 and entered in force on 25 September 1974.[31] The Convention has had about ninety contracting parties, including the United States, the European Union and its Member States, Hong Kong, and China.[32] Not all of these, however, are parties to all the relevant annexes, such as Annexe E.6 concerning temporary admission for inward processing, Annexe E.8 concerning temporary exportation for outward processing, and Annexe F.1 concerning free zones. These annexes contain the basic substantive rules, which are not legally binding but may take effect as standards, recommended practices, or notes.

China has ratified the Convention but has not accepted any of the three annexes. However, since the early 1980s, Chinese legislation, both central and local, on Special Economic Zones (SEZs) has had a direct influence on the concentration of production facilities in the international toy trade. Most toy factories are located in the Shenzhen SEZ. Shenzhen rules on foreign direct investment provide for Chinese–foreign joint ventures, Chinese–foreign contractual joint ventures, wholly foreign-owned enterprises, international leasing, compensation trade, and processing and assembling with materials and parts from foreign suppliers.[33] Recently, however, the fact that labour costs in Shenzhen are higher than in the rest of Guangdong Province, due partly to law, has encouraged toy companies to establish outside the SEZ, though still in Guangdong.

---

[29] On EU law, see Francis Snyder, *International Trade and Customs Law of the European Union* (London: Butterworths, 1998), 83–103.

[30] For case studies from an economic standpoint, see Folker Froebel, Juergen Heinrichs, and Otto Kreye, *The New International Division of Labour: Structural Unemployment in Industrialised Countries and Industrialisation in Developing Countries*, trans. Pete Burgress (Cambridge: Cambridge University Press; Paris: Editions de la Maison des Sciences de l'Homme, 1980).

[31] 1975 OJ (L100/2); Cmnd 5938.

[32] An updated version of the Convention was adopted on 25 June 1999. It has not yet been ratified by all parties, which now number 114. See the World Customs Organization website at http://www.wcoomd.org.

[33] For an introduction, see the Shenzhen SEZ Internet homepage at http://china-window.com/Shenzhen-w/shenzhen.html.

D. Membership in one or more chains

A third factor is membership in one or more chains. Is a box located in more than one commodity chain? If so, how many? Do specific sites, including institutions, norms, and processes, create a structure of incentives so that a particular box tends to be inserted in more than one commodity chain? To what extent, and how, is this insertion of a particular box in different commodity chains accomplished partly by the law? What role do law and other types of norms play in the management of relations between the different commodity chains in which a particular box is located?

E. Property arrangements

I turn, fourthly, to property arrangements. What property-like arrangements (such as use, ownership, management, control) are associated with the units of a specific box? Which sites of global legal pluralism are the most relevant to these arrangements? Which specific institutions, norms, and processes are determinative with regard to the arrangements in a particular site, and why? If different property-like arrangements prevail among the various units in a box, what institutions, norms, and processes encourage or tolerate diversity? How is such diversity managed?

F. Modes of labour control

Turning next to modes of labour control, what modes of labour control are found in each box? Which sites of global legal pluralism are most relevant, and why? Which specific institutions, norms, and processes are significant, and why? To what extent are different modes of labour control encouraged or facilitated by legal or other institutions, norms, and processes? Are there conflicts among different sites with regard to modes of labour control? If so, how are these conflicts resolved in institutional, normative, and processual terms?

The labour law of nation-states is not the only relevant law, or in the case of China even the most important. Far more significant are the codes of conduct elaborated under the aegis of multinational companies and sector-specific trade associations. These reflect the organization of power in the global toy commodity chain in two respects. First, the dominant buyers, whose power rests on their control of brands and marketing, are able in effect to determine the content of industry-wide codes of conduct and then to impose them on their suppliers. Codes of conduct are thus analogous to standard-form contracts laid down by the leading firms in a particular market.[34] Second, precisely because the dominant buyers are

[34] Peter T. Muchlinski, '"Global Bukowina" Examined: Viewing the Multinational Enterprise as a Transnational Law-making Community', in Teubner (ed.), *Global Law without a State* (above, n. 22), 86.

few in number, they are unusually susceptible to political pressure. Non-governmental organizations, such as the Toy Coalition, have successfully put pressure on the small number of powerful American buyers, and the national and international trade associations they control, to elaborate codes of conduct with regard to their mainly Asian workforce.

G. Links between different chains

A sixth set of questions concerns links between different commodity chains. How are the boxes within a particular commodity chain linked to each other? Which specific institutions, norms, and processes create, sustain, or transform these links? What role do different sites of global legal pluralism play in linking different boxes? Is there any overall coordination of these links? How is the discreteness of a particular commodity chain maintained, and what role does global legal pluralism play in this respect?

H. Relations between economic relations and specific sites

A seventh set of questions concerns specifically the relations between particular sets of economic relations (boxes) and specific sites of global legal pluralism. Do specific sites relate to particular aspects of specific boxes? For example, do certain sites deal with labour control, others with financial arrangements, others with marketing, others with dispute resolution, and so on? How, and why? To what extent are particular sites important in governing the social organization of the constituent units of a box, even when the sites are not geographically proximate to the box (in other words, when governance, economic processes, and territory are not congruent)?

I give four examples to illustrate the relationship between the marketing of toys and the European Union as a legal site. First, quotas were applied to imports into the European Union of toys from China until 1998, provoking a series of cases before the European Court of Justice.[35] Second, the EC 'toys directive'[36] provides that all toys sold in the European Union must meet essential safety requirements and bear a 'CE' mark indicating conformity. It conditions Chinese production of toys for export to Europe on the conduct of inspections in Hong Kong.[37] Third, with regard to EC environmental legislation, though no such legislation has yet been enacted in response to pressure from Greenpeace to ban all soft PVC toys for children in the European Union, the risk that it might be has already changed

---

[35] For a detailed analysis, see Snyder, 'Governing Economic Globalization' (above, n. 1).

[36] Council Directive 88/378/EEC, as amended.

[37] See 'Hong Kong's Toy Industry', *Hong Kong & China Economics*, on the Internet homepage of the Hong Kong Trade Development Council at http://www.tdc.org.hk/main/industries/t2_2_39.htm, last updated 2 July 1998.

the practices of some toy factories in China which export to the European Union.[38] Fourth, general EC trade legislation affects Chinese toy exports. As from January 1998, preferences for certain Chinese goods were removed under the EC's Generalised Scheme of Preferences (GSP), leading to an increase in the tariff rate for toys to levels varying between 3.4 and 6.3 per cent.[39]

I. Relations between sites and the chain as a whole

An eighth and last consideration is relations between sites and the chain as a whole. What types of relationships, for example horizontal or vertical, competitive or cooperative, market-based or state-based or convention-based, exist between the different sites that are relevant to a specific global commodity chain? Does any specific site concern the global commodity chain as a whole? To what extent does the plurality of sites provide an effective way of managing the chain as a whole? Would a single site or a small number of sites be more effective? What does 'effective' mean in this context? In other words, what are our criteria for evaluating the effectiveness of specific sites, and of the totality of sites which we call global legal pluralism, in the organization and management of the chain as a whole?

Certain sites concern several parts of the chain or the chain as a whole. The most well-known example is the Uruguay Round agreements associated with the World Trade Organization (WTO). This includes the General Agreement on Tariffs and Trade (GATT), the General Agreement on Trade in Services (GATS), and the Agreement on Trade-Related Aspects of Intellectual Property (TRIPS).

The GATT/WTO was a crucial conditioning element in the negotiation of the EU quota on toys from China in 1993–4 and the related litigation between 1994 and 1998.[40] It also cast a long shadow with regard to future disputes, notably by holding out, to China and multinational companies 'located' there, the promise of new norms, institutions, and processes which would become available on eventual Chinese accession. When China joins the GATT, the firms located there will benefit from Article XI GATT concerning the general elimination of quantitative restrictions. Also, the provision of services and the protection of intellectual property in brand names are likely to be affected by the eventual application of GATS and TRIPS. It may further be argued that the impact of the GATT on China is already real, even if China has not yet acceded to the WTO. Companies are already positioning themselves in anticipation of a further opening up of China's domestic market to imported toys and foreign toy

---

[38] Interviews in Guangzhou and Shenzhen Special Economic Zone, China.
[39] 'Hong Kong's Toy Industry' (above, n. 37).
[40] For detailed analysis, see Snyder, 'Governing Globalization' (above, n. 1).

retailers. One has only to note that in 1997, the same year it purchased a major competitor Tyco, Mattel launched Barbie in China.[41]

VI. CONCLUSION

I have argued here that global economic networks are governed by the totality of strategically determined, situationally specific, and often episodic conjunctions of a multiplicity of institutional, normative, and processual sites throughout the world. The totality of such sites represents a new global form of legal pluralism.

The development of the global economic relations involved in the international toy industry owes much to corporate strategies. But these strategies themselves have been pursued in light of the framework of the law and have been elaborated through use of the law. They take place, are conditioned by, and have contributed to the development of global legal pluralism. To put it more accurately, the development of global networks in the toy industry has occurred in conjunction with the development of a variety of structural sites throughout the world, each of which comprises institutions, norms, and dispute-resolution processes.

Taken together, these different but interwoven sets of norms, whether legally binding in formal terms or merely soft law, amount to a distinct regime for governing global economic networks. However, they are less a structure of multilevel governance than a conjunction of distinctive institutional and normative sites for the production, implementation and sanctioning of rules. In the specific case of the toy industry, they testify, in part, to the structure of authority and power within these inter-firm and intra-firm networks, which are characterized by a buyer-driven, rather than a producer-driven, governance structure. These new normative forms for governing global economic networks are among the reasons why US, EU, and Chinese firms and economies are so intimately linked in the internationalized production and distribution relations which are characteristic of globalization.

Several more specific hypotheses can be derived from this discussion. First, global legal pluralism is a way of describing the structure of the sites taken as a whole. Seen from the perspective of a specific global commodity chain, global legal pluralism may be described as a network, even if some segments of the network may be occupied alternatively by two or more possible sites.

Second, the sites of global legal pluralism may be classified provisionally into three rough categories. Some sites are market-based, i.e. generated by economic actors as part of economic processes. Some are

[41] See the history of Mattel on the company Internet homepage at http://www.snc.edu/baad/ba485/spr1998/group8/history.htm.

polity-based, in that they form a part of established political structures. Others are convention-based, in the sense that they are derived from agreements between governments. This classification scheme distinguishes between different types of sites according to their mode of creation.

Third, the various sites differ in decision-making structure, that is, in their institutions, norms, and processes. These factors affect the outcomes of the various sites, including the different ways in which they allocate risk. At the same time, however, it is important not to overlook the extent to which sites are interrelated, for example in relation to institutional arrangements such as jurisdiction, copying or borrowing of norms, and the interconnection of their dispute-resolution processes.

Fourth, the sites are not all equally vulnerable to economic pressures. It is going too far to say that the network of global legal pluralism which is put into play by the economic processes of any specific global commodity chain reflects the structure of authority and power in the global commodity chain in question. Some types of institutions, some types of processes, and some types of norms are more permeable to economic processes than others.

Fifth, the economic organizations occupying the same box in a global commodity chain are sometimes, if not often, in conflict. These conflicts involve and have important implications for sites. For example, conflicts over markets may pit foreign producers, exporters and importers, on the one hand, against domestic producers, on the other hand. Conflicts over markets also arise between companies occupying similar positions in the chain. The occupants of each of these segments try to enlist the norms, institutions, and processes of the various sites of global legal pluralism to improve their position, not only vis-à-vis their direct competitors but also in relation to the occupants of other segments of the global commodity chain.

Sixth, taken as a whole, the various sites are not necessarily hierarchically ordered in relation to each other. Instead, they reflect many other types of interrelationships, both symmetrical and asymmetrical, as is the case with many aspects of regulatory cooperation between the European Union and the United States. In other words, they do not make up a legal system, even viewed in a more general perspective. This contrasts strongly with the usual lawyer's view of the multilevel governance of international economic relations. On such a view, international economic relations involving EU and US firms are governed by a hierarchically ordered combination of EU, US, and WTO law. (If they involve EU firms, they are then governed mainly by a hierarchically ordered combination of WTO law, EU law, and the law of the EU Member States.) That is a normative perspective, quite different from the mainly sociological perspective that I have sought to develop here.

Seventh, these sites of global legal pluralism are not always, or even usually, alternatives in dispute resolution, as might be expected if one presumes that the norms governing global economic networks are ordered in a hierarchical arrangement. Instead, each site governs, or seeks to govern, a discrete part of the global commodity chain. Once a chain is established, its activities are subject to a given set of rules, emanating from a variety of linked sites, except to the extent that normal conflicts of law rules (that is, private international law) allow firms a choice of governing legislation or a choice of dispute resolution.

Numerous questions remain to be addressed by future research. For example, how are sites created? How are they constituted, developed, and legitimated as sites? Do sites have a specific location, and, if so, why? What decision processes are involved? Do these processes vary in their resemblance to state law (insertion in a hierarchy, reliance on case law, binding decisions, use of precedent, etc.), and why? To what extent do the norms of a particular site combine hard law and soft law? To what extent are sites interconnected, and how are they connected? What determines the modes and organization of dispute resolution? How are groups, hierarchies, and networks of sites created, and how are such processes connected to political and economic relations? Do certain sites tend to converge or become more uniform in their institutional characteristics, norms, or dispute settlement processes, and why? How do conflicts between sites arise, and how are they handled? The answers to these questions will help us to understand further how global economic networks are governed.

Part III

*Transatlantic regulatory cooperation:
theoretical perspectives*

International regulatory cooperation: a neo-institutionalist approach

Giandomenico Majone

Scholars in the fields of International Relations and International Political Economy have traditionally de-emphasized the role of formal institutions in favour of greater emphasis on national power, national interests, and informal regimes. Similarly, intergovernmentalist students of European integration maintain that only national preferences and resources are truly fundamental, while supranational institutions such as the European Commission and the European Court of Justice are largely epiphenomenal: their main function is to carry out the wishes of the more powerful Member States.

To hold such views is to repeat the mistake of the economic theory of politics as applied to the analysis of public regulation by George Stigler and other Chicago economists. The virtual ignorance of institutions which characterizes the economic theory of regulation is the direct consequence of a chain of control which is supposed to operate without any significant friction: interest groups control politicians and politicians control regulators, so the groups get what they want. Policy will reflect the underlying balance of power among the various interests.

As Terry Moe has pointed out, however, if one assumes such a chain of control then there is little to be gained from modelling politicians, regulators, and their complicated surrounding institutions, which simply operate to provide a faithful translation of interests into policy.[1] In fact, control is far from being unproblematic. Both domestic and international institutions have interests of their own, including survival, growth, and security; they take actions on their behalf, not simply on behalf of some underlying interests. Moreover, domestic and international regulatory policies lack credibility if the institutions responsible for their implementation appear to be captured by particular economic or political interests. In short, a unidirectional causal chain from domestic interests and state preferences to policy outcomes presupposes a world of negligible transaction costs.

Recent work in neo-institutionalist economics and political science is beginning to look inside the institutional black box of neoclassical economists to throw new light on such issues as the political control of

---

[1] Terry M. Moe, 'Interests, Institutions and Positive Theory: The Politics of the NLRB', *Studies in American Political Development*, vol. 2 (1987), 236–99.

administrative agents, the logic of delegation, and the design of mechanisms to achieve credible policy commitments. As the present contribution shows, these issues are highly relevant to the study of international regulatory cooperation. This is because deepening economic integration tends to be accompanied by the strengthening of existing institutions, such as the transformation of GATT into the World Trade Organization, or the creation of new institutions like the European Central Bank.

This is not to say that a higher level of institutionalization necessarily leads to more effective international regimes. For example, the 1946 International Convention for the Regulation of Whaling established an organization, the International Whaling Commission (IWC), with considerable formal powers. However, the record of the IWC since its creation has been largely the history of its inability to overcome the short-term interests of the whaling industry.[2] On the other hand, some international agreements, such as the Montreal Protocol on Substances that Deplete the Ozone Layer, have been fairly successful despite a low level of institutionalization.

Thus, a high level of institutionalization is neither a necessary nor a sufficient condition of regime effectiveness. Nevertheless, the presence or absence of delegation of formal powers to international organizations is an important criterion by which to classify and analyse various strategies of regulatory convergence. Accordingly, this contribution is divided into two parts. The first part deals with strategies of more or less spontaneous regulatory convergence: parametric adjustment; information exchange; mutual recognition; delegation to private organizations producing non-binding regulations and standards. The second part of this contribution considers the role of formal institutions in aiding international regulatory cooperation. Among the topics discussed in this part are: various modes of binding harmonization; problems of enforcement and dispute resolution; the logic of delegation; and the issue of public accountability.

Such institutional questions cannot be evaded if one wants to understand why sovereign states may wish to delegate significant regulatory powers to international bodies, and the resulting positive and normative problems. Strategies of spontaneous regulatory convergence, on the other hand, can be analysed without the full conceptual apparatus of neo-institutionalism. In this sense, and only in this sense, I speak of an 'elementary theory' and an 'advanced theory' of international regulatory cooperation.

---

[2] Lynton K. Caldwell, *International Environmental Policy* (Durham, N.C.: Duke University Press, 1984).

I. THE ELEMENTARY THEORY:
SPONTANEOUS REGULATORY CONVERGENCE

A. Parametric adjustment

Charles Lindblom defines parametric adjustment as a decision situation where decision-maker X adjusts his/her decision to Y's decisions already taken or to Y's expected decisions, without seeking to induce a response from Y.[3] A form of non-central coordination, parametric adjustment includes several strategies of more or less spontaneous regulatory convergence.

In the case of *unilateral harmonization* a country chooses to adapt its regulations to those of another country or group of countries.[4] This strategy is particularly important to small countries whose economies are heavily dependent on international trade and which therefore tend to be 'regulation takers'. For example, small European countries which are not members of the European Union, such as Switzerland, often conform their legislation to Community rules.

Policy imitation is another example of parametric adjustment. In looking for models to imitate rather than seeking originality, policy entrepreneurs behave like economic actors who in pursuit of profit follow the pricing or marketing leadership of successful enterprises. Imitation affords relief from the necessity of searching for conscious innovations which, if wrong, expose the policy-maker to severe criticism. Thus, in a complex and uncertain environment the strategy of adopting successful foreign models may be quite rational.[5]

Models emanating from economically and politically powerful countries are most likely to be imitated. The force exerted by a foreign model can be of two types: push or pull. American influence on the development of antitrust policy in Germany at the end of World War II exemplifies the first type. On the other hand, the American deregulatory policies of the 1970s have attracted the attention of European policy-makers without direct pressures, except those transmitted through the markets. In practice, policy imitation is often the resultant of both push and pull forces. Thus, the 1957 German Cartel Law reflects not only the American pressures on the German government, but also the attraction exerted by American antitrust policy on Erhard and other economic liberals.[6]

---

[3] Charles E. Lindblom, *The Intelligence of Democracy* (New York: The Free Press, 1965), 37.

[4] David W. Leebron, 'Lying Down with Procustes: An Analysis of Harmonization Claims', in Jagdish N. Bhagwati and Robert E. Hudec (eds), *Economic Analysis*, vol. 1 of *Fair Trade and Harmonization* (Cambridge: The MIT Press 1996), 41–117.

[5] Giandomenico Majone, 'Cross-National Sources of Regulatory Policymaking in Europe and the United States', *Journal of Public Policy*, vol. 11 (1991), 79–106.

[6] Ibid.

Also the anti-cartel clauses of the European Coal and Steel Community Treaty and of the Treaty of Rome were significantly influenced by American antitrust law and policy. These examples show that a good deal of regulatory convergence takes place as the result of the internationalization of politics no less than economics.

Private legislation is a special case of the pull model of policy imitation. Private legislatures are organizations—often professional bodies—that draft laws in the hope that other bodies will adopt them. They do not purport to enact legislation themselves, but they often enjoy sufficient prestige to make their recommendations attractive to other law-makers.[7] (The Model Penal Code promulgated by the American Law Institute in 1962, for example, had a profound influence on the reform of many individual state codes by establishing a logical framework for defining offences, and a consistent body of general principles in such matters as criminal intent and the liability of accomplices.)

In the field of international trade, private legislatures have enjoyed substantial influence by promulgating model laws that many national legislatures have enacted. The greater the success of a particular proposal, the greater the pressure individual states face to adopt them. This is an instance of the effect of network externalities: once a model law takes on the character of an international standard, states or private economic actors derive benefits from conforming to it that are independent of the intrinsic virtues of the particular rules contained in the law.[8]

While unilateral harmonization and policy imitation are parametric adjustments to existing regulatory models, *self-regulation* may be a strategy to pre-empt more restrictive regulations in the future. An example at national level is the decision of cigarette manufacturers to cease advertising on US television broadcasts, to avoid more general restrictions and the prospect of government-sponsored counter-advertising.[9]

In the European Community, self-regulation by the 'social partners' (employers and employees) has been advocated by the European Commission as an alternative to formal regulation. According to the Commission's proposal that has been partly implemented by the Agreement on Social Policy attached to the Treaty on European Union, where the Commission could legally propose regulatory measures in the area of industrial relations, it would first announce its intentions to do so to the social partners. These partners could then agree to negotiate in the area announced for legislation. If negotiations succeeded, their results could become a substitute for EC legislation. If the social partners did not

---

[7] Paul B. Stephan, 'Accountability and International Lawmaking: Rules, Rents and Legitimacy', *Northwestern Journal of International Law and Business*, vol. 17 (1996–7), 688.

[8] Ibid. 689–90.

[9] Jeffery Atik, 'Science and International Regulatory Convergence', *Northwestern Journal of International Law and Business*, vol. 17 (1996–7), 736–58.

reach agreement, then the Commission would proceed with its regulation.[10]

B. Information exchange

Growing interdependence among nations has the effect of strengthening the impact of domestic policies on other countries. Exchanges of information among policy-makers of different countries are useful for assessing the extent of policy externalities, for understanding the mechanisms through which they are transmitted, and for planning remedial action. An authoritative survey of policy coordination since 1945 comes to the conclusion that 'an appreciable amount of the benefits of discussions among national policy-makers derives not from explicit co-ordination, but rather from making governments aware of the consequences of their actions for other countries'.[11]

An important example of information exchange are the notification requirements for new national standards and regulations under GATT and EC rules. Strictly speaking, the EC notification system belongs to the advanced theory of regulatory cooperation since the Commission plays a central role in the operation of the system. It is discussed here, however, in order to contrast it with the GATT rules.

Directive 83/189, as amended by Directives 88/182 and 94/10, establishes a mandatory notification procedure which empowers the Commission and the Member States to block the adoption of draft technical regulations for a maximum of 18 months. During this time the Commission can assess the compatibility of new regulations with the prohibition of restrictions to trade contained in Article 30 of the Rome Treaty. After some initial difficulties, the system set up by Directive 83/189 as amended now seems to be evolving into a fruitful collaborative network among European and national regulators. Its greatest value is its contribution to diminishing the risk that national regulators will damage the process of market integration by making choices in isolation from regulators in other Member States.[12]

There are important differences between the European Community and the GATT notification systems. While in the European Community every new technical regulation is covered by the relative directives, under GATT rules only standards and regulations that in the judgement of the notifying country are likely to have a significant effect on trade must be notified.

---

[10] George Ross, 'Assessing the Delors Era and Social Policy', in Stephan Leibfried and Paul Pearson (eds), *European Social Policy* (Washington, DC: The Brookings Institution, 1995), 379.

[11] David Currie, Gerald Holtham, and Andrew H. Hallett, 'Does Policy Coordination Pay?' *Centre for Economic Policy Research Bulletin*, vol. 34 (1989), 7.

[12] Stephen Weatherill, *Law and Integration in the European Union* (Oxford: Clarendon Press, 1995), 146.

Other differences lie in the power of the Member States and the Commission to delay the implementation of new regulations if they object to them, and especially in the power of the Commission to propose harmonization directives when adverse effects on trade seem likely.

The last difference is inevitable given the absence in the GATT system of an institution with powers comparable to those of the European Commission. Yet, as Professor Alan Sykes has suggested, one can imagine GATT signatories agreeing to notify a central clearing house of all new product regulations, and to delay their implementation briefly while other countries have an opportunity to comment on them. Such a system would make non-compliance more obvious and thus more costly politically than under the current system. It could also reduce the trade impact of new regulations by giving foreign suppliers somewhat more time to adapt.[13]

Information exchange plays an important role in the 1991 agreement between the United States and the European Community to coordinate enforcement of antitrust policies. The agreement calls for mutual notification when one party's enforcement activities may affect important interests of the other party; the exchange of information on broad policies and enforcement actions; and a general willingness on both sides 'to take into account the important interests of the other Party', and avoid enforcement action conflicts. However, the agreement does not bind the US and EC authorities to engage in cooperative enforcement; each retains the option to demur.[14]

C. Mutual recognition

In many respects, the method of mutual recognition is the most interesting among the strategies of regulatory coordination covered by the elementary theory. It requires that jurisdictions accept for domestic purposes certain regulatory determinations of other jurisdictions, even though those determinations and the criteria on which they are based are not harmonized.[15] Thus, the European Court of Justice in the landmark *Cassis de Dijon* judgment of 1979 determined that the Member States could no longer prevent the marketing within their borders of a product lawfully manufactured and marketed in another Member State. The Court reasoned that the basic aims of national regulations, such as the protection of the health and lives of the citizens, are generally the same everywhere. The specific methods to achieve those aims may be different, but since they all try to achieve the same objectives they should normally be accepted, or 'mutually recognized', in all the Member States.

[13] Alan O. Sykes, *Product Standards for Internationally Integrated Goods Markets* (Washington, DC: The Brookings Institution, 1995), 93.
[14] F. M. Scherer, *Competition Policies for an Integrated World Economy* (Washington, DC: The Brookings Institution, 1995), 41.
[15] Leebron, 'Lying Down with Procustes' (above, n. 4), 91.

As a method of regulatory convergence, mutual recognition has two attractive features. First, as already noted, it does not require the delegation of formal powers to a supranational institution, but only restricts the freedom of action of national governments in certain respects. Second, mutual recognition provides a framework of general rules within which different regulatory philosophies can compete. Competition among rules should drive out rules that offer protection which consumers do not, in fact, require. The end result is *ex post* or bottom up harmonization achieved through market-like processes rather than being imposed by public authorities as in the case of *ex ante*, or top down, harmonization.

It is, however, important to realize how demanding the principle of mutual recognition actually is. An American analyst has pointed out that the principle requires a higher degree of comity among nations than the commerce clause of the US Constitution requires among individual states. The commerce clause has been interpreted by the Supreme Court to allow each state to insist on its own product quality requirements, unless the subject matter has been pre-empted by federal legislation, or unless state standards unduly burden interstate commerce.[16] As is shown in section E below, the requisite level of mutual trust cannot be assumed to exist even among closely integrated countries such as the members of the European Union.

Again, both the opinion of the Court of Justice and the interpretation of that opinion by the Commission make clear that 'mutual recognition' really means 'mutual recognition of equivalent rules'. There are, however, no objective criteria to determine whether or not two national regulations are in fact equivalent. The difficulty of establishing regulatory equivalence is shown, for example, by the judgment of the Court in the 'wood-working machines' case.[17] Here the Court was confronted with two national approaches to safety: German regulation was less strict and relied more on an adequate training of the users of this type of machinery, while French regulation prescribed additional protective devices on the machines. Departing from the sweeping assumptions of equivalence of the *Cassis* decision, the Court ruled against the Commission which had argued that both regulations were essentially equivalent. It found that in the absence of harmonization at EC level a Member State could insist on the full respect of its national safety rules, and thus restrict the importation of certain goods.

In fact, mutual recognition cannot work in an integrated market unless certain 'essential requirements' are harmonized. In the European Community these essential requirements are harmonized according to the so-called total method; that is, the original national provisions are replaced

---

[16] Gary C. Hufbauer (ed.), *Europe 1992* (Washington, DC: The Brookings Institution, 1990), 11.

[17] Case no. 188/84, *Commission v. France*, 1986 ECR 419.

by new European provisions and Community rules become the sole regulation governing the area. This is true not only of health and safety but also of economic regulation. Thus, the regulatory framework applied to banks is provided by Directive 89/646—the so-called Second Banking Directive—and by three narrower directives concerned with the definition of a bank's capital, with capital adequacy ratios, and with procedures for winding up credit institutions. These three technical directives aim to harmonize prudential standards in key areas, rather than to provide mutual recognition. They provide a firm basis on which mutual recognition can take place: central harmonization only of basic prudential rules, and of institutional and organizational conditions essential for the protection of consumers. All other conditions are defined and controlled by the home country of the bank, and must be accepted by the other Member States.

In this, as in all other applications of the new regulatory philosophy, harmonization and mutual recognition are not simply alternatives but are, in fact, complementary and mutually supporting.

D. Delegation to non-governmental bodies

This strategy of regulatory convergence is particularly important in the field of technical standardization. Standards promulgated by bodies such as the International Organization for Standardization, the Codex Alimentarius Commission, or the European standardization organizations are not legally binding. Member States are not obligated to follow or adopt these standards in their national markets, even if they vote in favour of adopting them in the international body.[18] For this reason, delegation to international standardization organizations falls within the scope of the elementary theory of regulatory cooperation.

The fact that international standards are voluntary is not in itself a disadvantage. On the contrary, voluntary standards are often more flexible, innovative, and cost-effective than mandatory ones. They are also less risky since firms can ignore them if they are obviously absurd. In terms of effective implementation the main problem of international standards is not their legal status but their credibility. The standards of prudential supervision of the Basle Committee on Banking Supervision are not legally binding yet they have been implemented by all the Member States, and even by many non-member countries. On the other hand, many international standards are simply ignored. It all depends on the credibility of the regulators, and this cannot be established by treaty.[19]

Some analysts argue that voluntary standards should play a larger role even at national level. Thus, it has been suggested that the US

---

[18] Sykes, *Product Standards* (above, n. 13), 60.

[19] Giandomenico Majone, 'Comparing Strategies of Regulatory Rapprochement', in *Regulatory Co-operation for an Interdependent World* (Paris: OECD, 1993), 155–78.

Occupational Safety and Health Administration (OSHA) should devote fewer resources to the development of mandatory standards and more to the development of flexible guidelines that can be easily modified in the light of new scientific information. Moreover, since mandatory standards can be, and often are, challenged in court, OSHA tends to wait until the evidence becomes strong before taking any action, while neglecting to address the much larger number of chemicals with less evidence of carcinogenicity. Thus reliance on formal rule-making leads to 'under-regulation'. On the other hand, a private body like the American Conference of Governmental Industrial Hygienists, which only recommends maximum exposure limits, can use new evidence of possible harm to cover a much larger number of hazards.[20]

In the European Community the 'New Approach to Technical Harmonization and Standardization', introduced in 1985, shifted the emphasis from mandatory standards to non-binding ones set by one of the European standardization bodies. Under the old approach, the Council produced detailed technical specifications for single products or groups of products. The approach failed completely. It could take as many as ten years to pass a single directive and in the meanwhile the Member States were producing thousands of new technical standards each year.

The new approach, under which binding standards are restricted to essential health and safety requirements, has considerably improved the situation, but problems remain. Some of these problems result from the ambiguity surrounding the relationship between harmonization and standardization. According to the Council Resolution of 17 May 1985 introducing the new approach, the essential requirements 'shall be worded precisely enough in order to create, on the transposition into national law, legally binding obligations which can be enforced'. Hence, the Resolution adds, the essential requirements 'should be so formulated as to enable the certification bodies straight away to certify products as being in conformity having regard to those requirements, in the absence of standards'.

However, in the majority of directives adopted under the new approach the essential requirements are expressed in such general terms that they cannot be applied without the support of standards. Hence the voluntary standards produced by the European organizations become, de facto, binding.[21] This is an awkward situation from the point of view of legitimacy—the European standardization organizations are private-law associations with which the Commission has only contractual relations as

[20] John M. Mendeloff, *The Dilemma of Toxic Substance Regulation* (Cambridge, MA.: The MIT Press, 1988), 79–99.

[21] Ernesto Previdi, 'The Organization of Public and Private Responsibilities In European Risk Regulation', in Christian Joerges, Karl-Heinz Ladeur, and Ellen Vos (eds), *Integrating Scientific Expertise into Regulatory Decision-Making* (Baden-Baden: Nomos, 1997), 225–41.

it has with hundreds of private consultants—and also with respect to liability, should a harmonized standard turn out to be defective.

Other problems arise in connection with testing and certification, and such problems are particularly significant for US–EU regulatory cooperation. Each new-approach directive sets out the procedures to demonstrate conformity with the essential requirements. Approval of products for the European market may only be granted by bodies 'notified' to the European Community by the Member States as being technically competent. To promote convergence of different techniques of conformity assessment, and to facilitate the mutual recognition of certifications in non-harmonized sectors, a European Organization for Testing and Certification (EOTC) was established in 1990 by the European Community, the European Free Trade Area (EFTA), and by the European standardization organizations CEN and CENELEC. Together with the 'Global Approach' to testing and certification introduced in 1989, the new organization should create the framework for a single testing and certification procedure, which in turn could be the model for the integrating world economy.

However, the global approach and the new approach are closely linked, in that much of the global approach presumes the existence of directives harmonizing the essential regulatory requirements. Absent a significant move towards regulatory harmonization internationally, therefore, much of the EC global approach is not transferable to the trading community at large.[22]

Other problems have been revealed by the US–EU negotiations started in 1994 to establish mutual recognition of testing and certification requirements. As noted above, under the new approach Member States must notify the Commission of acceptable testing and certification bodies. But this sort of monitoring of technical competence does not exist in the United States, where government agencies do not accredit or monitor testing and certification bodies.[23] It remains to be seen whether the US Government is prepared to give up the traditional reliance on manufacturer's self-declaration, and to start accrediting or monitoring testing and certification bodies on the basis of the 'ISO 9000' quality control standards, in order to meet the EU conditions for mutual recognition.

E. The limits of spontaneous regulatory convergence

As the discussion of the preceding sections suggests, a substantial part of international regulatory cooperation takes place more or less sponta-

---

[22] Sykes, *Product Standards* (above, n. 13), 95.

[23] Michelle Egan and Anthony Zito, 'Regulation in Europe and the Globalization of the Economy: European Standardization at a Crossroad', in Christian Joerges, Karl-Heinz Ladeur, and Ellen Vos (eds), *Integrating Scientific Expertise into Regulatory Decision-Making* (Baden-Baden: Nomos, 1997), 282.

neously and in a decentralized fashion. This conclusion parallels the emphasis of the new economics of organization on private, as opposed to court, orderings for the regulation of business transactions. Contract execution, it is pointed out, is normally a much more informal and cooperative process than legalistic approaches to contracting would suggest. Since courts are poorly suited to preserve continuity of relationships, private orderings tend to arise in support of transactions for which continuity is valued.[24]

Also at the international level the importance of informal agreements, both independently and in synergy with formal institutions, is likely to grow. This is because increasing economic interdependence among nations implies that international transactions are becoming both more frequent and longer-lasting. Thus countries have strong incentives to keep an agreement, even without the threat of formal sanctions, in order to cultivate a reputation which will be valuable in future transactions.

These considerations should not, however, obscure the fact that there are important situations where international regulatory cooperation cannot be sustained without the aid of formal institutions. Consider for example the strategy of information exchange discussed in section B. There it was argued that information strategies such as the GATT rules for the notification of national regulations and standards may be quite useful in correcting the tendency of national regulators to ignore the international consequences of their decisions. This is not, however, the only kind of policy externality relevant to international regulatory cooperation. A more serious type of externality is caused by the deliberate use of national regulations as a strategic weapon in international competition.

Even purely local market failures can give rise to such strategic externalities. Thus safety regulations for the construction of buildings in a certain locality can create trade barriers if they specify a particular material only produced in that locality. In general, any federal or multilevel system of governance faces a serious dilemma. Local authorities may be more attuned to individual tastes but they are unlikely to make a clear separation between providing public goods for their citizens and engaging in policies designed to advantage their jurisdiction at the expense of other jurisdictions. Centralization of regulatory authority at a higher level of government can correct such strategic externalities, but at the cost of homogenizing regulations across jurisdictions that may be dissimilar with respect to underlying tastes and needs.[25]

Also rule enforcement may be used strategically. Strategic behaviour in the enforcement of cooperative agreements gives rise to problems of

---

[24] Oliver E. Williamson, *The Economic Institutions of Capitalism* (New York: The Free Press, 1985).

[25] Roger G. Noll, 'Regulatory Policy in a Federalist System' (paper presented at the Conference on Regulatory Federalism, European University Institute, Florence, Italy, 1990).

credibility since agreements are not credible when the level of implementation is uncertain. Absent international monitoring institutions, governments may have problems of credibility not just in the eyes of each other but also in the eyes of third parties such as regulated firms. Thus where the fines prescribed by an environmental agreement impose significant disadvantages on firms that compete internationally, firms are likely to believe that national regulators will be unwilling to prosecute them as rigorously if they determine the level of enforcement unilaterally rather than under international supervision. Hence the delegation of monitoring powers to an institution such as the European Commission can make strict regulation more credible.

The effectiveness of mutual recognition, too, depends on the support of formal institutions. First, as already noted, in an integrated market it will usually be necessary to harmonize some essential regulatory requirements. In the European Community these essential requirements are harmonized according to the total method, see section C. Moreover, an institution like the Court of Justice is needed to determine whether or not two national regulations are sufficiently similar to allow mutual recognition without some prior harmonization.

Again, the effectiveness of mutual recognition depends crucially on a high level of mutual trust among national regulators. Where such mutual trust is not forthcoming, regulatory cooperation may have to be supported by formal institutions and centralized procedures. Thus the old EC procedure for the approval of new medical drugs relied on the mutual recognition of toxicological and clinical trials conducted according to standardized European protocols. Under the 'multi-state drug application procedure' introduced in 1975, a company that had received a marketing authorization from the regulatory agency of a Member State could ask for mutual recognition of that approval by five other countries. The agencies of the countries nominated by the company had to approve or raise objections within 120 days. The procedure did not work well. Actual decision times were much longer than those prescribed by the directive and national regulators did not appear to be bound by decisions of other regulatory bodies.

Because of these disappointing results the procedure was revised in 1983. Now only two countries had to be nominated in order to be able to apply for a multi-state approval. But even the new procedure did not succeed in streamlining the approval process since national regulators continued to raise objections against each other almost routinely.[26] These difficulties finally induced the Commission, supported by the European pharmaceutical industry, to propose the establishment of a European

[26] Erich Kaufer, 'The Regulation of New Product Development in the Drug Industry', in Giandomenico Majone (ed.), *Deregulation or Re-regulation? Regulatory Reform in Europe and the United States* (London: Pinter, 1990), 153–75.

Agency for the Evaluation of Medicinal Products and of a new centralized procedure, compulsory for biotechnology products and certain types of veterinary medicines, and available on an optional basis for other products, leading to an EC-wide authorization. Both the agency and the centralized procedure were established in 1993.

In sum, while spontaneous regulatory convergence has been, and will continue to remain, important, growing interdependence among national and regional economies is likely to require significant delegation of rule-making, enforcement, and adjudication powers to international organizations. Hence, there is an urgent need to understand the conceptual and normative problems raised by the partial transfer of regulatory sovereignty to independent institutions.

II. THE ADVANCED THEORY: REGULATORY CONVERGENCE AIDED BY FORMAL INSTITUTIONS

A. Harmonization and its modes

David Leebron provides an exhaustive classification of various types of harmonization.[27] Not all types require the delegation of formal powers to formal organizations. Thus non-mandatory harmonization, whether unilateral or multilateral, limits itself to the formulation of harmonized rules. Acceptance of such rules by a country does not necessarily entail an international obligation. In fact, as Professor Leebron points out, most international harmonization efforts have taken place without international obligation. A common methodology is the drafting of model laws and standards by a private body, as discussed in the first part of this contribution.

Non-mandatory processes may be particularly appropriate when the degree of harmonization required is relatively low.[28] When the goal is the creation of a single market out of a number of distinct national markets, however, harmonized rules are usually mandatory and are enforced by formal organizations such as the European Commission and Court of Justice. But even in the European Community there are several types of mandatory harmonization, while the relative importance of each type has changed considerably over time and across policy areas.

From the early 1960s to about 1973—the date of the first enlargement of the Community to the United Kingdom, Ireland, and Denmark—the European Commission's approach to harmonization was characterized by a distinct preference for detailed measures designed to regulate exhaustively the problems in question to the exclusion of previously existing national regulations—the approach known as *total harmonization*. Under

---

[27] Leebron, 'Lying Down with Procustes' (above, n. 4).   [28] Ibid. 61.

total harmonization, once EC rules have been put in place, a Member State's capacity to apply stricter rules by invoking the values referred to in Article 30 (ex Article 36) of the Rome Treaty—the protection of the health and life of humans, animals, and plants, and the preservation of national cultural treasures—is excluded.

For a long time the Court of Justice supported total harmonization as a foundation stone in the building of the common market.[29] From the point of view of market building, total harmonization has indeed the advantage of simplicity. Once the Community has acted, national regulations no longer apply: the common market operates under a common set of rules. In practice the situation is a good deal more complicated. First, EC directives, which are the main instrument of harmonization, leave to the national governments 'the choice of form and methods' for achieving the regulatory objectives. The discretion in implementation granted to the Member States, combined with the absence of *ex post* rewards and sanctions, leads to uneven implementation across the Union, generating a sense of legal uncertainty for producers, traders, and consumers.

Moreover, under Article 94 (ex Article 100) of the Treaty of Rome, harmonizing directives proposed by the Commission must be unanimously approved by the Council of Ministers before they become European law. This unanimity requirement forced the Commission and the Council to engage in lengthy and sometimes fruitless bargaining. It is easy to imagine the difficulty of totally harmonizing the laws and regulations of six, nine, twelve, and finally fifteen countries differing widely in political, legal, and administrative traditions. Even the process of adapting existing European regulations to technical progress was so slow as to produce a systematic regulatory lag.

It is possible that the lack of historical precedents led to a serious underestimation of the difficulties of total harmonization. While there are several examples of free trade areas and customs unions—such as the German *Zollverein* and the Austrian-Hungarian customs union, to mention two well-known cases from the nineteenth century—there are no previous instances of harmonization on the scale necessary to create a single European market out of the heavily regulated markets of sovereign welfare states. However, the main reason for the preference for total harmonization in the early days of the Community was political. In those days harmonization tended to be pursued not just to solve concrete problems but also to drive forward the general process of European integration. This political use of harmonization ran into increasing opposition from some Member States, especially after the first enlargement of the Community.

By the mid-1970s the limits of total harmonization had become clear. As the Commission was to write some years later, '[e]xperience has shown

---

[29] Weatherill, *Law and Integration* (above, n. 12).

that the alternative of relying on a strategy based totally on harmonization would be over-regulatory, would take a long time to implement and could stifle innovation'.[30] At the same time, mounting opposition to what many Member States considered excessive centralization convinced the Commission that the powers granted to it by the then Article 100 of the Rome Treaty had to be used so as to interfere as little as possible with the regulatory autonomy of the national governments. The emphasis shifted from total to 'optional' and 'minimum' harmonization—and to mutual recognition.

Optional harmonization aims to guarantee the right of free movement of goods while permitting the Member States to retain their traditional forms of regulation. Thus a food specialty, such as cheese made from non-pasteurized milk, not conforming to European standards may still be produced for the domestic market.

A particular form of optional harmonization is provided by the fourth paragraph of Article 95 (ex Article 100a), added to the Rome Treaty by the Single European Act in 1987. While Article 100—which deprived Member States of competence in the area covered by a harmonization directive— required the unanimous approval of the Council, the new Article 100a introduced qualified majority voting for internal market legislation. However, Member States were not prepared to give up their veto power without some weakening of total pre-emption. Hence, Article 95 (4) (ex Article 100a (4)) provides, in part, that:

If, after the adoption of a harmonization measure by the Council acting by a qualified majority, a Member State deems it necessary to apply national provisions on grounds of major needs referred to in Article 30 (ex Article 36), or relating to protection of the environment or the working environment, it shall notify the Commission of these provisions.

The Commission shall confirm the provisions involved after having verified that they are not a means of arbitrary discrimination or a disguised restriction on trade between Member States.

Thus Community harmonization does not necessarily exclude the possibility of regulatory action by the Member States, where this is shown to be justified. Fears were expressed at the time of entry into force of the Single European Act that Article 100a (4) represented a dangerous backward step from the model of a uniform European legal order. These predictions have not been borne out in practice, which suggests that Member States understand the damage that could be done by recourse to this escape clause.[31]

Article 100a (4) specified the permissible grounds for setting national rules that differ from the Community standard, and introduced a system

---

[30] Commission of the European Communities, *Completing the Internal Market*, COM(85)310 final (Luxembourg: Office for Official Publications of the European Communities, 1985), 17.

[31] Weatherill, *Law and Integration* (above, n. 12), 150–1.

of controls involving the Commission as well as the other Member States. Neither restriction applies to the method of *minimum harmonization*. Under minimum harmonization the national governments must secure the level of regulation set out in a directive but are permitted to set higher standards, provided the stricter national rules do not violate primary Community law. Like optional harmonization, minimum harmonization liberalizes trade without suppressing justifiable regulatory diversity.

It should be noted that the areas where minimum harmonization is the rule—environment, consumer protection, occupational health and safety—are not at the core of market building. Stricter national standards mainly affect production processes located in the regulating state, or methods of marketing products rather than the products themselves. By contrast, measures dealing with the safety or other aspects of traded goods directly affect market integration and hence must follow the traditional approach whereby Community rules pre-empt national rules.[32]

B. Enforcement and dispute resolution

Regulation is not achieved simply by making rules, or by harmonizing different national rules, but requires also an administrative infrastructure for rule enforcement and adjudication. The limits of a purely legislative approach to market integration are becoming increasingly clear in the EU. The area of telecommunications provides an instructive example of the present mismatch between increasingly sophisticated regulatory tasks and inadequate administrative instruments.

In this policy area a European regulatory framework is now in place, based on the principles of Open Network Provision (ONP). The framework Directive 90/387 is the basis of all ONP legislation. It deals with the harmonization of rules for access to, and use of, public networks and services, and calls for the mutual recognition of licensing procedures. The directive also sets up an 'ONP Committee', of which the members are drawn from the National Regulatory Authorities (NRAs). The Committee functions as an advisory body, except with respect to the adoption of rules for the uniform application of essential requirements of objectivity, transparency, equality of access and non-discrimination, and of decisions necessary to make the reference to European standards mandatory for services across national frontiers. In these cases the procedures of the ONP Committee are the more restrictive ones of a 'regulatory committee'. This means that where the Commission wishes to adopt measures not in accordance with the Committee's opinion, it must submit the proposed measure to the Council of Ministers. The Council decides whether to accept or reject the Commission's proposal by qualified majority. The Council's fail-

---

[32] Weatherill, *Law and Integration* (above, n. 12), 152–7.

ure to act within a given time limit results in the Commission adoption of the proposed measures.

Directive 92/44 on the application of ONP to leased lines is interesting from the point of view of harmonization of institutional structures and procedures. As David Leebron observes, rules will generally not be truly harmonized unless the procedures and institutions for implementing them are made more similar.[33] In fact, the directive introduces a number of harmonized principles concerning the way the NRAs should exercise their authority. These include notification and reporting arrangements, tariffing and cost accounting principles, and the establishment of appeal and conciliation procedures. Article 8 of the directive requires that the Member States establish a dispute-resolution procedure that should be easily accessible; capable of settling disputes in a fair, timely, and transparent manner; and respect due process and the rights of parties to be heard. Article 12 introduces a conciliation procedure for disputes which cannot be resolved at the national level, or involve telecommunications operators (TOs) from more than one Member State. Disputes are to be reviewed by a working group of the ONP Committee. Although the working group is charged merely with non-binding arbitration, this is nevertheless a significant step in the direction of centralized dispute resolution. Finally, the ONP Voice Directive sets out a regulatory hierarchy where the first level is formed by commercial agreements, the second level includes the NRAs, while the Commission, supported by the ONP Committee, forms a third level intended to represent Community interests with minimal intervention. Among other things, the Voice Directive extends the right of appeal against the decisions of the NRAs to all users, and promotes users' rights to institute legal proceedings against the TOs.[34]

The question is whether the innovative framework already in place will be sufficient to achieve a well-functioning internal market for telecoms equipment, services, and infrastructure. Among the shortcomings of the current, highly decentralized regulatory system are: imprecise obligations and pricing rules for interconnection; the absence of a one-stop-shop for licences; inconsistencies between competition policy and industry regulation at both national and European levels; mechanisms of dispute resolution that fall far short of the standards of judicial review; uneven quality of national regulators in terms of independence as well as expertise; and poor coordination of the national regulatory authorities among themselves and with the European Commission.[35]

---

[33] Leebron, 'Lying Down with Procustes' (above, n. 4), 46.

[34] Wolf Sauter, 'The ONP Framework: Towards a European Telecommunications Agency', *Utilities Law Review* (Autumn 1994), 140–6.

[35] Jacques Pelkmans, 'A European Telecom Regulator?' Paper presented at the Conference *Network Industries in Europe: Preparing for Competition*, Edinburgh, 10–11 July 1997.

While some of these shortcomings could be corrected by improved legislation, the deeper problems of the present regulatory system are institutional. This explains the recurrent demands for a European Telecommunications Agency (ETA). A well-publicized plea for such an agency was made by the High Level Group on the Information Society (Bangemann Group) in a report to the European Council meeting at Corfu in June 1994. According to this report, the European regulator would be charged with issues of a Community-wide nature, such as licensing, interconnection, frequency allocation, and numbering. It would also receive appeals from all users against the decisions of the national regulators.

In Spring 1997 the European Parliament demanded that the Commission study the merits of an ETA, and that the results of the study be used in the review of the existing regulatory system to be carried out in 1999. Thus the issue of the ETA is now on the political agenda, but opinions about the structure and powers of the new regulatory body still differ widely.

At one extreme, some analysts propose the creation of a powerful European regulator on the model of the US Federal Communications Commission: a regulatory body with all the necessary powers to coordinate state regulators effectively, if necessary by the use of federal preemption, and to settle disputes that cannot be resolved at state level. This model has a number of attractive features, but for political and legal reasons it cannot be exported to Europe. First, it is unrealistic to suppose that the Member States would be willing to delegate to a European regulator powers that they are not prepared to grant to their own regulatory authorities. It must be remembered that in most European countries regulatory agencies operating at arm's length from government are a new development, which many people still consider a constitutional and administrative anomaly.[36]

Moreover, the model of the independent agency raises serious problems for European law, since nothing in the founding treaties, or in the subsequent amendments, provides for the creation of such bodies. Article 7 (ex Article 4) of the Treaty of Rome lists the various institutions operating at Community level and specifies that each of them must act 'within the limits of the powers conferred upon them by this Treaty'. This has generally been read as a prohibition on the establishment of additional bodies, short of a treaty revision. As early as 1958 the European Court of Justice stated that the delegation of powers by Community institutions to ad hoc bodies not envisaged by the Treaty on the European Coal and Steel Community was possible only subject to strict conditions; in any event, the delegation of broad discretionary powers was not permitted. This 'Meroni Doctrine' is generally held to be applicable, *mutatis mutandis*, also in the broader context of the Rome Treaty.

---

[36] Giandomenico Majone, *Regulating Europe* (London: Routledge, 1996), 47–9.

These political and legal difficulties explain why the European agencies created in the early 1990s have been given only very limited regulatory powers. Even the European Agency for the Evaluation of Medicinal Products (EMEA), which comes closest to being a full-fledged regulatory body, does not take decisions concerning the safety and efficacy of new medical drugs, but must submit opinions concerning the approval of such products to the Commission. The present decentralized system of telecoms regulation does not raise any such political and legal problems, and for this reason it is supported by the Council—as well as by the incumbent operators and former monopolists, who are accustomed to deal directly with the national governments.

The Member States argue that the national regulators and the newly established regulatory regimes should be given a fair chance to prove themselves. Now, it is true that the compromise on a highly decentralized set-up was necessary in order to establish a liberalized European market for telecoms services in the first place. However, the present system suffers from serious credibility problems because of the shortcomings noted above, and also because of the very poor record of implementation and enforcement of non-voice liberalization measures.[37] Hence, the present decentralized regime should be considered a temporary arrangement. The stable solution which is likely to emerge will occupy an intermediate position between a European FCC and the loose framework of today; it will be neither a centralized body nor a collection of national representatives, but a network built around the ONP Committee. The above-mentioned EMEA provides the relevant model.

C. Transnational regulatory networks

A central role in EMEA's work is played by two committees of experts— the Committee for Proprietary Medicinal Products (CPMP) and the Committee for Veterinary Medicinal Products (CVMP)—which correspond to the ONP Committee, but are more powerful. They have the task of formulating the scientific opinions of the agency, and also of arbitrating disputes between pharmaceutical firms and national authorities, for example when the latter are unwilling to approve an application authorized in another Member State. In a number of important cases such arbitration is mandatory (it will be recalled that in the case of the ONP Committee arbitration is not binding), and applicants may also request the relevant committee to initiate mandatory arbitration.

The CPMP, like the CVMP, consists of two members nominated by each Member State, while the Commission is not represented in the committees. The committee members represent the national regulatory

---

[37] Pelkmans, 'A European Telecoms Operator?' (above, n. 35).

authorities and serve for renewable three-year terms. It would be wrong to assume that through their power of appointment the national governments effectively control the authorization process. In fact, both committees—which already played a role in the old multi-state drug application procedure, see section I.E—have become not only more important but also more independent since the creation of the EMEA. This is because it is in their interest to establish an international reputation for good scientific work, and for this purpose the degree to which they reflect the views of the national governments is irrelevant.

This change in the incentive structure of regulators operating in a transnational network deserves to be emphasized since such networks will probably play an increasingly important role in international regulatory cooperation. In his work on the sociology of science and the professions, Alvin Gouldner has introduced the distinction between 'cosmopolitans' and 'locals'. Cosmopolitans are likely to adopt an international reference-group orientation, while locals tend to have a national or subnational (e.g. an organizational) reference group orientation. Hence local experts tend to be more submissive to the institutional and hierarchical structures in which they operate than cosmopolitan experts, who can appeal to the standards and criteria of an international body of scientific peers.[38] Using Gouldner's terminology we may say that by providing an international focus at European level and important links to other organizations such as the US Food and Drug Administration, the EMEA is pioneering in the transformation of national regulators from 'locals' to 'cosmopolitans'.

Recent game-theoretic work on the role of reputation in repeated transactions leads to similar conclusions.[39] Let us start with the observation that teamwork can help to achieve credible commitments. Although people may be weak on their own, they can build resolve by forming a group. Any member of the group is open to peer pressure and thus places himself or herself in a situation where pride and self-respect are lost when commitments are broken. The success of organizations such as Alcoholics Anonymous and Weight Watchers is based on this insight.[40]

What is true of individuals in a team also applies to organizations in a network. Thus, an agency that sees itself as part of a transnational network of institutions pursuing similar objectives and facing analogous problems, rather than as a marginal addition to a large national bureaucracy pursuing a variety of objectives, is more motivated to defend its policy commit-

[38] Alvin W. Gouldner, 'Cosmopolitans and Locals: Toward an Analysis of Latent Social Roles', I and II, *Administrative Science Quarterly*, vol. 2 (1957–8), 281–306, 444–80.

[39] John Milgrom and Paul Roberts, *Economics, Organization and Management* (Englewood Cliffs, NJ: Prentice Hall, 1992), 138–43.

[40] Avinash K. Dixit and Barry J. Nalebuff, *Thinking Strategically* (New York: W. W. Norton 1991), 158–60.

ments and professional standards against external influences. As already noted, agency executives have an incentive to maintain their reputation in the eyes of the other members of the network. Unprofessional or politically motivated behaviour would compromise their international reputation and make cooperation more difficult to achieve in the future.[41]

In sum, a transnational network not only permits an efficient division of labour and the exchange of information among national regulators, but also facilitates the development of behavioural standards and working practices that create shared expectations and enhance the effectiveness of the social mechanisms of reputational enforcement. Knowledge about agencies that do not fulfil the expectations of their partners spreads through the network by formal and informal means. The network performs the crucial task of deciding which members are in good standing, and communicating this information to other members. Thus, it becomes an intangible asset carrying a reputation and conferring that reputation upon the agencies in good standing.[42]

EMEA is not the only example of a transnational regulatory network in the European Union. A network structure is also emerging in the field of competition policy. Recently the Commission's Competition Directorate (DG IV) has initiated a decentralization project with the long-term goal of having one EC competition statute applied throughout the European Union by a network including DG IV itself, national competition authorities, and national courts. Direct links already exist between Commission inspectors and national competition regulators as regards any investigation carried out by the Commission. Moreover, a high level of harmonization of national competition laws has already occurred spontaneously in the Member States, while national competition authorities are becoming more professional and increasingly jealous of their independence.

The European System of Central Banks represents an even more formalized model, but its function in banking regulation, as distinct from monetary policy, is not yet clear. At present, international cooperation on banking regulation is achieved mainly through the Basle Committee on Banking Supervision established in 1975 by the central bank governors of the Group of Ten (G-10) industrialized countries. The Committee was set up to establish guiding principles on international supervision and to work towards harmonization of regulatory policies following the world banking crisis caused by the failure of the German bank Herstatt in 1974.

Neither the G-10 nor the Committee has formal legal status as an international organization or supranational supervisory authority, and the

---

[41] Giandomenico Majone, 'The New European Agencies: Regulation by Information', *Journal of European Public Policy*, vol. 4 (1997), 262–75.
[42] David M. Kreps, 'Corporate Culture and Economic Theory', in James E. Alt and Kenneth A. Shepsle (eds), *Perspectives on Positive Political Economy* (Cambridge: Cambridge University Press, 1990), 90–143.

same is true of the International Organization of Securities Commissions (IOSCO) established in 1983. IOSCO has regular contacts with the Basle Committee, and includes the European Commission, the International Finance Corporation, and OECD as affiliate members. The most significant efforts of the international network of securities commissioners have been in the areas of developing minimum capital adequacy standards for securities regulators, encouraging exchange of information agreements, and common accounting and disclosure requirements.

While the Basle Committee and IOSCO are well established, although still evolving, structures, the International Conference on Harmonization of Technical Requirements for the Registration of Pharmaceuticals for Human Use (ICH) exemplifies an emergent international regulatory network. ICH participants include officials from drug regulatory agencies and pharmaceutical companies in the European Union, United States, and Japan. ICH's primary goal is to harmonize testing standards so as to speed the approval of medical drugs worldwide. At the first conference in 1991 a number of harmonization measures were adopted which United States, European Union, and Japanese regulators would use in order to revise their respective laws. In particular a 'minimum data blueprint' guideline was approved and subsequently incorporated into United States, European Union, and Japanese law. It defines data collection conditions acceptable to the three regulatory systems, thus allowing a firm to file the same data package with each regulator. While the data submitted are still evaluated by national officials (who may demand data beyond the scope of the minimum data blueprint), this guideline does eliminate the need for costly, essentially repetitive tests.[43]

In the opinion of many observers the most important accomplishment of the 1991 conference was that all three regulatory agencies were willing to commit publicly to harmonization principles. The FDA's participation was especially significant since, as recently as the mid-1980s, the American agency had publicly regarded foreign clinical data as 'too precarious' to base a marketing approval decision on them.[44]

These examples of European Union and more broadly based regulatory networks suggest that professionalism and political independence are crucial to the viability of the network model. Professionals are oriented by standards of conduct, cognitive beliefs, and career opportunities that derive from their professional community, giving them strong reasons for resisting interference and directions from political outsiders.[45] In turn, political independence is important for achieving credible commitment to internationally agreed regulatory objectives in spite of changing political

---

[43] David Vogel, 'Regulatory Interdependence in a Global Economy: The Globalization of Pharmaceutical Regulation' (paper presented at the annual meeting of the American Political Science Association, Chicago, Ill., 31 Aug. to 3 Sept. 1995).

[44] Ibid. 24.   [45] Moe, 'Interests, Institutions, and Positive Theory' (above, n. 1), 251–3.

and economic conditions at national level. The trade-off between regulatory commitment and responsiveness to majoritarian preferences is one of the central problems of the advanced theory of international regulatory cooperation.

D. The delegation problem

Why political sovereigns may choose to delegate regulatory powers to an independent agency, or to a network of independent agencies, is an issue which is receiving increasing attention by neo-institutionalist scholars. The existence of international market failures, such as transboundary pollution, is not sufficient to explain the phenomenon of delegation to supranational authorities. We know from Coase's theorem that it is not the externalities as such that constitute a problem for collective action, but positive transaction costs and imperfect information.[46] In a situation where transaction costs are zero and information is complete, affected parties can bargain among themselves to reach an efficient solution: either the externality is 'internalized' by the emitter or, if the costs of eliminating it outweigh the benefits, the externality persists but is shown, *ipso facto*, to be Pareto-irrelevant.

The same argument can be applied to problems of collective action at the international level. Without transaction costs and given complete information, there would be no need for sovereign states to delegate regulatory powers to supranational organizations. If national regulators were willing and able to take into account the external effects of their decisions, if they were well informed about one another's intentions, and the costs of organizing and implementing policy coordination were negligible, their international externalities could be managed by intergovernmental agreements, or even by some of the strategies of unilateral adaptation discussed in section I.A.

Of course, such conditions are never satisfied in practice; hence most international agreements are accompanied by the creation of a secretariat to facilitate the exchange of information and reduce the costs of organizing voluntary cooperation. The powers delegated to European institutions are much greater than this, however. In order to explain why the members of the European Union have accepted such far-reaching limitations of their regulatory sovereignty, and why other countries may soon wish to do the same in order to respond to the challenges of globalization, we must distinguish the different kinds of transaction costs that arise in the formulation and implementation of international regulatory agreements.

---

[46] Ronald H. Coase, 'The Problem of Social Cost', *Journal of Law and Economics*, vol. 3 (1960), 1–44.

Such costs may be grouped under three broad categories: search and information costs; bargaining and decision costs; and policing, enforcement, and measurement costs. The third category is the most significant one for the purpose of the present discussion. This is because any intergovernmental agreement involves search and bargaining costs, but enforcement costs are especially important in the case of regulatory agreements. The high level of enforcement costs explains the decision to delegate regulatory powers to a supranational authority rather than merely setting up an international secretariat.

Policy discretion is probably the most important reason why policing regulatory agreements is so costly. Unfortunately, discretion in regulation is unavoidable. First, regulation is heavily dependent on scientific, engineering, or economic knowledge, but the relevant knowledge is almost always insufficient to permit definite conclusions about the causes and feasible remedies of particular problems. Hence the regulator is forced to exercise scientific and policy discretion in choosing among several courses of action. Second, regulation consists of applying the general principles stated in a formal document (a statute or an international convention, for example) to particular, and often rapidly changing, circumstances, and this again entails a good deal of discretion.

Again, because regulators lack information that only regulated firms have, and because governments are reluctant, for political reasons, to impose excessive costs on industry, bargaining is an essential feature of regulatory enforcement. Regardless of what the law says, the process of regulation is not simply one where the regulators command and the regulated obey. A 'market' is created in which bureaucrats and those subject to regulation bargain over the precise obligations of the latter.[47] Since bargaining is so pervasive it may be difficult for an outside observer to determine whether the spirit of an international regulation has been violated. But when it is difficult to observe whether governments are making an honest effort to enforce a regulatory agreement, the agreement is not credible. Hence the delegation of regulatory powers to some independent organization, such as the European Commission, is an important means whereby governments can commit themselves to strategies of regulatory cooperation that would not be credible in the absence of such delegation.[48]

So far I have considered Coasean transaction costs—the costs of bargaining, of writing and especially of enforcing agreements. However, delegation to an independent agency or supranational organization is also a means of reducing *political* transaction costs. Such costs arise from the difficulty of electorally accountable politicians in making long-term contingent commitments. Because democracy is a form of government *pro*

---

[47] Alan Peacock (ed.), *The Regulation Game* (Oxford: Basil Blackwell, 1984), 12.

[48] Konstantine Gatsios and Paul Seabright, 'Regulation in the European Community', *Oxford Review of Economic Policy*, vol. 5 (1989), 37–60.

tempore,[49] the policies of the current majority can be subverted by a new majority with different and perhaps opposing interests. Hence political executives tend to have shorter time horizons than their counterparts in the private sector and lack good 'technologies of commitment'.

The point of insulating regulators from the political process is to enhance the credibility of regulatory commitments. Because agency heads tend to attach more importance to the agency's statutory objectives than the government or the median voter, they are more likely to pursue those objectives even when, because of changed economic or political conditions, they no longer enjoy popular support.[50]

So far the political-transaction-cost framework has been applied mostly to domestic policy-making,[51] but the approach throws additional light also on the logic of delegation at the supranational level. Thus, if the Treaty of Rome makes the decision-making powers of the Council of Ministers and of the European Parliament dependent on the proposals of the Commission, this is not to give a privileged position to a supranational bureaucracy against the democratically legitimated representatives of the Member States or the popularly elected members of the Parliament. Rather, the Commission's monopoly of legislative proposals is a mechanism for credibly committing the political branches of the EU to the basic goals of European integration defined by the Treaty.

E. Accountability as a design problem

The delegation of policy-making powers to politically independent, or non-majoritarian, institutions immediately raises the issue of democratic accountability. This issue has been debated extensively in connection with the problem of political control of the bureaucracy, and several lessons of general significance have been learned. Perhaps the most important lesson is that the possibility of reconciling political independence and democratic accountability depends crucially on the way the relationships between electorally accountable politicians, non-majoritarian institutions, and the general public are structured. Political principals create independent agencies, define their legal authority, objectives, and decision-making procedures, and appoint key personnel. Such powers can and should be used not only to provide *ex ante* legitimacy, but also to design institutional arrangements capable of ensuring democratic accountability over time.

---

[49] Juan J. Linz, 'Democracy's Time Constraints', *International Political Science Review*, vol. 19 (1998), 19–37.

[50] Majone, *Regulating Europe* (above, n. 36), 68–72.

[51] Douglass C. North, 'A Transaction Costs Theory of Politics', *Journal of Theoretical Politics*, vol. 2 (1990), 355–67; Avinash K. Dixit, *The Making of Economic Policy* (Cambridge, MA.: The MIT Press, 1996).

It is interesting to note that before the 1980s most research on political–bureaucratic relations tended to cast doubt on the possibility of effectively controlling the bureaucracy. Neither the legislature nor the top executives, it was argued, are capable or willing to effectively monitor their administrative agents. Legislators are more concerned with satisfying voters than with overseeing the bureaucracy. Budgeting was revealed to be decentralized and incremental, resulting in automatic increases that further insulate the bureaucracy from political control. Even presidents, it seemed, lack the resources to monitor the federal bureaucracy adequately.

More recent studies come to very different conclusions. Effective political control is possible; elected leaders can and do shape bureaucratic behaviour in systematic ways.[52] This new research is deeply influenced by principal–agent theory. Its more optimistic conclusions reflect the emphasis of agency theory on the variety of control instruments and incentives available to principals. In particular, political principals can use procedural rules and citizen complaints to offset information asymmetries, and when policy outcomes diverge significantly from desired results they have the means to bring their agents back into line.

It is true that direct monitoring, on which much of the older literature concentrated, is likely to be an imperfect mechanism of control. Such monitoring is expensive and most methods for imposing meaningful sanctions on bureaucratic agents lack credibility since they also entail serious costs for the principals. In addition, it may be difficult in practice to detect noncompliance. However, institutional design and administrative procedures are powerful additional mechanisms for helping elected politicians retain control of policy-making. Institutional choices concerning the extent of delegation, task specification, and the governance structure of the agency, together with rules defining the procedures to be followed in agency decision-making, can guide agencies to make decisions that are broadly consistent with the policy preferences of their elective principals.[53] In sum, it is up to the principals to structure relationships with their agents so that the outcomes produced through the agents' efforts are the best the principals can achieve, given the choice to delegate in the first place.

Procedural requirements, and especially the requirement that regulators give reasons for their decisions, are probably the most effective means of improving the transparency and accountability of international agencies. This is because the reason-giving requirement activates a number of other mechanisms for controlling regulatory discretion. In the words of

---

[52] Daniel B. Wood and Robert W. Waterman, 'The Dynamics of the Political Control of the Bureaucracy', *American Political Science Review*, vol. 85 (1991), 801–28.

[53] Matthew D. McCubbins, Roger G. Noll, and Barry R. Weingast, 'Administrative Procedures as Instruments of Control', *Journal of Law, Economics and Organization*, vol. 3 (1987), 243–77; Murray Horn, *The Political Economy of Public Administration* (Cambridge: Cambridge University Press, 1995).

Martin Shapiro, 'giving reasons is a device for enhancing democratic influences on administration by making government more transparent. The reason-giving administrator is likely to make more reasonable decisions than he or she otherwise might and is more subject to general public surveillance.'[54]

The framers of the treaties establishing the European Communities were well aware of the special importance of giving reasons for institutions not directly accountable to the voters or their elected representatives. Article 5 of the Paris Treaty establishing the European Coal and Steel Community states that 'the Community shall . . . publish the reasons for its actions', and Article 15 of the same treaty provides that '[d]ecisions, recommendations and opinions of the High Authority shall state the reasons on which they are based'. Similarly, Article 253 (ex Article 190) of the Rome Treaty requires that '[r]egulations, directives and decisions of the Council and of the Commission shall state the reasons on which they are based'. It should be noted that at the time these treaties were drafted there was no general requirement to give reasons in the law of most Member States, so that these European provisions were not only different from, but in advance of, national laws.[55]

Moreover, the European Court of Justice is quite prepared to impose the obligation of giving reasons upon the national authorities in order that individuals be able to protect their rights in so far as they arise under Community law. For example, in the *Heylens* case,[56] the Court reasoned that effective protection requires that the individual be able to defend his or her right under the best possible conditions. This would involve judicial review of the national authority's decision restricting that right (in the *Heylens* case, the right of free movement of workers). For judicial review to be effective, however, the national court must be able to call upon the authority to provide its reasons.[57] It remains to be seen whether Article 253 (ex Article 190) of the Rome Treaty—according to Shapiro 'one of the world's central devices for judicial enforcement of bureaucratic transparency'[58]—will be used by the ECJ to move beyond formal requirements towards substantive judicial review of regulatory decision-making in the European Community. At any rate, the EC experience shows how supranational regulatory cooperation, supported by appropriate institutions, may produce superior results not only in terms of efficiency but also of public accountability.

[54] Martin Shapiro, 'The Giving-Reasons Requirement', *University of Chicago Legal Forum* (1992), 183.
[55] T. C. Hartley, *The Foundations of European Communities Law*, 2nd edn (Oxford: Clarendon Press, 1988), 119.
[56] Case 222/86, *UNECTEF v. Heylens*, 1987 ECR 4097.
[57] Robert Thomas, 'Reason-Giving in English and European Community Administrative Law', *European Public Law*, vol. 3 (1997), 213–22.
[58] Shapiro, 'Giving-Reasons Requirement' (above, n. 54), 218.

The 'demand' for international regulatory cooperation: a public-choice perspective*

Jonathan R. Macey

I. INTRODUCTION

The idea of the state lies at the core of international relations and international law. The concept of sovereignty lies at the core of the notion of the state. Indeed, inherent in a system of states are the principles of political independence and sovereign equality that form the underpinnings of sovereignty.[1] Thus it is unsurprising that the United Nations Charter specifically addresses the concept of sovereignty and makes it clear that '[n]othing contained in the present Charter shall authorize the United Nations to intervene in matters which are essentially within the domestic jurisdiction of any state or shall require members to submit such matters to enforcement'.[2] The provision in the UN Charter, which is typical of international treaties,[3] was necessary because without it sovereign nation-states would have been reluctant to join the United Nations. Countries jealously protect their sovereignty, and under international law, have the right to use armed force to do so.

This devotion to sovereignty appears to be inconsistent with the increasing trend towards the establishment of international agreements and institutions, since they involve a surrender of some degree of sovereignty. After all, '[s]ince governments put a high value on the maintenance of their own autonomy, it is usually impossible to establish international institutions that exercise authority over states'.[4] This contribution attempts to reconcile this apparent inconsistency by examining the trend towards international agreements from a public-choice perspective. In order to provide some precision and focus to the enquiry, I concentrate on the fields of corporate finance and monetary policy. The starting point for

* This contribution is an adaptation of 'A Public Choice Model of International Economic Cooperation and the Decline of the Nation State', by Enrico Colombatto and Jonathan R. Macey, *Cardozo Law Review*, vol. 18 (1996), 925. The author wishes to thank Enrico Colambatto and Yeshiva University for permission to reproduce portions of that article.

[1] Barry E. Carter and Phillip R. Trimble, *International Law*, 2nd edn. (Boston: Little, Brown, 1995), 1366.

[2] UN Charter art. 2, ¶ 7.

[3] Carter and Trimble, *International Law* (above, n. 1), 1366–7.

[4] Robert O. Keohane, *After Hegemony: Cooperation and Discord in the World Political Economy* (Princeton, NJ: Princeton University Press, 1994), 88.

the analysis is that nations do not decide to cooperate or forge international agreements, rather the regulators, bureaucrats, and politicians
within nations do. And regulators will not agree to enter into international
agreements unless it is in their (private) interest to do so. Furthermore,
regulators are political-support-maximizing actors; they respond to political pressure and to self-interest.

All else equal, regulators would prefer not to cede or to share authority
with their counterparts from other countries. Thus regulators in a particular country do not want to coordinate their activities with regulators in
other countries because such coordination forces the regulators to sacrifice
autonomy. The thesis of this contribution, however, is that technological
change, market processes, and other exogenous variables can deprive the
regulators in a particular country of the power to act unilaterally. Such
change can cause regulators acting alone to become irrelevant. When this
happens, the regulators in a particular country will have strong incentives
to engage in activities such as international coordination in order to survive.
Viewed from this perspective, it is clear that the trend towards international
agreements and the formation of international institutions are consistent
with the basic desire of governmental actors to maintain their sovereignty.
Such agreements and institutions ought to be viewed as attempts to preserve as much national autonomy as possible in the modern world.

In this contribution, I apply my theory to the Basle Accords, the historic
documents which standardize minimum capital requirements among the
world's banks. In the context of the negotiations leading up to those agreements, my theory explains why the Japanese regulators were reluctant to
compromise with their bureaucratic colleagues from other nations, while
the regulators from the United States were quite eager to reach an agreement about capital levels. Unlike their counterparts in the United States,
the Japanese bureaucrats, who represented Japan's Ministry of Finance,
were quite powerful. Their autonomy was not being threatened by internal or external sources, and therefore the Japanese bureaucrats felt little
need to reach an international accord in order to protect either their autonomy or their bureaucratic turf. By contrast, the US banking regulators
were faced with serious challenges to their own power at home, and therefore had strong private incentives to reach an agreement.

Part I of this contribution describes the public-choice theory of international regulatory competition and coordination in more detail. It begins
by briefly distinguishing the two competing views of government regulation, public-interest theory and public-choice theory, to illustrate why
public-choice theory provides a useful perspective on recent international
coordination in financial regulation. Next, the contribution lays out the
framework of a public-choice theory for financial regulation.[5] In Part II, I

[5] For a more in-depth application of public-choice theory to international financial regulation, see Edward J. Kane, 'Tension Between Competition and Coordination in International

apply the insights of public-choice theory for financial regulation to the recent efforts to coordinate banking and monetary policy. First, I examine the Basle Accords on minimum capital requirements for financial institutions and demonstrate that coordination of such requirements makes little sense from a public-interest perspective. However, I show that international coordination can easily be explained from a public-choice view. Next, I turn to the European Union's formation of a common currency under the European Monetary Union (EMU). In this area, where regulators were faced with declining control over domestic monetary policy, we will see that in joining the EMU they successfully augmented their power in directing European monetary policy. Again, public-interest theory provides little guidance in explaining this activity, while a public-choice theory provides a useful explanation.

II. PUBLIC-CHOICE THEORY AND THE DECLINE OF THE NATION STATE

Political science and economics provide competing theories to explain the role of the government in regulating society. The traditional view of political scientists, formally known as the public-interest theory, generally posits that legal institutions and bureaucracies regulate in order to further the common good.[6] Adherents of the public-interest theory assert that a government seeks to achieve this basic goal of serving the public by solving collective action problems and intervening when private markets fail to properly allocate resources. 'Public-interest theory maintains that government should correct these failures through regulation, for example, through taxes or subsidies designed to push markets toward a "socially optimal" equilibrium.'[7]

A. An introduction to public-choice theory

To reach its conclusion about the role of government regulation, the public-interest theory makes some questionable assumptions about the abilities and nature of government. A major shortcoming of the theory is that it assumes that government has the superhuman ability to both identify and correct market failures without cost.[8] Moreover, as McCormick and

Financial Regulation', in *Governing Banking's Future: Markets vs. Regulation*, Catherine England (ed.), (Boston: Kluwer Academic Publishers, 1991).

[6] *See generally* A. C. Pigou, *The Economics of Welfare*, 4th edn. (London: Macmillan and Co., Ltd, 1932).

[7] Henry N. Butler and Jonathan R. Macey, 'Health Care Reform: Perspectives from the Economic Theory of Regulation and the Economic Theory of Statutory Interpretation', *Cornell Law Review*, vol. 79 (1994), 1434, 1436. For a full description of the public-interest model, see Robert E. McCormick and Robert D. Tollison, *Politicians, Legislation, and the Economy: An Inquiry into the Interest-Group Theory of the Government* (Boston: M. Nijhoff, 1981), 3.

[8] See Butler and Macey, 'Health Care Reform' (above, n. 7), 1436.

Tollison note, 'the [public-interest] approach assumes an all-knowing, benevolent government'.[9] Not surprisingly, the public-interest theory has been criticized as 'not a very *believable* theory of government'.[10]

Even more problematic, given its objective of explaining government regulation, is that public-interest theory fails to explain much of what we observe in the real world. Contrary to the predictions of public-interest theory, one often observes regulation where there is little evidence, if any, of market failure. One also observes governmentally coerced wealth transfers that benefit powerful, discrete interest groups at the expense of the general public.[11]

In contrast to the public-interest theory of political scientists, the public-choice or 'interest-group' theory of regulation uses the standard assumptions about human nature routinely employed by economists. Public choice assumes that politicians, bureaucrats, and other decision-makers in public life are rationally self-interested.[12] This means that, like individuals and firms in the private sector, politicians and bureaucrats attempt to maximize their personal power and wealth even when these selfish ends conflict with public-spirited goals.[13] Applied to what bureaucrats and politicians do, the assumption of self-interest means that law is traded for political support, money, power, and other things that politicians and bureaucrats demand. As Judge Richard Posner explains, public-choice theory 'asserts that legislation is a good demanded and supplied much as other goods, so that legislative protection flows to those groups that derive the greatest value from it'.[14]

The critical advantage of public-choice theory over public-interest theory is its superior predictive powers. For example, as Kenneth Scott has noted, '[i]n [public-choice theory's] light, much of banking regulation (such as restraints on entry or price fixing through the late and unlamented Regulation Q) can be explained as successful efforts by banks to obtain monopoly rents through a cartel administered by the government'.[15] Similarly, Geoffrey Miller and I have demonstrated elsewhere that the real beneficiaries of deposit insurance are financial institutions,

---

[9] McCormick and Tollison, *Politicians, Legislation and the Economy* (above, n. 7), 4.

[10] Ibid., 3.

[11] See Kenneth E. Scott, 'Commentary', in *Restructuring Banking and Financial Services in America*, William S. Haraf and Rose Marie Kushmeider (eds) (Washington, D.C.: American Enterprise Institute for Public Policy Research, 1988) (commenting on Edward J. Kane, 'How Market Forces Influence the Structure of Financial Regulation,' ibid. 343).

[12] See Butler and Macey, 'Health Care Reform' (above, n. 7), 1436–7 ('Thus, [public choice theory] analyzes decisions made by politicians, bureaucrats, and interest-groups in accordance with generally accepted principles of rational economic behavior.').

[13] See ibid. 1436.

[14] Richard A. Posner, 'Economics, Politics, and the Reading of Statutes and the Constitution', 49 *University of Chicago Law Review*, 263, 265 (1982); see also Butler and Macey, 'Health Care Reform' (above, n. 7), 1436.

[15] Scott, 'Commentary' (above, n. 11), 387.

because deposit insurance minimizes their cost of funds, and not the public, which pays for deposit insurance with forgone interest.[16]

B. Public-choice theory and financial regulation

The application of public-choice analysis to bureaucracies in general, and to the promulgation of financial regulation by such bureaucracies in particular, yields two insights. First, all regulatory entities will engage in wealth-maximizing behaviour. They will attempt to maximize the rough 'value of their (bureaucracies) subject to technological, market, and statutory restraints and principal-agent difficulties'.[17] Second, any given regulatory authority competes with other regulatory authorities for whatever it is that they are attempting to maximize. This competitive behaviour will occur on a national as well as an international level.

Thus, as Edward Kane has observed, 'like dominant firms in any domestic market, a country's dominant financial regulator must worry about foreign competition'.[18] Kane offers an important explanation for changes in financial market regulation. He observes that, even where capital flight is easy and financial service firms can do business across borders with little difficulty, regulated entities cannot easily change regulators, because doing so is very costly, due to 'substantial transition or switching costs'.[19] Regulators employ 'exit fees, administrative delays, and outright prohibitions'[20] to prevent the firms they regulate from leaving the regulatory fold and to preserve their market shares.[21]

However, 'technological change and increasing competition between foreign and state regulators'[22] have made it more difficult for regulators to protect their turf. Technological change and market developments have made it possible for banks and insurance firms and investment banks to compete directly, despite the fact that these firms traditionally have been regulated by rival regulators. Technology has increased competition, as travel and information costs have declined, making international competition increasingly easy. These changes 'have made it increasingly less costly for financial firms to penetrate US and foreign regulators' administrative fences by cleverly adapting their institutional structures to squeeze through loopholes in the system of prohibited activities'.[23] As Professor Kane observed:

The recent global acceleration of financial and regulatory change reflects the response of regulatees and regulators to exogenous and endogenous decreases in

---

[16] Jonathan R. Macey and Geoffrey P. Miller, *Banking Law and Regulation* (Boston: Little, Brown, 1992).

[17] Kane, 'Tension Between Competition and Coordination' (above, n. 5), 34 (citing Kenneth E. Scott, 'The Dual Banking System: A Model of Competition in Regulation', *Stanford Law Review*, vol. 30 (1977), 1).

[18] Ibid. 36.   [19] Ibid. 37.   [20] Ibid.   [21] Ibid.   [22] Ibid.   [23] Ibid.

the costs of entry and exit from various financial product markets. The microeconomic view is that the product line and geographic market expansion by suppliers of financial regulatory services follow and support rivalry between client financial services firms within and across countries, regions, and various kinds of administrative boundaries. Supplementing strictly bureaucratic theories of regulatory behavior . . . my conception is based on the premise that regulators attempt, subject to bureaucratic, market and technological constraints, to extend or defend their share of the market for regulatory services in the face of exogenous and endogenous disturbances in the economy.[24]

I made an argument analogous to Kane's in a recent article discussing administrative agency obsolescence.[25] In that article, I applied principles of firm or industry failure in a market economy to administrative agencies. In a competitive market when 'a firm misuses limited resources by "producing unwanted products, or overproducing, or using inefficient production techniques, at the extreme it will fail, and the resources will find more socially desirable uses".'[26] The argument there was that 'just as technological innovations in markets often cause whole industries to become obsolete—for example, the introduction of the automobile had disastrous consequences for the buggy whip industry—so too can technological innovation render administrative agencies obsolete'.[27] This argument concluded that while a competitive market allows firm or industry failure so that resources will flow to more efficient uses:

[W]hen administrative agencies become obsolete, they are likely to respond to their obsolescence in ways that impose very heavy costs on the firms they are supposed to regulate, or on society generally, or both. As obsolescence sets in, administrative agencies are likely to replace the publicly articulated goals that provided the initial justification for the creation of the agency with self-serving goals designed to ensure that the agency will remain a secure place for the officials who comprise its staff.[28]

Applying these obsolescence principles to the recent international coordination of financial regulation produces conclusions consistent with Kane's. Specifically, when technological change, market processes, or other exogenous variables threaten either to remove power from a nation's regulatory structure or cause it to become irrelevant, then the regulators in that nation will have strong incentives to engage in activities such as international coordination in order to protect their autonomy.

---

[24] Kane, 'Tension Between Competition and Coordination' (above, n. 5)

[25] Jonathan R. Macey, 'Administrative Agency Obsolescence and Interest Group Formation: A Case Study of the SEC at Sixty', *Cardozo Law Review*, vol. 15 (1994), 909.

[26] Ibid. 910 (quoting A. Dale Tussing, 'The Case for Bank Failure', *Journal of Law and Economics*, vol. 10 (1967), 129).

[27] Ibid. 911.   [28] Ibid. 913.

III. APPLYING PUBLIC-CHOICE THEORY IN SPECIFIC CONTEXTS:
THE BASLE CAPITAL ACCORDS AND THE EUROPEAN MONETARY
UNION

A. The Basle Capital Accords

1. *Background*

In theory, the purpose of capital adequacy rules is to protect depositors
from the damage caused by excessive risk-taking by financial institutions.[29] Generally speaking, a bank's capital is the difference between the
bank's assets and its liabilities. This sum is often characterized as a bank's
'cushion' against insolvency.[30] The higher a bank's level of capital, the
larger the cushion that protects depositors in case of financial stress.
Likewise, so long as a bank has a positive capital level, it is solvent: it has
sufficient assets to pay all of its outstanding liabilities, and the risk of loss
in case of failure falls solely on the shoulders of the shareholders.[31] Thus,
the presence of adequate capital provides protection for depositors, or in
the context of federal deposit insurance, for the federal deposit insurance
system.

Although the theory of capital adequacy is relatively straightforward,
implementation of a workable capital adequacy system is in reality quite
difficult to achieve. First, there is the problem of quantifying a financial
institution's base capital level. This process is made extremely difficult
due to the fact that capital takes many forms, ranging from more permanent and certain sources of value (e.g. common stock) to less certain and
less permanent sources of value (e.g. subordinated debt).

Even more problematic is the problem of asset risk. Any rational system
of capital adequacy rules must account in some meaningful way for the
risk present in the financial institution's asset portfolio. This is because the
riskier the firm's assets, the greater the risk of bankruptcy. For example, a
bank that simply accepts time deposits and invests the proceeds in short-
term government debt of matching maturities does not run any risk of
insolvency (so long as the return on the notes can cover the interest on the
deposits plus the bank's expenses). By contrast, a bank that takes deposits
and invests the proceeds in speculative assets like real estate loans or
derivatives presents a significantly higher risk of insolvency.

For these reasons, simple, bright-line capital rules are inappropriate and
ineffective. Ironically, for a long time, such crude, bright-line rules were
exactly what financial institutions in the United States operated under.
The original capital adequacy rules, known as leverage ratio, simply

---

[29] See Macey and Miller, *Banking Law* (above, n. 16), 284.   [30] See ibid.
[31] See ibid.

required that banks meet a gross ratio of capital to assets with no accounting for the risk of assets.[32] This allowed banks to operate at widely disparate levels of risk while remaining in compliance with the leverage ratio guidelines.

The inadequacy of the leverage ratio framework became increasingly apparent with the dramatic growth in banks' international and cross-border activities during the 1970s. The greatly varied capital adequacy rules throughout the world caused major banking nations to be concerned that countries with relatively strict capital guidelines were being placed at a competitive disadvantage as compared to those with more lenient guidelines.[33]

To illustrate, take two banks, Bank A and Bank B.[34] Assume that the cost of debt funding (e.g. what a bank must pay depositors or other creditors for the use of their money) for both banks is 7 per cent and that the cost of equity funding is 10 per cent. This is consistent with observed reality, since the cost of equity funding is higher than the cost of debt funding. Next, assume that Bank A is subject to a 4 per cent capital ratio and Bank B is subject to a 6 per cent capital ratio, and that in all other respects the banks are identical. This would mean that Bank A can fund up to 96 per cent of any given loan with deposits or other debt, and must fund only 4 per cent of the loan with some form of equity that meets the minimum capital requirements. Bank B, on the other hand, can fund only 94 per cent of the loan with deposits or other debt, and must fund 6 per cent of the loan with some form of equity that meets the capital requirements.

The cost to each bank of making a loan is shown by the following equation:

Loan Cost = [(% of loan funded by debt) × (cost of debt)] +
[(% of loan funded by equity) × (cost of equity)].

Applying this formula, one can easily calculate what it would cost each bank to make a loan of $100:

Bank A's Loan Cost = (96)(.07) + (4)(.1) = 7.12%
Bank B's Loan Cost = (94)(.07) + (6)(.1) = 7.18%

[32] See Macey and Miller, *Banking Law* (above, n. 16), 285. While leverage ratios remain in place under US banking regulation, their importance has effectively been trumped by the Basle Capital Accords guidelines.

[33] See ibid. See also, *Risk-Based Capital Requirements for Banks and Bank Holding Companies: Hearing Before the Subcommittee on General Oversight and Investigations of the House Committee on Banking, Finance and Urban Affairs, 100th Congress, 2d Sess.*, (Washington, DC: US G.P.O., 1988), 5 (statement of William Taylor, Division of Banking Supervision and Regulation, Federal Reserve Board) ('[W]e simply cannot ignore the impact of differing regulatory standards on US banks' ability to compete worldwide. More consistent supervisory standards among countries can contribute to competitive equality and, in the long run, to a safer and more stable banking system.').

[34] This example is drawn from Hal S. Scott and Shinsaku Iwahara, *In Search of a Level Playing Field: The Implementation of the Basle Capital Accord in Japan and the United States* (Washington, DC: Group of Thirty, 1994).

Thus, Bank A's lower capital requirements enable it to finance its lending activities more cheaply than Bank B, giving Bank A a competitive advantage. Put another way, because it faces lower capital requirements, Bank A can lend out more money for a given level of equity than Bank B. And, all else equal, Bank A will be more profitable than Bank B.

It was widely understood that the competitive advantage to be gained from more lenient capital standards was responsible for a reduction in the capital levels of international banks. This reduction became a source of concern for regulators, which 'was exacerbated by the emerging debt crisis in the major developing countries'.[35] In addition to the competitive inequality concern, regulators expressed concern over the striking development and growth in off-balance sheet activities by banks (e.g. standby letters of credit, and derivatives such as currency and interest rate swaps). These activities raised a new set of risks for financial institutions that were completely different from the traditional risk associated with the institution's loan portfolio.[36]

The concerns about banks becoming increasingly risky as a result of dangerously low capital levels and off-balance sheet activities made banks increasingly difficult to monitor. This initially led to a joint initiative between the United States and the United Kingdom in 1986, which was designed to achieve a common risk-weighted capital measuring system.[37] This initiative was followed in December 1987 with the Basle Capital Adequacy Accords.[38] The Basle Accords are essentially a 'gentleman's agreement' among central bankers in the countries that make up the Basle Supervisors Committee of the Bank for International Settlements (BIS).[39] In 1989, when the European Union adopted its own capital guidelines based on the Basle structure, the Accord were extended to several non-G-10 EU countries.[40] In addition to these countries, many other nations have adopted the Basle Accords in order to enhance their international reputation, and to 'enable them to operate in countries like the United States that require conformity with the Basle standards as a condition for entry'.[41]

---

[35] Peter Cooke, 'Excerpts from Bank Capital Adequacy', in Hal Scott and Philip Wellons, *International Finance: Transactions, Policy and Regulation* (Westbury, NY: Foundation Press, 1995), 216; see also, David Shirreff, 'The Fearsome Growth of Swaps', *Euromoney*, Oct. 1985, 247, 253 (quoting Charles Lucas of the Federal Reserve Bank of New York as stating that central banks must harmonize their regulation of swaps, for '[o]therwise the business will simply be driven to the least regulated markets').

[36] See Cooke, 'Excerpts' (above, n. 35), 216.   [37] See ibid. 217.

[38] See Ethan B. Kapstein, 'Resolving the Regulator's Dilemma: International Coordination of Banking Regulations', *International Organization*, vol. 43 (1989), 323, 323.

[39] See Hal S. Scott, 'The Competitive Implications of the Basle Capital Accord', *St. Louis University Law Journal*, vol. 39 (1995), 885, 888. The BIS Committee includes the Group of Ten (G-10) countries (Belgium, Canada, France, Germany, Italy, Japan, Netherlands, Sweden, United Kingdom, and the United States) plus Switzerland and Luxembourg. Ibid. 885.

[40] See ibid. This brought in Denmark, Greece, Ireland, Portugal, and Spain.

[41] Ibid.

Before looking at the Basle Accords from a public-interest and public-choice perspective, it will be helpful to provide a brief summary of how the Basle's risk-adjusted capital ratio framework operates. Under the Basle Accords, a bank's asset portfolio is divided into four categories. Each category is assigned a risk-weight percentage which in theory reflects the risk level of the assets within that category.[42] The higher the risk-weight percentage, the riskier the asset category. For example, the risk-weight percentage for private loans is 100 per cent, while the risk-weight percentage for government securities is 0 per cent.[43] Thus, no capital is necessary to offset government securities, while 100 per cent of the specified minimum capital levels must be held against a bank's loan portfolio because the total assets in each category are then multiplied by the appropriate risk-weight, and these products are summed.

The Basle guidelines also seek to account for the risks associated with financial institutions' off-balance sheet activities. Each off-balance sheet activity is multiplied by a credit conversion factor to determine a 'credit equivalent value' for the particular activity.[44] The 'credit equivalent value' is then adjusted for risk based on the identity of the borrower. The result is known as the bank's 'adjusted credit equivalent value'.[45] The sum of the risk-weighted assets is added to the adjusted credit equivalent value to reach the firm's 'total risk adjusted assets'.[46]

The next step is to calculate the bank's capital. The Basle Accords divide the bank's capital into two categories, called 'tiers'. Tier 1, commonly known as the firm's 'core' capital, generally consists of common stock, qualifying non-cumulative preferred stock, and minority interests in equity accounts of subsidiaries. Tier 1 does not include goodwill.[47] Tier 2, commonly known as the firm's 'supplementary' capital, generally includes allowances for loan and lease losses, perpetual preferred stock not in Tier 1, subordinated debt, intermediate-term preferred stock, and certain other hybrid capital instruments and notes.[48] Essentially, Tier 2 capital consists of items that have less certain or less permanent value than Tier 1 capital. Tier 1 is then added to Tier 2, with the exception that the Tier 2 level cannot exceed the Tier 1 level, and this sum is reduced by certain deductions. The result is the financial institution's total capital.[49]

The final step is to determine whether the bank's ratio of total capital to total risk-adjusted assets meets the Basle requirements. That ratio is currently at 8 per cent. Additionally, because a bank's Tier 2 capital cannot exceed its Tier 1 capital, the Basle guidelines effectively impose a 4 per cent ratio of Tier 1 capital to total risk-adjusted assets.[50]

[42] Macey and Miller, *Banking Law* (above, n. 16), 285.   [43] Ibid.   [44] Ibid. 286.

[45] Ibid.   [46] Ibid.   [47] Ibid.   [48] Ibid.   [49] Ibid.   [50] Ibid. 287.

2. The Basle Accords from the public-interest perspective

The public-interest based explanation for the Basle Accords is easily summarized. The globalization of financial markets that began in the 1970s brought a substantial increase in international competition. This increased competition, combined with the explosion in banks' use of off-balance sheet activities, is supposed to produce a need for international regulatory coordination. Coordinating internal regulations would provide for the safety and soundness of the banking industry and would promote competitive equality within the banking industry.[51] It is argued that without the Basle Accords, banks operating in countries with weak capital requirements would have a competitive advantage over banks operating in countries with stringent capital requirements. This competitive advantage would put pressure on bank regulators. A competition among regulators results in a 'race to the bottom' where regulators try to benefit their own constituents by lowering capital requirements. International coordination in the form of the Basle Accords solves this problem.

There are at least two problems with the public-interest analysis. First, the Basle Accords did not improve the safety and soundness of the financial system. Nor have they 'levelled the regulatory playing field' by eliminating the competitive inequities that can theoretically arise from differing capital guidelines. Second, the public-interest approach presumes that such 'harmonization' or 'cooperation' is beneficial to the public without offering a believable explanation of why a country such as the United States would be eager to sacrifice at least some of its national autonomy in the area of financial regulation.

Hal Scott and Shinsaku Iwahara have effectively demonstrated that the Basle Accords have not levelled the international playing field.[52] Scott and Iwahara explain that '[c]ompetitive advantages between banks in two countries are caused primarily not by differences in capital ratios, but by differences in comparative advantage, the fundamentals of each economy, and governmental support in the form of safety net policies'.[53] One of the principal reasons for Scott and Iwahara's conclusion arises from the existence of a 'bailout differential' between nations.[54] In an efficient market, the risk of debtor default would lead creditors of highly leveraged firms to demand higher interest payments than creditors of less leveraged firms. This does not occur in the banking industry because of the presence of a governmental 'safety net'. All major banking countries have some form of implicit or explicit guarantee/deposit insurance that the depositors in

---

[51] See, e.g. Cooke, 'Excerpts' (above, n. 35); Kapstein, 'Resolving the Regulator's Dilemma' (above, n. 38); Note, 'The Proposed Risk-Based Capital Framework: A Model of International Banking Cooperation?', *Fordham International Law Journal*, vol. 11 (1988), 777.

[52] See generally Scott and Iwahara, *In Search of a Level Playing Field* (above, n. 34).

[53] Ibid. 1.   [54] Scott, 'The Competitive Implications' (above, n. 39), 886.

financial institutions will be protected if the financial institution defaults.[55] The presence of this guarantee generally makes creditors indifferent to a financial institution's leverage ratio.[56]

However, the strength of this safety net varies from country to country.[57] For example, there is strong evidence to support the fact that the Japanese and European safety nets are stronger than that of the United States.[58] The implication of this is that 'creditors will demand higher interest rates from US banks than they do from European or Japanese banks with the same leverage because the overall risk of lending to United States banks is higher. . . . United States banks must have more capital to make up for the weaker government guarantees.'[59] The available data appear to confirm Scott and Iwahara's position. The average capital ratio for the ten largest US banks in 1993 was 13.6 per cent, as compared with 9.67 per cent for the ten largest Japanese banks.[60] Similarly, the average capital ratio for the ten largest European banks in 1993 was 10.12 per cent, also lower than the United States' 13.6 per cent.[61] Moreover, neither the capital ratio differentials between the United States and Japan nor those between the United States and Europe have narrowed since the inception of the Basle Accords.[62]

Not only have the Basle Accords not levelled the international playing field with respect to capital, 'it would be a total accident if it did so given the disparate effects of regulatory, market, accounting and tax differences among countries'.[63] Moreover, the Basle Accords's risk-weight categories create competitive distortions based upon differences between domestic economies. Japanese banks typically have higher levels of private loans relative to the US, which are risk-weighted at 100 per cent.[64] The United States, by contrast, has relatively higher levels of residential mortgages, which carry a risk-weight of 50 per cent.[65] Thus, the Basle standards themselves place Japan at a competitive disadvantage relative to the US banks. Residential mortgages, which are favoured by the Accords, are a more important part of the US banking market than the Japanese banking market, while private loans, which are disfavoured are more important to Japanese banks.

What about safety and soundness of the Basle Accords? While no systematic analysis has yet to provide a clear answer as to whether the Basle

---

[55] See Macey and Miller, *Banking Law* (above, n. 16), 745.
[56] See Scott, 'The Competitive Implications' (above, n. 39), 886–7.
[57] See ibid. 887–8.
[58] See ibid. Scott noted that '[n]o depositor in Japan has lost a single Yen due to bank failure since the end of World War II', while US depositors have often been required to absorb significant losses. Ibid. In addition, the safety net of European countries is also stronger than that of the United States because the European countries have either 'fewer but larger banks (too big to fail), or [they] have state-owned banks'. Ibid.
[59] Ibid. 887–8.
[60] See ibid. 888 (citing Federal Reserve, Japanese Securities Report).
[61] Ibid. 889 (citing *American Banker*).   [62] Ibid.   [63] Ibid.   [64] Ibid.   [65] Ibid.

Accords have achieved this objective, Robert Litan has shown that their framework can contribute to credit crunches in periods of economic downturn.[66] Litan's analysis casts a strong shadow over any claim that the Accords have improved the safety and soundness of the banking system. The Basle Accords have this effect because their 'risk weights tilted the incentives of banks heavily toward investing in government bonds [risk-weight of 0 per cent] rather than making loans'.[67] Assuming a bank must pay 3 per cent to attract deposits and 10 per cent for equity, the implication of these risk-weights is that a bank's cost of funding to invest in government bonds is 3 per cent, while its cost of funding for a private loan is 3.56 per cent.[68]

Thus, between December 1991 and July 1992, the volume of commercial bank loans in the United States fell by $20 billion, while the total bank investments in government bonds rose by $50 billion.[69] Litan concludes:

It is no doubt true that weak demand for commercial loans has contributed to this situation. But the undeniable fact remains that before the Basle Accord . . . the cost of funding both government bonds and loans were the same. . . . Moreover, by pushing banks into playing the government bond yield curve, the risk-weights are impelling banks to take on greater interest rate risk, which may come to haunt them when the yield flattens, as it eventually will.[70]

Thus the public-interest theory's safety and soundness and competitive equality arguments fall short. Moreover, public-interest theory fails to explain why a country would be willing to sacrifice its autonomy in order to take part in the Basle Accords.

3. The Basle Accords from the public-choice perspective

The public-choice model provides a much more useful perspective on the Basle Accords. Consistent with the public-interest view, the public-choice perspective traces the regulatory innovations that resulted in the Basle Accords to the market and technological innovations of the past twenty years. These exogenous market and technological forces posed a significant threat to the national regulatory structure of countries like the United States and the United Kingdom. In response to this threat, the bank regulators in those countries pushed the Basle agenda in an attempt to protect their autonomy in the face of international competition. Indeed, the Accords are entirely consistent with the desire on the part of regulators to avoid regulatory obsolescence.

The principal effect of the technological change and the globalization of markets over the past two decades has been to reduce the entry and exit

---

[66] Robert E. Litan, 'Nightmare in Basle', *The International Economy*, Nov./Dec. 1992, 7, 8–9.
[67] Ibid. 8 (commercial/private loans risk-weight of 100%; residential mortgages' risk-weight of 50%).
[68] Ibid.   [69] Ibid.   [70] Ibid. 8–9.

barriers which had maintained financial institutions within domestic boundaries.[71] This, in turn, has made it easier for regulated firms to migrate to more sympathetic regulators, and has caused increased competition among national regulatory authorities. In this competition, the United States has 'been losing market share in securities and banking to foreign regulators, particularly to the Japanese'.[72]

This emerging loss of market share to the Japanese has forced nations such as the United States and the United Kingdom to respond with demands for 'harmonization' in order to maintain some degree of autonomy.[73] From their position of relative strength, regulators in Japan's Ministry of Finance saw little need to enter into an international accord. Moreover, Japanese banks were not undercapitalized when the Basle Accords were being discussed. Rather the reverse: Japanese banks were solidly capitalized.[74]

But nonetheless, the Basle Accords still served the interests of Japanese regulators. Japanese bureaucrats could not obtain the power unilaterally to impose minimum capital requirements on their own banks because Japanese banks were able to resist this attempt. But while the Japanese banks could constrain the regulators domestically, the agency costs between the banks and the regulators were too high in the international context. Thus from the perspective of the Japanese, the Basle Accords represented a hands-tying strategy in which the Japanese bureaucrats were able to collude with bureaucrats from other countries in order to obtain more discretionary regulatory authority.

In this context, it is important to note that it was only after US regulators threatened to exclude Japanese banks from US markets that the Japanese were drawn into the fold.[75] In other words, Japanese regulators could report back to their bank clientele that they had no choice but to enter into the Accords, or else the consequences for Japanese banks would be even worse. The Japanese regulators at Basle probably could have resisted the threat of exclusion from the US markets by promising to protect depositors against loss. But they most likely did not want to do so because signing the Basle Accords increased the power and autonomy of Japanese regulators.

B. The European Monetary Union

1. Background

The EMU provides another example of how international cooperation is used to preserve sovereignty of governmental actors. On 1 January 1999,

---

[71] See Kane, 'Tension Between Competition and Coordination' (above, n. 5), 44.
[72] Ibid.   [73] Ibid. at 45.
[74] I am grateful to Raghuram G. Rajan of the University of Chicago for reminding us of this fact.
[75] See Kapstein, 'Resolving the Regulator's Dilemma' (above, n. 38).

eleven member states of the EMU adopted the Euro as their single currency. Germany, France, Italy, Spain, Portugal, Austria, Belgium, the Netherlands, Luxembourg, Ireland, and Finland have agreed to let the European System of Central Banks (ESCB) control their monetary policy in accordance with the Maastricht Treaty signed in 1992. Four remaining members of the European Union, including the United Kingdom, may adopt the Euro later.[76] The EMU resulted largely from the creation of a single common market in Europe.[77] The European Union expects this system to 'bring greater visibility and predictability to markets and investments'.[78] There are several other economic gains that possibly will result from the EMU. First, a single currency will make it much easier for Europe's citizens to compare the cost of goods. Second, the Euro will significantly reduce transaction costs for international trade. An indirect effect of these reduced transaction costs will be large cross-border capital flows.[79] All of these benefits are hoped ultimately to stimulate growth and employment across Europe. From a public-choice perspective, however, the question remains, what is in it for the bureaucrats and elites that have so strongly pressed for economic and monetary union? Put another way, whatever public benefits the Euro may bring come at the loss of a significant degree of autonomy for Europe's central bankers and other bureaucrats.

The EMU appears to contradict the theory that the individual nation-state actors would act to maintain their autonomy by retaining control over monetary policy. However, as was the case with the Basle Accords, the EMU reflects the rational response of central bankers confronted with obsolescence in a regulatory arena. 'The integration of the world's capital markets, driven by a combination of technological change and financial innovation, has increasingly constrained the ability of central banks to set and implement their own monetary policies.'[80] Specifically, continuing dissatisfaction with German dominance of European monetary policy was a major factor for several nations in entering into the EMU.[81] Thus, German central bankers would be expected to oppose relinquishing a system in which they had complete control over monetary policy.[82]

---

[76] Karen Horn, 'The ESCB Statute', *New Zealand Law Journal*, Feb. 1999, 3–4.

[77] Richard I. Fine and Francois Alland, 'Current Political and Economic Developments in the European Union', *Whittier Law Review*, vol. 18 (1997), 281, 284.

[78] Ibid.

[79] Ed Stevens, 'The Euro', *Economic Commentary, Federal Reserve Bank of Cleveland*, 1 Jan. 1999, 2.

[80] Brian K. Kurzmann, 'Challenges to Monetary Unification in the European Union: Sovereignty Reigning Supreme?', 23 *Denver Journal of International Law and Policy*, 135 (1994).

[81] Wayne Sandholz, 'Choosing Union: Monetary Politics and Maastricht', 47 *International Organization* 1, 30 (1993).

[82] Ibid. 31.

2. European Monetary Union from a public-interest perspective

According to the public-interest theory, the EMU was enacted to promote growth and employment in the Member States. In order to accomplish this, the ESCB established price stability as its primary objective.[83] Pro-inflation and currency devaluation policies, therefore, became incompatible with the ESCB's restrictive monetary plan.[84] Unfortunately, by many accounts, this monolithic monetary approach may in fact undermine the goals of growth and employment for members of the EMU.

Until now, individual NCBs (national central banks) could set overnight policy interest rates different from—and to some extent independently of—one another. Those that were experiencing cyclical softness in economic conditions (like Germany) relative to others that were not (like Ireland) could ease monetary policy. Faster money growth and lower interest rates could stimulate internal and external demand to offset whatever asymmetric economic shock was depressing conditions in one country relative to the other. Henceforward, however, participating nations cannot use monetary policy to offset such independent, asymmetric economic shocks.[85]

Finally, while the much anticipated free flow of capital will not be a zero sum game, certain national stock markets, industry sectors, and individual firms will win, while others will lose.[86] 'Member states with large institutional equity assets, but which represent only a small proportion of total euro-bloc market capitalization, will suffer an outflow of capital.'[87]

If the EMU is likely to exact harms in an unequal distribution among Member States, then the surrender of national monetary policy by the members cannot be consistent with public-interest theory. Moreover, it is not clear why any rational country would want to help rival nations by allowing the outflow of capital in light of the global competition for capital.

3. European Economic Union from a public-choice perspective

Public-choice theory provides a more persuasive explanation of the Member States' pursuit of the EMU. Perhaps the most important reason among the Member States for agreeing to a common currency was that they were dissatisfied with inequities present in the European Monetary

---

[83] Horn, 'The ESCB Statute' (above, n. 76), 4.

[84] Sandholz, 'Choosing Union' (above, n. 81), 5.

[85] Stevens, 'The Euro' (above, n. 79), 4.

[86] Peter Lee, 'Toward an Efficient Euro Frontier', *Euromoney*, Aug. 1998, 40 (quoting Peter Oppenheimer of HSBC Securities).

[87] Ibid. (quoting Peter Oppenheimer; The Netherlands, for example—which has nearly 60% of EMU pension fund assets allocated to local equities but with Dutch companies comprising only 20% of European market capitalization—will likely suffer large, net outflows of capital).

System (EMS). In particular, they perceived the German Bundesbank as having the dominant voice in European monetary policy, i.e. the monetary activities of other Member States were irrelevant.[88]

The EMS was a voluntary system set up by the European Union to ensure price stability among Europe's currencies. Regulators became dissatisfied with what they observed as a fundamental imbalance in the system, namely, that the countries with the weaker currencies were disproportionately burdened with adjustment so as to maintain parities.[89] 'Indeed, whereas other EMS countries sometimes faced major adjustments when the Bundesbank tightened policy (for example), the Germans needed only consider domestic objectives and consequences.'[90] Thus, regulators' push towards a common currency resulted from the belief that a greater voice in the EMU would be preferable to continued German dominance in the EMS.

Regulators in some of the Member States advanced a common currency to obtain policy results that were impossible via domestic politics. In particular, the fragmented Italian political environment made it virtually impossible for regulators to pursue macroeconomic discipline. Entry into the EMU would force macroeconomic discipline in Italy from without.[91] Again, regulators sought to enhance their own power by subscribing to a pan-European monetary policy in which smaller countries would have some voice.

This outcome is a net improvement from the perspective of non-German central bankers, whose power over monetary policy gradually had been eviscerated by post-World War II globalization and particularly Europeanization, as well as the growth of world foreign-exchange markets. These developments had made it impossible for European central bankers either to defend their own currencies against attack or to mount a successful monetary policy of their own. Thus, the enthusiasm of Europe's bankers for monetary union is consistent with modern public-choice theory.

This analysis, of course, does not explain Germany's decision to embrace monetary union. Germany stands to benefit from monetary centralization in several ways. First, Germany entered on the assurance that its own monetary policy of price stability would be maintained. The European Central Bank, located in Frankfurt, represents the Germanization of European monetary policy. Second, in addition to exporting its own monetary policy even more completely throughout Europe, this centralization allows German bankers to see their currency grow to rival and perhaps replace the US dollar as the world's reserve currency. Finally, this centralization allows Germany to reclaim centre stage in the world's political, diplomatic, and economic arenas after the country's devastating

---

[88] Sandholz, 'Choosing Union' (above, n. 81), 30.
[89] Ibid. 28.
[90] Ibid.
[91] Ibid. 4.

military and moral defeat in World War II, which destroyed for decades the country's reliability as a credible moral actor in world politics.

IV. CONCLUSION

It is clearly the case that nations try to maintain their sovereignty, and that bureaucracies try to protect their turf. We observe this on many levels, but it is certainly apparent at the limits. Countries fight to protect their borders, even when the odds of victory appear slight. The recent trend in international agreements is consistent with this view. As international borders have become virtually irrelevant in global capital markets, regulators have been forced to enter international agreements in order to remain relevant.

Over time, all bureaucracies will substitute private, bureaucratic objectives for the public objectives that characterized their origination. But it seems clear that this general problem becomes worse in the case of agencies facing obsolescence, since obsolescence makes the problem of bureaucratic self-interest far more immediate. Thus, it stands to reason that agency officials faced with the prospect of losing their ability to control the actions of the firms they are supposed to regulate will fight hard to find some way to retain their power.

Local bureaucracies will enter international agreements that sacrifice some of their national sovereignty in order to avoid the spectre of becoming irrelevant. This thesis, as exemplified in both the Basle Accords and the formation of the EMU, provides a new way to explain international economic coordination in an era of increasing global competition.

In sum, the purpose of this chapter has been to view international cooperation from a public-choice perspective. The hypothesis is that the behaviour of politicians, interest groups, and bureaucrats in the international arena is no different than their behaviour elsewhere. We live in a rent-seeking society and international agreements reflect this. This contribution has applied this perspective to two important sources of international cooperation: formation of a common currency and capital requirements for banks. In these settings international cooperation was driven by concerns on the part of regulators about the effect of the increasingly internationalization of capital markets on their ability to regulate. Financial market regulators are concerned about their ability to regulate in a world in which capital can be transferred around the world quickly, business can be conducted across borders at very low cost, and institutional structures can be changed in order to avoid regulation.

From the regulators' perspective, reaching international accords has two effects, one positive, the other negative. The positive effect is that such accords, by homogenizing regulation across borders, enables regulators in one country effectively to collude with their colleagues in other countries, thereby reducing the demand of the domestic firms they regulate to move their operations to more congenial jurisdictions. The negative effect of international accords is that they require compromise. Regulators in different countries champion different domestic interests (although I have argued here that they do not champion 'the national interest' in large part because that term has no real meaning). The process of compromise requires the bureaucrats to give up power and autonomy, which they would prefer not to do.

We can expect an international accord among financial regulators whenever an international agreement involves a smaller sacrifice of autonomy than the autonomy that would be lost by normal market processes as firms migrated to the most liberal regulatory environment. A major point of this chapter is that the increasing globalization of markets, brought about largely through exogenous technological developments, has increased the incentives of regulators to enter into international accords by raising the loss of power to bureaucrats who do not enter into such accords.

The claim in this chapter is not that all international accords are fuelled by concerns about losing regulatory turf. In many contexts, regulators, politicians, and interest groups have other concerns. The point here is simply that technological change has made concerns about relevance of great importance at the moment in the area of global corporate finance. In other areas where international accords are discussed, such as the environment, national security, and aid to developing nations, other concerns are likely to dominate.

Finally, the broader point of this chapter is that regulators and politicians must maximize political support in order to survive. This political support comes from interest groups. The international agreements, accords, structures, frameworks, and regimes negotiated by politicians and bureaucrats are going to reflect the preferences of these groups. In the end, all politics is local.

Regulatory cooperation and competition: the search for virtue

Paul B. Stephan

A conference devoted to regulatory cooperation must pay some attention to its absence. Here I explore the consequences of a decision not to cooperate in the regulation of multinational businesses. In particular, I want to expose the underappreciated advantages of a particular kind of non-cooperation. When states offer regulatory programmes but allow private parties to choose alternative legal systems, they may encourage desirable innovation in legal rules—'races to the top'. This contribution considers how states may promote such beneficial competition, and how regulatory cooperation may stifle it.

I. INTRODUCTION

States sometimes cooperate in their regulatory policy, as when the US Government and the European Union (EU) enter into an antitrust enforcement agreement or the fiscal authorities of the major economic powers agree on capital standards for banks.[1] Other times they compete, as when the United States permits the sale of bio-engineered food products and the European Union forbids it. All this seems familiar territory. But specialists in international economic law have not paid much attention to the issues that arise when states cooperate in their regulatory competition.

We normally think of regulatory competition as an adversarial process. In the conventional conception of the problem, states propose various regulatory regimes that each would wish to apply to all relevant activity. As a result, economic transactions that occur in multiple jurisdictions, such as farming in the United States that results in food exports to the European

---

[1] See Decision of the Council and the Commission of 10 Apr. 1995 Concerning the Conclusion of the Agreement Between the European Communities and the Government of the United States of America Regarding the Application of Their Competition Laws, 1995 Off. J.L. 95 (95/145/EC, ECSC) (cooperation on antitrust enforcement); Bank for International Settlements, Proposals for International Convergence of Capital Measurement and Capital Standards (Dec. 1987), *reprinted in* 27 I.L.M. 530 (1988); Enrico Colombatto and Jonathan R. Macey, 'The Decline of the Nation State and Its Effect on Constitutional and International Economic Law: A Public Choice Model of International Economic Cooperation and the Decline of the Nation State', 18 *Cardozo Law Review*, vol. 18 (1996), 925 (cooperation on bank capital adequacy standards).

market, lead to clashes as to whose rules should apply. Within the European Union, these disputes often wend their way to the European Court of Justice. Thus, in a conflict between standards over the production of beer, the Court upheld that of the producer jurisdiction over that of the consumer jurisdiction.[2] If the controversy involves World Trade Organization (WTO) members, the WTO Dispute Settlement Body (DSB) may end up handling the clash of standards. Thus, returning to bio-engineered food, the DSB so far has sided with the United States in its determination of what food consumers may buy.[3] What these examples of adversarial competition have in common is an assumed need to resolve the contest in favour of one regulatory regime or another to avoid imposing conflicting standards on a single transaction.

But regulatory competition can also exist in a cooperative framework that permits different regimes to coexist. Such systems encourage potential subjects of regulation to choose which regime they will follow. These choices in turn encourage states to offer regulatory packages that will attract transactions, from which they can extract taxes and other rents. The issue then becomes one of virtue: Does competition among regulatory jurisdictions lead to races to the bottom—downward spirals of increasingly dangerous and exploitative business environments—or to races to the top—optimization of regulation to maximize the total value of transactions to parties and society in general.[4]

The several states of the United States, for example, have come to accept that the law of the place of incorporation will govern most issues arising out of the internal governance of a corporation, even where the firm and its managers and investors have only a formal connection with that place. Universal acceptance of this jurisdictional principle in turn permits the states to compete for corporate charters by offering legal rules that will appeal to the persons who make the decision of where to incorporate. Similarly, something of a consensus exists over many, although by no means all, source rules with respect to property and sales (but not income) taxation. These source rules allow people to move themselves and their assets across jurisdictions in a way that gives a dynamic aspect to the tax choices that jurisdictions make.[5]

---

[2] In re Purity Requirements for Beer: *EC Commission v. Germany*, [1987] ECR 1227 (Case 178/84).

[3] Cf. EC Measures Concerning Meat and Meat Products (Hormones), WT/DS26/AB/R, WT/DS48/AB/R (upholding US claim that European prohibition of imports of meat produced using certain hormones violated US rights under Uruguay Round Agreements).

[4] For a useful overview of the issue, see William W. Bratton and Joseph A. McCahery, 'The New Economics of Jurisdictional Competition: Devolutionary Federalism in a Second-Best World', *Georgetown Law Journal*, vol. 86 (1997), 201.

[5] See Saul Levmore, 'The Case for Retroactive Taxation', *Journal of Legal Studies*, vol. 22 (1993), 265.

Scholars have engaged in fierce debate over the virtues of the races run under the US corporate law system.[6] More recently, academics and government officials have focused on potential harms from tax competition in the face of greater capital mobility.[7] In the midst of this controversy, two points seem clear: cooperation with respect to assignment of regulatory jurisdiction facilitates competition among state corporate laws and local tax regimes, and there is at least a possibility that in some instances the resulting competition may prove to be virtuous, in the sense that we end up with better law.

This contribution explores the capacity of international economic law to encourage races to the top. It first describes the structural elements of cooperative competition to determine what the formal aspects of such a race would look like. It examines both home-made jurisdictional allocations through choice-of-law and choice-of-forum clauses in contracts and more general jurisdictional rules, such as the place-of-incorporation norm and the territoriality principle. Next it examines the mechanisms that allow adversarial and cooperative competition to take place in international economic affairs today. It compares the approach taken by US courts to securities regulation, the rules of bankruptcy, the law of intellectual property and competition policy, where one can detect aspects of both adversarial and cooperative conduct. Viewed with sufficient optimism, contemporary judicial practice suggests that some of the elements necessary for conducting robust cooperative regulatory competition exist, although the edifice remains incomplete if not inchoate.

This contribution next considers the conditions under which competition for regulatory jurisdiction may lead to races to the top. It emphasizes two considerations that suggest the desirability of a weak presumption in favour of promoting cooperative competition in a variety of fields. First, this contribution argues that the distinctive and pervasive susceptibility of international law-making to government failure should encourage courts to help parties in their search for ways around at least some regulatory barriers. Second, recent studies by psychologists of risk assessment

---

[6] For an extensive discussion of the US system and the scholarly literature, see Roberta Romano, *The Genius of American Corporate Law* (Washington, DC, AEI Press, 1993), 87–99. For a recent ambitious restatement of the debate, see Ehud Kamar, 'A Regulatory Competition Theory of Indeterminacy in Corporate Law', 98 *Columbia Law Review* (1998), 1908. For an informative discussion of the approach of British Commonwealth countries to these questions, see Michael J. Whincop and Mary E. Keyes, 'Statutes' Domains in Private International Law: An Economic Theory of the Limits of Mandatory Rules', *Sydney Law Review*, vol. 20 (1998), 435.

[7] See Dani Rodrik, *Has Globalization Gone Too Far?* (Washington, DC, Institute of International Economics, 1997); Organization for Economic Cooperation and Development, *Harmful Tax Competition: An Emerging Global Issue* (Paris, Organization for Economic Cooperation and Development, 1998); Reuven S. Avi-Yonah, 'Globalization, Tax Competition and the Fiscal Crisis of the State', *Harvard Law Review*, vol. 113 (2000), 1573; Dennis C. Mueller, 'Constitutional Constraints on Governments in a Global Economy', *Constitutional Political Economy*, vol. 9 (1998), 171.

strengthens the argument that *ex ante* contractual allocations of regulatory risk generally may represent desirable adaptations to an uncertain world, and not exploitation by persons with superior information. It concludes by considering strategies for enhancing cooperative competition among regulatory jurisdictions.

II. THE FORMAL ELEMENTS OF COOPERATIVE COMPETITION

Cooperative regulatory competition requires certain conditions. Multiple jurisdictions must exist for any competition to occur. Increasing the number facilitates competition by thickening the market for regulatory packages. In the case of federal states, this means allowing lower-level bodies, and not the national state, to have primary or exclusive regulatory authority. In addition, economic actors must have the capacity to choose which jurisdiction will regulate their behaviour. They might make this choice formally and at little cost, as a US corporation does by deciding on a state of incorporation, or informally and at some considerable cost. The latter course typically means forgoing transactions that will trigger the regulatory authority of an undesired jurisdiction.

In the realm of private law, many countries have acceded to private decisions to choose which legal regime will govern business relations. They do this primarily by giving force to contractual clauses determining the governing law, the appropriate forum for resolving disputes between the parties, or both. Thus, a Texas business and a German carrier contracting to ship an oil-drilling platform from the United States to Europe may stipulate that the High Court in London will hear all complaints arising from the contract, conscious that the High Court will apply the substantive rules of maritime law it has developed over the centuries rather than the law of either the United States or Germany.[8] Similarly, many international loan contracts stipulate that the law of New York will govern all disputes, whether the lender and borrower do business in New York or not. A broad consensus about the enforceability of these commitments allows London and New York to offer highly developed and specialized bodies of private law to all persons engaged in international commerce.

---

[8] See *The Bremen v. Zapata Off-Shore Co.*, 407 US 1 (1972). Because the *Zapata* dispute involved federal admiralty law, the choice of choice-of-law rules also was federal. Claims arising out of Texan business transactions that do not have a federal component face certain legislative restrictions on the power of the parties to choose the governing law. Tex. Bus. & Com. Code secs. 1.105, 35.51 (1999) (limiting power to choose governing law to specified transactions). These restrictions are not typical of US law, but rather reflect the particular power of the plaintiff's bar in that jurisdiction. See generally Alex Wilson Albright, 'In Personam Jurisdiction: A Confused and Inappropriate Substitute for Forum Non Conveniens', *Texas Law Review*, vol. 71 (1992), 351 (reviewing attractions of Texas law for persons suing out-of-state corporations).

These private choices have public consequences. At a minimum, they allow contracting parties to avoid the assignment of rights and responsibilities prescribed by local legislation, and thus to thwart the regulatory objectives of those laws. For example, the enforcement of a contract of carriage calling for litigation in London might allow the carrier to avoid a duty of due care that US law would impose regardless of the terms of the agreement. But other factors also might be in play. A contractual optimist, i.e. someone who believes that persons engaging in international commercial transactions generally understand the implications of their commitments and can make reasonable guesses about the future, might conclude that respect for private choices of law allows parties to make optimal allocations of risks and responsibilities associated with these transactions. A contractual pessimist, on the other hand, might suspect that allowing unfettered choice of governing law too often leads to undesirable exploitation and wasteful misallocation of risk. A considerable body of legal scholarship expresses concern about the average person's ability to assess and manage unwanted outcomes.

In contrast to the popular position in the academy, the US judiciary has demonstrated some capacity for trusting parties to contracts to get it right. The Supreme Court in particular has admonished the lower courts to give contracting parties the benefit of the doubt when they elect which law or forum will govern their disputes.[9] To be sure, in none of these decisions did the Supreme Court endorse unfettered private power to choose governing law, and in cases involving arbitration the Court made a point of noting that a US court could require an arbitrator to take US regulation into account as a condition for the award's earning recognition or enforcement.[10] Even so, the Court's willingness to tolerate private allocations of risk at the expense of US law seems striking. At least some lower courts have taken up the implicit invitation to extend the domain of contractual optimism by allowing contracting parties to opt out of US protective regulation, such as the federal securities laws.[11]

---

[9] See *Vimar Seguos y Reaseguros, S.A. v. M/V Sky Reefer*, 515 US 528 (1995) (interpreting New York Arbitration Convention and Carriage of Goods at Sea Act); *Carnival Cruise Lines, Inc. v. Shute*, 499 US 595 (1991) (admiralty); *Mitsubishi Motors v. Soler Chrysler-Plymouth*, 473 US 614 (1985) (interpreting New York Arbitration Convention and Sherman Act); *The Bremen v. Zapata Off-Shore Co.*, 407 US 1 (1972) (admiralty). For further discussion of these cases and the trends they suggest, see Paul B. Stephan, 'The Futility of Unification and Harmonization in International Commercial Law', *Virginia Journal of International Law*, vol. 39 (1999), 788–96. For criticism of these trends, see Philip J. McConnaughay, 'The Risks and Virtues of Lawlessness: A "Second Look" at International Commercial Arbitration', *Northwestern University Law Review*, vol. 93 (1999), 453.

[10] *Mitsubishi Motors v. Soler Chrysler-Plymouth*, 473 US 614, 637 n.19 (1985).

[11] See, e.g. *Lipcon v. Underwriters at Lloyd's of London*, 148 F.3d 1285 (11th Cir. 1998); *Richards v. Lloyd's of London*, 135 F.3d 1289 (9th Cir. 1998); *Haynsworth v. The Corporation*, 121 F.3d 956 (5th Cir. 1997); *Allen v. Lloyd's of London*, 94 F.3d 923 (4th Cir. 1996); *Shell v. R. W. Sturge, Ltd.*, 55 F.3d 1227 (6th Cir. 1995); *Bonny v. Society of Lloyd's*, 3 F.3d 156 (7th Cir. 1993), cert. denied, 510 US 111 (1994); *Roby v. Corporation of Lloyd's*, 996 F.2d 1353 (2d Cir.),

These cases suggest a formal adjustment to, and a substantive judgment about, private choices of regulatory regimes. Formally, explicit commitments to a particular legal regime by all parties to a transaction invite respect, if not necessarily obeisance. Absent such a formal and explicit commitment, local regulators have less of a reason not to apply their own rules. Substantively, the willingness to consider alternative regulatory regimes suggests scepticism about the merits of local law. At least in the cases presented, the courts seem willing to believe that parties to a transaction might have good reason to prefer alternative risk allocations, and that the judgments underlying the allocations made by local law may not reflect society's best interests. The courts might believe, for example, that local law represents successful rent-seeking by discrete interest groups. Alternatively, courts might believe that the virtually unlimited power of private litigants to settle lawsuits in advance of judicial determination of their rights implies a power to commit to such settlements before any problems arise. The broader point is that in some cases the courts believe that norms advanced by party autonomy deserve greater weight than those norms expressed in local regulatory legislation.

In Part IV of this contribution I address arguments that courts might consider in deciding when to prefer party autonomy to enacted norms. Here I consider what forms courts might choose to respect as indicative of a choice of a particular legal regime. Most of the recent litigation has involved explicit contractual statements that left little room for interpretation. But a century ago in the United States, and to some extent in Europe today, the prevailing doctrine of conflicts of law allowed contracting parties a somewhat more robust vocabulary for expressing their preference for a governing legal regime. In a world where highly formal rules, in many cases subject to party manipulation, dictated the choice of law, people could determine governing law simply by their choice of transactional form. For example, when the location of a debtor determined which law governed a debt, one could have an entity formed in a jurisdiction with attractive law assume the role of debtor and thus fix the regulatory regime. The contemporary US rule that allows the place of incorporation to determine the law governing most disputes among managers, directors, and shareholders of a corporation is a survival of that earlier formalistic and manipulable conflicts-of-law regime. The rule limiting state usury laws to the lender's place of incorporation represents another example of a formal jurisdictional assignment that permits cooperative competition.

Formal and manipulable choice-of-law rules do not only provide an alternative to express contractual terms. Such rules have the capacity to allocate regulatory jurisdiction where a party does not participate in the initial choice of law. Consider, for example, the impact of a place-of-

cert. denied, 510 US 945 (1993); *Riley v. Kingsley Underwriting Agencies, Ltd.*, 969 F.2d 953 (10th Cir.), cert. denied, 506 US 1021 (1992).

incorporation rule on persons who later invest in a corporation. The purchase of corporate stock normally does not bring with it any express commitment to be bound by the law of the incorporation jurisdiction, but investors come to the corporation knowing, or at least having good reason to know, that this regime applies. The choice of law becomes part of a broader take-it-or-leave-it transaction: the investor can own stock and accept the designated law, but cannot invest and select a different legal regime. Similarly, later directors as well as the founding ones implicitly acquiesce in a particular body of legal rules when they accept their posts.

One could imagine conflicts-of-law rules of even broader scope, such as a norm that anyone suing a corporation for any reason had to accept the place of incorporation's law. Yet broad transactional-form rules of this sort do not exist in the contemporary world. An obvious explanation is that choice of law implies some kind of deliberation and consent, even if choice comes bundled in a larger take-it-or-leave-it deal. Some transactions seem so devoid of deliberation as to preclude imputing any kind of consent to the parties. Recall, for example, the Union Carbide Bhopal disaster. Only the most relentless determinist could argue that the impoverished Indian untouchables who gathered around the plant, hoping to subsist off secondary economic activity generated by the plant and its workers, thereby consented to the risk of toxic gases and the regulation of their tort claims by US law.[12] Somehow we regard people who come to environmental accidents as unable to commit in advance to governing law in a way that is different from the incapacity of those who make bad investments.

These reservations do not undermine the main point, however. Over time the law has demonstrated some capacity to assign regulatory jurisdiction based on formal considerations, such as the 'situs' of an intangible interest or a legal person.[13] The more formal and manipulable the predicate for allocating jurisdiction, the more the choice-of-law rule functions likes an express and enforceable contractual choice of law.

In this regard, consider how the territoriality principle can facilitate transactional regulatory choices. This concept, as ancient as the field of conflicts of law, rests on the premise that sovereign power should extend only as far as the sovereign's territory. To determine which law governs a transaction, thing, or person, the principle requires only that we supply a location. Once we can place the item, we will know which sovereign's law to use.

---

[12] I am putting aside the issue of veil-piercing, given that Union Carbide owned only a substantial minority interest in the Indian company that operated the plant at the time of the disaster. For more on the dispute, see In re Union Carbide Corporation Gas Plant Disaster, 809 F.2d 195 (2d Cir. 1987).

[13] On situs in international business law, see Paul B. Stephan, Don Wallace, Jr., and Julie A. Roin, *International Business and Economics—Law and Policy*, 2d edn (Charlottesville, VA: Michie, 1996), 381–3.

This simple concept carries with it deep indeterminacies. To take one example, during the early years of the twentieth century many courts attempted the Sisyphean task of determining where people and firms had their 'presence' for purposes of asserting jurisdiction over absent persons. But the difficulty of this task stemmed in large part from judicial efforts to restrain individual autonomy so as to bolster state regulatory power. When a sovereign cedes to parties the power to choose a situs, these problems disappear (although others then emerge). If a sovereign determines, for example, that a person or a physical thing is 'present' only where it can be found currently, or that a sale takes place where the parties designate that title passes, then it becomes simple to decide which territory has regulatory jurisdiction—perhaps too simple, if parties exercise this power to locate transactions away from a state that has a significant interest in what they do and wants to impose regulatory norms that transactors wish to avoid.

To summarize, the formal prerequisite of a cooperative approach to regulatory competition is the existence of a consensus about either the enforceability of explicit choices of law or the content of choice-of-law rules that turn on transactional forms that parties can manipulate. A good example of the latter approach is a rule that ties the governing law to the place of a party's incorporation. More generally, the territorial principle that dominated most discussion of regulatory jurisdiction until the middle of the twentieth century may lend itself to formal manipulation, depending on what rules sovereigns use to determine the situs of things and transactions. But unless some shared commitment to rules such as these exists, cooperative competition becomes difficult if not impossible.

III. ADVERSARIAL AND COOPERATIVE COMPETITION FOR REGULATORY POWER: THE CONTEMPORARY ENVIRONMENT

We can find regulatory competition almost everywhere. The debate over non-tariff barriers and the role of environmental and labour standards in trade disputes reflects a recognition of the obvious fact that domestic regulatory choices about product content and production methods have international consequences in a global marketplace. Alongside these issues, which for the most part get addressed in state-to-state negotiations such as NAFTA and the Uruguay Round, there exist a variety of what I will call firm-structure issues. These regulatory choices involve the nature of ownership interest in firms, the kinds of intangible property firms can employ in business, and the manner in which firms can organize particular markets.

Most scholars and policy-makers concerned with regulatory cooperation and competition focus on rules governing production and product content.[14] One can understand this focus, given the importance and complexity of these questions. But concentrating on these issues may discourage any effort to reconceptualize the problem. Often disputes over different standards entail intractable issues of technological optimism, cultural norms, and political expectations. Firm structure questions, by contrast, seem more clearly the province of legal specialists and thus to some extent divorced from broader technological, cultural, and political concerns. By looking at how cooperative competition works with respect to firm structure, we may get at least hints about how we might address the more elusive production and product-content debates.

In the United States, we address questions of firm structure largely through securities, bankruptcy, intellectual property, and antitrust law. Each has an international dimension, and judicial creativity rather than legislative mandate has produced much of the law. Both similarities and contradictions exist in this judicial practice, and such patterns as one may discern with respect to cooperative competition sometimes seem engulfed by general background noise. A separate examination of each body of law may bring things into better focus.

A. Securities law

Those who surrender control of their capital to others in the pursuit of profit can look to two bodies of US law for protection of their interests. States provide rules governing the rights of shareholders in relation to the officers and directors of a corporation. In addition, federal securities statutes address the rights of persons who buy or sell interests in firms.

[14] In addition to the papers published in this volume, see, e.g. Jagdish Bhagwati and Robert E. Hudec (eds), *Fair Trade and Harmonization: Prerequisites for Free Trade?* (Cambridge, MA: MIT Press, 1996); Robert Howse & Michael J. Trebilcock, 'The Free Trade–Fair Trade Debate: Trade, Labor, and the Environment', in Jagdeep S. Bhandari and Alan O. Sykes (eds), *Economic Dimensions in International Law—Comparative and Empirical Perspectives* (Cambridge, UK: Cambridge University Press, 1997), 186; Joel R. Paul, 'Competitive and Non-Competitive Regulatory Markets: The Regulation of Packaging Waste in the EU', in William W. Bratton, Joseph A. McCahery, Sol Picciotto, and Colin Scott (eds), *International Regulatory Competition and Coordination: Perspectives on Economic Regulation in Europe and the United States* (New York, NY: Oxford University Press, 1996), 378–9; Richard B. Stewart, 'Environmental Regulation and International Competitiveness', *Yale Law Journal*, vol. 102 (1993), 2039; Alan O. Sykes, Regulatory Protectionism and the Law of International Trade, University of Chicago Law Review, vol. 66 (1999), 1; 'The (Limited) Role of Regulatory Harmonization in the International Goods and Services Markets,' *Journal of International Economics Law*, vol. 2 (1999), 49; Joel P. Trachtman, 'International Regulatory Competition, Externalization, and Jurisdiction', *Harvard Journal of International Law*, vol. 34 (1993), 105; 'Externalities and Extraterritoriality: The Law and Economics of Prescriptive Jurisdiction,' in Bhandari and Sykes (eds), *Economic Dimensions in International Law* (above), 642. For seminal work in the development of the law and economics of regulatory protectionism, see Edmund W. Kitch, 'Federalism and the American Common Market', in A. Dan Tarlock (ed.), *Regulation, Federalism, and Interstate Commerce* (Cambridge, MA: Oelgeschlager, Gunn and Hain,1981), 7; Saul Levmore, 'Interstate Exploitation and Judicial Intervention', *Virginia Law Review*, vol. 69 (1983), 563.

Although substantial overlap between these regulatory systems exists, and federal law always will trump state law in the event of any inconsistency, the federal courts and Congress have preserved some areas for exclusive state regulation.[15] These exclusively state domains, such as the rules governing corporate opportunity and self-dealing among officers and directors, are sufficiently important that, when coupled with the place-of-incorporation rule for allocating regulatory authority, they have a clear effect on decisions where to incorporate. Defenders of this system argue that because investors take the rules governing their rights into account at the time that they invest, and because managers have incentives both to lower the firm's cost of capital and to ward off hostile takeovers by maximizing share value, managers will choose to incorporate in those states whose rules are most likely to produce positive effects on shareholder value. Critics argue that the ways in which managers and investors attach value to these rules are not symmetrical, and that managers are more likely to attach greater significance to rules that increase their opportunities for exploitation of shareholders than are shareholders. These two accounts, based on contradictory beliefs about shareholder assessments of future risks, produce conflicting race-to-the-top and race-to-the-bottom explanations for the evolution of state corporation law.

Competition among the several states is not the only means for determining the law governing corporations. Nations also can compete for regulatory jurisdiction. State law accommodates the possibility of foreign regulation by respecting the choice to incorporate in a foreign jurisdiction. Federal securities law presents a more complex picture. On the one hand, courts have tended to give the relevant statutes extraterritorial effect. This approach discourages competition by making it more difficult (although not impossible) to structure transactions so as to avoid federal regulation. On the other hand, courts have tolerated some efforts to avoid the application of US regulation through contract.

The federal securities statutes do not specify the scope of their jurisdiction. Courts have responded to this gap by constructing their own rules for determining when US rules will apply to transactions with offshore elements. In the absence of any guidance by the Supreme Court, the courts of appeals have taken various approaches. They agree that these laws apply not only to persons who reside or transact in the United States, but also those whose transactions have a significant effect on US persons. Formally, the courts call these the 'presence' and the 'effects' tests, and use them as independently sufficient standards for enforcing US regulation. The details of this extraterritoriality vary, with courts differing both as to what kind of US conduct constitutes 'presence' and what kinds of offshore

[15] *Santa Fe Industries, Inc. v. Green*, 430 US 462 (1977); cf. *Blue Chip Stamps v. Manor Drug Stores*, 421 US 723 (1975) (standing under federal securities laws); *Birnbaum v. Newport Steel Corp.*, 193 F.2d 461 (2d Cir.), cert. denied, 343 US 956 (1952) (same).

activity produces US effects sufficient to justify application of these laws. The broad picture, however, is clear. At least some US investors who engage in transactions outside the country, and some foreigners whose investment activities have some connection to the United States, may invoke the federal regulatory regime against those who take their capital.[16]

Yet in spite of its regulatory nature, federal securities law does not always apply to these transactions. For many decades now, US securities regulators have not pushed their extraterritorial jurisdiction as far as it might go. In particular they have distinguished their authority to enforce rules governing the formal and disclosure requirements for issuing new securities, especially the rules pertaining to registration, from the standards governing fraud in securities transactions. The regulators have shown some willingness to surrender their jurisdiction to enforce the registration rules while maintaining their right to attack fraud more widely. Through several administrative rules and decisions, the Securities and Exchange Commission has allowed issuers who undertake reasonable efforts to isolate their securities from the US market to avoid complying with the extensive reporting rules that US law imposes on US issuers. This approach limits 'presence' in the United States to deliberate persistent activity and ignores the 'effects' prong of jurisdictional power; it resembles the territorial principle as courts applied it in the first half of this century and earlier. Thus the Eurobond market has grown up as an offshore alternative for US firms to raise capital, and English securities law has emerged as an alternative regulatory system for shaping new issues of US securities.[17]

This competition for rules governing new issues requires firms to make important choices about the form of a transaction. They may not directly address potential US investors, employ the services of securities professionals working in the United States to close the transaction, or take other steps that indicate an intent to market their securities domestically. Given the sophisticated nature of the industry and the existence of a significant number of knowledgeable US investors who can work through intermediaries to participate in this market, compliance with these rules has not proved excessively burdensome.

Many issuers seem to find the benefits derived from non-compliance with US registration rules sufficiently great, and the costs associated with fitting within the offshore exemption sufficiently low, to justify structuring their transaction in a way that falls within the exemption. But evidence

---

[16] See *Kauthar SDN BHD v. Sternberg*, 149 F.3d 659, 663–67 (7th Cir. 1998) (reviewing authorities).

[17] See generally Norman S. Poser, *International Securities Regulation* (Boston: Little, Brown and Co., 1991); Samuel Wolff, 'Offshore Distributions under the Securities Act of 1933: An Analysis of Regulation S', *Law and Policy in International Business*, vol. 23 (1991–2), 101.

exists that some would like to do even more. The registration rules have two drawbacks: they require firms to absorb some transactions costs caused by seeming to isolate their securities offering from the US market, and they fail to call off US antifraud rules. Thus we also see contracts involving the sale of securities to US customers that purport to substitute foreign law for US regulation in all respects.

The enforceability of these contracts in the context of fraud claims presents deep issues. On the one hand, fraud is tantamount to theft and thus antithetical to any market, including that for capital. On the other hand, some firms and investors regard the US system of antifraud protection as over-inclusive and, when embedded in a civil litigation system that permits class actions and broad if not unlimited discovery, a source of substantial deadweight losses. At least in limited circumstances, contracts that would displace the US antifraud system with that of another jurisdiction have enjoyed judicial support. A recent line of cases, all involving litigation against Lloyd's of London by disgruntled 'names', has enforced contracts under which investors agreed to substitute British securities regulation for that of the United States.[18] The courts attached great significance to the clarity of the investor's *ex ante* commitment to apply British law, the relative wealth and sophistication of the investors, and the reassuring aspects of British investor protection policy. The courts may have inferred from the size and durability of the British securities industry that its legal underpinnings must have something to offer investors.[19]

Given the unique relationship of the British and US legal systems and the fact that the Lloyd's investors all had to pass a minimum-wealth test, these cases do not necessarily signal a fundamental shift in US regulatory jurisdiction. The implications, however, are intriguing. London is a great financial centre, but so are Frankfurt, Singapore, and Tokyo. Lloyd's is famous for allowing only deep-pocket investors to become 'names', but as a general matter sophisticated investors play a pervasive role in world capital markets. Were courts to let the contractual dimension of these cases—the fact that the investors explicitly agreed to accept British jurisdiction—dominate their interpretation, one could foresee a world where at least sophisticated parties would have the freedom to choose among several well-developed regulatory systems.

At least one prominent scholar has welcomed the prospect of greater party freedom to select regulatory regimes involving securities. Roberta

---

[18] See above, n. 11.

[19] A parallel development involves the increased willingness of US courts to enforce arbitration agreements where one party claims a violation of the federal securities laws. See *Rodriguez de Quijas v. Shearson/American Express*, 490 US 477 (1989); *Shearson/American Express v. McMahon*, 482 US 220 (1987). Resort to arbitration in lieu of litigation may not replace the substantive law governing a claim but will produce significant changes in the dispute resolution process that can have an asymmetrical impact on the parties' incentives to pursue a grievance.

Romano would let a firm commit to a particular State or nation's securities laws and require the federal government to respect these commitments. She believes that investors would benefit from competition among regulatory jurisdictions to provide optimal combinations of paternalism and laissez faire, and that such competition would determine what laws the potential regulatory jurisdictions would enact.[20]

At present Romano's vision of a virtuous competition to offer the optimal package of securities regulation remains more of a thought experiment than a concrete project to restructure the law. But her arguments lend support to the trends that have manifested themselves in the judiciary. At the core of her proposal are two propositions: (1) the persons with the authority to select regulatory regimes in general will internalize the costs and benefits of those choices; and (2) competition among regulatory authorities will restrain rent-seeking that otherwise might manifest itself through regulation. The arguments for enforcing contractual choices of law and forum rest on the same foundations.

In sum, US investor protection law supports cooperative regulatory competition in two respects. Where state law applies, the place-of-incorporation rule for selecting applicable law directly promotes competition among regulators. Even in areas subject to federal jurisdiction, a willingness to enforce *ex ante* choices of regulatory jurisdiction through transactional form or express contracts may displace otherwise mandatory federal regulation. At least one distinguished scholar supports extension of the range of permitted choices and the manner of making them to promote further competition among jurisdictions.

B. Bankruptcy

Bankruptcy law determines ownership and governance of firms in a particular set of circumstances, namely those times when a business finds itself unable to pay its creditors. Because all firms face some risk of insolvency, one can envision bankruptcy regimes as the background to all transactions in which a firm engages. In this sense, bankruptcy pervasively affects firm structure.

The rules determining what happens to defaulting debtors represent a mixture of contractual choices and mandatory terms. Borrowers can influence the outcome of insolvency proceedings by extending security, locating assets in particular jurisdictions, and separating risky operations

---

[20] Roberta Romano, 'Empowering Investors: A Market Approach to Securities Regulation', *Yale Law Journal*, vol. 107 (1998), 2359. For proposals to extend this approach internationally, see Stephen J. Choi and Andrew T. Guzmán, 'Portable Reciprocity: Rethinking the International Reach of Securities Regulation', *Southern California Law Review*, vol. 71 (1998), 903; Andrew T. Guzmán, 'Capital Market Regulation in Developing Countries', *Virginia Journal of International Law*, vol. 39 (1999), 607.

from assets through separate incorporation, franchising, and other contractual devices. But bankruptcy law also contains mandatory rules that constrain the power of debtors to provide for the consequences of a default, including exemptions, statutory liens, mandatory stays on enforcement of debts, and prohibitions of fraudulent conveyances.

The allocation of jurisdiction to determine which bankruptcy rules apply to which transactions is remarkably complex. Superficially, the US system rests on a federal statute that pre-empts all other regimes. But federal law looks to both state and foreign law with respect to many issues, such as how a creditor may obtain security or what assets the debtor may own. Perhaps the most important example of non-federal law incorporated into federal bankruptcy are state and foreign rules determining when a firm can insulate its owners from recourse for its debts. Moreover, in deciding which state or foreign law to apply, the US bankruptcy regime relies on many formal and manipulable choice-of-law rules. Firms, for example, may shift assets to take advantage of local laws that facilitate separation of ownership from the use of property in potentially liability-generating activity. The most obvious technique involves creating separate subsidiaries in different jurisdictions to cabin liabilities resulting from particular operations.[21] Individuals have similar flexibility, and in particular can obtain the protection of the US bankruptcy regime simply by moving to this country after becoming insolvent.[22]

Given the substantial flexibility business people have to influence bankruptcy outcomes through choice of form, one might expect to see a corresponding power to precommit to non-standard bankruptcy outcomes through contract. Such precommitments might take the form of either home-made rules, such as waivers of rights otherwise bestowed by the bankruptcy statute, or a choice to apply the laws of another jurisdiction to a transaction. But the courts generally have resisted such innovations. In spite of dicta in some bankruptcy court opinions, the weight of authority seems to stand against either waivers or contractual choice of alternative law.[23] The scholarly literature reflects a greater diversity of opinion, rang-

---

[21] For a debate over the extent to which debtors avail themselves of these strategies and for what purposes, see Lynn M. LoPucki, 'The Death of Liability', *Yale Law Journal*, vol. 106 (1996), 1; James J. White, 'Corporate Judgment Proofing: A Response to Lynn LoPucki's The Death of Liability', ibid., vol. 107 (1998), 8; Lynn M. LoPucki, 'Virtual Judgment Proofing: A Rejoinder', ibid. 1413.

[22] In re Simon, 153 F.3d 991 (9th Cir. 1998).

[23] The waiver cases are reviewed in Steven L. Schwarcz, 'Rethinking Freedom of Contract: A Bankruptcy Paradigm', *Texas Law Review*, vol. 77 (1999), 524–8. For an especially striking refusal to accept a foreign choice of law, in a case where both the creditor and the debtor resided in the contracted-for jurisdiction at the time of the contract, see In re Simon, 153 F.3d 991 (9th Cir. 1998). Cf. In re Rimsat, Ltd., 98 F.3d 956 (7th Cir. 1996) (US bankruptcy court not obligated to defer to injunction issued by court in place of debtor's incorporation that would have given control over debtor to a particular US shareholder); *Ma v. Continental Bank, S.A.*, 905 F.2d 1073 (7th Cir. 1990) (bank not liable for turning asset over to foreign receiver in bankruptcy where receiver had valid appointment from country with jurisdiction to make

ing from allowing debtors to contract around some, but not all, bankruptcy rules and to choose some, but not all, foreign regimes, to unwavering enforcement of the statutory mandate.[24]

The balance between contractual autonomy and mandatory rules in bankruptcy cases presents an interesting contrast to that struck in the securities laws. Although parties to debt contracts can use security interests, situs rules, and corporate form to determine what will happen upon insolvency, they may not contract in advance for any jurisdiction's laws. Once insolvency becomes likely, debtors have some flexibility to move themselves and their assets around to choose unilaterally the legal regime that will determine the effect of a bankruptcy. In other words, US bankruptcy law provides the greatest flexibility to choose a regulatory regime exactly in those circumstances where one party is most likely to behave opportunistically and in a fashion that detracts from overall welfare, and resists *ex ante* efforts to limit the debtor's power to behave in such a fashion.

C. Intellectual property

Intellectual property law, or more precisely the law specifying rights in valuable information, permits an extension to the realm of ideas of the separation of ownership and control inherent in the concept of a firm. For ease of analysis, I will divide these rights into two categories—those generated by an ongoing relationship, such as employer–employee, licensor–licensee, or corporation-officer, and those bundled with a discrete and resaleable product, such as a text, image, sound, or physical configuration. Contracts law, along with the law of corporations, agency, and fiduciary duty, normally governs the former.[25] Copyright, trademark and patent, all

appointment; question of whether claim against bank belonged to bankrupt or to estate, or whether ownership of that claim rested on Hong Kong or US law, left open).

[24] See Edward S. Adams and James L. Baillie, 'A Privatization Solution to the Legitimacy of Pre-petition Waivers of the Automatic Stay', *Arizona Law Review*, vol. 38 (1996), 1; Lucian Arye Bebchuk and Andrew T. Guzmán, 'An Economic Analysis of Transnational Bankruptcies', *Journal of Law and Economics*, vol. 42 (1999), 775; Daniel B. Bogart, 'Games Lawyers Play: Waivers of the Automatic Stay in Bankruptcy and the Single Asset Loan Workout', *UCLA Law Review*, vol. 43 (1996), 117; Lynn M. LoPucki, 'Cooperation in International Bankruptcy: A Post-Universalist Approach', *Cornell Law Review*, vol. 84 (1999), 696; Robert K. Rasmussen, 'Free Contracting in Bankruptcy at Home and Abroad', in Francis Buckley (ed.), *The Fall and Rise of the Freedom of Contract* (Durham: Duke University Press, 1999); 'A New Approach to Transnational Insolvencies', *Michigan Journal of International Law*, vol. 19 (1997), 26; 'Debtor's Choice: A Menu Approach to Corporate Bankruptcy', *Texas Law Review*, vol. 71 (1992), 51; Robert K. Rasmussen and David A. Skeel, Jr., 'The Economic Analysis of Corporate Bankruptcy Law', *American Bankruptcy Institute Law Review*, vol. 3 (1995), 85; Schwarcz, 'Rethinking Freedom of Contract' (above, n. 23); Alan Schwartz, 'A Contract Theory Approach to Business Bankruptcy', *Yale Law Journal*, vol. 107 (1998), 1807; 'Contracting About Bankruptcy', *Journal of Law, Economics and Organization*, vol. 13 (1997), 127.

[25] See Ronald J. Gilson, 'The Legal Infrastructure of High Technology Industrial Districts: Silicon Valley, Route 128, and Covenants Not To Compete', *New York University Law Review*,

of which rest on statutes, more often determine the scope of rights in the latter category. The more robust the protection of intellectual property, the greater the flexibility that firms have to diversify the forms of their operations.

Historically, nations have differed in the kinds of intellectual property they have recognized, with capital-exporting countries tending to offer more extensive and stronger protection than importers of capital. The Uruguay Round Agreement on Trade-Related Aspects of Intellectual Property (TRIPS Agreement) seeks to stamp out some of these differences by requiring members of the World Trade Organization (WTO) to meet minimum standards of patent, copyright, and trademark protection. But even where substantive standards have converged, significant differences in administration and enforcement remain. Moreover, none of these projects has addressed the category of rights that rest on the law of contracts and other non-statutory doctrines.

Disregarding the obvious conflicting interests of producers and consumers of intellectual property and differences in the distribution of producers and consumers across nations, one still might predict some variation in the level of intellectual property protection among jurisdictions. A general *ex ante* specification of the optimal level of ownership rights seems unattainable, given the irreducible conflict between the need to encourage innovators to invest in the search for new ideas and the need to propagate new learning as rapidly as possible. Ideally, the balance should shift in response to changes in technology, information production and dissemination, and market structure.[26] Law-makers might implement the local judgment about this balance not only by varying the content of property rights embodied in patent, copyright, and trademark, but also by choosing different regimes, e.g. for the duties owed firms and employers by their officers and employees.

In the United States, one finds a mixture of jurisdictional rules that both encourage and discourage cooperative competition with respect to intellectual property. That part of the law that turns on common law doctrine readily facilitates jurisdictional competition, because parties generally remain free either by express contractual terms or through formal choice to decide which law will apply to their relationship.[27] That part which

---

vol. 74 (1999), 575; Edmund W. Kitch, 'The Law and Economics of Rights in Valuable Information', *Journal of Legal Studies*, vol. 9 (1980), 683.

[26] On the relationship between technological innovation and the openness of the market, see Richard R. Nelson and Gavin Wright, 'The Rise and Fall of American Technological Leadership: The Postwar Era in Historical Perspective', *Journal of Econ. Lit.*, vol. 30 (1992), 1931; Paul M. Romer, 'Endogenous Technological Change', *Journal of Pol. Econ.*, vol. 98 (1990), S71.

[27] Although old authority suggests that the policies of the jurisdiction where an employment contract is entered into might prevail over an express choice-of-law clause in that contract, *Alaska Packers Ass'n v. Industrial Accident Com'n*, 294 US 532 (1935), more modern cases support the power of parties to choose which jurisdiction's laws will govern the terms of an

rests, in whole or part, on a federal statute—patent, copyright, and trade-mark—presents a more complex picture. Patent, copyright and, to a certain extent, trademark rest on a uniform national legal structure. The courts have interpreted two of these systems—patent and copyright—as having largely a territorial basis.[28] This territoriality means that transactions occurring within any particular nation will implicate only that jurisdiction's laws, a necessary if not sufficient condition for cooperative competition. But judicial interpretation of US trademark law violates territoriality in two important respects: when US producers export their goods and when US importers bring back to the country goods sold overseas subject to a US trademark. At least in some circumstances, copyright law also abandons territoriality with respect to imports.[29] The most that firms owning US copyrights and trademarks can do to protect themselves against parallel imports is to insert a contractual clause imposing some costs on dealers and consumers who violate the territorial allocations set out by the owner.[30] By contrast, EU law mandates that national governments protect intellectual property owners from parallel imports, except in the case where the country of export also belongs to the EU.[31]

Territoriality aids cooperative competition in the common instance where an intellectual property right accompanies a concrete transaction,

employment contract, including the enforceability of a covenant not to compete. *PHP Healthcare Corp. v. EMSA Limited Partnership*, 14 F.3d 941 (4th Cir. 1993); *Vaske v. Ducharme, McMillen & Associates Inc.*, 757 F. Supp. 1158, 1163 n.9 (D. Col. 1990). Cf. *Steinke v. Sungard Financial Systems, Inc.*, 121 F.3d 763 (1st Cir. 1997) (effectiveness of choice-of-law clauses in employment contracts). Older California decisions hold that an employee resident in that State may apply California law to invalidate covenants not to compete in the face of an express choice of law in favour of a jurisdiction that would uphold such covenants. *Scott v. Snelling*, 732 F. Supp. 1034, 1039–40 (N.D. Cal. 1990); *Frame v. Merrill Lynch*, 20 Cal. App. 3d 668, 673, 97 Cal. Rptr. 811 (1971). But cf. *Nedlloyd Lines B.V. v. Superior Court*, 3 Cal. 4th 459, 834 P.2d 1148, 11 Cal. Rptr. 2d 330 (1992) (choice-of-law clauses enforceable as long as jurisdiction chosen has some connection to the transaction; presence of strong California policy not determinative).

  [28] See Curtis A. Bradley, 'Territorial Intellectual Property Rights in an Age of Globalism', *Virginia Journal of International Law*, vol. 37 (1997), 505.
  [29] See *Steele v. Bulova Watch Co.*, 344 US 280 (1952) (exports); *K-Mart Corp. v. Cartier, Inc.*, 486 US 281 (1988) (imports); *Quality King Distributors, Inc. v. L'Anza Research International, Inc.*, 118 S. Ct. 1125 (1998) (goods manufactured in the United States and sold abroad subject to 'first sale' doctrine, which bars copyright holder from treating subsequent resale as an infringement, even where the resale is the first transaction within the United States). For lower court approaches to the export issue, compare *Reebok International, Ltd. v. Marnatech Enterprises, Inc.*, 970 F.2d 552 (9th Cir. 1992); *American Rice, Inc. v. Arkansas Rice Growers Coop. Ass'n*, 701 F.2d 408 (5th Cir. 1983), with *Nintendo of America, Inc. v. Aeropower Co.*, 34 F.3d 824 (4th Cir. 1994), and *Totalplan Corp. of America v. Colborne*, 14 F.3d 824 (2nd Cir. 1994).
  [30] See *Continental T.V., Inc. v. GTE Sylvania, Inc.*, 433 US 36 (1977) (territorial restrictions on retail distribution do not violate antitrust laws if reasonable); Antitrust Div., US Dep't of Justice, Antitrust Guidelines for International Operations, 53 Fed. Reg. 21,584, 21,607 (exclusive vertical distribution arrangements) (1988).
  [31] Compare *Silhouette International Schmied GmbH Co. KG v. Hartlauer Handelsgesellschaft mbH*, [1998] ECR 4799 (Austrian law providing for exhaustion of trademark after first sale to non-EU customer conflicts with law of EU), with *Consten v. Commission*, [1966] ECR 299 (territorial restrictions on trademark use within EU violate Treaty of Rome).

whether the purchase of a physical commodity (e.g. buying a videotape) or the consumption of a service (e.g. attending a film). Under these circumstances, one can associate the specified right with definite markets. *Ceteris paribus*, producers and consumers both can choose to enter particular markets taking the intellectual property into account. To be sure, the decision whether to transact in a particular jurisdiction is not as formal and easy to manipulate as, say, a choice of where to incorporate, but on the margin parties can shift their business in response to the legal environment. For example, the refusal of producers of intellectual-property-intensive commodities such as pharmaceuticals to set up manufacturing facilities in the absence of what they regard as adequate intellectual property protection has led to the enactment of strong laws in at least some jurisdictions. Similarly, a consumer interested in the authenticity of a protected good is more likely to buy it in a jurisdiction that provides strong protection.

I do not mean to argue that the problems of extraterritorial enforcement and of parallel imports are identical. Limitations on remedies against parallel imports undermine the value of the intellectual property right involved, while extensions of protection extraterritorially expand the right. But what is important for my purposes is that both moves break the link between territory and level of protection. The weaker the tie between territory and the right, the less likely that parties will choose where to exploit the rights based on the level of protection. In this sense, both outbound and inbound departures from territoriality impede cooperative competition.

D. Antitrust law

The need to suppress monopolies seems so closely associated with the premises of a market economy that many readers may conceive of suboptimality as synonymous with underenforcement. The law-and-economics literature has used antitrust law generally, and the Sherman Act in particular, as a model of welfare-enhancing government intervention in the market. This body of work presents the legislative edifice as an ideal solution to market failure and tends to regard judicial interpretations of the law that fail to advance welfare as dishonouring legislative intent.[32] Implicit in this literature is a judgment that other nations' antimonopoly regimes, which differ in material respects from the US system, must reflect

---

[32] Fred S. McChesney and William F. Shughart II, 'Introduction and Overview', in Fred S. McChesney and William F. Shughart II (eds), *The Causes and Consequences of Antitrust* (1995), 1. For further work documenting the interest-group politics involved in the enactment of US antitrust legislation, see Carlos D. Ramírez and Christian Eigen-Zucchi, 'Why Did the Clayton Act Pass? An Analysis of the Interest Group Hypothesis' (George Mason University Working Paper No. 98.03, 1998).

unfortunate concessions to entrenched economic interests rather than stand as alternative pathways to virtuous market regulation.

Yet a closer look at the structure of competition laws both within the United States and internationally suggests that, as with intellectual property, specifying *ex ante* an optimal market structure is impossible. As a matter of *a priori* logic, it seems implausible that any one balance between cooperation and competitive activity should fit all organized economic behaviour.[33] Various production and sales processes will have different needs for information sharing, will present differing opportunities for economies of scale and scope, and otherwise will face organization challenges too diverse for any one form to dominate.

A review of international practice bolsters the intuition that people prefer a variety of competition policies. US antitrust law reverses the normal presumption in a federal system that national legislation prevails over state or local law. Pursuant to the *Parker* doctrine, the Sherman Act does not apply to cooperative business behaviour organized by a lower-level governmental body.[34] This rule allows states to offer competition regimes that displace the federal law's presumption against cartelization.[35] And a review of competition laws in most advanced industrial countries reveals considerable convergence as to professed ends but substantial divergence in terms of enforcement mechanisms. Almost all countries have a government agency with authority to forbid mergers and other organizational strategies that present too great a risk of anticompetitive consequences. But the United States stands alone in its reliance on private lawsuits, bolstered by access to punitive damages, the class action device, and wide-ranging discovery, as a mechanism for scourging would-be monopolists. Were these aspects of the US system even close to optimal, one might expect to find at least one other country appropriating them.

Another sign that the contemporary legal status quo in the United States may not represent an optimal competition policy is the instability over time of the territoriality principle as applied to the Sherman Act. In the early years of the century the Supreme Court attempted to cabin the antitrust laws by excluding from their ambit all conduct that could be said to have taken place outside the United States.[36] Later cases relaxed this rule, requiring only that some part of the offensive conduct occur on US soil.[37] Only in the last decade has the Court embraced the opposite position—that no conduct need occur in the United States as long as the

---

[33] See generally Saul Levmore, 'Competition and Cooperation', *Michigan Law Review*, vol. 97 (1998), 216.

[34] *Parker v. Brown*, 317 US 341 (1942).

[35] See Frank H. Easterbrook, 'Antitrust and the Economics of Federalism', *Journal of Law and Economics*, vol. 26 (1983), 23; John Shepard Wiley, Jr., 'A Capture Theory of Antitrust Federalism', *Harvard Law Review*, vol. 99 (1986), 713.

[36] *American Banana Co. v. United Fruit Co.*, 213 US 347 (1909).

[37] *United States v. Sisal Sales Corp.*, 274 US 268 (1927).

actions complained of have an effect on the US economy—and then only by the narrowest of margins.[38]

If no one antitrust policy is clearly optimal, does the law allow transactors to choose which regime to live under? The question poses considerable difficulty. First, to a greater extent than the bodies of firm structure law that I examined above, antitrust law concerns itself with injuries to third parties. In the case of cartels, for example, the arrangement typically involves only producers and excludes exactly the consumers that antitrust law seeks to protect. More generally, many of the kinds of agreements that implicate antitrust law involve transactions with significant negative externalities and no good mechanism that would force the transactors to internalize these costs. Not surprisingly, then, the law does not give a lot of weight to the choices transactors make in structuring these relationships. But some residuum of transactor flexibility remains. First, the continuing instability over the applicability of the territoriality principle, when combined with the federalism approach embodied in the *Parker* doctrine, holds out the prospect of at least some jurisdiction-shopping by multinational firms. Second, the endorsement by the Supreme Court of foreign arbitration of antitrust claims allows parties to shed some of the unwelcome procedural aspects of antitrust litigation and in certain circumstances may allow them to avoid US antitrust law entirely.

Hartford Fire Insurance Co. endorsed the principle that US antitrust laws applied wherever one could find a direct and intended effect on the US economy, but three other justices joined Scalia's strong dissent. The relevant aspect of the case involved the market for reinsurance contracts, which the United Kingdom subjected to industry self-regulation. The reinsurers carried out these transactions in the United Kingdom, but their decisions as to what risks to reinsure had a direct impact on the array of insurance products available in the United States. Scalia noted that, pursuant to specific legislation, US insurers enjoy an exemption from the antitrust laws and instead must submit to local regulation. He would have extended this deference to foreign oversight, including the kind of government-sponsored industry self-regulation that the United Kingdom had embraced. Generalizing his point, one might argue that firms still might make use of the territorial principle to choose their antitrust regime, much as transactors in intellectual property have some power to locate the rules determining their rights, as long as they pick a jurisdiction with some regulatory programme in place. Of course, a Court dissent is not the law, but it does sustain hope.

In *Mitsubishi Motors v. Soler Chrysler-Plymouth*, the Court upheld the right of contractual parties to choose to arbitrate antitrust claims arising

---

[38] *Hartford Fire Insurance Co. v. California*, 509 US 764 (1993). See Larry Kramer, 'Note: Extraterritorial Application of American Law After the Insurance Antitrust Case: A Reply to Professors Lowenfeld and Trimble', *American Journal of International Law*, vol. 89 (1995), 750.

out of their relationship.[39] The Court noted that the arbitration body would have to address the US statutory claims, and that a failure to do so would result in a refusal by a US court to enforce the award. But where the disputants have assets outside the United States, non-enforcement by a US court is not much of a sanction. The prevailing party simply may go to another jurisdiction where assets exist and obtain enforcement there. Thus for many multinational firms, arbitration can become a route to home-made competition rules.[40]

IV. MARKET FAILURE, GOVERNMENT FAILURE, AND VIRTUOUS COMPETITION

I have identified the formal requirements for cooperative competition across jurisdictions and established that elements of the prerequisite legal doctrines exist, albeit in nascent form, in securities regulation, bankruptcy, intellectual property, and antitrust. Now I consider whether legislatures, administrators, and courts should expand the opportunities for business people to choose which regulatory systems by which they will abide. This question implicates two broad issues: under what circumstances can parties to transactions internalize the costs and benefits of their choices, thereby ameliorating market failure for which State regulation may be desirable; and under what circumstances do parties possess sufficient capacity for sophisticated assessments of the likelihood of undesired outcomes when calculating the value of a transactional relationship. I then discuss the application of these insights to firm-structure law.

A. Market failure and government failure

Legal regulation of economic activities inevitably implicates two stories. On the one hand, we can envision regulation addressing market failure, which in turn could stem from any of a number of structural deficiencies such as cartelization, network effects, public goods, negative externalities, or collective action problems. On the other hand, we can depict regulation as the product of government failure, caused by principal–agent issues between bureaucracies and law-makers or successful rent-seeking by cohesive interest groups. A vast literature addresses these questions, although unambiguous answers and clear guidance for policy-makers remain hard to come by.

---

[39] 473 US 614 (1985).

[40] For more on the use of arbitration to avoid local competition laws, see Eric A. Posner, 'Arbitration and the Harmonization of International Commercial Law: A Defense of Mitsubishi', *Virginia Journal of International Law*, vol. 39 (1999), 647.

When economic activities extend over more than one jurisdiction, these stories take on an added dimension. Where we see market failures caused by the inability of a single State to regulate a complete transaction, we would want regulators to cooperate in promulgating and administering rules. Where we see multijurisdictional regulation leading to government failure, we might want States to compete among each other to offer the best regulatory package. Putting the point a little more formally, where the costs of market failure otherwise would exceed those of government failure, we would wish to see regulatory cooperation. Where the costs of government failure produced by such cooperation exceed the costs of market failure, we would want States to accept regulatory competition.

The difficulty comes in predicting the instances in which market failures will outweigh government failures, and vice versa. Economists have developed some theoretical models that point towards predictions about the optimal level of government for the undertaking of particular functions, but at present none has sufficient robustness to give much specific guidance to policy-makers.[41] Instead, one must both make guesses based on second-order observations about the structure of particular industries and remain open to ongoing revision of these guesses in the face of new experience.

In light of these limitations, I offer three propositions that may seem acceptable to a broad range of opinion, although none commands unanimous support. First, some market failures doubtless exist at the international level, so some form of international regulatory cooperation seems desirable in some instances. Second, international governance presents particular problems of government failure because of the absence of direct political controls over international decision-makers and the difficulty of opting out of worldwide regulatory decisions. Third, the dynamic nature of the global economy and the relatively recent onset of global economic regulation suggest that what we do not know dwarfs what we do know. This last point suggests a special need for flexibility in choosing among global, national, and subnational regulatory jurisdiction. I will elaborate on each point.

Market failure. Collective action problems surely exist at the international level. International cartels have played an important role in the economic history of the last century; tax havens and bank secrecy regimes exist because the jurisdictions that offer succour to other nation's economic scofflaws do not have to bear the cost of the lawlessness they encourage; international securities swindles have undermined the global financial system from the time of the 1929 stock market crash to the 1998 collapse of the Russian economy; variations in national bankruptcy law

---

[41] But cf. Levmore, 'Case for Retroactive Taxation' (above, n. 5) (optimal level of government for taxation).

create creditor insecurity because of debtor incentives to move assets into jurisdictions with attractive rules; dangerous products enter the stream of commerce because producer nations do not consume them. The examples abound. Perhaps not all of these problems will disappear in the face of successful regulatory cooperation, but surely some will. This point needs underscoring, because scepticism towards regulatory cooperation too easily can lead to a form of market nihilism.

International cooperation and government failure. I will summarize here arguments that I and others have made previously.[42] International lawmakers do not face the same kind of political discipline that national and local ones do. None stands for election, and all can hide behind what I have called a veil of collective mandate. The governments that conduct international negotiations and frame questions for domestic parliamentary approval may have institutional reasons for wishing international law-making to proceed that are independent of the content of the laws produced. Thus we have reason to suspect that in many cases internationally imposed regulatory regimes not only will promote rent-seeking rather than welfare enhancement, but will do so to a greater extent than comparable national schemes.

I must emphasize that the vulnerability of international regulatory cooperation to rent-seeking does not mean that all projects are doomed to failure. Just as the existence of market failure in the global economy seems indisputable, so the potential for technocratic expertise, unencumbered by political constraints, to reach desirable and otherwise unattainable regulatory choices seems clear. The point is only cautionary: the hidden dangers of regulating internationally have received insufficient attention. Collaterally, and perhaps obviously, it takes more to justify an international regulatory project than demonstrating the existence of some market failure. One still must address the risks attendant upon the fabrication of rules and norms through international action, even where those rules respond to a genuine problem.

Flexibility and international regulation. We should pay special attention to the lock-in problem that international regulation presents. It takes time and effort to construct an international regulatory regime, as each party's government negotiates both with its counterparts and with domestic lawmakers and interest groups. Once these edifices are erected, the parties may find them quite difficult to dismantle. Yet we have no reason to believe that the technological, organizational, and social problems that prompt calls for regulatory cooperation remain static during the time that governments build and implement regulatory systems. Thus it seems

---

[42] See, e.g. Stephan, 'The Futility of Unification' (above, n. 9); 'Accountability and International Lawmaking: Rules, Rents and Legitimacy', *Northwestern Journal of International Law & Business*, vol. 17 (1996–7), 681.

likely that international regulation runs a greater risk of becoming out-moded more quickly than does normal national or subnational legislation.

The lock-in problem admits of two solutions. First, governments might delegate substantial law-making powers to international administrative agencies to permit flexible responses to changes in the regulatory environment. The problem then would become retracting such delegations. Presumably reversing an assignment of regulatory power through international negotiations would be as difficult and cumbersome a process as extending the authority in the first place. Second, governments could explore alternatives to regulatory cooperation at the international level. Here the possibility of races to the top becomes critical.

B. Transactor rationality

For races to the top to have any chance of occurring, the person or entity that controls the decisions that determine the regulatory regime must internalize a substantial portion of the costs associated with the particular regime. The process of cost internalization occurs only if the persons with whom the choosing entity comes into contact recognize those costs and can bargain over them. Thus, if the choosing entity has monopoly power and prefers imposing costs on its customers to charging them higher prices, cost internalization cannot take place and races to the top become impossible.

The monopoly story, however, is not especially interesting. Firms that attain monopoly power without the help of government usually prefer extracting monopoly rents in the form of higher prices rather than by shifting costs. A more common scenario involves rate-regulated firms that, working behind the barrier to entry that this government intervention creates, gouge their customers by the imposition of unfriendly terms because they do not have the option of raising prices.[43] But this type of welfare loss results from the relationship between firms and their regulators, and thus can be portrayed as a form of government failure. Because more regulation does not seem the inevitable response to unsuccessful regulation, we can disregard this problem in considering when transaction-based cost-shifting can proceed.

A more compelling concern is that systematic biases in the way people transact will free regime-choosers from internalizing the costs of that choice. If decision-makers regularly and substantially do a better job than others of assessing the risks associated with a particular regime, we might expect them to impose most of the costs of their choices on others. One might believe, for example, that some parties to international commercial contracts—say, carriers or banks—have far greater experience with the

---

[43] See Stephan, 'The Futility of Unification' (above, n. 9), at 768.

underlying transaction than do their customers and thus have a better sense of the likelihood of unfortunate events. They might exploit their superior knowledge by assigning to customers risks that less-informed persons will seriously underestimate, and by assuming at an inflated price those risks that the other parties systematically overestimate. If so, the race to the top would never begin, because no one would have an incentive to press the choosers towards better regulatory systems.

This pessimistic story about transactions pervades the academic literature. Many scholars attach particular importance to the work of Daniel Kahneman and Amos Tversky, psychologists whose experiments suggest the existence of persistent and pervasive misconceptions on the part of otherwise intelligent decision-makers who attempt to predict future events. This research claims to document a number of heuristics that people use to manage incomplete information and to generate guesses about the future. These heuristics produce consistent and significant errors that vitiate the capacity of transactional choices rationally to manage risk.[44]

But psychologists do not provide undiluted support for contractual pessimism. Recent work by a research team led by Gerd Gigerenzer suggests that humans have evolved fairly effective pragmatic approaches for grappling with uncertainty, and that Kahneman's and Tversky's experimental evidence for systematic cognitive failures results from testing the wrong capacities. Gigerenzer begins with the assumption that human cognitive

---

[44] See, e.g. 'Symposium—Legal Implications of Human Error: Cognitive Imperfections: Consumer Law Inferences', *Southern California Law Review*, vol. 59 (1986), 225; 'Symposium—The Legal Implications of Psychology: Human Behavior, Behavioral Economics, and the Law', *Vanderbilt Law Review*, vol. 51 (1998), 1499; Victor Brudney, 'Corporate Bondholders and Debtor Opportunism: In Bad Times and Good', *Harvard Law Review*, vol. 105 (1992), 1821; John C. Coffee, Jr., 'Shareholders Versus Managers: The Strain in the Corporate Web', *Michigan Law Review*, vol. 85 (1986), 1; Melvin Aron Eisenberg, 'The Limits of Cognition and the Limits of Contract', *Stanford Law Review*, vol. 47 (1995), 211; Jon D. Hanson and Douglas A. Kysar, 'Taking Behavioralism Seriously: The Problem of Market Manipulation', *New York University Law Review*, vol. 74 (1999), 632; 'Taking Behavioralism Seriously: Some Evidence of Market Manipulation', *Harvard Law Review*, vol. 112 (1999), 1420; Henry T. C. Hu, 'Illiteracy and Intervention: Wholesale Derivatives, Retail Mutual Funds, and the Matter of Asset Class', *Georgetown Law Journal*, vol. 84 (1996), 2319; Thomas H. Jackson, 'The Fresh-Start Policy in Bankruptcy Law', *Harvard Law Review*, vol. 98 (1985), 1393; Russell Korobkin, 'The Status Quo Bias and Contract Default Rules', *Cornell Law Review*, vol. 83 (1998), 608; Bailey Kuklin, 'The Gaps Between the Fingers of the Invisible Hand', *Brooklyn Law Review*, vol. 58 (1992), 835; 'The Asymmetrical Conditions of Legal Responsibility in the Marketplace', *University of Miami Law Review*, vol. 44 (1990), 893; Timur Kuran and Cass R. Sunstein, 'Availability Cascades and Risk Regulation', *Stanford Law Review*, vol. 51 (1999), 683; Donald C. Langevoort, 'Selling Hope, Selling Risk: Some Lessons for Law from Behavioral Economics About Stockbrokers and Sophisticated Customers', *California Law Review*, vol. 84 (1996), 627; Howard A. Latin, '"Good" Warnings, Bad Products, and Cognitive Limitations', *UCLA Law Review*, vol. 41 (1994), 1193; 'Problem-Solving Behavior and Theories of Tort Liability', *California Law Review*, vol. 73 (1985), 677; Cass R. Sunstein, 'Legal Interference with Private Preferences', *University of Chicago Law Review*, vol. 53 (1986), 1129; Eyal Zamir, 'The Efficiency of Paternalism', *Virginia Law Review*, vol. 84 (1998), 229.

abilities reflect an evolutionary process, and that present capacities should reflect adaptive responses to the environment in which humans evolved over the last million or so years. He posits that humans have a good capacity to draw inferences from observed frequencies, a talent that might have helped survival in the evolutionary environment, but not to frame questions in terms of base-ten probabilities:

Probabilities and percentages are quite recent forms of representations of uncertainty. . . . I propose that the original format was *natural frequencies*, acquired by *natural sampling*. . . . Natural sampling is the sequential process of updating event frequencies from experience. A foraging organism who, day after day, samples potential resources for food and learns the frequencies with which a cue . . . predicts food, performs natural sampling by updating the frequencies *a* [positive outcomes] and *b* [negative outcomes] from observation to observation. . . . Natural frequencies report the final tally of a natural sampling process.[45]

Gigerenzer and his colleagues tested this proposition by replicating the experiments that had seemed to support the dysfunctional-heuristics model, but restating the questions in terms of frequency rather than probability. This research consistently demonstrates that the supposed cognitive errors detected by the earlier research disappear. His later work documents the existence of what he terms 'fast and frugal' heuristics that enable humans to manage uncertainty and effectively to extrapolate to the future in many circumstances.[46]

The significance of Gigerenzer's work for regulatory policy is twofold. First, many, although by no means all, of the more recent arguments for restricting consumer choice in situations where cooperative competition may take place have rested on research that he has undermined. His new evidence does not disprove all the justifications for regulatory intervention, but it does knock out one of its important props. Second, his concept of fast and frugal heuristics suggests that experience transactors can do a satisfactory job of assessing future risks.

Of course, evidence that people with frequentist experience—what we usually call repeat players—have some capacity to assess and manage risk does not make the case for transactional autonomy. If many transactors in a market lack experience, firms still might exploit their ignorance. But this exploitative power faces a strong constraint whenever two significant conditions are satisfied. Where firms both lack the power to discriminate between experienced and naive customers due to product standardization and seek to capture the marginal customer due to competitive market con-

[45] Gerd Gigerenzer, 'Ecological Intelligence: An Adaption for Frequencies', in D. D. Cummins and C. Allen (eds), *The Evolution of the Mind* (New York: Oxford University Press, 1998), 9, 12–13.

[46] Gerd Gigerenzer and Peter M. Todd, 'Fast and Frugal Heuristics: The Adaptive Toolbox', in Gerd Gigerenzer *et al.* (eds), *Simple Heuristics That Make Us Smart* (New York, Oxford University Press, 1999), 3.

ditions, the firms must make their product attractive to the sophisticated customer.[47] Many of the markets of interest to international regulators have these characteristics.

This new support for optimism about transactional rationality, when coupled with the arguments about the potential of international regulation for government failure, does not imply that we should do away with all efforts to come up with harmonized international regulatory regimes. It does suggest, however, that we need to explore alternatives to regulatory cooperation, if only to assess the respective merits of each approach. What would cooperative regulatory competition look like, if we were to pursue the potential for races to the top in different areas of law?

C. Implications for the law of firm structure

Earlier I noted how four areas of regulatory law mix contractual choices and formal choice-of-law rules with strategies that advance substantive regulatory strategies at the expense of party autonomy. In each instance we need to ask to what extent it is plausible to believe that persons who can choose the regulatory regime will internalize the costs of that choice and, if so, how might the law allow them to choose.

Securities regulation. The debate over the merits of cooperative regulatory competition has gone further in securities regulation than in any other. The central question involves the efficiency of capital markets and the extent of investor rationality. Substantial evidence exists that investors respond to regulatory regimes much as they do to brand names, with choices among brands dependent on the investor's tastes for risk and cost. Investors respond to the brand by insisting on a return commensurate with the regulatory regime, which in turn affects the price that a firm must pay for capital. Thus efforts by firms to chisel investors by lowering protection can result in greater costs to firms and, where a takeover market exists, firm managers.

Those firms that pursue capital seem to understand the implications of investor tastes for a regulatory regime. Rather than exploiting the technological changes that facilitate the flight of international capital to the most lax jurisdiction, at least some firms have sought to upgrade their product by choosing to market their securities in high-regulation jurisdictions. Perhaps the most prominent recent example involves Daimler-Benz, which chose to list its securities on the New York Stock Exchange precisely to makes itself more attractive to investors.

---

[47] See David M. Grether, Alan Schwartz, and Louis L. Wilde, 'The Irrelevance of Information Overload: An Analysis of Search and Disclosure', *Southern California Law Review*, vol. 59 (1986), 277; Alan Schwartz and Louis L. Wilde, 'Imperfect Information in Markets for Contract Terms: The Examples of Warranties and Security Interests', *Virginia Law Review*, vol. 69 (1983), 1387.

Given the reasonable, although surely not clear-cut, case for cooperative competition among securities regulators, one should not be surprised to find elements in securities law that facilitate this process. As I observed above, US law demonstrates a remarkable willingness to enforce choice-of-forum and -law clauses (what I will call choice clauses) in securities contracts, even when the result divests the United States of regulatory authority. The SEC also has shown some willingness to regard its authority to regulate the registration of new issues as bounded by a fairly formal conception of the territorial principle. What may be more difficult to explain is the seemingly contradictory tendency of the courts in other cases to reject a formal version of the territoriality principle in favour of the more amorphous 'presence' and 'effects' tests. Why do the courts protect the boundaries of US regulatory authority with remarkable vigilance if they permit investors to contract out of that regulation and allow issuers to avoid US registration requirements?

Surely the courts cannot believe that contractual clauses indicate a degree of advertence on the part of the investor that cannot be expressed in any other way. Sellers of securities typically include choice clauses as standardized terms offered on a take-it-or-leave-it basis. How does this differ from, say, a firm's insistence that the investor use an offshore brokerage account so as to give a transaction a foreign situs?[48]

One response is historical: the courts developed the 'presence' and 'effects' tests in the 1960s and 1970s, before global financial mobility really took off. At that time, regulators and courts may have believed that the dominant US position in the world financial market made regulatory competition inconsequential, and thus permitted unilateral imposition of US regulatory terms. Once the existence of regulatory competition became apparent, the courts have trimmed their response. This perspective would suggest that the acceptance of choice clauses represents only a first step towards a generally more formalistic approach to regulatory jurisdiction. Courts may yet allow vendors of securities to avoid national regulation simply by complying with a few (non-contractual) formalities, such as the appointment of an offshore agent. And as the Internet makes assigning a location to any statement connected with a security more difficult, courts may come to disregard the question of where misrepresentations took place as a factor in establishing regulatory jurisdiction.

Bankruptcy. At first glance, the argument that bankruptcy lends itself to a race to the top should closely track that for securities regulation. Bankruptcy only emerges as an issue with respect to persons who stand in a debtor–creditor relationship, and one might think that persons can enter

---

[48] Cf. *Leasco Data Processing Equipment Corp. v. Maxwell,* 468 F.2d 1326 (2nd Cir. 1972) (purchase of stock in British company through British brokers on London Stock Exchange covered by US securities law because allegedly misleading statements were made in the United States).

into that relationship as mindful of the regulatory environment as persons who invest in securities. But recall the discussion of the Bhopal disaster in Part II of this contribution. As that case illustrates, an important class of persons can become creditors without adverting to the debtor–creditor relationship, simply by becoming victims of a wrongdoing. Only by stretching the meaning of 'transact' to the breaking point can we say that persons who expose themselves to harms caused by others choose to transact with such persons.

Yet the present bankruptcy regime does allow firms considerable control over their obligations to involuntary creditors. The corporate form, to the extent courts respect it, allows firms to segregate risky activities. In the Bhopal case, Union Carbide protected itself from liability for the plant's operation, although perhaps not responsibility for its design, by conducting its Indian operations through a subsidiary in which it had only a minority interest. Franchising and other contractual arrangements similarly allow firms to receive a return from risky activities without possessing the formal attributes of ownership or the substantive responsibility of liability for harms caused. At a minimum, these formal arrangements put firms in an arms race with plaintiffs' attorneys, with theories about separation of ownership competing with liability theories.

Given these sources of flexibility in the law of firm structure, the case against allowing firms to precommit to a bankruptcy regime for involuntary as well as voluntary creditors seems weak. Moving to a more formal system based on up-front choices likely would promote transparency and lower legal and accounting fees without significantly reducing the protection accorded involuntary creditors. Moreover, although some involuntary creditors may find themselves helpless, as were the Bhopal victims, others might have sufficient bargaining power to deter a firm from choosing an egregiously exploitative regime.

One approach that might prove useful would borrow from US corporation law and assign bankruptcy jurisdiction to the place of incorporation.[49] Jurisdictions concerned about protecting local creditors, including potential victims of wrongdoing, could insist that firms incorporate locally and place a specified level of assets within that jurisdiction. Bank regulation at the international level already takes this form in many instances.[50]

Such an approach would not lack drawbacks. Any regime that insisted on local incorporation would involve the State more heavily in licensing business activity, at least in the United States where such requirements

[49] Cf David A. Skeel, Jr., 'Rethinking the Line Between Corporate Tax and Corporate Bankruptcy', *Texas Law Review*, vol. 72 (1994), 471 (proposing corporate charter competition for bankruptcy).

[50] See Stephan *et al.*, *International Business and Economics* (above, n. 13), at 346–8, 416–17; cf. Henry Hansmann and Reinier Kraakman, 'Toward Unlimited Shareholder Liability for Corporate Torts', 100 *Yale Law Journal*, vol. 1879, 1922–3 (1991) (proposing bond as a condition of doing business for foreign corporations).

now are comparatively lax. Administrative decisions as to what would constitute sufficient local assets might invite rent-seeking. But benefits might also arise: this regime could lead to the creation of an industry offering bankruptcy insurance for involuntary creditors on reasonably attractive terms.

If a place-of-incorporation approach to bankruptcy seems too visionary, lesser changes in the law still might improve the chances for cooperative regulatory competition. Rethinking the enforceability of choice clauses would be a good place to start. Even if one wished to resist the application to third parties of a choice clause in a debt contract, as when a debtor commits to apply the law of a stated jurisdiction to all of its future obligations, no good reason exists not to apply such a clause to the debt created by the contract. At a minimum, courts should regard with suspicion the one US appellate decision refusing to honour such a clause in an international transaction.[51]

Intellectual property. As I noted above, rights that arise out of relationships present different legal issues than do product-related interests such as copyright, patent, and trademark. If an employee or business associate appropriates a right to valuable information, the question of ownership normally will depend on the terms of their prior relationship. In most cases the issue becomes whether explicit or implicit commitments not to appropriate exist and, if so, whether such commitments are enforceable.

At first blush, one might think that simple enforcement of contracts as written would enable parties to internalize the costs of any particular assignment they might make of rights in information. Absent some systematic inability to guess about the future or differentials in bargaining power, the parties should assign rights to the person who best can optimize their value. If so, then courts might promote a virtuous cooperative competition simply by upholding these arrangements, including any choice clauses they might contain.

But in one important respect, comprehensive contractual enforcement might undermine cooperative competition. Unfettered use of choice clauses may take away the power of jurisdictions to address potential collective action problems in cases where the ideal solution is uncertain. In 'new economy' industries where human capital dominates as a factor of production, we do not know for sure whether allowing employees to move among firms without restriction enhances or diminishes overall welfare. Employers would prefer an unfettered power to hire new employees, but also to retain a veto over current employees' departures. Because these objectives are irreconcilable, and because it would be costly for industries with numerous employers to negotiate compacts encouraging free movement, employers might default to a regime of enforced

---

[51] In re Simon, 153 F.3d 991 (9th Cir. 1998).

restrictions on employee movements. Some jurisdictions respond to this strategy by refusing to enforce covenants not to compete, but this response works only if employers cannot use choice clauses to avoid the non-enforcement rule.

In this instance, an alternative approach exists that permits virtuous competition without honouring choice clauses. The territoriality principle works in most cases, because one usually can determine the place of employment without too great difficulty. As long as jurisdictions apply consistent, non-overlapping rules for determining in whose territory an employment relationship exists, they can test various approaches to restrictions on mobility. Because high-human-capital employees seem to resist emigration less than do other workers, a natural experiment can proceed as to which regime works best.[52]

Intellectual property rights bundled with products present different issues. Typically the owner of the right has no prior dealings with either the person who infringes it or those who do business with the infringer. The owner instead must make non-contractual decisions that have choice-of-law consequences. In most cases, the producer of products to which intellectual property rights may attach can take the level of protection of those rights into account only when it decides whether to enter a market or not. A market boycott may have third-party effects, and thus serve as a sanction for inadequate levels of protection, in cases where the rights holder can withhold collateral benefits when it stays out of a market.

A traditional analysis of intellectual property rights assumed that importing jurisdictions—countries whose citizens did not own patents, copyrights, or trademarks—had little to lose from refusing to protect these interests and should bargain for compensation to the extent that they assumed any obligation to respect them. As long as these countries did not reasonably expect their citizens to originate intellectual property, they would do better to harbour pirates. But the rise of the post-industrial economy has complicated this picture. In at least some economic sectors, the originator of assets protected by intellectual property law possesses know-how that has value independent of those interests expressed in its property rights and can choose whether to share this knowledge. Where this holds true, a firm's decision where to locate direct investment has important consequences for host countries, which can derive not only taxes but learning and other spillover benefits from serving as a base for foreign-owned production. Countries faced with this trade-off might choose to forgo the fruits of piracy to harvest the benefits of hosting.

---

[52] For observations of this natural experiment, see Gilson, 'Legal Infrastructure' (above, n. 25).

The possibility that this dynamic exists might justify experimenting with different approaches to intellectual property protection. But competition among jurisdictions to reach optimal levels would proceed more readily if each could define clearly what rights existed within its territory. As with labour relationships, the territorial principle provides an effective means of achieving this definition. Locating this kind of intellectual property seems easy enough, because the product with which it is bundled typically has an obvious situs. And the presence or absence of these products within a country's territory is directly related to the boycott mechanism through which the owner of intellectual property can pass on some of the costs of piracy to the pirating jurisdiction.

US law already embraces the territoriality principle with respect to many aspects of intellectual property, but two significant exceptions exist. First, the courts have extended US trademark protection to foreign markets, albeit in an episodic and unpredictable fashion. Second, the courts have not fully enforced either trademark or copyright rights with respect to products sold overseas by the US rightholder and then imported into the United States. Both exceptions undermine cooperative competition by thwarting each country's effort to control the level of protection it will extend.

Extraterritorial protection of US rights clouds the message that host countries send by substituting US enforcement for what rights otherwise would exist. The host country to some extent can free ride on the US regime and thus does not have to confront the trade-off between piracy and investment spillovers. Tolerance of parallel imports similarly confuses a jurisdiction's choice about the level of protection by making local rights depend on overseas events, which may unfold in a different regulatory climate.

Both of these exceptions rest on judicial decisions rather than deliberate legislative choices, although at this point Congress may have to intervene to undo the case law. Neither exception exists in EU law, at least if one regards the territoriality principle as embracing the entire European Union as an integrated legal space. Thus relatively modest legal changes could advance a form of cooperative international competition over intellectual property law that may prove beneficial to both producers and consumers of valuable information.

Antitrust. Competition law deals with many of the same underlying issues as does intellectual property law, but these legal regimes differ in two significant respects. First, antitrust law focuses on industrial structure rather than on product location; indeed, the absence of products in a particular market is one of the evils that antitrust law seeks to combat. Second, competition law depends much more heavily on public enforcement; outside the United States private enforcement of competition law tends to be non-existent or insignificant. Both of these features affect the opportunities for cooperative competition.

The focus on industry structure means that the territoriality principle must play a diminished role in competition law. When an industry carries out production in one jurisdiction, marketing and distribution in a second, and sales in a third, one cannot say that the industry exists only in one place. Formal assignments of territory, such as a place-of-incorporation rule, make little substantive sense. In the case of securities regulation and bankruptcy law, we have plausible arguments that persons who contract with firms, and who therefore may take choice of law into account, have some capacity to force firms to internalize the costs of their choices. But in the case of competition policy, it is often the persons with whom firms do not do business—competitor producers as well as consumers subject to a producer cartel—who have the most legitimate concerns about anticompetitive behaviour.[53]

Nor is it reasonable to expect government regulators, such as those who approve mergers, to stay their hand when firms that claim some other jurisdiction as home seek to obtain a dominant position in the local market. Whether motivated by consumer welfare or rent-seeking, these regulators have no reason not to use competition rules to harass offshore firms, especially if those firms have domestic competitors. In particular, one cannot expect regulators to avoid the seduction of strategic trade theory, which counsels a nation simultaneously to attack monopolists in other jurisdictions while protecting its own.[54]

But even if competition policy does not readily lend itself to races to the top, some modest opportunities to promote cooperative competition may exist. First, the territoriality principle is not meaningless even with respect to industry structure. Some monopolies are local, even if they have economic effects beyond their borders. Recall, for example, the Supreme Court's response to the argument that the cartelization of the retail market for consumer electronic products in Japan gave US producers a claim under the Sherman Act: 'American antitrust laws do not regulate the competitive conditions of other nations' economies.'[55] Even though the line between US competition and that in other economies may blur, the principle seems sound enough. The consumers of the country tolerating the cartel bear the costs of the monopoly, giving their government an incentive to find the right balance between cooperation and competition in the

---

[53] When, however, potential antitrust claimants do enter into contractual relations with their putative oppressors, the present presumption in favour of enforcing choice-of-forum clauses makes sense. Unless the imposition of the clause itself represents an exercise of monopoly power—unlikely for the reasons discussed above—the parties presumably agree to such terms because they reduce the overall cost of the relationship.

[54] For the dubious real-world benefits of such a policy, compare Paul Krugman, 'Increasing Returns, Monopolistic Competition, and International Trade', *Journal of International Economics*, vol. 9 (1979), 9, with Paul Krugman, 'Is Free Trade Passé?', *Journal of Economic Perspectives*, vol. 1 (1987), 131.

[55] *Matsushita Electric Industrial Co. v. Zenith Radio Corp.*, 475 US 574, 582 (1986).

industry. If the balance struck causes significant long-term harm, presumably those consumers will do a better job of calling their government to account than any litigation in US courts.

A related point can be made with respect to inbound transactions. The decision of countries where production takes place to permit or encourage monopolies normally should not justify antitrust measures against those who buy those products offshore and then import them. Under US law, for example, the *Parker* doctrine already allows states to substitute cooperative regulatory regimes for the Sherman Act's competition policy. These local monopolies may end up collecting rents from out-of-state consumers, but the government-supervised organization of the industry also might produce collateral benefits due to economies of scale, scope, or the solution of collective action problems.

The Court regards the Sherman Act as too weak a mandate to justify undoing state-supervised cooperation. It has not extended this courtesy to the actions of foreign governments, but one wonders why not.[56] The logic of the *Parker* doctrine applies just as well to a foreign government's decision about how to structure production taking place within its territory. In both cases, Congress remains free to check the extraction of excessive rents from non-local consumers, either by directly intervening to overturn state regulation or by retaliating against a foreign government with trade measures.

To be sure, distinguishing a local monopoly from a transnational one may prove difficult in particular cases. As an economic matter, one may have difficulty distinguishing price-fixing—a classic example of international anticompetitive behaviour with clear and pernicious local consequences—from restrictions on supply at the point of production. Yet antitrust regimes in most countries regularly attack the former and tend to leave the latter alone. (Think of OPEC and the DeBeers cartel.) The difference may reflect only practical considerations; offshore producers offer less of a purchase to domestic regulators than do multinational firms operating in the local market. But the difference may also reflect different levels of concern about potential harm. Local limits on production work best in industries where the product is tangible and dependent on location, which is to say agricultural and extractive industries. Given the already high level of State intervention in these economic sectors around the world, producer cartelization may not pose much incremental harm. Restrictions on manufacturing and services, by contrast, would impede the more dynamic and innovative part of the world economy.

In short, the implications of Justice Scalia's dissent in *Hartford Insurance* deserve further exploration. Scalia argued that because US antitrust law subjects the insurance industry to local rather than federal competition

[56] See Stephan *et al.*, *International Business and Economics* (above, n. 13), at 661–2.

regulation domestically, the courts should not regard industry activity subject to foreign regulation as within the scope of the antitrust laws.[57] As Scalia framed it, this argument applies only to the business of insurance, which enjoys a specific statutory exemption from the Sherman Act. But surely other occasions exist where local regulation, including government-approved industry self-regulation, may substitute for US antitrust jurisdiction.

V. RUNNING RACES TO THE TOP

I have left until last the most difficult questions that this chapter raises. If the possibility of government failure counsels caution towards international regulatory cooperation, what about the kind of cooperation that cooperative competition requires? If, as I contend, interest groups enjoy an advantage in the international law-making process and if the laws we see reflect rent-seeking, why should we expect to see governments embrace strategies that reduce rents? In particular, why should governments, including courts, embrace cooperative competition without some payoff to the government decision-maker?

The difficulty arises because, as I indicated in Part II of this chapter, cooperative competition works only if some uniformity exists among jurisdictions as to the appropriate choice-of-law rules. If a few economically significant countries defect from the regime, the consequences to the remainder of pursuing either virtuous or harmful policies diminish and the race breaks up without a victor. We have, in short, a classic collective action problem at an international level, seemingly no different from the kinds of problems that Part IV asserts often will lead to government failure.

Other than recognizing the difficulty of this conundrum, I do not have a completely satisfactory response. Rather, I identify three arguments that defuse, even if they do not completely dispel, the force of the objection.

First, public-choice theory, which lies at the heart of the concern about government failure, depicts the struggle over government action as a kind of competition between discrete groups and the general welfare, with information serving as the principal weapon. Cohesive interest groups can generate and share information at a relatively lower cost than can diffuse and disorganized groups. But propagation of information, including information about the virtue of particular government actions, may redress the imbalance at least temporarily. Thus scholarship has a role in shifting perceptions about the desirability of particular governmental choices, even if scholarship itself may exhibit its own form of rent-seeking.

---

[57] *Hartford Fire Insurance Co. v. California*, 509 US 764, 819 (1993) (Scalia, J., dissenting).

Second, judicial decision-making offers the advantages of technocratic rule-making along with the drawbacks. Conflicts-of-law rules on which cooperative regulatory competition depends engage the specialized expertise of jurists. Because these rules work in the background, they tend to be less transparent than rules that address primary conduct. The largely unchecked power of the legal profession to construct these rules makes it more difficult for the political process to correct poor choices of rules, but paradoxically it also enables the profession to impose outcomes that powerful interest groups might oppose.

I do not intend to suggest that empowering judges to make choice-of-law rules means that good rules—for purposes of my argument, rules that promote cooperative regulatory competition—will result. This contribution stands for the proposition that many of the judge-created rules now in force in the United States impede the search for virtuous regulation. Rather, I simply believe that the judicial process remains more open to influence through scholarly argument than does the political system. Which arguments succeed in persuading judges turn on many factors, not all of which include the inherent force of the argument made.

Third, one should recall the context of this contribution. The topic, and in some sense the agenda, is regulatory cooperation. By almost any standard of measurement, international regulatory cooperation has grown significantly in the last two decades and promises to expand even further. Most regulators and many academics on both sides of the Atlantic seem to believe that cooperation is good and more would be better.

Against the force of this trend, my chapter stands as a brake, not a roadblock. For my arguments to succeed, it would not be necessary for the move towards greater internationalization to reverse itself. I do not wish to freeze regulatory cooperation at current levels, much less end it. Rather, I intend to introduce a note of cautious scepticism and invoke a response of hesitation. The audience of rule-makers does not have to come away from this chapter convinced of the benefits of cooperative regulatory competition. It would suffice if judges, legislators, and academics were to consider seriously the possibilities that competition may present, and to measure alternative regulatory approaches against this strategy.

Part IV

Transatlantic regulatory cooperation, international trade, and competition law

Reconciling transatlantic regulatory imperatives with bilateral trade

Mauro Petriccione

I. INTRODUCTION

The interrelationship between international trade, on the one hand, and regulation of the production and sale of traded products and/or services, on the other, is rapidly becoming a key feature of international trade relations. Moreover, it is at the heart of many, if not most, serious trade conflicts that have exploded in the recent past or threaten to do so in the near future. Nowhere is this more apparent than in transatlantic relations. The purpose of this contribution is to explore the impact of domestic regulation in both the United States and the European Union on transatlantic trade, as well as some of the solutions that are being sought to the tensions between the two, which revolve directly or indirectly around the concept of regulatory cooperation.

This contribution is written unashamedly from a trade perspective. The underlying question is: How can we ensure that domestic regulation, or differences in regulatory approaches between the two sides of the Atlantic, will not impede the development of bilateral trade or, worse, degenerate into open trade warfare? To provide an answer, this contribution reviews some of the initiatives and instruments that are being used or explored, in particular in transatlantic relations. Before doing so, I would like to touch briefly on two issues that are of crucial importance but are somewhat outside the link between trade and regulation: (a) the purpose of regulation, and (b) the basis of regulation.

A. The purpose of domestic regulation

It would appear to be relatively easy to justify regulating the production and sale of a product or a service in general terms, for instance as being functional to the protection of human health, workers' safety, consumer interests, or the environment. In reality the question of what interests are worthy of protection and of whether regulation is useful, necessary, or appropriate to that end, is extremely difficult to answer. It keeps our legislators and regulators in full employment, making public opinion more and more attentive to their activity. Today this is happening not only at the domestic level but increasingly at the international level as well.

For the purpose of this contribution, however, it will be assumed that, in each given case, a good choice has been made as to whether to regulate and how. This may appear to be a rather unrealistic assumption, in light of the controversy that regulatory issues have caused of late in transatlantic relations, especially (but not exclusively) in relation to food-safety issues. I would submit, nevertheless, that this is a classic case of not being able to see the forest for the trees. Cases and even whole areas of activity certainly exist where there is a genuine divergence of views between Europe and the United States as to the need to regulate. By and large, however, both sides share an overall commitment to maintaining high standards of protection for health and safety of workers, consumers, and the environment. The question then becomes how to pursue this commitment while avoiding adverse impacts on our bilateral trade relations that are neither necessary nor useful to achieve our regulatory aims. In this respect, as will become clearer later, the crucial issue becomes the manner in which regulation is made and implemented.

B. The basis for domestic regulation

By 'basis' of regulation I mean the *knowledge* or the *information* that informs the primary choice to regulate as well as the manner of regulation. This brings us to the question of how this knowledge is created (in other words, to the question of the scientific basis for regulation), as well as to the question of the criteria for choosing what knowledge/information is *relevant* for a given regulatory purpose.

Again, this contribution will refrain from examining this issue in any depth and will assume that domestic regulation is based on adequate, sufficient, and relevant information. When considered in the context of this contribution, this assumption is somewhat more arbitrary than the previous one, since it ignores the issue of *scientific cooperation*, in spite of its close links with regulatory cooperation. The main reason for this assumption, therefore, is one of maintaining the focus of the paper on the instruments to solve actual or potential trade problems arising from differences in regulation. The role of scientific cooperation (and, more generally, of knowledge-sharing or knowledge-pooling mechanisms) will of course need to be kept in mind, especially when looking at regulatory cooperation as a means of developing similar, or at least compatible, regulatory approaches.

II. THE IMPACT OF REGULATION ON INTERNATIONAL TRADE

In international trade, the progressive elimination of tariff barriers has made the impact of non-tariff barriers (NTBs) more apparent than before.

Likewise, the successes of the multilateral trade system (first GATT,[1] and now the World Trade Organization) in tackling those NTBs more directly related to trade, such as quantitative restrictions or subsidies, has uncovered a 'third generation' of trade barriers. To be more precise, it is now more apparent than ever that international trade can be seriously hampered by the trade effects of domestic regulation, whether or not these effects are intended. Obstacles to trade of a regulatory character are commonly lumped together under the heading 'technical barriers to trade' (TBTs). In general, all TBTs arise from domestic regulatory requirements or from the difference between the respective regulatory requirements of two trading partners. Not all TBTs are the same, however, and the differences call for different policy responses.

In a number of cases, a TBT is such because it has been deliberately set up to have an impact on trade *or* because, while pursuing perfectly legitimate goals other than trade, it has an unnecessarily trade-restrictive effect. These TBTs are not very different, in fact, from more directly trade-related forms of NTBs such as those mentioned above. Thus, they should be dealt with in very much the same manner, i.e. establishing multilateral disciplines and enforcing them, irrespective of their regulatory nature. This is the approach enshrined in Articles 30 *et seq.* of the EC Treaty,[2] in the Tokyo Round GATT Agreements,[3] and then in the Uruguay Round WTO Agreements,[4] as well as in many of the EU's bilateral agreements. Key instruments needed for this purpose are, for instance, the principles of non-discrimination and of proportionality of the WTO TBT Agreement.[5]

The EU's experience with the Internal Market, however, illustrates that this kind of trade liberalization, necessary and valuable as it is, sooner or

---

[1] General Agreement on Tariffs and Trade. The original GATT, concluded in 1947 in provisional form and modified over the years, has been 're-concluded' as a result of the Uruguay Round of multilateral trade negotiations and dubbed 'GATT 1994' in order to distinguish it from the original 'GATT 1947'. Legally speaking, the 're-concluded GATT' is different, as it is linked to a number of other legal texts adopted at the same time. The actual text of the GATT, however, is unchanged and is reproduced in GATT Secretariat, *The Results of the Uruguay Round of Multilateral Trade Negotiations—The Legal Texts* (Geneva, 1994), 485.

[2] Now Articles 28–31 of the Treaty Establishing the European Community, as amended by the Treaty of Amsterdam (which also changed the numbering of the EC Treaty provisions).

[3] As a result of the Tokyo Round of multilateral trade negotiations, the then-Contracting Parties of GATT concluded a number of Agreements that went further than GATT in dealing with certain NTBs, but which were not signed by all GATT Contracting Parties. A good example was the Agreement on interpretation and application of Articles VI, XVI, and XXIII of the General Agreement on Tariffs and Trade (so-called Subsidies Code), GATT Basic Instruments and Selected Documents, 26th Supplement (Geneva, 1980), 56, that elaborated to a very considerable extent on previous GATT disciplines on subsidies and countervailing duties.

[4] The Subsidies Code was then replaced by the *Agreement on Subsidies and Countervailing Duties* as part of the Uruguay Round undertaking. GATT Secretariat, *The Results of the Uruguay Round* (above, n. 1), 264.

[5] Agreement on Technical Barriers to Trade, GATT Secretariat, *The Results of the Uruguay Round* (above, n. 1), 138.

later hits a glass ceiling. Fully legitimate, non-discriminatory, and proportionate domestic regulatory requirements can and do hamper trade, simply because they exist and/or because they differ from one another. In international trade this becomes more apparent as trade relations intensify and are liberalized (that is, tariffs and other NTBs have a diminishing impact). This effect is glaringly obvious vis-à-vis developed trading partners in Europe, North America, and Japan. It can also be detected, however, in many other cases (Korea, ASEAN, Latin America, etc.).

Before proceeding further, however, it is worth looking at the terminology that is commonly employed in this field. The distinction between the terms 'standards' and 'technical regulations' used in the remainder of this contribution follows the approach established in the WTO TBT Agreement. 'Standards' is a generic term that designates technical (product or process) specifications aimed at ensuring that a product presents certain characteristics in terms of its physical nature or its performance and/or that a process produces certain results. Normally standards are of private origin and the TBT Agreement uses the term in this sense. They are also normally developed by consensus among interested parties and their use is voluntary. 'Technical regulations' means the same, but designates the standards issued or mandated by, or under the authority of, a public body, normally for the purpose of ensuring the safety and quality of products/processes for users and workers, the public at large, or the environment. 'Regulatory requirements' is a wider and more general expression, not consecrated in any text. It can be taken to include technical requirements, the imposition of certification obligations and conformity assessment procedures (whether or not by third parties such as independent laboratories), documentary requirements, or labelling requirements. For the sake of simplicity, however, the term 'standards' alone will often be used, except where it would clearly be inappropriate.

III. THE PHILOSOPHY OF THE INTERNAL MARKET IN THE EUROPEAN UNION

In the European Union, harmonization of standards and technical regulations, together with the mutual acceptance of products originating in another Member State regardless of applicable standards (the so-called *Cassis de Dijon*[6] principle), is a cornerstone of the Internal Market, giving substance to the EC Treaty's principle of free circulation of goods. Looking briefly at how the relationship between regulatory objectives and trade concerns has evolved in Europe, the protection of a number of interests of a public nature today figures prominently among the objectives of the

---

[6] Judgment of the Court of 20 Feb. 1979, Case 120/78, 1979 ECR, 649.

European Union as set out in the Treaty.[7] Thus, regulation at the European level, in a number of areas, is enacted to fulfil these objectives, while ensuring the least (and ideally the absence of) impact on intra-Community trade.

Originally, however, the emphasis was much more on achieving and preserving the goal of free intra-Community trade, and harmonization was a means of ensuring that differences in Member States' regulation would not interfere with this goal. Almost in parallel with this evolution, the Community moved from a traditional approach to harmonization, which was largely based on the issuance of detailed regulations by public agencies, to an approach which, in most sectors, is better suited to combining the fulfilment of regulatory objectives with the flexibility that the competitiveness of European industry requires: the so-called 'new approach' or 'global approach'.[8] Basically, this approach abandons the detailed and prescriptive regulation of products or production processes and limits itself to laying down essential requirements, leaving it to the market to choose the means of implementing them. At the same time, the creation of European standards (with the highest possible degree of identity or similarity with international standards) is encouraged, not least by granting to users of these standards a presumption of conformity with a directive's essential requirements. Lastly, a key feature of the European regulatory system is a mix of regulation at the European and Member State (or even sub-national) levels, varying from sector to sector and across different regulatory objectives.

A rough summary of the philosophy of the system, as it has developed from this evolutionary process, could therefore be: (a) a strong commitment to free trade within the Internal Market; (b) an equally strong commitment to the protection of essential public interests, such as health and safety, consumer protection, and the environment; (c) a commitment to using the lightest type of regulation that would still fulfil the objectives of that regulation (notably by resorting to the combination of essential requirements and market-developed European standards); (d) resorting to regulation at the European level (as opposed to the Member States or

---

[7] In general, see Article 2 of the EC Treaty. More specifically, see Article 137.1, 1st indent, for workers' health and safety, Title XIII for public health, Title XIV for consumer protection, Title XIX for environment. All references are to the *Consolidated Version of the Treaty Establishing the European Community* (Luxembourg: Office for Official Publications of the European Communities, 1997).

[8] See, *inter alia*, Council Resolution of 7 May 1985 on a New Approach to Technical Harmonization and Standards, OJEC No. C 136 of 4.6.1985, p. 1; Council Resolution of 18 June 1992 on the Role of European Standardization in the European Economy, OJEC No. C 137 of 9.7.1992, p. 1; Communication from the Commission to the Council and the European Parliament on the Broader Use of Standardization in Community Policy, COM(95) 412 final, 30.10.1995; Report from the Commission to the Council and the European Parliament, 'Efficiency and Accountability in European Standardization under the New Approach', COM(1998) 291 final, 13.5.1998.

sub-national level) when necessary to fulfil the regulatory objectives of the Treaty or when differences in regulation among Member States threaten to disrupt intra-EU trade; (e) an effective administrative and judicial mechanism to weed out abuses in relation to either Member State or European regulation.

IV. THE INTERNATIONAL TRADE PERSPECTIVE

Outside the institutional and legal environment of the European Union, a mechanical transposition of these instruments is obviously not possible. Nevertheless, their underlying philosophy provides useful guidance for the purposes of addressing the negative side effects of domestic regulation on international trade relations. There have been a growing number of initiatives in recent years aimed at addressing this problem. These range from the establishment of informal discussion fora to full-fledged international agreements, but they can all be reduced to two broad concepts. In layman's terms, we can either achieve common standards and regulatory requirements with our trading partners by changing both our standards and theirs; or we can accept the differences in our respective standards and regulatory requirements and find a way to deal with the trade effects that these differences produce.

It is important to bear in mind, however, that these two approaches are not separate from one another and that there may be a considerable degree of overlap between them depending on several factors, namely the number and nature of trading partners involved, the sector or product involved, the nature of the regulatory problems we want to tackle, the time-scale within which we want to achieve certain results, and the resources we and our partners wish to devote to the task.

A. Achieving common standards

1. International harmonization

We can achieve common standards with our trading partners by harmonizing those standards that already exist. This can be done bilaterally or multilaterally, informally or through a multitude of international institutions and/or ad hoc fora. In light of the slow, time- and resource-consuming nature of this task, the European Union has always preferred multilateral harmonization, where the prize of broader application of harmonized standards better justifies the effort.

2. International standardization

The role of international standards bodies in this context is, of course, crucial. One of the lessons of the European experience with regard to technical harmonization has been that in order to be effective, the process must be flexible and adapted to changing market conditions and technological innovation. Regulation must be clear as to what it seeks to achieve, while leaving an acceptable margin of manoeuvre to producers of regulated goods. Consequently, one of the urgent challenges we face in this area is precisely how to revitalize international standards bodies in order to make them more effective, more open and accountable, and more responsive to the (often conflicting) demands for international standards.

There are a number of issues that await clarification in this respect. There is a difference of views, notably between the European Union and the United States, as to what an international standard is (and therefore as to the nature of an international standardization body). Agreement on the features that characterize standards as international would enable both of us to improve compliance with our commitment under the TBT Agreement, which requires that preference be given to international standards when adopting technical regulations. The relationship between international, regional, and national standardization bodies also deserves to be clarified. On the one hand, closer cooperation and common programmes would encourage greater transposition of international standards as regional and national standards. On the other hand, their respective roles are in need of clarification and the relationship between these different levels of standardization should be organized, paying particular attention to the transparency and accountability of these bodies as well as to the possibility of conflicts of interest.

In terms of expanding the application of international standards as a trade-facilitation instrument, we are faced with the serious challenge of bringing developing countries on board. This is all the more important as we (and other developed countries) are under increasing domestic pressure to adopt stricter standards (including standards for production processes) to protect health, safety, and the environment. Developing countries, however, increasingly see this as a denial of market access. In many cases, while this is not the objective, denial of access to our market may well be the outcome. Hence the need to anchor our standards to international ones, and to involve developing countries in the process of formation of those standards.

The other main challenge that the international standardization process faces, of course, is the traditional 'aloofness' of the United States. This is linked to a perception of international standardization bodies as being foreign- (and more specifically European-) dominated, either because of voting rights, or because of too close links with European standards bodies. On the other hand, the United States is perceived as not being able to 'deliver' the effective domestic application or transposition of international standards.

3. Regulatory cooperation

Common standards can also be achieved through cooperation between domestic regulatory authorities. This avenue may attempt to deal with existing regulatory requirements, for instance in order to explain them and facilitate compliance, but its real value lies in creating the conditions for the development of similar, or at least compatible, regulatory requirements by two or more trading partners as and when the need to regulate arises.

In fact, regulatory cooperation potentially offers the greatest long-term rewards to prevent technical regulations and standards from creating unnecessary trade barriers. Its aim should be to foster dialogue among regulatory agencies on both sides of the Atlantic regarding problems that industrial products may pose for the health and safety of users, the environment, consumers or the public at large, as well as regarding the appropriate policy response to these problems. In other words, the ideal outcome of regulatory cooperation would be to arrive at a shared analysis of an actual or potential problem, on the basis of which both US and European regulators would adopt similar or at least a compatible set of policy responses (for instance, in terms of technical standards or requirements, or of certification requirements).

Regulatory cooperation could be multilateral, but it is more likely to produce results in a bilateral context, or among a small group of countries, because it presupposes a minimum level of development of domestic regulatory structures. This is not to say that bilateral or multilateral cooperation is not possible or not useful between countries with regulatory systems that are unevenly developed, but it would have a different focus in such a case. For instance, we should encourage developing countries (and perhaps some developed countries as well) to deregulate and/or rely on self-regulation, unless public regulation is indispensable. One way of doing this, for instance, would be to explore and encourage 'best practices'.

In the bilateral EU–US context, however, our ultimate goal is that regulators should first share an assessment of the need to regulate, and then work towards compatible, trade-friendly, regulatory requirements.

Regulatory cooperation should not interfere with the institutional responsibilities of any of the regulators involved or with their ability to carry out their tasks. These agencies are normally entrusted with the protection of important public policy interests and their role and authority should be preserved. However, in the areas in which these agencies are normally involved (health and safety of consumers, quality of products, and their effect on the environment) there are often a variety of policy responses available. The choice is partly a consequence of the level of knowledge of the underlying problem: the pooling and sharing of knowledge with regard to product hazards and the sensitivity of the public to certain hazards should in fact improve the regulators' effectiveness. Moreover, to the extent that the choice between equivalent responses may be influenced by economic considerations, similar or compatible choices by EU and US regulators would avoid unnecessary barriers to transatlantic trade.

For regulatory cooperation to work in practice, it is crucial that it should take place at a very early stage in the process that leads from the identification of a potential threat to a public interest to the adoption of preventive or remedial regulation. The later the stage at which dialogue takes place, the greater the obstacles it will face for a number of reasons. In particular, it may be more difficult for regulators who have invested more or less heavily (intellectually, politically, or otherwise) in a particular policy response to a perceived problem to change what has already become their preferred course of action. Moreover, at the later stages of the process, the perception—or even the actual risk—of interference with the institutional mandate of a regulatory agency is likely to be greater than at the earlier stages.

B. Dealing with differences

The other, complementary avenue open to us is to accept the differences that exist in our respective regulatory requirements and approaches and find a way to eliminate or at least reduce their trade effects, in particular by reducing the transaction costs associated with them.

1. Transparency

One key instrument for doing this, of course, is transparency of domestic requirements. Quite apart from the cost of complying with additional or different requirements, lack of knowledge of applicable standards or other regulatory requirements, especially if this is added to distance and language factors, can have a seriously chilling effect on trade. Formal publicity requirements and opportunities for public comment, however, are only the beginning of a solution. Transparency is of limited value if it is not accompanied by effective openness of the regulatory process to take into account the legitimate views of all stakeholders. Thus, there is a need to ensure that interested parties can make meaningful contributions to the regulatory process, in the expectation that these will be duly taken into account.

2. Mutual recognition and equivalence

a. Mutual recognition of conformity assessment

The question of testing and certification has often been addressed as a first step in the attempt to reduce the impact of different regulatory requirements. Although these requirements normally exist to ensure compliance of a product or process with applicable standards and regulations, the impact of conformity-assessment requirements on international trade is in fact quite distinct from the impact of the standards themselves. Even in the presence of identical standards, the fact that each importing country requires conformity assessments to be performed locally adds considerably to the costs and difficulty of trading. Unilateral recognition or acceptance of test data, test results, and even certificates is well established, and regulators in various countries often have procedures for unilaterally recognizing data and/or certificates of certain foreign laboratories. Bilateral arrangements between regulatory bodies or between accreditation bodies in different countries also exist. There are even some multilateral examples, like the interestingly named OECD MAD (Mutual Acceptance of Data) Decision concerning Good Laboratory Practices (GLPs) for testing chemical products.[9]

Mutual Recognition Agreements (MRAs) constitute a further development and considerably add to legal certainty for manufacturers and traders. Their reciprocally binding nature gives greater guarantees as compared with unilateral recognition procedures, and their intergovernmental nature signal a higher degree of legal (and political) commitment than arrangements between private accreditation bodies or more administrative arrangements between regulators. The European Union has spearheaded developments in this area, with its expanding network of MRAs[10] and of PECAs (Protocols on European Conformity Assessment) that have been appended to the Europe Agreements concluded between the European Union and Central and Eastern European countries.[11]

[9] The two relevant Acts of the OECD Council are the 1981 Council Decision [C(81)30/Final] on Mutual Acceptance of Data in the Assessment of Chemicals, and the 1989 Council Decision-Recommendation on Compliance with Principles of Good Laboratory Practice [C(89)87/Final, as amended].

[10] 'Agreement on Mutual Recognition in Relation to Conformity Assessment, Certificates and Markings between the European Community and Australia', OJEC No. L 229 of 17.8.1998, p. 3; 'Agreement on Mutual Recognition in Relation to Conformity Assessment between the European Community and New Zealand', ibid., p. 62; 'Agreement on Mutual Recognition between the European Community and Canada', OJEC No. L 280 of 16.10.1998, p. 3; 'Agreement on Mutual Recognition Between the European Community and the United States of America', OJEC No. L 31 of 4.2.1999, p. 3.

[11] PECAs are similar agreements to MRAs, in that one of their objectives is the mutual recognition of conformity assessment between the parties. These agreements, however, are being negotiated between the EU and a number of countries which are candidates for accession to the EU (currently negotiations are under way with Hungary, the Czech Republic, Latvia, and Estonia). Thus, they aim at preparing these countries for eventual accession and, in a sense, anticipate their integration in the Internal Market, albeit on a sectoral basis. In practice, this translates into two main differences with an MRA. First, PECAs also aim, in certain sectors, at complete mutual acceptance of products (i.e. irrespective of the technical regulations applicable in either party, subject to safeguards—contained in the Europe Agreements that the European Union has with all Central and eastern European Countries— similar to those contained in the EC Treaty. Secondly, where mutual recognition (in the sense of an MRA) applies, it does so in sectors where these countries have already aligned their legislation and their regulations on those of the European Union (the 'Community *acquis*').

The MRA between the European Union and the United States,[12] which entered into force on 1 December 1998, is rather typical, even though it is not the original model.[13] A framework agreement sets out principles and lays down general provisions, whereas six Sectoral Annexes provide details of the procedures for the mutual recognition of the conformity assessments in each sector (telecommunications equipment, electrical safety, electro-magnetic compatibility (EMC), recreational craft, pharmaceutical goods manufacturing practices (GMP), and medical devices). The existence of such an agreement clearly has value in itself, even in the presence of different technical regulations in the European Union and in the United States, because it allows assessments of conformity with the requirements of the importing country to be made in the exporting country before exports take place. This will make the conformity assessment process more transparent and predictable, and will reduce its costs as well.

The key to the good functioning of an MRA is that each of the parties has confidence in the ability of the laboratories of the other party (or conformity assessment bodies or CABs, as they are called) to carry out testing, not only in relation to their own country's applicable standards, but also in relation to those of another country. For this reason, the MRAs contain extensive provisions on confidence-building and verification: reciprocal information, training of inspectors and of laboratory personnel, reciprocal or joint inspection programmes, etc., as well as (often but not always) transitional periods. For this reason, there is a limit to the number of countries that can usefully negotiate and successfully implement this kind of agreement, because a precondition for doing so is a high degree of sophistication of the 'conformity assessment industry', as is the ability of public authorities to monitor it.

An MRA is of real interest only for products/sectors where both parties impose mandatory third-party certification requirements (that is, conformity assessment by a public entity or a recognized/accredited laboratory). However, the trend in most developed countries, notably in the European Union and in the United States, is towards deregulation, with a supplier's declaration of conformity (SDoC) replacing third-party certification in many cases (although by no means in all). In fact, one of the challenges of an MRA is to deal with sectors where there is an imbalance in the certification requirements between the two sides. The extreme case is where one party imposes a certification requirement and the other does not, but there are other variants: one party may require a certification by an accredited laboratory whereas the other requires the intervention of a public authority or, at the opposite end of the spectrum, accepts a

---

[12] 'Agreement on Mutual Recognition between the European Community and the United States of America', OJEC No. L 31 of 4.2.1999, p. 3.
[13] The 'honour' belongs to the twin Agreements with Australia and New Zealand.

supplier's declaration. Supplier's declarations, in turn, may or may not be backed by a Quality Assurance System (QAS).

b. Mutual recognition of technical regulations and (functional) equivalence

The concept of mutual recognition can be applied beyond the issue of conformity assessment to the substantive technical regulations themselves. Because harmonization is a slow and complex process mutual recognition is the instrument capable of bringing the greatest substantive results in the short term. Without going as far as the mutual acceptance of products in the Internal Market of the European Union, this concept aims to create the conditions for goods legally produced and marketed in the territory of one side to move across the Atlantic and be marketed on the other side as far as possible without facing further formalities or duplicative requirements. It would allow firms on both sides of the Atlantic to produce to a single set of product specifications. If also coupled with mutual recognition of conformity assessment, it would fulfil the slogan of 'one standard, one test' that industry in Europe and the United States has been championing for some time.[14]

Stated in simple terms, the mutual recognition of technical regulations must begin with an analysis and comparison of standards and regulatory requirements applicable to a given product (in itself not an easy task). This is then followed by a judgement on whether the two sets of technical regulations and/or standards are both equally apt to reach the intended result in terms of product safety/quality, protection of public health, or of the environment. In other words, the technical requirements or specifications of the regulation are equivalent for the purpose of fulfilling the objectives of the regulation itself; they can also be said, therefore, to be 'functionally equivalent'.[15]

There is, however, a certain conceptual difference between the notions of 'equivalence', on the one hand, and of 'mutual recognition,' on the other. The latter describes the process whereby regulators recognize the validity of technical regulations issued by a foreign country for the fulfilment of domestic regulatory objectives. On the other hand, equivalence applies to the technical content of the regulation: as such, this is a notion that also applies to standards of private origin. This conceptual

---

[14] The Transatlantic Business Dialogue (TABD) has been particularly vocal in this respect, urging governments on both sides of the Atlantic to act in this direction.

[15] The WTO TBT Agreement gives a concise but rather clear definition of functional equivalence of technical regulation as a means to avoid or reduce negative trade effects. Article 2.7 of the Agreement reads: 'Members shall give positive consideration to accepting as equivalent technical regulations of other Members, even if these regulations differ from their own, provided they are satisfied that these regulations adequately fulfil the objectives of their own regulations.' GATT Secretariat, *The Results of the Uruguay Round* (above, n. 1), 140.

distinction has practical implications because of the role that market-developed standards play in the regulatory process both in the European Union and in the United States. It is conceivable that regulators would recognize each other's requirements even where these are based on market-developed standards, provided they are equivalent.

The rewards of this instrument in terms of trade facilitation, however, should not overshadow the difficulty of making the equivalence judgement in the first place, nor the fact that there are many cases where that judgement will be negative. In particular, equivalence will be more difficult—or impossible—to establish for products/sectors subject to very detailed requirements, in particular where the products are potentially hazardous. Equivalence should be easier (although not necessarily easy) for products/sectors where mutual recognition is already the norm within the Community and/or where at least a degree of international harmonization already exists or where the use of international standards is widespread. Nevertheless, and in spite of the difficulties, the Transatlantic Economic Partnership (TEP) Declaration and Action Plan accords mutual recognition of technical regulations a key place.

Mutual recognition of technical regulations and equivalence of standards also raises a peculiar problem of enforcement in the transatlantic context. Where two countries develop their technical regulations through regulatory cooperation or align them to international standards there is nevertheless a single set of applicable requirements that a product—whether manufactured locally or imported—must meet in order to be lawfully put on the market. Enforcement of those requirements is carried out by the administrative and judicial authorities of that country. The fact that the requirements may be identical in the exporting country does not change the nature or the content of the regulations to be enforced. However, where mutual recognition of technical regulations applies, the administrative and judicial authorities of a country are confronted with products that meet a different set of requirements (those of the exporting country). This raises the question of how these authorities can understand, interpret, and enforce foreign requirements within their own jurisdiction when a controversy concerning imported products arises.

Moreover, the question of the equivalence itself may give rise to controversies, the volume and technicality of which may make it inappropriate to resort to any mechanism known in international agreements (such as consensual resolution or dispute settlement). A similar set of problems arises in the Internal Market of the European Union in relation to the mutual acceptance of products. The problem there is solved through the administrative and judicial enforcement of the European Commission and the European Court of Justice, respectively. In the transatlantic context this question will need careful attention.

V. THE EUROPEAN UNION AND THE UNITED STATES: CONFLICT OR
JOINT LEADERSHIP?

Turning to the interplay between our bilateral relationship and the rest of
the world, it would be complacent to assume that the trend in many parts
of the world is towards less regulation. Indeed, much as this runs contrary
to our deeply held belief as to what governments around the world should
be doing, the trend may well be towards more, rather than less, regulation.
Speaking in very rough terms, the direct and indirect effects that the products (and production processes) we use have on our life and our environment increase and multiply with the increase in sophistication of those
products/ processes. At the same time, our knowledge, as citizens and consumers, has grown enough for us to be aware of, or suspect, or simply fear,
the existence of negative effects, but not enough to be sure of the implications, let alone to master them. Hence, there may well be a demand for public authorities to provide more (and stricter and 'better') regulation.

In most developed countries, long experience with the downside of
excessive regulation has made public authorities wary of such demands
and has prompted regulators to examine with care both the need to regulate and the form of regulation. This is the fruit of experience, however,
and requires a high degree of sophistication of regulatory authorities. In
countries where a proper regulatory culture is still relatively new (developing countries or countries in transition from a non-market economy),
there is a much higher risk of a knee-jerk reaction: when the public opinion perceives a risk, the response of the public authorities is to enact more
and 'stricter' regulations, which often means more bureaucratic regulations and not necessarily more effective regulations.

Better regulation, however, must not necessarily mean heavier regulation. In fact, at least in developed countries there is a balance between
more and stricter regulation on the one hand, and 'lighter' regulatory
approaches on the other. 'Heavy' regulation hampers economic activity.
There are fields where strict administrative controls are inevitable, given
the risks involved, but even then 'techniques' for regulation may be
more—or less—intrusive. Even in sectors such as pharmaceuticals (one of
the most heavily regulated and controlled sectors in all countries, due to
the potential risks for human life and health), there are ways of making life
easier for economic operators without compromising health and safety.

More to the point, however, there are many products/sectors where this
type of approach is not necessary and/or would prove unfeasible. The
shift in the technical harmonization policy of the Community over the
years provides a clear example of this. The New Approach directives[16] lay

[16] The new approach is described here in its basic form, but there are several variations on
the theme, not all necessarily consistent with each other or with the overall 'model'. This is

down a minimum number of 'essential' requirements with which a product must comply, usually expressed in terms of performance of the products. Manufacturers have the choice of how to fulfil these requirements, but they are normally provided with a 'shortcut' since, in most cases, compliance will be presumed if the manufacturer adopts certain available standards, normally set by one of the European-level standards bodies (CEN, CENELEC, ETSI). In many cases, in fact, the Community will give one of the standards bodies a specific mandate to elaborate standards for this purpose. This approach combines the need for regulation by the public authorities with flexibility for economic operators as to the means to comply with regulation. For instance, manufacturers of special or 'niche' products, for which available standards are not appropriate, have the right to argue (and, of course, the onus to show) that their product nevertheless meets the requirements laid down in Community law. Under a more detailed and prescriptive approach to regulation (one where technical regulations prescribe in greater detail how a product should be manufactured) this right would not exist unless expressly provided for in the regulation.

It is interesting to compare this with the philosophy of the United States. The United States, of course, has the same problem as the European Union, namely finding a balance between the need to regulate and the need to avoid placing its economic operators in a straightjacket. At the risk of oversimplifying, the American solution appears to be to regulate fewer sectors/products and to rely more on self-regulation and purely private sector standard setting. However: (a) manufacturers of unregulated products are subject to a rather harsh regime of product liability that, arguably, should make them careful enough to make regulation unnecessary; and (b) when US regulators do intervene they tend to be rather prescriptive. This illustrates the difficulty of reconciling these different approaches in the transatlantic relationship while, at the same time, underlining the fact that we have very similar ultimate objectives, which makes the exercise all the more worthwhile in spite of the difficulties.

One can also see a similar trend in respect of conformity-assessment procedures. Here there is a 'deregulation path', going from certification by public authorities, to third-party certification (by an accredited laboratory), to self-certification (supplier's declaration of conformity—SDoC). Another element worth mentioning here is the development—and the growing effectiveness—of Quality Assurance Systems (QAS) employed by manufacturers to guarantee the quality and safety of their products. Generally based on statistical process control (SPC) techniques and normally comprising audits by third parties (public agencies or private

---

due partly to the specificity of certain products/sectors, and partly to the fact that this approach has developed gradually over time.

bodies), QAS are nowadays one of the keys to effective self-regulation and/or self-certification mechanisms. They enable regulators to diminish their certification requirements, reduce the economic burden of regulation for economic operators and make better use of the regulators' own scarce resources.

The general trend in the European Union and in the United States, as well as in most other developed countries, is therefore towards 'lighter' forms of conformity assessment. However, differences between the European Union and the United States still exist and generate unnecessary costs. In addition, it cannot be taken for granted that our trading partners elsewhere will follow this trend. Under these circumstances, the European Union and the United States face a choice. On the one hand, they can stress their differences and run a high risk of trade wars that will be all the more intractable because they will be rooted in genuine beliefs in respect of issues such as health, safety, or the environment. Or, alternatively, they can develop mechanisms that reconcile trade imperatives with a high commitment to protection of the public interest. If we follow this second path, an added bonus would be the leadership role that the European Union and the United States would jointly play vis-à-vis other trading partners, both in the developed and in the developing world.

VI. CONCLUSION

The United States and the European Union must aim for the right balance between an increased 'demand' for regulation and the need to avoid stifling economic activity. A balance that works at the domestic level, however, does not necessarily work at the international level. The philosophy of the Internal Market in the Community can be said to be inherently 'trade friendly'. This is hardly surprising, since it is born of the need to facilitate intra-Community trade. The philosophy of the United States produces a generally trade-friendly situation, but the regulated sectors are more difficult to penetrate for foreign firms. However, both require reliance on a developed legal and business environment. Self-regulation cannot work without product liability and judicial enforcement; self-certification cannot work without market surveillance and product recall mechanisms.

The 'philosophy' of most governments in the economic field is, in contrast, more 'interventionist' than that of either the European Union or the United States. Faced with the need to regulate for safety, health, and environmental reasons, on the one hand, and the inadequacy of their legal and business environment, on the other, there is a real danger of many countries over-regulating their economies. This may be so particularly in the case of emerging economies in Asia and Latin America.

Faced with this situation, the conclusions I draw are the following:

- The European Union and the United States share very similar regulatory objectives in terms of desired levels of protection of essential public interests: health, safety, the environment, etc.
- They also share the desire to achieve a balance between these objectives and the need to avoid stifling economic activity.
- Differences in regulatory approaches and culture exist and are not easy to overcome, but in the light of these shared objectives, it would be irresponsible not to tackle them. The alternative would be to continue to burden our industries and consumers with unnecessary costs and to deprive our citizens of the benefits of more effective regulation.
- The instruments required to achieve this result also exist and we are attempting to give them a concrete shape. Regulatory cooperation will permit better understanding of the differences that exist today and enable the development of a more shared approach in the future. Mutual recognition and equivalence would help at least to reduce the impact of those differences today and in the immediate future.
- The European Union and the United States should exercise joint leadership vis-à-vis our trading partners elsewhere and encourage international harmonization, reform of international standardization, and deregulation.

Transatlantic regulatory cooperation from a trade perspective: a case study in accounting standards

Joel P. Trachtman*

This contribution examines the problem of varying national financial accounting requirements from a trade in services perspective. This problem, which has deterred listing of foreign securities and public offering of securities by foreign issuers in the United States, has been considered mainly as a financial accounting or free movement of capital issue: how and why should financial accounting standards be modified to facilitate cross-border securities transactions? This consideration has not generally reflected a trade-regulation perspective, which asks to what extent does diversity of accounting standards present a barrier, not to listing or offering per se, but to cross-border trade in accounting, investment banking, stock exchange, and legal services.

This contribution examines the WTO's General Agreement on Trade in Services (GATS) to assess the way in which diversity of accounting standards in connection with securities regulation may be disciplined under that agreement. It finds that the transactional focus of this type of securities regulation does not fit neatly into the more institutional categories of GATS. It thus concludes that GATS provides limited potential disciplines capable of application by a WTO dispute resolution tribunal. This limited potential applicability of disciplines by dispute resolution bodies has the effect of referring the problem either to the more political fora of GATS, or to more specialized functional fora such as the International Accounting Standards Committee or the International Organization of Securities Commissions.

I. INTRODUCTION: THE ACCOUNTING STANDARDS PROBLEM IN GLOBAL SECURITIES OFFERINGS

Once problems of discrimination have been addressed, as they generally have been in transatlantic relations, the leading barrier to trade in services

* This contribution is based, in part, on research by the author previously published as 'Accounting Standards and Trade Disciplines: Irreconcilable Differences?', *Journal of World Trade*, vol. 31 (1997), 63.

is variation of regulation. The globalization of capital markets also is impeded by access restrictions that prevent or impede issuers from offering securities globally. A leading, and most intractable, type of access restriction is the requirement that the financial statements of issuers of securities comply, in whole or in part, with specified local requirements. While free flow of capital is an important component of international economic integration, and is increasingly viewed as related to the free flow of goods, services, and workers, this contribution focuses on the direct trade issues arising from varying accounting standards. The particular problem that this contribution will use as a case study is the fact that US accounting standards tend to be more demanding than, or at least different from, those in many foreign countries,[1] and that the US moderation of these standards for foreign issuers is criticized as insufficient. Due to the size and efficiency of the US capital markets, they tend to be attractive to foreign issuers that want to increase the breadth and depth of their sources of financing, as well as for issuers that seek to enhance their name-recognition in the United States for other reasons.[2]

There are three main types of responses to the problem of varying accounting standards: (i) harmonization, (ii) recognition, and (iii) inaction. In addition, a combination of these three responses is possible, and more likely. Indeed, harmonization is rarely total, leaving room for a measure of local diversity. In the European Community, policy-makers speak of 'essential harmonization': sufficient harmonization to form the predicate for recognition. Recognition is the acceptance, for local regulatory purposes, of compliance with non-local regulatory regimes. The structure under most active consideration today is one of recognition, not of foreign national accounting standards, but of a set of international accounting standards. While some refer to this approach as harmonization, it would not, at least initially, amount to complete harmonization, as it would not affect rules for offerings by domestic issuers. This would raise some interesting issues. For example, would a US issuer need to comply with US accounting standards at home but with international accounting standards for foreign offerings? As a practical matter, most foreign states seem to accept financial statements prepared in accordance with US standards. Further, it is arguable that, to some extent, a rule of recognition will result in some degree of harmonization through regulatory competition or

---

[1] For an assessment of the diversity of accounting standards, see Emmanuel N. Emenyonu and Sidney J. Gray, 'International Accounting Harmonization and the Major Developed Stock Market Countries: An Empirical Study', *Journal of International Accounting*, vol. 31 (1996), 269; Bernhard Grossfeld, 'Comparative Accounting', *Texas International Law Journal*, vol. 28 (1993), 233.

[2] See, e.g. 'Survey: Accessing US Capital Markets', *Financial Times*, 2 May 1997. William E. Decker, 'The Attractions of the US Securities Markets to Foreign Issuers and the Alternative Methods of Accessing the US Markets: From the Issuer's Perspective', *Fordham International Law Journal*, vol. 17 (1994), S10, S12.

simply through pressure from domestic-regulated persons seeking to be subject to rules similar to those applied to foreign-regulated persons.

Considering the problem of diverse accounting standards from a trade perspective, the question arises: Trade in what? The first and most obvious answer is trade in services, which is the principal concern of this chapter. But then a second question arises: Whose services? There are at least three industry groups:

Accounting. First, and most directly, is the accounting profession. Under the auspices of the WTO, the GATS is currently working to facilitate trade in accounting services. While varying accounting standards raise some issues of professional mobility, the largest accounting firms have long ago adapted to overcome any barriers. Varying accounting standards also raise some barriers for cross-border services: for example, because of the differences between US GAAP and Indian GAAP, an Indian accounting firm cannot provide accounting services to US companies, in the way that an Indian software firm can provide software development services to US companies. Finally, varying accounting standards is a barrier to establishment by a foreign accounting firm, in so far as it will need to develop expertise, and obtain licensing, in local accounting standards.

Financial services firms and law firms. Second, financial services firms and law firms are hindered in performing global services by virtue of the fact that barriers to entry for their clients make their clients less interested in these services. Cross-border services are impeded precisely because cross-border transactions are impeded. Barriers to internationalization of capital markets are barriers to international financial services and legal services. Larger financial service firms, like larger accounting firms, have adapted to some extent, offering services internationally, rather than globally (serving a number of local markets, rather than a single global market). Law firms, hindered to a greater extent than at least financial service firms by licensing requirements, have moved more slowly.

Stock exchanges. Finally, and perhaps most interestingly, is the stock exchange or other trading entity (such as the NASDAQ). These entities compete for volume. They are competing to be the most liquid market for securities. Perhaps this competition will loosen its geographic anchors and develop into a delocalized virtual industry, but until it does, and as it does, international competition will continue. In fact, to some extent the geographic competition is carried out by delocalization: by enabling persons in varying geographic locations to participate. It is this competition which is the major motivation for liberalization of US requirements.

A final introductory issue must be addressed: even given the obstacles facing these industry groups just discussed, is diversity of accounting standards properly considered a trade issue? Because diversity of accounting standards is a mixed issue—combining trade concerns with investor protection, free movement of capital, and other concerns—thus far the institutions addressing diversity and harmonization of accounting standards are not those one thinks of in connection with free trade. The GATT, the WTO, the GATS, and the NAFTA have so far remained on the sidelines of this issue. Furthermore, the institutions that have been more active, such as the International Accounting Standards Committee (IASC) and the International Organization of Securities Commissions (IOSCO), have even more limited mandates, focusing more on accounting and protection of investors than on free trade in services. Certainly, from a finance (as opposed to a financial services) standpoint, the issue is not an international trade issue but a domestic regulatory issue. However, as explained above, it is no longer possible to ignore the trade and free movement of capital ramifications of these domestic regulatory issues.

It seems increasingly clear that the pure mandates for 'full disclosure' or unmoderated 'investor protection' that have served as guiding epithets for the US Securities and Exchange Commission (SEC) since the 1930s are no longer sustainable. Both the methods of achieving these goals and the degree to which we seek to achieve them must be revised. The question of diversity, harmonization, and recognition of accounting standards is thus *both a trade issue and a regulatory issue*. Neither perspective can eclipse the other. Rather, it is necessary to make trade-offs between trade values and regulatory values. The goal of this chapter is not to suggest how the trade-offs should be made, but rather to show how trade disciplines are structured to invoke a rough and incomplete analysis, leaving the question of how to make these trade-offs very much open to further negotiations.

This contribution therefore takes the view that accounting standards are indeed standards cognizable from a trade-law perspective. This trade-law perspective, at its most rigorous (and where it is applicable), evaluates standards to determine whether they should be permitted to be maintained despite their trade-inhibiting effects. The utility of accounting standards must be understood not only in terms of their capacity to achieve certain regulatory and efficiency goals, but also in terms of their impact on trade. Accounting standards are like any other regulatory standards subject to trade-law disciplines—i.e. they are ostensibly designed, or maintained, to achieve non-trade social policy in the state applying the measures but they also hinder trade, intentionally or unintentionally.

In short, the conflict between accounting standards on the one hand, and free trade in financial services on the other hand, is comparable to the generalized problem of accommodating trade goals to other social goals, such as environmental protection, labour standards, competition policy, etc. Recently, the WTO, in its Singapore Ministerial conference, deferred definitive action on allocation of responsibility for trade and environment issues, and referred responsibility for trade and labour standards issues to the International Labor Organization. Also at the Singapore Ministerial, the WTO stated that '[w]e encourage the successful completion of international standards in the accountancy sector by IFAC [International Federation of Accounting[3]], IASC and IOSCO'.[4] This signals the WTO's deference, and in effect delegation (at least in part) to specific functional organizations the task of establishing standards to facilitate the free movement of accountancy services. These disciplines apply to all Member States that have made specific commitments in accountancy but do not apply to national measures listed as exceptions under Articles XVI and XVII. This particular delegation is similar to practices in other regulatory domains, such as food safety standards (Codex Alimentarius Commission) and general product standards (International Organization for Standardization (ISO)). We can begin to see emerging a general institutional solution to the 'trade and . . . problem' utilizing delegation to specialized functional international organizations. The further question, however, is how will the WTO ensure that these organizations reflect appropriately the trade perspectives that concern the WTO?

Part II describes the principal accounting requirements and issues, explains the relationship between these requirements and trade concerns, and describes the role of the IOSCO and the IASC as standards-setting bodies. Part III examines the role and law of the WTO and GATS, and the potential application of this law to a hypothetical failure by the United States to recognize IASC standards. Part IV summarizes the regulatory alternatives available to address the relevant concerns. Part V concludes by outlining the contours of a cost–benefit analysis to determine the level of integration appropriate in the accounting area.

II.   ACCOUNTING REQUIREMENTS: DOMESTIC AND INTERNATIONAL CONCERNS

A. US GAAP requirements and international accounting standards: the FASB, the IASC, the SEC, and IOSCO

Accounting standards vary by jurisdiction. The US Financial Accounting Standards Board (FASB), under the supervision of the SEC, maintains the

---

[3] This body is closely related to the IASC but is concerned more with international auditing standards than international accounting standards.

[4] World Trade Organization, Singapore Ministerial Declaration Adopted on 13 Dec. 1996, WT/MIN(96)/DEC, para. 17. On 29 May 1997 the WTO adopted guidelines for recognition of qualifications in the accountancy sector as part of the work programme mandated under GATS. These guidelines are suggestive of the structure of mutual recognition agreements regarding the qualifications of accountants. See http://www.wto.org/new/press73.htm. The WTO Committee on Trade in Services adopted on 14 Dec. 1998 the *Disciplines on Domestic Regulation in the Accountancy Sector*, developed by the WTO Working Party on Professional Services. *WTO Focus*, Dec. 1998, 10–11.

US Generally Accepted Accounting Practices (US GAAP). While the SEC has responded to the internationalization of the securities markets by moderating the applicability of the full panoply of US disclosure require-ments to non-US issuers of securities, foreign issuers are still required either to comply with US GAAP or to reconcile their financial statements to US GAAP and Regulation S-X (the SEC's master accounting regulation). Such reconciliation requires that significant line items such as net income and earnings per share be analysed to show what they would be if US GAAP were applied. The most complete level of reconciliation requires a level of work that approaches the complete conversion of the financial statements to US GAAP.

In 1995 IOSCO set a goal of endorsing a 'core' set of international accounting standards for use in connection with cross-border securities offerings by June 1999 (subsequently changed to March 1998), assigning the IASC the task of developing fifteen new standards.[5] When these revised standards were finished on 16 December 1998, it was hoped (at least by the IASC) that they would form the basis for national regulators to permit global public offerings without different financial statements in different countries. As of this writing, the United States had not responded to the IASC standards.

On 17 May 2000, IOSCO endorsed thirty core standards prepared by IASC.[6] While the United States participated in this endorsement, the endorsement itself is qualified. It provides that multinational issuers may use the IASC standards as supplemented by requirements of reconcilia-tion, disclosure, and interpretation, 'where necessary to address outstand-ing substantive issues at a national or regional level'.

The leading reason for developing international accounting standards is to facilitate access to the US market, as (i) the US capital market is the largest in the world, and (ii) foreign regulators are often not so discrimi-nating as the SEC. The current SEC chairman has stated that acceptance by the SEC is 'not a foregone conclusion', and that the IASC principles must 'measure up' to FASB's standards.[7] A former chairman of the SEC has observed that '[t]he SEC's expressed reservation makes it seem unlikely that the IASC principles will be embraced in full by the SEC as acceptable

---

[5] The SEC may delay a decision. See 'Global Accounting Rules Goal Remains Elusive', *Insurance Accounting*, 10 May 1999, 1.

[6] IOSCO, IASC Standards—Assessment Report, Appendix A: Resolution and List of IASC 2000 Standards, available at http://www.iosco.org/docs-public-2000/2000-iasc_standards-document04.html.

[7] Jim Kelly, 'Accounting Code on Track to Meet Deadline, Says Carsber', *Financial Times*, 13 Jan. 1997. But see Jim Kelly, 'A Foot on the Brake: The US Standard Setter Fears that Global Harmonization is Moving Too Fast', *Financial Times*, 13 Mar. 1997, at 32 (FASB expresses con-cerns that the IASC process either will fail to produce the standards proposed by mid-1998, or that if it does, they will be unacceptable to the United States).

substitutes for US GAAP'.[8] If this occurs, and the United States rejects foreign registrants that comply with the revised group of international accounting standards, will foreign states have any remedies under GATS? Should they?

B. The role of IOSCO and the IASC as international standards-setting bodies

On the multilateral level, little has been done to address disparities in disclosure or accounting requirements in connection with public offerings. IOSCO and the IASC are the leading protagonists in the multilateral sphere. IOSCO is the leading multilateral organization that addresses securities regulation. It differs from GATS by virtue of the specificity of its focus, and by virtue of its emphasis on regulation rather than trade as a motivation. Its institutional character is similar to the Basle Committee with respect to bank regulation,[9] in so far as it does not legislate in a legally binding sense (as GATS may do through further treaty development), but issues consensual recommendations that its members are bound, in an ethical or political sense, to implement. IOSCO functions to assemble comparative information regarding national securities regulation and to provide a forum for cooperation and coordination among securities regulators, culminating in annual meetings. The comparative information that it assembles can be used as a basis for efforts at harmonization, mutual recognition, or unilateral law reform. As of May 1997, IOSCO had eighty-two ordinary members, ten associate members, and forty-four affiliate members.

IOSCO has sought to address disclosure regulation in connection with public offerings,[10] and is continuing this process. In October 1993 some of the work of the working party on multinational disclosure and accounting

---

[8] David S. Ruder, 'Reconciling US Disclosure Policy with International Accounting and Disclosure Standards', *Northwestern Journal of International Law and Business,* vol. 17 (1996), 1, 11.

[9] IOSCO was founded in 1974 as the Inter-American Association of Securities Commissions and Similar Agencies. It originally lacked any secretariat and functioned as a club for organizing meetings of securities regulators from the Western Hemisphere. It became an international forum in 1983, and established a secretariat, in Montreal, Canada, in 1986. 'Organization's Fundamental Mission to be Focus of Meeting in Mexico City', *International Securities Regulation Reporter,* 19 Oct. 1993. IOSCO was reformed under Quebec law as a not-for-profit organization in 1987. IOSCO Ann. Rept. 1992, at 21.

On the Basle Commitee, see Joseph J. Norton, *Devising International Bank Supervisory Standards* (London, Boston: Graham and Trotman/M. Nijhoff; Norwell, MA: Kluwer Academic Publishers, 1995); Joseph J. Norton, 'The Work of the Basle Supervisors Committee on Bank Capital Adequacy and the July 1988 Report on International Convergence of Capital Measurement and Capital Standards', *International Lawyer,* vol. 23 (1989), 245.

[10] Technical Committee of the International Organization of Securities Commissioners, 'International Equity Offers', app. A, in *Documents of the XVth Annual Conference, International Organization of Securities Commissions, Venice, Italy, September 1989* (1989).

resulted in a recommendation (via a resolution of the Presidents' Committee of IOSCO, its main decision-making organ) that:

members of IOSCO take all steps that are necessary in their respective home juris-dictions to accept cash flow statements prepared in accordance with IAS 7 [International Accounting Standard 7], as amended, as one alternative to state-ments prepared in accordance with the regulators' domestic accounting standards relating to cash flow statements in connection with cross-border offerings and con-tinuous reporting by foreign issuers.[11]

This recommendation is notable for several reasons. First, it is an initial step towards a coordinated international disclosure system. Second, it is a small step, addressing only a single, relatively less significant, aspect of accounting practice. Third, it only relates to international offerings, and does not allow domestic issuers to use these standards, although it is pos-sible that implementing countries would permit domestic issuers to do so. Finally, it is in the form of a non-binding recommendation.

More recently, the IASC and the FASB agreed on new standards, under IAS 33, for disclosing earnings per share, an important component of dis-closure. Interestingly, the technique used here is parallel adoption by both the international organization and the national member, resulting in har-monization in this particular standard. However, the FASB standard requires some additional disclosures. Therefore, compliance with IAS 33 alone would not satisfy US GAAP requirements.

Except for a brief period during 1994 and 1995, IOSCO has worked cooperatively with the IASC. This cooperation brought forth an agreement in July 1995 that, by 1999 (subsequently changed to March 1998[12]), the IASC would develop 'a comprehensive set of core principles which would allow the IOSCO Technical Committee to endorse them for cross-border capital raising and listing purposes in all global markets'.[13] It is expected that IOSCO will require a unanimous vote of its members to recommend the IASC standards.[14]

The IASC is the leading professional international accounting organiza-tion.[15] Unlike IOSCO, it is not an intergovernmental organization. Thus, it

[11] Final Communique of the XVIIIth Annual Conference of the International Organization of Securities Commissions (IOSCO), 29 Oct. 1993, in *Documents of the XVIIIth Annual Conference, International Organization of Securities Commissions, Mexico City, Mexico, 24–28 October 1993* (1994).

[12] 'IASC Will Complete Accounting Standards by 1998', *Journal of Accountancy*, July 1996, 24–5.

[13] See A. A. Sommer, 'IOSCO: Its Mission and Achievement', *Northwestern Journal of International Law & Business*, vol. 17 (1996), 15, citing IOSCO, 1995 Annual Report, 13. See also 'Special Report: The Future of Financial Accounting: Universal Standards', *Journal of Accountancy*, May 1996, 20.

[14] 'SEC and FASB Remain Cautious About International Standards', *Journal of Accountancy*, Mar. 1997, 16. Of course, IOSCO only has power to recommend, not to bind.

[15] The IASC was established in London in 1973 by a group of nine professional account-ing organizations, and as of January 1996, had 116 member organizations in 86 countries. See

does not purport to represent the general public interest. Its objectives are '(a) to formulate and publish in the public interest accounting standards to be observed in the presentation of financial statements and to promote their worldwide acceptance and observance, and (b) to work generally for the improvement and harmonization of regulations, accounting standards, and procedures relating to the presentation of financial statements'.[16]

III. THE WTO AND GATS

One leading goal of the WTO is to liberalize trade in services. In financial services, as in other areas, the goal of trade liberalization must be tempered by regulatory concerns,[17] as well as by monetary policy concerns. The WTO system has no particular expertise in either of these areas. However, in order to liberalize trade in financial services, it is necessary to address regulatory and monetary concerns. GATS has only begun this process.

The GATS, by its terms, applies to measures by Member States that affect trade in services. Accounting standards set by government entities must be viewed as affecting trade in accounting, investment banking, stock exchange, and legal services. Of course, in some countries, accounting standards are set by non-governmental bodies, such as professional accounting organizations or stock exchanges. Where such standards are not given the force of law and do not otherwise amount to measures by Member States, they would not be subject to the GATS. Accounting standards would not necessarily prohibit trade in services, but might make it more difficult and expensive for foreign service suppliers to compete. The effect on investment banking and legal services would be ameliorated by comparison to the effect on accounting services and stock-exchange services, but still present.

We review here both the provisions of GATS itself, and the additional provisions of (a) the GATS Annexe on Financial Services (the Annexe) and

'The Standard Setters: As the Influence of the International Accounting Standards Committee Grows, Christopher Nobes Explains How it Works', *Financial Times*, 10 Oct. 1996, 12; 'Accountancy: Turning the Multinationals Inside Out: Paul Pactor on the International Accounting Standards Committee's Efforts to Require Better Information about "Segments" in Companies', *Financial Times*, 30 May 1996, 28.

[16] Lee H. Radebaugh and Sidney J. Gray, *International Accounting and Multinational Enterprises* (New York, NY: John Wiley & Sons, Inc., 1997), 188, citing International Accounting Standards Committee.

[17] See, e.g. Joel P. Trachtman, 'International Regulatory Competition, Externalization and Jurisdiction', *Harvard International Law Journal*, vol. 34 (1993), 47; Joel P. Trachtman, 'Recent Initiatives in International Financial Regulation and Goals of Competitiveness, Effectiveness, Consistency and Cooperation', *Northwestern Journal of International Law and Business*, vol. 12 (1991), 241.

(b) the GATS Understanding on Commitments in Financial Services (the Understanding). GATS annexes are an integral part of the GATS itself, and in circumstances of conflict the provisions of the Annexe that deal more specifically with financial services would be expected to control the more general provisions of GATS.

The Annexe applies to 'measures affecting the supply of financial services'. 'Financial services', in turn, is defined to include, *inter alia*, '[p]articipation in issues of all kinds of securities, including underwriting and placement as agent . . . and provision of services related to such issues' and '[a]dvisory, intermediation and other auxiliary financial services on all the activities listed [above], including credit reference and analysis, investment and portfolio research and advice, advice on acquisitions and on corporate restructuring and strategy'. This definition is in part circular (financial services includes 'advisory, intermediation and other auxiliary financial services'), and it is difficult to say the extent to which preparation of financial statements required for a public offering or listing would be included. It is clear that investment banking, including both dealing and underwriting securities, is included. Of course, one argument would be that the *expressio unius* principle of interpretation would seem to exclude auxiliary services beyond those listed. Without rehearsing all the interpretive arguments, suffice it to say here that while it is not clear that accounting, legal, and stock-exchange services relating to a public offering or listing of securities are excluded from the definition of financial services, the better argument is probably that they are. However, in order to be covered by the Annexe, preparation of financial statements need not be a financial service. Rather, the requirement is that the 'measure' (in this case the regulatory requirement) affect the 'supply of financial services'. As argued above, it seems reasonably clear that these regulatory requirements do affect the supply of investment banking and stock-exchange services. Thus, it appears that the Annexe would apply to such regulatory requirements.

A. Article VI of GATS: domestic regulation

First, much of Article VI only covers sectors in which specific commitments have been undertaken. Within such sectors, Article VI(1) imposes requirements for reasonable, objective, and impartial administration of all measures of general application, as well as procedural safeguards.

Article VI(4), which appears to be applicable regardless of the member's commitments, is forward-looking, calling on the WTO's Council for Trade in Services to develop any necessary disciplines 'with a view to ensuring that measures relating to qualification requirements and procedures, technical standards and licensing requirements do not constitute unnecessary barriers to trade in services . . . '. Such disciplines would ensure, *inter alia*, that such requirements are 'not more burdensome than necessary to ensure the quality of the service . . . '. This, of course, is not a proportionality requirement per se, but an agreement to develop disciplines based on a proportionality standard. Given the indefiniteness of the proportionality standard, it is difficult to see this provision as strongly binding in a legal sense.

The Uruguay Round Decision on Professional Services calls for the work programme under Article VI(4) to be put into effect immediately as to professional services, and calls for the establishment of a Working Party on Professional Services to develop 'the disciplines necessary to ensure that measures relating to qualification requirements and procedures, technical standards and licensing requirements in the field of professional services do not constitute unnecessary barriers to trade'. The Decision on Professional Services also establishes work in the accountancy sector of professional services as a priority, calling *inter alia* for establishment of disciplines referenced in Article VI(4) and the use of international standards. It further calls on the Working Party on Professional Services to 'encourage the cooperation with the relevant international organizations as defined under paragraph 5(b) of Article VI, so as to give full effect to paragraph 5 of Article VII'.[18] The CTS adopted on 14 December 1998 the *Disciplines on Domestic Regulation in the Accountancy Sector*,[19] developed by the WTO Working Party on Professional Services. These disciplines apply to all Member States that have made specific commitments in accountancy but do not apply to national measures listed as exceptions under Articles XVI (market access) and XVII (national treatment). They generally articulate further and tighten the principle of necessity: that measures should be the least trade-restrictive method to effect a legitimate objective.

The provision of Article VI that imposes present disciplines of interest here is Article VI(5), which is limited to sectors in which the Member has undertaken specific commitments,[20] and is further limited to the period prior to the entry into force of disciplines developed under Article VI(4): it is an interim device. During this period, 'the Member shall not apply licensing and qualification requirements and technical standards that nullify or impair such specific commitments in a manner which' *inter alia*, is more burdensome than necessary to ensure the quality of the service, and

---

[18] Article VII(5), as discussed below, calls for recognition based on multilaterally agreed criteria, requiring that states 'work in cooperation with relevant intergovernmental and nongovernmental organizations towards the establishment and adoption of common international standards and criteria for recognition . . . '. GATS Article VII (5).

[19] WTO Focus, Dec. 1998, 10–11.

[20] It should be noted here that the US schedule of commitments stated that the non-insurance financial services subsector is 'unbound' with respect to market access through cross-border supply and commercial presence for expansion or new activities. This exception could be the basis for an argument by the United States that the disciplines of Article VI(5) do not apply to new or expanded services in this subsector.

'could not reasonably have been expected of that Member at the time the specific commitments in those sectors were made'.[21] In determining whether a Member is conforming with these obligations, account is required to be taken 'of international standards of relevant international organizations applied by that Member'.[22] The elements of this test thus include (i) nullification or impairment of a concession, (ii) proportionality, and (iii) reasonable expectations. The reference to international standards presumably amplifies the proportionality test.[23]

These provisions represent a limited set of disciplines, a compromise, and an agreement to engage in further work in the future regarding the application of standards to services. This treatment reflects concerns that the services sector is heterogeneous enough to confound attempts to apply generic disciplines on standards. The remainder of this subsection considers the application of these disciplines to the IASC standards project, and to a *hypothetical* future failure by the US SEC to accept IASC standards for listings or public offerings.

B. Application of Article VI of GATS to hypothetical US failure to accept IASC standards

It is at least possible that the US SEC may reject the IASC standards. Perhaps a German or Malaysian company would then seek to list or engage in a public offering in the US on the basis of the IASC standards and be refused. Or perhaps a British accounting firm would find that one or more of its clients begin preparing their financial statements in accordance with US GAAP, and replace the UK firm with a US-based accounting firm. Of course, in the latter case, it might be argued that there is no impediment to trade in services, as the British firm would have provided the services locally, or it may be that the services provided by the US-based accounting firm are provided from London, again raising the question of whether any trade in services issue is presented. Let us assume for purposes of this analysis that a trade in services issue is presented sufficiently for application of GATS to this hypothetical.

---

[21] GATS Article VI(5). For economy of exposition, I have not included here the criteria that do not seem applicable to accounting standards: whether the requirements are based on objective and transparent criteria and, in the case of licensing procedures, whether they are themselves restrictions on the supply of the service.

[22] GATS Article VI(5) (citation omitted). The omitted footnote defines the term 'relevant international organizations' as 'international bodies whose membership is open to the relevant bodies of at least all Members of the WTO'. It appears that the Council of Ministers, at the Singapore Ministerial, designated the IFAC, IASC, and IOSCO as the 'relevant international organizations'.

[23] That is, a measure may be viewed as disproportionate in relation to the fact that international measures exist, whereas if the international measures did not exist, the measure might be proportionate. This concept is clearly expressed in the jurisprudence of the European Court of Justice under former Articles 30 and 36 of the Treaty of Rome. It is also specifically included in the Standards Agreement.

As noted above, assuming that the WTO Council for Trade in Services has not acted as to accounting standards under Article VI(4) of GATS, the operative discipline would be provided by Article VI(5): this test includes (i) nullification or impairment of a concession, (ii) lack of proportionality, and (iii) unexpectedness.

Nullification or impairment. The structure of this provision makes it possible to argue that the 'nullification or impairment' prong of this test should be deemed satisfied, by virtue of the fact that a measure satisfies the second and third prongs. However, a strong counter-argument would recall that in GATT, nullification or impairment is only presumed where there is a violation of the agreement itself. Here, there is no separate violation. Thus, it may be necessary to show trade effects—in our case, to show that the US regulatory requirements actually nullify or impair the US commitments under GATS. As discussed above, due to the structure of the commitments, it may be less than clear that US accounting standards have effects on *trade* in services.

Proportionality. The 'proportionality' prong of the test, enquiring whether the requirements are 'more burdensome than necessary to ensure the quality of the service', invokes a significant GATT and WTO jurisprudence. The 'necessity' qualifications contained in Article XX(b) and (d) of GATT have been interpreted to require the national measure to be the least trade-restrictive alternative reasonably available. The language contained in Article VI(4) of GATS, and incorporated by reference in Article VI(5), seems designed to invoke this jurisprudence (although it does not explicitly include the reasonableness criterion). The proportionality of requirements for compliance with or reconciliation to US GAAP would be argued by the SEC to be 'not more burdensome than necessary' to protect investors. Several arguments would be raised in response.

The first type of argument is relatively simple. It is the argument, raised by economists like William Baumol and Burton Malkiel,[24] to the effect that reconciliation is unnecessary. This argument, based on the efficient capital markets hypothesis (ECMH), argues that price-setters in liquid markets do not need reconciliation, but are capable of comparing financial statements on their own (presumably at lower cost than that associated with reconciliation by the issuer). Therefore, for the rest of us, we can rely on market prices and need investigate no further. Of course, the ECMH has its limitations.[25] Moreover, this argument proves too much. It suggests that regulatory requirements for US GAAP are unnecessary for domestic issuers

[24] William J. Baumol and Burton G. Malkiel, 'Redundant Regulation of Foreign Security Trading and US Competitiveness', in Kenneth Lehn and Robert W. Kamphuis (eds), *Modernizing US Securities Regulation: Economic and Legal Perspectives* (Burr Ridge, Illinois: Irwin Professional Publishing, 1992).

[25] See generally Andrew W. Lo (ed.), *Market Efficiency: Stock Market Behaviour In Theory and In Practice* (Cheltenham, Glos., UK; Lyme, NH: Edward Elgar Pub., 1997).

as well as for foreign issuers. While this may (or may not) be correct, repeal of this requirement for domestic issuers is not a serious prospect at the moment. A similar analytical perspective might consider changes in stock price as indicators of regulatory utility, suggesting that the reconciliation requirement does not pass the simple means-ends rationality test. 'It is interesting to note,' argues one observer, 'that when Daimler-Benz agreed with the SEC to flow through to their profit and loss statement some $2.5 billion of reserves, the stock did not budge on the Frankfurt Stock Exchange. Apparently, in their own way, investors already knew of the presence of these reserves.'[26]

The second type of argument is more nuanced. It is that exceptions to requirements for reconciliation suggest that the requirement is unnecessary where it is maintained: selective application indicates lack of necessity. Consider the following two exceptions. First, issuers that have not effected a US public offering, the securities of which trade on the 'pink sheets',[27] i.e. are not traded on an exchange or on NASDAQ, under Rule 12g3–2(b) pursuant to the Exchange Act, are not required to provide any reconciliation. However, these securities present the same risks of unreconciled financial statements as listed companies. Perhaps the SEC's argument here would be that the location on the pink sheets put investors on notice that there is limited disclosure regarding these companies. Second, foreign issuers may effect public offerings abroad under Regulation S, combined with private placements in the United States, and subsequent trading of those privately placed securities under Rule 144A, without required reconciliation. A similar argument recalls the fact that US investors can go abroad and frustrate protections. The SEC, under Regulation S, has in effect deemed the decision of a US investor to purchase abroad (under certain circumstances described in Regulation S) a kind of waiver of at least the protections of the registration requirements under the Securities Act. However, the SEC has not viewed this action as a waiver of the protections of the antifraud laws.

Subject to the exceptions discussed below, these types of arguments regarding proportionality or necessity could well be successful in an attack on US reconciliation requirements, especially after an international standard is set in place by the IASC, as suggested by Article VI(5)(b) of the GATS. IOSCO's endorsement on 17 May 2000 of thirty core standards

---

[26] William C. Freund, 'Two SEC Rules in an Era of Global Equities Trading', ch. 23 in Robert A. Schwartz (ed.), *Global Equity Markets: Technological, Competitive, and Regulatory Challenges* (McGraw Hill Professional Book Group, 1995), 371, 375.

[27] See, e.g. James L. Cochrane, 'Are US Regulatory Requirements for Foreign Firms Appropriate?', *Fordham Journal of International Law*, vol. 17 (1994), S58, S60: 'Retail investors are certainly not being protected by current SEC policy, which forces the securities of world-class foreign companies that have not reconciled to US GAAP to trade on the over-the-counter electronic bulletin board where no financial information is made available to investors' (citations omitted).

would, if unqualified, support an attack on US reconciliation requirements, as it would set a multilateral standard to which a dispute resolution panel or the Appellate Body might refer. However, the qualifications included in IOSCO's endorsement of the standards would substantially weaken this attack.

Reasonable expectations. Under this third prong, it seems relatively clear that there would be little ground for attack against pre-existing regulations. It does not seem possible to argue that the US system for reconciliation 'could not reasonably have been expected' of the United States 'at the time the specific commitments in those sectors were made'.

Thus, there seems little potential basis for a successful attack under Article VI(5) against the application of US accounting standards to foreign issuers.

C. Article 2 of the Annexe on Financial Services and Article XIV of the GATS

Even so, Article 2(a) of the Annexe, if applicable, would cut a wide swath in any disciplines otherwise imposed by Article VI of GATS. It provides that:

[n]otwithstanding any other provisions of the Agreement, a Member shall not be prevented from taking measures for prudential reasons, including for the protection of investors . . . or to ensure the integrity and stability of the financial system. Where such measures do not conform with the provisions of the Agreement, they shall not be used as a means of avoiding the Member's commitments or obligations under the Agreement.

These are broad justificatory bases, and this provision is not qualified by a necessity or other proportionality requirement. It is possible that it would be argued that the requirement that measures under this provision be 'for prudential reasons' imposes at least a requirement of simple means-ends rationality, but it does not impose a least-trade-restrictive alternative requirement, as might result from a 'necessity' qualifier, nor does this provision contain a reasonableness requirement. Interestingly, here, the necessity qualifier is already included in the prohibition: Article VI(5) of GATS prohibits requirements that are more burdensome than 'necessary to ensure the quality of the service'. Thus, the intent is clearly that even 'unnecessary' prudential regulation is to be protected from scrutiny. Only financial regulation so unnecessary that it lacks 'prudential reasons' is subject to discipline.

The only clear limitation on regulation under Article 2(a) of the Annexe is quite limited and is provided in the last sentence: regulation may not intentionally be used as a means of defection. Interestingly, some argue that US reconciliation requirements may actually harm the competitiveness of US financial service providers such as investment banks and stock exchanges. If this is true, these measures might not be viewed as a means by which the United States seeks to avoid its commitments in these sectors. However, the reference at the end of Article 2(a) is to 'means of avoiding the Member's commitments or obligations under the [GATS]', and thus may refer to commitments in the accounting sector or other service sector. To the extent accounting services in connection with securities offerings are included, there is at least a colourable argument that the reconciliation requirements have the effect of protecting US accounting firms, and perhaps some evidence could be adduced to the effect that this protection is intentional.

Because of the wide scope of Article 2(a) of the Annexe, it becomes important to know whether the Annexe is applicable to measures setting financial accounting standards. The Annexe purports to apply to 'measures affecting the supply of financial services'. As noted above, the definition of 'financial services' does not provide a clear resolution to this question. However, as outlined above, it would appear that the better argument is that the establishment of financial accounting standards required by law is a 'measure' affecting the supply of financial services, despite the fact that it also affects, also indirectly, the supply of accounting services. This interpretation would comport with a view that the WTO agreements should be interpreted narrowly in order to avoid constraints on sovereignty that have not been undertaken expressly. A similar argument would suggest that the exception in Article 2(a) of the Annexe be interpreted broadly to include all measures affecting financial services, regardless of whether they affect other services.

If Article 2(a) of the Annexe were found inapplicable, domestic regulation might still be protected from challenge under Article XIV of GATS. Article XIV plays a similar function in the GATS to Article XX in the GATT: it delineates some areas of permitted exceptions from the obligations otherwise imposed by GATS. The relevant part of Article XIV for our purposes is Article XIV(c), which provides an exception for measures that, in relevant part, (i) are not applied in a manner which would constitute a means of arbitrary or unjustifiable discrimination or a disguised restriction on trade, and (ii) are necessary to secure compliance with laws or regulations not inconsistent with the provisions of the GATS including those relating to the 'prevention of deceptive and fraudulent practices or to deal with the effects of a default on services contracts'.[28] There may well be circumstances in which national accounting standards would satisfy these criteria: perhaps the argument would go that these standards are necessary to secure compliance with the antifraud laws.

Interestingly, the very promulgation of international accounting standards may reduce the ability of a state to rely on this provision, as the

---

[28] GATS Article XIV(c)

maintenance of differing accounting standards might no longer be the least trade restrictive means to achieve the regulatory goal. On the other hand, it might be argued by states such as the United States that the global diversity of accounting standards alone renders its requirement of reconciliation necessary to prevent deceptive practices. The success of this argument would depend, *inter alia*, on the definition of deceptive practices. For example, does the use of hidden reserves constitute a deceptive practice? This argument would also be subject to refutation by efficient capital markets theory, holding that price-setters in capital markets do not rely on compliance with US GAAP.

IV. SUMMARY OF REGULATORY ALTERNATIVES

Negotiation of international accounting standards adds multiple levels of complexity to the process of establishing domestic accounting standards. Both international trade concerns and foreign prudential concerns must be incorporated in the decision process. There are substantial issues of path dependency and coordination. From the standpoint of a national securities regulator, such as the SEC, or from the standpoint of a regional or multilateral community, there are several regulatory alternatives:

National treatment. The status quo prior to the conclusion of the Uruguay Round for accounting standards would include in most cases autonomously provided national treatment—application of local accounting standards to foreign firms, plus ad hoc findings of equivalence and progressive unilateral liberalization. It is important to recognize that the SEC has already taken a number of steps, both in specific cases, and in rules of general applicability, to moderate the difficulty experienced by foreign registrants. This action is taken autonomously, pursuant to pressure from domestic and foreign sources.

Disciplined autonomy. At this moment, it appears that GATS provides only marginally disciplined autonomy, in the form of proportionality requirements or specified market access requirements, to states in the accounting standards sector. The scope and effect of these disciplines remains to be worked out.

Harmonization. GATS provides a facility for harmonization or other similar activities that has not yet been utilized in the accountancy sector (or any other). We have distinguished between harmonization of rules applicable to foreign issuers only, and harmonization of rules applicable to all issuers, foreign and domestic.

Recognition and market segmentation. GATS also permits recognition. Recognition is different from harmonization, although it may operate in synergy with harmonization, as in the European Community. Segmentation in this context refers to the creation of exceptions from reconciliation, such as those for companies that trade in the pink sheets or those traded under Rule 144A. Another example of segmentation is the New York Stock Exchange proposal for an exemption from reconciliation for certain 'world class' issuers.[29]

Essential harmonization combined with mutual recognition. Essential harmonization is sometimes a predicate for mutual recognition regimes in the European Community. The US–Canadian Multijurisdictional Disclosure System is another (limited) example of this model. Of course, regional or other non-multilateral regimes for mutual recognition raise MFN ('most favoured nation') issues. The IASC programme may be viewed not as essential harmonization, but as a type of sectoral harmonization, intended only for international issuers. Furthermore, the IASC programme does not involve direct recognition of national regimes, but recognition of international standards.

V. CONCLUSIONS: TOWARDS A COST–BENEFIT ANALYSIS METHODOLOGY

The foregoing analysis has indicated that a WTO or NAFTA dispute resolution tribunal would be likely to have little mandate to evaluate domestic accounting standards. Elsewhere, I have suggested that cost–benefit analysis would be the obvious methodology to be applied to the question of whether autonomy in accounting standards should be maintained, or sacrificed by harmonization or recognition to values of economic integration, and more realistically, to what extent this sacrifice should take place.[30] Where dispute resolution tribunals are not empowered to engage in an evaluative analysis of national regulation, we may read this disempowerment as a determination to address these issues in a more political forum. Political fora have significant advantages (and disadvantages) in relation to adjudicative fora as cost–benefit analysts. For one, they have significantly greater ability to award compensation of one sort or another to those harmed by the adoption of a standard. This contribution cannot suggest how political fora should finally decide these questions, but it can suggest some categories of costs and benefits for evaluation. Non-governmental organizations, such as IOSCO (an intergovernmental organization) and IASC (a private-membership organization) act as agents of States to enter into agreements, or to prepare the way for States to enter into agreements.

[29] See James L. Cochrane, 'Assessing and Evaluating the Current Directions of Transnational Listings', New York Stock Exchange Working Paper 93-03, 29 June 1993.

[30] See Joel P. Trachtman, 'The Theory of the Firm and the Theory of the International Economic Organization: Toward Comparative Institutional Analysis', *Northwestern Journal of International Law & Business*, vol. 17 (1997), 470–555.

A. Accounting standards and diverse regulatory goals

'You manage what you measure.'[31] Different societies, with different economic systems and structures, emphasize different management goals, and accordingly, have different expectations with respect to their accounting standards. Without evaluating or quantifying these different goals, it seems evident that there is some value to diversity. However, to the extent that the consumers of financial statements are the capital markets, the internationalization of capital markets would appear to diminish the value of customization of accounting standards for the local capital market: the local capital market will only consume a part of the financial statements. Thus, the value of diversity may change based on variations in financing and other business patterns. In addition, standardization always favours some and disfavours others. Standardization in the financial accounting field will no doubt move towards a US GAAP, but the important question is how far will it move in that direction.

B. Accounting standards and path dependency

It is also important to recognize that, while national accounting standards are designed to address particular national economic goals, they are a product of history. The development of national accounting standards is thus affected by path dependency. Path dependency may be interpreted as a particular category of optimization of institutions: optimization of fit taking the institutional context into effect. The institutional context represents the accretion of social capital over time: path dependency is largely another term for recognition of the value of that capital. However, the fact remains that national accounting standards become costly to change simply because they exist and are used: they generate positive network externalities. Changing to a new system produces local losses, especially to local accounting firms whose intellectual capital becomes less valuable. These local losses may be countervailed by local benefits, or if they are not, presumably they will only be accepted where the foreign benefits are great enough to provide the capacity for compensation to the losers.

C. Trade in services benefits of harmonization and/or recognition

The benefits of harmonization are of two main kinds. First, harmonization produces broader economies of scale and reduces the costs of learning new accounting standards for different systems. Second, and in part arising from the first, harmonization produces greater scope for competition, presumably reducing prices and enhancing quality. Recognition provides similar trade in services benefits, by a different mechanism. Recognition allows foreign service providers to provide competitive services under different rules, thus allowing them to compete with local service providers. In fact, as we have seen in Europe and in the MDS, recognition is often predicated on a degree of harmonization.

D. Other economic integration benefits of harmonization/recognition: free movement of capital

Of course, the analysis of international accounting standards would be incomplete without considering the goal of free movement of capital. Diversity of accounting standards for securities offerings or listings impedes free movement of capital by segmenting capital markets. Thus, even if there were no trade benefits arising from international cooperation with respect to accounting standards, capital movement benefits might provide a justification.

E. Institutions and transaction costs of regulatory cooperation and integration

Finally, cost–benefit analysis of the utility of international cooperation with respect to accounting standards must consider the costs of cooperation itself. Without organizations such as IASC or IOSCO, cooperation would presumably be more difficult. These organizations gather data as well as promote discussion and agreement. Of course, they involve costs themselves. The decision of States to fund these organizations or participate in them is presumably a transaction costs-economizing decision. Presumably, cooperation through these organizations is cheaper and/or more effective than cooperation without them.

It is of interest that the WTO has deferred to specialized functional organizations, such as IFAC, IASC, and IOSCO in the accounting standards field, for implementation of the WTO mandate to negotiate the reduction of barriers to trade in services. These specialized organizations certainly have expertise that the WTO lacks. However, they also lack some of the useful features that the WTO provides, such as the ability to facilitate cross-sectoral negotiations, as well as cross-sectoral retaliation, strengthened dispute resolution, and sensitivity to trade effects. It will be of further interest to examine how links between the WTO and these functional organizations are developed to utilize the beneficial features of each.

These institutional costs and benefits must be considered along with the substantive costs and benefits of harmonization or recognition of accounting standards, and the distributive effects of harmonization or recognition.

Competition law: linking the world

Eleanor M. Fox

I. INTRODUCTION

Competition law is uniquely related to market systems. The law helps to remove artificial business restraints on trade and competition and thereby to make markets work. But the question arises: to what end and for whose benefit? Answers to this question have differed over time and among nations. They derive from both political economy and economics. Prominently, they include: (1) freedom of enterprise, which may be both a value in itself and an instrument to assure that markets, not men and not autocrats, govern the economy, (2) economic efficiency, and (3) protection of weak economic actors from abuses of powerful firms. Whatever the mix of goals, there is a large degree of harmony among them in the sense that competition rules designed to effectuate any one of these goals overlap significantly (but by no means completely) with competition rules designed to effectuate the other goals.

Nations increasingly are adopting competition laws; and economic problems are increasingly transnational. The increasing incidence of problems that transcend national borders and the attendant conflicts of national legal systems have led to calls for greater cooperation among nations' antitrust authorities and convergence of legal rules, on the one hand, and for international conceptions of law and of process, on the other. Indeed, these events and conflicts have led to 'warring factions'; those who argue passionately that answers must be found in internationalization (higher law or principles), and those who insist, with equal passion, that antitrust must and should remain national.

In this contribution I will review the state of play and the existing tools available for addressing the problems. I will then propose a conception for internationalization that retains as much subsidiarity as possible,[1] consistent with realizing synergies from an open trade-and-competition system among nations.

---

[1] That which can be done as well or better at the lower level of government should remain at the lower level.

II. CONFLICT, COOPERATION, AND COMITY

The early issues of international antitrust were issues of conflict and cooperation. Jurisdictions cooperated in information sharing when they had common interests, as was the case in connection with the European-based quinine cartel, which was discovered by the Americans when the Dutch ringleader overbought quinine bark from the US stockpile. The US authorities not only prosecuted the cartelists but gave the incriminating tip to the European authorities.[2]

The notorious cases, however, were predictably not those of cooperation but those of conflict. The early conflicts involved extraterritorial use of US antitrust law, allegedly invading the sovereignty of US trading partners. In this period, before the end of the 1980s, the preferred way to resolve conflicts, if they were to be resolved, was respect and retreat in the interests of comity (negative comity). After balancing interests, however, the United States virtually never respected or retreated.[3]

In any event, antitrust clashes of the 1970s, and particularly the perception that the US agencies and courts had exceeded jurisdictional bounds and tread on other nations' sovereignty, led to the negotiation and adoption of three memoranda of understanding (MOUs). Agreements were signed by the United States and Germany (1976), the United States and Australia (1982), and the United States and Canada (1984, superseded by an expanded agreement in 1995). These agreements provide for notification by one authority of its actions that may affect the important interests of the other party, consultations if there is a conflict of interests, and cooperation in gathering and sharing information of mutual benefit. The major purpose of the MOUs was to resolve or modulate conflicts of interest by the exercise of restraint.

Meanwhile, however, the number of free-enterprise nations grew. The antitrust community of nations grew. A critical mass of nations began to accept the legitimacy of 'inbound' extraterritoriality: i.e. the notion that a regulating State may reprehend an offshore cartel targeted at the regulating nation, and possibly also other offshore anticompetitive conduct or transactions having a direct, substantial, and foreseeable effect on competition within the regulating nation. Indeed, absent such a rule, national competition policy would be so limited and the law would be so toothless in the face of harms launched in the global economy that an international law of antitrust would surely already have been put into place.

---

[2] See Case 41/69, ACF *Chemiefarma v. Commission (Quinine)*, 1970 ECR 661.

[3] See Eleanor M. Fox, 'Extraterritoriality, Antitrust, and the New Restatement: Is Reasonableness the Answer?', *New York University Journal of International Law & Politics*, vol. 19 (1987), 565.

A new initiative evolved—one of *positive* comity. A second generation of bilateral agreements was designed principally to enhance positive measures; i.e. assistance in investigation and enforcement. The era of positive comity blossomed in 1991,[4] when the United States and the European Commission signed a Cooperation Agreement Regarding the Application of their Competition Laws.[5] The most innovative article (Article V) lays the groundwork for one party to take action to protect market access of the other. If one party believes that anticompetitive acts taken on the territory of the other are adversely affecting its important interests, it may request the other to initiate enforcement activities. The notified party will consider the request and advise the notifying party of its decision, and of developments. The Cooperation Agreement (Article II) provides also for notification of enforcement activities that may affect the other's important interests. Notification should be given far enough in advance of a complaint or settlement for the enforcing party to take the other's views into account. The parties agree to exchange information in order to promote understanding, to assist enforcement and coordination of parallel enforcement, and, based on comity factors, to avoid conflicts.

In 1998 the United States and the European Union clarified and strengthened Article V. The scope and purpose clause of the 1998 Agreement (which excludes mergers from its purview) explains:

1. This Agreement applies where a Party satisfies the other that there is reason to believe that the following circumstances are present:

(a) Anticompetitive activities are occurring in whole or in substantial part in the territory of one of the Parties and are adversely affecting the interests of the other Party; and

(b) The activities in question are impermissible under the competition laws of the Party in the territory of which the activities are occurring.

2. The purposes of this Agreement are to:

(a) Help ensure that trade and investment flows between the Parties and competition and consumer welfare within the territories of the Parties are not impeded by anticompetitive activities for which the competition laws of one or both Parties can provide a remedy; and

(b) Establish cooperative procedures to achieve the most effective and efficient enforcement of competition law, whereby the competition authorities of each Party will normally avoid allocating enforcement resources to dealing with anticompetitive activities that occur principally in and are directed principally towards the other Party's territory, where the competition authorities of the other Party are able and prepared to examine and take effective sanctions under their law to deal with those activities.[6]

---

[4] The United States had already entered into a number of Mutual Legal Assistance Treaties (MLATs), whereby nations agree to assist one another in the enforcement of criminal law. The Canadian MLAT (1988) specifically includes assistance in criminal antitrust enforcement.

[5] Reprinted at CCH Trade Reg. Rep. ¶ 13,504.   [6] Ibid.

Seeds of the 1998 Agreement were sown in 1992, following on the heels of the Strategic Impediments Initiative between the United States and Japan.[7] The United States announced that it may use US antitrust law to open foreign markets closed by anticompetitive restraints (e.g. if a boycott or exclusionary restraints in Japan keep American exports out of Japan) if the host country fails to enforce its own antitrust laws. An implicit purpose of the 1998 agreement on the part of the European Union was precisely to forestall US 'outbound' extraterritorial enforcement of US antitrust laws to pry open the EU market if it is allegedly closed by private restraints.[8]

Under the 1998 agreement, a party may request enforcement by the competition authority of the territory wherein competition is allegedly lessened, and the two parties may then agree that the requesting party will suspend its contemplated enforcement. The requesting party will normally suspend its enforcement if: (a) the challenged acts 'do not have a direct, substantial and reasonably foreseeable impact on consumers in the Requesting Party's territory', or the acts 'occur principally in and are directed principally towards the other Party's territory' (Article IV.2(a)(i) and (b)), the adverse effects on the Requesting Party are likely to be adequately remedied in the Requested Party's jurisdiction (2(b)), and (c)), and the Requested Party agrees to devote adequate resources, use best efforts, and notify the Requesting Party of intentions and status and take into account its views (2(c)).

The United States made one referral to the European Commission in anticipation of, and then under, the 1998 agreement: the claim that SABRE, a US-based computer airline reservation system, has been blocked from effective competition in the French, German, and Spanish markets for computer airline reservation services as a result of anticompetitive refusals to supply current flight information by the French, German, and Spanish airlines that own the competing (and dominant) computer reservation system, Amadeus. After two years of investigation, the European Union commenced proceedings against (only) Air France.

Other cooperation has proceeded simply because the agencies have common interests and the investigated party cooperates by allowing the agencies to share its business documents for purposes of the investigation, proceedings, and settlement. Microsoft I (the 1995 consent decree) and the MCI/WorldCom merger were products of such cooperation between the

---

[7] See Mitsuo Matsushita, *The Antimonopoly Law of Japan*, chap. 5 at 151, 155, 184, and Eleanor M. Fox and Robert Pitofsky, chap. 7 at 235, 239, 265, in E. M. Graham and J. D. Richardson (eds), *Global Competition Policy* (Institute for International Economics 1997).

[8] See Karel van Miert, 'International Cooperation in the Field of Competition: A View From the EC', chap. 2 in B. Hawk (ed.), *International Antitrust Law & Policy 1997*, Annual Proceedings of the Fordham Corporate Law Institute, vol. 11 (Yonkers, NY: Juris Publishing, 1998).

US Department of Justice and the Competition Directorate of the European Commission.[9]

Meanwhile, the US Department of Justice has faced a different problem. It has been frustrated in its enforcement against international cartels because of the difficulty of obtaining evidence located abroad. To facilitate the obtaining of foreign-located evidence, it proposed and Congress enacted the International Antitrust Enforcement Assistance Act of 1994. The act authorizes the Attorney General of the United States and the Federal Trade Commission to conduct investigations and provide antitrust evidence to foreign authorities regarding a possible violation of the foreign antitrust laws (even if the conduct does not violate the US antitrust laws, as through an export cartel) if the US authorities are confident that the foreign authorities can and will reciprocate in providing information to the US authorities and that the foreign authorities will safeguard the confidence of the information provided. The act contemplates that reciprocating countries will enter into mutual assistance agreements pursuant to the act. Nations have been reluctant to enter into such agreements, for they fear that the United States, not they, will be the beneficiaries, and they fear that the shared information might be used against their firms for purposes that go beyond the US request (e.g. for private class actions and treble-damage cases). It was not until 1999 that a trading partner—Australia—entered into such an agreement with the United States.

III. INTERNATIONALIZATION

In 1992 Sir Leon Brittan, European Commissioner in Charge of External Relations for the European Union and previously Commissioner in Charge of Competition, gave a now-famous speech at Davos, Switzerland. He noted that, in the shrinking world, private restraints of trade and competition are a pressing problem; they distort the playing field as public restraints recede. He called for an internationalization of competition law and integration of competition law with issues of trade. Thereafter Karel van Miert, European Commissioner in Charge of Competition, appointed a Group of Experts, who studied the issues. Their Report, submitted in 1995, supports an international initiative.[10] The Report proposes that the

---

[9] See *United States v. Microsoft Corp.*, 1995–2 Trade Cas. (CCH) ¶ 71,096 (DDC 1995); European Commission Press Release, 'Commission Clears WorldCom and MCI Merger Subject to Conditions' (8 July 1998); US Department of Justice Press Release, 'Justice Department Clears WorldCom/MCI Merger After MCI Agrees to Sell Its Internet Business' (15 July 1998).

[10] Report of the Group of Experts, *Competition Policy in the New Trade Order: Strengthening International Cooperation and Rules* (reproduced for discussion purposes, European Commission, 1995). The members of the group of experts are, as external experts, Ulrich Immenga, Frédéric Jenny, and Ernst-Ulrich Petersmann; and, as Commission experts,

initiative be built upon a foundation of agency cooperation, including bilateral agreements with positive comity, and that at later stages it should proceed to the adoption of common minimum rules for acts and transactions of international dimension, with a system for dispute resolution.

The Report of the Group of Experts and ensuing related proposals were not well received in the United States. The US antitrust authorities opined that their own tools for enforcement combined with bilateral cooperation were adequate to deal with international problems, and that a multilateral or plurilateral initiative would lead to the corruption of antitrust principles (which aid consumers) by trade principles (which protect competitors); to the watering down of US antitrust rules to the lowest common denominator as a result of bargaining with nations not committed to efficient competition; and to a distant and growing bureaucracy and the settlement of disputes by unknown and untrusted jurists or bureaucrats. Moreover, if the enterprise should be brought within the purview of the World Trade Organization, officials say, this would increase the threat of reducing antitrust to trade law, and it would place a burden on the WTO that it cannot bear.[11]

On the other side of the ocean, the European Union vetted the Experts' ideas through the various interested directorate generals of the European Commission and through the European Commission and Council, and proposed the launching of an initiative on trade and competition at the Singapore Ministerial Meeting of the WTO in December 1996. While the United States at first opposed the initiative, it ultimately agreed with a recommendation—which was adopted—that a Working Group on the Interaction Between Trade and Competition Policy be created and given a two-year life, on condition that the group be empowered only to *discuss* the issues and enhance mutual knowledge, and on condition that formation of the group did not imply a next step.

As the WTO Working Group began its meetings, the US antitrust authorities proposed an initiative within the Organization for Economic Cooperation and Development—its preferred forum because the OECD members are 'like' (industrialized) nations, and because the OECD has no dispute resolution mechanism. The United States proposed and secured a Recommendation Concerning Effective Action against Hard Core Cartels. Such a recommendation, which could facilitate soft convergence of law, was adopted at the OECD ministerial meeting in Paris in April 1998.[12] The

Claus-Dieter Ehlermann, Jean-François Pons, Roderick Abbott, François Lamoreux, Jean François Marchipont, and Alexis Jacquemin.

[11] See Joel Klein, 'Anticipating the Millennium: International Antitrust Enforcement at the End of the Twentieth Century', chap. 1 in Hawk (ed.), *International Antitrust Law* (above, n. 8).

[12] Recommendation of the Council Concerning Effective Action Against 'Hard Core' Cartels, C(98)35, adopted at Paris, 27–8 Apr. 1998. The recommendation bears strengthening to narrow the exceptions.

document recommends to Member countries that they ensure that their competition laws effectively halt and deter hard-core cartels. The recommendation is subject to any exceptions and authorizations in the Member countries' laws, but, it provides, those derogations should be transparent and should be reviewed periodically to assess whether they are necessary and tailored to overriding policy objectives.

Meanwhile, since the end of the Uruguay Round, the WTO has been expanding its competences, and some of its new or extended competences touch upon issues of antitrust. The Agreement on Trade-Related Aspects of Intellectual Property (TRIPs), Article 40, states that members are authorized to enact laws against intellectual property licensing practices 'having an adverse effect on competition'. The General Agreement on Trade in Services (GATS), Article 9.1, requires each member to prohibit suppliers of monopoly services in its territory from abusing their market power in conflict with the obligation of most-favoured-nation treatment (thus the article forbids discriminatory abuse of dominance, as by giving local telephone networks preferred or exclusive access to a telecom bottleneck). The Agreement on Technical Barriers to Trade (TBT), Article 3.4, forbids a member from encouraging private testing and certification organizations to discriminate against foreign products contrary to the national treatment principle. The Antidumping Agreement, Article 3.5, requires the administering authority, when determining injury to a domestic industry, to take into account any restrictive business practices by members of the industry. The Safeguard Agreement, Article 11.1, prohibits members from encouraging or supporting private firms' adoption of measures equivalent to voluntary export restraints; thus members may not encourage or support export cartels.[13] Thus the seeds of competition are already planted within the WTO. The new competences suggest that, to nurture them coherently, we may need a point of reference.

In December 1998 the WTO Working Group on the Interaction Between Trade and Competition Policy issued its report. The report summarizes the work of the group, including the 104 submissions by WTO members, takes stock of existing instruments and standards regarding trade and competition, and recommends that the group continue its discussions to the end of 1999 on issues including: (1) the relevance of fundamental WTO principles of national treatment, transparency, and most-favoured-nation treatment, (2) approaches to promoting cooperation among members, and (3) the contribution of competition policy to promoting international trade. As discussions continue within and among nations, consensus seems to be developing that world competition demands concepts that reach beyond national borders and national law, that conversations should continue, but that solutions are not at hand.

---

[13] See Mitsuo Matsushita, 'Reflections on Competition Policy/Law in the Framework of the WTO', chap. 4 in Hawk (ed.), *International Antitrust Law* (above, n. 8).

IV. COSMOPOLITANISM WITH SUBSIDIARITY

There is both a broad and a narrow claim of need for international antitrust. The broad claim invokes the fact that so many problems are international, and the crazy quilt of the laws of nations is costly, incoherent, lacks a holistic grasp, and is geared towards conflict of egocentric systems rather than nurture of harmonious premises. All of this is true, but there are serious problems of a practical, political, and conceptual nature: What will be the forum for hammering out this world antitrust law? Can a law be hammered out to the satisfaction of nations? Will nations (and the relevant political actors within them) withstand this 'transfer of sovereign power' (even if a 'good' law can be adopted)? What will be the institutions to enforce the law? change it as needed? apply it? Who will be the enforcers, legislators, judges of the world? Will too much be lost, in terms of national context and needs? Regulatory competition among nations? Democratic participation?

The narrow claim for internationalization is a claim of opportunity that focuses on the most persistent trade and competition problem: market access. When markets are closed discriminatorily, nationalistically, or excessively by the *state*, the problem is a trade problem and it falls within the existing purview of the WTO. When markets are so closed by *commercial market actors*, the problem is a competition problem. It is beyond the reach of most harmed (excluded) nations.[14] The exclusion is not now caught by the WTO, although it can totally undermine WTO member nations' open-market commitments. The WTO is a proper and logical home for these market-blocking restraints. If problems about formulation of law, top-down imposition of law, and (fear of excessive or untrusted) dispute resolution can be surmounted, the market access competition problem has a reasonable chance of easy assimilation into the competences of the WTO.

There are in fact practical means of solving these institutional and sovereignty problems. One solution would provide an overarching conception to which (one could expect) liberal nations would agree, and it would then defer to national choice and be largely self-executing, much like European framework directives. Consensus might be formed around the following principles, for example, applicable to transactions and conduct with significant transnational effects:

1. Nations should have and enforce laws against anticompetitive [or unreasonable] blockage of markets.

---

[14] US law is the one nation's law that might extend so far; but it is, as noted, subject to criticism as impermissibly extraterritorial.

The laws should be applicable to state-owned enterprises and to privileges granted by the state except to the extent necessary for the enterprise to perform an obligation of the state, as in the EC Treaty of Rome Article 86 (ex Article 90).

2. Nations should enforce and apply their laws without discrimination as to nationality

(a) While nations should be free to regulate their economies in ways that derogate from competition policy, nations should agree not to use nationalistic policies (such as national champion policies) to trump anticompetitive restraints that have significant negative international spill-overs.

(b) In analysing competition problems with substantial international effects, nations should endeavour to count the costs and benefits imposed and realized abroad as if those costs and benefits occurred within their borders.

3. Transparency

(a) Conduct or transactions challenged as anticompetitive should be analysed first and separately under competition criteria. Non-competition criteria that are admissible and applied (e.g. environment, national security) should be clearly stated in decisions and opinions.

(b) Each nation should ensure that its rule of law is clear, e.g. by the use of guidelines or policy statements.

4. Jurisdiction and comity

(a) Nations should recognize that all nations have subject-matter jurisdiction over transactions and conduct that directly and significantly threaten harm to competition within their markets.

(b) Nations should refrain from ordering relief that is unreasonably extraterritorial.

5. Cooperation, process, and due process:

(a) As in TRIPs and as in positive comity agreements (e.g. US–EU), nations should provide in their laws opportunity for harmed nations and persons to complain to the authorities of an allegedly excluding nation, and protocols should be established for agency cooperation in discovery and enforcement.

(b) The allegedly excluding nation should be obliged to provide an accessible litigation or administrative system accompanied by the safeguards of due process, thus assuring effective recourse to harmed nations and persons (as in TRIPs). If this rule is violated, the harmed nation or person should be free to bring suit in its own country, subject to the choice-of-law principle below.

6. Choice of law

(a) Where the harm is to a nation's exports or foreign investment and the challenged conduct and the directly harmed consumers are in the importing/excluding nation, the law of the latter nation should apply (unless waived by defendants), as long as it prohibits anticompetitive market blockage and is non-discriminatory.

(b) If a nation does not have an antitrust law against market blockage or that law is discriminatory on its face, the harmed nation should be free to apply its own law.

7. Dispute resolution

Dispute resolution should be available for conflicts arising from provable breaches of the above obligations (as in TRIPs).

(a) A dispute resolution panel should be comprised of antitrust experts chosen by the disputing nations for their expertise and their freedom from nationalistic bias.

(b) The panel should not have power to second-guess application of national law by any national authority or court, as long as the nation has and has applied its own non-discriminatory antitrust law. The panel should, however, have the right to determine that a nation has not credibly applied its own law, as in NAFTA Article 19.

(c) Where the dispute is not resolved by the rule in (b), the panel should be empowered to develop a common law of conflict resolution, guided by the following two guideposts: (1) respect as much as possible for the law and policy of each involved nation/region, and (2) economic welfare of a geographic community that includes all affected parties, as if no national frontiers separated the disputing parties. Where necessary, the panel should develop principles to reconcile these two objectives.

(d) Alternative models for dispute resolution include:

(i) Mediation.

(ii) Rule-based dispute resolution, applying the rules above, in which case the panel should be required to submit a reasoned opinion and that opinion should be published and should be available as guiding authority.

(e) Binding nature? The resolution of the panel under rule-based dispute resolution should be in the nature of a recommendation only for a first term of years while experience is developed.

V. CONCLUSION

Unilateral and bilateral solutions to world competition problems are evolving and will continue to evolve. Cooperative efforts are strong and, usefully, are deepening. But the global economy makes poignant the limits of the nation-state as actor and regulator in the field of competition law. In the interests of world welfare and a stronger peace,[15] we are likely to, and we should, move towards the acceptance of cosmopolitan principles that link the world.

[15] See Joel P. Trachtman, 'L'Etat, C'est Nous: Sovereignty, Economic Integration and Subsidiarity', *Harvard International Law Journal*, vol. 33 (1992), 459.

Transatlantic regulatory cooperation in competition policy: the case for 'soft harmonization' and multilateralism over new bilateral US–EU institutions

Merit E. Janow

I. INTRODUCTION

Recent years have shown a significant increase in cooperation between US and European competition authorities. Cause and effect are difficult to unravel, but it appears that this has resulted from the effects of the M & A market as well as new policy initiatives. The increase in the number of cross-border transactions or transactions that are reviewed by both the United States and Europe is causing repeat interaction between US and European officials. This is, by its very nature, creating incentives for improved cooperation. New bilateral antitrust cooperation agreements between the United States and the European Union are providing more structure and predictability to the official interaction that occurs. Recent years have also produced several heated disputes, most notably the tense and acrimonious Boeing–McDonnell Douglas merger. Such direct conflicts, at least in competition policy, are quite rare; however, that case in particular may have proven instructive as to the costs of conflict.

Looking ahead, the need for new bilateral institutions is not apparent. There is both a need and an opportunity to maximize the gains from cross trade and investment and improve economic relations through 'soft' convergence measures and experimentation with enhanced comity initiatives. The brief discussion that follows shall assess the record to date and identify some possible directions for the future. And, if we look beyond the bilateral agenda, there is broad scope for cooperation between the United States and the European Union to facilitate the development of competition policy in a global economy. This cooperation could occur at the World Trade Organization (WTO), the OECD, or even take the form of new global initiatives, but should not take the form of a new US–EU bilateral regulatory institution.

II.   A QUICK LOOK AT COOPERATION BETWEEN COMPETITION
AUTHORITIES

In contrast to earlier decades, there have been notable positive achievements in US–EU cooperation in the field of antitrust or competition policy
enforcement during the 1990s. During this decade, the United States and
the European Community entered into two antitrust cooperation agreements: a 1991 Agreement and a 1998 Positive Comity Accord that builds
upon the 1991 Agreement. The 1991 Agreement embodies two themes—
enforcement cooperation, on the one hand, and the avoidance or management of disputes, on the other.[1] Under US law, the 1991 Agreement is
considered an 'executive agreement'; it is a binding international agreement, but since it has not been ratified by the US Senate, it does not override domestic law.

The 1991 Agreement was the first accord related exclusively to competition law to include a provision covering the notion of positive comity.
Positive comity refers to the principle that a country should give serious
consideration to another country's request to investigate and remedy anticompetitive conduct occurring within its borders that is harming another
country's important interests. This differs from the traditional comity,
which refers to the general principle that a country should take other
countries' important interests into account in its own law enforcement in
return for their doing the same. In essence, positive comity means that
either the United States or the European Community can request the other
jurisdiction to enforce its laws with respect to conduct occurring within its
borders that is harming the other jurisdiction. Such cooperation remains
voluntary and discretionary.

Building on these features of the 1991 Agreement, in June 1998 the
United States and the European Union entered into a separate positive
comity agreement that supplements the 1991 Agreement and sets forth
principles for implementation in certain types of cases. It clarifies the situations that would presumptively call for referrals between agencies and
seeks to further articulate the report-back and consultation mechanisms
that would be triggered once a referral has been made.

Positive comity has inherent limitations. For example: neither the 1991
Agreement nor the more elaborated 1998 Accord permits the sharing of
confidential information without the provider's consent, and both agreements exclude mergers. Neither of these agreements provide a mechanism

---

[1] The earliest bilateral agreement in this field was entered into between the United States
and the Federal Republic of Germany in 1976. Later agreements involved Australia (1982 and
1999), and Canada (1984, superseded by a new agreement in 1995). In the spring of 1999 the
United States and Japan announced the conclusion of a new bilateral competition policy
agreement. See http://www.usdoj.atr.pressrelease

for resolving disputes that continue after the end of consultations and in the event that a positive comity referral is seen as unresponsive. Furthermore, neither of these agreements implicates substantive law nor seeks to reach any formal procedural harmonization between the two jurisdictions. Both the United States and the European Community retain their full sovereign rights to accept or reject a referral.

One might reasonably ask: why do we need these procedural agreements, which do not in any event override domestic law? The answer has as much to do with political economy as it does with formal law. Although cooperation could occur legally without the 1991 and 1998 Accords, these agreements have been helpful in bringing some order to the cooperation that transpires, in introducing a degree of transparency into the process of cooperation, and in establishing agreed upon notions of what are important interests of a nation that need to be coordinated. The record of cooperation to date suggests that there is considerable scope for deepening bilateral cooperation still further under existing instruments. For argument's sake, let us posit three areas where meaningful cooperation could occur, and then ask whether US–EU authorities have attained that degree of cooperation.

In the enforcement context, one expression of 'close' cooperation occurs when a jurisdiction is prepared to undertake or apply its compulsory powers at the request of another jurisdiction, and then share the fruit of that investigation with the foreign requesting jurisdiction. Put concretely, one could posit a scenario where the European Union (or the United States) applies its compulsory powers to obtain documentary evidence from European- (or US-) based companies and then shares that information with US (or European) competition authorities.

Can or does this occur? At present, the answer is no. The United States and the European Union are not parties to an agreement that permits the exchange of confidential information. Because, as noted earlier, neither the 1991 Agreement nor the more recent 1998 Positive Comity Accord permits either US or European authorities to exchange confidential information, such exchanges of confidential information pursuant to an enforcement action has not occurred except in circumstances where the affected party voluntarily agrees to waive its rights to protect information obtained by authorities in each jurisdiction. There have, however, been parallel investigations between US and EU authorities in civil as well as criminal antitrust matters.

A second expression of cooperation in the antitrust enforcement context could, in theory, occur when a jurisdiction is prepared to devote its own resources to investigate a case that has been referred by a foreign jurisdiction and take any necessary remedial measures. As of this time, there has only been one formal referral between the United States and the European Community. Indeed, this is the only formal referral that has occurred between *any* two jurisdictions. Given that track record, the United States and the European Community have already embarked down an important and pathbreaking road. But, clearly we are still in the early days of positive comity.[2]

A third area for potential cooperation between authorities arises in merger review. As noted earlier, the number of transatlantic mergers is growing. As a result, while US and European law differ markedly both as to the substance and the procedural aspects of merger review, it has now become commonplace for US and EU authorities to discuss and share non-confidential information and exchange ideas about many aspects of a proposed merger that is being reviewed in both jurisdictions. Cooperation appears to be particularly useful in those cases where the merging parties have granted waivers to the exchange of confidential information. As of this writing, the Worldcom/MCI merger is often mentioned by lawyers and officials as the recent case that produced the greatest cooperation between US and EU authorities. One US official describes the cooperation that occurred as follows:

Division staff and DGIV staff worked closely to share their independent analyses of the transaction as they evolved and we and the EC Commission ultimately reached essentially the same conclusions. With the parties' consent, obtained through written waivers of confidentiality, the agencies shared confidential information with one another and held joint meetings with the two US companies to discuss the issues and possible solutions. In addition, before announcing its approval of the transaction in July, the European Commission formally requested, pursuant to the 1991 US–EU antitrust cooperation agreement, the Division's cooperation and assistance in evaluating and implementing the proposed divestiture.[3]

Of course, to say that authorities cooperate and even exchange information does not mean that they will reach the same conclusions. Recent years have produced a number of mergers where US and EU authorities came to different conclusions as to the competitive effects of a proposed merger, and hence called for different remedial measures by the affected parties to the transaction. Direct conflicts may be rare, but they have been known to occur. The most dramatic case in recent time was the proposed merger of McDonnell Douglas and Boeing, which the United States cleared and the European Community blocked, absent certain adjustments by Boeing. Politicians in both the United States and the European Community accused each other of supporting their own national champion. The dis-

---

[2] For a more complete discussion of this concept and its application in the US–EU context, see Merit E. Janow, 'A Look at US–EU Cooperation in Competition Policy', in *TransAtlantic Cooperation* (Washington, DC: Brookings Institution, forthcoming).

[3] See statement by A. Douglas Melamed, Principal Deputy Assistant Attorney General, Antitrust Division, US Department of Justice, 'Antitrust in a Global Economy' before Fordham Corporate Law Institute 25th Annual Conference on International Antitrust Law and Policy, 22 Oct. 1998. Published in Barry Hawk (ed.), *International Antitrust Law and Policy* (New York: Juris Publishing Inc., 1998).

pute nearly escalated into a trade war, as European authorities threatened to impose very high fines if the merger went forward and some US officials threatened to bring the case to the WTO, which may not have been much of a threat. The record suggests that this case was exceptional; the incidence of conflict is quite limited although it can recur. The ongoing and repeat nature of the cooperation between US and EU authorities, driven by the international merger boom, may keep brinkmanship at bay and create the incentives for enhanced cooperation between authorities. Indeed, the extent of communication that does now occur between authorities may also be reducing the opportunities for lawyers to a transaction to 'game it' or attempt to play off US or EU timetables or procedures against each other.

III. POSSIBLE NEXT STEPS: CONSTRAINTS AND OPPORTUNITIES

I am not of the view that a new institution is needed between the United States and the European Union to facilitate economic cooperation in general or in this arena of competition policy. There remains, I believe, ample scope for expanding cooperation in the field of competition policy still further under existing structures. The United States and the European Community represent two of the most mature competition authorities in the world today. Yet US and EC competition law differs both as to substance and as to procedure in many important areas. Hence, it is unrealistic to expect that formal harmonization of law could occur and even sillier to imagine that either jurisdiction would be willing to entrust competition policy enforcement to a supranational, bilateral agency.

Looking at European economic integration more broadly, it may be the case that, motivated by underlying political considerations, the European approach to cooperation has relied on the drafting and ratification by all participants of legally binding international agreements or treaties. The factors driving cooperation in the field of competition policy, while not devoid of political content, have chiefly been economic in nature and have occurred in a legal environment of sufficient similarity in approach to competition policy as to make cooperation possible. In other words, such cooperation has developed in response to the growing investment flows.

I am not of the view, however, that there is an overwhelming argument that the collective interests of the United States and the European Community require that both jurisdictions subsume a meaningful degree of economic autonomy in the design and implementation of their competition policies to the greater good of both jurisdictions. No such shared underlying sense of community or vision of collective interest presently exists between the United States and the European Community. Moreover, with over eighty jurisdictions in the world having some form of competition policy in place, full bilateral convergence only between the United States and the European Community may not make sense, even if it were achievable.

While substantive convergence may neither be desirable nor achievable, as EC Competition Commissioner Karel van Miert has noted, cooperation is producing a degree of 'soft harmonization' and a spirit of deference as foreign authorities see that in some instances US responses are addressing some of the same competition policy concerns as those of foreign jurisdictions. Promotion of such 'soft harmonization' is constructive, where possible. To facilitate this process, both US and EU authorities might usefully take a hard look at the procedural features of their merger-control regimes and consider whether there are steps that each could take to address some of the defects of their system that might also bring their regimes into greater convergence.

Let me mention several examples in the area of merger review. A first area for consideration is with respect to merger-review procedures that can apply equally to those transactions which raise no competition policy questions as well as those which raise very complex questions of this type. Practitioners often remark on differences between US and EC review periods and triggering events. The European Community for its part requires definitive agreements and filing within seven days, while the US Hart Scott Rodino (HSR) statute is more flexible, and permits notification as early as execution of a letter of intent. That little example may illustrate an area where it may be more efficient to see the harmonization of procedures—in this case perhaps the elimination of the definitive agreement requirement.

Lawyers engaged in transatlantic merger practice often complain about what is perceived as an excessive amount of information required by EC authorities in the initial notification, which can be especially burdensome in those transactions that raise no significant competition policy questions. But even more burdensome on the parties and complex for the agencies is the tendency of US authorities to require a vast amount of information and documentation in the back end or second request stage of an investigation.[4] Narrowing the information requirements in complex cases is no easy task, for US authorities will surely feel that they must be able to obtain the necessary information to conduct a thorough review of the competitive effects of the transaction. Yet this may be particularly costly and burdensome on international transactions where documents are located in many jurisdictions and in many languages. Such complaints should encourage officials in both the United States and the European

---

[4] These points were repeatedly stressed during the November hearings of the International Competition Policy Advisory Committee (ICPAC), in Washington DC. See November Hearings, available at: http://www.usdoj.gov/atr/icpac

Community to look at their own merger review policies and practices and consider whether there is scope for improvement.

An even more important direction for cooperation in the merger context could occur through the further development of teamwork or work-sharing arrangements in complex transatlantic cases. As the Worldcom/MCI merger illustrates, cooperation and teamwork between US and EC authorities is deepening. But there is still a long way to go before the enforcement efforts of one agency are viewed as sufficient to remedy the antitrust concerns of another jurisdiction. Yet, that may be a goal that authorities should aspire towards, even if it may not be realistic or achievable in any given case. To facilitate the maturation of a more integrated approach to reviewing the facts, competitive overlap, remedies, and other aspects of a transaction, it is conceivable that the US and the EC authorities could develop some form of protocol to permit a more fully coordinated process. This approach would need on the one hand, to allow the participation by representatives from the other agency, while on the other, preserve the right of all participants to take their own measures, as necessary, if they believe that the substantive analysis or remedies diverge from preferred national approaches. Consideration and exploration of such approaches would go a long way towards creating a more nearly seamless merger-review system between the United States and the European Community.

Over time, and with successful shared experience, collaboration on merger cases might produce sufficient trust to even consider the application of proportionality principles, whereby in cases of overlapping review, authorities might consider which jurisdiction has the greater interest in the matter. And, in some circumstances, and with sufficient basis for confidence, they may even allow that agency to serve as the lead agency. Although we are a long way from this development at present, the United States and the European Community are moving constructively down a path towards deeper cooperation. I believe that successful collaboration is likely to be a more potent facilitator of the maturation of bilateral cooperation than the creation of new bilateral institutions as such.

Of course, improved cooperation in other areas is also possible and desirable. As noted, there has been but one formal positive comity referral. One logical next step to enhance effective communication and cooperation between antitrust authorities might be for the United States and the European Community to negotiate and enter into an agreement that permits the intergovernmental exchange of confidential information in antitrust matters, along the lines of the International Antitrust Enforcement Agreements Act (IAEAA) in place between the United States and Australia. If the United States and the European Community were to enter into an IAEAA-type agreement, authorities will need to address concerns about leakage that have frequently been raised by business groups on both sides of the Atlantic.

A final area for cooperation between the United States and the European Community that is vast and extremely important has to do with global rather than bilateral competition policy matters. At present, the United States and the European Union are headed into the Seattle trade summit with different official positions on the appropriateness of the WTO as a forum for the negotiation of horizontal competition rules subject to WTO dispute settlement. US authorities have argued that the time is not ripe for such WTO rules and raised a number of concerns regarding the WTO. Antitrust officials in the United States argue that bilateral cooperation agreements and expanded and intensive cooperation between competition authorities are the most useful way to advance the practical enforcement agenda.

The European Community also acknowledges the positive contribution of bilateral arrangements but is forcefully on the record as advocating the negotiation of competition rules at the WTO. The European Community has suggested that early efforts at negotiation oblige countries to have competition laws, enforce them in a transparent and non-discriminatory fashion, provide for international cooperation, and over time consider efforts at broader substantive coverage. The EC proposal also suggests that these rules should be subject to dispute settlement, but that individual cases would not be examined, but rather 'patterns' of cases. So far, the EC proposal has received some public support from Canada, Japan, and Australia.

As of this juncture, there does not appear to be sufficient consensus around the world—and certainly insufficient consensus within the United States—to support the negotiation of horizontal competition rules at the WTO.[5] I am also uncomfortable with the EC position that countries should be obliged to have competition laws and enforce them. A more central objective that is shared broadly in the world is the further development of market-oriented, open and transparent economic systems. To the extent that countries have chosen to introduce competition laws as part of the fabric of their economic laws and policies, then the WTO can probably play a constructive role in supporting the development of transparent and non-discriminatory competition policies. This may be particularly useful with respect to those areas where trade and competition policy concerns overlap.

---

[5] In the United States, for example, the International Competition Policy Advisory Committee (ICPAC) held hearings in the autumn of 1998 and in the spring of 1999 on this and other competition policy questions. Interestingly, none of the US business groups that testified before ICPAC argued in favour of horizontal competition rules at the WTO. Those testifying included important US groups such as the Business Roundtable, the National Association of Manufacturers, the US Council for International Business, several sectoral trade associations, and a number of individual business interests. See transcripts from 17 May 1999 hearings of the ICPAC available at: http://www.usdoj.gov/atr/icpac

Hence, this may be the opportune time to consider incremental steps at the WTO that would make it more 'competition policy' friendly as an institution. Several activities are illustrative: the Trade Policy Review Mechanism (TPRM), which regularly reviews a nation's trade policies, could also include a review of competition policies and their application. The Trade and Competition Policy Working Group that was established as part of the Singapore work programme has had a productive period of engagement. Hopefully, it can continue for a period of years and further explore areas of trade and competition policy overlap.

But international collaboration between the United States and the European Community on competition policy should not stop at the WTO. Since many competition problems are international in nature but not all competition problems are trade problems, this suggests that there may be areas where the United States and the European Community can cooperate. For example, differences in law and practice notwithstanding, it is likely that the United States and the European Community could agree on what constitute 'best practices' in competition law and enforcement and work with newer regimes in implementing such policies. As the recent agreement at the OECD on hardcore cartels illustrates,[6] there are areas where the United States and the European Community share views on appropriate policies and could work together in a global arena to achieve consensus on approaches to competition problems. Any such global initiatives do not require new bilateral institutions; more useful may be the establishment of a new and more inclusive multilateral competition policy fora to promote for consultations among countries on best practices, technical assistance programmes, and other global-competition issues as they arise.

[6] OECD Document No. C (98) 35/Final.

Transatlantic regulatory cooperation: exclusive club or 'open regionalism'?

Petros C. Mavroidis

INTRODUCTION

It is perhaps a sign of the times that regional integration schemes are becoming increasingly widespread. Does this trend towards regional integration indicate a general dissatisfaction with the way the World Trade Organization (WTO) has handled its portfolio so far? I would suggest not. Rather, I would suggest that governments move towards regionalism for reasons of political expediency, and that the overwhelming majority of regional integration schemes (the European Union excepted) lack real substance. Moreover, the WTO control of regional integration is anything but tight, so these schemes can happily co-exist alongside the WTO.

What, then, are the benefits of schemes to promote regional integration? Are they welfare maximizing instruments? Economic science does not always provide us with a clear answer to these questions, largely because it is simply too difficult to construct the counterfactual case. Nevertheless, the insights of economics may give rise to some degree of scepticism towards such schemes. There is little doubt that cooperation should be pursued in fields where gains can be derived. Where there is doubt, however, is whether beneficial cooperation requires strict limitations on membership, as is often the case. Jagdish Bhagwati has time and again suggested that 'open regionalism' (in which governments would be allowed to integrate faster than the WTO process but which any other government would have the opportunity to join if it can meet the membership thresholds) is a preferable option to limited membership. An explicit commitment to such open regionalism would remove doubts relating to the true intentions of the participating states, but so far Bhagwati's proposal has found no adherents in practice.

The Transatlantic Economic Partnership (TEP) between the European Community and the United States should be viewed from the economic perspective of the gains it will produce. The United States and the European Community are also members of the WTO and, consequently, are bound by its disciplines. While their cooperation can extend to fields outside trade liberalization, such cooperation is meaningful only when it takes place in fields where gains can be derived, and thus, it makes sense to prioritize those sectors where benefits are probable. Feasibility is a central concern, though existing international obligations (such as through the WTO) have to be acknowledged as well. The TEP agenda suggests that the two domains in which the potential economic gains of coordination between the European Community and the United States are the greatest are in trade and competition policy.

The political will to deepen transatlantic cooperation in these domains clearly exists, but the question arises as to whether new, exclusively 'transatlantic' institutions are needed in order to realize the potential economic gains. This institutional question is the focus of this contribution. First, we must evaluate what precisely is the nature of the existing cooperation in the trade and competition policy. Second, we must take into account the existing legal constraints. In the field of trade, the WTO imposes an unambiguous obligation to extend any regional advantages to all WTO Members (the most-favoured-nation clause, MFN). On competition policy issues, however, the two participants in principle enjoy greater freedom to choose between any form of cooperation they deem appropriate, although the trade impact of competition policy is increasingly recognized. In either case, the existing institutional background cannot be overlooked, and the question of exclusivity versus open regionalism must be addressed.

I. US–EU TRADE POLICY COOPERATION: THE TRADE COMPONENT OF THE TRANSATLANTIC ECONOMIC PARTNERSHIP

A. The focus on non-tariff barriers to trade: the Mutual Recognition Agreements

Since its inception, the GATT/WTO process has led to a substantial reduction in customs duties. Given this success, over the last years trade negotiators have slowly shifted their attention towards disciplining trade-inhibiting non-tariff barriers (NTBs). This is not to say that customs duties are no longer an issue in trade liberalization. To the contrary, the tariffication process in agriculture (undertaken during the Uruguay round) reminds us that tariff peaks do exist (the textiles sector is another confirmation of this fact). NTBs essentially stem from regulatory diversity. The WTO is not, on its face, an instrument for harmonization of this diversity, and thus WTO Members are essentially free to pursue any regulatory policy they deem appropriate to the extent that they do not violate the non-discrimination principle.[1] However, regulatory diversity, as the very

---

[1] Interestingly, the European Court of Justice (ECJ), in the famous *Keck & Mithouard* judgment, interpreted the provisions of the EC Treaty relating to free movement of goods as an instrument prohibiting discrimination and refused to adhere to the thesis that they are an instrument of deregulation, see 1993 ECR I-6097 as well as the analysis in Peter Oliver, *Free Movement of Goods in the European Community* (London: Sweet & Maxwell, 1996), 130 ff.

recent *Hormones* dispute between the European Community and the United States shows, can easily lead to trade friction.[2]

Hence, it is understandable that the US–EU regulatory cooperation (via the recently concluded Mutual Recognition Agreements (MRAs)) has placed significant emphasis on the mutual recognition of standards (the outcome precisely of regulatory diversity). The mutual recognition of standards in the transatlantic context is a product of political will, as opposed to the strictly intra-European context, where it was in the first instance the product of a judicial mandate by the ECJ in its famous *Cassis de Dijon* jurisprudence. This case law essentially paved the way for an automatic mutual recognition of production processes among EC Members.

As Richard Baldwin correctly points out, this judicial mandate (and more precisely its subsequent interpretation by the EC Commission) removed the argument from domestic European lobbies to 'press' for regulatory interventions 'mirroring' domestic production processes, because foreign regulatory interventions would have to be accepted as equivalent to domestic ones unless compelling reasons (mandatory requirements) existed supporting the opposite conclusion.[3] In the case of the MRAs concluded between the United States and the European Community nothing of the sort is envisaged: the two participants agree that their domestic laboratories can perform conformity assessment to ensure that a domestic product corresponds to the other party's standards.

In so far as the US–EU MRAs are concerned, therefore, the pressure to impose domestic regulatory requirements on foreign products is not removed. Standards and technical regulations remain a credible barrier to trade liberalization.[4] It is not by coincidence that they have given rise to a significant amount of WTO litigation. Consequently, their inclusion in the TEP agenda is entirely justified, especially because regulatory activity on both sides of the Atlantic is very much alive.

B. Do we need specifically 'transatlantic' institutions to attack the problem of non-tariff barriers?

At first glance, one is tempted to answer definitively in the negative. Since conformity assessment will not take place in a centralized/harmonized manner, nothing suggests that new institutions are needed to implement

---

[2] See WTO Doc. WT/DS26/AB/R (26 Jan. 1998).

[3] See Richard Baldwin, 'Mutual Recognition in the WTO' (paper presented at the CEPR London Conference on 'The Next Negotiating Round: The New Issues', Feb. 1999).

[4] See on this issue Alan O. Sykes, *Product Standards for Internationally Integrated Goods Markets* (Washington, DC: Brookings Institution, 1996); see also, Sylvia Ostry and Richard R. Nelson, *Techno-Nationalism and Techno-Globalism: Conflict and Cooperation* (Washington, DC: Brookings Institution, 1995).

the current content of the TEP agenda in this respect. To answer this question definitively, however, we must consider the WTO Agreement on Technical Barriers to Trade (TBT).

Article 2.7 of the TBT gives an opportunity to WTO Members to negotiate mutual recognition agreements (MRAs). Since the WTO contract in this respect is about regulatory diversity, WTO Members are, in principle, free to set their standards as high or as low as they wish. Then, in accordance with Article 2.7 TBT, they can proceed to MRAs with other Members having intervened in the similar area. These MRAs, however, cannot be negotiated in disrespect of the overarching MFN obligation. WTO case-law has time and again made this point clear.

Hence, the question of compatibility of MRAs with the MFN principle arises. The MFN principle imposes on WTO Members the obligation to extend 'automatically' and 'unconditionally' any advantage they have accorded to another country. There is no doubt that standards do constitute an advantage, since nonconformity with them could easily lead to market exclusion. On the other hand, the terms 'automatically' and 'unconditionally' come into play only when likeness between the two foreign products concerned has been previously established. Consequently, the real issue is how to establish likeness between a product corresponding to a standard for which an MRA exists and another product corresponding to a standard for which no MRA exists.

As a preliminary remark, it must be noted that an MRA and the MFN principle are not mutually exclusive: any interpretation of the WTO agreements that the MFN principle precludes MRAs must be rejected, because it runs counter to the principle of 'effective interpretation' of the treaties as laid down in the Vienna Convention on the Law of Treaties. According to this principle, the role of the interpreter is to give meaning to each and every provision of an international treaty and to avoid reading out any one of them. From early on, the Appellate Body of the WTO has interpreted the WTO contract in conformity with the Vienna Convention. The conclusion so far is that MRAs and MFN can, in principle, co-exist.

But the next question is: under what conditions? WTO case-law provides little guidance on this question. One could reasonably advance the argument, however, that one should not read too much into the words 'automatically' and 'unconditionally', otherwise the *effet utile* of MRAs would disappear. At the heart of an MRA lies some notion of 'trust', which means that, at least initially, governments will not pursue MRAs unless they have some trust in the regulatory process abroad.

Moreover, one should not forget that the TBT is in fact the other side of a possible Article XX defence. This means that WTO Members have, in principle, the option to either defend a market-access restriction through a TBT or through an Article XX GATT defence. In the latter case, they can block trade with respect to all products not conforming to their standard of protection which as such cannot be put into question.[5] In addition, when applying their legislation, a WTO Member is only obligated to ensure even-handedness with respect to those countries where the same conditions prevail.[6] The argument here is that the TBT should not be read as imposing extra conditions on those already laid down in Article XX, otherwise governments will have an incentive to switch their defence to Article XX GATT. In both types of cases, the focus will be on the words 'where the same conditions prevail'.

Where does all this leave us? I suggest that one could expect to see the WTO case-law evolving in the following way (using the standards for catalysts for cars as an example):

(a) Assume that the US–EU MRA provides that each of the two participants accepts each other's standards with respect to catalysts for cars;

(b) assume further that Japan turns to Brussels arguing that its own catalysts are as good as the US catalysts and that the EC refuses to accept the Japanese argument;

(c) in pursuing the case before the WTO, Japan would have to prove that the European Community violates the MFN obligation; hence it would have to prove that its catalysts can satisfy the norms set by the EC regulatory intervention in the same way as US catalysts do;

(d) does this mean that the European Community must sign an MRA with Japan as well? Does this mean that Japanese laboratories must be accepted by the European Community to be competent to do conformity assessment with EC standards in the same way as US laboratories are? Clearly not. Japan, even if it wins its case, will have only won with respect to one particular product and not with respect to the capacity of their laboratories. Hence, most likely MRAs on conformity assessment per se cannot be put into question before WTO adjudicating bodies, but their impact on trade in particular products can be put into question.

In such a case, if the European Community and the United States want to continue to benefit from their MRA *inter se*, they will have to give serious consideration to the forgotten idea of a Transatlantic Free Trade Area (TAFTA). In other words, were the WTO panel to find that Japanese catalysts are a like product to US catalysts, and assuming that the European Community and the United States do not want to grant Japan the treatment they have reserved for themselves, they will have to look for a WTO permissible exception, and the only one that can guarantee long-term exemption from pertinent WTO rules is the exception offered by Article XXIV GATT (V GATS), governing regional integration.[7] Hence, as for

[5] See the panel report on 'United States—Section 337 of the Tariff Act of 1930', adopted on 7 Nov. 1989, published in BISD 36S/345.

[6] Appellate Body report on United States—Import Prohibition of Certain Shrimp and Shrimp Products, WTO Doc. WT/DS58/AB/R (12 Oct. 1998).

[7] I do not suggest that a TAFTA is the first-best for the United States and the European Community. I only suggest that *legally* this is the most appropriate option.

whether new institutions are necessary to realize the gains of deepened EU–US regulatory cooperation, the transatlantic partners may need a new institutional 'umbrella' to the extent that they want to keep a privileged relationship among themselves.

II. TRANSATLANTIC COOPERATION IN THE FIELD OF COMPETITION POLICY

The European Union and the United States have over the years developed significant experience in the field of cooperation on antitrust issues. Their first agreement in this respect laid down the 'positive comity' principle, whereby, contrary to the traditional 'comity' principle, each of the two participants could request from the other to take into account its interests when exercising its competence on competition-policy matters.

In principle, the two participants are unconstrained by the GATT/WTO regime in the field of competition-policy cooperation. However, the argument could be made that Article III of the GATT requires national treatment in the application of all domestic regulations, including competition laws, affecting internal sale and offer for sale of goods. Based on a traditionally wide reading of the term 'affecting',[8] the argument could be made that competition laws are indeed covered by Article III of the GATT. If this is the case (this argument has not been sanctioned in GATT/WTO case-law), then competition laws will have to obey the principle of national treatment but only to the extent that they deal with the scope of Article III:4 of the GATT relating to the treatment of products. Consequently, in the absence of international disciplines, the United States and the European Union are largely unconstrained to pursue 'deepened integration' in this area.

The question, however, arises as to how far the two participants may go in this area? Is it meaningful to go beyond the disciplines already laid down in the EU–US Cooperation Agreement in the field of antitrust? This question clearly relates to the ongoing discussion in the WTO on the relationship between trade and competition. Following the Singapore Ministerial Conference in 1996, a WTO group was created to examine this relationship, based on the assumption that restrictive business practices do constitute a major obstacle in trade liberalization. For a number of good reasons, however, this assumption can be put into question: (a) several commentators have noted that it is practically impossible to quantify the externalities stemming from lax enforcement of competition laws;[9] (b) oth-

---

[8] Panel report on Italian Discrimination against Imported Agricultural Machinery, adopted on 23 Oct. 1958, B.I.S.D. at 7S/60 (1958).

[9] See Marc Bachetta, Henrik Horn af Rantzien, and Petros C. Mavroidis, 'Do Negative Spillovers from Lax Enforcement of Competition Laws Argue for an International

ers have suggested that, if at all, practice shows that competition-related disputes are not much of a problem as far as trade liberalization is concerned;[10] (c) still others explain why a substantial part of the problem can be taken care of within the existing legislative framework.[11]

Aside from these criticisms, it should be noted that the European Union and the United States participate actively in the ongoing discussions on trade and competition that take place in the context of the WTO group, which means that they will have to implement the results if and when tangible results are achieved. Hence any institutional issues will be handled in a multilateral framework. At this stage, one can only speculate about the shaping of the final outcome. Most likely, it will be a minimalist intervention leaving ample room for intervention in the field of competition laws to WTO Members, although the WTO will likely prove to be at least an indirect constraint in the future.

Pending the completion of the work of the WTO group, the European Union and the United States are thus free to pursue the TEP agenda in the domain of competition-policy cooperation. As currently formulated, the TEP agenda requires little additional institutional infrastructure; rather, the participants are acknowledged to have the right to request from each other, when applying their domestic competition laws, to take care of the other party's interests. The only difference between the traditional 'comity' as we know it from public international law and the 'positive comity' as laid down in the EU–US Agreement is a change in the initiative: it is no longer the *ratione materiae* competent authority that will decide whether to defer; rather, it is the affected authority that places such a request. 'Comity' functioned for years without any need for institutional intervention, and there is no need to change this practice simply because of a change in the initiative.

In addition, the other obligations laid down in the Agreement have to do essentially with facilitation of collection of information about allegedly illegal practices. To perform this task, each participant will have recourse to its own domestic laws and administrative procedures. New, exclusively transatlantic, institutions would only be needed where one or both parties' laws were deemed to be inefficient. At this point, this is hardly the case.

Agreement on Competition?', in Claus-Dieter Ehlermann and Laura Laudati (eds), *Robert Schuman Centre Annual on European Competition Law 1997* (London, UK: Hart Publishing, 1998), 313ff.

[10] J. Michael Finger and K. C. Fung, 'Can Competition Policy Control 301?', *Aussenwirtschaft*, vol. 49 (1994), 379–416.

[11] See the following: Eleanor Fox, 'Toward World Antitrust and Market Access', *American Journal of International Law*, vol. 91 (1997), 1–25; Diane P. Wood, 'International Standards for Competition Law: An Idea Whose Time Has Not Come' (paper presented at Graduate Institute of International Studies, Geneva, 19 June 1996); and Bernard M. Hoekman and Petros C. Mavroidis, 'Competition, Competition Policy and the GATT', *The World Economy*, vol. 17 (1994), 121–50.

What is essentially requested from each party is to put into work an effective domestic machinery for the benefit of the other party's competition authorities. Again, there seems to be no need to add to the existing institutional framework.

A number of areas, however, have been singled out as candidates for future discussions. Most of them relate (in one way or another) to the question of the permissible scope of national competition laws, the infamous extraterritoriality issue. Conceptually, with an agreement on extraterritoriality one could take care of a number of issues ranging from merger notifications to vertical/horizontal restraints to abuse of dominance. Is a formal transatlantic institution necessary for an agreement to be reached? Practice and especially communication between the competent authorities when practising competition law can largely take care of the problem. Moreover, it is difficult to imagine what criteria could help solve the problem permanently. It is true that, in the context of the Agreement on the European Economic Area (EEA), threshold criteria were established which provided an *ex ante* response as to which authority should a merger be notified to. It is also true, however, that the EEA Agreement operated between participants having essentially identical competition laws. A 'lock, stock, and barrel' transposition of the EEA recipe to the EU–US context is hardly recommendable.

III.   SOME CONCLUDING REMARKS

This contribution aimed to show that there is no need to add to the existing institutional framework in order to ensure the gains from the existing TEP agenda. Rather, it points to the multilateral perspective: the TEP is about opening up our minds to knowledge and experience from abroad so vital to maximize our own welfare. It is nonsensical to restrict the openness. The TEP should be used as the vehicle to move all willing countries forward towards enhanced communication and integration and should avoid serving as another 'limited membership group' inaccesible to the many. Then and only then it will have served its real purpose.

Part V

Transatlantic regulatory cooperation in selected sectors

Telecommunications and 'Cyberspace': transatlantic regulatory cooperation and the constitutionalization of international law

Klaus W. Grewlich

Transatlantic regulatory cooperation in communications should contribute to a successful transition of our societies to the age of 'cyberspace'. This emerging digital environment is an invisible, intangible world of electronic information and processes stored at multiple interconnected sites, with controlled access and manifold interaction.[1]

Regulatory (and de-regulatory) cooperation in the transatlantic dimension should aim at the development of an 'international law of cooperation',[2] eventually to the 'constitutionalization'[3] of international relations and international law. An empirical assessment of the legal and institutional mechanisms for transatlantic cooperation and coordination in communications requires an analysis of regulatory challenges, of commonalities and disparities, of institutions and principles, and of courses of action.

Thus, the following contribution comprises first, a conceptual understanding of regulatory approaches, second, an empirical analysis of commonalities and disparities pertaining to the perception of interests, political rationales, and cooperative and non-cooperative attitudes in the European Union and North America, third, some considerations on institutions and normative principles, and fourth, reflections on courses of action to achieve regulatory cooperation.

---

[1] Klaus W. Grewlich, *Governance in 'Cyberspace'—Access and Public Interest in Global Communications* (The Hague, Boston, and London: Kluwer Law International, 1999), 1 f.

[2] Wolfgang Friedmann, *The Changing Structure of International Law* (New York: Stevens 1964); P. Verloren Van Themaat, *The Changing Structure of International Economic Law* (The Hague: Nijhoff 1981); Rüdiger Wolfrum, 'International Law of Cooperation', in Rudolf Bernhardt (ed.), *Encyclopedia of Public International Law*, Instalment 9 (Amsterdam: Elsevier 1986); Maurice Bourquin, 'Pouvoir Scientifique et Droit International', *Hague Recueil*, vol. 70 (1947), 359 f.

[3] David J. Gerber, 'Constitutionalizing the Economy: German Neo-Liberalism, Competition Law and the "New Europe"', *American Journal of Comparative Law*, vol. 42 (1994), 25; Ernst-Ulrich Petersmann, 'How to Constitutionalize International Law and Foreign Policy for the Benefit of Civil Society?', *Michigan Journal of International Law*, vol. 20 (1998), 1.

I. CONCEPTUAL REGULATORY CHALLENGES

In the endeavour to create a favourable regulatory framework for the transition to the age of cyberspace, a number of key legal and regulatory responses are required. In developing such responses for telecommunications, cyberlaw, and policies, on both sides of the Atlantic we have many regulatory challenges in common, and there also exist important cultural, technological, and legal similarities.

A. Free market philosophy

Forward-looking action has to be taken, either to regulate or—even more important—not to regulate in order to preserve and widen the areas of freedom and free choice. This fundamental understanding of a liberal philosophy of deregulation and freedom of creation[4] has allowed information technologies and communications to thrive and the information economy to blossom.[5] Liberalization and deregulation has been one of the major causes for growth in telecommunications and particularly the new innovative dynamics on the multimedia value chain, encompassing content production, content packaging, service provision, network operation, and consumption.[6]

B. Digitalization—Convergence

The notion of convergence relates to telecommunications, the audiovisual sector, and computers. Traditionally telecommunications and broadcasting are subject to separate regulatory regimes while the information technology and computer sector was not regulated at all.

In telecommunications the regulators saw the different networks, services, and pertinent regulatory schemes as more or less congruent. Thus, a telecom service was linked to a specific infrastructure and both the specific infrastructure and the service were covered by specific regulatory regimes. However, these regulatory delineations are now dramatically changing: as a result of the revolutionary impact of *digitalization*, telecommunications, com-

---

[4] Ernst-Joachim Mestmäcker, introduction to Walter Eucken, *Grundsätze der Wirtschaftspolitik (Principles of economic policy)*, 6th edn., (Tübingen: Mohr 1990) V–XVI; Gerber, 'Constitutionalizing the Economy' (above, n. 3); Wolfgang Fikentscher, *Recht und wirtschaftliche Freiheit* (Tübingen: Mohr, vol. 1, 1992, vol. 2, 1993).

[5] Alain Dumort and John Dryden, *The Economics of the Information Society* (Brussels: European Commission 1997).

[6] KPMG, *Report to the European Commission: Public Policy Issues Arising from Telecommunications and Audiovisual Convergence* (Brussels: European Commission 1996) or Squire, Sanders, and Dempsy/Analysis (EU-DGXIII), Study on Adapting the EU Regulatory Framework to the Developing Multimedia Environment (Summary Report, Main Report, Annexes 1 and 2) (Brussels/Luxembourg: EU Commission 1998).

puters, and broadcasting are seen as rapidly converging. The most impressive phenomenon in this development is that different services, such as voice, data and video, can be stored at multiple places, retrieved and manipulated and delivered over any kind of network (i.e. fixed, wireless, or satellite.) This network-independent delivery is called platform independence.

As a result, varying qualities of voice may be transmitted via the Internet and switched telephone networks can, on the other hand, become a medium for delivering video. When audiovisual products become generally available over interactive digital communication networks this is quite different from broadcasting as a point to multipoint service. Print media can be accessed online in addition to their physical distribution. While in the past corporate networks were closed data networks with more or less adequate gateways to other networks and network layers, today we see a mixture of IP-networks[7] Internet/Intranet/[8]Extranet, PSTN/ISDN/GSM/UMTS[9] with larger capacity data lines, multimedia integration, different layers of voice quality, and 'click to call'.[10]

C. Regulatory complexity in the transition to cyberspace

Competition is the Magna Carta of free enterprise[11] and 'interconnection' is the fundamental ordering principle for freedom in cyberspace. The removal of obstacles to interconnection and market access as a result of liberalizing regulation is recognized as having a strong positive impact on technological innovation and the emergence of new products and markets. This interrelation between technological innovation, sustained economic growth, and regulatory action or regulatory self-restraint becomes particularly evident when analysing the phenomena of interconnectivity and interoperability of networked communication applications.[12]

---

[7] Internet Protocol: IP defines the structure of data, or 'packets', transmitted over the Internet. The higher-level 'transmission control protocol' (TCP) and 'user-defined protocol' (UDP) control the routing and transmission of these packets across the network. Most Internet services use TCP, and thus the Internet is often referred to as a 'TCP/IP' network. IP is a higher-level application protocol that contrasts with protocols at the basic transport level (such as ATM—Asynchronous Transfer Mode); IP may ride on top of transport protocols such as ATM.

[8] A dedicated computer network (either a local- or wide-area network) within a corporation or other private institution intended to serve its own needs for data exchange, electronic mail, bulletin boards, etc. with reliability, performance, and security beyond that provided by the public Internet.

[9] Public Switched Telephone Network; Integrated Services Digital Network; Global Standard for Mobile Communication; Universal Mobile Telecommunication System.

[10] For an introduction into the technologies of the age of 'Cyberspace', see Michael Dertouzos, *What Will Be—How the New World of Information Will Change Our Lives* (San Francisco: Harper 1997).

[11] *United States v. Topco*, 405 US 596, 610 (1972); see contribution of Ernst-Ulrich Petersmann to this volume.

[12] Carl Shapiro and Hal Varian, *Information Rules—A Strategic Guide for the Network Economy* (Boston: Harvard Business School Press, 1999).

The challenge of creating the appropriate regulatory conditions, i.e. the challenge of 'quality regulation', is not only addressed to the public regulator. The agenda for private self-regulation, particularly for international standardization bodies, is impressive.[13] As to the public regulators' tasks, there is an unprecedented increase in complexity in the various fields of action. As already explained, for regulatory agencies it will be less possible to separate telecommunications from networked computer-based communications and global-information networks such as Internet and electronic media and content in the dynamics of the multimedia value chain. These will melt down into something deeply converging, a stream of data. But this stream is likely to flow not in one pipe but in many pipes or communication systems competing with each other. There is likely to be as much interdependence as competition of business activities in global communications networks and cyberspace, both at the transport and content level. In the new phase of communications development described as cyberspace, the telephone service, for instance, might become a by-product of global communication networks (Internet) that are 100 times the current performance/cost levels in transmission capacity and speed to the final user with basically unlimited worldwide distribution capacity. Eventually, electronic commerce might become a reality in almost every household![14]

Thus, the question comes up, whether technological and possibly market 'convergence' needs to be replicated at the regulatory level. Can regulatory policies and law be any longer confined to well-delineated vertical industrial sectors? Should they not be reorganized alongside horizontal cross-sectoral issues instead? Would this lead to undesirable overregulation or would it rather promote transparent and lean regulation?

In fact a cross-sectoral approach followed in lieu of sector-specific legislation could eventually result in the rebalancing of the present 'dual system'[15] of *ex ante* sectorspecific regulation and *ex post* regulation to the advantage of competition rules. However, legal adjustments of some concepts such as 'essential facilities'[16] and the evolution of an international competition framework may be key conditions for the success of such a reshaping. Proponents of this view may argue that *ex post* regulation, i.e. the application of competition rules, would suffice to curb market abuses

[13] Paul A. David, *Standards, Markets and Network Evolution* (New York: Cambridge University Press, forthcoming).

[14] Herbert Ungerer, 'Ensuring Efficient Access to Bottleneck Network Facilities: The Case of Telecommunications in the European Union', http://europa.eu.int/en/comm/dg04/dg4home.htm.

[15] Klaus W. Grewlich, '"Cyberspace": Sector-Specific Regulation and Competition Rules in European Telecommunications', *Common Market Law Review*, vol. 36 (1999), 937–69.

[16] John Temple-Lang, 'Defining Legitimate Competition—Companies' Duties to Supply Competitors and Access to Essential Facilities', *Fordham International Law Journal*, vol. 18 (1994), 437–524; Philip Areeda, 'Essential Facilities—An Epithet in Need of Limiting Principles', *Antitrust Law Journal*, vol. 58 (1990), 841–53.

and that the presently increasing advocacy for 'self-regulation' appears to enhance the need of an effective competition law framework. In any case, the future regulatory framework must be 'technology neutral', i.e. position itself at a high level of abstraction, conceptual consistency, and clarity. Obviously, there is a need for widely accepted orientations to guide this deep regulatory reshaping.

D. 'Creating' markets and 'sustaining' competition—*ex ante* and *ex post* regulation

As regards the theory of regulation pertaining to 'networked' sectors[17] such as telecommunications, air transport, rail transport, electricity, gas, post, and certain financial services, two different types of regulatory activities may be distinguished. The first type, that of market-making regulation, is designed to create markets and competition by establishing a framework of appropriate rules. In sectors such as communications, that were dominated by monopolies, market-making regulations imply the abolition of fixed prices, cross subventions, and of different obstacles to market access, i.e. the introduction of full competition and the transfer of public utilities to private ownership (privatization).[18] In the European Union the primordial *ex ante* market-making instruments in the field of communications comprise the Full Competition Directive[19] and the Open Network Provision (ONP) Interconnection Directive.[20] The comprehensive basis for sector specific regulation in the United States, that redefined the communications industries in many ways,[21] is the Telecommunications Act of 1996.

There is a second type of regulation. Once market processes have been originated and the offer-and-demand mechanism is functioning, the regulatory framework of markets will need to be sustained and corrected to prevent anti-competitive behaviour. This is the field of *ex post* regulation, notably in terms of cross-sector competition rules.

[17] Shapiro and Varian, *Information Rules* (above, n. 12); Adrienne Héritier, *After Liberalisation—Public-Interest Services in Utilities*, Reprint Max-Planck-Projektgruppe Recht der Gemeinschaftsgüter (Bonn 1998), 3f.

[18] Giandomenico Majone, *Regulating Europe* (London: Routledge, 1996).

[19] EU Commission Directive 96/19/EC of 13 Mar. 1996, amending Directive 90/388 with regard to the implementation of full competition in telecommunications markets, 1996 O.J. (L74/13), 22.03.1996.

[20] The ONP framework consists of a series of Directives issued since 1990 when the ONP Framework Directive was adopted. In the present context, the most important ONP Directive is the ONP Interconnection Directive; EU, European Parliament and Council, Directive 97/33/EC of 30 June 1997 Interconnection in Telecommunications with Regard to Ensuring Universal Service and Interoperability through Application of the Principles of Open Network Provision (ONP), 1997 O.J. (L 199/32, 26.7.1997) (ONP Interconnection Directive).

[21] For instance, the Act permits one licensee to own a greater number of television stations and radio stations, cable TV operators are subject to less rate control, and the regulatory oversight of the Federal Communications Commission (FCC) is redefined.

E. Rationale for liberalization and deregulation in telecommunications

What was the practical rationale that led legislators and policy-makers to dismantle the national monopolies? Taking for illustrative purposes the example of Europe, at least four reasons may be identified.[22] First, because of the pervasive force of digitalization a heavily regulated market (telecommunications) and an almost unregulated market (computers, information technology) were coming close to each other, even starting to integrate. But, what regulatory regime should prevail—the liberal or the heavily regulated? Secondly, the existence of national monopolies was not compatible with the EC Treaty's legal objective of a single internal market. With national barriers, telecommunication costs were higher within the European Union, putting European companies at a disadvantage as they compete on global markets. In addition, the less than satisfactory performance of monopolies, not only in cost but also in quality, was recognized, as the monopolies were unable to provide at high quality and low price the plethora of new products and services available elsewhere. Thirdly, some Member States had recognized the necessity to privatize their 'PTT monopolies' in order to finance the huge capital outlays required in the telecommunications sector. Fourthly, the United States, having liberalized to some extent the American communications market and particularly divested AT & T,[23] started an effort to open foreign markets in terms of 'reciprocity'. This trade diplomacy was named 'Market Access Fact Finding Missions' (MAFF).[24] In fact, via these MAFF talks (a particular form of argument about trade matters and at the same time 'regulatory cooperation') the United States put pressure on the institutions of the European Communities and its Member States. Following the example of the United Kingdom, the majority of EC countries agreed in the second half of the 1980s to the liberalization of the European telecommunications markets. Some EC Member States, like Germany and the Netherlands, became strong supporters of liberalizing efforts in the pursuit of enlightened economic self-interest, as some key personalities had understood that adequate liberalization in communications might become a comparative advantage in 'systems competition'.

---

[22] I. Van Bael and J.-F. Bellis, *Competition Law of the European Community* (3rd edn.) (Bicester: CCH Europe, 1994); Ernst-Joachim Mestmäcker, Hrsg., *Kommunikation ohne Monopole II—Ein Symposium über Ordnungsprinzipien im Wirtschaftsrecht der Telekommunikation und der elektronischen Medien, Law and Economics of International Telecommunications* (Baden-Baden: Nomos 1995), 116 ff.

[23] Steve Coll, *The Deal of the Century—The Breakup of AT&T* (New York: Atheneum, 1986).

[24] This name was used by the United States in order to avoid the impression of (bilateralized) anticipated 'Trade in Services'-negotiations.

F. 'Access' regulation and 'public-interest' regulation

Assuming the issues pertaining to market access and the removal of obstacles are basically well addressed by 'market creating *ex-ante* regulation', there still remain other regulatory challenges that may pertain to 'public-interest' objectives, such as human dignity, security, and privacy. What shape, for instance, should copyright protection take as instantaneous undetectable copying becomes possible? Should the 'right to receive and impart information and ideas' (Article 10 of the European Convention on Human Rights,[25] respectively the First Amendment to the US Constitution)[26] encompass a right to send encrypted messages that are for all intents and purposes immune to eavesdropping by law enforcement? What standard of liability should be imposed on system operators and service providers in regard to the availability of 'obscene' material?[27] An additional question is: Will and should these questions be answered with a focus on 'legal centralism' in substantive rulemaking, or is 'decentralized' law-making and social control, i.e. self-regulation—both in industries and network communities—possible and more adequate?

Thus, another distinction, from the point of view of regulatory theory, is the one between *access* regulation (both *ex ante* and *ex post*) and regulation to safeguard *public-interest* objectives, often relating to content and implying fundamentals such as human dignity, privacy, and security. Indeed, the integration of human dignity and fundamental rights with economic liberalism by the 'rule of law', i.e. the juxtaposition and synergy of 'free access' regulation and 'public-interest' regulation, may not only require liberalization, de(re)regulation, economic freedom, and various forms of access to protect the market mechanism in order to generate wealth. There are circumstances where, in the public interest, limits have to be imposed on economic and political freedom, even on freedom of expression,

---

[25] European Convention on Human Rights, 4 Nov. 1950; P. Van Dijk and G. J. H. Van Hoof, *Theory and Practice of the European Convention on Human Rights* (2nd edn.) (Boston: Deventer, 1990).

[26] 'Congress shall make no law abridging the freedom of speech, or of the press.' US Const. amend. I.

[27] The US Telecommunications Act of 1996 imposed new obscenity and indecency requirements on broadcast and cable systems and the industry was required to develop a rating system for the transmission of violent material; see in this context *Reno v. ACLU*, 117 S. Ct. 2329 (1997). The Administration underlines that the Supreme Court decision did *not* affect US laws and regulation against obscenity and child pornography, and that it remains committed to the vigorous enforcement of federal prohibitions against the transmission of child pornography and obscenity and the use of the Internet by paedophiles; see http://www. whitehouse.gov/WH/New/Ratings/index.html; it is argued that the *ACLU* opinion fails to confront the critical normative judgement about the real sacrifice that free speech demands, see Eugene Volokh, 'Freedom of Speech, Shielding Children, and Transcending Balancing', http://www.law.ucla.edu/Faculty/volokh/shield.html.

because of other countervailing public-interest objectives such as human dignity.[28]

Therefore, even if deregulatory action may eventually lead to the phasing out of many regulatory instruments, certain forms of *public-interest regulation* will have to remain in place to protect the *ordre public*. However, this should be kept to a minimum, following the principle of proportionality,[29] as governments could best protect personal and economic freedom and other fundamental rights where the market is allowed to produce wealth prosperity and stability.[30]

G. Phasing out sector specific *ex ante* regulation—competition rules

In the European Union a 'dual system' has developed concerning the treatment of access to bottleneck situations. First, concerning sector-specific regulation of access, the existing National Regulatory Agencies (NRAs) can act *ex ante* and impose, as necessary, and in substantial detail, interconnect provisions regarding prices and technical elements. Second, at the same time the cross-sector rules of EU competition law are directly effective so that competition rules are also enforceable in the national courts. Thus, NRAs must ensure that actions taken by them within the ONP framework are consistent with EU competition law.[31] They may therefore not approve arrangements which are contrary to EU competition rules.[32] The competition law's substantive rules focus on 'eliminating excessive economic power from the market or, where this is not practicable, preventing the use of such power to distort competition'.[33] Following this logic, the 'dual regime' for sectorspecific regulation (notably the ONP Interconnection framework) and competition rules in European telecommunications aim at ensuring the attainment of the objectives of the Community as enshrined in Article 3 of the EC Treaty: i.e. the establish-

[28] See Josef Isensee, 'Das Grundrecht als Abwehrrecht und als staatliche Schutzpflicht', in Josef Isensee and Paul Kirchhof (eds), *Handbuch des Staatsrechts (HdbStA) V*, 1992, 163 ff.; Charles Firestone and Amy Garmer (eds), *Digital Broadcasting and the Public Interest* (Washington DC: Aspen, 1998); Eugene Volokh, 'Freedom of Speech' (above, n. 27); W. B. Lockhart *et al.*, *Constitutional Law* (6th edn.) (St Paul: West, 1986).

[29] See Art. 3b (3) EC Treaty; Hauer—Cases 44/79, ECR 79/3727; Case 122/78, Buitoni— ECR 1979/677; Hoechst—Cases 46/87 and 227/88 ECR 1989/2859; see also Christopher Bellamy and Graham Child in Vivien Rose (ed.), *Common Market Law of Competition* (4th edn.) (London: Sweet & Maxwell, 1993), 24 f.; Matthias Herdegen, *Europarecht* (2nd edn.) (München: Beck, 1999), 124.

[30] See Gerber, 'Constitutionalizing the Economy' (above, n. 3), 83 f.

[31] See Cases 66/86 *Ahmed Aaeed* ECR 838 (1989); Case 153/93 *Federal Republic of Germany v. Delta Schiffahrtsges.* ECR I-2517 (1994); Case 267/86, *Van Eycke*, ECR 4769 (1988).

[32] Case 13/77, *GB-Inno-BM/ATAB* ECR 2115 (1977), at paragraph 33: '. . . while it is true that Article 86 is directed at undertakings, nonetheless it is also true that the Treaty imposes a duty on Member States not to adopt or maintain in force any measure that could deprive the provision of its effectiveness'; for further duties of national authorities see Case 103/88 *Fratelli Costanzo* ECR 1839 (1989).

[33] Gerber, 'Constitutionalizing the Economy' (above, n. 3), 74.

ment of a system 'ensuring that competition in the internal market is not distorted' and of 'an internal market characterized by the abolition, as between Member States, of obstacles to the free movement of goods, persons, services and capital'.[34]

Access to bottleneck issues may eventually change in nature with the advent of cyberspace.[35] As convergence threatens to outpace sector-specific regulatory systems, is the dual regime of sectorspecific regulation and competition rules in European telecommunications sustainable in the age of cyberspace? New types of service providers will require new types of resources and access to new types of bottleneck holders. These may range from state-of-the-art network resources to access to set-top boxes, conditional access systems, Application Program Interfaces (relevant for the programming of set-top boxes), browsers and navigation software and content rights. As a result, market definitions will change profoundly. A range of new access issues will emerge, such as those pertaining to 'Internet-domain names'. Thus, there is likely to be an increasing number of cases which will not be covered by *ex ante* sectorspecific regimes that cannot anticipate and plan ahead casuistically.

Thus, it is likely that competition law will increasingly have to address manifold bottleneck situations. The 'dual system' of access regulation will have to be rebalanced to the advantage of competition rules. A substantial part of sectorspecific *ex ante* regulation is likely to phase out gradually. Cross-sector competition rules will prevail, together with public-interest regulation that is essential and proportional from the point of view of constitutional law and common values.

II. EMPIRICAL COMMONALITIES AND DISPARITIES IN 'CYBER'-REGULATION

In an empirical perspective, what entices legislators to legislate and regulators to regulate in the field of communications? Mainly citizens and users rights, the particular nature of network economics, industry relationships including the emergence of alliances, and the competitive situation (also in terms of 'national or public interest')[36] are in the forefront. The latter may lead to 'systems frictions' and international conflict. The critical question is, whether the development of new services and new business opportunities, will be hindered by a range of barriers, including regulatory barriers existing or introduced at different levels of the value chain

---

[34] See George A. Bermann *et al.*, *Cases and Materials on European Community Law* (St Paul: West, 1993 and Supps. 1995, 1998).

[35] Grewlich, *Governance in 'Cyberspace'* (above, n. 1), 133f.

[36] See Paul Krugman, 'Competitiveness—A Dangerous Obsession', *Foreign Affairs* (Mar./Apr. 1994), 28–44.

and converging markets; or whether governments and regulators will be wise enough to avoid such constraints?

In the transatlantic relationship some commonalities and disparities in regulatory action may be recognized in analysing key policy documents,[37] e.g. 'A European Initiative in Electronic Commerce' (EU, 1997) and the 'Framework for Electronic Commerce' (US, 1997). The US policy statement refers to the 'Global Information Infrastructure' (GII), the European document to the 'information society'. A comparative analysis of these policy documents and the actual legislative and regulatory practice leads to the distinction between:

(i) areas of a basically common approach or transatlantic agreement in reach, e.g. pertaining to intellectual property rights (IPRs);[38] telecommunications regulation; the balancing of freedom of expression, human dignity,[39] and privacy; and

(ii) fields of existing or potential transatlantic disparities, e.g. cryptography, protection of personal data, peering agreements, the domain-name issues, foreign direct investment restrictions pertaining to communications, trade in media products.[40]

Thus, there exist a number of possibly conflicting telecommunication regulations and 'cyber' laws and policies. To investigate all potential conflicts in the transatlantic relationship that may result from regulatory disparities is not possible here. However, while there appears to be public awareness on some issues, there may still exist a lack of solution-oriented analysis pertaining to some major conflicting developments,[41] such as the WIPO draft Data-Base Treaty,[42] export controls relating to cryptog-

---

[37] See Klaus W. Grewlich, 'The Power of Global Communication—Data Highways and Multimedia. Competition and Cooperation', in Donald M. Lamberton (ed.), *Communication & Trade—Essays in Honor of Meheroo Jussawalla* (Cresskill, New Jersey: Hampton Press, 1998), 77 ff.

[38] With the exception of problems relating to the 'WIPO—Draft Data Base—Treaty'; see National Research Council, US National Academy of Sciences, *Bits of Power—Issues in Global Access to Scientific Data* (Washington: National Academy Press, 1997).

[39] European Parliament Resolution of 24 Apr. 1997 on the Commission communication on illegal and harmful content on the Internet, http://www2.echo.lu/legal/en/internet/communic.html; European Parliament Resolution of 24 Oct. 1997 on the Commission Green Paper on the protection of minors and human dignity in audiovisual and information services, COM(96)483; see also Commission of the European Communities, Communication to the European Parliament, the Council, the Economic and Social Committee and the Committee of the Regions, Action Plan on Promoting Safe Use of the Internet, COM(97)582 (available online at http://www2.echo.lu/legal/en/internet/actplan.html); *Reno v. ACLU*, 117 S. Ct. 2329 (1997); see also *ACLU et al. v. Reno*, Civ. Act., 929 F. Supp. 824 (E.D. Pa. 1996): 'Just as the strength of Internet is chaos, so the strength of our liberty depends upon the chaos and the cacophony of the unfettered speech the First Amendment protects.'

[40] Helmut Baumann, *Die Dienstleistung auf dem Gebiet der Audiovisuellen Medien im Rahmen des GATS im Spannungsfeld von Marktfreiheit und kultureller Selbstbestimmung der Staaten der Europäischen Union* (Berlin: Duncker & Humblot, 1998).

[41] These are discussed in Grewlich, *Governance in Cyberspace* (above, n. 1), part two.

[42] See National Research Council, *Bits of Power* (above, n. 38); after an 'unholy alliance' the European Union and the United States might now develop partly opposing positions.

raphy,[43] the EC Directive on the Protection of Personal Data,[44] the regime for domain names, the issues pertaining to the liberalization of media products in the next WTO/GATS review rounds (including the European policy in the field of *télévision sans frontières*),[45] and the notion of 'universal access' with regard to cyberspace. Some of these examples are dealt with in the following pages to illustrate the need for solution-oriented transatlantic regulatory cooperation.

A. Example: systems competition—liberalization, re-regulation, and 'neo-protectionism'

It is recognized that deregulation and competition are major driving forces towards convergence and the creation of wealth in the multimedia value chain. But conversely, as the emerging new reality of convergence feeds back to the regulatory environment and as this may result in regulatory inconsistencies, a certain amount of re-regulation, i.e. an adjustment of existing regulatory schemes might be required. The ensuing search for optimization in regulatory action may enhance the ongoing competition among systems[46] and have an impact on trade in goods and services and foreign direct investment flows.[47]

Particular 'arbitrary' comparative advantages may result from a combination of pro-active generous liberalization of communication markets and simultaneous aggressive opening of foreign markets, so to speak, to 'make the world safe' for information and communication products and services. 'Optimum policy mixes', taking advantage of existing 'pull effects' of lead markets and a collective will to maintain the advantages of 'information power' and high-tech superiority,[48] together with widely shared political visions,[49] may possibly be perceived as neo-protectionism,

---

[43] Kenneth W. Dam and Herbert S. Lin (eds), *Cryptography's Role In Securing the Information Society* (Washington: National Academy Press, 1996).

[44] EU, European Parliament and Council Directive 95/46/EC of 24 Oct. 1995 on the protection of individuals with regard to the processing of personal data and the free movement of such data, 1995 O.J. (L 281/31), 23.11.1995.

[45] Faced with competition by the major US producers, the European film industry has undergone a dramatic decline, and in response governments have set up various support schemes for European productions. What is under such circumstances the potential for conflict and cooperation in the field for e-commerce? Notably, how do US and EU antitrust policies compare pertaining to the issues of vertical integration (audiovisual (Internet/telecoms))?

[46] See Joel Trachtman, 'International Regulatory Competition—Externalisation and Jurisdiction', *Harvard International Law Journal*, vol. 34 (1993), 48–104.

[47] Klaus W. Grewlich, *Direct Investment in the OECD Countries* (Sijthoff & Noordhoff: Alphen aan den Rijn, 1978).

[48] Joseph S. Nye and William A. Owens, 'America's Information Edge', *Foreign Affairs*, vol. 75, no. 2 (1996), 20–36; Klaus W. Grewlich, *Europa im globalen Technologiewettlauf—Der Weltmarkt wird zum Binnenmarkt* (Gütersloh: Bertelsmann Foundation, 1992).

[49] Such as 'global information highway' or 'global information society'.

notably if combined with judicious trade policies and if certain obstacles such as regulatory foreign direct-investment restrictions[50] are not removed. One rationale occasionally advanced for maintaining a higher degree of regulation over international services than domestic services, for instance, is 'the need to preserve leverage when dealing with supposedly less pro-market administrations abroad'.[51]

To the extent that certain limitations on direct foreign ownership have been explicitly retained in the pertinent WTO/GATS offers and schedules, such regulatory restrictions are not covered by the liberalizing obligations of GATS Agreement on Telecommunication Services.[52] Thus, there would be no infringement. Nevertheless, such cases are instances of regulatory disparities that may lead to conflict. Therefore, issues as, for instance, Article 310 of the US Communications Act ('public-interest analysis') should be addressed in bilateral regulatory cooperation and/or eventually in future multilateral negotiation rounds.

B. Example: domain names

To take the example of the regulation of Internet domain names, the following position is certainly not uncontroversial but might be a good starting point for a candid transatlantic regulatory discussion: 'It is improbable that the US will surrender the control of "Internet domain names" until there is full deregulation. Because the Internet is the brainchild of the US it is unlikely that the US will give up governance to simply see it fall into the domination of other countries who will also treat the registries as their own natural monopolies.'[53]

---

[50] There exist various restrictions in the telecommunications market that impede competition in a number of sectors, such as Art. 310 of the (US) Communications Act of 1996 which limits foreign direct investment in common carrier radio licences to 20% (the regime for indirect ownership is more liberal); see Klaus W. Grewlich, *Konflikt und Ordnung in der globalen Kommunikation—Wettstreit der Staaten und Wettbewerb der Unternehmen (Conflict and Order in Global Communications—Struggle among States and Competition between Enterprises)*, Law and Economics of International Telecommunications, vol. 33 (Baden-Baden: Nomos, 1997), 152f.; see, on the other hand, Stefan M. Meisner, 'Global Telecommunications a Reality—United States Complies with WTO Pact', *American University International Law Review*, vol. 13 (1997), 111ff.

[51] See Kenneth G. Robinson, *Building a Global Information Society* (Washington: Aspen, 1996); see also 'consent decrees' (DOJ) and decisions in the cases 'Concert' and 'Global One' analysed in Grewlich, *Konflikt und Ordnung* (above, n. 50), 129ff., notably FCC, MCI Communications Corp., British Telecommunications plc, 9 FCC Ecd 3960 (1994).

[52] World Trade Organisation (WTO) Agreement on Telecommunications Services (Fourth Protocol to General Agreement on Trade in Services), 15 Feb. 1997, 36 I.L.M. 354 (1997) (with introductory note by Laura B. Sherman); Phillip L. Spector, 'The World Trade Organisation Agreement on Telecommunications', *International Lawyer*, vol. 32, no. 2 (1998), 217ff.

[53] Aurora Rodriguez Aragón, 'Competing Telecommunications and Cyber Regulation—Is there a Need for a Transatlantic Regulatory Framework?' (paper presented in the seminar 'Technology and International Competition—Conflict and Order in Global Communications', Bruges, College of Europe, 1999 [http://mars.coleurop.be/infosoc]); see also the US State Department Instruction (Secretary of State M. Albright) to the US—'Internet Ad-hoc

It is correct that, with the agreement on the Internet Corporation for Assigned Names and Numbers (ICANN), a structure has become operational that is distinguished by an improved international participation (although US representatives hold six out of eleven seats on the 'Initial Board'). It is also true that in the new structure European registrars were assigned an upgraded role in the administration of domain names. But, on the other hand, the US Department of Commerce's National Telecommunications and Information Administration (NTIA) still retains important rights of interference regarding ICANN[54] and the administration of domain names. How much regulatory cooperation is realistically desired from the point of view of established leadership positions?

C. Example: peering agreements

In opposition to the settlement payments mechanism of the telecommunications world, the Internet Service Provider (ISP), which initiates the call, so far—following the Internet communities' 'sender-keeps-all' (SKA) methodology—does not pay anything to the ISP which terminates the call. Money changes hands only from the user to the access provider and from access providers to the nearest backbone operator. The Internet has, in fact, evolved rapidly on the basis of this model.

The problem with this network business model, however, is that there is no real contribution to balanced organic network growth. This is not only because of the SKA methodology, but also because of the simple fact that ISPs wanting to connect to the most vital Internet backbones in the United States did not pay 'half-circuit costs', but 'full-circuit costs' (both half circuits) of the leased line that performs the connection. This commercial situation reflected the fact that non-US connecting networks benefit greatly from connecting to the US backbone, the centre of the Internet empire, while US backbone networks benefit much less from connecting with 'peripheral' networks outside the United States.[55] Trying to impose an accounting rate system under such circumstances would be detrimental for the commercial working of this global information network. For instance, in many cases it probably would cost more to implement and maintain a billing system than to deliver the traffic. But as usage in 'peripheral' countries and regions increases, production of successful content augments and pertinent networks mature, traffic flows will become more balanced. At this point, it would then seem fair to advance

Committee' (IAHC)—Delegation advising against the signing of the 'Generic Top Level Domain' (gTLD)-MOU, as reported by Dan Brekke, *Wired* (30 Apr. 1997).

[54] 47 USC. §902; see also Memorandum of Understanding Between the US Department of Commerce and ICANN, http://www.ntia.doc.gov/ntiahome/domainname/icann-memorandum.htm.

[55] ITU, *Challenges to the Network—Telecoms and the Internet* (Geneva: ITU, 1997), 25f.

to a half-circuit settlement system to avoid a 'sender-pays-all' situation for ISPs which are not based in the United States.

Because ISPs based outside the United States could not avoid paying the full cost of both 'half circuits' of the leased line required to connect into the US backbone—even though the traffic flows both ways over the circuit—a number of observers and parties involved have begun to question the right of the United States to dictate the terms for the expansion of the Internet and to treat cyberspace as if it were a 'US Territory'. Subsequent to the US Federal Communication Commission's (FCC) Notice of Proposed Rule Making on International Settlement Rates[56] issued in December 1996, the pertinent issues have been highlighted in the comments submitted by Telstra Corporation Ltd., an Australian telecommunications organization.[57] Telstra points out that Internet traffic to the United States is growing at a compound rate of 10 per cent per month. Originally the majority of traffic flowing over the line was from Australian consulting databases and websites in the United States, i.e. traffic flowing from the United States to Australia. But as many users from the United States now consult websites based in Australia, US multinational enterprises offload traffic to Australia, as convenient, and as Internet telephony becomes a reality, the balance of traffic flows is considerably changing in favour of Australia. Thus Telstra claims that it is actually cross-subsidizing US Internet users. Telstra, therefore, requests a more rational pricing system for transborder Internet traffic.[58] The company reported that as a result of the unfair system US providers would gain every year US$9.6 million from Telstra, and worldwide US$2.5 billion until the year 2000.[59]

In view of the oligopolistic developments that now take place as a result of the disappearance of small ISPs and the possibly ensuing conflicts, private parties would have to negotiate reasonable peering schemes and states should be willing to provide a light but stable and effective international framework.[60] Possible bilateral solutions, to be globalized at a later stage, could be elaborated via transatlantic regulatory cooperation that includes governments, business, and representative civil society entities.

[56] FCC, *International Settlement Rates*, IB Docket No. 96-261, *Notice of Proposed Rulemaking*, FCC No. 96-484 (rel. 19 Dec. 1996).

[57] The text of Telstra's comments is available from the FCC As to the Report and Order: see FCC, *International settlements rates*, IB Docket No. 96-261, *Report and Order*, FCC No. 97-480 (rel. 18 Aug. 1997).

[58] Telstra lost its case in Court, because the Court held that the *Notice of Proposed Rulemaking* (No. 96-484 rel. 19 Dec. 1996) concerned only the 'message telephone service' but not the Internet; the phenomenon of convergence was not taken into consideration!

[59] FCC, Telstra Corp. Ltd., Comments of Telstra Corporation Limited regarding IB Docket No. 96-261, 4f.

[60] Robert Frieden, 'Without Public Peer—The Potential Regulatory and Universal Service Consequences of Internet Balkanisation', *Virginia Journal of Law and Technology*, vol. 3 (1998) (available at http://vjolt.student.virginia.edu/graphics/vol3/vol3_art8.html); Christian von Hammerstein, 'US-Gericht—Höchstpreise für internationale Zusammenschaltungsentgelte bestätigt', in *Multimedia und Recht* (MMR), vol. 2 (1999), XIIf.

D. Example: 'tragedy of the commons' in cyberspace—'unholy trans-atlantic regulatory cooperation' in the case of the draft WIPO Data Base Treaty?

Part of the public domain that anyone can freely appropriate are any non-copyrightable or subpatentable materials, i.e. any publicly disclosed information that does not meet the threshold of legal requirements for protection under patent or copyright law. To illustrate this statement in more detail, we may, for example, immediately use data and ideas disclosed in books or articles. Copyright law does not protect against use as such but only protects against certain uses: notably adaptation, reproduction, and public performance. The digital environment, however, has made the traditional balancing of public interest and private rights more complex. To protect non-copyrightable databases internationally and nationally in a tailor-made legal regime, a 'sui generis protection' for data banks (possibly a new type of unfair competition law) was proposed in the 1996 WIPO Diplomatic Conference by the EC Commission and EC Member States.[61] The EC Commission had developed a 'database policy', as it found that information lies at the core of social advancement and economic competitiveness, and that consequently European database producers had to expand their market share to catch up with US database industries, perceived as the 'OPEC of information'.

In the 1996 WIPO Diplomatic Conference's deliberations on a possible Data Base Treaty,[62] the US delegation came forward with a counterproposal (based on regulatory cooperation with the EC Commission). The US proposal did not differ in substance too much from the EC text. This US proposal must be seen against the background of domestic legislative developments in the United States: bill H.R. 3531[63] proposing to protect non-copyrightable databases. Under H.R. 3531 and the 1996 EC Directive, a compiler, having expended resources, would be granted exclusive rights to prevent extraction and re-uses of the whole or substantial parts of any database.[64] The WIPO Diplomatic Conference postponed immediate action on the Draft Data Base Treaty, seeing the matter as not yet sufficiently 'mature', although it qualified for WIPO follow-up work.

---

[61] On the basis of EU, European Parliament and Council Directive 96/9/EC on the legal protection of databases of 11 March 1996, 1996 OJ L (77/20) 27 Mar. 1996, WIPO-Doc. BCP/CE/VI/13.

[62] Gisbert Hohagen, 'WIPO-Sitzung zum zukünftigen internationalen Schutz von Datenbanken', Gerwerblicher Rechtsschutz und Urheberrechte, Internationaler Teil, vol. 47, no. 1 (Jan. 1998), 54ff.; Grewlich, in Governance in 'Cyberspace' (above, n. 1), ch. 8, sec. 4.4.

[63] Database Investment and Intellectual Property Antipiracy Act of 1996, H.R. 3531, 104th Cong. (1996).

[64] The provision is seen as ignoring the constitutional enabling clause, which requires intellectual property rights to be limited in time, US Const. art. I, §8, cl. 8; see National Research Council, Bits of Power (above, n. 38), 157.

I am not convinced that the 1996 EC Directive on the legal protection of databases, the US bill H.R. 3531 (ultimately rejected in the US Congress), and the present deliberations pertaining to a WIPO Draft Data Base Treaty adequately take into account the public interest in not impeding the full and open flow of basic science data. As a matter of fact, access to scientific data which are already largely collected, managed, and distributed in electronic form would be affected by the new legal framework for the protection of non-copyrightable databases that seems to be evolving. Should the needs of data users, such as scientists, working in the public interest in the fields of basic scientific research and education become subordinate to the desires and interests of those seeking protection of, and return on, investment in creating and maintaining databases? Is there a danger of conferring market power and monopolies on database developers far broader and stronger than is needed to avert market failures?[65]

It is true that the EC Directive gives EU Member States the option of allowing authorized extraction from non-copyrightable databases 'for the purpose of illustration for teaching or scientific research, as long as the source is indicated and to the extent justified by the noncommercial purpose to be achieved'.[66] This exception, however, is available only to a 'lawful user' and only for the purpose of 'extraction' but not for that of re-utilization, and only to the extent that the different EU Member States opt to enact it. It is doubtful whether the notion of 'illustration' comprises uses for other scientific and educational purposes, such as browsing and extractions from collected data to reach new scientific conclusions that then may be illustrated. The critical question in this 'tragedy of the commons' is whether and how to create fair use zones in cyberspace that would protect the public interest in ensuring that certain users, notably science, research, and education, are not priced out of the market or forced to cut back on basic research.[67]

The pertinent fora of transatlantic regulatory cooperation should scrutinize to what extent the growing scope of patents and patent protection is contrary to the original idea of balancing private and public interests. True, a patent is a legal monopoly. To deny a patentee freedom of pricing would undercut the rationale for patent protection. But there is evidence of a proliferation of exclusive rights in the United States and in Europe that

---

[65] National Research Council, *Bits of Power* (above, n. 38), 8 ff., 132 ff.

[66] EU, European Parliament and Council Directive 96/9/EC on the legal protection of databases of 11 March 1996, art. 9(b), 1996 O.J. (L 77/20), 27 March 1996.

[67] Marci A. Hamilton, 'The TRIPS Agreement—Imperialistic, Outdated and Overprotective', *Vanderbilt Journal of Transnational Law*, vol. 27 (1996), 623 f.: proposing 'free use zones' in the online area. Such 'zones' would not mean that the Internet should be 'free' or that copyright would effectively be emasculated; see Kenneth W. Dam, 'Self-Help in the Digital Jungle,' in Chicago Working Papers in Law & Economics no. 59, 2nd Series (Chicago: University of Chicago School of Law, 1998), 2; National Research Council, *Bits of Power* (above, n. 38), 145.

are neither quite copyright nor quite patent. Is the notion of *sui generis* protection of databases and the ensuing shrinking fair use the bankruptcy of systematic legal interpretation?[68]

Transatlantic regulatory cooperation should forcefully address such issues, possibly beginning with the following reference frame work: First, the protection of databases, as important as it is on the whole, should be distinguished by a balance between public and private interests. There is a public interest to promote free competition between public goods and private intellectual property (which might imply some pro-competitive policies); second, the pertinent treaties and laws to be conceived, enacted, and implemented should preserve and create *fair use zones*, specifically designed to facilitate, encourage, and enhance both the national and notably the transborder scientific enterprise.

E. Example: protection of personal data—'adequacy'?

An example for both regulatory disparities and possible cooperation is the EC Directive on the Protection of Personal Data.[69] When it was first drafted in 1990, data communication took place mainly between big mainframe computers. The explosion of global communications, the spread of personal computers and global information networks were not anticipated by the Directive. But because, in fact, the Directive covers now all such traffic ('any information relating to an identified or identifiable natural person') it may disturb trade-related data flows and transborder data-exchange between economic actors and even inside transnational enterprises and business alliances.[70]

The Directive lays down the conditions which must be fulfilled for legally processing personal data. The conditions include that personal data must be 'processed fairly and lawfully', 'collected for specified, explicit and legitimate purposes', must be 'accurate and, where necessary, kept up to date', and 'kept in a form which permits identification of "data subjects" for no longer than is necessary for the purposes for which the data were collected' (Article 6). 'Member States shall prohibit the processing of personal data revealing racial or ethnic origin, political opinions, religious or philosophical beliefs, trade-union membership, and the processing of data concerning health or sex life' (Article 8). Processing may only take place if the person concerned agrees or if processing is otherwise

---

[68] See The National Academy of Sciences/German–American Academic Council Foundation, *The Changing Character, Use and Protection of Intellectual Property* (forthcoming).

[69] EU, European Parliament and Council Directive 95/46/EC (above, n. 44).

[70] Grewlich, *Konflikt und Ordnung* (above, n. 50), 67 f. See the analysis regarding possible extraterritorial effects of the European Data Privacy Directive by Henry H. Perritt and Margaret G. Stewart, 'False Alarm?', *Federal Communications Law Journal*, vol. 51 (1993/3), 811 ff.

necessary because of legal reasons or contractual obligations of the person ('data subject') concerned (Article 7).

If the network computers, notably the Web servers,[71] are within the European Union they must comply in every respect with the national data-protection law implementing the Directive. In those cases where servers are located in third countries outside the European Union and personal data are transferred for processing, the third country must, according to Article 25 of the Directive, ensure an adequate level of protection: 'Where the Commission finds, under the procedure provided for in Article 31 (2),[72] that a third country does not ensure an adequate level of protection within the meaning of paragraph 2[73] of this Article, Member States shall take the measures necessary to prevent any transfer of data of the same type to the third country in question.'

'Adequacy', however, may not only refer to governmental legislation and regulation, but from the point of view of the United States, also to effective systems of self-regulation (even if these are based on independent initiative and do not refine a framework that has been preconceived by public institutions). Here again, it is far from clear what the term 'effective' precisely means.

Even if the application of certain critical rules may be waived for a number of years, the problem with the EC Directive is that there is the Scylla of 'draconian application' and the Charybdis in terms of a possible 'credibility gap'. In plain language: if there are no exemplary cases, the threat that (transatlantic) data flows may be cut will not be taken seriously and business might eventually ignore the Directive. Such a development would be detrimental for the rule of law and the European Union's legal culture. If, however, there are cases where data streams are cut, this would create a delicate and unstable international situation and could trigger a trade war between the European Union and third countries, such as the United States. This is an excellent example of a legal and political constellation, where transatlantic regulatory cooperation is a vital condition for solving the problem and avoiding conflict.

It appears now as a considerable disadvantage for the community of nations, particularly for the transatlantic relationship, that the efforts to promote an international framework for privacy and data protection in the

---

[71] Central computer where software packages are stored. A computer on a network that performs functions (for instance computation, storage, and retrieval) for other computers, terminals, and peripheral devices on the network.

[72] The EU Commission shall be assisted by a Committee composed of representatives of the Member States chaired by the representative of the Commission. The Committee (acting by qualified majority) shall adopt measures. These shall normally apply immediately. Application may be deferred for a period of three months.

[73] '2. The adequacy of the level of protection afforded by a third country shall be assessed in the light of all the circumstances surrounding a data transfer operation or set of data transfer operations; . . .'

digital environment which took place for many years in the OECD (and which were strongly supported by many European countries) were met with reluctance by some OECD partners, notably the United States.

However, more recent developments show that it is not too late for a solid international framework regarding privacy. In the United States attitudes pertaining to data protection are changing and pertinent policies are under review. In the framework of the OECD Ministerial Conference 'A Borderless World: Realising the Potential of Global Electronic Commerce' that took place in Ottawa in October 1998,[74] OECD ministers adopted a declaration on continuing to work on the protection of privacy.[75] It was agreed that 'the OECD, in cooperation with industry and business, should provide practical guidance on the implementation of the OECD privacy guidelines[76] based on national experiences and examples'. Thus, in a field where until now disparities prevailed, transatlantic regulatory cooperation could develop important overriding commonalities.

III. NORMATIVE PRINCIPLES — 'CONSTITUTIONALIZATION' OF INTERNATIONAL LAW

The insights offered here into some transatlantic commonalities and disparities regarding the regulation of communications point to the need for a more developed bilateral and—given the global nature of cyberspace—international regulatory framework. International law was expected to evolve from a law of coexistence to a law of cooperation.[77] Given the present reality of international affairs (as illustrated by the allied force initiative for protecting human rights in Kosovo, the global environmental syndrome, development crises, migration, ethnic and fundamentalist conflicts, the promises and threats of global information networks), as well as the level of effective multilateral cooperation that has been reached (e.g. in WTO, WIPO, ITU, and many other international organizations), the objective of an international law of cooperation may have to be

[74] See OECD News Release, 'Ottawa Conference on Electronic Commerce', 13 Oct. 1998, http://www.oecd.org/news-and-events/release/nw98-95a.htm.

[75] OECD Ministerial Conference A Borderless World: Releasing the Potential of Global Electronic Commerce—Conference Conclusions 7–9 Oct. 1998, Ottawa, Canada, SG/EC(98)14/REV6, 26 Oct. 1998 (Annexe 1), 12ff.; see Dimitri Ypsilanti, 'A borderless world—the OECD Ottawa Ministerial Conference and initiatives in electronic commerce', *info*, vol. 1 (1999), 23–33.

[76] The Objectives set forth in the following OECD-instruments were reaffirmed: The Recommendation Concerning Guidelines Governing the Protection of Privacy and Transborder Flows of Personal Data, adopted by the Council of the OECD on 23 September 1980 (*OECD Privacy Guidelines*); The Declaration on Transborder Data Flows, adopted by Governments of OECD Member Countries on 11 April 1985; and the Recommendation concerning Guidelines for Cryptography Policy, adopted by the Council of the OECD on 27 March 1997 (available at the OECD Secretariat, Paris).

[77] Friedmann, *Changing Structure* (above, n. 2).

complemented and superseded by the more ambitious but timely objective of 'constitutionalizing' international law. Transatlantic cooperation could constructively contribute to reaching the objective of a qualitative jump in modernizing both international economic law and the UN legal system by integrating human rights, democratic accountability, the rule of law and justice[78] in a multi-actor and multi-level approach.

The notion of governance might be used to characterize the present transitional phase. I understand governance not as a final stage of development nor as an objective in itself, but rather as an important step towards an improved international legal scheme (i.e. a constitutionalized international law). This development comprises not only bilateral and multilateral governmental cooperation but also encompasses the activities of transnational business[79] and of influential and representative non-governmental civil society actors (multi-actor analysis). The required effort should reflect that in harmony with the principle of 'subsidiarity', regulatory and self-regulatory action in the age of cyberspace may have to take place at different levels of competence, i.e. regional, multiregional, or global.

In this transition to constitutionalization, today's increasingly networked[80] legislators, regulators, conference diplomats, business and civil society entities need a common mental framework, in terms of shared essentials of governance (and a vision of constitutionalization) including normative principles, to safeguard both competition and public policy objectives, at a scale congruent to cyberspace.

A. Normative principles—elements of governance in cyberspace

With a view to enhancing competition between economic actors and to minimize conflict between states, the OECD was looking for the subjects of trade and direct investment[81] and also global information networks (information society and electronic commerce) for some time. The Ministerial Conference in Ottawa (October 1998) on 'A Borderless World—Realising the Potential of Global Electronic Commerce'[82] was a

[78] Ernst-Ulrich Petersmann, 'How to Reform the United Nations—Lessons from the International Economic Law Revolution', UCLA Journal of International Law and Foreign Affairs, vol. 2 (1997), 185; Gerber, 'Constitutionalizing the Economy' (above, n. 3); see contribution of Ernst-Ulrich Petersmann to this volume.

[79] Klaus W. Grewlich, Transnational Enterprises in a New International System (Alphen aan den Rijn and Rockville, Md.: Sijthoff & Noordhoff, 1980).

[80] See Anne-Marie Slaughter, 'Liberal International Relations Theory and International Economic Law', American University Journal of International Law & Policy, vol. 10 (1995), 717, see also contribution of Anne-Marie Slaughter to this volume.

[81] OECD, Open Markets Matter—The Benefits of Trade and Investment Liberalisation (Paris: OECD, 1998).

[82] OECD, Ministerial Conference—A Borderless World: Realising the Potential of Global Electronic Commerce, Ottawa 7–9 Oct. 1998, Paris 1998; for a critical position arguing that the

'multi-actor' event. It brought together governments, international organizations, business leaders, representatives of labour, consumer and civil society groups. Though not legally binding, but normative in nature and possibly a starting point for the development of 'soft law',[83] the operational results of the OECD Ottawa Conference typically pertain not only to governments, but also to business and civil society groups. This effort, in terms of multi-actor and multi-level governance, might give some guidance for further developments. It is, however, still far away from a grand design such as the constitutionalization of international relations and international law.

Transnational economic and civil society actors are generally not treated as subjects of international law like states or international organizations. However, they may become (necessary) partners in approaches of regulatory cooperation and viable systems of *governance*. Are we heading towards an enlargement of the international society as a legal community?[84] Will a 'mature' international law eventually evolve into 'constitutionalization' comprising not only schemes of democratic legitimation and accountability, fully incorporating fundamental rights, but for instance also the international law of development and international environmental law? Will such a modernized international law also perform normative 'umbrella functions' such as covering not only the relations between nations but also business actors (transnational companies, consortia, and business confederations), transnational labour and civil society groups? Will the various 'subjects of international law' be equal in all respects or is a double standard appropriate acknowledging and guaranteeing the higher legitimacy of states? Indeed, some sort of two-tier legal community may emerge, with actors such as business and civil society entities recognized as subjects of international law but with states being privileged as they possess, so to speak, the 'framework powers' or 'constitutional prerogatives'.

The core of the issues pertaining to the institutional aspects of governance is the transformation of the sovereignty of states resulting from globalization. This not only implies the well-known phenomenon of 'Sovereignty at Bay',[85] i.e. the perception that the power of sovereign states is diminishing as a result of reallocation of powers in favour of other international actors such as transnational enterprises and recently civil society groups. There is another related development, to be observed inside countries: that is the shift of the power distribution in national

OECD-Ottawa meeting was dominated by big business see James Love, 'Democracy, privatization and the governance of cyberspace', *info,* vol. 1 (1999), 16–22.

[83] Richard Baxter, 'International Law in Her Infinite Variety,' *International and Comparative Law Quarterly,* vol. 29 (1980), 549 ff.

[84] Hermann Mosler, *The International Society as a Legal Community* (Alphen aan den Rijn: Sijthoff & Noordhoff, 1980); see also Myres McDougal, 'International Law, Power and Policy—A Contemporary Conception', *Hague Recueil,* vol. 82 (1953), 137.

[85] Raymond Vernon, *Sovereignty at Bay* (New York: Basic Books, 1971).

governmental institutions because of the necessary participation of competent state agencies, such as central banks, ministries of finance, specific committees, etc., in the implementation of 'globality'.[86] As a result, such institutions may become more outward looking and networked in a global 'peer system', each component thus transgressing the limited national perspective and growing into an additional role (*dédoublement fonctionnel*).[87]

B. Policy principles and substantive principles

The issues pertaining to governance as a step towards constitutionalization in the transition to the global information society comprise, apart from regulatory elements in terms of creating and correcting markets (bottleneck problems) and safeguarding access/competition and the public interest, the questions of what policy principles should be followed and of what substantive principles should be applied.

1. Policy principles

Core-policy principles, calling on governments to ensure an appropriate framework aiming at stimulating private investment in, and usage of, global information networks have been agreed, for instance, at the G7 Brussels Conference in February 1995. These principles are: promoting dynamic competition; encouraging private investment; defining an adaptable regulatory framework; providing open access to networks; ensuring universal provision of and access to services; promoting equality of opportunity to the citizen, enhancing diversity of content, including cultural and linguistic diversity; recognizing the necessity of worldwide cooperation with particular attention to less-developed countries.

A number of political activities and international events such as the 1997 Ministerial Conference on Global Information Networks, in Bonn,[88] and the 1998 OECD Ministerial Conference on Borderless World: Realising the Potential of Global Electronic Commerce, in Ottawa,[89] have contributed to the refinement of these principles. Besides fundamental policy questions, the latter conferences notably also addressed legal issues such as security and confidentiality, authentication and integrity of messages, data protection, intellectual property rights, the facilitation of trading in multimedia content, and taxation.

The Ministerial Declaration ensuing from the Bonn Conference as well as a collateral 'Industrial Declaration' put forward by the private sector and a declaration from 'user groups' contain key principles for further progress: regulation should be as light-handed and flexible as possible;

---

[86] Saskia Sassen, 'Global Financial Centers', *Foreign Affairs*, vol. 78 (1999), 82.

[87] Georges Scelle, *Précis de droit des gens* (Paris: Pedone, 1934).

[88] Ministerial Conference Bonn 6–8 July 1997 ('Global Information Networks').

[89] Conference Conclusions, OECD Document SG/EC(98)14REV6 26 Oct. 1998, Paris 1998.

legal rules applicable to global information networks should be consistent across the borders; telecommunication markets should be opened up rapidly to effective competition; market forces must be allowed to rapidly develop open technical standards; discriminatory tax costs should not be imposed on the use of these networks; a high level of intellectual property rights protection is necessary for the creation, storage, and distribution of cyber-content.

In the framework of the OECD Ottawa Conference, business proposed a set of principles 'to shape the policies that govern electronic commerce, if the promises of electronic commerce are to be fulfilled'.[90] Many civil society entities were opposed to a 'privatized' Internet that would be mainly governed by self-regulation. They rather advocated clear public/governmental authority and responsibilities on the basis of democratic legitimation, as the pertinent issues were perceived as being 'too important to be left to a handful of trade officials and corporate lobbyists'.[91]

2. Substantive principles

Substantive principles of governance that should contribute to creating a level playing field to reduce the potential for international conflict and to guarantee a thriving transborder information society may distinguish between, first, specific (sectorial) and, second, general (horizontal) principles:

(i) The more specific principles turn around three main themes of cyber-law and policies:[92]

- Strengthening trust for consumers: i.e. the protection of personal data, security, confidentiality and privacy. In particular, trust also means that buyers and sellers are able to authenticate and verify the integrity of messages and on-line transactions.
- Evolving ground rules for the new digital environment (electronic market place). This effort would include: avoiding market distortion resulting from ruinous tax competition between countries taxing at the points of output or consumption of electronic products; trade policy issues; market access and the protection of intellectual property rights.
- Enhancing state-of-the-art infrastructures: affordable access to infrastructures is needed. Internet governance (e.g. domain names) and technical standards are salient issues. Regulatory reform and more

---

[90] OECD Ministerial Conference, 'A Borderless World: Realising the Potential of Global Electronic Commerce', A Global Action Plan for Electronic Commerce Prepared by Business with Recommendations from Governments, 7–9 October 1998, Ottawa, Canada, OECD Document SG/EC(98)11/REV2, 5 Oct. 1998, (9).

[91] See James Love, 'Democracy, privatization and the governance of cyberspace', *info*, vol. 1 (1999), 16 ff.

[92] See in detail Grewlich, *Governance in 'Cyberspace'* (above, n. 1).

competition in communication markets might help further to decrease prices for service provision.

(ii) *General* (horizontal) 'principles' may contain:

- first, policy principles, notably including 'international cooperation,' 'open markets' and 'quality of national regulation' and
- second, principles derived from international economic law and comparative administrative law. Apart from transparency, these principles would primarily comprise subsidiarity and proportionality and non-discrimination (i.e. national treatment and most-favoured-nation treatment (MFN)) and estoppel,[93] etc.

The principles of subsidiarity and proportionality[94] applied to the practice of regulation mean that regulation, to the extent that it is necessary, first, should take place at the appropriate level (international, regional/ European, national, provincial, local): i.e. the higher level should only become active to the extent that the lower is unable to effectively deal with the issues at hand[95] (once the principle of subsidiarity is applied as a matter of routine the complex system of governance may be assessed in terms of 'multi-level analysis'); and second, should not exceed what is necessary to achieve the objective sought, i.e. be clearly focused, transparent, and minimally interventionist.

IV. COURSES OF ACTION FOR REGULATORY COOPERATION

Considerable efforts are being made at present to deal with pertinent issues of cyberlaw and policies in a number of international organizations (e.g. WTO, OECD, WIPO, ITU), in bilateral regulatory cooperation and in innovative business fora (Transatlantic Business Dialogue;[96] Global Business Dialogue), in the Internet community and various civil society groups, and in the research community, partly on the basis of self-regulation.

---

[93] As to the latter and additional general principles see e.g. Hans Van Houtte, *The Law of International Trade* (London: Sweet & Maxwell, 1995), 3ff.

[94] See Article 3b (3) EC-Treaty; *Hauer*—Cases 44/79, ECR 79/3727; Case 122/78, *Buitoni*— ECR 1979/677; *Hoechst*—Cases 46/87 and 227/88 ECR 1989/2859; see also Bellamy and Child, *Law of Competition* (above, n. 29), 24f.; Herdegen, *Europarecht* (above, n. 29), 113. When deciding whether to enact binding or non-binding measures, the Community has to assess both the importance of uniform regulatory conditions and the technical complexity involved. Even if legislation is judged necessary at the European level, it may be expedient to leave margins of manoeuvre to national authorities in transposing EU legislation into national laws.

[95] The principle of subsidiarity is enshrined in Article 5 (ex Article 3b (2)) of the EC Treaty: 'In areas which do not fall within its exclusive competence, the Community shall take action, in accordance with the principle of *subsidiarity*, only if and in so far as the objectives of the proposed action cannot be sufficiently achieved by the Member States and can therefore, by reason of the scale or effects of the proposed action, be better achieved by the Community'.

[96] Cf. Transatlantic Business Dialogue, Mission Statement 1998.

A. Self-regulation

The efforts of self-regulators may be important, notably in the field of standards. There is a decentralized power structure in the Internet. But as a pure anarchy, global networks could not function. The definition of protocols, for instance, must be coordinated. Technical compatibility of networks must be ensured; otherwise content would not be able to pass seamlessly between different networks. Participants in the Internet communicate on the basis of a common protocol, the 'open standard TCP/IP'. This protocol is first written, then freely distributed to any individual or entity who wants to use it. Revisions of the protocol take account of the experience of the users. Business and other stake holders should ensure that effective self-regulation pertaining to open standards is maintained and no restrictions on free competition and access arise.

B. Formal and informal regulatory cooperation

Bilateral governmental regulatory cooperation may be formal or informal. The present transatlantic negotiations on domain names or a framework for private peering schemes for the sharing of Internet traffic basically are informal approaches. On the other hand, a formal bilateral scheme of regulatory cooperation is, for instance, the 'Agreement Between the Government of the United States of America and the European Communities on the Application of Positive Comity Principles in the Enforcement of their Competition Laws'.[97]

C. Bilateral and multilateral cooperation

Transatlantic regulatory cooperation may be bilateral. It may also be part of a wider multilateral effort to avoid undue national regulatory differentials that might hinder international economic and cultural exchange and to ensure that the rule of law prevails on the regional and global level with the objective to improve the international framework towards reaching the objective of constitutionalization.

Regarding multilateral governmental efforts in communications and cyberspace, a number of international agreements and arrangements have been concluded that are of importance as a basis for international cooperation in the digital environment. The Ministerial Declaration on Trade in Information Technology Products agreed upon in Singapore on 13 December 1996 provides for the enhancement of trade in information technology products. This agreement covers approximately 90 per cent of

---

[97] Available at http://www.usdoj.gov/atr/public/international/docs/1781.htm; for further discussion see Alexander Schaub, 'International Cooperation in Antitrust Matters', *Competition Policy Newsletter* no. 1 (1998), 2 ff.

world trade in IT products.[98] Follow-up negotiations have produced the result that tariffs on IT products will gradually be reduced to zero by 1 January 2000. The WTO Agreement on Basic Telecommunications Services[99] comprising sixty-nine countries, accounting for 90 per cent of the world's US$650 billion basic telecoms market came into force on 5 February 1998. The WIPO Diplomatic Conference held at Geneva in December 1996 adopted two treaties in the field of copyright and neighbouring rights.[100]

V. SUMMARY AND CONCLUSIONS

The digital revolution leads to convergence (of telecommunications, computers/global information networks, and broadcasting) and to dynamic multimedia value chains (comprising content origination—content packaging—service provision—and communications infrastructure/distribution). In the new digital environment traditional sectorspecific regulation looks outdated. Adjusted schemes of regulation (including self-regulation) are under consideration. The objectives are to provide access, under conditions of platform independence, notably interconnection, transparency, and flexibility, to free and sustain competition and to redress imbalances; at the same time to safeguard public-interest objectives, such as security and human dignity.

Regulatory and self-regulatory action may take place at different levels of competence (local, national, supra-national, 'multi-regional', global) and imply various actors (notably governments, transnational business, and civil society entities).

Deregulation and competition are the major driving forces towards convergence and the creation of wealth in the multimedia value chain. But conversely, as the emerging new reality of convergence feeds back to the regulatory environment and as this may result in regulatory inconsistencies, a certain amount of re-regulation, i.e. an adjustment of existing regulatory schemes, might be required. Arbitrary national comparative advantage may emerge from 'optimum policy mixes' (for instance 'pull effects' of lead markets resulting from proactive liberalization, R&D superiority together with widely shared political visions) combined with judicious trade policy (market opening); it may possibly be perceived as 'neo-protectionism' if certain obstacles remain (e.g. critical foreign direct-investment restrictions).

[98] World Trade Orgnisation (WTO), Agreement of the Implementation of the Ministerial Declaration on Trade in Information and Technology Products, 36 I.L.M. 375 (26 Mar. 1997).
[99] Agreement on Telecommunications Services (above, n. 52).
[100] WIPO Copyright Treaty, WIPO Doc. CRNR/DC/94 and WIPO Performances and Phonogramm Treaty, WIPO Doc. CRNR/DC/95.

As an important step towards the constitutionalization of international relations and international law legislators, regulators, conference diplomats, business and civil society entities need a common mental framework, in terms of shared essentials of governance to safeguard both competition and public-policy objectives, at a scale congruent to cyberspace.

A number of attempts are being made at present to deal with pertinent issues in a number of international organizations (WTO, OECD, WIPO, ITU), in bilateral cooperation and in innovative business fora (Transatlantic Business Dialogue; Global Business Dialogue), in the Internet community and civil society groups, in the research community, and other entities.

Such efforts, particularly, pertain to *ex ante* and *ex post* access regulation, public interest/*ordre public* principles (e.g. privacy, human dignity, security) and consumer protection (e.g. fair trading, fraud, breach of contract), network economics (external effects, essential facilities) and other matters such as trademarks and copyright, fair use, and the shrinking 'public domain'.

Future transatlantic regulatory cooperation may particularly focus on:

- the essentials of *governance* in the secular transition towards constitutionalization in a multi-actor/multi-level/multi-instrument digital environment (particularly including an understanding on the notion of 'light-handed' or bottleneck regulation and the principle of regulatory self-restraint); with international law serving as a normative umbrella for the multi-level and multi-actor environment, i.e. covering also business and NGOs in the process towards constitutionalization of international relations;
- the WIPO efforts on the protection of databases, the arrangements pertaining to Internet domain names, peering schemes for the sharing of traffic, settlements of accounts, frameworks for the IP standard family, shared public–private efforts tied to schemes of cooperative self-regulation for the protection of minors or arrangements on information and communication security/intergovernmental issues pertaining to the export of encryption keys and 'lawful access or non-access';[101]
- 'sunset' schemes for phasing out sectorspecific regulation and at the same time conceiving a viable (WTO) international competition framework living up to the challenges of both cyberspace and the necessary process towards constitutionalizing international law.

[101] Grewlich, *Governance in 'Cyberspace'* (above, n. 1), 193–300.

Biotechnology and regulatory risk assessment

Matthias Herdegen

I. INTRODUCTION

A. Biotechnology

Almost 10,000 years ago, man was already producing foods using techniques that nowadays would be considered applications of biotechnology. Typical examples are the production of wine, beer, and bread by fermentation—fermentation being a natural process based on the biological activity of micro-organisms such as bacteria, yeasts, and moulds.[1]

Based on thousands of years of experience, such traditional biotechnological techniques are considered to be safe. By contrast, modern techniques of biotechnology have often been fiercely criticized as allegedly posing novel, unprecedented risks. This is particularly true for 'recombinant DNA' technology (rDNA), also known as genetic engineering. Within the context of biotechnology and regulatory risk assessment, the following reflections focus on genetic engineering as a paradigm for modern biotechnological techniques.

Genetic engineering is the intentional new programming of living cells designed to optimize the cells' products.[2] Each cell may be viewed as a production unit which synthesizes molecules such as amino acids and proteins. The production programme is encoded in a molecule, the deoxyribonucleic acid (or DNA). A DNA section encoding for the synthesis of a whole protein is called a gene. Since the structure of DNA is identical among all organisms, a gene can be transferred between different species, invariably leading to the production of the same protein for which the transferred gene provides the code.

In very general terms, genetic engineering may be described as a four-step-process: a gene is cut from the DNA of a donor cell (step 1); the gene is combined with a specific DNA molecule[3] forming recombinant DNA (rDNA) (step 2); the rDNA is inserted into the recipient cell (step 3); and

---

[1] See e.g. Hans-Jürgen Rehm and Paul Präve, 'Biotechnologie—Geschichte, Verfahren und Produkte', in Paul Präve, Uwe Faust, Wolfgang Sittig, and Dieter A. Sukatsch (eds), *Handbuch der Biotechnologie*, 2nd edn./students' edn. (Munich: R. Oldenbourg Verlag, 1984), 1 et seq.

[2] Fonds der Chemischen Industrie (ed.), *Biotechnologie/Gentechnik*, 1st edn (Frankfurt am Main: Fonds der Chemischen Industrie, 1989), 4.

[3] I refer to the so-called vector which is the vehicle necessary for the transfer of the gene into the recipient cell.

finally, those cells have to be identified which actually contain the rDNA (step 4).[4] An understanding of these steps is important for the risk regulation of genetic engineering, since all risks related to the process of genetic engineering are necessarily associated with these steps.

B. Transatlantic trade and investment

Biotechnology, rightly considered one of the key high technologies for the twenty-first century, is destined to contribute enormously to progress in the fields of medicine, agriculture, nutrition, and environmental protection.[5] Thus, in Germany, biotechnology is expected to provide up to 110,000 jobs by the year 2000. Forty thousand of these jobs are expected to be in the field of commercial biotechnology, representing a twofold increase since 1992. The turnover in commercial biotechnology is estimated to be 4.1 billion Deutschmarks in the year 2000, compared to 2.16 billion Deutschmarks in 1995, with a growth rate of up to 25 per cent per year, depending on the sector of biotechnological application.[6]

However, the potential of modern biotechnology is likely to be realized only if domestic as well as foreign private investors are willing to invest their capital in start-up companies. The supply of venture capital in particular requires a regulatory climate free from unscientific risk perceptions and other forms of purely psychological irrationalities.

European regulation of biotechnology could hamper not only the free flow of capital across the Atlantic, but also transatlantic free trade in biotechnological products. US biotechnology companies constitute the world leaders in the commercialization of biotechnology, particularly in the field of agricultural biotechnological products. At the same time, the United States has traditionally been an important global exporter of agricultural products. Thus, Europe faces hard export pressure especially from US firms. As figures on product approvals in the United States and Europe demonstrate, a veritable tidal wave of biotechnological products is rolling across the Atlantic.

In North America, transgenic plants such as soybeans, cotton, corn, tobacco, and canola were grown on almost one-third of all agriculturally cultivated areas in 1998. It is estimated that within five years genetically modified plants will comprise up to two-thirds of all agriculturally cultivated plants.[7] All of these products, however, may only be placed on the European market with specific European product approvals.

[4] See e.g. Stanley N. Cohen, 'Genmanipulation', in *Erbsubstanz DNA, Vom genetischen Code zur Gentechnologie* (Heidelberg: Spektrum-der-Wissenschaft-Verlagsgesellschaft, 1985), 108 et seq.

[5] See e.g. STI Review No. 19, *Special Issue on Biotechnology* (Paris, OECD, 1996).

[6] Bundesministerium für Bildung, Wissenschaft, Forschung und Technologie (ed.), *Rat für Forschung, Technologie und Innovation. Biotechnologie, Gentechnik und wirtschaftliche Innovation. Chancen nutzen und verantwortlich gestalten* (Bonn: BMBF, 1997), 9 et seq.

[7] 'Gentechnisch maßgeschneidertes Saatgut verändert Herbizid-Markt', *Frankfurter Allgemeine Zeitung*, 6 Apr. 1999, 29.

C. Risks of biotechnology

From the beginning, genetic engineering has been associated with novel, unique risks specific to the process of genetic engineering, and it is on the basis of such risks that critics have called for a moratorium or even a ban on genetic engineering activities.

However, scientists have yet to prove the risks specific to the technical processes of genetic engineering. From the current scientific point of view, such risks constitute mere 'phantom risks', or at most conventional risks, namely risks which have always attached to the application of breeding techniques, regardless of whether the technique is genetic engineering, cell fusion, or for that matter simply traditional mating. Such conventional risks include the risks of gene transfer, physiological changes in the recipient organism, invasiveness, as well as so-called 'evolutionary' risks. There is no basis for supposing that genetic engineering entails a novel potential to produce unprecedented and catastrophic adverse consequences. This potential cannot be attributed to genetic engineering merely on the basis of an argument that the position of the transgene in the recipient organism's genome influences the synthesis of the transgene, or that the integration of the transgene in the recipient organism's genome may influence the synthesizing function of other genes. Again, these consequences are not specifically related to genetic engineering, but rather are related to any other conventional breeding technique.[8]

What is specific to the process of genetic engineering, however, is the possibility of carrying out a highly precise risk assessment—one that correlates risks to the different steps of the genetic engineering process. A 'phased' risk assessment will take into account the characteristics of the donor organism (step 1), the vector (step 2), the recipient organism (step 3), and the genetically modified organism itself (step 4).

II. REGULATORY PHILOSOPHIES IN THE FIELD OF BIOTECHNOLOGY

Protection of human health and the environment is the driving force behind regulation in the field of biotechnology. From the constitutional perspective prevailing in Germany and elsewhere in continental Europe, this protection is warranted by the State's constitutional responsibility for the life and physical integrity of human beings.

---

[8] Cf. Wolfgang van den Daele, Alfred Pühler, Herbert Sukopp (eds), *Grüne Gentechnik im Widerstreit. Modell einer partizipativen Technikfolgenabschätzung zum Einsatz transgener herbizidresistenter Pflanzen* (Weinheim: VCH Verlagsgesellschaft, 1996), 59 et seq.

A. 'Process approach' (European Union) v. 'product approach' (United States)

The choice of regulatory philosophy depends essentially on a regulator's perception of risk. In the area of biotechnology, the basic choice is between, on the one hand, a *process approach* which assumes that certain processes such as genetic engineering are intrinsically risky (and therefore entail 'phantom risks') and, on the other hand, a *product approach* which focuses on the risks presented by the products used in, or resulting from, the genetic engineering process. The difference between a product approach and a process approach is important in practice. A process approach will normally lead regulatory authorities to impose a new 'horizontal' regulation, i.e. a comprehensive regulatory framework covering all genetic engineering activities; a product approach will direct them to new or already existing 'vertical' (or 'sectoral') regulations, such as those peculiar to certain product sectors such as drugs, food, seed, feed, pesticides, toxic substances, or plant pests.

The process approach represents an expression of the precautionary principle, according to which regulatory measures should be taken to prevent risks to human health and the environment posed by the application of a new technology even though it is empirically uncertain whether such risks really exist. The precautionary principle legitimizes regulatory restraints under conditions of empirical uncertainty, though this legitimacy is subject to challenge as science disputes the existence of any such risk. On the other hand, purely speculative risks cannot justify the application of the precautionary principle as a basis for risk regulation.[9]

In the United States, the NIH-Guidelines (first issued in 1976) initially followed the process approach, on account of the uncertainty surrounding the novel risks specifically posed by the novel process of genetic engineering. By the mid-eighties, US regulatory practice had come to the view that an assumption of risks specifically inherent in the process of genetic engineering could not be sustained on an empirical basis. Accordingly, since then, regulation in the United States has in principle followed the product approach, particularly in the field of deliberate releases and the marketing of genetically engineered organisms. The federal administration implemented a 'vertical' regulatory framework based on administrative rules that had been issued pursuant to existing product-specific legislation. Several attempts in Congress to pass a 'horizontal' process-specific genetic engineering law have failed.[10]

---

[9] Cf. Olivier Godard, 'Social Decision-Making under Conditions of Scientific Controversy, Expertise and the Precautionary Principle', in Christian Joerges, Karl-Heinz Ladeur, and Ellen Vos (eds), *Integrating Scientific Expertise into Regulatory Decision-Making* (Baden-Baden: Nomos Verlagsgesellschaft, 1997), 65.

[10] On the development of the US regulatory framework for biotechnology, see e.g.

In sharp contrast to the United States, the European Community has chosen the process approach. The resulting 'horizontal' regulatory framework consists of Directive 90/219/EEC on the contained use of genetically engineered micro-organisms (hereinafter Contained Use Directive)[11] and Directive 90/220/EEC on the deliberate release, including marketing, of genetically engineered organisms (hereinafter Deliberate Release Directive).[12] The reaction of German and other European firms upon shifting their research and development activities to the United States is painful evidence of the difficulties for private enterprise of competition between different regulatory systems.[13] It is only recently, on the occasion of revising the Contained Use Directive towards the end of 1998,[14] that the European legislator cautiously—almost timidly—recognized that the genetic engineering of micro-organisms does not of itself necessarily entail a risk. Whether a future reform of the Deliberate Release Directive[15] will bring Europe more closely in line with the product approach is still an open question.

B. Socio-economic and ethical concerns as a barrier to free trade

No less important in a transatlantic perspective on regulation is the cultivation of socio-economic and ethical concerns as a present and future barrier to the marketing of products. The role of socio-economic and ethical concerns is especially invisible within the framework of the current Deliberate Release Directive. The consent procedure for the placement on the market of products containing or consisting of genetically engineered organisms permits every EU Member State to raise objections. Some EU Member States almost routinely raise objections based on socio-economic or ethical grounds, even though such objections are clearly beyond the scope of the directive.[16] Occasionally, Member States disguise socio-economically or ethically motivated objections in terms of the alleged adverse effects of a product on human health.

Hans-Georg Dederer, *Gentechnikrecht im Wettbewerb der Systeme. Freisetzung im deutschen und US-amerikanischen Recht* (Berlin: Springer-Verlag, 1998), 176 et seq.

[11] 1990 O.J. (L 117) 1.

[12] Ibid. 15.

[13] See also Henry I. Miller, 'Concepts of Risk Assessment: The "Process versus Product" Controversy Put to Rest', in Dieter Brauer (ed.), *Biotechnology*, vol. 12, 2nd edn. (Weinheim: VCH Verlagsgesellschaft, 1995), 55 et seq.

[14] 1999 O.J. (L 25) 1.

[15] The European Commission initiated a 'Proposal for a European Parliament and Council Directive 90/220/EEC on the deliberate release into the environment of genetically modified organisms' in February 1998, COM(98)85 final at COD 98/0072. The first reading in the European Parliament took place in February 1999 (PE 276.723).

[16] Matthias Herdegen, *Internationale Praxis Gentechnikrecht*, vol. 1 (Heidelberg: C. F. Müller Verlag, 1996 et seq.), Part 3, I.2. (EG-Recht/Erläuterung, 2. Richtlinie [90/220/EWG]), n. 31.

A prominent example is Novartis's herbicide-tolerant and insect-resistant corn containing an antibiotic resistance gene.[17] Despite the vote of the scientific committees, confirming the safety of the genetically engineered corn and discounting the risk of transfer of the antibiotic resistance to humans, thirteen Member States out of fifteen objected to the grant of marketing consent. (Only one state—France—voted in favour of the corn's marketing, and one state abstained.) The European Commission nevertheless gave the French Ministry of Agriculture a green light to issue the marketing consent. However, the producer is still facing protracted battles with Greenpeace and its associates before French tribunals.[18] As European and American producers alike have learned, producers seeking consent to the marketing of their transgenic products under the Deliberate Release Directive need great patience and steady nerves.[19] US Deputy Secretary of Agriculture, Richard Rominger, as well as the US Trade Representative, Charlene Barshefsky, claim that shipments of transgenic corn from the United States to Europe have been blocked due to excessively long approval procedures under European law leading to a potential loss to American farmers in the region of US$200 million.[20]

Measures demanding ethically responsible treatment of genetic engineering have played a prominent role in national legislation within the European Union, particularly in former EFTA-countries like Sweden and Austria. Within the proposed Swiss gene law, ethical clauses implementing the constitutional guarantee of the dignity of all 'creatures'[21] require respect for the dignity of animals and even plants. It is accordingly likely that genetic engineering of the slipper animalcule will be challenged on the basis of ethical concerns regarding the slipper animalcule's untouchable dignity.[22]

The Austrian Law on Genetic Engineering dramatically illustrates how even grave genetic defects of an individual's genome may be understood

---

[17] For details, see Philippe Sands, *In the matter of directive 90/220/EEC and in the matter of the authorization by the European Commission of the placing on the market in the Community of Novartis Bt. maize. Preliminary opinion* (Greenpeace, 1998), 1 et seq.

[18] See 'Organismes génétiquement modifiés. Dissémination volontaire dans l'environnement et mise sur le marché d'organismes génétiquement modifiés', in *Dictionnaire permanent bioéthique et biotechnologies* (Montrouge: Editions Législatives, 1998), bulletin no. 69, p. 8298.

[19] Cf. the open-ended history of the product approval for Novartis Bt. maize in ibid. 1637.

[20] See 'Amerika droht der EU mit weiteren Strafzöllen', *Frankfurter Allgemeine Zeitung*, 22 Mar. 1999, 19; Scott W. Morrison and Glen T. Giovannetti, *Bridging the Gap: Ernst & Young's 13th Biotechnology Industry Annual Report 1999* (Palo Alto: Ernst & Young, 1999), 51.

[21] Cf. Swiss Federal Constitution art. 24.

[22] In fact, a Swiss doctoral dissertation came to the conclusion that genetic engineering of animals as well as the use and patenting of genetically engineered animals violates their constitutionally protected dignity: Peter Krepper, *Zur Würde der Kreatur in Gentechnik und Recht. Thesen zum gentechnischen Umgang mit Tieren in der Schweiz unter Berücksichtigung des internationalen Rechtsumfelds* (Basel: Helbing & Lichtenhahn, 1997), 436.

as part of Creation and as thus entitled to protection against genetic engineering. Human somatic gene therapy is not permitted, if the risk of an unintended modification of the germ line cannot be completely excluded.[23] This will ultimately force certain patients, even in cases of the worst genetic defects, to undergo sterilization before being treated with somatic gene therapy.

The Austrian Law on Genetic Engineering also provides a good example of socio-economic reservations against the marketing of products containing genetically engineered organisms. Placement of such products on the market may be prohibited if they are 'socially intolerable',[24] in the sense of imposing an unacceptable burden on society for economic, social, or moral reasons. The concern for 'social intolerability' of gene products obviously flows from doubts as to whether society really needs transgenic products. A 'necessity approach' clashes with fundamental liberties.

US genetic engineering regulation has never paid tribute to mere socio-economic or ethical concerns. The federal administration strictly adheres to a regulatory approach based on the scientifically provable risk of products. Given the direction of ongoing revisions of the Deliberate Release Directive, the regulatory approaches of the European Union and the United States are becoming less and less compatible.

C. Labelling of novel foods

Conflict in regulatory approach is also apparent in the field of genetically modified foods, or so-called novel foods, particularly regarding the labelling of such foods. In the European Union, under the Novel Foods Regulation,[25] labelling of a novel food is generally obligatory if the presence of recombinant DNA or recombinant proteins are scientifically provable in the food. The label must then indicate clearly and explicitly that genetic engineering has been used within the production chain. At the same time, the label must not be understood as constituting a warning about health risks, since according to the Novel Foods Regulation novel foods must not be placed on the market if they pose a risk to consumers. The labelling requirement is obviously a reaction to widespread distrust among European consumers over genetic engineering in the food chain. Such labelling in turn nurtures socio-economic and ethical concerns of consumers, if only by enabling those opposed to genetic engineering as such, because of its interference with God's creational order, to make a choice against novel foods.

From the US regulatory perspective, such concessions to consumer idiosyncrasy are highly curious. In the field of novel foods, the US authorities

---

[23] Austrian Law on Genetic Engineering Sec. 74 cl. 2.   [24] Cf. ibid., Sec. 63.
[25] Cf. Regulation 258/97 of the European Parliament and of the Council of 27 Jan. 1997 Concerning Novel Foods and Novel Food Ingredients, art. 8 (1997 OJ (L 34) 1).

have maintained their science- and risk-based product approach. Novel foods must be labelled only if they differ substantially from existing conventional foods. While differences in the composition of food resulting from genetic engineering may be regarded as substantial, the mere presence of recombinant DNA or recombinant proteins in food does not necessarily mean that the food's composition is substantially different. Thus, labels on novel foods need not explicitly and specifically indicate the use of genetic engineering. Only a substantially different composition (e.g. the reduced content of vitamin C in a genetically engineered tomato) or a specific health risk to parts of the population (e.g. the risk of allergenic reactions due to a peanut protein in a genetically engineered tomato)[26] is required to be labelled.

EC Regulation 1139/98 relating to the labelling of food products made of genetically engineered corn (Novartis Bt. maize) or soybeans (Monsanto Roundup Ready™ soybeans), requires that the use of genetic engineering be spelled out to the consumer regardless of the presence of any risk to consumer health. The US Government considers such deference to scientifically unsupported consumer interest in information relating to the food production method to be excessive and a violation of WTO law.[27]

III. CONFRONTATION IN REGULATORY RISK ASSESSMENT: IMPLICATIONS OF THE 'HORMONES' CASE

The WTO dispute settlement body is an appropriate forum for resolving transatlantic trade conflicts over biotechnology. The legal yardstick for determining the permissibility of trade barriers is the SPS Agreement[28] or, if the SPS Agreement is not applicable, the TBT Agreement.[29] Evidently, the European Commission does not anticipate a concrete transatlantic confrontation within the WTO in the area of biotechnological products. This may be unrealistic.

The famous 'hormones' case (in which the European Union found itself confronting the United States and Canada) offers some guidance as to a WTO Member's margin of appreciation in the light of fragmentary empirical evidence. In this case, the European Union banned the import of 'hormone meat', i.e. meat from cattle treated with hormones in the United

---

[26] For details see 'Statement of Policy: Foods Derived from New Plant Varieties', 57 Federal Register 22992 (1992).

[27] Cf. Rudolf Streinz, 'The Novel Foods Regulation—A Barrier to Trade?', *European Food Law Review*, vol. 9 (1998), 286.

[28] Agreement on the Application of Sanitary and Phytosanitary Measures, 1994 OJ (L 336), 40.

[29] Agreement on Technical Barriers to Trade, 1994 OJ (L 336), 86.

States and Canada.[30] At first instance, the European Union suffered a heavy defeat,[31] but the Appellate Body then gave the European Union one more opportunity to justify its import ban of hormone meat in terms of a risk assessment which takes full consideration of the requirements of the SPS Agreement.[32]

The necessity of a risk assessment derives directly from the SPS Agreement. The EU's import ban on hormone meat must be viewed as constituting a higher level of sanitary protection than that found in international standards of the Codex Alimentarius Commission. The Codex standards establish certain maximum residue limits for artificial hormones in meat,[33] while the EU's import ban constitutes practically a zero-residue standard. This higher level of protection on part of the European Union had to be justified on the basis of a risk assessment, in particular an assesment of the risks to human health posed by the consumption of hormone meat.[34] The risk-assessment itself had to be based on risk-assessment methods developed by the competent international organizations.[35]

Under the SPS Agreement, the risk to be assessed is not the theoretical uncertainty of adverse effects of a substance on human health, since it is scientifically impossible to exclude the possibility that a given substance will never be harmful to human health.[36] On the other hand, the risk need not be provable in a laboratory under strictly controlled scientific conditions. The risk assessment has to focus on the risk as it actually exists in human society.[37]

To prevent risk to human health and the environment, each WTO Member retains the sovereign right to take any precautionary measures it deems necessary and adequate for its territory.[38] However, when opting for a level of protection exceeding international standards, a WTO Member must provide empirical scientific evidence to substantiate the need for stricter precautionary measures. The relationship between the risk assessment and the higher sanitary measure must be a rational one.[39]

---

[30] Cf. Directive 88/146/EEC, art. 6 para. 1, 1998 OJ (L 70), 16; and Directive 88/299/EEC, 1998 OJ (L 128), 36. Both directives were replaced by Directive 96/22/EC, 1996 OJ (L 125), 3).

[31] See WTO Panel Reports 'EC Measures Concerning Meat and Meat Products (Hormones)', WT/DS 26/R/USA, and 'EC Measures Concerning Meat and Meat Products (Hormones)', WT/DS 48/R/CAN.

[32] See Report of the WTO Appellate Body, 'EC Measures Concerning Meat and Meat Products (Hormones)', WT/DS 26/AB/R; WT/DS 48/AB/R, n. 255.

[33] Report of the 21st Session of the Joint FAO/WHO Codex Alimentarius Commission, Rome, 1995, ALINORM 95/37, Appendix 4, p. 2.

[34] Cf. SPS Agreement, art. 3.3, 5.1.   [35] Ibid., art. 5.1.

[36] Report of the WTO Appellate Body (above, n. 32), n. 186.

[37] Ibid. (above, n. 32), n. 187.

[38] Cf. e.g. Vern R. Walker, 'Keeping the WTO from Becoming the "World Trans-science Organization": Scientific Uncertainty, Science Policy, and Fact Finding in the Growth Hormones Dispute', *Cornell International Law Journal*, vol. 31 (1998), 273.

[39] Report of the WTO Appellate Body (above, n. 32), nn. 186, 193.

Accordingly, mass hysteria against genetic engineering will hardly constitute the rational basis required for sanitary measures.

IV. COOPERATION AND COORDINATION IN BIOTECHNOLOGY RISK ASSESSMENT

There needs to be coordination of efforts and cooperation on both sides of the Atlantic as early as the negotiation stage in relation to international standard-setting for sanitary measures within the relevant international organizations. This is because sanitary measures introduced in conformity with established international standards are irrebuttably deemed to be in accordance with the SPS Agreement and the GATT,[40] so that a risk assessment is not necessary for individual sanitary measures. If no mutual understanding can be achieved concerning international standards for sanitary measures, it is equally important to cooperate and coordinate efforts within the framework of those international organizations entrusted with developing risk-assessment methods. This in turn is due to the requirement that WTO Members must base their sanitary measures on risk assessments carried out in accordance with risk-assessment techniques developed by international organizations.[41]

A. Cooperation and coordination within international organizations

1. FAO/WHO Codex Alimentarius Commission

The SPS Agreement refers to the international standards of the Codex Alimentarius Commission in so far as food-safety measures adopted by a WTO Member are concerned.[42] WTO Members are supposed to base their food-safety measures on the Codex Standards for the purposes of international harmonization of sanitary measures.[43] If a Member's food-safety standards comply with the Codex Standards they are considered to be in accordance with the WTO law,[44] and the unilateral resort by another WTO Member to a higher level of protection than the level stipulated by the Codex Standards must be rationally based on a risk assessment.[45] The Codex Standards do not become directly binding on WTO Members by means of the SPS Agreement. However, the requirement that a risk assessment must meet the relatively strict requirements of the SPS Agreement, as construed by the Appellate Body in the 'hormones' case, may induce WTO Members to adhere to the Codex Standards.

---

[40] SPS Agreement art. 3.2.
[41] Ibid. cf. art 5.1.
[42] Ibid., art. 3.1, annexe A.
[43] Ibid., art. 3.1.
[44] Ibid., art. 3.2.
[45] Ibid., art. 3.3, 5.1.

The Codex standards also constitute international norms as referred to in the TBT Agreement.[46] But under the TBT Agreement, the Codex Standards do not exercise the same gentle pressure on WTO Members as under the SPS Agreement. According to the TBT Agreement, WTO Members must merely use the Codex Standards as a basis for their technical regulations at home. What is more, WTO Members are permitted to set the Codex Standards aside if these standards constitute ineffective or inappropriate means to fulfil a legitimate purpose.[47]

However, the Codex Alimentarius Commission is not well equipped to serve as a forum for effective transatlantic cooperation and coordination. The Codex Alimentarius Commission is an international organization created by both the FAO and the WHO. Only the EU Member States are members of the Codex Alimentarius Commission. The European Community itself is not; it is restricted to observer status.

Even more problematic is the decision-making process within the Codex Alimentarius Commission. The Codex Alimentarius Commission has established four principles of decision-making, the fourth of which is crucial: 'When the situation arises that members of Codex agree on the necessary level of protection of public health but hold differing views about other considerations, members may abstain from acceptance of the relevant standard without necessarily preventing the decision by Codex.'[48] Such 'other considerations' of Codex Members, which are not necessarily related to the protection of human health, may be of a socio-economic or ethical nature or simply concern the negative attitude of consumers. Under this fourth principle, the fact that Codex Members have taken such considerations into account does not prevent acceptance of the standard by other Codex Members. Nevertheless, the adopted Codex Standard may have an indirect binding effect, through the SPS Agreement, even on those Codex Members that did not vote in favour of the Codex Standard or simply abstained. Moreover, decisions of the Codex Alimentarius Commission may be taken by a simple majority, with a quorum of only 20 per cent of all Codex Members casting their vote. Thus, only 69 out of 144 Codex Members took part in the final decision on residue limits for growth hormones in beef. The residue limits were accepted by thirty-three Codex Members only, with seven Members abstaining.[49] This is far from a satisfactory procedure for establishing normative standards.

---

[46] TBT Agreement art. 2.4, annexe 1. [47] Ibid., art. 2.4.

[48] Statements of Principle Concerning the Role of Science in the Codex Decision-Making Process and the Extent to which Other Factors are Taken into Account (http://www.fao.org/WAICENT/faoinfo/economic/esn/codex/Manual/decide.htm E10E1).

[49] Christine Godt, 'Der Bericht des Appellate Body der WTO zum EG-Einfuhrverbot von Hormonfleisch', Europäisches Wirtschafts- und Steuerrecht, vol. 9 (1998), 204 et seq.

So far, there is no Codex Standard specifically for biotechnological food products. Only an amendment to the 'General Standard for the Labelling of Prepackaged Foods'[50] concerning the labelling of foods produced through biotechnology is still under discussion. The original draft of the proposed amendment seems to be based on the US model for regulating the labelling of novel foods.[51] The outcome of the decision-making, however, is still open due to the submission of an alternative proposal supported by the European Community observer as well as by delegations from outside the European Union.[52] The alternative proposal is consumer-oriented in that it would allow consumers to make an informed choice. This in turn may trigger the applicability of the fourth principle of the decision-making procedure,[53] implying that those Codex Members in favour of the alternative proposal should abstain from accepting the new labelling standard for novel foods because the alternative is not restricted entirely to health considerations. Consequently, the original draft, based strictly on food-safety considerations, may well become the final Codex Standard.

2. OECD working group on the harmonization of regulatory oversight in biotechnology

In 1995 the OECD established a Working Group on the Harmonization of Regulatory Oversight in Biotechnology, composed of experts in the field of biotechnology regulation nominated by their OECD Member States.[54] Through its efforts, the OECD was able to launch a Programme of Work on the Harmonization of Regulatory Oversight in Biotechnology for the period from 1997 to 1999. The harmonization envisaged by the programme focuses on the assessment of environmental and health risks, with a view to avoiding non-tariff trade barriers resulting from excessively burdensome risk regulations by OECD Members.[55]

The most important component of the programme is the drafting of so-called consensus documents, containing technical information for use in regulatory risk assessments of biotechnological products.[56] Whether these documents have a harmonizing effect depends on their mutual acceptance by the OECD Members. At the same time, consensus documents are intended to enhance deregulation, for instance through the introduction of simplified administrative procedures. So far, four consensus documents

---

[50] Codex Alimentarius, vol. 1A, 2nd edition, 21 et seq.
[51] Report of the 26th Session of the Codex Committee on Food Labeling, ALINORM 99/22, Appendix VIII, 67 et seq.
[52] ALINORM 99/22, 6 et seq.   [53] See above, n. 48.
[54] OECD, 'OECD's Working Group on the Harmonization of Regulatory Oversight in Biotechnology' (http://www.oecd.org/ehs/experts.htm).
[55] OECD, 'OECD's Programme of Work on the Harmonization of Regulatory Oversight in Biotechnology' (http://www.oecd.org/ehs/projects.htm).
[56] OECD, 'Consensus Documents' (http://www.oecd.org/ehs/cd.htm).

have been published, with additional documents currently in preparation. The consensus documents are product specific, focusing either on the organism (e.g. Pseudonomas, oilseed rape, potato) or on the introduced gene (e.g. coat protein gene ensuring protection of plants against viruses).

The Working Group is also examining the long-term effects of releasing genetically engineered plants and micro-organisms. Its first report of this type relates to a transgenic tree, the Norway Spruce. Ancillary to this and its other activities, the Working Group has assembled important information sources, the heart of the information network being a BioTrack Online which disseminates information on the World Wide Web (particularly on legislative developments throughout the OECD) and provides databases of field trials of genetically engineered organisms in OECD Member States.[57]

3. United Nations Environment Programme (UNEP)

(a) UNEP International Technical Guidelines for Safety in Biotechnology

The UNEP International Technical Guidelines for Safety in Bio-technology[58] (hereinafter referred to as UNEP Guidelines), issued in December 1995, represent a non-binding international regulatory instrument. As explicitly stated in their introduction,[59] the guidelines do not release governments from national, regional, or international legal obligations. Rather, their purpose, on the national, regional, and international level, is to contribute significantly to safety in all fields of biotechnology applications, including the marketing of products consisting of or containing genetically engineered products.[60] The UNEP Guidelines are meant to bring a sound scientific approach to biotechnological risk assessment and risk management, with a focus not on the process, but rather on the products (i.e. the organisms and their novel traits) and on the products' intended fields of application.[61] The Guidelines reflect the principle of familiarity, meaning that risk assessment and risk management should take into account expanding knowledge and experience.[62] Assuming the international community eventually embraces the risk assessment, risk management, and capacity-building provisions laid down in the UNEP Guidelines, the Guidelines will promote the sustainable development of biotechnology and free world trade in biotechnological products.[63]

On the other hand, the UNEP Guidelines do not require governments to adhere to a purely scientific regulatory approach, for the guidelines expressly state that socio-economic, ethical, and other impacts of biotechnology may be taken into consideration on the national or regional level.[64]

---

[57] Cf. OECD, 'OECD's Working Group on the Harmonization of Regulatory Oversight in Biotechnology' (http://www.oecd.org/ehs/experts.htm).

[58] Reprinted in part in Herdegen, *Internationale Praxis* (above, n. 16), vol. 2, pt. 5, II.3.

[59] Above, n. 17.   [60] Above, nn. 10, 11.   [61] Above, n. 19.

[62] Cf. above, n. 20.   [63] Above, n. 14.   [64] Cf. above, n. 16.

Socio-economic and ethical impact assessments may, of course, operate as a counterpoint to free international trade since they are generally invoked to justify non-tariff trade barriers.

Implementation of the UNEP Guidelines, like other international legal instruments on biotechnology regulation, depends heavily on the capacity to carry out risk assessment and risk management at the national and regional level. Developing countries in particular may lack the required institutional and infrastructural capacities, human and financial resources, and information. Capacity-building has thus become a key-word in discussions of biotechnological risk regulation in international fora.

(b) Biosafety Protocol

If adopted, the Biosafety Protocol will constitute a protocol under Article 19, para. 3 of the Biodiversity Convention.[65] Given the failure of the Extraordinary Conference of the Parties of the Biodiversity Convention to reach agreement on the Biosafety Protocol at its February 1999 meeting in Cartagena, the Conference will resume its deliberations in light of discussions in the Open-ended Ad hoc Working Group on Biosafety. Disagreement at Cartagena centred on the issue of minimizing socio-economic impacts, on concern over the capacity of developing countries to address biosafety, and even on the protocol's scope, including the question of liability. Indeed, the negotiating parties were not even able to define the relationship between the Biosafety Protocol and the WTO.[66]

4. United Nations Industrial Development Organization (UNIDO) Voluntary Code of Conduct for the Release of Organisms into the Environment

The goal of the UNIDO Voluntary Code of Conduct for the Release of Organisms into the Environment[67] (hereinafter referred to as Code of Conduct) is 'to set forth the minimum acceptable components necessary for international cooperation'.[68] From the UNIDO's point of view, the deliberate release of genetically modified organisms into the environment demands international cooperation, due to the strong potential for 'trans-fontier impacts'.[69] This will explain why the Code of Conduct does not, on the other hand, address the contained use of transgenic organisms.

The Code of Conduct expressly states that 'regulatory oversight and risk assessment should focus on the characteristics of the product rather

---

[65] Reprinted in part in Herdegen, *Internationale Praxis* (above, n. 16), vol. 2, pt. 5, II.2.

[66] For further details see UNEP Press Release, 'Governments Postpone Adoption of Biosafety Treaty', 24 Feb. 1999; DG XI Press Release, 'Differences between Main Exporters and Developing Countries Prevent Finalization of Biosafety Protocol Negotiations', 24 Feb. 1999 (BIO/99/80).

[67] Reprinted in Herdegen, *Internationale Praxis* (above, n. 16), vol. 2, pt. 5, II.4.

[68] Preamble, cl. C.   [69] Preamble, cls. D. and E.

than the molecular or cellular techniques used to produce it'.[70] But, while the Code adheres to the 'product approach' to regulation, it nevertheless remains voluntary, as its title suggests. Notwithstanding the rational scientific aura surrounding the Code, UN Member States are not thereby obliged to adjust their existing regulations.[71]

B. Bilateral Cooperation and Coordination

1. Existing bilateral fora

The 1995 Transatlantic Agenda between the United States and European Union set up a High Level Environment Consultation Group, to which a Permanent Technical Working Group has been attached. The working group consists, on the European side, of DG XI (Environment, Nuclear Safety, and Civil Protection) and DG I (External Relations, especially with North America) and, on the US side, the United States Trade Representative (USTR), the Environmental Protection Agency (EPA) and, where appropriate, the US Department of Agriculture's Animal and Plant Health Inspection Service (APHIS). While striving to meet twice a year, the Permanent Technical Working Group has found its work eclipsed somewhat by the Biotech Group[72] organized under the newer Transatlantic Economic Partnership (see below).

There are two other transatlantic fora for bilateral discussions on biotechnology. The Agrifood Biotech Group is an ad hoc group for the exchange of information that meets once a year and consists of representatives of DG VI (Agriculture) and DG III (Industry), on the one side, and USDA and USTR, on the other. (Depending on the subject of its meetings, other services of the European Commission may participate, as may representatives of the US EPA and, occasionally, the US FDA (Food and Drug Administration).)

Yet another bilateral institution is the US–EC Task Force on Biotechnology Research whose activities, for the European Commission, are centred in DG XII (Science, Research, and Development). This working group, too, operates on the basis of an information exchange between the United States and the European Union on biotechnology research programmes—an exchange carried out within the specific framework of workshops among ten European and ten US scientists. The prospective agreement between the United States and the European Union on transatlantic research cooperation would be fully applicable to biotechnology research.

2. Transatlantic Economic Partnership

With the more recent establishment of the Transatlantic Economic Partnership of 1998, there has been set up a new working group on

---

[70] Section II-C-1.a.   [71] Preamble, cl. C.   [72] Below, n. 73.

biotechnology, namely the TEP Biotech Group.[73] Rather than supersede the existing bilateral groups, the TEP Biotech Group specifically draws its membership from them. What distinguishes the new working group on biotechnology is its deliberate purpose to coordinate the discussions and work of the existing bilateral fora, so as to ensure consistency and full coverage. A more particular mission of the new bilateral working group on biotechnology is to review the progress of the bilateral dialogue on technical issues with regard to their potential effects on transatlantic trade. In so doing, the working group should strengthen information exchange and, more generally, scientific and regulatory cooperation between the United States and the European Union, while promoting transparency and the provision of information of use to consumers. The initial meeting of the new working group was largely restricted to practical steps: the exchange of current information on product approvals, on revision of the Deliberate Release Directive, and on consumer views and monitoring. But discussions also turned to the prospects for a pilot project on the simultaneous evaluation of biotechnological products.

3. Future Perspectives: Mutual Recognition Agreements and Bilateral Panels

Following this consolidation of knowledge about the risks associated with specific organisms and products, a logical next stage might seem to be the establishment of bilateral admission mechanisms for placing genetically modified products on the market. However, the European Union's complex decision-making structures suggest that this will not easily be achieved. Failing a truly internationalized admission procedure, the establishment of bilateral panels of experts may continue to be the most appropriate forum for pre-dispute cooperation.

A model for successful 'bilateralism' in the biotechnology field may be found in the institutionalized bilateral discussions on agricultural biotechnology between the United States and Canada. The two countries had previously exchanged information within the framework of bilateral discussions and concurrent reviews of genetically modified plants intended to be placed on the market. But, on 15 and 16 July 1998, US and Canadian officials met specifically in order to identify genetic molecular characterization data relevant to the review of genetically modified plants being undertaken by the USDA's Animal and Plant Health Inspection Service, on the one hand, and the Canadian Food Inspection Agency (CFIA) and Health Canada, on the other. Their aims included, in addition to general discussion of fields of cooperation and exchange of information, the identification of common approaches to molecular genetic characterization.[74] The meeting

---

[73] 'Transatlantic Economic Partnership Action Plan' (DG E VI, Doc. 12272/98), 3.5.2.

[74] 'Summary Report, Canada–US Bilateral Discussions on Agricultural Biotechnology 15–16 July 1998, Ottawa, Ontario, Canada' (http://www.cfia-acia.agr.ca/english/plant/pbo/usda02_e.html).

produced a mutual understanding of 'similarities and differences in the critical elements of the molecular genetic characterization of transgenic plants
considered during the review process',[75] as well as specific so-called
'reviewers' checklists' to be used by reviewers in the assessment process. [76]

V. THE TRANSATLANTIC DIALOGUE: IMPULSE FOR RATIONALITY

Globalization—currently a key word in national and international politics—has several distinct aspects. One aspect is certainly the effort of
industrial enterprises, as well as academic and research institutions, to
find shelter from the cold winds of irrational regulations, preferably in a
place where the regulatory climate is sunny and warm. This development
has forced Europe into a relationship of regulatory competition with the
other great global players. Such competition among regulatory systems
will inevitably push each player in the direction of a more rational
approach to risk regulation in biotechnology, under threat of falling even
further behind its global competitors. In the words of the WTO Appellate
Body in the 'hormones' case, the risk to be evaluated is 'the actual potential for adverse effects on human health in the real world where people
live and work and die'.[77] As influenced by WTO law, the transatlantic
dialogue should provide a further impetus to rationality. Of all the facets
of globalization, this enhancement in rationality is perhaps the most
appealing.

[75] 'Canada–US Bilateral on Agricultural Biotechnology, Appendix I: Molecular Genetic
Characterization Data' (http://www.cfia-acia.agr.ca/english/plant/pbo/usda03_e.html).
[76] 'Canada and United States Bilateral on Agricultural Biotechnology, Reviewers'
Checklist' (http://www.cfia-acia.agr.ca/english/plant/pbo/usda04_e.html).
[77] Report of the WTO Appellate Body (above n. 32), n. 187.

Existing legal and institutional mechanisms for cooperation and coordination: the case of intellectual and industrial property

Josef Drexl

INTRODUCTION

Transatlantic regulatory cooperation in the field of intellectual property is far from new. Bilateral agreements between the United States and European countries relating to patents, trademarks, and copyrights date back to the nineteenth century.[1] These have been complemented by the multilateral WIPO Conventions and the Paris and Berne Conventions.[2] This type of cooperation is designed to guarantee mutual protection of intellectual property rights to the nationals of the contracting parties. The impact of intellectual property protection on international trade, however, did not emerge as an important issue until the end of the 1980s, finding its most noticeable expression in the TRIPs Agreement (Agreement on Trade-Related Aspects of Intellectual Property Rights) as an integral part of the WTO package signed in 1994 by the former Contracting Parties of GATT.[3]

Although there is a long history of progress in the field of intellectual property, especially in recent years, trade tensions over intellectual property cannot be excluded for the future. This contribution examines the existing system of transatlantic protection of intellectual property, attempting to identify some issues of potential dispute and, finally, to

[1] See, e.g. the Bilateral Copyright Agreement between the United States and the German Reich of 15 January 1892. This Agreement, which is still in force, gives nationals of the other party full national treatment. On its current scope of application, see Josef Drexl, 'Duration of Copyright Protection Accorded US Authors in the Federal Republic of Germany— Changes Due to the US Accession to the Berne Convention', *International Review of Industrial Property and Copyright Law*, vol. 22 (1991), 204.

[2] However, the Berne Convention became effective for the United States only on 1 March 1989; see Jane Ginsburg and John Kernochan, 'One Hundred and Two Years Later: The US Joins the Berne Convention', *Columbia–VLA Journal of Law and the Arts*, vol. 13 (1988), 1. Before, copyright relations between the United States and European countries were governed by the Universal Copyright Convention of 6 Sept. 1952 (revised in 1971). The Universal Copyright Convention was designed to bridge the gap between the Berne Convention countries, which followed the continental author's right approach, and the United States with its copyright approach.

[3] For a commentary on the Agreement, see especially Friedrich-Karl Beier and Gerhard Schricker (eds), *From GATT to TRIPs: The Agreement on Trade-Related Aspects of Intellectual Property Rights* (Weinheim and New York: VCH, 1996).

make a few suggestions on how to resolve these potential problems. Consequently, we shall first look at the interrelationship between trade and intellectual property (I), then analyse the current system of international protection (II), address some aspects of patent (III) and copyright law (IV), and close with some remarks on the issue of parallel and grey market imports (V).

I. INTELLECTUAL PROPERTY AND WORLD TRADE

A. Intellectual property as part of the regulatory system of nation states

Protection of intellectual property rights constitutes an important part of the economic policy of states. Patents, trademarks, copyrights, and other intellectual property rights are designed by national legislatures to fulfil certain functions in the framework of national regulatory systems. The US Constitution, for example, gives Congress the power 'to promote the Progress of Science and useful Arts, by securing for limited Times to Authors and Investors the exclusive Right to their respective Writings and Discoveries'.[4] National laws on the protection of intellectual property, created in particular economic, historical, and philosophical environments, reflect slightly different goals but, even more importantly, different legal concepts applicable to infringements taking place within their national territory (principle of territoriality).[5]

More and more, the export of technology is replacing the export of manufactured goods in highly developed states. Increasing dependence on exports of this kind is the reason why the United States in particular has started to integrate intellectual property protection into its trade policy, as a means of protecting US right holders according to US legal standards.[6] The national interest in giving uniform protection against any infringement has even been extended to infringements taking place abroad.

---

[4] US Const. Article 1, sect. 8.

[5] The principle of territoriality is sometimes questioned, especially for the continental copyright author's-rights approach with its protection of the personal interests of the author (moral rights); for the German copyright law, see Haimo Schack, *Urheber- und Urhebervertragsrecht* (Tübingen: Mohr-Siebeck, 1997) 338 et seq., proposing a 'principle of universality'. However, the German Federal Supreme Court rightly continues to uphold the principle of territoriality, justifying it with the economic interest of the State to create a uniform legal environment; Bundesgerichtshof (Federal Supreme Court) of 16 June 1994, *International Review of Industrial Property and Copyright Law*, vol. 26 (1995)—'Droit de suite with Respect to Sales Abroad' (English translation). But see *Itar Tass Russian News Agency v. Russian Kurier*, 153 F.3d 82 (2d Cir. 1998).

[6] Cf. the very thorough analysis of the US trade policy with respect to copyrights, Maximilian Haedicke, *Urheberrecht und die Handelspolitik der Vereinigten Staaten von Amerika* (Munich: Beck, 1997). Cf. also Josef Drexl, 'Urheberrecht und Handelspolitik: Zweckehe oder Mesalliance', *Gewerblicher Rechtsschutz und Urheberrecht Internationaler Teil* (1999), 1.

B. Intellectual property laws as non-tariff trade barriers

There is an increasing realization that, in a globalized economy, differing standards of protection create barriers to trade. On the one hand, barriers to trade exist in cases of deficient domestic protection. A State that does not protect intellectual property rights forces other countries to tighten import controls on infringing goods.[7] At the same time, high-priced patented, branded, and copyrighted goods from the developed world have trouble entering markets with a low level of protection.

On the other hand, strong protection of intellectual property rights may also restrict trade. An instructive example can be found in the 1998 decision of the European Court of Justice in the *Silhouette* case, which dealt with parallel imports from outside the European Union.[8] The Court made clear that even genuine goods produced in the European Union and exported to a third country may not be re-imported without the consent of the trademark owner.

C. Intellectual property laws as a means of furthering regional integration

Beyond the issue of excessively weak or strong forms of protection of intellectual property rights as barriers to trade, there are differences in the design of intellectual property regimes which may also restrict trade. This is why the European Community, as a means of establishing the internal market, has started to harmonize intellectual property laws and has even introduced genuine Community rights, such as the Community trademark.[9]

---

[7] Therefore, nations started to enact special laws providing for particular border measures to seize infringing goods. Such legislation, among other problems, gave an incentive to the GATT negotiations on intellectual property, leading to the conclusion of the TRIPs Agreement as part of the WTO package. TRIPs contains special rules on border measures (Art. 51 et seq.), balancing the interests of the right holder and the importer. For the law of the United States, see Sect. 337 US Trade Act; for the Community law, see Regulation No. 3295/94 of 22 Dec. 1994 laying down measures to prohibit the release for free circulation, export, re-export, or entry for a suspensive procedure of counterfeit and pirated goods, 1994 OJ (L 341/8).

[8] ECJ of 16 July 1998, C-355/96, *Silhouette International Schmied GmbH & Co. KG v. Hartlauer Handelsgesellschaft mbH*, *International Review of Industrial Property and Copyright Law*, vol. 29 (1998), 920.

[9] Regulation No. 40/94 of 20 Dec. 1993 on the Community trade mark, 1994, OJ (L 11/1). See also Regulation No. 2100/94 of 27 July 1994 on Community plant variety rights, 1994 OJ (L 227/1). A Community Patent Regulation is currently being discussed.

II. THE EXISTING INTERNATIONAL REGULATORY SYSTEM FOR THE
PROTECTION OF INTELLECTUAL PROPERTY: WHERE HAVE WE
COME FROM? WHERE ARE WE GOING?

A. International protection of intellectual property—a historical outline

International protection of intellectual property rights developed as an early field of international law. Following some bilateral trade agreements dealing with intellectual property, the existing international system started to develop with the conclusion of the Paris[10] and Berne Conventions[11] at the end of the nineteenth century. These Conventions protect industrial property and copyright respectively. They prohibit any discrimination of foreign nationals under the national treatment clause and establish an obligation to grant certain minimum rights. Both Conventions have been administered by the World Intellectual Property Organization (WIPO) since 1967.

This multilateral system underwent a fundamental change in 1994 with the conclusion of the already mentioned TRIPs Agreement as an integral part of the WTO Agreement.[12] The TRIPs Agreement follows the so-called 'Paris plus' and 'Berne plus' approach adding new rules to the existing principles of international protection and making a violation of the Paris and Berne Conventions a violation of TRIPs.[13] One important consequence of this approach consists in the application of the WTO dispute settlement rules to a violation of Convention rules.[14] But the TRIPs

[10] Paris Convention for the Protection of Industrial Property, original version of 20 Mar. 1883, last revision of 14 July 1967, for further information see G. Bodenhausen, *Guide to the Application of the Paris Convention for the Protection of Industrial Property as Revised at Stockholm in 1967* (Geneva: BIRPI, 1968). For the Convention's genesis, see Yves Plasseraud and François Savignon, *Paris 1883, Genèse du droit unioniste des brevets* (Paris: Litec, 1983).

[11] Berne Convention for the Protection of Literary and Artistic Works, original version of 9 Sept. 1886; last revision of 24 July 1971. For further information see Sam Ricketson, *The Berne Convention for the Protection of Literary and Artistic Works: 1886–1986* (London: Sweet & Maxwell, 1987).

[12] According to Article XIV (1), WTO Agreement, TRIPs is a so-called Multilateral Trade Agreement that is automatically accepted with accession to the World Trade Organization (WTO).

[13] Article 2 (1), TRIPs: Paris plus; Art. 9, (1) TRIPs: Berne plus. The first intellectual property case to be decided by WTO dispute settlement bodies dealt with the so-called pipeline protection of inventions in India under Art. 70 (8) (a) and (9), TRIPs; WTO Appellate Body of 19 Dec. 1997, WTO Doc. WT/DS79/R, see www.wto.org/wto/dispute/79r.doc. See also Gail Evans, 'Issues of Legitimacy and the Resolution of Intellectual Property Disputes in the Supercourt of the World Trade Organization', *International Trade Law Review*, vol. 4 (1998), 81.

[14] On 4 Feb. 1999, the European Community has brought in a request for consultation against the United States under the WTO dispute-settlement procedure, giving rise to the first case dealing with the Berne-plus approach. The European Community argued that Sect. 110 (5), US Copyright Act, as amended under the 'Fairness in Music Licensing Act' of 1998, violates Article 11 *bis* (1) of the Berne Convention; see WTO Doc. WT/DS160/1

Agreement is also important for underlining the impact of intellectual property rights on trade and, it is important to add, for the introduction of specific obligations relating to domestic enforcement.[15] Such enforcement rules were unknown to the pre-existing Conventions.

B. European protection of intellectual property protection—a late development

The Paris and Berne Conventions have played, and still play, an important role within the European Community. By stipulating minimum standards of protection they create a kind of de facto harmonization in Europe. Harmonization under secondary Community law only goes back to 1986, when the European Community passed the Directive on the protection of topographies of semiconductor products.[16] This harmonization continued with the adoption of the Trademark Harmonization Directive[17] in 1988 and was extended in the 1990s in the field of copyright law.[18] This 'positive' protection of intellectual property law under Community law, however, was preceded by the case-law of the European Court of Justice that dealt, in a negative sense, with the conflict of domestic intellectual property laws and the European principle of free movement of goods.[19] The Court of Justice thereby recognized the principle of European exhaustion of rights as a genuine Community intellectual property principle, which was later enacted in some Community legislation[20] as well as national laws.[21]

IP/D/16. Section 110 (5), US Copyright Act, under certain circumstances, permits the playing of radio and television music in public places such as bars, shops, restaurants without the consent of the right holders of the musical works and without any obligation to pay royalties. In contrast, Art. 11 *bis* (1), Berne Convention not only stipulates a right of transmission, but in addition a right of public communication of the transmission.

[15] See Thomas Dreier, 'TRIPs and the Enforcement of Intellectual Property Rights', in Beier and Schricker (eds), *From GATT to TRIPs* (above, n. 3), 248.

[16] Directive No. 87/54 of 16 Dec. 1986 on the legal protection of topographies of semiconductor products, 1987 OJ (L 24/36).

[17] First Directive No. 89/104 of 21 Dec. 1988 to approximate the laws of the Member States relating to trade marks, 1989 OJ (L 40/1).

[18] See Directive No. 91/250 of 14 May 1991 on the legal protection of computer programs, 1991 OJ (L 122/42); Directive No. 92/100 of 19 Nov. 1992 on rental right and lending right and on certain rights related to copyright in the field of intellectual property, 1992 OJ (L 346/61); Directive No. 93/83 of 27 Sept. 1993 on the coordination of certain rules concerning copyright and rights related to copyright applicable to satellite broadcasting and cable retransmission, 1993 OJ (L 248/15); Directive No. 93/98 of 29 Oct. 1993 harmonizing the term of protection of copyright and certain related rights, 1993 OJ (L 290/9); Directive No. 96/9 of 11 Mar. 1996 on the legal protection of databases, 1996 OJ (L 77/20). See also Directive No. 98/71 of 13 Oct. 1998 on the legal protection of designs, 1998 OJ (L 289/28).

[19] See ECJ of 8 June 1971, C-78/70, *Deutsche Grammophon v. Metro*, [1971] ECR 487, establishing the European principle of exhaustion of copyrights.

[20] See Art. 7 of the First Trademark Harmonization Directive No. 89/104 of 21 Dec. 1988. A similiar Europe-wide principle of exhaustion of copyrights is now contained in Article 4 (2) of the Commission's proposal for a Directive on the harmonization of certain aspects of copyright and related rights in the Information Society.

[21] See, e.g. Sect. 17 (2), German Copyright Act.

Even today, however, international regulation of intellectual property in many respects goes beyond the current state of harmonization under secondary Community law. This is especially true for patent law, as well as to some extent for copyright law. It is most true, however, with respect to internal enforcement where there is no secondary Community law at all. Consequently, the law of the Member State applies even if Community rights, like a particular Community trademark, need to be enforced.

C. International protection of intellectual property as a European issue

Negotiation of TRIPs as a trade agreement gave rise to a particular problem for the Community. In the past, only EC Member States (as opposed to the Community) were interested in and parties to the WIPO Conventions. But reforming the GATT system—and consequently negotiating the contents of TRIPs—appeared to be an issue for the exclusive competence of the European Community over commercial policy.[22] In addition, the Community interest to conclude TRIPs was also generated by its own expanding secondary legislation. At the end of the negotiations, the European Community and the Member States concluded the WTO trade package as a mixed agreement and became equal Members to the WTO.[23]

In 1994 the European Court of Justice was asked to express its opinion on the external competence to conclude TRIPs.[24] The EC Commission argued that, given the trade-related aspect of TRIPs, the EC had exclusive power to conclude the TRIPs Agreement. In fact, the Commission argued that the whole body of TRIPs, with its Paris and Berne plus approach, was part of Community law, thereby creating an enforceable Community obligation for the Member States to harmonize their law according to international standards. The Court of Justice rejected this attempt, concluding that there was only joint competence of the European Community and the Member States to conclude TRIPs.[25]

---

[22] Article 133, EC Treaty (Amsterdam version).

[23] Mixed agreements are concluded where exclusive external power of the European Community does not exist or is in dispute. See, in general, Nanette Neuwahl, 'Joint Participation in International Treaties and the Exercise of Power by the EEC and its Member States: Mixed Agreements', *Common Market Law Review*, vol. 28 (1991), 717.

[24] ECJ of 15 Nov. 1994, Opinion 1/94, [1994] ECR I-5267.

[25] The precise understanding of the concept of joint competence is still unclear; for an interpretation, see Josef Drexl, 'The TRIPs Agreement and the EC: What Comes Next After Joint Competence?', in Beier and Schricker (eds), *From GATT to TRIPs* (above, n. 3), 23 et seq., followed by Mark Miller, 'The TRIPS Agreement and Direct Effect in European Community Law: You Can Look . . . But Can You Touch?', *Notre Dame Law Review*, vol. 74 (1999), 607 et seq. In a recent decision, the European Court of Justice concludes in favor of a broad scope of competence at least of the Court itself to interpret the provisions of TRIPs, i.e. even with respect to domestic enforcement rules relating to the enforcement of national trademarks. See ECJ of 16 June 1998, C-53/96, *Hermès International v. FHT Marketing Choice BV*, *International Review of Industrial Property and Copyright Law*, vol. 30 (1999), 292. The Court argues that uniform interpretation of TRIPs has to be guaranteed in the case when a national trademark as well as when a Community trademark is enforced.

The Court's finding of joint competence creates several potential difficulties for the United States in so far as transatlantic cooperation is concerned. Whether the United States has to negotiate with the European Commission or the governments of the Member States depends on the specific issue to be regulated. Perhaps the Uruguay Round negotiations leading up to the conclusion of the WTO Agreement also points to a way out of the problem. The United States should negotiate with the European Community and then conclude the Agreement with both the Community and its Member States as a mixed agreement, leaving it to the European Court of Justice to solve the problem within the European Union.

III. THE CASE OF PATENT LAW

Transatlantic regulatory cooperation is essential in the field of patent law. However, differing legal concepts may cause serious conflicts between the United States and Europe.

A. Cooperation of patent offices

The majority of patent applications in Europe are filed by US citizens and firms, and a large part of applications in the United States are filed by European inventors. Thus, cooperation between the US Patent and Trademark Office (PTO) and its European counterparts, especially the European Patent Office (EPO), is of primary importance. Patent offices nowadays consider themselves as service institutions for industry, providing relatively cheap, fast, and uncomplicated procedures as well as high-quality research and patent protection.

Based on the so-called 'Kyoto Action Plan', the European Patent Office and the patent offices of the United States and Japan cooperate closely to achieve these goals in a globalized economy.[26] The Patent Cooperation Treaty (PCT) of 1970 allows international filing of patent applications. The WIPO proposals for a Patent Law Treaty, which as of this writing are about to be accepted,[27] will harmonize procedural laws in the United States and Europe.

B. Problems confronting Europe and the United States

The WIPO proposals for a Patent Law Treaty were initially designed to harmonize not only procedural law, but also material patent law

[26] Cf. Brian Derby, 'Perspectives on the European Patent System', *Journal of World Intellectual Property*, vol. 1 (1998), 961 et seq.
[27] See Draft Patent Law Treaty and Draft Regulations of 15 Feb. 1999, WIPO Doc. SCP/2/3.

worldwide. This ambitious project unfortunately had no success, because of the resistance it encountered in the United States.[28] Consequently, some fundamental conceptual differences between patent laws in Europe and the United States persist.

1. First-to-invent or first-to-file

A first issue, relating to the patentee, can be summed up under the catchwords of first-to-file and first-to-invent. The law of the United States follows the first-to-invent approach. If two persons make the same invention independently and file a patent application in the United States, the patent will be granted to the person who first made the invention.[29] In contrast to US law, under the law of most other countries—and this is also true of EC Member States as well as under the European Patent Convention[30]—the patent will be granted to the person who first filed the patent application. This difference causes trade problems when patents for the same invention may well belong to different persons in the United States and the European Union. One solution would be to harmonize patent laws, which the WIPO has tried for several years but without success. The first-to-file system is the more practicable one, and the one preferred by larger firms. However, in the United States many inventions are still made by independent inventors and universities that, often slow in filing their inventions, defend the first-to-invent principle. It remains to be seen when and even if the United States will be ready to talk about harmonizing substantive patent law again.

2. The Hilmer doctrine in the United States

Closely tied to the principle of first-to-invent is the so-called Hilmer doctrine of US patent law. According to Article 4B of the Paris Convention, a person filing a patent application somewhere in the Paris Union acquires a priority right throughout the Union. According to the priority right, the date of first filing is decisive in determining the state of the art throughout

---

[28] Cf. Heinz Bardehle, 'A New Approach to Worldwide Harmonisation of Patent Law', *International Review of Industrial Property and Copyright Law*, vol. 29 (1998), 876; Joseph Straus, 'Implications of the TRIPs Agreement in the Field of Patent Law', in Beier and Schricker (eds), *From GATT to TRIPs* (above, n. 3), 176 et seq.

[29] Sect. 102 (g), US Patent Act. In the past, the first-to-invent rule was modelled in a discriminatory way, forbidding an applicant to establish prior invention by referring to knowledge or use of or other activity with respect to the invention that took place abroad (former Sect. 104, Patent Act). This rule had to be brought into conformity with Art. 27 (1), TRIPs, which prohibits any discrimination as to the place of the invention. See Straus, 'Implications of the TRIPS Agreement' (above, n. 28), 189 et seq.

[30] Article 60 (2), EPC. Note that the European Patent Convention is not only concluded by EU Member States, but has additional Members (currently Switzerland, Liechtenstein, Monaco, Cyprus). The European Patent Convention does not create a uniform Community-wide patent, but a number of national patents that are granted in a single administrative procedure. See Friedrich-Karl Beier, 'The European Patent System', *Vanderbilt Journal of Transnational Law*, vol. 14 (1981), 1.

the Paris Union in order to establish novelty. Under the Hilmer doctrine, first developed by the US Court of Customs and Patent Appeals in 1966,[31] a US filing prevails even over an earlier filing in another country establishing a priority right for the Paris Union.[32]

The Hilmer doctrine thereby creates a strong incentive to file in the United States at an early date, discriminating against foreign filings. In the process of implementing TRIPs, the Clinton administration made a conscious decision to maintain this kind of discrimination.[33] Whether the Hilmer doctrine can be considered to be in conformity with the Paris Convention still needs some consideration[34] and could be tested under the Paris-plus approach in the framework of a WTO dispute settlement procedure.

3. Patentability of biotechnological inventions

Another issue relates to the patentability of biotechnological inventions. In Europe, there have been vivid emotional discussions and opposition around the idea of 'patentability of human life'. With the Directive on biotechnological inventions, adopted last year,[35] Europe has accepted in substance the patentability of biological material containing genetic information, provided that the general requirements for the grant of a patent are met.

Proponents of the directive argued that patent law is neutral in moral terms. Accordingly, the recitals of the Directive clearly express that a patent gives a right only to prevent economic exploitation of the patent by another party, but it does not give a right to the patentee to use the patent unconditionally (recital 14). Nevertheless, the Directive makes a few exceptions for moral reasons, excluding from patent protection, for example, the cloning of human beings.

---

[31] *US Patent Quarterly*, vol. 149 (1966), 480.

[32] The details of the US first-to-invent system are rather complex. There is the legal fiction that the invention was completed upon the filing of a complete and adequate patent application (so-called *constructive* reduction to practice). Despite recognition of the foreign priority right (Sect. 119, US Patent Act), foreign filings must meet US disclosure requirements in order to prove constructive reduction to practice. The applicant with a priority right based on a foreign application, however, may still prove *actual* reduction to practice even before the date of the US filing. But this evidence may be difficult to adduce. See Bardehle, 'A New Approach' (above, n. 28), 880 et seq.; Richard Schwaab and Harold C. Wegner, 'Harmonization and Priority of Invention', in Joseph Straus (ed.), *Aktuelle Herausforderungen des geistigen Eigentums. Festgabe von Freunden und Mitarbeiter für Friedrich-Karl Beier zum 70. Geburtstag* (Köln *et al.*: Carl Heymanns Verlag, 1996), 165 et seq.

[33] See Steve Charnovitz, 'Patent Harmonization under World Trade Rules', *Journal of World Intellectual Property*, vol. 1 (1998), 136, with further references.

[34] Cf. Bardehle, 'A New Approach' (above, n. 28), 882 et seq., arguing that the doctrine does not violate the national treatment obligation, but the spirit of the Paris Convention.

[35] Directive 98/44/EC of 6 July 1998 on the legal protection of biotechnological inventions, 1998 O.J. (L 213) 13. See Robin Nott, '"You Did It": The European Biotechnology Directive At Last', *European Intellectual Property Review*, vol. 20 (1998), 347.

The European legislator was well aware that genetic engineering and research requires high-risk investment and that, in order to encourage such investment, effective protection under patent law is needed. Consequently, the legislator made this conscious decision for patent protection, leaving the question of whether in principle the patent can actually be used for other parts of the law. Because of Europe's fear of losing technology-intensive industry to the United States, the Directive may well be considered to be the result of transatlantic regulatory competition.

Because creating a favourable business and investment environment appears to be a leading goal of current patent laws, one can expect that competition of regulatory systems in many instances will lead to an increasing harmonization of the legal environment in Europe and the United States, one which is best adapted to furthering inventive efficiency. However, as we have seen in the case of the first-to-file/first-to-invent problem, regulatory competition does not always further approximation of national laws.

IV. THE CASE OF COPYRIGHT LAW

A. Copyright or *droit d'auteur*: works made for hire or moral rights

Copyright law is an even more delicate transatlantic issue than patent law. With respect to patent law, there is a consensus that protection is designed—as the US Constitution tells us—'to promote the progress of science and useful arts'. In short, investment has to pay. The situation is different for copyright law, for which we can identify very different traditions in Europe and the United States. The law in the United States gives protection against the copying of works as an incentive for the labour and effort necessary to increase the public good.[36] By contrast, according to the continental 'author's rights' approach, the copyright derives directly from the personality of the author as a natural property right.[37]

This fundamental theoretical difference manifests itself in the design of laws. For example, whereas under the European approach the author's rights can only come into existence in the person of the creator of the work,

---

[36] The US copyright approach is based on the philosophy of John Locke who considered copyright protection as a tool to convince the author/investor to contribute to the common stock of mankind; see Justin Hughes, 'The Philosophy of Intellectual Property', *Georgetown Law Journal*, vol. 77 (1988), 296 et seq.

[37] The Continental view of copyright has its beginnings in France where this different concept is best expressed by the traditional title of the former Copyright Act: '*loi sur la propriété littéraire et artistique*' (Act on Literary and Artistic Property). The Continental tradition was further developed by German philosophers (Fichte, Hegel, Schopenhauer, Kant). See Hughes, 'Philosophy of Intellectual Property' (above, n. 36), 330 et seq. See also Josef Drexl, *What Is Protected in a Computer Program? Copyright Protection in the United States and Europe* (Weinheim and New York: VCH, 1994), 1 et seq.

under US law, notably the so-called 'works-made-for-hire' doctrine,[38] an employer may be regarded as the original author of a commissioned work. Another difference consists in the range of rights conferred. Under the European tradition, a distinction has to be made between the economic rights and the moral rights of the author,[39] whereas such moral rights, which protect the personal interests of the author, are traditionally unknown under the US copyright approach.[40]

Both issues create considerable problems for the movie industry. Under US law, the producer of the movie is considered to be the original author of a cinematographic work; under European law the work is co-authored by different people, notably the director and the author of the script. Consequently, in Europe these co-authors, as part of their moral rights, have a right to object to a 'distortion' or 'mutilation' in the case of a later colorization of a black-and-white movie. Understandably, therefore, the US movie industry does not particularly admire the European author's rights approach. When trade diplomats from the United States claim stronger copyright protection abroad they most likely have the US copyright approach in their mind. And, in fact, it may well be true that nowadays the economic importance of copyright to modern society comes from its capacity to enhance the useful arts, as the US Constitution puts it, thereby describing the function of copyright to protect investment.

But here, two caveats need to be introduced: first, recognition of the moral rights of the author and of the creator of a work as the original author does not affect crossborder investment. Problems can be solved by contract law; exploiters simply have to pay for such additional rights that they encounter in Europe. Secondly, the European author's rights approach poses no greater problem in the copyright/trade context. In many instances, the European Court of Justice has accepted moral rights of the author as part of the specific object of copyright protection justifying an exception to the free-movement-of-goods principle.[41]

In fact, moral rights have never been a difficult problem for the European Court of Justice, because moral rights grounded in the obligation under Article 6 *bis* of the Berne Convention are recognized

---

[38] See Sect. 201 (b), US Copyright Act.

[39] See, e.g. Sect. 11, German Copyright Act: 'The copyright protects the author in his intellectual and personal relations to the work and in the exploitation of the work.' The following provisions are headed by the terms 'Moral rights of the author' (*Urheberpersönlichkeitsrechte*, Sect. 12 et seq.) and 'rights of exploitation' (*Verwertungsrechte*, Sect. 15 et seq.).

[40] However, US law is changing. According to Sect. 106A, US Copyright Act, enacted under the Visual Arts Act of 1 Dec. 1990 (Pub. L. No. 101–650, 104 Stat. 5128), the Copyright Act protects the attribution and the integrity of works of visual arts.

[41] See especially ECJ of 20 Oct. 1993, C-92/92 and 326/92, *Phil Collins v. Imtrat Handelsgesellschaft*, [1993] ECR I-5145 (para. 20).

throughout the European Union. This same article also applies to the United States after its accession to the Convention became effective in 1989.[42]

B. Copyright and the protection of investment: the MAI lesson

Copyright issues recently caused a transatlantic conflict in the framework of the OECD. With the support of the United States, the OECD had drafted the Mulilateral Agreement on Investment, the so-called MAI.[43] At first glance, the MAI's goal of enhanced protection of transborder investment appeared unproblematic. However, the very broad definition of the term 'investment' under the MAI would have included any investment relating to copyrighted works, thereby affecting the European author's rights approach to the benefit of the economic interests of investors in copyrighted works.[44] Moreover, neither the WIPO nor the WTO nor intellectual property specialists were considerably involved in the Agreement's negotiations. As a consequence, the MAI came under heavy criticism in the European Parliament as well as some national parliaments in Europe. In October 1998 France withdrew from the negotiations, making the conclusion of the agreement impossible.

The MAI lesson is a painful, but maybe fruitful one: we have to respect different copyright traditions on each side of the Atlantic and discuss them openly where it is necessary.

V.   THE CASE OF PARALLEL IMPORTS

A. The 'parallel import prohibition' versus 'international exhaustion of rights'

The most intriguing issue in international intellectual property law is how to deal with parallel and grey market imports. Trade lawyers do not like intellectual property protection since national protection creates barriers

---

[42] Whether US law provides sufficient protection of the personal interests of the author through legal rules outside copyright law, be it under the Lanham Act (especially Sect. 43(a)) and State tort law, is a difficult question to be answered. See the analysis by Ginsburg and Kernochan, 'One Hundred and Two Years Later' (above, n. 2), 31 et seq.

[43] See Riyaz Dattu and John Boscariol, 'A Quick Primer on the Multilateral Agreement on Investment', *International Business Lawyer*, vol. 27 (1999), 50.

[44] According to the Draft, 'investment' means any kind of asset owned or controlled directly or indirectly by an investor, including direct investments, portfolio investments, real estate, intellectual property rights, rights under contract and rights conferred by authorizations or permits. See Maximilian Haedicke, 'Urheberrecht als Investitionsschutz?', *Gewerblicher Rechtsschutz und Urheberrecht Internationaler Teil*, vol. 47 (1998), 632; Joachim Karl, 'Das Multilaterale Investitionsabkommen (MAI)', *Recht der Internationalen Wirtschaft*, vol. 44 (1998), 432 f.

to the import of goods. In Article 6 TRIPs the issue of international exhaustion of rights, which has an obvious impact on trade, has been left unregulated. Under current international law, it is still up to domestic law to decide whether imports of grey market goods are legal.

At the Community level, there is a large body of case-law affirming a principle of European exhaustion. If the right holder in the country of importation distributes or agrees to the distribution of a protected good in the territory of another EU Member State, the right holder cannot rely on the intellectual property right in order to prevent the importation.[45] Whether the same or a similar principle should be applied internationally, is a very disputed issue. In order to find the answer, the specific goals of a given intellectual property right need to be taken into account.

B. Parallel imports under trademark law

The issue of international exhaustion is mostly discussed in the field of trademark law. Europe has harmonized trademark law under its Directive of 1988 that also addresses the issue of exhaustion (Art. 7).[46] Whether the Directive excludes a principle of international exhaustion, which was, for example, recognized under former German case-law,[47] had been much in dispute.[48] In 1998, in the *Silhouette* case noted above,[49] the European Court of Justice decided that the Directive should be understood in the sense that Member States may no longer recognize a principle of international exhaustion.[50]

From a US perspective, *Silhouette* should be regarded as a remarkable decision because under US law the right holder may not invoke the

---

[45] See especially ECJ of 8 June 1971, C-78/70, *Deutsche Grammophon v. Metro*, [1971] ECR 487 (on copyrights); of 14 July 1981, C-187/80, *Merck v. Stephar*, [1981] ECR 1981, 2063 (on patents); of 17 Oct. 1990, C-10/89, *S.A. CNL-Sucal NV v. Hag GF AG*, [1990] ECR I-3711 (on trademarks).

[46] Above, n. 17.

[47] Bundesgerichtshof (Federal Supreme Court), BGHZ 41, 84—'Maja'; Bundesgerichtshof (Federal Supreme Court), *Gewerblicher Rechtsschutz und Urheberrecht Internationaler Teil* (1973), 562—'Cinzano'. The Federal Supreme Court changed its position under the new Trademark Act implementing the Community Directive: Bundesgerichtshof (Federal Supreme Court), *International Review of Industrial Property and Copyright Law*, vol. 28 (1997), 131—'Dyed Jeans' (English translation).

[48] Cf. Wilhelm Nordemann *et al.*, *Wettbewerbs- und Markenrecht*, 8th edn. (Baden-Baden: Nomos, 1996), 246 et seq., with further references.

[49] Above n. 8.

[50] Most interestingly, a few months before the *Silhouette* decision, the EFTA Court of Justice adopted a quite different interpretation of Art. 7, EC Trademark Directive with respect to imports from third countries to Norway as a partner in the European Economic Area, accepting a principle of international exhaustion; EFTA Court of Justice of 3 Dec. 1997, C-2/97, *Mag Instrument Inc. v. California Trading Company Norway, Ulsteen, Gewerblicher Rechtsschutz und Urheberrecht Internationaler Teil* (1998), 309. On both decisions, see Gallus Joller, 'Zur territorialen Reichweite des Erschöpfungsgrundsatzes im Markenrecht. Silhouette einer Zwischenbilanz', *Gewerblicher Rechtsschutz und Urheberrecht Internationaler Teil* (1998), 751.

trademark to prevent the import of genuine goods that were legally manufactured in the United States. On the other hand, US trademarks may be
invoked against importation of branded goods that are manufactured in a
third country with the consent of the US right holder only in the case that
those goods do not meet the quality expectations of US consumers.[51] In a
comparable situation, under the principle of European exhaustion, trade
in branded goods between EU Member States may not be restricted,
whereas imports from third countries into the European Union would be
illegal. In fact, the US approach seems very reasonable. Trademark law
protects the goodwill of the right holder. Therefore, trademark protection
against genuine goods or branded goods produced abroad, but with similar quality, appears as a disguised restriction on trade.

The European Court of Justice is well aware of these arguments and
suggests an alternative solution to the problem. According to the Court,
the principle of international exhaustion can only result from negotiation
and agreement with third states.[52] Hence, for the development of transatlantic trade relations, a principle of transatlantic exhaustion of rights
would necessarily have to be part of a trade agreement to be negotiated in
the future. As to its contents, a solution approaching the principle of
European exhaustion would likely be adequate. If the trademark holder
agreed on the production and distribution of branded goods on the other
side of the Atlantic, there should be no possibility to oppose parallel
imports. Consumer expectations, the general level of product safety, and
the willingness of consumers to pay are largely comparable in Europe and
the United States. A need to discriminate between European and the US
production with respect to the quality of goods should not be recognized.

C. Parallel imports under copyright law

The situation is different for copyright law. National laws, including the
laws of the EU Member States, recognize the so-called first-sale doctrine,
which is, in substance, the copyright equivalent to the exhaustion of rights
principle. Once a copy of a protected work has been distributed legally for
the first time, the distribution right is exhausted and the person who
bought the copy can resell it.[53] European Community law also applies this
principle in the situation when the copy is sold in one EU Member State
and then resold in the territory of another Member State.

However, the first-sale doctrine appears problematic with respect to
third countries. A goal of copyright law is to provide the author with a just

---

[51] See, e.g. *Original Appalachian Artworks, Inc. v. Granada Electronics, Inc.*, 816 F.2d 68 (2nd
Cir. 1987). See also Lynda Zadra-Symes and Joseph Basista, 'Using US Intellectual Property
Rights to Prevent Parallel Imports', *European Intellectual Property Review*, vol. 20 (1998), 220 et
seq., reviewing the US case-law of trademarks.

[52] ECJ (above, n. 8), para. 28.   [53] See Sect. 109(a), US Copyright Act.

remuneration for the creation. Trade lawyers argue that the first-sale doctrine should also apply to transborder situations since the right holder has already been rewarded when the copy is sold for the first time.[54] However, copyright lawyers rightly indicate that the decision of the right holder where to sell a copy of the work depends on a broad range of economic and legal circumstances.[55] According to this view, an advanced level of economic and especially legal integration, including harmonization of copyright laws, is required for the application of a principle of international exhaustion. Given the fundamental differences between copyright laws in Europe and the United States, such a principle should not be applied in transatlantic relations.

There is, however, an exception to be made. For copyrightability, US law only requires a modicum of creativity.[56] This opens the door to using copyright protection for labels in order to restrict imports of genuine goods that cannot be restricted under trademark law. In the L'anza case decided in 1998 by the US Supreme Court,[57] the US manufacturer of hair-care products opposed re-importation of US products that were sold at a relatively low price in the United Kingdom. The manufacturer thereby tried to protect the goodwill of the trademark in the United States which the manufacturer had achieved through cost-intensive promotional activities in the United States not equalled by those in the United Kingdom. Nevertheless, the Supreme Court decided that the first-sale doctrine applies to this particular situation of products manufactured in the United States.

It follows from the reasoning that the decision would be different if the imported goods were produced abroad.[58] In this latter situation, US copyright law may well create barriers to trade which would not exist under trademark law. It seems that there is no particular justification for using copyright protection for product labels or the general trade dress when the intellectual property right is only used to restrict parallel imports and to protect promotional efforts exclusively deployed in the country of importation. Copyright protection would otherwise work as an instrument to discriminate against foreign production.

---

[54] F. Abbott, Second Report of the Committee on International Trade Law, in: International Law Association, *Report of the Sixty-Seventh Conference, Helsinki* (London: 1996), 258 et seq.

[55] Drexl, 'Urheberrecht und Handelspolitik' (above, n. 6), 10 et seq.; Ulrich Joos, *Die Erschöpfungslehre im Urheberrecht* (Munich: Beck, 1991), 141 et seq.

[56] See *Feist Publications, Inc. v. Rural Telephone Service Company, Inc.*, 111 S. Ct. 1282 (1991).

[57] *Quality King Distributors, Inc. v. L'anza Research International, Inc.*, 118 S. Ct. 1125 (1998). See Daniel De Vito and Benjamin Marks, 'Preventing Gray Market Imports After *Quality King Distributors, Inc. v. L'anza Research International, Inc.*', *Journal of Proprietary Rights*, vol. 10, no. 5 (1998), 2; Zadra-Symes and Basista, 'Using US Intellectual Property Rights' (above, n. 51).

[58] In the same sense De Vito and Marks, 'Preventing Gray Market Imports' (above, n. 57), 4.

D. Multilateral or bilateral regulation of the parallel import prohibition

Given the discriminatory effect of bilateral agreements, regulating intellectual property law in transborder situations should preferably be done multilaterally. However, the issue of parallel imports cannot be disconnected from the level of economic development national economies have attained and the level of integration to be achieved. Parallel imports would therefore be an issue for a bilateral trade agreement between the United States and the European Community.

E. A case for harmonization?

Another (and last) issue in this context is whether accepting a principle of transatlantic exhaustion requires harmonization of intellectual property laws. This is a very important question with respect to copyright law. The European Court of Justice has been very reluctant to apply the principle of exhaustion to situations where persisting differences of domestic copyright laws were at stake.[59] This case-law triggered harmonization of copyright laws in Europe, including, for example, the Europe-wide introduction of a rental right and of the 70-years term of protection.[60]

A similar harmonization in transatlantic relations can most adequately be achieved in multilateral fora. For example, recognition of a rental right has been agreed upon in 1996 as part of the new WIPO Copyright Treaty.[61]

VI. CONCLUSIONS

1. International regulation and harmonization of intellectual property protection in some respects go beyond what has already been achieved within the European Union. Multilateral regulation is the best way to create an adequate regime for the transatlantic protection of intellectual property.

2. Regulatory systems in Europe and the United States, expecially in the field of patent law and copyright law, are based on different historically generated concepts that need to be respected.

---

[59]   ECJ of 17 May 1988, C-158/86, *Warner Brothers v. Christiansen*, [1988] ECR 2605; of 24 Jan. 1989, C-341/87, *EMI Electrola GmbH v. Patricia Im- und Export Verwaltungsgesellschaft mbH*, [1989] ECR 79.

[60]   Directive No. 92/100 of 19 Nov. 1992 on rental right and lending right and on certain rights related to copyright in the field of intellectual property, 1992 OJ (L 346/61); Directive No. 93/98 of 29 Oct. 1993 harmonizing the term of protection of copyright and certain related rights, 1993 OJ (L 290/9).

[61]   Article 7, WCT. For the text, see the WIPO website: www.wipo.org.

3. In the field of patent law, competition of regulatory systems will, to some extent, help to create a legal environment in Europe and the United States which is adequate to further inventive efficiency.

4. In the field of copyright law, the European author's rights approach and the US copyright approach can co-exist in a globalized economy. The European approach, as is demonstrated by the experience within the European Union, does not contradict the protection of transborder investment and, in principle, the free movement of goods.

5. The issue of international exhaustion of rights needs to be discussed separately for different intellectual property rights.

6. In the field of trademark law, the principle of international exhaustion, as it is currently established under internal Community law, should be agreed upon in a bilateral trade agreement between the European Community and the United States.

7. In the field of copyright law, the first-sale doctrine should not be applied in transborder cases between the United States and the European Union. An exception has to be made in cases in which US copyright law is relied upon solely for the purpose of protecting the integrity of a method of marketing particular products.

International governance for voluntary standards: a game-theoretic perspective

Walter Mattli

I. INTRODUCTION

The nature and institutional geography of standardization is diverse and complex. Standards are commonly defined as documented agreements containing technical specifications or other precise criteria to be used consistently as rules, guidelines, or definitions of characteristics to ensure that materials, products, processes, and services are fit for their purpose. Put differently, standards are about levels of safety, performance, conformity, interoperability, interconnectability, properties of materials, systems of classification, methods of test, the operation of equipment or systems, quality assurance, definition of terms, and so on.

Standardization institutions are many too. The most notable institutions at the international level are the International Standardization Organization (ISO) and the International Electrotechnical Commission (IEC), but there are an additional forty international intergovernmental organizations (IGOs) and about 450 international non-governmental organizations (INGOs) involved in standardization as well.[1] At the regional level, the most prominent bodies are the European Committee for Standardization (CEN), the European Committee for Electrotechnical Standards (CENELEC), and the European Telecommunications Standards Institute (ETSI), although other regional institutions can be found in Latin America (COPANT), Africa (ARSO), and the Pacific Rim (PASC). At the national level, there exist 21 African, 15 Latin American, 21 Pacific Rim, and 18 European standards bodies, including such influential organizations as the *Deutsches Institut für Normung* (DIN), the British Standards Institute (BSI), and the *Association Française de Normalisation* (AFNOR). Many of these national organizations have close ties to national firms, industry groups, professional and scientific organizations, trade associations, consumer groups, trade unions, and public bodies.

This contribution will primarily focus on the institutional relationship between the ISO/IEC and standardization bodies in Europe and the

---

[1] Thomas Loya and John Boli, 'Standardization in the World Polity: Technical Rationality over Power', in John Boli and George Thomas (eds), *Constructing World Culture: International Nongovernmental Organizations Since 1875* (Stanford: Stanford University Press, 1999), 169–97.

United States. It will examine this relationship, enquire into the causes of transatlantic tension, and conclude by listing institutional proposals for a smoother working relationship between Americans and Europeans in international standardization bodies. The solutions discussed here are thus limited in two important ways: (1) they do not address problems faced by developing countries or non-Western developed countries, notably Japan; and (2) de facto standards and proprietary standards are outside the scope of this study.

The contribution considers the questions of optimal institutional design with the help of a simple game-theoretic model which describes a 'mixed preference coordination' game between two states. Each state imposes costs or benefits on the other contingent upon the other's policy. The collective action problem is that neither state can choose its best policy without knowing what the other intends to do, but there is no obvious point at which to coordinate. The game suggests different sets of institutional solutions that maximize the chances of lasting cooperation.

The study argues that in international standardization, the choice of equilibria institutions and practices (particularly in ISO and IEC) has been made primarily by the Europeans; that is, European states have acted as first-movers in the coordination game. Americans, on the other hand, have been the laggards, the second-movers (one possible measure of this is the small number of secretariats held by Americans compared to Europeans). First-movers define a problem and set the agenda for resolving it. This may give them the advantage of being able to produce standards that fit their own production profiles better than those of second-movers.

Two reasons explain the American position. First, standards setting in the United States has traditionally been focused on the domestic market and organized along sectoral lines. Given the size of the US market and its relative independence of international trade (measured in terms of value of trade as a percentage of GNP), there was little need for many industries to become involved in international standards processes. Tellingly, the American National Standards Institute (ANSI) was able to assume the position of national representative body within the ISO, not because of its stature in standards setting but rather because ASTM (the American Society for Testing Materials)—the most prominent standards development organization at the time—made a clear policy decision not to get involved in international standardization.

A second reason for the relative weak American position in ISO and IEC has to do with deep conflicts in the American standards community. ANSI is today the national coordinating body for US standards development organizations, and the national member body within the ISO. However, ANSI's status is not fully accepted by major players in the US standards community, and a number of organizations continue to act independently in their dealings with other national standards organizations. Nor have these organizations been willing to defer to ANSI leadership in domestic-standards activities. Competition and turf battles among American standards-setting bodies often revolve around the issue of revenues from the sales of standards, which for some organizations can account for up to 80 per cent of their income. Failure to bring American standards-setting organizations together and work out their relationship has been a real problem and has repeatedly foiled attempts to define a coherent national-standards strategy at the international level.

Game theory shows that equilibria in 'mixed-preference coordination' games are fragile if the games are played repeatedly, primarily because of tensions raised by distributional issues (i.e. question of equitable distributions of the gains from cooperation). This suggests that ISO and IEC will have to undergo significant institutional reforms if they are to carry out their missions effectively in the future. The study concludes with a discussion of possible reforms, including introduction of weighted voting; a cooperation agreement between ISO/IEC and the standards-developer organizations on a sectoral basis; use of Dresden or Vienna Agreement as a model, depending on sector.[2]

II. COORDINATION GAMES AND INSTITUTIONAL DESIGN

In the theoretical literature on standards, reference is often made to coordination games. They are generally less well understood as examples of collective-action problems than the more familiar Prisoners' Dilemma (PD) game. As Snidal puts it, 'the problem in PD is that in pursuing its self-interest, each state imposes costs on the other independent of the other's policy, whereas in the coordination game each imposes costs or benefits on the other *contingent upon the other's policy*. The collective action problem is that neither state can choose its best policy without knowing what the other intends to do, but there is no obvious point at which to coordinate.'[3]

In the coordination game of Figure 1, State B prefers policy y_1 if State A chooses policy x_1 but prefers policy y_2 if A chooses x_2, and vice-versa. Once a cooperative solution is achieved, it is self-enforcing. Neither state

---

[2] On the Dresden and Vienna Agreements, see generally n. 32 below, and accompanying text.

[3] Duncan Snidal, 'Coordination versus Prisoners' Dilemma: Implications for International Cooperation and Regimes', *American Political Science Review*, vol. 79 (Dec. 1985), 931–2. See also Arthur Stein, 'Coordination and Collaboration: Regimes in an Anarchic World', in Stephen Krasner (ed.), *International Regimes* (Ithaca, NY: Cornell University Press, 1983), 115–40; Robert Keohane, *After Hegemony: Cooperation and Discord in the World Political Economy* (Princeton: Princeton University Press, 1984); Lisa Martin, 'Interests, Power, and Multilateralism', *International Organization*, vol. 46 (Autumn 1992), 765–92; and Geoffrey Garrett and Barry Weingast, 'Ideas, Interests, and Institutions', in Judith Goldstein and Robert Keohane (eds), *Ideas and Foreign Policy: Beliefs, Institutions, and Poltical Change* (Ithaca: Cornell University Press, 1993), 173–206.

has an incentive to defect.[4] In other words, the problem in the coordination game is one of choice between multiple stable and efficient equilibria over which states have opposed interests, whereas in the Prisoners' Dilemma game the problem is how to get away from a single stable but inefficient equilibrium.[5]

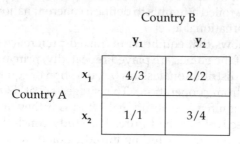

Figure 1. Coordination Game

A. Coordination in the presence of an undisputed leader

Typically the collective-action problem underlying an n-person coordination game is solved if there is one state (a regional leader) whose cooperation in the group is perceived, by all or by a majority within the group, to be more important to the group than that of any other state. Germany is arguably such a leader in Europe. The German economy represents almost one quarter of the Community's GDP and contributes about one-quarter to the EU's external and internal trade. Germany is the main trading partner of thirteen EU Member States, as well as Switzerland, Turkey, and the former Yugoslavia; and it is the second most important economic partner after Russia for most East European states. Germany's centrality to Europe is of course not a new fact. John Maynard Keynes wrote before World War I: 'Round Germany as a central support the rest of the European economy system group[s] itself, and on the prosperity and enterprise of Germany the prosperity of the rest of the Continent mainly depend[s].'[6]

Adaptation to the proposals of the leader makes not only political but also economic sense; that is, it is likely to be the least-costly change within the group. For example, switching to German safety standards is, in the aggregate, less costly to the European Union than switching to Dutch stan-

---

[4] The same result holds in an n-person coordination game.

[5] Snidal, 'Coordination Versus Prisoners' Dilemma' (above, n. 3), 932.

[6] Quoted in Simon Bulmer, 'Germany and European Integration: Toward Economic and Political Dominance?', in Carl Lankowski (ed.), *Germany and the European Community* (New York: St Martin's Press, 1993), 88. See also William Wallace, 'Germany's Unavoidable Central Role: Beyond Myths and Traumas', in Wolfgang Wessels and E. Regelsberger (eds), *The Federal Republic of Germany and Beyond* (Bonn: Europa Union Verlag, 1988), 276–85.

dards, for example.[7] Unsurprisingly, DIN (*Deutsches Institut für Normung*) standards have long set the tone in a wide range of European industries. Germany has also been a key-initiator and agenda-setter in many areas of European standardization. Its influence is felt, notably, through DIN's participation in European standards-setting organizations such as CEN and CENELEC.[8] A measure of this influence is DIN's control of the largest number of secretariats for technical committees within CEN and CENELEC.[9] For example, in March 1989, DIN held 75 out of 212 CEN/CENELEC secretariats for technical committees, that is, 35.4 per cent. The British Standards Institution (BSI) held 18.4 per cent and the *Association Française de Normalisation* (AFNOR) 17.9 per cent.[10]

Considerations about switching costs aside, regional leadership can also help ease distributional issues which arise as coordination games are played over time. Repeated play makes coordination more difficult because it gives states incentives to be more concerned with the *distributional consequences* of coordination. If x_1y_1 (in Figure 1) is the repeated outcome of an iterated coordination game, State A will be quite satisfied (it obtains 4 on each round), whereas State B only gets its second-best solution, namely 3. Small differences add up over time. Questions of fairness and equitable distribution of the gains from cooperation will need to be addressed to prevent discontent from derailing standardization and integration processes more broadly.[11] A dominant Member State of a regional

---

[7] Note, however, that even the 'least-costly' coordination arrangement involves typically immense switching costs. Russell Hardin recently wrote that 'the cost of re-coordination is the chief obstacle to moving to any supposedly superior order, even if it would be in virtually everyone's interest to be in the new order'. See Russell Hardin, *Liberalism, Constitutionalism, Democracy* (forthcoming).

[8] European Standards Committee and European Electrical Standards Committee; both are known by their French acronyms.

[9] Stephen Woolcock, Michael Hodges, and Kristin Schreiber, *Britain, Germany and 1992* (London: Pinter, 1991), 48–9.

[10] Germany's leadership is, of course, not only felt in the field of technical standards. It is credited with launching the European Monetary System (see Peter Ludlow, *The Making of the European Monetary System: A Case Study of the Politics of the European Community* (London: Butterworth Scientific, 1982), 290). It also played central roles in the initial outline of the budget compromise at the Stuttgart Council summit in June 1983; in relaunching the EMU at the Hannover summit in June 1988; and in calling for an inter-governmental conference (IGC) on political union paralleling the proposed EMU. Germany's contribution to the institutional architecture of the Union further includes the strengthening of common macroeconomic, social, and environmental policies, as well as the introduction of concepts such as subsidiarity and multi-tiered governance. Another illustration of Germany's influence is the widespread acceptance of the Bundesbank as the model for the statute of the European Central Bank, and the adoption by the Union of the 'Rhineland model of capitalism', a form of economic liberalism with strong provisions for social-policy cushioning. See Simon Bulmer and William Paterson, *The Federal Republic of Germany and the European Community* (London: Allen & Unwin, 1987), 12; and Michael Hodges and Stephen Woolcock, 'Atlantic Capitalism versus Rhine Capitalism in the EC', *West European Politics*, vol. 16 (July 1993), 329–44.

[11] Distributional issues have generally been neglected by students in International Political Economy, while scholars of the Realist School have exaggerated their importance. Realists argue that states refrain from cooperation because they fear the security implications

grouping may be able and willing to assume the role of regional paymaster, easing distributional tensions and thus smoothing the path of integration.[12]

The relevance of these considerations to the European case is obvious. The shaping of institutional arrangements within EU standardization and beyond has arguably favoured German interests more directly than those of other Member States, thus possibly giving rise to distributional concerns. Simon Bulmer notes: 'The adoption of German institutional rules . . . mobilizes a procedural bias that should facilitate the articulation of German interests. There is, of course, a time-lag in how this institutional power comes into play. Shaping the EU's constitutive politics in one time period will only mobilise bias enabling Germany to advance its interests in the regulative politics of the EU in a subsequent time period.'[13]

Nevertheless, German leadership has largely been gentle rather than imposing.[14] Germany strongly prefers to build consensus and readily offers concessions to preserve that consensus. This is true not only in standardization but in other domains as well. Standardization games in Europe are frequently connected to parallel games played by the Member States in other issue-areas, and thus can be thought of as nested in the meta-game of economic integration. A general measure of Germany's willingness to ease distributional tensions in the meta-game is its generosity as regional paymaster. Germany is by far the largest net contributor to the EU budget (measured both in absolute and per capita terms) which redistributes substantial resources, notably through the European Regional Development Fund, the European Social Fund, and more recently the Cohesion Fund. The primary beneficiaries of these funds are the poorer EU Members. The existence of the funds depends much on continuing German prosperity and generosity. Germany's net contribution to the budget has increased from DM 10.5 billion in 1987 to DM 22 billion in 1992. It is estimated to exceed DM 30 billion by the end of this decade. In 1996 Germany's financial contribution to the European Union amounted

---

of unbalanced distribution of the gains from cooperation. (See Joseph Grieco, *Cooperation Among Nations* (Ithaca, NY: Cornell University Press, 1990); and Stephen Krasner, 'Global Communications and National Power: Life on the Pareto Frontier', *World Politics*, vol. 43 (Apr. 1991), 336–66.) I argue that distributional issues matter—not primarily because of security reasons but because they can affect domestic politics or raise questions of fairness.

[12] Note that this account is different from hegemonic stability theory (see, for example, Keohane, *After Hegemony* (above, n. 3)). The latter is based on an analysis of public goods, a special case of the Prisoners' Dilemma, and deals with the implications of free-riding. The present account, however, refers to the coordination game, where the issue is not free-riding but how to overcome distributional inequities.

[13] Simon Bulmer, 'Shaping the Rules? The Constitutive Politics of the European Union and German Power', in Peter Katzenstein (ed.), *Tamed Power: Germany in Europe* (Ithaca: Cornell University Press, forthcoming).

[14] 'Gentle giant' is how Simon Bulmer characterizes Germany in his writings. See, e.g., above, nn. 6 and 13.

to about two-thirds of the net income of the Union, double the relative size of the German GDP in the European Union.[15]

Why has Germany assumed the role of institutional leader and regional paymaster? In part, the answer is that Germany acts out of economic self-interest. Germany depends economically on its European partners as much as they depend on Germany, and thus any measure that improves stability and security in trade and investment in Europe is likely to suit Germany. More generally, unobstructed access to a single and prosperous European market is of obvious interest to Europe's most powerful and efficient economy. It enables German firms to expand through increased exports, mergers, and acquisition. Regional production networks, in turn, reduce production costs and raise the international competitiveness of German firms.[16]

In sum, the European example illustrates how the presence of an undisputed leader among a group of countries seeking closer ties can help resolve coordination problems in standardization, and economic integration more broadly. A dominant state can serve as focal point in the coordination process, while also helping to ease distributional tensions through, for example, side-payments.

B. Coordination in the absence of an undisputed institutional leader

In the absence of an institutional leader, coordination problems may be quite difficult to solve, as has repeatedly been illustrated, for example, in the case of ASEAN or the Andean Pact. Likewise, coordination difficulties will arise when two or more potential leaders belong to the same group. For example, within APEC, the United States and Japan are contending leaders. Their differing economic institutions and policy preferences in many technical and economic domains make coordination very difficult.[17]

Charles Kindleberger has put forth a similar idea by arguing that when countries are evenly matched in size and importance, agreement on international standards for output regulation, taxation, and the like is likely to be weakened by compromise. Thus he concluded in an essay written in the early 1980s: 'In today's . . . international economy with no one country any longer leading or dominant, there is risk of market failure in the sense of

---

[15] Peter Katzenstein, 'United Germany in an Integrating Europe', in Katzenstein (ed.), *Tamed Power: Germany in Europe* (above, n. 13). See also Michael Shackleton, 'The Budget of the European Community', in Juliet Lodge (ed.), *The European Community and the Challenge of the Future* (London: Pinter, 1989), 129–47.

[16] Rudolf Hrbek and Wolfgang Wessels, 'National Interessen der Bundesrepublik Deutschland und der Integrationsprozess', in Hrbek and Wessels (eds), *EG-Mitgliedschaft: Ein Vitales Interesse der Bundesrepublik Deutschland?* (Bonn: Europa Union Verlag, 1984), 29–69.

[17] For a full discussion, see Walter Mattli, *The Logic of Regional Integration* (Cambridge: Cambridge University Press, 1999).

failure to adopt widely accepted standards in new goods, to keep old standards up to date as improvements become possible, and especially to achieve the international public good of world standards.'[18]

Nevertheless, in the absence of an undisputed leader, standards setting is still possible, particularly if one party is in a first-mover position, for systemic reasons or due to historical accident. Suppose State A in Figure 1 is a first-mover and thus gets to choose a strategy before B makes up its mind. State A will naturally pick strategy x_1; faced with this choice, country B will also opt for y_1, thus securing payoff 3 which is better than 2, the payoff it would obtain by responding with strategy y_2. If the game is played not just one time but repeatedly, questions of fair and equitable distribution of the gains from cooperation will have to be addressed lest discontent disrupt the integration process.

III. FIRST-MOVERS AND LAGGARDS IN INTERNATIONAL STANDARDIZATION

Since World War II, and arguably even before, European countries have been in a position of first-movers in international standardization, a position that has given them considerable influence in shaping standards institutions, processes, and outcomes. The United States, by contrast, has been somewhat removed from the process (though there are signs that this is now changing). The American position can thus be characterized as one of second-mover or laggard. There are two possible explanations of this position.

The first explanation is functional and is based on a well-known finding that the size elasticity of foreign trade is negative; that is, the smaller the state the higher its economy's degree of openness, or the larger a country, the less its dependence on foreign trade. Given the huge size of its domestic market, the United States has traditionally been a relatively closed economy (measured in terms of trade as a percentage of GNP). It follows that many US industries have not had much of an incentive to get involved in international standardization (with notable exceptions, including telecommunications and information technologies). The European countries, by contrast, have always had a vital interest in participating and investing by international standardization given the relative high degree of openness of their economies (see Figure 2).

[18] Charles Kindleberger, 'Standards as Public, Collective and Private Goods', *Kyklos*, vol. 36 (1983), 393. Kindleberger finds that the same logic applies at the domestic level and argues, for example, that in nineteenth-century England industrial standards failed to emerge in many areas because the country's industries typically were not dominated by a single large firm. By contrast, standardization in France and Germany was achieved because of the presence of dominant firms.

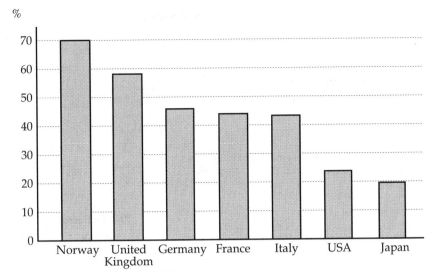

Figure 2. Foreign Trade as % of GNP (1996)

Source: *International Monetary Fund, Directions of Trade Statistics Yearbook,* various issues.

A second and perhaps more important reason for the pro-European institutional bias has to do with the structure of the American standard-ization system. Unlike the European system with its national standards monopolies, the American system is market driven, decentralized, sector-oriented, and characterized by a high degree of competition among the various standardization bodies. As shown in Figure 3, on the private sec-tor side, 300 trade associations, 130 professional and scientific societies, 40 general membership organizations, and approximately 150 consortia have set a total of about 51,000 standards. The US government has typically abstained from getting involved in standards setting for the private mar-ket and has instead focused its efforts on the fairness and effectiveness of standards-setting processes. Uppermost in this regard have been concerns about antitrust infringements and due process. The 1975 Trade Act for-mally recognized the private sector's role in standards setting and affirmed the preference for voluntary consensus standards.[19]

This decentralized and market-driven system has served the American domestic market well, but its lack of unity and the at-times acrimonious turf battles among standards-setting bodies have weakened the position of the United States abroad. At the international level, US interests are typ-ically represented by the American National Standards Institute (ANSI).

[19] US Congress, Office of Technology Assessment, *Global Standards: Building Blocks for the Future,* TCT-512 (Washington, DC: US Government Printing Office, Mar. 1992), 14–15.

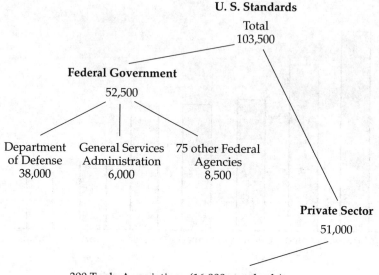

U. S. Standards

Total
103,500

Federal Government
52,500

Department
of Defense
38,000

General Services
Administration
6,000

75 other Federal
Agencies
8,500

Private Sector
51,000

300 Trade Associations (16,000 standards)

- *National Electrical Manufacturers Association (NEMA)*
- *American Petroleum Institute (API)*
- *Computer Business Equipment Manufacturing Association (CBEMA)*

130 Professional and Scientific Societies (16,000 standards)

- *American Society of Agricultural Engineers (ASAE)*
- *American Society of Automotive Engineers (ASAE)*
- *Institute of Electrical and Electronics Engineers (IEEE)*

40 General Membership Organizations (SDOs) (17,000 stds)

- *American Society of Testing Materials (ASTM)*
- *National Fire Protection Association (NFPA)*

150 Consortia (2,000 de facto standards)

- *[primarily in information and communications technologies]*

Figure 3. U.S. Standardization System

However, ANSI is a relatively weak institution, mainly for two reasons: First, its status has not been fully accepted by major players in the American standards community and a few organizations keep acting independently of ANSI at the international level. Frequently tensions arise because of issues concerning the revenues from the sales of standards, which for some organizations can account for up to 80 per cent of their income. In a revealing memo of 1991, ASTM explained its reluctance to cooperate with ANSI as follows:

If the ANSI prescription prevailed . . . ASTM would, over time, decline from the largest voluntary consensus standards developer in the world to a 'bit player' in a system dominated by the ISO and ANSI. ASTM would become solely a feeder of US consensus standards and positions into ANSI for blessing as US 'national' standards and into ISO for blessing as 'international standards'. And ASTM might not even be able to play that limited role. If Europe and the US agreed to adopt and require the use of ISO standards in their respective markets, sales of ASTM standards, nationally and internationally, might be so eroded that ASTM could no longer support itself.[20]

A second reason is that ANSI's resources are modest compared to those of national standards bodies in Europe, thus limiting ANSI's ability to play a role commensurate to the size of the American economy. A comparison between ANSI and just one of the European national standards-setting organizations, the DIN, conveys a sense of the striking difference between the Americans and the Europeans in the institutional resources allocated to international standardization (see Figure 4). ANSI has a full-time staff of ninety-eight, DIN's staff counts over one thousand employees. ANSI's budget is $18 million, DIN's budget is more than seven times as big. While ANSI's activity is evenly split between domestic and international standardization work, nine-tenths of DIN's standards activity is directly related to international and regional standardization; only one-tenth of DIN's focus is on new and purely German standards.

IV. INTERNATIONAL STANDARDIZATION BODIES AND ASYMMETRIC
INVOLVEMENT

A. The institutions

The International Organization for Standardization (ISO) is a worldwide federation of national standards bodies for 132 countries, one from each country.[21] The ISO was created in 1947 from the union of two organizations, the International Federation of National Standardizing Associations (ISA), established in 1926, and the United Nations Standards Coordinating Committee (UNSCC) of 1944. The ISA was primarily dominated by European organizations from the Continent. The UNSCC had been set up by the United States, the United Kingdom, and Canada to bring the benefits of standardization to bear on the war effort and the work of reconstruction.[22] Many of the statutes and rules of procedure of ISO were adopted from ISA and of the sixty-seven Technical Committees which ISO

---

[20] US Congress, Office of Technology Assessment, *Global Standards*, 23.

[21] Of the 132 Member countries, 88 are full Members (Member bodies), 35 are correspondent Members, and 9 are subscriber Members.

[22] ISO, *Friendship Among Equals: Recollections from ISO's First Fifty Years* (Geneva: ISO Central Secretariat, 1997), 15.

	ANSI	*DIN*
Full Time Staff	98	1,040
Budget	$18 m	$132 m
Governmental Financial Support	none	12% of budget
Status	– Private non-profit federation	– Association under private law
Activities	– Coordinates US standards position in the international arena; sole US representative at ISO/IEC.	– Represents German interests at the international and regional levels.
	– Clearing House and Coordinating Body. Certifies that members have arrived at standards through one of three ANSI accredited procedures. About 25% of private standards have been processed through ANSI.	– 9/10 of DIN's standards setting activity is directly related to international and regional standards (i.e., only 1/10 of its focus is on new, purely German standards).
		– DIN committee work is performed by 33,000 external experts participating in one or several committees. There are 4,000 Technical Committees.

Figure 4. A comparison of ANSI and DIN

set up initially, the majority were previously ISA committees.[23] The ISO achieved only modest results in its early years but began to move more rapidly and play a bigger role in the 1960s. Dramatically, it more than doubled the number of standards between 1968 and 1971. Membership grew from fifteen nations in 1947 to seventy in 1971. The ISO also began in the 1970s to cooperate with several regional associations and made a particular effort to attract Japan and other Asian countries to the organization.[24]

The technical work of ISO is highly decentralized, carried out today in a hierarchy of some 186 technical committees, 576 subcommittees, and 2,057

[23] ISO, Friendship Among Equals.
[24] Samuel Krislov, *How Nations Choose Standards and Standards Change Nations* (Pittsburgh: University of Pittsburgh Press, 1997), 51.

working groups. In these committees and working groups, qualified representatives of industry, research institutes, public organizations, and consumer groups gather to tackle standardization issues.

There are three main phases in the ISO standards-development process. The need for a standard is usually expressed by an industry sector which communicates this need to a national member body that, in turn, proposes the new work item to ISO. If ISO accepts the mandate, it will ask a working group comprising technical experts from countries interested in the subject matter to elaborate a definition of the technical scope of the future standard. Once the working group reaches an agreement on the technical aspects to be covered by the standard, a second phase is entered during which a committee works out the detailed specifications of a standard. The main responsibility for administrating a standards committee is with one of the national standards bodies that comprise ISO membership. Finally, an agreement reached by a technical committee is submitted as a draft international standard to the ISO member bodies for voting and publication as ISO International Standard.[25] As of the end of 1998, ISO had adopted and published 11,950 standards.

The main cost of standardization is borne by the member organizations: member firms in national bodies furnish and support the experts who comprise the various committees. Some 30,000 experts participate annually in ISO standardization. The technical work is coordinated from the ISO Central Secretariat in Geneva which has a full-time staff of 165.[26]

In sum, ISO standards are market-driven. They are developed on the basis of international consensus among experts from the sectors which have expressed a requirement for a particular standard. Since ISO standards are voluntary, they are only used to the extent that people find them useful.

The ISO covers most technical fields, although one exception is the electrotechnical domain which falls under the responsibility of ISO's sister organization, the International Electrotechnical Commission (IEC).[27] The IEC was founded in 1906 and membership consists of more than fifty countries. The supreme authority of the IEC is the Council, which is the

---

[25] For the adoption of an ISO international standard, voting rules require a two-thirds majority of the ISO Members that participated actively in the standards development process and no more than one-quarter negative votes of the total votes cast. If these conditions are not met, the draft standard is sent back to the relevant committees for reconsideration in the light of the technical reasons submitted in support of negative votes.

[26] Membership fees provide the bulk of the budget of the ISO Central Secretariat. National standards bodies supply 80% of the operating expenses of ISO, the remainder coming from the sale of subscriptions and publications.

[27] The IEC charter embraces all electrotechnologies, including electronics, magnetics and electromagnetics, electroacoustics, telecommunication, and energy production and distribution, as well as associated general disciplines such as terminology and symbols, measurement and performance, dependability, design and development, and safety and the environment.

general assembly of National Committees (who are the members of the IEC). Its organizational structure closely resembles that of the ISO, and its standards work is carried out by some 200 technical committees and sub-committees and some 700 working groups. In all, about 10,000 experts worldwide participate in the technical work of the IEC. After an enquiry stage, during which National Committees can vote a proposal up or down and propose technical amendments, a revised version called the Final Draft International Standard (FDIS) is circulated to the members. A FDIS is approved if a majority of two-thirds of the votes cast by participating members is in favour, and if the number of negative votes by all National Committees does not exceed one quarter of all the votes cast.

B. Asymmetric involvement

An examination of the involvement of various national bodies in ISO standardization shows a significant asymmetry between the United States and key European countries.[28] One statistic is the number of ISO standards developed on the basis of a mandate submitted by particular nationals, expressed as a percentage of all ISO standards. The number for the United States is 10.9 per cent; France, Germany, the United Kingdom, Sweden, and the Netherlands account for 57 per cent.[29] Another statistic is the number of secretariats held by various countries. The United States held in the mid-1990s a total of twenty-seven secretariats, second only to Germany with thirty-two. However, a more telling comparison is that between North America and Europe. The United States and Canada, which together represent 27.1 per cent of World GNP, held thirty-three secretariats; Western European countries, which together account for about 29.4 per cent of World GNP, controlled 110 secretariats.[30] Also remarkable is the relatively insignificant role played in international standardization by other regions of the world, notably Asia-Pacific. Japan, China, Australia, and New Zealand, which represent 21.9 per cent of world GNP, held only eleven secretariats.[31]

A subsidiary piece of evidence of the greater commitment of Europe to international standards are the reciprocity agreements between European and international standardization bodies; these are the Vienna Agreement of 1991 between the ISO and CEN, and the Dresden Agreement of 1996 (which is a revision of the Lugano Agreement of 1991) between the IEC and CENELEC.[32] Under the Vienna Agreement, for example, CEN and

---

[28] ISO, *Participation in technical committees and other ISO committees* (Geneva: ISO, 1994).
[29] US Congress, Office of Technology Assessment, *Global Standards: Building Blocks for the Future*, TCT-512 (Washington, DC: US Government Printing Office, Mar. 1992), 87.
[30] ISO, *Participation* (above n. 28).   [31] Ibid.
[32] A working agreement also exists between the IEC and the European Telecommunications Standards Institute (ETSI).

ISO agreed to exchange information and to cooperate during the drafting stage of standardization, thus avoiding duplication of work. CEN also agreed to adopt already existing international standards as European standards. Such adoption can happen in several ways. CEN may determine that an ISO standard is in need of revision. ISO may revise the standard before it is processed as a new standard at both the international and the European levels. If ISO declines to revise the standard, CEN can simply adopt the ISO standard with modifications made under the normal CEN procedure.

The reciprocity agreements also contain provisions about adoption procedures and division of labour. For example, when CENELEC considers a new work, it consults the IEC to determine whether the latter is in a position to complete the work within the target dates given. The work is begun in CENELEC in parallel with the consultation with the IEC, which may last up to six months. Thereafter, it is only continued in CENELEC if the IEC either rejects a request or is unable to meet the target date. After completion of the work, voting forms are sent simultaneously to the IEC National Committees and to CENELEC. If the results are positive, the standard will be adopted both as the international and European standard.[33] Similarly, CEN may propose that ISO carry out a new work item, or vice-versa, with parallel approval conducted in ISO and CEN.

Despite some difficulties in the implementation of these agreements caused by the failure to synchronize the work between the various standardization bodies,[34] cooperation has overall been remarkably successful, bringing about a high degree of convergence in standardization between the international and the European levels. Indeed, 35 per cent of CEN standards are today identical to ISO standards, and 80 per cent of CENELEC standards are identical to IEC standards. Such convergence is conspicuously absent in the case of international and American standards. Helmut Reihlen, director of the German national standards institute DIN, noted in 1992 that 'fewer than 30 of the more than 38,700 privately developed standards in the United States . . . were ISO/IEC standards'.[35]

C. Proposals for institutional reform

In conclusion, it is worth pondering what steps ought to be taken to reform the current system and attract more American investment and expertise,

---

[33] International Electrotechnical Commission, *Inside the IEC* (Geneva: IEC Central Office, 1990), 22–4.

[34] For example, requests have been received to submit texts for parallel processing without there being relevant work items in both ISO and CEN. In such circumstances the work must either be delayed while the other organization fulfils its procedural requirements for approval of a new work item, or continued independently in the lead organization, although the procedures may be synchronized at a later stage.

[35] US Congress, Office of Technology Assessment, *Global Standards* (above, n. 19), 85.

thus achieving a more balanced representation of national interests at the international level. At a major international conference entitled 'Standardization for the 21st Century' that took place in Berlin in March 1999, policy-makers and scholars debated how to reform the system. The two main recommendations can be summed up as follows. First, the introduction of a cooperation agreement between ISO/IEC and the American standards-developers organizations (SDOs) on a sectoral basis, and the use of the Dresden and Vienna Agreement as model, depending on sector.[36] Such an arrangement would align international and national standards and improve transparency, while also reducing the cost of standards development as well as products and tests. Second, the introduction of weighted voting in ISO and IEC. The weight could be a function of GNP, trade, population, and number of national standards. Such a reform would also require a change in the dues structure. Weighted voting, however, has one major drawback: it is likely to further marginalize developing countries.

These reforms would increase the influence of the United States in international standardization but also impose certain obligations on the Americans, most notably an agreement to implement international standards as national standards and withdraw conflicting national standards. Further, ANSI would have to become a stronger and better-funded organization in order for the United States to be able to assume a greater international role.

A final issue that reformers will have to grapple with is the question of the role of consumer groups in international standardization, particularly as the scope of standards in support of trade liberalization and public-policy objectives widens to include areas such as services, environmental protection, and the 'information society'. In Europe, participation of consumers has become a political precondition for the acceptability and further development of European standardization. The European association for the coordination of the representation of consumers in standardization (ANEC) is a member of several European standardization bodies, including CEN and CENELEC; further, it is financially supported by the Commission.[37] As a member of these regional standards bodies, ANEC is accepted into the technical boards and general assemblies and can even play a role in the administrative boards.

---

[36] A pilot project between ISO and four American standards-developing organizations (ASTM, ASME, API, and IEEE), launched in 1998, may be followed up by a formal Dresden/Vienna-like agreement on a sectoral basis.

[37] ANEC was set up by national consumer bodies from the European Community and EFTA Member States to coordinate consumer representation in standardization in response to the adoption of the New Approach in 1985. The New Approach gave standards an important role in the elimination of technical barriers to trade and thus the regulation of safety and other consumer issues.

This level of consumer participation contrasts sharply with the experience at the international level. The only group that is allowed to represent consumer interests at the international level is Consumers International (CI), an umbrella organization representing over 200 independent consumer organization from almost 100 countries.[38] Within the international standards bodies, however, CI cannot appoint its own representatives above the level of technical committees, depriving it of real influence at the critical technical management and policy levels. Further, no funding is made available at the international level, which seriously hampers CI's ability to send observers to all important committees. This dissatisfactory situation needs to be remedied. In particular, the ISO and the IEC need to open up their own structures to organize and support consumer representation in a way that is similar to the European example.

In sum, at the international level reformers will have to pay more attention to the guiding principles of openness and transparency—for it is these principles that create the basis for political acceptability of international standardization. Some guarantees and checks and balances will be necessary to ensure that the results of international standardization processes reflect not only the interests of industry but of all major societal players.

---

[38] CI status as sole representative of consumers at the international level is a consequence of its observer status on the UN Economic and Social Committee.

Part VI

The interface between international regulatory initiatives and the domestic legal environment

US and EU structures of governance as barriers to transatlantic regulatory cooperation

Jonathan R. Macey

I. INTRODUCTION

With the globalization of the world's capital markets, domestic regulators are finding that maintaining and enforcing rules both within their own borders and abroad is becoming an increasingly difficult task. The need for international regulatory cooperation is acutely felt by regulators whose interests are threatened by the increasing internationalization of capital markets. For the United States and Europe, this changing landscape has particular implications because of the extent to which Europe and the United States are linked economically.[1]

For US companies, the European market is twice as large as Japan and Canada combined.[2] Moreover, 'American companies in Europe, if aggregated, would represent the fourth largest economy on the continent'.[3] European investment in the United States is on a similar scale: US$145 billion, generating US$900 billion in annual sales. Additionally, 8 per cent of US factory workers are employed by European companies.[4] 'Because European industry is at the same time American industry's single most important business competitor, regulatory policy in the US and EC [European Community] is a major determinant of those industries basic competitiveness. . . . [Thus, Europe] is, at the present time, the clearest candidate for partnership with the US in a collaborative rulemaking process.'[5]

The problems faced by US agencies dealing with Europe are complicated by the divergence in the political and economic interests of individual European Member States. The basic issue is the lack of a centralized decision-maker.[6] As Henry Kissinger asked, 'When you want to talk to Europe, who do you call?'[7] The European Union, with its apparent emphasis on economic and political aggregation, aims to answer this

---

[1] George A. Bermann, 'Regulatory Cooperation Between the European Commission and US Administrative Agencies', *Administrative Law Journal of American University*, vol. 9 (1996), 933, 935.

[2] Speech by Robert Mallett, Deputy Secretary of the United States Department of Commerce, to the British American Business Council, 12 Apr. 1999, *FDCH Federal Department and Agency Documents*.

[3] Ibid.   [4] Ibid.   [5] Bermann, 'Regulatory Cooperation' (above, n. 1), 935.

[6] Mallet, Speech to British American Business Council (above, n. 2).   [7] Ibid.

question. Unfortunately, the European Union is an evolving entity, and it is yet to be seen whether its policy-making will become more centralized. As of now, 'Europe lacks an FDA, an FAA, and SEC and other regulatory institutions essential for a unified market to function efficiently.'[8]

This contribution does not claim that regulatory coordination is hampered by the lack of a centralized policy-making structure in Europe. Rather, it acknowledges this fact but points out that European regulators face similar problems when dealing with the United States. Furthermore, it attempts to clarify some of the impediments that regulators in the United States and Europe face in trying to adopt, or even negotiate, new rules. The first part of the contribution briefly examines how public opinion tends to effect the rule-making process in democracies. Next, it reviews the obstacles that confront regulators dealing with the evolving European Union, including adoption and enforcement of EU directives, and the principle of subsidiarity. Finally, the contribution examines the special problems that the United States poses to foreign and domestic bureaucrats. This section looks at the diffusion of power within the United States, which has the important effect of raising the costs of negotiating and reaching international agreements, including agreements about international regulatory cooperation. Accordingly, this contribution examines the structure of the US constitutional system, parallel government structures, the US federalist system, and, finally, the historically omnipresent notion of the 'policy window' in the passage of financial rules in particular.

II. DEALING WITH PEOPLE IN DEMOCRACIES

In democracy there is the problem of dealing with public opinion, because in democracies, the people have views about the desirability of regulatory cooperation that may not comport with the views of the elites. Regulations are the by-products of the legislative process. However, 'as an indispensable surrogate to the legislative process, rulemaking has a fundamental flaw that violates basic democratic principles. Those who write the law embodied in rules are not elected; they are accountable to the American people only through indirect and less-than-foolproof means. Our elected representatives have confronted this dilemma on numerous occasions and decided that one answer is direct participation by the public in rulemaking.'[9]

It is the participation of the public that gives the rule-making process legitimacy. Regulators rely on information that the public provides in order to formulate rules. Therefore, if public participation is stymied by

---

[8] Mallett, Speech to British American Business Council (above, n. 2).

[9] Cornelius M. Kerwin, *Rulemaking: How Government Agencies Write Law and Make Policy*, 2nd edn (Washington, DC: C.Q. Press 1999), 157.

the regulatory agency, the rule will lack authority and will, therefore, not be respected by the affected community. This, in turn, creates problems with compliance and enforcement after the rule has been implemented.[10] As several commentators, including Professor Malecha, have noted, 'All regulatory agencies are public agents and as such must accept and reflect public opinion'.[11] In addition to the direct input of the public, regulatory policy in the United States is strongly influenced by the Congress. The US Congress is highly sensitive to public opinion, and therefore, often demands the various agencies to tailor their rules to deal directly with the problems that create the most public outcry.[12]

A recent example of the impact of the power of public opinion on regulatory decision-making can be seen in the attempted takeover of Telecom Italia by Deutsche Telekom. Telecom Italia had initially agreed to merge with Deutsche Telekom, but the deal faced strong political opposition from the Italian government, which could ultimately prevent the acquisition by the German company. The Italian government was in this position because it held a 'golden share' in Telecom Italia, and could effectively prevent any merger by refusing to relinquish this share. The merger of Telecom Italia with Deutsche Telekom would have effectively given the German government a 40 per cent share of the new company. The Italian people saw the potential takeover of Telecom Italia as a threat to their national sovereignty and therefore found it unacceptable. Although the CEO of Telecom Italia was adamant in his opposition to a hostile takeover by Olivetti, a domestic company, government officials nevertheless supported Olivetti since it would keep the country's primary telecommunications operator under Italian control.[13]

Olivetti was successful in its takeover effort largely because of political opposition to a proposed German merger. Public opinion, especially when dealing with concerns of compromising national sovereignty, must therefore be entered into the regulatory equation. This is not to say that public opinion will always coalesce around such concerns. Indeed, the public must first perceive the proposition as a significant concern, and second, public outcry must be resounding enough that public officials will take notice.

---

[10] Ibid., at 158.

[11] Lorena Bark Malecha, John Moffet, and Natasha Zalkin, 'San Francisco Bay Area Boatyards: A Case Study in Regulating Small Polluters', *Boston College Environmental Affairs Law Review*, vol. 20 (1993), 453, 467.

[12] Alan B. Horowitz, 'Terminating the "Passive" Paradox: A Proposal for Federal Regulation of Environmental Tobacco Smoke', *American University Law Review*, vol. 41 (1991), 183, 195.

[13] Michael Harrison, Business Editor, 'Olivetti Clinches Victory in Pounds 40BN Telecom Italia Battle', *Independent* (London), 22 May 1999, 19.

III. STRUCTURES OF GOVERNANCE AND UNCERTAINTY IN REGULATORY
NEGOTIATIONS WITH THE EUROPEAN UNION

The Maastricht Treaty signed in 1992 was a major step in Europeans' effort
to establish 'ever closer union' among the Member States. The treaty contained provisions, among others, for the establishment of economic and
financial union and also for the creation of the Common Foreign and
Security Policy (CFSP), and for Cooperation in the Fields of Justice and
Home Affairs (CJHA). While the notion of economic and financial
unification has progressed with the establishment of the Euro as the common currency, the idea that Europe now acts as a single entity is not yet a
reality in many major regulatory domains. The hope is that the currency
unification will be the first step in forming a real political union. With
regard to CFSP and CJHA, however, the European Union does not have
the mandate to make policy choices binding on Member States.
Furthermore, the judicial branch of the European Union, the European
Court of Justice, does not have jurisdiction to enforce decisions in these
areas.[14] Regulators hoping to deal with EU regulatory bodies must keep
these limitations in mind in establishing a strategy for regulatory cooperation with European nations.

Another consideration that agencies must keep in mind is that Member
State administrations bear the primary responsibility for executing and
enforcing EU policy. In the United States, by contrast, federal policy is
implemented and enforced by federal agencies. Thus, enforcement oversight is logistically much more difficult to carry out.[15] Another barrier to
regulatory efficacy results from the fact that most EU rules are issued as
directives and not regulations. This distinction is important, since unlike
regulations, which directly and immediately bind the Member States
upon their passage, directives require the Member State to modify their
national law to bring it into line with the content of the EU directive. This
procedural mandate may ultimately complicate the promulgation of the
rule. Thus, an agency that engages in regulatory cooperation with the
European Union will not only have to concern itself with the passage of
the rule by the European Union, but it will also have to evaluate the extent
to which the Member States have each incorporated and enforced the
directive.[16]

There is an additional legal hurdle that must be overcome before the
European Union can enter into international regulatory agreements.
Unlike US regulatory agencies which need not seek the legislative
approval of each and every international agreement that is entered, the

---

[14] Dieter Kugelmann, 'The Maastricht Treaty and the Design of a European Federal State',
Temple International and Comparative Law Journal, vol. 8 (1994), 335, 343.
[15] Bermann, 'Regulatory Cooperation' (above, n. 1), 939.   [16] Ibid., at 940.

European Commission, the EU institution responsible for regulatory proposals, cannot by itself ratify a binding international agreement. Instead the Commission must submit the proposed directive to the Council for approval. This limitation derives from the fact that international regulatory agreements under EU law are subject to specific treaty-making procedures established by the EU.[17] In *France v. Commission*,[18] the Court of Justice ruled that in the context of the EU–US competition law agreement, the Commission did not have the authority to enter into an agreement with the United States without ratification by the Council.[19] Thus:

[u]nder the Court's ruling, arguably, the Commission lacks authority to commit itself to following any particular form of cooperation with foreign authorities, including consultation in the preparation of draft regulatory texts or even the sharing of underlying data, without observing the treaty-making procedures laid down in the EC [European Community] Treaty. Under this reading, the Commission may cooperate as fully as it wishes with overseas authorities, without observing any prior formalities, but may not, on its own, obligate itself to do so.[20]

Finally, it is important to note that the European Union operates under the principle of subsidiarity, which states that the European Union can act only if the aim of the proposed legislation cannot be accomplished by the Member States themselves, and that the European Union can more effectively achieve the aim of the policy. Thus, subsidiarity acts to ensure that the Member States' autonomy is respected.[21]

Arguably, each participant in the legislative process of the Community—the Commission in proposing (and in some cases issuing) a rule, the Parliament and other bodies in expressing an opinion on a proposed rule, and the Council in adopting a rule—can determine whether the measure comports with the principle of subsidiarity, before, respectively, proposing, commenting on, or adopting it.[22] Thus, in adhering to the principle of subsidiarity, multiple levels of the legislative process are burdened with determining the subsidiarity impacts of proposed laws.

---

[17] Ibid., at 959.   [18] Case C-327/91 [1994] E.C.R. I-3666.   [19] Ibid.
[20] Bermann, 'Regulatory Cooperation' (above, n. 1), 960.
[21] Kugelmann, 'The Maastricht Treaty' (above, n. 14), 349.
[22] George A. Bermann, 'Taking Subsidiarity Seriously: Federalism in the European Community and the United States', *Columbia Law Review*, vol. 94 (1994), 331, 366.

IV. DEALING WITH THE UNITED STATES: STRUCTURAL IMPEDIMENTS
TO INTERNATIONAL REGULATORY COOPERATION

A. US constitutional system

An important goal of a well-developed legal system is to promulgate rules that reduce the transaction costs facing privately contracting parties.[23] Mutual agreements reached by privately contracting parties work to the benefit of both parties. Therefore, to the extent that the legal system can facilitate these transactions by reducing their costs, everyone is made better off. By way of contrast, another important goal of a legal system that desires to promote social stability and welfare is to increase the transaction costs facing parties who seek enactment of legislation that would employ the machinery of the state to effect coercive wealth transfers from one group to another. Even the possibility of such transfers reduces the wealth of society as a whole, as people are driven to consume resources to block such transfers.[24] Arguably, the Framers of the US Constitution intended to impede rather than to facilitate such 'rent-seeking' activity by incorporating several provisions that raise the transaction costs of interest groups. Regulators are therefore faced with a system which inherently impedes the rule-making process.

The modern economic theory of legislation can be summarized easily. To use Judge Richard Posner's description, the economic (or 'interest-group') theory of legislation asserts that legislation is a good demanded and supplied much as other goods, so that legislative protection flows to those groups that derive the greatest value from it, regardless of overall social welfare.[25] A basic presumption of the economic theory of legislation is that, all else equal, increasing levels of expenditures by an interest group on a particular issue increase that group's influence on that issue.[26] The structure of government, however, greatly affects the marginal price that an interest group must pay to obtain the passage of a particular statute. Thus, constitutional drafters who are concerned about the welfare-reducing influence of special-interest groups can design a governmental structure that makes it relatively costly to obtain passage of a statute.

---

[23] Charles J. Goetz and Robert E. Scott, 'The Limits of Expanded Choice: An Analysis of the Interaction Between Express and Implied Contract Terms', *California Law Review*, vol. 73 (1985), 261, 266.

[24] This article embraces the assumption that wealth creation and wealth transfers are mutually exclusive. I do not, however, mean to suggest that wealth transfers cannot enhance overall societal utility.

[25] Richard A. Posner, 'Economics, Politics, and the Reading of Statutes and the Constitution', *University of Chicago Law Review*, vol. 49 (1982), 263, 268.

[26] Robert E. McCormick and Robert D. Tollison, *Politicians, Legislation, and the Economy: An Inquiry into the Interest-Group Theory of Government* (Hingham, MA: Kluwer Boston, 1981), 30–1.

A venerable and straightforward application of the notion that altering the structure of government can affect the cost and thus the production function of legislation was offered by Montesquieu.[27] Montesquieu argued that a separation of powers between the various functions of government would control governmental abuse by providing a check on the law-making ability of rival branches. The principle of separation of powers, advocated by Montesquieu and incorporated in many governmental organizational structures, is a way of increasing the costs to discrete special interest groups of achieving their legislative goals. Establishing a system of government with a separation of powers not only raises the equilibrium price for obtaining passage of a law, it also imposes varying costs on different interest groups, depending on the characteristics of each group and the nature of the legislation.

Establishing several independent branches of government that can block or impede the enactments of rival branches is a means of raising the cost of obtaining legislative enactments for all groups. If a two-thirds vote must be obtained in one elected body to override the veto of the executive, for example, the costs to an interest group of obtaining passage of a statute of which the executive disapproves must also go up. Similarly, if the judicial branch of the government can invalidate or misconstrue (either intentionally or unintentionally) a legislative enactment, then the expected benefit of a statute is necessarily decreased.[28] Thus, the American constitutional system sets up a system of checks and balances by creating both a federal judiciary that is insulated from political pressure because its judges have life tenure and salaries that cannot be reduced, and a federal executive with authority to veto acts of Congress.

In addition to the regime of checks and balances, the Constitution employs a bicameral legislature, with houses of widely different sizes, which also raises the price to interest groups of obtaining favourable legislation.[29] As

---

[27] See Charles de Montesquieu, Nugent trans., *The Spirit of the Laws* (New York: Hafner Publishing Company (1949), 151–2) (discussing the values of separation of powers). Ample evidence contemporary with the drafting of the Constitution suggests that Montesquieu's ideas greatly influenced the framers. See Alexander Hamilton, *The Federalist*, No. 9, C. Rossiter (ed.) (1961), 76 (quoting Montesquieu); James Madison, ibid., No. 47, 301 (citing Montesquieu); Alexander Hamilton, ibid., No. 78, 468 (quoting Montesqieu) (New York: New American Library, 1961).

[28] Jonathan R. Macey, 'Promoting Public-Regarding Legislation through Statutory Interpretation: An Interest Group Model', *Columbia Law Review*, vol. 86 (1986), 223, 253–4.

[29] In addition, having a bicameral legislature is a low-cost device for implementing a system of diverse representation that, as described above, serves to reduce the incidence of special interest legislation. As James Buchanan and Gordon Tullock have observed:

[I]f the basis of representation can be made significantly different in the two houses, the institution of the bicameral legislature may prove to be an effective means of securing a substantial reduction in the expected external costs of collective action without incurring as much added decision-making costs as more inclusive rule would involve in a single house.

James Buchanan and Gordon Tullock, *The Calculus of Consent* (Ann Arbor: University of Michigan Press, 1971), 236.

Mancur Olson has shown, the cost of making collective decisions goes up in a non-linear fashion—the costs increase at a faster rate than the growth in the size of the legislature.[30] As a result, if the total size of the legislature is held constant, increasing the size of one house (with a concomitant decrease in size of the other house) raises the cost to an interest group in obtaining agreement in that house by an amount that is greater than the group's savings in the other house.[31]

Finally, each of the three branches of government must appeal to different constituencies for political support, which bolsters the efficacy of the separation of powers.[32] For example, the nature of the underlying transaction costs may be such that the representative of a particular subdivision is easily influenced by a particular interest group to support a particular statute. If influencing this legislator is all the interest group has to do to prevail, the costs of interest-group influences will be very low. If, however, an interest group must put together a large number of coalitions representing different constituencies to influence political outcomes, the cost of obtaining such influence will increase.

In sum, the US constitutional system makes it much harder for bureaucrats to achieve their regulatory goals. That is, regulators seeking to harmonize with their foreign counterparts are faced with a system that intrinsically impedes the rule-making process by various mechanisms.

B. Disaggregation of regulatory power in the United States: the example of the dual banking system

The disaggregation of regulatory power that is characteristic of US bureaucracies poses a particular problem for those seeking to establish regulatory cooperation between the United States and Europe. Regulatory turf of rival agencies often overlaps. Moreover, a system of checks and balances is in place which monitors the rule-making process. The various contingencies that effect rule-making in the United States invariably complicate efforts for foreign and domestic regulators.

[30] See Mancur Olson, *The Logic of Collective Action: Public Goods and the Theory of Groups* (Cambridge, MA: Harvard University Press, 1971) 53–65.

[31] See McCormick and Tollison, *Politicians, Legislation, the Economy* (above, n. 26), 44. Begin with the assumption of a bicameral legislature consisting of a house and senate. If there are 200 legislators equally divided between the two houses, then an interest group must provide sufficient political support to fifty-one people in each body to gain passage of a statute. Assume also that the statute is not vetoed or subsequently declared to be unconstitutional. If the structure of the government is altered so that the senate has forty members and the house has 160, the 'logic of collective action' dictates that the cost to the interest group of obtaining passage of its statute will go up, because the increase in the cost of influencing the outcome in the house will be greater than the decrease in the cost of influencing the outcome in the senate. In other words, the cost of making collective decisions will, with the shift in the two houses' sizes, increase in a non-linear fashion—i.e. it will increase at an increasing rate. See Olson, *The Logic of Collective Action* (above, n. 30), 53–65.

[32] Buchanan and Tullock, *The Calculus of Consent* (above, n. 29), 233–48.

The banking system within the United States is an excellent example of the disaggregation of regulatory power. The United States is unique in its dual banking system. Indeed, no other country has a banking system in which the central government and its constituent states charter and regulate the same financial institutions.[33] There are a number of entities that oversee banking activity in the United States. These include the Federal Reserve, the Comptroller of the Currency, the FDIC, state banking agencies, the House and Senate Banking Committees, and various other federal agencies which affect banking operations such as the Securities and Exchange Commission and the Department of Justice.[34] Additionally, banking regulations are subject to executive and Congressional oversight, and ultimately are subject to judicial review.[35] The multitude of regulatory institutions can create problems in that regulatory jurisdiction will often overlap. Moreover, since the agencies and branches are accountable to different constituencies, there often exist quite diverse, and often conflicting, motivations in creating and reviewing banking regulations.[36]

The dual nature of the US banking system often leads to contention between state and federal law-makers. For example, establishing a bank, be it state or federal, no longer depends on acquiring a charter. Instead, a bank must procure federal deposit insurance. The FDIC is the sole government agency responsible for granting federal deposit insurance.[37] Moreover, the FDIC 'has the authority to override state legislation relating to bank powers where the Corporation believes that its deposit insurance fund might be threatened'.[38] On the other hand, there are federal laws that yield to state banking laws in the areas of branch banking, and trust and fiduciary powers.[39]

There is also significant overlap of federal and state regulatory turf. One example of this overlap is the aforementioned requirement that all state chartered banks have federal deposit insurance. Three more federal laws brought state banks under the fold of the federal government: first, the Federal Reserve Act of 1913 provided that the federal government could regulate state banks that were part Federal Reserve System; second, the Glass–Steagall Act prohibited all banks, state and federal, from engaging in both commercial and investment banking; finally, the Depository Institutions Deregulation Act required all banks to directly or indirectly have reserves with the Federal Reserve.[40] 'As a consequence, the current

---

[33] Carter H. Golembe, 'Are the States Still Part of the Dual Banking System?', *Banking Policy Report*, vol. 13, no. 8 (1994), 2.

[34] Roger G. Noll, *Reforming Regulation* (Washington, DC: The Brookings Institution, 1971), 58.

[35] Kerwin, *Rulemaking* (above, n. 9), 70.

[36] See Buchanan and Tullock, *The Calculus of Consent* (above, n. 29), 233–48.

[37] Golembe, 'Are the States?' (above, n. 33), 2.   [38] Ibid., at 3.

[39] Edward L. Symons, Jr., 'The United States Banking System', *Brooklyn Journal of International Law*, vol. 19 (1993), 1, 9.

[40] Ibid., at 5.

dual banking system consists of two interrelated regulatory systems rather than two independent regulatory systems.'[41]

While the US banking system is an excellent example of the regulatory morass that is often created by multiple agencies with overlapping authority, this complex regulatory scheme also functions as a system of checks and balances that has limited the concentration of economic power among banks.[42] This system of checks and balances also includes the mechanisms used by the Congress, the President, and the judiciary to hold regulators accountable.[43]

Congress employs several devices to keep regulators in check. First, it can construct laws so precisely and thoroughly that the need for rules is eliminated.[44] 'Alternatively, Congress can establish clear expectations regarding the types of rules agencies write, the content of those rules, the methods by which they are developed, and the time taken to complete the rulemaking task.'[45] In addition to the procedural guidelines that Congress creates for these agencies, they can also use *hammers*. Hammers are statutes that will take effect on a specified date unless an alternative regulation can be crafted by the agency. This type of provision places pressure on the regulator to expedite the crafting process. Next, Congress has the power of the purse. It can supply agencies with more or less money depending on their expected performance. More significantly, Congress has available to it many direct oversight tools, including staff communication, oversight hearings, and the infrequently used legislative veto.[46] Furthermore, the Small Business Regulatory Enforcement Fairness Act, passed in 1996, mandates that all rules must be offered to both Houses of Congress and to the General Accounting Office for review.[47]

Presidents have come to realize that keeping a watchful eye on the rulemaking of agencies is the most effective way of controlling regulation.[48] 'Since the Carter administration, each president has articulated a set of principles, often in the form of an executive order, that has become the basis for review of individual rules by White House staff.'[49] Review of most rules by the executive branch is conducted through the Office of Management and Budget (OMB). The OMB can suggest changes to the rules, the most extreme result of this scrutiny being withdrawal of the rule by the sponsoring agency.[50] The President also has the power to appoint the commissioners who head the various independent regulatory agencies. He does not have the power to fire commissioners, but can deny their reappointment at the end of their terms.[51] 'The regulators thus occupy an

---

[41] Symons, 'The United States Banking System' (above, n. 39).
[42] Noll, *Reforming Regulation* (above, n. 34), 58.
[43] Kerwin, *Rulemaking* (above, n. 9), 70.   [44] Ibid., at 207.
[45] Ibid., at 209–10, 214.   [46] Ibid.   [47] Ibid., at 220, 5 USC, e.g. 801–8.
[48] Ibid., at 221.   [49] Ibid.
[50] Jefferey S. Lubbers, *A Guide to Federal Agency Rulemaking*, 3rd edn (Chicago: ABA Publishing, 1998), 19–20.
[51] Louis M. Kohlmeier, *The Regulators* (New York: Harper and Row, 1969), 36–7.

ill-defined and varying position in relation to the President, somewhere between the subordinate status of cabinet officers and the independence of judges.'[52]

The judiciary also plays a large role in the review of rules. The judiciary need not act for its presence to be felt by the executive offices, the Congress, and the regulatory agencies. The possibilities of litigation and of the courts striking down a regulation loom in the background during the rule-making process. Thus, one of the ways in which the judiciary exerts its influence is extremely subtle.[53] Of course, the courts have a more direct method of exerting their influence, which is to invalidate a rule. The Administrative Procedure Act defines the scope of judicial review of rules.[54] Its terms include criteria that define invalid rules, including rules that are found to be 'arbitrary, capricious, an abuse of discretion, or otherwise not in accordance with the law' or 'in excess of statutory jurisdiction, authority, or limitations, or short of statutory right'.[55] The Act covers nearly every aspect of rule-making, and therefore gives the courts broad power in overseeing regulators.

The ramification of all of the above-mentioned interplays is that enacting statutes or rules that will regulate an industry is an arduous, and often convoluted affair. Regulators usually must deal with a host of US agencies and will, inevitably, have to deal with the three branches of government in establishing new rules.

C. The US system of federalism

The Framers of the Constitution intended that foreign relations were the exclusive domain of the federal government. And yet state and local governments are increasingly involved in a multitude of activities that have international impact. Examples of this activity abound. There are numerous state-run trade and investment offices in foreign countries. State officials routinely travel abroad to secure foreign investment and to increase exports. Countries that violate human rights are frequently subject to state- or city-sponsored divestment policies.[56] Thus, '[t]he nation has been disaggregated, so that the channels of contact across national boundaries are now myriad where they used to be singular'.[57] Regulators must be able to deal with policy ramifications at the national level as well as the subnational level in the United States.

---

[52] Ibid., at 38.   [53] Kerwin, *Rulemaking* (above, n. 9), 234.   [54] Ibid., at 237.

[55] Ibid., at 239, quoting from the Administrative Procedure Act, Section 706, USC Section 551 et seq.

[56] Richard B. Bilder, 'The Role of States and Cities in Foreign Relations', *American Journal of International Law*, vol. 83 (1989), 821.

[57] Peter J. Spiro, 'Foreign Relations Federalism', *University of Colorado Law Review*, vol. 70 (1999), 1223.

There are several Constitutional obstacles to the states' ability to engage in dealings with other nations. First, the Constitution prevents states from making treaties or generally engaging in war with foreign nations. Nor may states engage in negotiations that implicate US foreign policy. Second, Article VI of the Constitution contains the Supremacy Clause, which clearly states that the laws and treaties of the United States supersede state law. Third, the Constitution prevents states from taxing imports or exports without the consent of Congress. Furthermore, states regulations or taxes are invalid if they impede interstate or foreign commerce.[58]

The courts have in the past generally barred any state activity that even hints at complicating US foreign relations. The US Supreme Court held in *Zschernig v. Miller*[59] that the Constitution prohibits 'an intrusion by the State into the field of foreign affairs which the Constitution entrusts to the President and Congress'.[60] Professor Spiro has characterized this validation of federal power by the courts as the 'exclusivity principle'.[61] However, he goes on to assert that '[i]nsofar as the states are recognized as autonomous players in global politics within their independent spheres of authority, and are subject to the discipline of a globalized international economy, there should no longer be a need to suppress their discrete preferences on international issues'.[62] Indeed, Professor Spiro's hope finds some support in *Clark v. Allen,* in which the Supreme Court held that the preclusive effect of federal authority in matters of foreign policy does not apply if a state's law has only 'some incidental or indirect effect on foreign countries'.[63]

The growing role of state and local governments in the globalized economy calls into question the legitimacy of federal exclusivity:

> In the old world order, the nation could not tolerate the unconstrained action of, say, California, because that state's misconduct might unleash retaliatory action by other countries against the nation as a whole. The stakes in that world were high, implicating core national security concerns and, at least in theory, national survival itself. Today, not only do other countries understand that when California acts on certain matters, it is acting alone, they also enjoy the capacity to retaliate directly and discretely.[64]

Thus, the notion of 'targeted retaliation' has highlighted the states' ability to apply divergent law without endangering national interests. The need to balance state interests against federal interests is therefore diminishing. An excellent example of the courts' gradual acceptance of this prin-

---

[58] Bilder, 'The Role of States' (above, n. 56), 824.
[59] 389 US 429, rehearing denied, 390 US 974 (1968).
[60] Bilder, 'The Role of States' (above, n. 56), 824, quoting from 389 US at 432.
[61] Spiro, 'Foreign Relations Federalism' (above, n. 57), 1225.   [62] Ibid.
[63] Bilder, 'The Role of States' (above, n. 56), 826, quoting from Clark, 331 US at 517.
[64] Spiro, 'Foreign Relations Federalism' (above, n. 57), 1225.

ciple was seen in *Barclays Bank International v. Franchise Tax Board*.[65] At the time of the case, California was applying unitary apportionment to multinational companies under the worldwide combined reporting system (WWCR). The system essentially factors in the parent company's total income in calculating the tax for that part of the company doing business in California. That is, multinational companies are treated as a unit, and therefore, a unitary tax is applied. This type of system places multinational companies at a distinct disadvantage. Moreover, the WWCR unitary accounting clashes with separate federal accounting methods that multinational companies must use. The added cost in maintaining two separate accountings can be extraordinary.[66] Nevertheless, the Supreme Court validated the state's WWCR system in the face of clear international fervour.[67]

State law still has the unfortunate quality of occasionally compromising US foreign relations. A recent example is seen in a Massachusetts law barring public agencies from conducting business in Burma, which allegedly perpetuates severe human rights abuses. The European Union and Japan both appealed to the World Trade Organization (WTO) in response to the law. They contended that the statute violated US obligations under the rules governing international trade.[68] If the WTO decides the Massachusetts law violates WTO provisions then they 'could authorize other countries to respond with proportional sanctions that could well affect US entities outside of Massachusetts'.[69]

International law as of yet does not recognize subnational governments. Thus, under the international rule of state responsibility, states in the United States bear no responsibility for breaking international law. Additionally, with the rise of subnational governments in the global marketplace, the need for legislative and procedural reforms both in the United States and internationally is strongly needed.[70] The implications for regulatory cooperation are obvious and must be entered into any decision-making process when dealing with the United States.

---

[65] Barclays, 225 Cal. App. 3d at 1370, 275 Cal. Rptr. at 641.

[66] See James M. Kane, 'International Tax Treaties and State Taxation: Can the Federal Government Speak with One Voice?', *Virginia Tax Review*, vol. 10 (1991), 765.

[67] *Barclays Bank OLC v. Franchise Tax Bd.*, 512 US 298, 1994.

[68] Brian Owens, 'The World Trade Organization and States' Rights: Will Foreign Threats Over Massachusetts' Burma Law Lead to a Domestic Backlash Against International Trade Agreements?', *Hastings International and Comparative Law Review*, vol. 21 (1998), 957, 959.

[69] Spiro, 'Foreign Relations Federalism' (above, n. 57), 1250.

[70] See Peter J. Spiro, 'The States and International Human Rights', *Fordham Law Review*, vol. 66 (1997), 567.

V. CONCLUSION

In addition to their strong economic ties, the United States and the European Union have become 'mutual frames of legal and policy reference'.[71] For example, the European Union crafted its own directive on insider trading after carefully considering US policy in that area. The United States has also looked towards the European Union in certain instances. The recent call for uniform products liability law in the United States will likely take into account the 1985 EU directive that established uniform products liability law for Member States. That is to say, legal reform on either continent is likely to proceed in light of the other's policy on the same matter.[72]

All of these ties point towards an ever increasing need for international regulatory cooperation between the United States and the European Union. Cooperation can be justified on several accounts. First, regulators may realize that they stand to benefit by sharing information and expertise. Moreover, with the globalization of capital markets, regulators can take advantage of their foreign counterparts' enforcement resources by harmonizing their regulatory standards.[73] Second, 'private industry ordinarily prefers to operate in a reasonably uniform regulatory environment of the sort that international regulatory cooperation may be capable of producing; it may find as a result that the overall cost of conducting multinational business is lowered'.[74]

These incentives for regulatory cooperation are offset to some extent by the barriers with which foreign and domestic regulators are faced. Perhaps the most significant obstacle is public opinion within the democracies of Europe and the United States. The nature of the agency rule-making in these democracies is designed to take public opinion into account. Public concerns over national sovereignty, for example, can often stymie or at least alter regulatory policy.

Working through the European Union would, at first, seem to facilitate the incentives for regulatory cooperation mentioned above. However, the European Union is still in its nascent stage. While monetary union has been realized, there are a host of other areas in which the European Union has yet to develop a unified policy, including a common security policy. There are also questions as to the enforceablilty of EU directives among Member States. Finally, the principle of subsidiarity creates a tension between the EU and Member States similar to federalism concerns in the United States.

---

[71] George A. Bermann, 'European Community Law From a US Perspective', *Tulane Journal of International and Comparative Law*, vol. 4 (1995), 1, 9.
[72] Ibid.   [73] Ibid., at 10.   [74] Ibid.

Dealing with the United States also poses its own problems for bureaucrats. The Constitutional system is designed to raise the decision-costs of government. Perhaps a larger obstacle is the disaggregation of policy-making power in the United States. In many areas, there is no one singular agency that is controlling. Indeed, agencies' regulatory turf tends to overlap. Moreover, each of the three branches of government all have oversight powers in the rule-making process, further complicating the maze which regulators must negotiate. The globalization of the world's economies has also given rise to the phenomenon where subnational governments are establishing their own foreign policies. This in turn makes the task of international regulatory cooperation a much more difficult proposition, since regulators must now account for the actions of states, and in many cases, cities.

In conclusion, with the advent of the global economy, there is a new emphasis on international regulatory cooperation. Bureaucrats looking to harmonize rules, however, should be acutely aware of the potential barriers that they face in forging ahead in this new paradigm. This contribution has attempted to delineate some of those barriers.

International regulatory cooperation and US federalism

George A. Bermann

I. INTRODUCTION

As many papers in this volume illustrate, it has become customary in the United States to measure the effect of international regulatory regimes on such values of the American regulatory system as transparency, participation, diversity, representativeness, accountability, and the rule of law.[1] Correlatively, it has become customary to question whether our commitment to these values permits full US participation in the emerging regimes. This paper specifically addresses a different interface, namely the interface between the processes of international regulatory cooperation, on the one hand, and US federalism, on the other. Attention to the impact of these processes on federalism—and, conversely, to the impact of federalism on these processes—is especially timely. American federalism has not only proved to be an enduring value over time, but is in the process of becoming, from a legal point of view if no other, more deeply entrenched than ever.[2]

As with transparency, participation, diversity, representativeness, accountability, and the rule of law, the federalism problem is a mirror-image one. First, one may ask, do the modalities of international regulatory cooperation tend to impair or prejudice the values associated with American federalism? Second, are the constraints that flow from US federalism themselves apt to prejudice the workability and effectiveness of regulatory cooperation, at least in its most typical forms?

A threshold question is, of course, whether the values of federalism should figure at all in the international regulatory equation in the first place. Assuming this question is answered in the affirmative, there is a fur-

---

[1] See also William W. Bratton *et al.*, *International Regulatory Competition and Coordination: Perspectives on Economic Regulation in Europe and the United States* (Oxford, 1996); *The Limits of Liberalization: Regulatory Cooperation and the New Transatlantic Agenda* (Washington, DC: American Institute for Contemporary German Studies, 1997); Paul B. Stephan, 'Accountability and International Lawmaking: Rules, Rents and Legitimacy', *Northwestern Journal of International Law and Business*, vol. 17 (1996–7), 681.

[2] See, notably, the decisions of the United States Supreme Court cited below in nn. 15 and 16. See generally, George A. Bermann, 'Regulatory Federalism: European Union and United States', 263 *Recueil des Cours* (The Hague: Hague Academy of International Law, Martinus Nijhoff Publishing, 1997), 100–16.

ther threshold question as to whether the proved or assumed consequences of international regulatory cooperation for federalism are
weighty enough to require that the architects of international regulatory
regimes take them into consideration. It is only if both questions are
answered in the affirmative that one needs to proceed further. I do answer
both questions in the affirmative.

II. INTERNATIONAL REGULATORY COOPERATION'S IMPACT ON FEDERALISM

A. Modes of regulatory cooperation

The question of the impact of transatlantic regulatory cooperation on US
federalism is highly elusive, if only because its impact is bound to depend
on the particular mode of regulatory cooperation that is being employed.
As the papers in this volume show, those modes are numerous and quite
different.

Take mutual recognition agreements, for example.[3] Suppose the United
States were to commit itself by agreement to an international regime of
conditional mutual recognition of professional licences. In passing upon
licence applications within the profession covered, US states would presumably become constitutionally bound to extend 'full faith and credit',
within the limits of the agreement, to the professional certifications given
by overseas regulators—possibly even to the advantage of US nationals
who may have benefited from licensing overseas. This would actually
impose a greater recognition burden on the states than they currently bear
under dormant commerce clause jurisprudence with regard to professional licensing applicants established in sister states. It may be that the
gains in international freedom of establishment are well worth the loss in
the states' traditional professional licensing freedom; still the states would
have ceded this measure of freedom and, until such time as sister-state
mutual recognition comes to be required as a matter of federal law, international regulatory cooperation will have eroded that freedom uniquely
to the benefit of persons professionally established in the territory of US
treaty partners as opposed to sister-state soil.[4]

Consider, by way of another example, transatlantic regulatory cooperation through the kind of informal, multi-centred regulatory networks
described by Anne-Marie Slaughter.[5] As we have learned, such networks,

---

[3] See the contribution of Kalypso Nicolaïdis to this volume.
[4] The situation in which, as a result of international agreements, non-nationals of the regulating State receive preferential treatment as compared to nationals is commonly described
as 'reverse discrimination'. See George A. Bermann et al., Cases and Materials on European
Community Law (St Paul, MN: West Publishing Company, 1993), 514 et seq.
[5] See the contribution of Anne-Marie Slaughter to this volume.

while anything but tidy, have the advantage of flexibility and improved access by interest groups, policy communities, and sub-national populations. How much they do so depends, of course, on the way in which networks are constructed and the resourcefulness with which interest groups approach the challenge of entering and exploiting them. The potential for access by the kinds of interests that federalism is supposed to champion—more or less local communities—would seem to be considerable, although their effective use of these networks will inevitably be met with challenge by competing entrants and exploiters in pursuit of opposing policies. Indeed, the capacity of informal, multi-centred regulatory networks to accommodate the interests of sub-national units and their populations is a positive reason for supporting their use.

If we permit federalism values to count for a great deal in the context of transatlantic regulatory cooperation, then we might logically select modes of cooperation in part—how big a part I do not know—by reference to the capacity of those modes to promote the values supported by federalism, for example, to give voice to the distinctive interests of sub-national communities.

B. Participation and 'ratification'

At the end of the day, it is difficult and indeed artificial to separate the safeguard of federalism values in the international regulatory cooperation context from the safeguard of participation values in that context. Indeed, of all the values associated with federalism—transparency, participation, diversity, representativeness, accountability, and the rule of law[6]—it is participation that the architects of regulatory cooperation have it most within their power to promote.

As shown by the discussion of modes of cooperation above, opportunities for participation by sub-national interests (whether defined by geography or by private or public interest) vary with the regulatory cooperation vehicle chosen. Even within a single vehicle, real participation opportunities will depend on the specific ways in which cooperation is structured and conducted. Once having determined that some combination of trade and regulatory policy suggests the advisability of international regulatory cooperation, federal officials may seek to ensure that the institutions that conduct the cooperation, or that comprise the relevant networks, as the case may be, include representation of sub-national governments and their constituencies. The test will be whether these governments and constituencies enjoy an opportunity to be heard in the

---

[6] See George A. Bermann, 'Taking Subsidiarity Seriously: Federalism in the European Community and the United States', *Columbia Law Review*, vol. 94 (1994), 331.

cooperation process and to influence outcomes—in other words, to become 'political safeguards of federalism'.[7]

If the results of international regulatory cooperation are to constitute 'hard law' within the participating states, they will at a minimum have to receive domestic political approval—whether express or tacit—by the relevant domestic authorities. For simplicity's sake, we may call this express or tacit approval 'ratification', provided that that term is not taken literally to denote necessarily in all cases the senatorial ratification procedure of the US Constitution. It is open to all states that participate in international regulatory cooperation to subject regulatory agreements that are reached to a ratification procedure designed to ensure that representatives of sub-national political units are heard.

It is beyond the scope of this contribution to determine whether Congress (and more particularly the Senate) performs an adequate federalism safeguard function in this regard. To the extent that it does not, various other mechanisms—'state and local government impact analyses',[8] advice and/or consent of a relevant federal advisory committee,[9] to name just two—come to mind. In a sense, 'ratification', as I use the term, represents a prolongation of the participation by state and local government interests that the prevailing modes of international regulatory cooperation themselves may entail.

C. Subject matter

It goes without saying that sub-national governments (and the interests they represent) have a stronger or weaker claim to be heard in international regulatory cooperation depending on the nature and scale of the problem being addressed and of the solutions being advanced. In this way, determining the voice to be reserved for those governments in the international regulatory arena is not very different from determining the voice to be reserved for them in Washington DC, in cases where the problem and solution are sought to be 'federalized' through the enactment of legislation at the national level. Perhaps the only difference is that, while in Washington sub-national groups stand to share power and voice with other US sub-national groups, in the international regulatory arena they stand to share power and voice with foreign governments and the various sub-national units within foreign countries for which foreign govern-

---

[7] See Herbert Wechsler, 'The Political Safeguards of Federalism: The Role of the States in the Composition and Selection of the National Government', *Columbia Law Review*, vol. 54 (1954), 543.

[8] See, for example, the State and Local Government Cost Estimate Act of 1981, 2 USC sect. 653.

[9] See, for example, the role of the United States Advisory Commission on Intergovernmental Relations under the Unfunded Mandates Reform Act of 1995, 2 USC sects. 658d et seq.

ments purport to speak. The risk that local power and voice will be 'diluted' is of course that much greater.[10]

Even allowing for this greater risk, some regulatory matters make compelling cases for moving the main deliberative situs from the national to the international arena. Aviation regulation—particularly international aviation regulation—is a good example.[11] Public education policy, by its nature, probably is not.[12] Many regulatory initiatives fall in between. Even matters as to which states have a very considerable claim to self-determination—state income-tax policy (e.g. freedom to 'double tax' foreign-earned income)[13] or state and local procurement policy (e.g. 'buy-local' legislation),[14] for example—may be ones as to which the United States has an overriding federal interest in curtailing the states' freedom of action. As a practical matter, the decision whether a regulatory issue is an appropriate one for international regulatory cooperation will be made in national institutions in which state and local governments and their constituencies will be more or less well represented. Depending on the decision that is made, those institutions may then turn to the business of selecting an appropriate vehicle for international regulatory cooperation (addressed in the previous section) and to questions of regulatory content (addressed in the section that follows).

Determining the proper scope of international regulatory cooperation is in part, but only in part, a legal (indeed, a constitutional) question. Notwithstanding the Supreme Court's recent reinvigoration of the Tenth[15]

---

[10] Joseph Weiler and others raise this issue when enquiring into the existence of a European *demos*. Joseph H. H. Weiler, 'The European Union Belongs to Its Citizens: Three Immodest Proposals', *European Law Review*, vol. 22 (1997), 150; Joseph H. H. Weiler and Joel P. Trachtman, 'European Constitutionalism and Its Discontents', *Northwestern Journal of International Law and Business*, vol. 17 (1996–7), 354.

[11] See George A. Bermann, 'Regulatory Cooperation with Counterpart Agencies Abroad: The FAA's Aircraft Certification Experience', *Law and Policy in International Business*, vol. 24 (1993), 669. See also George A. Bermann, 'Regulatory Cooperation between the European Commission and US Administrative Agencies', *Administrative Law Journal of American University*, vol. 9 (1996), 933.

[12] See Koen Lenaerts, 'Subsidiarity and Community Competence in the Field of Education', *Columbia Journal of European Law*, vol. 1 (1994–5), 1. See also Paul B. Stephan, 'The Futility of Unification and Harmonization in International Commercial Law', *Virginia Journal of International Law*, vol. 39 (1999), 743.

[13] See, for example, US Model Convention for the Avoidance of Double Taxation, Article 2(1), discussed in Klaus Vogel, *Double Taxation Conventions* (Deventer: Kluwer Publishing, 1991), 79–80.

[14] See, for example, US Schedule Attached to the 1994 GATT Agreement on Government Procurement, annexe 2, reprinted in House Doc. 103-316, 103d Cong., 2d Sess., vol. 1, pp. 1989–95.

[15] The Tenth Amendment reads: 'The powers not delegated to the United States by the Constitution, nor prohibited to it by the States, are reserved to the States respectively, or to the people.' For recent Supreme Court rulings on the Tenth Amendment, see *Printz v. United States*, 521 US 98 (1997); *New York v. United States*, 505 US 144 (1992). See also *Reno v. Condon*, 2000 WL 16317 (USSC., 12 Jan. 2000).

and Eleventh Amendments,[16] there is good reason to suppose that a determination by federal authorities that one or another form of international regulatory cooperation will promote interstate and foreign commerce will, if challenged, be judicially sustained.[17] It should be easy enough for Congress and the Executive to avoid the regulatory forms (viz. 'commandeering' of state apparatus[18] and unconsented suits against the states,[19] respectively) that have received the Supreme Court's specific constitutional disapproval under the Tenth and Eleventh Amendments. But a determination that a particular international regulatory arrangement can escape constitutional censure is not enough. Policy-makers should not feel free to enter into whatever international arrangements suit them from a trade and regulatory policy point of view, irrespective of the federalism implications that those arrangements may have.

D. Regulatory content

Regulatory cooperation's impact on federalism does not turn exclusively on the type of vehicle of cooperation that is chosen. Regulation is a matter of substance as well as form, and so too is regulatory cooperation. Negotiators of cooperative regulatory regimes may achieve certain of the objectives pursued by federalism by ensuring that, in their content, regulatory norms reflect the diversity, flexibility, and opportunity for public choice that US federalism is designed to favour.

The European Union, probably more than any other entity, has explored the possibilities for tailoring regulation to the interests of sub-units, without causing undue prejudice either to the Common Market or to the larger polity's basic social or economic objectives. To an extent, the notion of regulatory diversity is embedded in the very notion of a directive, which according to the EC Treaty 'shall be binding, as to the result to be achieved, upon each Member State to which it is addressed, but [which] shall leave to the national authorities the choice of forms and methods'.[20] It is also reflected in legislative language specifically precluding Community law from establishing a regulatory 'ceiling' even as it prescribes a regulatory

---

[16] The Eleventh Amendment reads: 'The Judicial power of the United States shall not be construed to extend to any suit in law or equity, commenced or prosecuted against one of the United States by Citizens of another State, or by Citizens or Subjects of any Foreign State.' For recent Supreme Court rulings on the Eleventh Amendment, see *Kimel v. Florida Bd. of Regents*, 120 S.Ct. 631 (2000); *Alden v. Maine*, 527 US 766 (1999); (1999); *College Savings Bank v. Florida Prepaid Post-Secondary Educ. Expense Bd.*, 527 US 666 (1999); *Florida Prepaid Post-Secondary Educ. Expense Bd. v. College Savings Bank and United States*, 527 US 627 (1999); *City of Boerne v. Flores*, 521 US 507 (1997); *Idaho v. Coeur d'Alene Tribe of Idaho*, 521 US 261 (1997); *Seminole Tribe of Florida v. Florida*, 517 US 44 (1996).

[17] See *United States v. Lopez*, 514 US 549 (1995). See also *Reno v. Condon*, 120 S.Ct 666 (2000). But see *United States v. Morrison*, 120 S.Ct. 1740 (2000).

[18] *New York v. United States* (above, n. 15); *Printz v. United States* (above, n. 15).

[19] See the Eleventh Amendment and decisions thereunder (above, n. 16).

[20] EC Treaty, art. 249 (ex art. 189).

'floor'.[21] It is still further reflected in the variety of options (including 'opt-in' or 'opt-out' provisions) that EC legislation may provide to Member States.[22] The entire range of techniques associated with the EC's now-not-quite-so-'new' approach to harmonization,[23] according to which the European institutions should confine themselves to addressing the bare 'essentials' of the regulatory solution at hand, are potentially relevant. 'Subsidiarity' is obviously an important part of this picture as well.[24]

E. Conclusion

The place that federalism deserves to occupy in deliberations over international regulatory cooperation should neither be underestimated nor overestimated. While federalism values may have been insufficiently visible up to now in public debates over international regulatory cooperation by comparison with such other 'domestic' concerns as transparency, participation, diversity, representativeness, accountability, and the rule of law, it does not follow that federalism should drive the debates. Efficiency considerations (naturally viewed in light of the specific substantive values and policies being pursued) still stand to tell us most about whether international regulatory cooperation is indicated and, if so, what international regulatory avenues are the most promising.[25] What is called for is merely attention to the federalism costs—alongside the transparency, participation, diversity, representativeness, accountability, and rule-of-law costs—that the choice of international regulatory cooperation and the choice among modes of international regulatory cooperation entail.

III. FEDERALISM'S IMPACT ON INTERNATIONAL REGULATORY COOPERATION

If modes of international regulatory cooperation have an impact on the condition of federalism within the United States, as they seem to do, it is

[21] See, for example, *Ministère public v. Grunert*, Case 88/79, [1980] ECR 1827 (concerning Council Directives 64/54 and 70/357 on the use of preservatives and antioxidants in foodstuffs).

[22] See, for example, Council Directive 85/374 on Member State liability for defective products, O.J. L. 210/29 (7 Aug. 1985).

[23] See Bermann *et al.*, *Cases and Materials* (above, n. 4), 442–7.

[24] EC Treaty, art. 5 (ex art. 3b): 'In areas which do not fall within its exclusive competence, the Community shall take action, in accordance with the principle of subsidiarity, only if and insofar as the objectives of the proposed action cannot be sufficiently achieved by the Member States and can therefore, by reason of the scale or effects of the proposed action, be better achieved by the Community.' See Bermann, 'Taking Subsidiarity Seriously' (above, n. 6).

[25] See generally David Vogel, *Barriers or Benefits? Regulation in Transatlantic Trade* (Washington, DC: Brookings Institute Press, 1997); John Braithwaite, 'Prospects for Win-Win International Rapprochement of Regulation', in Scott H. Jacobs (ed.), *Regulatory Co-operation for an Interdependent World* (Paris: OECD, 1994), 201.

also the case that federalism affects the capacity of the United States to engage in such cooperation and to comply with the undertakings made in its wake. In other words, federalism points not only to a set of virtues that may or may not be put at risk by international regulatory cooperation, but also to a set of data that say something about how effective the international regulatory cooperation practised by the United States can be.

A. Political safeguards of federalism in fashioning cooperative arrangements

A first question—easier to state than to answer—is whether sub-national governments (or their constituencies) actually influence the decision whether and to what extent federal authorities should pursue international regulatory cooperation, and the modes by which they should do so.[26] About this we know rather little. To some extent the answer will depend on whether federal agencies have existing legislative authority to engage in cooperation in the form that is envisaged or whether such cooperation will require separate and subsequent Congressional approval (if only in the form of senatorial ratification). It seems safe to say that, all else being equal, state and local government reservations about commitments made pursuant to international regulatory cooperation are apt to receive a more sympathetic ear within Congress than within the agencies. Depending on the version of the theory of the political safeguards of federalism at hand, either the President or Congress offers sub-national governments the greatest hope for official representation of their interests;[27] under no version of the theory do the federal agencies offer it.

On the other hand, effective representation of sub-national governments and their constituencies in the federal regulatory process does not depend exclusively upon their having specific advocates within federal officialdom. The state and local government 'lobby' is itself a powerful one, not only in Washington but also in the capitals of the nations or regions that constitute the US's international regulatory cooperation partners.[28] Depending on its perception of the regulatory stakes, as well as its prediction of cooperation's likely outcome, this lobby may act energetically for or against the cooperation effort. State income-taxation policy and State- or local-government procurement policy, invoked earlier by way of example,[29] exemplify matters on which the state and local government stake and the prediction of outcome have combined to produce serious obstacles to comprehensive international agreements against double

---

[26] See generally, Bermann, 'Taking Subsidiarity Seriously' (above, n. 6), 431–6.
[27] See generally, Wechsler, 'The Political Safeguards of Federalism' (above, n. 7).
[28] See generally, Bermann, 'Taking Subsidiarity Seriously' (above, n. 6).
[29] See above, nn. 13 and 14, and accompanying text.

income taxation[30] and favouritism in government procurement,[31] respectively. Where its stake in the regulatory outcome coincides with that of powerful private or public interests, or certain well-established policy communities, the state and local government lobby will enjoy heightened influence.

B. Enforcement constraints

Even if federalism issues do not get in the way of negotiating satisfactory international cooperative arrangements, they may surface significantly in the execution of those arrangements. Enforcement gaps are not unknown in any Member State or in any regulatory sphere within the European Union,[32] and enforcement of the EU's international engagements is no exception. While the supremacy of binding EU commitments over contrary Member State policy is beyond question,[33] it cannot be assumed that all such commitments have direct effect in the sense that private parties can be assumed to derive from them judicially enforceable rights that all Member State authorities—and ultimately Member State courts—must enforce.[34] And even if both supremacy and direct effect may be assumed, daily enforcement of claims based on such commitments is entrusted to the Member State administrations, with all the weaknesses that such a system entails.[35]

Although the legal landscape in the United States is considerably different, the federalism-related enforcement problems are not by their nature dissimilar. While federalism should present no difficulties in cases where the US's international regulatory arrangements intervene in spheres already within the ambit of federal legislation and federal administrative machinery, these are not the only cases. For example, US friendship, commerce, and navigation treaties impose many more practical constraints on the freedom of state and local authorities than they do on the freedom of action of federal authorities, and their effectiveness depends in the first instance on the readiness of state and local administrative and judicial authorities to act in compliance with them.[36] Recent controversies over state law-enforcement officers' non-compliance with

[30] See above, n. 13, and accompanying text.
[31] See above, n. 14, and accompanying text.
[32] See generally Raffaele Petriccione, 'A New Mechanism for the Implementation of Community Law', *European Law Review*, vol. 14 (1989), 456.
[33] See, e.g. *Costa v. ENEL*, Case 6/64, [1964] ECR 585.
[34] See, e.g. *Faccini Dori v. Recreb Srl*, Case C-91/92, [1994] ECR I-3325.
[35] See Bermann *et al.*, *Cases and Materials* (above, n. 4), 277–8.
[36] See Elizabeth Landry, 'States as International Law-Breakers: Discrimination against Immigrants and Welfare Reform', *Washington Law Review*, vol. 71 (1996), 1095.

the requirements of the Vienna Convention on Consular Relations[37] provide a still more vivid example. Since criminal law and criminal law
enforcement are mostly a state and not a federal responsibility, and since
federal law does not prescribe specific remedies for the violation of such
agreements, the enforcement gap has proved to be considerable.

In the case of certain major international undertakings of the United
States (notably the North American Free Trade Agreement and the
Uruguay Round Agreements of 1994), such gaps are visible on the face of
the federal implementing legislation[38] and, occasionally, on the face of the
terms of the underlying international agreement itself.[39] Much has been
written about 'federal–state' clauses found, in various guises, both in
treaty texts and in implementing legislation.[40] While the precise import of
such clauses may be far from clear,[41] they cast at least some doubt on the
accountability of federal authorities for treaty violations by sub-national
authorities. More telling are provisions of federal implementing legislation that specifically deny the 'self- executing' character of the underlying
treaty,[42] or that specifically protect state and local authorities from legal
claims based upon the treaty except through a direct 'infringement action'
brought, in his or her discretion, by the US Attorney General.[43]

To put the matter differently, international regulatory arrangements
have a vital enforcement and remedial aspect that is too often overlooked,
and yet upon which the effectiveness of those arrangements very much
turns. Depending on the allocation of authority within federal states, not
only the enforcement of claims deriving from these arrangements, but also
the availability of remedies for their non-enforcement may effectively
reside in the hands of sub-national authorities.

C. Conclusion

While the emergence of diverse forms of international regulatory cooperation may produce shifts in the balance of authority within participating
federal states, the converse is also true. Existing allocations of authority
within those states help to shape the regulatory understandings that are
capable of being achieved. Through the operation of a variety of political

---

[37] See, e.g. *Breard v. Greene*, 523 US 371 (1998).
[38] See, e.g. North America Free Trade Agreement Implementation Act, Pub. L. No. 103-
182, 107 Stat. 2057 (1993), codified at 19 USC. sects. 3301 et seq.; Uruguay Round Agreements
Act, Pub. L. No. 103-465, 108 Stat. 4809, codified at 19 USC sects. 3501 et seq.
[39] See above, nn. 13 and 14, and accompanying text.
[40] See generally *Restatement (Third) of Foreign Relations Law of the United States*, sect. 313,
reporter's note 5.
[41] See, e.g. US Senate Resolution of Advice and Consent to Ratification of the International
Covenant on Civil and Political Rights, Understanding no. 5, 138 Cong. Rec. (1992), S4784.
[42] See. e.g. North America Free Trade Agreement Implementation Act (above, n. 38) and
Uruguay Round Agreements Act (above, n. 38).
[43] Ibid.

safeguards at the national level, and in possible combination with assorted other interest groups, sub-national constituencies may be in a position to curtail the scope of international regulatory arrangements into which the United States enters or otherwise alter the tenor of the commitments made. This pattern may be less conspicuous in the United States than the European Union (if only on account of the unapologetic assertion of Member State interests within the Council of the European Union[44] and within the committees that the Council establishes to review the Commission's exercise of delegated powers).[45] It is nevertheless very much in play.

Federalism fault lines do not only surface at the time that cooperative arrangements in the international regulatory arena are negotiated and achieved. Such arrangements also invariably contemplate enforcement of some sort. While the United States does not systematically entrust the enforcement of international undertakings to sub-national authorities, if we look at the full range of arrangements, we will find that it does so often enough. Moreover, when administrative responsibility resides at that level, responsibility for remedying non-compliance more often than not resides there as well.

IV. CONCLUSION

International regulatory cooperation is only one among many factors shaping the future of federalism in federal states. But federalism nevertheless belongs in the constellation of values—alongside transparency, participation, representativeness, diversity, accountability, and the rule of law—that the choice to participate in such cooperation, and the choice of modes of cooperation for doing so, is likely to affect. While federalism, even in doggedly federal states, may not be an end in itself, many of the values with which it is associated are indeed independently prized.

Conversely, federalism is only one among many factors that shape both the general prospects for international regulatory cooperation and the specific regulatory outcomes to which such cooperation leads. As the contributions in this volume illustrate, the kind of cooperation, if any, that commends itself to regulators in any given regulatory context depends on a host of variables. So too does the efficacy of the regulatory cooperation that is undertaken, whether in terms of advancing specific substantive objectives, creating a reasonably level international regulatory playing field, inducing cooperative regulatory behaviour, or accommodating

---

[44] See Koen Lenaerts, 'Some Reflections on the Separation of Powers in the European Community', *Common Market Law Review*, vol. 28 (1991), 11.

[45] On so-called 'comitology', see Christian Joerges and Ellen Vos (eds), *EU Committees: Social Regulation, Law and Politics* (Oxford: Hart Publishing, 1999).

relevant differences among participating States and their populations. Among those variables, the allocation of regulatory authority within divided-power systems is not to be overlooked. To the extent that federalism manifests itself in a pattern of leaving both daily administration of regulatory policy and remedial responsibility in the hands of sub-national authorities, it is a variable of considerable importance.

Implementing regulatory cooperation through executive agreements and the problem of democratic accountability

Joel R. Paul

Constitutional principles and domestic politics both structure the character of regulatory cooperation and, conversely, often reflect the significance of the cooperative relationship. How internal politics and law affect transatlantic relations is readily apparent. Less obviously, regulatory cooperation also shapes internal political and legal structures. The subject of this contribution, executive agreements, exemplifies both the impact of domestic politics and constitutional principles on regulatory cooperation and the effect of regulatory cooperation on US political and constitutional structures. Since the end of World War II, the United States has relied almost exclusively upon executive agreements as the primary vehicle for executing international regulatory cooperation. The ease of ratifying such agreements in US law has facilitated ever-increasing regulatory cooperation, but at the same time, the uncertain constitutional status of executive agreements has contributed to the 'soft' quality of regulatory commitments under US law. Conversely, the perceived need for regulatory cooperation has justified in large part the expanded use of executive agreements and, as a consequence, regulatory cooperation has helped to transform the executive's power over foreign relations at the expense of congressional authority.

An executive agreement is an international compact signed by the executive without the advice and consent of two-thirds of the Senate as required for treaties under Article I of the United States Constitution. Congress may, by a simple majority vote of both houses, approve executive agreements, which are called, 'congressional-executive agreements'. Examples of these congressional-executive agreements include the North American Free Trade Agreement and the Charter of the World Trade Organization. Alternatively, the executive may unilaterally ratify executive agreements, which are called, 'sole executive agreements'. Examples of sole executive agreements include the 1947 General Agreement on Tariffs and Trade (GATT), the 1991 Agreement Between the United States and the EC Commission Regarding the Application of Competition Laws, and the 1998 Agreement between the United States and the European Communities on the Application of Positive Comity Principles in the

Enforcement of Competition Laws. The President alone decides whether to submit an agreement to the Senate as an Article I treaty or whether to ratify it as an executive agreement with, or without, congressional approval.

Today, almost all agreements concerned with trade, commerce, or economic regulation are executive agreements. In fact, foreign partners often prefer an executive agreement over a treaty, because an executive agreement may be either ratified by the executive without congressional interference or rushed through Congress on the 'fast track'. The fast track refers to a special legislative procedure that Congress authorizes for some trade agreements. Fast-track agreements require that Congress must vote within strict time limits on the agreement and without any opportunity to amend it.[1] The growing reliance upon executive agreements represents a collective judgment among the federal branches that primary responsibility for managing international affairs rests with the executive. The concomitant growth of executive power has facilitated the projection of US power globally since 1945. The imperatives of US global hegemony in the military and economic spheres has greatly facilitated executive hegemony within the internal US constitutional structure.

I. THE RISE OF THE EXECUTIVE AGREEMENT: AN HISTORICAL OVERVIEW

The Constitution did not mention executive agreements, but some commentators have argued that executive agreements were implied.[2] Article I (10) of the United States Constitution prohibited States from entering into 'an Agreement or Compact with another State, or with a foreign Power', without congressional authorization. The reference to 'an Agreement or Compact' indicated that the Constitution's Framers foresaw alternative forms of international agreements to Article II treaties. There is no evidence, however, that the Framers actually anticipated that the executive could make such agreements. Indeed, Alexander Hamilton argued that the President would be required to submit all international agreements to the Senate.[3] Hamilton pointed out that 'The King of Great Britain is the sole and absolute representative of the nation in all foreign transactions. He can of his own accord make treaties of peace, commerce, alliance, and of every other description.' The king could act without parliament's

---

[1] See Harold Hongju Koh, 'The Fast Track and United States Foreign Policy', *Brooklyn Journal of International Law*, vol. 18 (1992), 143.

[2] Wallace McClure, *International Executive Agreements*, 255–9 (New York: AMS Press, 1967); Myers S. McDougal and Asher Lans, 'Treaties and Congressional-Executive or Presidential Agreements: Interchangeable Instruments of National Policy: I', *Yale Law Journal*, vol. 54, (1945), 181.

[3] Camillius Letters, in J. C. Hamilton (ed.), *The Works of Alexander Hamilton*, vol. VII (New York: J. F. Trow, 1851), 518.

approval of an agreement, but '[i]n this respect, therefore, there is no comparison between the intended power of the President and the actual power of the British sovereign. The one can perform alone what the other can only do with the concurrence of a branch of the legislature.'[4]

More likely, the reference to 'an Agreement or Compact' in Article I(10) derived from Emerich de Vattel's influential treatise, *The Law of Nations*, which was first published for the American market in 1775. Many of the Framers were familiar with Vattel's writing and relied on it in drafting and discussing the Constitution.[5] Vattel defined a treaty as a 'pact made with a view to the public welfare by the superior power, either for perpetuity, or for a considerable time'. By contrast, Vattel defined an 'Agreement or Compact', as 'accomplished by one single act, and not by [repeated acts]. These pacts are perfected in their execution once for all.'[6] In the context of Article 1(10) this definition made sense. The Framers anticipated that some states would need to readjust disputed borders with sister states and foreign powers, and therefore provided that the states could make such one-time contemporaneous exchanges of property with the consent of Congress.[7] Thus, Article 1(10) reinforced the idea that there were only two forms of international agreements: Article II treaties undertaken to bind the nation in perpetuity under international law requiring the approval of two-thirds of the Senate, and other agreements and compacts which

[4] Alexander Hamilton, 'The Federalist No. 69', in Benjamin F. Wright (ed.), *The Federalist Papers* (Cambridge, MA: Belknap Press of Harvard University Press, 1961), 448.

[5] Emerich de Vattel, *The Law of Nations* (London: J. Newberry *et al.*, 1760). Vattel's work was cited during the Constitutional Convention by three of the most prominent Framers: James Wilson, one of the principal drafters of the Constitution, John Rutledge, who chaired the committee of detail that finalized the draft, and Oliver Ellsworth, a prominent jurist and later Chief Justice of the US Supreme Court. Others, like Luther Martin, delegate from Maryland, also cited Vattel during the Constitutional Convention. Max Farrand (ed.), *The Record of the Federal Convention of 1787*, vol. 1 (New Haven: Yale University Press, 1966), 437–42. Throughout the Constitution and the ratification debates that followed, Vattel's influence was evident. See Arthur Schlesinger, *The Imperial Presidency* (Boston: Houghton Mifflin, 1973), 85–6; Bernard Bailyn (ed.), *The Debate on the Constitution: Federalist and Antifederalist Speeches, Articles, and Letters During the Struggle Over Ratification* (New York: Library of America, distributed to United States and Canada by Viking Press, 1993), 348; Abraham C. Weinfeld, 'What Did the Framers of the Federal Constitution Mean By "Agreements or Compacts"?' *University of Chicago Law Review*, vol. 3 (1936) 458–9; Peter Haggenmacher, 'Some Hints on the European Origins of Legislative Participation in the Treaty-Making Function', *Chicago-Kent Law Review*, vol. 67 (1991) 313, 325–6.

[6] Vattel, *The Law of Nations* (above, n. 5), sects. 152–3.One of the early commentators on the Constitution and a contemporary of the Framers, St. George Tucker, cited these sections of Vattel in his discussion of the meaning of the treaty clause. St. George Tucker, *Blackstone's Commentaries With Notes of Reference to the Constitution and Laws of the Federal Government of the United States and the Commonwealth of Virginia*, vol. 1 (Philadelphia: William Young Birch and Abraham Small, 1803), app. 309.

[7] During the Confederation period there were numerous agreements between States pertaining to boundary lines and navigation, subject to congressional consent as permitted by the compact clause. See Felix Frankfurter and James M. Landis, 'The Compact Clause of the Constitution—A Study in Interstate Adjustments', *Yale Law Journal*, vol. 34 (1927), 685.

merely effected contemporaneous exchanges of rights or property requiring congressional authorization.

For the first quarter-century of the republic, US presidents relied exclusively on Article II treaties to embody international agreements. When President Thomas Jefferson was negotiating the acquisition of the Louisiana Purchase from France, he considered the possibility of an executive agreement, but determined he had no such authority.[8] In 1817, without seeking the Senate's advice and consent, President James Monroe signed the Rush–Bagot Agreement with Britain to limit military forces along the Great Lakes. After signing, President Monroe questioned whether he had the constitutional authority to make this executive agreement. One could argue that as commander-in-chief of the armed forces, President Monroe had clear authority to make agreements related to military forces. Nevertheless, Monroe subsequently submitted the agreement for the Senate's advice and consent.[9]

Throughout the nineteenth century, presidents following Monroe used executive agreements rarely and only to effect a contemporaneous exchange. Presidents understood that an executive agreement, unlike an Article II treaty, could not bind a president's successors. By 1900, presidents had concluded only 124 executive agreements over 111 years, and none of these agreements bound the United States prospectively.[10] President Theodore Roosevelt relied on executive agreements with greater frequency as he aggressively projected US hemispheric hegemony. Yet, even President Roosevelt respected the traditional limits on the usage of executive agreements. Roosevelt, for example, concluded an executive agreement to assume responsibility for Santo Domingo's customs house, but he later decided that since the agreement might operate prospectively, he needed the Senate's advice and consent.[11]

By the 1930s presidents increasingly relied on executive agreements. President Franklin Roosevelt signed more than 600 executive agreements in his four terms in office. Still, Roosevelt respected the traditional distinction between treaties and executive agreements. When Roosevelt considered the exchange of US destroyers for bases owned by Great Britain, he was advised that it could be accomplished by executive agreement. Then Attorney-General Robert Jackson counselled Roosevelt that when 'negotiations involve commitments as to the future', they 'are customarily submitted for the ratification by a two-thirds vote of the Senate before the

---

[8] Dumas Malone, *Jefferson and His Time*, vol. 4 (Boston: Little, Brown, 1948), 311–32.

[9] Samuel B. Crandall, *Treaties: Their Making and Enforcement* (New York: Columbia University Press, 1916), 102–3.

[10] Lawrence Margolis, *Executive Agreements and Presidential Power in Foreign Policy* (New York: Praeger, 1986), 101–6.

[11] Theodore Roosevelt, *An Autobiography* (New York: McMillan Co., 1920), 551–2.

future legislative power of the country is committed'.[12] In this case, Jackson concluded that the agreement had no prospective binding legal effect, and therefore, it could be accomplished by sole executive agreement.

President Harry Truman used executive agreements for the first time in lieu of treaties to bind the nation prospectively when he signed the Bretton Woods Agreements in 1945. These agreements established the International Monetary Fund and the World Bank. In addition, President Truman approved a protocol in 1947, which bound the United States to the GATT. Congress approved the Bretton Woods Agreements as congressional-executive agreements, but neither the Senate nor Congress ever approved the 1947 GATT. Since 1947 presidents have relied almost exclusively on executive agreements in place of Article II treaties.

It is clear that the presidential usage of executive agreements has changed dramatically since the end of World War II. This transformation occurred as a consequence of the expansion of presidential control of foreign relations generally. The executive's role expanded as a response to the perceived security threat posed by the Soviet Union during the Cold War. Both the increased global responsibilities of the United States and the greater danger posed by nuclear weapons appeared to foreclose any opportunity for democratic deliberation in foreign policy-making. Commentators and policy-makers argued that for the United States to confront the Soviet threat credibly, authority for conducting foreign policy must be concentrated in the President, who alone could respond expeditiously in crisis. Senator William Fulbright, the powerful chair of the Senate Foreign Relations Committee characterized the Cold War as 'an entire era of crisis in which urgent decisions have been required, decisions of a kind the Congress is ill-equipped to make with . . . the requisite speed . . .'. Senator Fulbright reasoned that 'The President has the means at his disposal for prompt action: the Congress does not. When the security of the country is endangered . . . there is a powerful premium on prompt action, and that means executive action.'[13] The Cold War became a permanent crisis that courts and legal scholars used to justify giving the President vast new executive powers that were previously thought extra-constitutional, including the power to use executive agreements as a

---

[12] Acquisition of Naval and Air Bases in Exchange for Over-Age Destroyers, *Opinion of the Attorneys General*, vol. 39 (1940), 484, 485–6.

[13] United States Commitments to Foreign Powers, Hearings Before the Subcomm. on Separation of Powers of the Senate Comm. of the Judiciary, 90th Cong. (1967) (statement of J. William Fulbright, US Senator), reprinted in Congressional Oversight of Executive Agreements: Hearings on S. 3475 Before the Subcomm. on Separation of Powers of the Senate Comm. on the Judiciary, 92d Cong. 370 (1972).

substitute for treaties.[14] I will refer to this form of justificatory rhetoric as a 'discourse of executive expediency'.[15]

One example of expediency discourse which was particularly influential was an article by Yale Law School Professors Myres McDougal and Asher Lans arguing that executive agreements should be interchangeable with Article II treaties.[16] They wrote that in the aftermath of World War II the people of the United States would insist on a more effective foreign policy. Developments in military technology, increased economic interdependence and the greater post-war responsibilities of the United States all justified empowering the President to use executive agreements in lieu of Article II treaties. A powerful executive unconstrained by Congress could best defend democracy. The values of efficiency, flexibility, and secrecy must supersede deliberative democracy:

[E]xecutive officers, who are charged with the tasks of conducting negotiations with other governments, must be able to treat the national body politic as a whole, and must be able to canvas it promptly and efficiently as a whole for the majority will, without being subject to delays, obstructions and disintegrating efforts by minorities . . . A leisurely diplomacy of inaction and of deference to dissident minority interests supposedly characteristic of past eras when economic and political change proceeded at a slower pace and the twin ocean barriers gave us an effortless security is no longer capable, if it ever was, of securing the interests of the United States.[17]

Expediency discourse justified President Truman's decision to sign the Bretton Woods Agreements and the protocol on the GATT as executive agreements. The Truman Administration negotiated the Protocol on Provisional Application as an interim measure to bring GATT into effect while continuing to draft the Charter of the International Trade Organization (ITO), for Congress' approval. By the time the ITO Charter was concluded, broad opposition to it had coalesced: labour and industry feared that foreign competitors enjoyed unfair advantages from government subsidies and low labour standards. Members of Congress questioned

---

[14] Professors Bruce Ackerman and David Golove suggest another theory about how the executive agreement became interchangeable with Article II treaties after World War II. Bruce Ackerman and David Golove, 'Is NAFTA Constitutional?', *Harvard Law Review*, vol. 108 (1995), 799. According to Ackerman and Golove, the 1944 presidential election represented a popular mandate for amending Article II to permit the President to use an executive agreement approved by Congress in lieu of an Article II treaty approved by two-thirds of the Senate. They view the 1944 election as a 'constitutional moment', which amended the Constitution. Professor Ackerman's theory of constitutional moments has been widely discussed. Professor Laurence Tribe, for example, has criticized Professor Ackerman's interpretive methodology. Laurence H. Tribe, 'Taking Text and Structure Seriously: Reflections on Free-Form Method in Constitutional Interpretation', *Harvard Law Review*, vol. 108 (1995), 1221. See Joel R. Paul, 'The Geopolitical Constitution: Executive Expediency and Executive Agreements', *California Law Review*, vol. 86 (1998), 742–6.

[15] See Paul, 'The Geopolitical Constitution' (above, n. 14).

[16] McDougal and Lans, 'Treaties and Agreements' (above, n. 2).   [17] Ibid., at 185–6.

whether an international body regulating trade threatened US economic sovereignty. Some critics charged that trade preferences extended by the British and the French to former colonies, discriminated against US products and perpetuated colonial dependence. Southern advocates of states' rights resisted any international regimes that might interfere with state autonomy.[18] The domestic opposition to the ITO proved overwhelming. In 1950 President Truman acknowledged defeat and withdrew the ITO Charter from consideration by the Senate, leaving only the Protocol of Provisional Application in place. In each trade bill from 1951 to 1979 authorizing and implementing successive rounds of the GATT agreements, Congress reiterated that it had never formally approved the GATT and that any subsequent legislative acts should not be construed as doing so.[19] Despite clear congressional reservations, every president from Truman to Clinton continued to rely upon the Protocol as the constituent act of the international trading system. Thus, a sole executive agreement bound the United States to the international structure of world trade for almost 50 years without congressional approval.[20]

Article I of the Constitution empowered Congress to tax imports and 'regulate Commerce with foreign Nations'.[21] Even prior to the Constitution, and throughout US history, tariffs and trade policy have been a source of tension and rivalry among the states. The Framers wisely empowered Congress alone as the representative of the states and the people to legislate trade policy. GATT's defenders employed expediency discourse to justify the use of presidential authority over congressional opposition by pointing to the twin national interests in stabilizing Western democracies and resisting the expansion of Soviet hegemony during the Cold War. Cold War rhetoric closely linked security interests and the growth of free markets.[22] President Truman, for example, in calling for

[18] See John H. Jackson, *The World Trading System* (Cambridge, MA: MIT Press, 1991), 32–7; Richard N. Gardner, *Sterling–Dollar Diplomacy* (New York: McGraw-Hill, 1969), 348–61; John H. Jackson, 'The General Agreement on Tariffs and Trade in United States Domestic Law', *Michigan Law Review*, vol. 66 (1967), 249, 251–3; William Diebold, Jr., 'The End of the ITO', in *Essays in International Finance*, No. 16, at 21–4, Princeton University, International Finance Section, Department of Economics and Social Institutions (1952).

[19] Five times from 1951 to 1988, Congress provided that the legislation 'shall not be construed to determine or indicate approval or disapproval by the Congress of the Executive Agreement known as the General Agreement on Tariffs and Trade'. See, e.g. Trade Agreements Extension Act of 1951, Pub. L. No. 82-50, sect. 10, 65 Stat. 72, 75 (1951) (codified at 19 USC, sect. 1351). The 1974 Trade Act provided that it did not imply approval or disapproval 'of all articles of GATT'. Moreover, Congress did not even appropriate funds to pay US fees to the GATT Secretariat until 1974. See Ronald A. Brand, 'The Status of the General Agreement on Tariffs and Trade in US Domestic Law', *Stanford Journal of International Law*, vol. 26 (1990), 486.

[20] See Stephen D. Cohen, Joel R. Paul, and Robert A. Blecker, *Fundamentals of US Foreign Trade Policy* (1996), 162–72, 260–73.

[21] US Const. arts. I(8)(1) and (3).

[22] See John L. Gaddis, *The United States and the Origins of the Cold War, 1941–1947* (New York: Columbia University Press, 1972), 342.

foreign aid to Europe, argued that 'we ourselves cannot enjoy prosperity in a world of economic stagnation. . . . [E]conomic distress anywhere in the world is a fertile breeding ground for violent political upheaval.'[23]

The urgency of economic aid and reducing trade barriers would not, in itself, appear to justify the executive acting without congressional approval. Unlike security policy, economic policy did not require the same secrecy and speed to react to Soviet provocations. Why then should the executive act alone in making executive agreements like GATT? Implicitly, the executive has viewed Congress as too insular, parochial, and partisan to entrust it with authority to negotiate trade relations. Executive agreements were expedient because they allowed the President to sidestep the Senate. The rhetoric of expediency had established that presidential power could grow in response to perceived geopolitical necessity. Economic necessity readily substituted for threats to the national security. The opportunities and need for regulatory cooperation legitimated a fundamental change in the constitutional roles of the executive and Congress concerning trade policy.

As regulatory cooperation has justified expanding the President's powers over trade and commerce, executive agreements have displaced Article II treaties as the primary vehicle for facilitating trade relationships. Unilateral executive power now substitutes for the Senate's advice and consent. This displacement, however, raises serious questions about democratic accountability, an issue I take up immediately below.

II. EXECUTIVE AGREEMENTS AND DEMOCRATIC ACCOUNTABILITY

If the President is contemplating an agreement with the European Union to reduce barriers to trade in services he has three choices: he may submit the agreement to the Senate as an Article II treaty for approval by two-thirds of its members; he may send it to Congress for approval by a simple majority of both houses; or he may approve it as a sole executive agreement.

If the President ratifies the agreement as a sole executive agreement, the agreement is unlikely to be subjected to democratic scrutiny. I am not arguing that the President is less representative than the Senate; rather, the executive deliberative process is inherently less transparent than are the open deliberations of the Senate. A constituent surely has a larger voice in how his or her senator will vote than in how the President negotiates an executive agreement. The President has many more constituencies than a senator; he is responsible to Congress, the public, foreign governments,

---

[23] Harry S Truman, *Public Papers of the President of the United States*, vol. 2 (Washington, DC: US Government Printing Office, 1962), 186–9.

and future generations. The voters get only one chance to dismiss a president seeking re-election, and it seems improbable that the voters would fail to re-elect a president who approved an unpopular agreement with a foreign government. Voters hold their senators accountable every six years, and interest groups closely monitor how senators vote on foreign trade and commerce issues that affect their constituents.

Some defenders of the executive agreement power have acknowledged that sole executive agreements might be undemocratic, but they insist that approval of an executive agreement by a majority of both houses of Congress is at least as democratic as approval of an Article II treaty by a two-thirds super-majority of the Senate.[24] On its face, it might seem that allowing all 535 members of Congress to vote would be more representative than allowing thirty-four senators to block an otherwise popular treaty. This argument is simplistic for two reasons: it fails to take into account why one ratifying procedure is used over another, and it overlooks how different legislative processes affect outcomes.

First, the President decides how an agreement will be adopted depending upon the politics of the situation. Obviously, senators and members of Congress may pressure the President to submit the agreement to one or both houses. However, since 1945 neither presidential practice nor case law has produced a principled distinction between congressional-executive agreements and sole executive agreements. If the President believes he is likely to encounter strong opposition in the Senate, he may decide to present the agreement to both houses; if he does not have a majority of both houses, he may decide to ratify it as a sole executive agreement. In other words, the decision not to submit an agreement for the Senate's advice and consent is a strong indication that the President does not have the requisite support.

Second, even when the President submits an agreement to both houses, the process of adoption is not necessarily governed by the same procedural rules as ordinary legislation. If Congress were considering a new tax, for example, it would follow the ordinary procedure: legislation is introduced on the house floor; one or more house committees and subcommittees hold hearings on the legislation over a period of many months; members offer amendments and publicly debate before they vote on the record; the Senate follows a parallel process, but there senators may delay or filibuster legislation for many months; after more amendments and another public debate, senators vote on the record; then joint committees of both houses negotiate compromise language, and each chamber votes again on the final bill before it is presented to the President for his signature or veto. Almost the entire legislative process, which may take years,

---

[24] e.g. Ackerman and Golove, 'Is NAFTA Constitutional?' (above, n. 14); Louis Henkin, *Foreign Affairs and the US Constitution* (Oxford: Clarendon Press, 1996), 215–26.

is publicly recorded, televised, and scrutinized by the media, interest groups, and lobbyists, who may mobilize constituents to contact their representatives. The public record of the legislative history is then subject to further scrutiny by courts seeking to interpret the legislation in light of congressional intent.

Now imagine the President negotiates a new tariff arrangement by executive agreement and presents it to Congress for its adoption as a congressional-executive agreement. The tariff may have the same economic impact as the tax bill, but the procedure is radically different. Typically, congressional-executive agreements are governed by extraordinary 'fast-track' procedures. The agreement would be negotiated secretly with some participation by a few congressional leaders, but without much public input. The finished agreement would be presented to Congress under a strict deadline that limits the time for hearings and congressional debate. Congress is not permitted to amend the agreement; the President tells Congress 'to take it or leave it'. In sum, the adoption of a congressional-executive agreement does not bear the indicia of the ordinary democratic legislative process.

Process has normative consequences, of course. An executive agreement may facilitate cooperation with foreign governments, particularly in lowering barriers to trade and investment. In that sense executive agreements are expedient, but expediency is not a measure of democracy. Surely, if the Framers of the Constitution had wanted to expedite foreign relations they would have empowered the President to act on his own. The Constitution diffused and checked power to protect us from our own worst impulses and to allow more time for mature, calm deliberation. Regulating trade and commerce has stirred intense regional antagonism since the early days of the republic. The Constitution compelled the Federal Government to take into account these concerns in setting trade policy. The Framers knew that it would be more difficult to obtain the votes of two-thirds of the Senate than it would be for the President to act alone or with a simple majority of one or both houses, but the Framers wanted to make it more difficult for the Federal Government to override state law and prior inconsistent federal law. The Framers also feared entangling alliances that would threaten domestic peace and security. By giving the advice and consent power to the Senate, where each state is represented equally, the Framers ensured that states would be represented when foreign influence threatened state autonomy. By requiring a supermajority, the Framers also made it more difficult to commit the nation to foreign conflicts.

Moreover, the advice and consent requirement may strengthen the President's negotiating position. The President must insist on negotiating terms that command broad public support and can withstand the close scrutiny of the Senate. Foreign governments may be more inclined to compromise in order to give the President terms that two-thirds of the Senate will support. In that sense, the requirement of Senate approval may strengthen the President's negotiating position relative to a foreign partner. The Senate's advice and consent does not ensure a better agreement, but it does mean that our international commitments have greater credibility. The United States is more likely to uphold an agreement ratified with the imprimatur of two-thirds of the Senate than an agreement ratified under ad hoc rules that do not appear in the Constitution. The public is more likely to support for the long term international commitments which have been publicly scrutinized and undertaken with broad public support.

III. A EUROPEAN PARALLEL: 'ADMINISTRATIVE AGREEMENTS'

A parallel debate over the process of implementing regulatory cooperation has occurred in the European Community. The Commission has taken the position that it has authority to approve at least some forms of 'administrative agreements' without the participation of the Council. The Commission has argued that such administrative agreements would facilitate regulatory cooperation which is an important goal of the Community. In a sense, the Commission is appealing to the executive expediency rationale. This issue emerged in the European Court of Justice's decision regarding the EC–USA Competition Laws Co-operation Agreement.[25] That decision vividly demonstrated how regulatory cooperation has shaped, and been shaped by, internal constitutional and political structures.

The Commission and the United States negotiated the Competition Laws Co-operation Agreement to limit conflicts over extraterritorial application of competition laws and to facilitate cooperation in enforcement. The Commission approved the Agreement despite objection from some Member States that only the Council had the legal authority to approve an international agreement under the then Article 228 of the EC Treaty. The Commission characterized the cooperation as an 'administrative agreement' between two regulatory enforcement bodies. In the Commission's view, an administrative agreement did not require the same Article 228 procedure as a treaty.

The Commission acknowledged that the Agreement had 'legal effects',[26] but it argued it could act without the consent of the Council. The Commission had approved similar administrative agreements with other states concerning the privileges and immunities of diplomatic missions,

---

[25] C-327/91, *France v. Commission*, 1994 ECR I-3641.
[26] Ibid., Advocate Gen. Op. I-3647, para. 7.

economic relations with members of the GATT, standards for the protection of plant life, and scientific and technical co-operation. These agreements were distinguishable from Article 228 treaties, in the Commission's view, for three reasons: the agreements only obligated the Commission to act; the agreements did not impose any financial liability on the Community; and the Community could not be held liable for non-performance.[27] These indicia all refer to the executive's functional authority to implement and enforce the law. In effect, the Commission defined the administrative agreement as the functional equivalent of the executive agreement. The Commission argued *inter alia* that these precedents had established over time its power to adopt administrative agreements in much the same way that the US President claimed his authority to make executive agreements was based in part on well-established practice.[28]

The structure of the Commission's claim in this case mirrored the expediency argument made by the US President with regard to executive agreements. Like the discourse of executive expediency, the Commission argued in terms of its relationship to another sovereign state. The Commission relied on the fact that both the US executive, and at least some of the Member States' executives, had authority to approve certain international agreements without the consent of the legislative branch.[29] The Commission claimed this power as an attribute of its authority to represent the Community in negotiations with other states. The Commission in part based its claim on the sovereign equality of states. For example, the Agreement identified the Commission, rather than the Community, as the party to the Agreement; the Commission pointed out that the other contracting party was the government, rather than the people, of the United States and that the Commission was therefore the most appropriate analogous party to represent the Community.[30] By drawing a parallel between its role and the reciprocal roles of other executives, the Commission tried to mask the underlying internal power struggle between the Commission and the Council. Similarly, in the United States, the executive justified its foreign-relations powers in terms of its relations to other states, masking the power conflict between the executive and the Congress.

The Advocate General pointed out that administrative agreements were not an existing class of international agreements. The Advocate General reasoned that in international law, all agreements are either binding as treaties or non-binding 'gentleman's agreements' or 'understandings'.[31] He opined that since the obligations were binding, they did in fact impose liability on

---

[27] C-327/91, *France v. Commission*, 1994 ECR I-3657–59, paras. 27–30.

[28] In the Advocate General's opinion, he rejected the Commission's argument that the Commission's prior administrative agreements had established a practice, but he declined to decide whether these prior administrative agreements were void. Ibid., I-3657–60, paras. 28–32.

[29] Ibid., I-3659–60, para. 32.   [30] Ibid., I-3652–53, para. 19.

[31] Ibid., I-3654, para. 22.

the Community, even if the United States had no specific remedy against the Community.[32] Clearly, the parties intended the Agreement to be binding since they provided a clause for revocation, which would be superfluous if the Agreement were not binding.[33] Having determined that the Agreement was indistinguishable from other binding international agreements, the Advocate General had no difficulty concluding that under Article 228 the Council's authority to approve external agreements precluded any claim by the Commission of an inherent authority to make binding international agreements without the Council's consent.[34]

The Court reached the same conclusion that the Commission had no explicit or inherent executive authority under the Treaty to make administrative agreements without the Council's consent. The Court rejected the Commission's appeal to expediency. In the Court's judgment neither necessity nor convenience justified the Commission's action. Thus, the Court foreclosed the Commission's attempt to draw a parallel between the expediency argument in the United States and the Community. The Court voided the Agreement.

The Court's judgment calls into question executive expediency discourse in the United States. As we have seen, the President's executive agreement power was premised on the idea that the President needed such authority to be effective in negotiating agreements to cooperate with other partners, like the Community. The European Court of Justice found that there was no real need or urgency to conclude a cooperation agreement that would justify the Commission's action. Thus, one might reasonably ask, why did the US executive perceive such urgency as would justify trespassing on the Senate's Article II powers?[35]

IV. THE LEGAL EFFECTIVENESS OF EXECUTIVE AGREEMENTS IN US
DOMESTIC LAW

The European Community rejected the Commission's claim of authority to make administrative agreements without the Council or the Parliament;

---

[32] Ibid., I-3659, para 31.   [33] Ibid., I-3653, para. 21.

[34] Interestingly, the Advocate General carefully left open the possibility that the Commission might have some authority to adopt an agreement that did not prospectively bind the Community, that is, an agreement which Vattel might call a 'compact', as opposed to a treaty. That interpretation of Article 228 would be consistent with the traditional interpretation of Article II treaties in the United States.

[35] The ECJ has accepted the idea that authority to make certain 'mixed agreements' may be shared between the Council and the Member States and it has tried to accommodate the different functions served by the Community and the Member States. The Court's willingness to interpret the provisions of the Treaty liberally somewhat parallels the US Court's willingness to permit the President to use some executive agreements in place of treaties. See Joseph Weiler, 'The External Legal Relations of Non-Unitary Actors: Mixity and the Federal Principle', in D. O'Keeffe and H. Schermers (eds), *Mixed Agreements* (Boston: Kluwer Law and Taxation Publishers, 1983).

by comparison, most US courts and legal scholars have brushed aside doubts about the democratic accountability of allowing the President to act by executive agreement. The binding legal effectiveness of the Co-operation Agreement at issue was never doubted by the ECJ, the Advocate General, or the Commission. By contrast, in the United States, the domestic legal effectiveness of the Co-operation Agreement and other executive agreements remains uncertain, and that uncertainty means that regulatory cooperation agreements may not have the same legal consequences in the United States as they have in the Community. Article VI of the US Constitution provides that treaties are the 'supreme law of the land', meaning treaties supersede contrary state law or prior inconsistent federal law. It is questionable whether the Supremacy Clause applies with equal force to executive agreements. The Supreme Court has never clearly resolved that question, lower courts have reached diverse conclusions, and legal authorities have disagreed.

In 1933 the United States re-established diplomatic relations with the Soviet Union through a sole executive agreement known as the 'Litvinov Assignment'. According to this executive agreement, the Soviet Government assigned to the United States Government all its assets in the United States, which had been frozen since the Russian Revolution. In consideration for these assets, the US executive released the Soviet Government from all claims by private individuals arising out of the Soviet nationalizations. When the Federal Government tried to enforce its rights under the Litvinov Agreement, other claimants challenged the enforcement of the executive agreement. The courts of New York State sided with the claimants' arguments that the Litvinov Agreement gave effect to a confiscation of private property contrary to New York State's public policy. The Supreme Court in two related opinions held first that state courts could not apply state public policy over federal policy as established by the Litvinov Assignment.[36] In the Court's view the decision to settle claims was part of a single transaction to recognize a foreign government and establish diplomatic relations. As such, the President as the 'sole organ' of foreign relations had exclusive authority to settle claims.[37]

In the second case, the Court found that the President's Article II power to 'receive foreign ministers,' included removing obstacles to recognition.[38] The Court described the power to settle claims by taking property rights as 'a modest implied power of the President who is the "sole organ of the federal government in the field of international relations"'.[39] Later authorities broadly read these two opinions as establishing the principle that *any* sole executive agreement might be supreme over state law or pub-

---

[36] *US v. Belmont*, 301 US 324 (1937).   [37] Ibid. 331.
[38] *US v. Pink*, 315 US 203 (1942).
[39] Ibid. 229. The reference to the President as the 'sole organ' comes from *US v. Curtiss-Wright Export Corp.*, 299 US 304, 320 (1936).

lic policy and could be directly effective without implementing legislation. However, the Court did not suggest that the President had plenary power to supersede state law by sole executive agreement. A strict reading of these opinions leads only to the narrow conclusion that executive agreements that settled claims to establish diplomatic relations may supersede state law.

Through World War II most legal authorities agreed that executive agreements did not directly affect domestic law.[40] The consensus of opinion changed during the Cold War as the executive gained greater power over foreign relations.[41] By the 1960s the drafters of the *Restatement (Second) of the Foreign Relations Law of the United States* opined that at least some congressional-executive agreements could have a domestic legal effect and override inconsistent state law or prior federal law.[42] The *Restatement* concluded that the President had a qualified authority to make sole executive agreements pertaining to the President's narrowly defined constitutional powers, such as the power to receive foreign ministers, and that some sole executive agreements might possibly override inconsistent state law, but not federal law.[43]

Executive agreements continued to gain legal status under domestic law as a consequence of the growing significance of the GATT. Some legal authorities and US courts began to treat the GATT as if it were a treaty for purposes of domestic law.[44] Professor John Jackson convincingly advocated that GATT was the functional equivalent of a treaty.[45] Section 30 of the Trade Act of 1945 had authorized the President to negotiate reciprocal agreements to lower tariff rates and then to 'proclaim' these new rates as

[40] e.g. Edwin Borchard, 'Shall the Executive Agreement Replace the Treaty?', *Yale Law Journal*, vol. 53 (1944), 616.

[41] Wallace McClure, *International Executive Agreements* (1967) 350–3; *Restatement (Second) of the Foreign Relations Law of the United States* (1962), sects. 117–20.

[42] *Restatement (Second)* (above, n. 41), sects. 117–20.

[43] Ibid., sects. 121, 141–4.

[44] *Restatement (Third) of the Foreign Relations Law of the United States*, sect. 303; Robert Hudec, 'The Legal Status of GATT in the Domestic Law of the United States', in Meinhard Hilf *et al.* (eds), *The European Community and GATT* (Boston: Kluwer Law and Taxation Publishers, 1986), 195–226; Jackson, 'General Agreement on Tariffs and Trade' (above, n. 18), 280–92.

See *Bercut-Vandervoort & Co. v. US*, 151 F. Supp. 942 (C.C.P.A. 1957) (holding that a federal tax on wine was consistent with GATT); *George E. Bardwil & Sons v. US*, 42 C.C.P.A. 118 (1955) (sustaining the President's authority to suspend tariff concessions); *K.S.B. Technical Sales Corp. v. North Jersey Dist. Water Supply Comm'n of New Jersey*, 75 N.J. 272 (N.J. 1977) (opining that GATT is a treaty for purposes of domestic law), appeal dismissed, 435 US 982 (1978); *Bethlehem Steel Corp. v. Board of Comm'rs*, 276 Cal. App. 2d 21 (Cal. Ct. App. 1969) (holding that state procurement law was pre-empted by the federal power over foreign affairs); *Baldwin–Lima–Hamilton Corp. v. Superior Court*, 209 Cal. App. 803 (Cal. Ct. App. 1962) (holding that California's procurement law violated GATT); *Hawaii v. Ho*, 41 Haw. 565 (Haw. 1957) (holding a state law requiring stores that sold imported eggs to give public notice violated GATT); see also 40 Op. Att'y Gen. (Cal.) 650 (1962) (opining that GATT overrides inconsistent state law).

[45] Jackson, 'General Agreement on Tariffs and Trade' (above, n. 18).

effective, replacing the existing rates. Jackson argued that the power to proclaim tariff rates had given the President authority to proclaim GATT as domestic law. Jackson justified this exceptional delegation of legislative authority by cautioning that 'to disown GATT at this point would be a jolt to this nation's foreign policy and indeed to the stability of international economic relations throughout most of the world'.[46] Jackson's argument again appealed to the expediency of the geopolitical situation to legitimate the expansion of executive power.

Professor Jackson distinguished the GATT from all other executive agreements based upon the textual provisions of the Trade Act of 1945 and the importance of the GATT to world trade. Some legal authorities and courts have cited Jackson's argument to support the general proposition that executive agreements are functionally equivalent to Article II treaties for purposes of domestic law.[47] Nevertheless, real doubt remains about the legal status of executive agreements.[48]

The Supreme Court considered the domestic legal status of sole executive agreements in a case arising out of the Iranian hostage crisis in 1979. Acting under the International Emergency Economic Powers Act (IEEPA),[49] President Carter froze the assets of the Government of Iran following the seizure of US diplomats by Iranian militants. On 20 January 1981, as he was preparing to leave office, President Carter signed the Declaration of Algiers, which provided for the release of hostages in exchange for the frozen assets and the termination of all litigation against Iran.[50] Pursuant to the Declaration, the President issued a series of executive orders which *inter alia* transferred Iran's assets out of the country and voided any attachments or liens on those assets.[51] A US company, Dames & Moore, had previously obtained a pre-judgment attachment against the property of certain banks owned by the Government of Iran to settle outstanding contractual claims. The Foreign Sovereign Immunities Act of 1976 (FSIA) conferred jurisdiction on the federal district court to hear

---

[46] Jackson, 'General Agreement on Tariffs and Trade' (above n. 18), 260.

[47] See, e.g. *Coplin v. US*, 6 Cl. Ct. 115; 84–2 US Tax Case (CCH) 9693 (1984); Henkin, *Foreign Affairs* (above, n. 24), 173–87; see Paul, 'The Geopolitical Constitution' (above, n. 14), 755–66. The drafters of the Third Restatement in 1986 concluded that any executive agreement, with or without congressional approval, could supersede both state and federal law. *Restatement (Third)* (above, n. 44), sects. 111 cmts. D, h; 303); see Peter J. Lesser, 'Superseding Statutory Law by Sole Executive Agreement: An Analysis of the American Law Institute's Shift in Position', *Virginia Journal of International Law*, vol. 23 (1983), 671.

[48] For example, Professor Louis Henkin, who was the reporter for the Third Restatement, has since questioned whether executive agreements are substitutes for Article II treaties. See Louis Henkin, *Constitutionalism, Democracy and Foreign Affairs* (1990), 57; Henkin, *Foreign Affairs* (above, n. 24), 215–26.

[49] IEEPA of 1977, Pub. L. 95–223, sect. 201, 91 Stat. 1625, 1626 (1977) (codified at 50 USC, sect. 1701).

[50] Declaration of the Government of the Democratic and Popular Republic of Algeria, initiated 19 Jan. 1981, US–Iran–Algeria, reprinted in 20 I.L.M. 224 (1981).

[51] Exec. Order Nos. 12276–85, Fed. Reg. 7913-32 (1981).

claims against foreign governments arising out of commercial transactions, like Dames & Moore's claim against Iran.[52] On 27 January 1981 a district court awarded summary judgment to Dames & Moore. The district court subsequently stayed execution as a result of the executive orders. Dames & Moore then sued the United States for declaratory and injunctive relief claiming that the executive orders were *ultra vires* and violated due process rights.[53]

The Supreme Court upheld the Declaration, even though it acknowledged that the President had no statutory authority to bar a claim in federal court that was expressly authorized by the FSIA. Instead the Court relied upon two sets of circumstances: First, the Court noted that there was a history of Congress approving settlements of claims against foreign governments, and that in this case Congress had by its silence 'acquiesced' in the executive agreement.[54] Second, the Court emphasized the exigent circumstances under which the President negotiated the executive agreement.[55] The Court stressed 'the narrowness of our decision', concluding only that

where, as here, the settlement of claims has been determined to be a necessary incident to the resolution of a major foreign policy dispute between our country and another, and where, as here, we can conclude that Congress acquiesced in the President's action, we are not prepared to say that the President lacks the power to settle such claims.[56]

The Court's analysis explicitly relied upon executive expediency. By interpreting congressional silence as approval, the Court elevated executive primacy over foreign affairs at the expense of congressional control. Although the Court expressly limited the scope of its opinion to the extraordinary facts of the case, the opinion has been relied upon as authority for the broader proposition that a sole executive agreement may have binding domestic legal effects. Federal Court of Appeals Judge Alex Kozinski, then sitting on the US Claims Court, opined in a subsequent case that

the president had ample authority to bind the United States [by executive agreement] . . . *Dames & Moore* . . . established— if doubt existed before— that the President has significant powers to bind the United States to international agreements without the advice and consent of the Senate. Such agreements supercede prior United States law to the extent it is inconsistent. In *Dames & Moore* . . . [t]he Supreme Court ruled that the President's action 'effected a change in the substantive law.' . . . [I]t upheld the President's authority to unilaterally change domestic law by executive agreement with a foreign state . . .[57]

[52] FSIA of 1976 (codified at 28 USC, sect. 1330, 1602–11).
[53] *Dames & Moore v. Regan*, 453 US 654 (1981).   [54] Ibid. 678.   [55] Ibid. 660–2.
[56] Ibid. 688.
[57] *Coplin v. US* (above, n. 47), 122 (upholding a sole executive agreement with Panama that exempted from US tax the income of US nationals employed by the Canal Commission).

Other courts and commentators have questioned Judge Kozinski's extraordinary conclusion that the President has the power to repeal existing federal law or make new law merely with the consent of a foreign government.[58] The Constitution limited the power of each branch in order to prevent the abuse of power. Allowing the executive to make an agreement that displaces state or federal law means the executive could exercise virtually unchecked legislative authority, unbalancing the constitutional structure.

Some legal scholars insist that executive agreements are merely a source of customary international law, which can be displaced by any inconsistent executive, judicial, or congressional decision.[59] Yet, it is still difficult to defend the proposition that state laws concerning traditional state authority, such as education, family law, or property rights, could be swept away by the action of the executive without pursuing the constitutionally mandated process for an Article II treaty. The Constitution preserves state sovereignty because some government functions are best provided at a sub-national level. The diversity of states allows experimentation and pluralism to flourish, and rightly or wrongly, most citizens believe that state government is closer to their interests, more responsive to their complaints, and more open to citizen participation and reform. To the extent then that executive agreements displace state laws, such agreements undermine federalism. The single overriding justification for executive agreements is to concentrate authority in the executive to respond to perceived geopolitical threats that have long ceased with the end of the Cold War.

V. CONCLUSION

In the present circumstance of uncertainty over the legal status of executive agreements and the lack of democratic accountability, executive agreements are a poor instrument for implementing regulatory cooperation. Historical practice, constitutional law, and sound policy all argue against reliance on executive agreements. Executive agreements frustrate democratic accountability by removing the process of undertaking foreign commitments from public discourse and scrutiny. Without public discourse, neither the public nor Congress are likely to be committed to our international undertakings. Executive agreements may be expedient in the sense that they facilitate foreign commitments, but to the extent that such

---

[58] Henkin, *Foreign Affairs* (above, n. 24), 221–2; *Swearingen v. US*, 565 F. Supp. 1019, 1021 (D. Colo. 1983) (holding that the sole executive agreement with Panama exempting from US tax the income of US nationals employed by the Canal Commission cannot supersede the Internal Revenue Code).

[59] *Restatement (Third)* (above, n. 44), 111, cmt. D.

commitments are undertaken lightly, they are likely to fail. When the public is not fully committed to a course of conduct, our foreign policy is weak and ineffectual, and our partners are frustrated. The wisdom of our Constitution lies in the requirement of a broad congressional consensus favouring international commitments. Policies that command broad support are more likely to be effective because the public will stay the course.

It is inherently unfair to our foreign partners to undertake commitments by executive agreements that may have no binding effect in domestic courts. When the President ratifies an executive agreement with the European Community, the Community and the United States are not assuming reciprocal obligations. If the United States is serious about a foreign commitment, we should dignify that commitment with an Article II treaty.

Integrating regulatory cooperation into the EU system

Gerhard Lohan*

This contribution examines the three main questions relevant to the interface between international regulatory initiatives and the domestic legal
and institutional environment on the EU side. These questions are: (1)
what the regulatory process in the European Union looks like, (2) what
kind of regulatory cooperation exists between the European Union and
the United States, and (3) what issues arise in integrating international cooperation into the EU system. My focus is on the life-cycle of product
and product-related requirements: production methods, performance and
design requirements, testing and conformity assessment, labelling and,
finally, recycling and waste management.

I. REGULATORY PROCESSES IN THE EUROPEAN UNION

A. General characteristics, differences between the EU and the US systems

Summarized below are the most relevant parts of the process, from the
identification of regulatory needs to the formal legislative process, including the transparency of that process. My account reveals one fundamental
difference: In the United States, rule-making at the federal level is largely
performed by agencies pursuant to a delegation of powers from Congress
through enabling legislation ('administrative rule-making'). By contrast,
EU regulations on product safety and product-related environment or
consumer protection are enacted by the EU legislative bodies themselves,
and they almost always do so by means of the generally applicable law-
making procedures. While the European Union does have a number of
agencies,[1] their mandate is ordinarily limited to analysis and advice—an

---

* The opinions expressed in this contribution do not necessarily reflect the position of the
European Commission.

[1] European Environment Agency, Copenhagen; European Training Foundation, Turin;
Office for Veterinary and Plant-Health Inspections and Control, Dublin, Ireland; European
Monitoring Centre for Drugs and Drug Addiction, Lisbon; European Agency for the
Evaluation of Medicinal Products, London; Agency for Health and Safety at Work, Bilbao,
Spain; Office of Harmonisation in the Internal Market (trademarks, designs, and models),
Alicante, Spain; Europol and the Europol Drugs Unit, The Hague; see Decision 93/C323/01,
1993 OJ (C 323/1).

exception being the European Agency for the Evaluation of Medicinal Products in London, which has a clear regulatory function, albeit in the issuance of product approvals rather than rule-making as such. Political discussion has begun on the utility of creating more agencies with operational powers (as, for example, in the food health field, or in competition policy), but no results are expected in the near term.

Accordingly, administrative rule-making at the EU level is very exceptional. It is found only in those cases where the Council has assigned certain powers to the Commission for the implementation of legislation adopted at a higher level.[2] In such cases, the Commission is empowered to issue implementing rules which are as binding on the Member States as the basic rules adopted by the Council. Member States become most closely involved in this procedure through participation in committees, pursuant to a Council Decision of 1987.[3] The three main types of committees—advisory, management, and regulatory—vary according to the degree of influence which they enable national delegates to exercise over the measure in preparation. Delegation is mainly used to modify the technical requirements laid down in Annexes to Council Directives, such as environmental and safety requirements for motor vehicles. (See Annexe 1, a comparative table showing the role of EU and US institutions in the rule-making process.)

B. The gist of EU regulatory procedures

The product-related requirements covered by this paper are laid down in secondary Community legislation as defined by Article 249 (formerly Article 189) of the EC Treaty, i.e. mainly in regulations and directives.[4] Regulations are binding in their entirety and are directly applicable in all Member States. Directives, on the other hand, are binding on Member States only as to the results to be achieved; the form and method for implementing directives are left to the Member States, which have a specific length of time in which to transpose them into national law, and which are responsible for their implementation.

The formal legislative process, in which the European Commission, the European Parliament, and the Council of Ministers work closely together, involves three basic activities: initiative, consultation, and decision-making. The Commission, based on its exclusive right of initiative, is responsible for the preparatory work. Once legislation is initiated, all three institutions then take part in the following process during which consultation and decision-making alternate with each other, until a measure is finally adopted.

---

[2] See EC Treaty Article 211 (ex Article 155), fourth indent.

[3] Council Decision 87/337/EEC, 1987 OJ (L 197) 33.

[4] This note reflects the situation under the Treaty prior to the coming into effect of the Amsterdam Treaty.

C. Main instruments of transparency

1. Regulatory planning

In establishing the need for a regulatory measure—say, in response to health, safety, or consumer protection concerns or environmental protection requirements—the Commission engages in a permanent dialogue with a great many segments of society. It both actively seeks opinions from such segments on the need for legislative measures and is approached by those segments on their own initiative.

Once it has identified a broad area for action, the Commission may make the political decision to publish a Green Paper setting out its ideas on possible courses of action. Green Papers also provide a framework for interest groups to make their views known and, in doing so, fix deadlines for the presentation of written views and raise the possibility of participating in hearings. Green Papers have been used, for example, in the context of liberalizing the telecommunications sector,[5] in regulating electronic commerce,[6] and in food law.[7]

On the basis of opinions canvassed, the Commission may then produce White Papers which, like Green Papers, are based on political decisions by the Commission, but which are more detailed and focused and may actually lay out concrete suggestions for directives. The best-known example is certainly the White Paper of June 1985 on completion of the internal market by 1992. Another important example is the White Paper on the preparation of the associated countries of Central and Eastern Europe for integration into the internal market.[8]

The Commission has further means of ensuring transparency as to its objectives and intended actions. Its Annual Work Programme[9] lists political priorities and new legislative initiatives envisaged for the year concerned, with more detailed information provided in a related 'Indicative List of Action Envisaged'.[10] The Commission also issues Communications to the Council and the European Parliament to analyse a particular situation, highlight policy options and developments, and more generally make the opinion of the Commission known to the public. While Communications serve to set out the Commission's general lines of policy, they often provide early information on the Commission's intended regulatory activities as well. All the documents mentioned are public documents, and their wide distribution is ensured through a multitude of communication channels.

[5] Green Paper on the Convergence of the Telecommunications, Media and IT Sectors and the Implications for Regulation, COM(97)623.

[6] Green Paper on Commercial Communications in the Internal Market, COM(96)192.

[7] COM(97)176.   [8] COM(95)163.

[9] The Commission's Work Programme 1999: COM(98)604 (political priorities) and COM(98)609 (new legislative initiatives).

[10] For 1999, see Document SEC (1998) 1901 of 5 Nov. 1998.

2. Initiating legislation

The Commission has the exclusive right to initiate EC legislation in most areas of regulatory cooperation between the European Union and the United States, and the Council can only enact legislation on the basis of a Commission proposal.[11] Nevertheless, the first impetus towards legislation can come from many different sources: Member States, industry, pressure groups, consumer associations, and others. Both the Council[12] and Parliament[13] may of course also state their views on the need to introduce legislation. When the time comes to draw up specific legislative proposals, the Commission will consult with working parties, independent experts, representatives from interested constituencies, and officials from Member States, with the latter in turn consulting interest groups at the national level. In many cases, extensive research is necessary into the technical, legal, economic, and social circumstances which may influence legislation to be adopted at the EU level. Where studies are commissioned to outside experts, the Commission services will naturally take their findings into account, but will obviously never feel bound by their regulatory proposals.

Interservice consultation involving all potentially interested Directorates-General of the Commission is another important step on the road towards a formal proposal. It is governed by the Commission's internal rules. Since formal proposals are adopted by the Commission as a whole, the agreement of all services concerned is a prerequisite and a formal decision is not likely to be taken in its absence. Consulted services may, in turn, consult interested parties during this process. Draft proposals accordingly go through a much wider scrutiny than would have been possible by the originating service alone.

Formal Commission proposals, which are commonly identified by their 'COM' reference number, contain an explanatory memorandum for the draft legislation and the draft legislative text itself. The text, but not the explanatory memorandum, is published in the *Official Journal of the European Communities* (C Series). In addition, the internet is increasingly being used to enhance transparency and to permit feedback from relevant parties. All existing legislation as well as formal legislative proposals are available on the EC web-sites.[14]

An example of the overall process can be seen in the preparation of a proposal for a directive concerning noise emissions from outdoor equipment, a proposal whose initial impetus came from Member States. The Commission circulated a Green Paper on Future Noise Policy (COM(96)

---

[11] See EC Treaty Articles 211 (ex 155) and 250–2 (ex 189a, b, c) concerning the Commission's right of initiative.
[12] EC Treaty Article 208 (ex 152).   [13] EC Treaty Article 192 (ex 138b), second paragraph.
[14] See The Europa server (http://EUROPA.eu.int.) and the services offered there (EUR-Lex, CELEX, and EUDOR).

540) and empanelled a consultation group comprising representatives from different Commission Directorates-General, national experts, non-governmental environmental organizations, industry, and local authorities. The group met several times over a two-year period and eventually considered the Commission services' first draft of proposed legislation. Upon redrafting and formal interservice consultation, the text became a Commission proposal.[15]

3. *Procedures through Parliament and Council*

The legislative processes under the EC Treaty differ according to the impact of the European Parliament on the possibilities of the other two institutions—the Commission and Council—for taking decisions. They are the Consultation Procedure, the Co-operation Procedure (Article 251, ex 189b), and the Co-decision Procedure (Article 252, ex 189c). Legislation on product requirements is mainly based on Article 95 (ex 100a) of the EC Treaty and is subject to the Co-decision Procedure. Article 300 (ex 228) of the EC Treaty specifies the role of the European Parliament with respect to the conclusion of international agreements, but Parliament's involvement in negotiations and decision-making on trade policy measures is specifically defined in Article 133 (ex 113). All the relevant meetings (including voting records) in the European Parliament are public and widely broadcast, and the basic documents are fully in the public domain.

Once adopted, all EC legislation is published in the eleven official languages in the *Official Journal of the European Communities* and available via the Celex system.

4. *Other bodies involved*

Principles of transparency apply equally to the participation of other EU bodies in the legislative process. More specifically, the Economic and Social Committee is a vehicle for the expression of views of workers, employers, and consumers. The Committee of the Regions acts, in appropriate cases, as an advisory body to the other institutions, giving voice to the interests of Europe's regions.

D. Right of public access to documents

In the past, documents of the Commission, the Council, and the Parliament were made available to the public at large as a matter of good policy and, after the 1993 Maastricht amendments to the EC Treaty, through a Code of Conduct for the Commission[16] and the Council[17] and a subsequent decision on public access by the Parliament.[18] The

---

[15] COM(98)46; 1998 OJ (C 124) 1.   [16] 1994 OJ (L 46).   [17] 1993 OJ (L 340).
[18] 1997 OJ (L 263).

amendments introduced by the Amsterdam Treaty confer further access rights on the public.

Article 1 of the EC Treaty, as amended, establishes as a general principle that decisions are to be taken as openly as possible and as closely as possible to the people. Article 255 (ex 191a) gives any Union citizen, as well as any natural or legal person residing or having a registered office in a Member State, the right of access to European Parliament, Council, and Commission documents. All three institutions are also required to include specific rules on access to documents in their Rules of Procedure, subject to general principles to be fixed by the Council and Parliament within a two-year period, following a proposal from the Commission. That work is underway. The basic idea is to give the right of access the widest possible interpretation, while at the same time safeguarding legitimate needs of confidentiality.

Still more specifically, a new provision (added as a third paragraph to what is now Article 207) requires the Council to grant access to all documents relating to its legislative activities, with required public indication of the results of votes, an explanation of votes, and statements in the minutes.

E. Transparency of national regulatory projects at EU level

In an effort to prevent Member States from adopting national technical regulations on products (as well as, more recently, on 'Information Society' services) which might create barriers within the internal market, a 'Transparency Directive'[19] (98/34/EC) requires Member States to inform and consult each other, and the Commission, before adopting any such measures. Notification triggers an initial three-month standstill period for examination by the Commission and the Member States, extendable where appropriate for an additional 3 to 15 months to permit modification of national measures imposing unjustified restrictions on EU trade or to enable the Commission to take the necessary legislative initiatives. The Commission has also published a guide to the Transparency Directive for the public.[20]

More specifically regarding standards, Directive 98/34/EC mainly obliges national standardization bodies to inform both the European Standardization Bodies and the Commission of their standards programme and their new or amended standards (unless identical or equivalent to an international or European standard). This should enable the

---

[19] Former Directive 83/189/EEC, abrogated and codified by Directive 98/34/EC of the European Parliament and of the Council laying down a procedure for the provision of information in the field of technical standards and regulations and of rules on Information Society Services. Available at http://www.europa.eu.int/comm/dgo3/tris/.

[20] Luxembourg, Office for Publications of the EC, 1998 ISBN 92-828-2785-2.

Commission, when necessary, to mandate that one of the European Standardization Bodies develop a common standard. Each week the Commission publishes in the *Official Journal of the European Communities*, Series C, the titles of draft national technical regulations notified to it under Directive 98/34/EC. Notifications should also soon be made available on-line on the EUROPA web site, thus enabling industry to be heard by the national authorities and by the Commission on a timely basis. Standardization activities are also available on line on the CEN, CEN-ELEC, and ETSI web sites.

F. Transparency of EU and national regulatory projects under the WTO–TBT Agreement

The Agreement on Technical Barriers to Trade (TBT), first reached in the Tokyo Round and then modified in the Uruguay (WTO) Round, likewise seeks to ensure that technical regulations and standards, as well as testing and certification procedures, do not create unnecessary obstacles to trade. Under the notification procedure that has been set up, TBT Members must under certain conditions notify all draft technical regulations, testing and certification procedures, as well as labelling rules, that have a significant effect on the trade of other Members.

The TBT Agreement has been made applicable for the European Union by way of a 1980 Council Decision approving the results of the Tokyo Round[21] and a 1994 Council Decision approving the modifications made during the Uruguay Round.[22] The Commission, which has overall responsibility for managing the Agreement, has set up the EU TBT Enquiry Point in DG III. Details on the handling of TBT procedures by the Commission and the Member States are set out in the EU's so-called 'Article 15.2 Report', most recently updated in July 1998.[23]

The TBT Agreement serves the purpose of transparency in the EU regulatory process in two particular ways:

- Both Commission proposals and relevant texts from the Member States are regularly notified to the WTO in Geneva, and made publicly available on the WTO web-site: http://www.wto.org/wto/ddf. Moreover, the Commission is developing a section on the EUROPA web-site that will contain all the relevant notified draft regulations that are not, as such, available on the WTO web-site, as well as all internal EU notifications made under the Transparency Directive 98/34/EC. The European Union is by far the largest single notifying entity of all the WTO signatories. In 1998 the European Union made 245 notifications

---

[21] Council Decision 80/271/EEC, 1980 OJ (L 71).
[22] Council Decision 94/800/EEC, 1994 OJ (L 336).
[23] TWO document G/TBT/Add.12/Rev.1, 1 July 1998.

(36 from the Commission, and 209 from the Member States), with all remaining WTO Members together accounting for the other 403 notifications (with 32 from the United States, 28 from Japan, and 19 from Canada).

- The European Union and the Member States' Enquiry Points provide information about existing regulations upon request to EU and non-EU parties alike. Although this facility is part of the TBT Agreement, enquiries are actually directed to Enquiry Points only in relatively few cases, since many other, often more specialized, information services are available for exporters to the European Union.

II. SURVEY OF EXISTING EU–US REGULATORY COOPERATION

A. Background and coverage

Within the context of the Transatlantic Economic Partnership (TEP) project, the European Commission and the US Administration agreed to establish an inventory of existing regulatory cooperation, with a view to identifying ways and means of improving access to each other's regulatory procedures. Moreover, joint general principles and guidelines governing those procedures were to be developed.

On the EU side, the first phase is a 'stocktaking' table (Annexe 2), covering ten industrial sectors for which DG III is the lead department. The table covers the following sectors: electrotechnical products, information technology, chemicals, medical equipment, recreational craft, foodstuffs, agri-food biotechnology, human pharmaceuticals, veterinary medicinal products, automobiles, and cosmetics. This list is not, however, exhaustive. Other sectors, especially those where contacts are only about to begin (such as road-safety equipment), have not been included. Moreover, the Commission is launching a second phase of 'stocktaking' for matters not primarily within DG III's purview.

On the US side, some federal agencies have prepared short summaries, and others have been invited to do likewise.

B. Main characteristics of regulatory cooperation

Even though in its early stages, the stocktaking exercise already permits a number of interesting observations.

First, in most sectors, cooperation is taking place in a multilateral context. Only two sectors—medical equipment and recreational craft—involve purely bilateral cooperation.

Second, regulatory cooperation is a relatively recent phenomenon, dating to within the last ten years, for most sectors. The most prominent exception is the automobile sector where cooperation can be traced to 1984 in the context of the 1958 UN–ECE Agreement.

Third, an important milestone in this decade of EU–US cooperation was the launch in 1989 of annual regulatory meetings with the US Food and Drug Administration. Almost all sectoral contacts now find the US Department of Commerce as a key participant.

Fourth, an important culmination in this period is the Mutual Recognition Agreement (MRA), which went into effect on 1 December 1998. The preparatory work for the MRA, starting with the first negotiations in 1991, was the occasion for creating many closer links between the two sets of regulators.

Fifth, modern communication tools such as video-conferences and audio-conferences hold out the promise of making the 'meetings' on which this cooperation depends less costly and time-consuming.

In addition to conducting sector-based cooperation, DG III has for many years maintained close contacts with the US Administration (mainly USTR) on matters related to the WTO–TBT Agreement. These communications, whether bilateral or in the context of so-called 'QUAD' meetings (European Union, United States, Japan, Canada), have generally been held on a strictly informal basis prior to formal Committee meetings in Geneva. They have mainly addressed the management of the TBT Agreement, the triennial review of the Agreement that was carried out in 1997, and follow-up on the latter. Detailed discussion of specific issues, however, tends to take place outside the TBT Agreement, in exchanges that parallel or amplify written comments under TBT. In several cases, particularly in the food sector, the European Union criticized US deviations from international standards. The US side has called attention to trade restrictions relating to genetically modified organisms as well as national measures to ban asbestos.

C. Prospects for achieving success in regulatory cooperation

Experience to date in the sectors mentioned suggests certain strategies for making cooperation work effectively:

Upstream: international cooperation efforts between regulators produce better results when they take place prior to formalization of legislative or regulatory proposals. Once proposals pass into the channels of formal rule-making, many other factors may come into play and override cooperation at the expert level.

Sectoral: because modern regulatory activity tends to be highly specialized, cooperation between real experts is indispensable. While horizontal approaches will not work, it is nonetheless useful to have an overall framework for reviewing progress in general.

Reciprocal: the potential for cross-fertilization in bilateral cooperation is greatest where both sides intend to regulate. Where only one side is actively pursuing a regulatory initiative, comments made by the other side, like the comments permitted by the WTO–TBT Agreement, may be perceived as part of trade policy and 'market-access' strategies more particularly, rather than as cooperation.

Similar concepts: where one side intends to regulate while the other is inclined to leave the subject matter to voluntary standards, the prospects for regulatory cooperation are small. Government regulators are not likely to enter into substantive cooperation with private standard-setters from other regions of the world.

Same level: cooperation is at its most feasible when both sides intend to regulate at the central or federal level, since regulators at different levels do not easily cooperate. US state regulators do not talk to the Commission; EU Member States are actually prohibited from cooperating with the US Federal Government on matters falling within the EU's legislative competence.

Incentives, not obligations: constructive international cooperation cannot be forced on the experts. Rather, regulators need to be convinced that cooperation produces better results, or produces good results more efficiently, in terms of achieving the underlying regulatory objectives, such as health, safety, or environmental protection. An additional incentive, though one that is sometimes less obvious for regulators, may be the positive international trade effects brought about through regulatory cooperation.

D. New issues

Beyond these general prescriptions, there is a growing political focus on the question of the extent to which regulations need to be based on scientific evidence. The issue is particularly relevant for the food sector, including the authorization of genetically modified organisms and the EU ban of growth hormones in animal feed. Is science able to answer all the questions that regulators may have? To what extent should principles of international regulatory cooperation permit recognizing aspects other than scientific evidence? How do political leaders exercise their obligation of risk management under circumstances of scientific uncertainty? These issues are still under discussion.

The TEP Action Plan raises another new issue by calling for the mutual recognition of technical regulations (as opposed to mutual recognition of product conformity certificates under the current MRA). Under this requirement, both sides should identify sectors in which such extended mutual recognition would be useful and achievable, and should establish a framework for achieving it.

In addition to identifying sectors and engaging in the necessary conceptual thinking, regulators must ask themselves questions such as the following: At what level of generality should such functional equivalence be established: entire regulations or detailed provisions? Is explicit recognition of equivalence between regulatory objectives a prerequisite? Should regulators address all aspects of a given product? Through what means should decisions on recognition be formalized? In any case, there is widespread agreement that what is feasible in the transatlantic relationship may be fundamentally different from the principle of recognition as applied in the context of the internal market under the *Cassis de Dijon* doctrine developed by the European Court of Justice.

III. HOW TO INCORPORATE REGULATORY COOPERATION IN THE EU SYSTEM

Integration of regulatory cooperation along the lines described above should not pose major problems for the European Union of either a legal or an institutional nature. As described above, the relevant processes are already taking place in many instances, all of which have proved to be fully compatible with, and supportive of, the EU regulatory objectives. The 1995 New Transatlantic Agenda and the TEP Action Plan constitute an appropriate framework for implementing and monitoring regulatory cooperation within the EU context.

With regard to the new elements currently envisaged or under discussion, it is useful to distinguish between new rules concerning *the process of regulatory cooperation,* on the one hand, and *results of such cooperation,* on the other.

The process of regulatory cooperation: the TEP Action Plan calls for developing jointly agreed upon general principles and guidelines on the procedures to be followed by regulatory authorities in pursuing cooperation between the United States and the European Union. A first step in this direction was already made in late 1997 when the EU/US Summit adopted a short statement, highlighting a number of procedural objectives, such as consultations in the early stages of drafting regulations, greater reliance on one another's technical resources and expertise, harmonization of regulatory requirements, and mutual recognition. The contemplated general principles and guidelines might usefully build on that text. There is agreement on both sides, however, that the 'transparency' and 'inventory' phases described above need to be accomplished first. It would be premature at the current time to predict the form in which the general principles and guidelines will be formalized. Clearly, an appropriate form would be one that, without creating disproportionate legal or procedural difficulties, produces an appropriate binding effect on regulatory agencies. The EU system is flexible enough to make this possible.

Results of cooperation: when we turn to the question of incorporating into the EU system substantive provisions which have been influenced by regulatory cooperation with other partners, our assumption must be that the rules of the EC Treaty have to be applied. No particular difficulties will arise in those cases in which the Commission services and the US Administration (possibly along with other partners) have cooperated in an informal manner. All sides are free to use the results of such cooperation in their usual domestic procedures, without further complication and possibly without even any need to refer specifically to the fact that cooperation has taken place.

The situation is legally more complex, however, when cooperation takes place in an international organization which issues 'Codes', 'Recommendations', or other formally adopted texts requiring transposition into the domestic regulatory system. Where such texts need to be formally transposed into the body of EC law, this needs to be done by way of Council decisions, and this in turn may necessitate the adaptation of existing rules.

Ultimately, concern is likely to arise in the European Union, as in the United States, over a perceived loss of sovereignty on account of the processes of international cooperation. The legislature may consider that its role in the rule-making process has become unduly limited when requirements that have been developed at the international level are presented to it on 'take-it-or-leave-it' basis. In the European Union, this may raise such serious questions as the legal basis for regulatory measures (Articles 95 and 133, ex 100a and 113) and the role of the European Parliament under the provisions of Article 300 (ex 228). Many of these questions remain at the moment unanswered.

Transparency in Rule-making Procedures in the European Union and the United States
Salient points raised in the attached papers on EU (Appendix 1) and US (Appendix 2) procedures

Phase	European Union	United States
General		
Type of rule-making Status of regulation	Legislative Mainly EU Directives to be transposed and implemented by Member States.	Administrative Administrative rules which have the force and effect of law.
Planning		
Pre-initiation process	Permanent dialogue with society, Green Papers, White Papers, Annual Work Programme, Commission communications to Council and Parliament.	Impact analyses of rules (small business, environment, information collection). Executive Order 12866 on Regulatory Planning and Review (cost-benefit assessment, consensual mechanisms, review by OMB).
Initiation		
Right to initiate	Exclusively the European Commission	Each agency concerned. Congress in certain cases under APA.
Consultation		
Directives	Consultations with experts, Member States, interservice consultation with relevant services, consultation with Economic and Social Committee and Committee of the Regions.	Public consultations by either formal hearing or informal written procedure.

over./

Transparency in Rule-making Procedures in the European Union and the United States *cont.*

Phase	European Union	United States
Decision-making		
Adoption of regulation	Council and European Parliament following Consultation, Co-operation or Co-decision procedure.	Each agency concerned.
Adoption of implementing rules	European Commission in case of powers delegated by the Council, subject to comitology procedures.	Each agency concerned.
Publication	Official Journal (proposals and adopted law), Green Papers, White Papers, and Annual Work Programme are all publicly available in print and on-line. Notification to, and consultation between, Member States and the Commission prior to adoption of technical regulations.	Notice of proposed rule-making and adopted measures (with some exceptions) published in Federal Register in print and on-line. Public comments received available for public review. OMB's Unified Regulatory Agenda of April and October. Code of Federal Regulations (all adopted regulations). APA as amended by Freedom of Information Act (public access to documents) and Executive Order 12600 (right to notice prior to release of information).
Judicial review	Court of Justice. Amendments of Directives through normal legislative procedures.	Public right to petition for the issuance, amendment, and repeal of a rule, to which agencies must respond. Also judicial review by courts. Congress petition process or instruction under APA.

DG III-Led Regulatory Cooperation with US Authorities
Table A: Basic Facts

	Basis/Framework	Commission service(s) involved	US agency(ies)	Cooperation started in:
Information technologies	Annexe to the WTO Ministerial Declaration on Trade in Information Technology Products, of 1997 TABD	ITA: DG III/C/12 with DG I	ITA: USTR	ITA: 1997
Electrotechnical products	MRA TABD	DG III/D/1 with DG I	OSHA (Electrical Safety) FCC: (EMC and Network Protection)	MRA: 1991
Chemicals	OECD Joint Committee on Chemicals and its subgroups UN-IOMC and the International Forum on Chemical Safety (IFCS) TABD	DG III/C-4 with DG XI	EPA	1992 (Rio Summit)
Medical devices	MRA TABD Global Harmonization Task Force	DG III/D-2	FDA	1991 1989

cont./

DG III-Led Regulatory Cooperation with US Authorities *cont.*

	Basis/Framework	Commission service(s) involved	US agency(ies)	Cooperation started in:
Recreational craft	MRA TABD	DG III/D/5	DOC, EPA, and US Coastguard	1994
Foodstuffs	Bilateral initiative at service level Codex Alimentarius OECD Food Safety and Quality Committee TABD TEP	DG III/E/I with DGs I, VI, XXIV	Priority: FDA	FDA bilateral: 1989
Agri-food biotechnology	Initiative at service level TABD (preliminary discussions) TEP	DG III/E/2 with DGs I, VI, XI	USDA, EPA, FDA, USTR	1996
Human pharmaceuticals	ICH (International Conference on Harmonization) Bilateral initiative at service MRA TABD	DG III/E/3 with DG I	FDA, DoC, USTR	ICH: 1989 FDA bilateral: 1989 MRA: 1991

Sector	Basis for Cooperation	Commission services involved	US agencies	
Veterinary pharmaceuticals	VICH (International Cooperation on Harmonization of Technical Requirements for Registration of Veterinary Medicinal Products)	DG III/E/3 with DG I	FDA, USDA, DoC, USTR	VICH: 1994
	Bilateral initiative at service level			FDA bilateral: 1989
	MRA			MRA: 1991
Automobiles	UN-ECE	DG III/E/5 with DGs VII, XI	EPA and NHTSA	UN/ECE Agreement: 1984
	IHRA (International Harmonized Research Agenda)			IHRA: 1996
	TABD			
Cosmetics	TABD	DG III/E/3	FDA	1998
	TEP			
	CHIC (Cosmetics Harmonization and International Cooperation)			

Explanatory Notes

1. Basis for Cooperation:

—Along with strictly bilateral bases (such as the MRA) the table lists only those international fora which DG III considers as the most important ones and where substantive regulatory discussions with the US authorities take place.

—TABD and TEP are only mentioned in those cases where the sector concerned has been positively included and where government-to-government contacts have started.

2. Commission services involved:

The information given in this column is without prejudice to the formal distribution of competencies between DGs.

3. US agencies:

In some cases, not all agencies with which there are contacts have been mentioned; the intention of this column is to indicate the primary interlocutors.

Table B: Objectives, Content, and Working Methods

	Objectives and content of EU/US cooperation	Methods
Information technologies	Objectives: All ITA signatories to allow the use of 'Supplier's Declaration of Conformity' (SDoC)	• Mainly informal QUAD meetings for comparison of positions prior to the ITA Committee meetings
Electrotechnical products	Objectives: Recognition of conformity assessment certificates; best use of confidence-building period Content: —Conformity assessment procedures such as laid down in the EMC Directive and the Low Voltage Directive —Use of international standards on electrical safety (IEC 950) and on electromagnetic compatibility (CISPR 22)	• Meetings of the Sectoral Committee in December 1998 (on EMC and electrical safety) and end April 1999 (on EMC). Workshop on regulatory systems in Brussels in December 1998 • Exchange of technical/scientific information, of information on regulatory approaches and on overall policy orientations
Chemicals	Objectives: —Simplification of notification of new chemicals —Equivalent methodologies of hazard and risk assessment Content: Directive on Classification, Packaging, Labelling of Dangerous Substances (67/548/EEC) and the US Toxic Substances Control Act	• OECD Joint Committee: 2 meetings per year • UN-IFCS: 1 meeting per year and subgroups • TABD: the Quadripartite Group has met 5 times and the next meeting will be in Italy in May 1999. Two horizontal TABD meetings per year • Exchange of technical/scientific information, of information on regulatory approaches and on overall policy orientations

- Several bilateral projects with EPA such as case studies on notification of new substances, cost/benefit analysis on new regulations, the precautionary principle

- MRA: mostly informal contacts (e.g. using video-conferences) and meetings (e.g. meeting held in Washington in February 1999). Member States and industry participate whenever relevant. Joint sectoral committee meeting to be scheduled

- GHTF: Plenary meetings every 18 months, next on 27 June 1999. Chair currently held by the US. Meetings of study groups held 3–4 times per year. GHTF website created by the US will include information on as well as documents from GHTF

- Informal meetings on implementation of the MRA will start in May 1999. Audio-/video-conferences may also be used

Medical devices

Objectives:
—MRA: make full use of the confidence-building period. Consider possibilities for expansion of the product coverage

GHTF: Information exchange and comparison of regulatory systems with particular regard to best regulatory practice, the equivalence of systems, and to the use of international standards. Utilization of work done in the GHTF for the purpose of the MRA

Content:
Directive 90/385/EEC on Active Implantable Medical Devices and Directive 93/42/EEC on Medical Devices; the relevant parts of the US Federal Food, Drug, and Cosmetics Act; the Public Health Services Act; relevant FDA regulations and other federal laws

Recreational craft

Objectives:
—full implementation of the MRA which covers production characteristics of pleasure boats but not exhaust emissions or noise standards

Table B: *cont.*

Objectives and content of EU/US cooperation	Methods
—achievement of equivalent regulatory solutions, possibly their harmonization, with regard to exhaust emission standards Content: Amendment to Directive 94/25/EEC and EPA measures on exhaust emission standards	• Regular meetings twice a year under TABD process • Exchange of technical/scientific information, on new regulatory initiatives, and on overall policy orientations
Foodstuffs Objectives: To improve knowledge for taking measures in specific areas, including the removal/prevention of technical barriers to trade Monitoring of worldwide developments with regard to keeping EC food law up to date and to improving the competitiveness of European food industry Content: Management of the EC food law and consideration of possible new measures	• Two formal meetings per year and several informal opportunities in international fora • Exchange of technical/scientific information, on new regulatory initiatives and on overall policy orientations
Agri-food biotechnology Objectives: Promotion of better understanding of how the regulatory systems work on both sides. Identification	• Since 1996, the frequency of bilateral contacts has considerably intensified. Such contacts took place notably in the following fora: Agri-food bio-

- technology working group: 2 meetings, TABD: 4 meetings, TEP: 1 meeting, bilaterals with FDA: 1 meeting. Beyond these, numerous informal contacts have taken place

- Exchange of technical/scientific information, exchange of information on existing regulatory frameworks and on new regulatory initiatives as well as on overall policy orientations

of major differences/underlying technical/scientific reasons. Exchange of economic information on the development of the biotechnology sector in the EU and the US.

Under TEP, the biotechnology group intends to monitor progress in various existing groups, to take into account potential trade effects, to enhance scientific and regulatory information exchange, and to promote transparency

Ultimate goal is arrive at compatible regulatory requirements leading to full consensus on mutual recognition of safety assessments

Short-term goals are
—a 'Process Guide' detailing the regulatory steps needed for product approval on both sides, to be prepared by industry with the help from governments (underway)

—a review of EU and US risk assessment and data requirements and encouragement of a simultaneous application for scientific assessment in the US and in a Member State, as a pilot project

Content:
Directives and Regulations covering the placing on the market of genetically modified organisms used in agri-food biotech (e.g. Directives 90/220/EEC and Regulation 258/97), and the corresponding instruments in the US

Table B: *cont.*

	Objectives and content of EU/US cooperation	*Methods*
Human pharmaceuticals	Objectives: ICH: Harmonization of —regulatory guidelines (quality, safety, efficacy) —a common format for submission of regulatory information —common electronic standards for the transmission of safety (pharmacovigilance) information and for submission of regulatory information —an internationally acceptable medical terminology in order to avoid duplication of testing, save resources, reduce testing on animals, and to facilitate sharing of information FDA Bilateral: Promotion of better understanding of how the regulatory systems work on both sides. Identification of major differences/underlying technical/scientific reasons and if appropriate possible areas where compatible legislation would be of benefit	Methods: ICH: Twice yearly meetings of a Steering Committee and Expert Working Groups also involving Japan and the industry associations from the three regions International conferences held in 1991 (EU), 1993 (US), 1995 (Japan), 1997 (EU) and 2000 (US) Additional meetings of experts and communication by telephone as necessary FDA Bilateral: Exchange of technical/scientific information, exchange of information on existing regulatory frameworks and on new regulatory initiatives as well as on overall policy orientations. Meetings normally held annually and eight formal meetings have been held since 1989. Meeting venue rotates between Europe and the US. MRA: Teleconferences and videoconferences to prepare for formal Joint Sectoral Committee. First Joint Sectoral Committee to be held in the US on 18 and 19 May 1999

TABD:
Annual Conference meeting of senior industrial and governmental representatives from both EU and US—focused on trade and business aspects. Mid-term reporting and progress-chasing meetings take place between the annual Conference which was held in Charlotte in 1998 and the next one to be held in Berlin in 1999

MRA:
Mutual recognition of results of GMP inspections performed in the EU and the US in order to facilitate trade and market access. Full recognition is preceded by an equivalence determination phase which aims to compare existing practices and verify effective implementation of legislation and procedures

TABD:
The state aim of TABD is to boost transatlantic trade and investment opportunities through the removal of costly inefficiencies caused by excessive regulation, duplication, and differences in the US and EU regulatory systems and procedures

Content:
A substantial body of directives, regulations, and supporting guidelines dating back to 1965 concerning applications for marketing authorization of pharmaceuticals, and the post-marketing surveillance of these pharmaceuticals (e.g. Directive 75/318/EEC, Directive 75/319/EEC, and Regulation 2309/93) and the corresponding instruments in the US

Table B: *cont.*

	Objectives and content of EU/US cooperation	*Methods*
Veterinary pharmaceuticals	Objectives: VICH: Harmonization of regulatory guidelines (quality, safety, efficacy) and cooperation on regulatory policy, in order to avoid duplication of testing, save resources, reduce testing on animals, and to achieve a common post-marketing framework for veterinary pharmaceuticals FDA Bilateral: Promotion of better understanding of how the regulatory systems work on both sides. Identification of major differences/underlying technical/scientific reasons and if appropriate possible areas where compatible legislation would be of benefit MRA: Mutual recognition of results of GMP inspections performed in the EU and the US in order to facilitate trade and market access. Full recognition is preceded by an equivalence determination phase which aims to compare existing practices and verify effective implementation of legislation and procoedures. Ongoing negotiation on veterinary immunologicals which are currently excluded from the scope of the MRA	Methods: VICH: Twice yearly meetings of a Steering Committee and Expert Working Groups also involving Japan and the industry associations from the three regions. First International Conference scheduled for November 1999 in Brussels. Additional meetings of experts and communication by telephone as necessary FDA Bilateral: Exchange of technical/scientific information, exchange of information on existing regulatory frameworks and on new regulatory initiatives as well as on overall policy orientations. Meetings normally held annually and eight formal meetings have been held since 1989. Meeting venue rotates between Europe and the US. In view of the current level of activity in VICH, the most recent FDA bilateral did not address veterinary pharmaceuticals MRA: Teleconferences and videoconferences to prepare for formal Joint Sectoral Committee. First Joint Sectoral Committee to be held in the US on 18 and 19 May 1999

Content:
A substantial body of directives, regulations, and supporting guidelines dating back to 1981 concerning applications for marketing authorization of veterinary pharmaceuticals, and the post-marketing surveillance of these veterinary pharmaceuticals (e.g. Directive 81/851/EEC, Directive 81/852/EEC, and Regulation 2309/93) and the corresponding instruments in the US.

- Comparison of existing positions and establishment of common positions 3 times per year at the UN/ECE WP 29 meetings (Geneva) and twice a year for each of 6 working group (Geneva)

- Exchange of technical/scientific information and of information on new regulatory initiatives as appropriate, as well as on overall policy orientations

- Several major international conferences such as under the TABD (1996), and ESV (Enhanced Vehicle Safety) conferences every two years

Automobiles and tyres

Objectives:
Revised 1958 Agreement: Harmonization at international level of technical regulations for components and parts of wheeled vehicles, notably on active/passive safety and environment protection; reciprocal recognition of certificates

Parallel Agreement: same, except for recognition of certificates

IHRA: Pre-regulatory cooperative research in particular with respect to safety requirements

Content:
There is a mutually beneficial interlinkage between EC Directives and UN-ECE Regulations in these areas

Table B: *cont.*

	Objectives and content of EU/US cooperation	Methods
Cosmetics	Objectives: CHIC: Alignment of requirements for safety substantiation of ingredients; Agreement on framework and processes for exchange of data between administrations; Alignment of criteria for assessment of safety and efficacy of sunscreens FDA bilateral: Promotion of understanding of the respective regulatory systems; Discussion of key issues, e.g. animal testing and acceptance of alternatives TEP: Alignment of criteria for approval of certain materials; Acceptance of in vitro data for the safety assessment of cosmetics TABD: as per Charlotte conclusions Content: Directives on cosmetic products 76/768/EEC and EU Inventory of Cosmetic Ingredients; corresponding US legislation	• CHIC: First meeting in 1999, to be held annually in the future • FDA bilateral: Annual meetings since 1998 • Exchange of scientific/legislative information and upstream work programmes

The respective powers of the European Community and Member States in transatlantic regulatory cooperation*

Paul Demaret

INTRODUCTION

In order to understand how the Transatlantic Economic Partnership could be implemented on the European side, it is important, particularly for the American reader, to keep in mind that the European Union is not a federal entity, but a complex and evolving structure composed of the European Community and fifteen Member States. This contribution is divided into five sections. The first briefly compares the external powers of the United States and of the European Community (I). The second deals with the Community's external powers which have gradually increased but still vary in nature and do not cover all areas directly relevant to the internal market (II). The third section discusses the manner in which the Community concludes external agreements in the light of the different procedures which depend on the subject matter covered by the agreement (III). The fourth section summarizes the relationship between international agreements and the Community legal order (IV). The fifth and last section stresses how, in practice, joint action by the Community and the Member States characterizes the external relations of the European Union, outside the narrowly defined commercial field. This does not always serve the external coherence of the internal market, but reflects the present stage of the European political integration process (V).

I. THE EXTERNAL POWERS OF THE UNITED STATES AND THE EUROPEAN COMMUNITY: A BRIEF COMPARISON

A. The limited external powers of the European Community

Under the US Constitution, the treaty-making power is exclusively vested in the United States and the external powers of the Federal Government

* This contribution has been written in the framework of the Interuniversity Poles of Attraction Programme P4/04—Belgian State, Prime Minister's Office—Federal Office for Scientific, Technical and Cultural Affairs.

are broader than its purely domestic powers.[1] By contrast, the EC Treaty does not vest the European Community with plenary treaty-making power. Except in those areas where the Community has been granted or has acquired exclusive competence, the Member States remain competent to enter into international agreements. In sum, the external powers of the European Community are more limited than its internal powers.

The external relations of the European Union as a whole are conducted either through the European Community, or the latter and the Member States acting jointly, or the Member States acting collectively. The Amsterdam Treaty[2] confers upon the European Union, seen as distinct from the European Community, a limited capacity to negotiate and conclude agreements with third countries in the framework of the second and third pillars of the Treaty on European Union.[3] However, matters subject to regulatory cooperation at the multilateral or bilateral level fall in the main within the scope of the EC Treaty.

B. The Community institutions and the Member States

The US Federal Government and its three branches are clearly distinct from the States. There is not such a clear separation between the European Community and the Member States. It is important to keep in mind that, whilst the European Commission, the European Central Bank, the European Parliament, and the European Court of Justice are supranational institutions which do not take instructions from the Member States, the Council of the European Union is a body made of representatives of Member State governments. Thus, the debate concerning the respective role of the Community and the Member States in the external field to a large extent takes place within the Council itself. The debate focuses on three main questions. First, is the Community competent to act? Second, if it is, will it act alone or will the Member States also intervene? Third, in so far as Community action is concerned, will the Council act by a qualified majority or unanimously? In the latter case, each Member State through its veto power has the capacity to influence the content of Community action. For example, in spring 1998, the New Transatlantic Market initiative put forward by the Commission was thought to require the Council's unanimous approval. It was rejected because of strong French opposition, with other Member States expressing reservations.[4]

---

[1] See *Missouri v. Holland*, 252 US 416 (1919); *US v. Curtiss-Wright*, 299 US 304 (1936).

[2] The Amsterdam Treaty entered into force on 1 May 1999.

[3] See Treaty on European Union, Article 24. Concerning the external relations of the European Union after the Amsterdam revision, see Marianne Dony (ed.), *L'union européenne et le monde après Amsterdam* (Bruxelles: Editions de l'Université de Bruxelles, Editions européennes, 1999).

[4] See *Europe*, 27 and 28 Apr. 1998, 8.

II. THE EXTERNAL COMPETENCE OF THE EUROPEAN COMMUNITY:[5]
A CHANGING AND INCREASINGLY COMPLEX PATCHWORK

In the original EEC Treaty of 1957, the external powers of the European Community were rather limited. They have increased through time, but still fall short of what the external coherence of the Single European market would require. They are fragmentary, and they vary in nature.

A. The gradual broadening of the Community's external competence

The EEC Treaty of 1957 provided for the establishment of a common external policy only in the commercial sector,[6] if one leaves aside the CAP which involves both an internal and an external component. The Community had the power to conclude agreements with third countries only in two cases: commercial agreements[7] and association agreements.[8] Since then, the external powers of the Community have been expanded first as a result of the interpretation of the Treaty by the Court of Justice, second as a result of the successive revisions of the Treaty.

In the 1970s, the Court of Justice established the doctrine of implied powers. The existence of external powers of an implicit nature, ruled the Court, could be inferred from the existence and the prior exercise of internal powers,[9] or, in exceptional cases, from the mere existence of internal powers.[10] The Court also ruled that in the commercial field only the

[5] On the external competence of the European Community, see Dony (ed.), *L'Union européenne* (above, n. 3), Christine Kaddous, *Le droit des relations extérieures dans la jurisprudence de la Cour de Justice des Communautés européennes* (Basle: Helbing & Lichtenhahn, 1998); Luis Norberto Gonzales Alonso, *Politica Comercial y Relaciones Exteriores de la Union Europea* (Madrid: Tecnos, 1998); Dominic McGoldrick, *International Relations of the European Union* (London, Longman, 1997); Daniel Dormoy (ed.), *L'Union européenne et les organisations internationales* (Bruxelles: Bruylant, Editions de l'Université de Bruxelles, 1997); Jacques Bourgeois, Jean-Louis Dewost, and Marie-Ange Gaiffe (eds), *La Communauté européenne et les accords mixtes* (Bruxelles, Presses interuniversitaires européennes, 1997); Ian MacLeod, I. D. Henry, and Stephen Hyett, *The External Relations of the European Communities* (Oxford: Clarendon Press, 1996); Nicolas Emiliou and David O'Keeffe (eds), *The European Union and World Trade Law* (London: Wiley, 1996). See also David O'Keeffe, 'Community and Member State Competence in External Relations Agreements of the EU', *European Foreign Affairs Review*, vol. 4 (1999), 7–36.
[6] See EC Treaty, Articles 110 to 116 (now Articles 131 to 135).
[7] See EC Treaty, Article 113 (now Article 133).
[8] See EC Treaty, Article 238 (now Article 310).
[9] See ERTA, European Court of Justice, 31 Mar. 1971, case 22/70 (1971) ECR 263. The concept of internal powers may be ambiguous in some cases. The internal competence to which reference is made to justify the competence of the Community to conclude agreements with third countries is sometimes the competence to take autonomous measures bearing on the Community's external relations. This was indeed the situation in the *ERTA* case, see Article 75 (now Article 71), para. 1(a) of the EC Treaty. Strictly speaking, it might be more appropriate to refer in such a case to the Community competence to take autonomous measures than to the Community internal competence.
[10] See Opinion 1/76, European Court of Justice, 26 Apr. 1977 (1977) ECR 741.

Community was competent to act.[11] Later, provisions were inserted in the EC Treaty allowing the Community to conclude agreements concerning environmental matters,[12] research matters,[13] monetary or foreign exchange regime matters,[14] and development cooperation.[15] Furthermore, since the Maastricht Treaty, the Community is competent to take autonomous measures regarding movements of capital between Member States and third countries.[16] In 1994 the Court of Justice ruled that the common commercial policy extended to cross-border services.[17] With the entry into force of the Amsterdam Treaty, the Community has also become competent to regulate the circulation of third-country citizens.[18] These new external powers may in turn serve to build the competence of the Community to conclude agreements with third countries relating to movements of capital or to movements of natural persons.

The principle of subsidiarity is meant to apply in areas where the Community is not exclusively competent. The Community is supposed to act only when 'by reasons of the scale or effects of the proposed action', the objectives pursued can 'be better achieved by the Community'.[19] The subsidiarity principle is often said to limit the Community sphere of action, as action is to be taken at the lowest possible level consistent with efficiency. However, in external matters, at least outside the commercial field,[20] application of the subsidiarity principle could and should lead to an expansion of the Community sphere of action. Indeed, in the external field, action by Member States will not promote efficiency and may even disrupt the functioning of the internal market. Actually, in the framework of the Community external relations, there do not appear to be many references to the subsidiarity principle in order to justify Community action. As indicated below, the Member States are in fact party to most important agreements concluded by the Community.

B. The less than complete external dimension of the internal market

Despite the fact that the Community's external powers have increased in the course of the past forty years, today the Community is not yet explicitly competent to conclude agreements with third countries covering all

---

[11] See Opinion 1/75, European Court of Justice, 11 Nov. 1975 (1975) ECR 1355.
[12] See EC Treaty, Article 130r (now Article 174).
[13] See EC Treaty, Article 130m (now Article 170).
[14] See EC Treaty, Article 109 (now Article 111).
[15] See EC Treaty, Article 130y (now Article 181).
[16] See EC Treaty, Articles 73b and sq (now Articles 56 and 59).
[17] See Opinion 1/94, 15 Nov. 1994 (1994) ECR I-5267.
[18] See Articles 61 to 69 of the EC Treaty as revised by the Amsterdam Treaty.
[19] See EC Treaty, Article 5 (formerly Article 3B).
[20] With respect to commercial matters in the sense of Article 133 (ex Article 113), the Community is exclusively competent, see above n. 11, and the principle of subsidiarity does not apply.

areas of direct relevance to the internal market, except on the basis of Article 310 (formerly Article 238) which provides for the conclusion of 'association agreements' between the Community and third countries.[21]

The present EC Treaty does not explicitly vest the Community with the power to conclude with third countries agreements intended to regulate either trade in services involving commercial presence or movement of workers, the access and treatment of foreign direct investments or various aspects of intellectual property rights. According to Opinions 1/94[22] and 2/92[23] of the Court of Justice, the Community must have made extensive use of its internal (or domestic) powers in these fields in order to become exclusively competent to conclude with third countries agreements covering the same fields. Where this is not the case, Member States need to be party to the agreement. The agreement establishing the WTO (together with the related Uruguay Round agreements) was concluded by both the Community and the Member States. The recent WTO agreement on financial services was also concluded by the Community and the Member States. Recent practice thus raises doubts as to whether the Community alone would be competent to conclude agreements dealing with a number of subject matters covered by the Transatlantic Economic Partnership.

It seems a bit odd that with respect to trade in goods and cross-border services, the Community competence is exclusive,[24] whereas with respect to trade in other services, investments, or intellectual property, the Community lacks competence as long as detailed internal measures have not been adopted. It is worth pointing out that, in the monetary field, most Member States (i.e. the members of the 'Eurozone') have forgone their national sovereignty.

Admittedly, the situation could change under the Amsterdam Treaty, since the latter allows the Council to extend the scope of Article 133 (formerly Article 113), the trade policy provision, to agreements concerning services the supply of which implies a commercial presence or movement of workers or to agreements concerning intellectual property rights. However, the Council can extend the scope of Article 133 only by a unanimous decision whereas, for other purposes under Article 133, it acts by a qualified majority. In addition, the Council could decide to proceed on a case-by-case basis instead of enlarging the scope of Article 133 on a permanent basis. Finally, international agreements dealing with foreign

---

[21] This results from the broad interpretation given by the Court of Justice to Article 238 of the EC Treaty (now Article 310 of the EC Treaty) in *Demirel*, 30 Sept. 1987, case 12/86, (1987) ECR 3719.

[22] European Court of Justice, 15 Nov. 1994 (1994) ECR I-5267.

[23] European Court of Justice, 24 Mar. 1995 (1995) ECR I-521.

[24] Several agreements between the United States and the European Community, all concerning goods, were concluded on the basis of Article 113 (now Article 133). These include the agreements on aircraft subsidies, 1992 OJ (L 301/31), on mutual recognition of certain distilled spirits, 1994 OJ (L 157/36), on customs cooperation and mutual assistance, 1997 OJ (L 222/16) and on mutual recognition, 1998 OJ (L 31/1).

investments are not mentioned. Despite representing a half-hearted measure, the new Article 133 could serve the external coherence of the European Union.[25] It will be interesting to see whether the Council will take advantage of Article 133 for the purpose of implementing parts of the Transatlantic Economic Partnership.

C. The fragmentary character and the diverse nature of the Community external powers

The preceding considerations reveal the fragmentary character of the Community external powers. In addition, the Community competence is diverse in nature. Depending on the case, it is explicit or implicit, exclusive, non-exclusive, or simply potential.

Strictly speaking, the Community is, as already indicated, exclusively competent to act externally only with respect to commercial matters in the sense of Article 133 (ex 113). The exclusive nature of the Community competence in the commercial field does not depend on the prior adoption by the Community of autonomous or domestic measures. However, the Court of Justice has construed the scope of former Article 113 somewhat narrowly: according to Opinion 1/94, the concept of commercial policy is restricted to trade in goods and to cross-border services.[26]

The EC Treaty gives the Community explicit competence to conclude agreements concerning environmental protection, research programmes, development cooperation, monetary matters. However, in these sectors, the Community competence is not exclusive: the Member States are also competent to conclude agreements with third countries. Three possibilities may arise: the agreement is concluded by the Community acting alone or by the Member States alone or by the Community and the Member States acting together. Although the Community is now explicitly competent to conclude external agreements in the environmental field, the Council practice in this area is not really different from the practice it follows in fields where the Community competence is based on the doctrine of implied powers. In the environmental field, the Community competence is also defined by reference to internal measures adopted by the Community. Actually, where the Community competence is explicit, reference to internal measures seems justified only in order to determine whether these measures have not pre-empted the field and whether, as a result, the Community has not become sole competent to intervene exter-

---

[25] This would be particularly the case if the Council were ever to decide to extend the scope of Article 133 (ex 113) to agreements already concluded, such as the WTO; otherwise, the following situation might occur: an agreement on services concluded in the GATS framework would qualify as a commercial agreement in the sense of Article 133 whereas GATS itself would not.

[26] See above, n. 22.

nally. In the area of development cooperation, the Community-specific competence is of a rather limited nature.[27] With respect to monetary matters, the Community holds the dominant role since the establishment of the EMU.

In the absence of explicit Treaty provisions, the doctrine of implied powers applies.[28] As indicated before, the Community competence to conclude international agreements then depends on the prior exercise by the Community of explicit internal powers. Different possibilities exist.[29] First, a Community regulation or directive may explicitly have delegated the task to deal with third countries in areas within the subject-matter of the regulation or directive to the Community. Second, the power to conclude agreements with third countries may result from the fact that Community secondary legislation regulates the situation of third-country nationals in the Community. In the third (and most frequent) case of implied powers, a certain field of activity has been made subject to common rules. Assuming these common rules to be exhaustive and not to leave room for the intervention by the Member States, the Community then becomes exclusively competent to act externally and to conclude agreements with third countries in the area covered by the common rules. However, if the common rules only consist of minimum standards, intervention by the Member States is not precluded. In this case, the Community and the Member States share competences.[30]

Whether or not internal rules are exhaustive and exclude external action by the Member States will often be a subject of debate. A good illustration is provided by the long-standing quarrel between the Commission, on the one hand, and the Council and the Member States, on the other with respect to the so-called 'open-sky' agreements. The Council having refused to give the Commission a new mandate to negotiate with the United States an 'open-sky' agreement on behalf of the Community, the Commission recently decided to bring an action before the Court of Justice

[27] The Community is competent to conclude cooperation agreements with developing countries, based on Article 181 (ex 130y) of the EC Treaty (qualified majority), only in so far as they provide for the establishment of a general framework. If, within that framework, concrete measures have to be taken concerning trade in goods or cultural matters for example, other more specific provisions of the EC Treaty need to be relied on, see *Portugal v. Council*, European Court of Justice, 3 Dec. 1996, Case 268/94 (1996) ECR I-6177.

[28] In Opinion 1/94 (above, n. 17), the Court of Justice took a restrictive view of Article 235 of the EC Treaty (now Article 308), since it made recourse to this legal basis for the conclusion of external agreements subject to the doctrine of implied powers. This means that external agreements can be concluded on the basis of Article 308 only to the extent that their subject matter is already governed by internal rules adopted by reference to the same provision. It is worth mentioning that before Opinion 1/94, the Council had used Article 235 as the legal basis for the agreement between Japan, the United States, Russia, and the EC establishing an International Center for Science and Technology, which had obvious security implications, see Council Regulation 3955/92 of 21 Dec. 1992, 1992 OJ (L 409/1).

[29] See *ERTA* (above, n. 9) and Opinion 1/94 (above, n. 17).

[30] See Opinion 2/91 (ILO), European Court of Justice, 19 Mar. 1993 (1993) ECR I-1061.

against the eight Member States which had concluded bilateral 'open-sky' agreements with the United States. The Commission relies (except in the case concerning the United Kingdom) on the doctrine of implied powers. It claims that the Community was exclusively competent to conclude this type of agreement as a result of the adoption of internal rules in the sector of air transport.[31]

III. THE COMMUNITY PROCEDURES TO CONCLUDE EXTERNAL AGREEMENTS: COMMON ELEMENTS AND DIFFERENCES

Article 300 (formerly Article 228) defines the conditions under which the Community concludes external agreements. Certain conditions apply to all agreements: the Commission makes recommendations to the Council, which then decides to authorize the Commission to open negotiations (in consultation with special committees appointed by the Council and within the framework of directives issued by the latter). The Council is, as a rule, the only organ competent to conclude international agreements. The Court of Justice therefore annulled in 1994 the act by which the Commission had concluded the 1991 agreement with the government of the United States on the application of Community and US competition law.[32] However, under Article 300 (ex 228), para. 4, the Council may delegate to the Commission, subject to conditions it determines, the power to approve modifications where the agreement provides for them to be adopted by a simplified procedure or by a body set up by the agreement. For instance, in the framework of the Mutual Recognition Agreement concluded by the Community and the United States, the Commission has received authority regarding modifications of the sectoral annexes.[33]

Other conditions vary according to the type of agreement. External agreements are normally concluded by the Council acting by a qualified majority. However, the Council is to act unanimously in the case of association agreements or when the agreement covers a field for which unanimity is required for the adoption of internal rules. For example, this will be the case when the Community, relying on the doctrine of implied powers, refers to internal rules based on Article 94 (formerly Article 100) or Article 308 (formerly Article 235). Agreements covering tax matters or the circulation of third-country nationals also require unanimity.

[31] See 1999 OJ (C 71/7).

[32] See *France v. Commission*, European Court of Justice, 3 Aug. 1994, case 327/91, (1994) ECR I-3641.

[33] See Article 3, para. 2, of Council Decision of 22 June 1998 concerning the conclusion of an agreement on mutual recognition between the European Community and the United States of America, 1998 OJ (L 31/1). The agreement was concluded on the basis of Article 113 of the EC Treaty (now Article 133), the commercial policy provision. For the text of the agreement, see 1998 OJ (L 31/3).

The European Parliament plays a more or less important role in the conclusion of external agreements according to the importance of the latter. On agreements of minor importance, the European Parliament is simply to be consulted. This, however, does not apply to commercial agreements. For important agreements, which are defined in Article 300 (formerly 228), the prior assent of the European Parliament has to be obtained. First among those are association agreements based on Article 310 (formerly Article 238) of the EC Treaty, such as, the Lomé IV Convention, the agreement on a European Economic Area or the Europe agreements with Central European countries. In addition, Article 300 provides that agreements establishing a specific institutional framework by organizing cooperation procedures, agreements having important budgetary implications for the Community, and agreements entailing amendment of an act adopted under the so-called co-decision procedure must also receive the Parliament's approval. As the Parliament is not directly involved in the negotiations of international agreements, its influence on the content of such agreements is limited. But, in some cases, it has threatened to use its veto power and even did use it, in order to block the conclusion of agreements with countries where, in its view, human rights were not sufficiently protected.

It is hardly surprising that the existence of significant differences between the procedures leading to the conclusion of international agreements by the Community has given rise to disputes between either the Community institutions themselves (Council, Commission, Parliament) or between the latter and the Member States. The European Parliament understandably tends to interpret the notion of 'commercial agreement' rather narrowly and the notion of 'important agreement' quite broadly. In 1996, in the wake of Opinion 1/94, the Court of Justice annulled, at the Parliament's request, the decision by which the Council had concluded an agreement with the United States relating to public procurement on the ground that the decision had been based solely on Article 113 (now Article 133), the trade policy provision, although the agreement extended to services involving movement of persons.[34] The Council had to rely on additional legal bases which allowed the Parliament to play a role.

Actually, the EC Treaty provides for a specific mechanism to ensure that the Community only concludes agreements which conform to the Treaty both in terms of procedure and in terms of substance. Under Article 300, para. 6 of the Treaty (formerly Article 228, para. 6), the Council, the Commission, or a Member State may consult the Court of Justice on whether an agreement envisaged is compatible with the Treaty. If the opinion of the Court is negative, the agreement may enter into force only

---

[34] See *Parliament v. Council*, European Court of Justice, 7 Mar. 1996, case C-360/93 (1996) ECR I-1195.

after a revision of the Treaty. This procedure has been used in many instances, some of which have already been mentioned. In several cases, the issue that was raised related either to the respective competence of the Community and the Member States or to the proper legal basis for the conclusion of the agreement.[35] There have been other cases, of a more sensitive nature from the standpoint of the Community external relations, where the discussion bore on the very compatibility—in terms of substance—of agreements with the Community institutional structure[36] or with principles of Community law.[37]

It is quite obvious that the preventive procedure provided by Article 300, para. 6 of the Treaty serves its purpose only if the Court of Justice renders its opinion before the date intended for the conclusion of the agreement[38] or if the Community delays its decision to conclude the agreement. Otherwise, the only remedy left is for a Member State or a Community institution to challenge the legality of the decision whereby the agreement was concluded by the Community.[39] This is the only avenue open to the European Parliament since it has been deliberately omitted from the institutions entitled to consult the Court of Justice before agreements are concluded.

IV. INTERNATIONAL AGREEMENTS AND THE COMMUNITY LEGAL ORDER

A. The primacy of international law

The primacy of international law over Community law is, as matter of principle, undisputed. Article 307 (formerly Article 234) of the EC Treaty explicitly provides that its provisions do not affect the rights and obliga-

[35] See Opinion 1/75, (1975) ECR 1355; Opinion 1/78, (1979) ECR 2871; Opinion 2/91 (above, n. 30); Opinion 1/94 (above, n. 17); Opinion 2/92, (1995), ECR I-521; Opinion 2/94, (1996) ECR I-1759. The latter concerned the competence of the European Community to adhere to the European Convention on Human Rights.

[36] See Opinion 1/76, (1977) ECR 741; Opinion 1/91, (1991) ECR I-6079; Opinion 1/92, (1992) ECR I-2821. The two latter opinions concerned the consistency with the EC Treaty of the draft agreement establishing a European Economic Area.

[37] See some of the arguments raised by Germany in its request for an opinion from the Court of Justice on the 1994 'framework agreement' covering trade in bananas between the Community and some third countries. However, the request was ruled inadmissible by the Court of Justice, see Opinion 3/94, (1994) ECR I-4577.

[38] In this regard, the speed with which the Court of Justice rendered its opinion regarding the conclusion of the Uruguay Round package, see Opinion 1/94 (above, n. 17), contrasts with the time it took the Court to proceed with the German request relating to the framework agreement on bananas signed at Marrakech at the same time as the Uruguay Round agreements. This resulted in the Court of Justice declaring the German request inadmissible under Article 228, para. 6 (now Article 300, para. 6), see above n. 37, on the ground that the agreement had already been concluded by the time the Court delivered its opinion.

[39] This is the course which Germany followed in the case of the framework agreement on bananas, see *Germany v. Council*, European Court of Justice, 10 Mar. 1998, case C-122/95, (1998) ECR I-999.

tions arising from agreements concluded before the entry into force of the Treaty by Member States and third countries.[40] Article 300 (formerly Article 228), para. 7 of the Treaty states that agreements concluded by the Community are binding on the Community institutions and on Member States. The primacy of international norms, whether of a customary or of a contractual character, over Community norms has also been acknowledged by the Court of Justice.[41] However, as indicated hereinafter, the superiority of international law over Community law needs to be qualified in certain respects.

B. The consistency of external agreements with the EC Treaty

The Community may conclude agreements with third countries only if they are compatible with the provisions of the EC Treaty and, more generally, with Community law. Normally, this question of compatibility is dealt with before the conclusion of the agreement in the framework of the procedure described above. However, in at least three cases, it was only after the agreement had entered into force that a determination of inconsistency was made by the Court of Justice in the framework of Article 230 (formerly Article 173) proceedings.[42] Even though the Court of Justice only annulled the decisions on the basis of which the Community concluded the agreements in question, without referring to the agreements themselves, this nevertheless did put the Community in a rather awkward position vis-à-vis the other parties to these agreements.[43]

C. The binding character of external agreements on the institutions of the Community and on Member States

Agreements concluded by the Community are binding on the Community institutions and on Member States.[44] That Member States should be bound

---

[40] In case there are incompatibilities between these agreements and Community law, the Member States are invited to seek to eliminate these through appropriate means. When applying agreements pre-dating the Treaty, Member States are also invited to take into account the special nature of the EC Treaty, the implication being that the advantages shared by the Member States under the Treaty ought not to be extended to third countries. In other words, the MFN treatment which Member States may have promised to third countries should be interpreted in the light of the *clausula rebus sic stantibus*.

[41] See *Racke*, European Court of Justice, 16 June 1998, case 162/96, (1998) ECR I-3688; *International Fruit*, European Court of Justice, 12 Dec. 1972, cases 21–24/72, (1972) ECR 1219.

[42] See *France v. Commission* (above, n. 32); *Parliament v. Council* (above, n. 34); *Germany v. Council* (above, n. 39). In the first two cases, the inconsistency concerned the procedure followed by the Community for the conclusion of the agreements. In the third case, and this may seem a more serious matter, the inconsistency was between a part of the agreement and the Community principle of non-discrimination.

[43] See below.

[44] See EC Treaty, Article 300, para. 7, whose full text reads as follows: 'Agreements concluded *under the conditions set out in this Article* shall be binding on the institutions of the

by international commitments undertaken by the Community is but logical. If Member States do not comply with agreements concluded by the Community, the latter will be responsible vis-à-vis third countries for such non-compliance.

In the context of the Community legal order, external agreements are treated as acts of the Community institutions.[45] As such, their interpretation and their enforcement are governed by the usual procedures provided by the EC Treaty. The fact that external agreements are ultimately interpreted by the Court of Justice helps to ensure the external coherence of the internal market. This was indeed the reason why the Court of Justice ruled that it was competent to interpret the GATT of 1947 in so far as it could affect the Community legal order, despite the fact that the GATT of 1947 was not an act of the Community institutions, since it had not been ratified by the Community, which did not even exist in 1947.[46]

Community measures not in conformity with agreements concluded by the Community or with customary international law can be challenged through the procedures provided by the EC Treaty in order to control the legality of Community measures.[47] Private individuals on several occasions,[48] and Member States much less frequently,[49] have indeed challenged the legality of Community measures on the ground that they were not in conformity with the Community international obligations.

Community and on Member States' (emphasis added). The qualification resulting from the words 'under the conditions . . .' should be understood by reference to the Community institutional framework. It cannot mean that external agreements concluded by the Community without complying with one of the conditions prescribed by Article 228 are not binding on the Community and its Member States as a matter of international law. In the three cases previously mentioned—*France v. Commission* (above, n. 32); *Parliament v. Council* (above, n. 34); *Germany v. Council* (above, n. 39)—where decisions relating to the conclusion of external agreements were annulled by the Court of Justice, the latter did not deal with the issue. On this issue, see Christine Kaddous, 'L'arrêt *France c. Commission* de 1994 (Accord concurrence) et le contrôle de la "légalité" des accords externes en vertu de l'article 173 CE: la difficile réconciliation de l'orthodoxie communautaire avec l'orthodoxie internationale', *Cahiers de droit européen* (1996), 613–33.

[45] See *Haegeman*, European Court of Justice, 30 Apr. 1974, case 181/73, (1974) ECR 449.

[46] See *International Fruit* (above, n. 41); *Michelin*, European Court of Justice, 16 Mar. 1983, cases 267–269/81, (1983) ECR 801.

[47] See Articles 230 (formerly Article 173), 234 (formerly Article 177), and 241 (formerly Article 184) of the EC Treaty.

[48] See, for instance, *International Fruit* (above, n. 41); *Fediol v. Commission*, European Court of Justice, 22 June 1989, case 70/87, (1989) ECR 1787; *Nakajima v. Council*, European Court of Justice, 7 May 1991, case 69/89, (1991) ECR I-2069; *N.M.B. v. Commission*, European Court of Justice, 10 Mar. 1992, case 188/88, (1992) ECR I-1689. See also, on the conformity of Community measures with customary international law, *Alström (Wood Pulp)*, European Court of Justice, 27 Sept. 1988, joint cases 89, 104, 114, 116, 117, and 125 to 129/85, (1988) ECR 5193. *Opel Austria*, Court of First Instance, 22 Jan. 1997, case T-115/94, (1997) ECR II-43; *Racke*, European Court of Justice, 16 June 1998, case C-162/96, (1998) ECR 1998 I-3688.

[49] See *Germany v. Council (Bananas)*, European Court of Justice, 5 Oct. 1994, case C-280/93, (1994) ECR I-4973; *Italy v. Council*, European Court of Justice, 12 Nov. 1998, case C-352/96, (1998) ECR I-6937.

To secure conformity of measures taken by Member States with Community agreements, the Commission may rely on infringement proceedings.[50] Actually, the Commission has not often resorted to infringement proceedings for that purpose.[51] There is perhaps an understandable reason for this: violations by Member States of the Community's international obligations may engage the international responsibility of the Community itself. The issue is of practical importance when a dispute-settlement mechanism exists at the international level, such as for instance in the WTO framework.[52]

On the basis of former Article 177 (now Article 234), national courts, for their part, have referred a significant number of questions which concerned possible conflicts between national measures and bilateral or multilateral agreements concluded by the Community to the Court of Justice.[53]

D. The effectiveness of Community agreements in the Community legal order

At the international level, the effectiveness of agreements concluded by the Community depends on whether or not there is an effective dispute-settlement mechanism as recent cases brought against the Community before the WTO illustrate. In the Community context, the effectiveness of agreements concluded by the Community depends, first, on whether the provisions of these agreements will be given direct effect or at least can be invoked before a court and, second, on how these provisions will be interpreted in terms of substance.

The Court of Justice has given direct effect to the provisions of several preferential agreements concluded by the Community.[54] However, the Court consistently denied direct effect to the provisions of GATT 1947. The latter could be invoked before a court only if Community legislation either

---

[50] See Article 226 (formerly Article 169) of the EC Treaty.

[51] See *Commission v. Greece*, European Court of Justice, 21 June 1988, case 127/87 (1988) ECR 3545; *Commission v. Greece*, European Court of Justice, 14 Oct. 1992, case C-65/91, (1992) ECR I-5245; *Commission v. Italy*, European Court of Justice, 25 May 1993, case C-228/91, (1993) ECR I-2701. In these three cases, the violation of a Community agreement was only one of the grounds on which the Article 169 proceeding was based.

[52] See, nevertheless, *Commission v. Germany* (*International Dairy Agreement*), European Court of Justice, case C-61/94, (1996) ECR I-3989. This case raised the interesting issue of whether the Commission could bring an infringement proceeding against a Member State for not complying with a Community agreement when Community legislation itself was perhaps not in conformity with the agreement. This issue is dealt with in the submissions of Advocate General Tesauro. The Court of Justice ruled that Community legislation was in conformity with the agreement.

[53] There have been more than twenty-five such referrals.

[54] One of the few instances where it refused to declare a provision of a preferential agreement directly applicable was the *Demirel* case (above, n. 21), where the issue concerned the right of Turkish workers to free circulation.

intended to implement GATT provisions or referred to the latter.[55] The Court of Justice has recently decided that the same case law, which reciprocity considerations underlie, had to be followed with respect to WTO provisions.[56]

Assuming that provisions of external agreements are either given direct effect or, at least, can be invoked under certain circumstances, their effectiveness in the Community legal order (in relation to Community law or to Member States law) will still depend on how they are construed by the Court of Justice. The practice of the Court indicates that provisions of external agreements are not necessarily given the same broad interpretation as identical or similar provisions of the EC Treaty.[57] The underlying rationale is that agreements with third countries, with the exception of the European Economic Area, are not meant to liberalize trade and other economic exchanges or to free movements of persons to the same extent as the EC Treaty.

Thus, with respect to agreements that the United States and the European Community might conclude for the purpose of implementing the Transatlantic Economic Partnership, two issues arise. The first is whether the Court of Justice would give direct effect to provisions of such agreements or would rather apply its GATT/WTO case law concerning

[55] See in particular *International Fruit* (above, n. 41), *Fediol* (above, n. 48), *Nakajima* (above, n. 48), *N.M.B.* (above, n. 48), and *Germany v. Council* (*Bananas*) (above, n. 49).

[56] See *Portugal v. Council*, 23 Nov. 1999, case C-149/96, not yet reported. This is the first case where the question of whether WTO provisions, including the GATT 1994, are capable of producing a direct effect was squarely addressed by the Court of Justice. Before, in *Hermes* (16 June 1998), case C-53/96, (1998) ECR I-3637, the Court answered a question concerning the interpretation of Article 50 of the TRIPs agreement, after bypassing the issue of direct effect. In *Italy v. Council* (above, n. 49), where the question concerned the interpretation of Article XXIV §6 of GATT 1994 and Article 5 of the Memorandum on Understanding, the Court followed the *Nakajima* approach (cited above, n. 48), considering that through the adoption of a regulation the Community had intended to implement a GATT obligation.

[57] On association agreements with ACP countries (the Yaounde and Lomé Conventions) and trade in goods, see *Bresciani*, 5 Feb. 1976, case 65/77, (1976) ECR 129; *Chiquita*, 12 Dec. 1995, case C-469/93, (1995) ECR I-4553.

On the association agreement with Turkey and the rights of workers, see *Demirel* (above, n. 21) and *Sevince*, 20 Sept. 1990, case C-192/89, (1990) ECR C-3641.

On the cooperation agreements with Maghreb countries and the right of workers to equal treatment, see *Bahia Kziber*, 21 Jan. 1991, case 18/90, (1991) ECR I-199, confirmed by several other judgments.

On respectively the association agreements with *Greece* and *Cyprus* and trade in goods, see *Pabst&Richarz*, 24 Sept. 1982, case 17/81, (1982) ECR 1331, and *Anastasiou*, 4 July 1994, case C-432/92, (1994) ECR I-3087.

On the free trade agreements of 1973 with EFTA countries and trade in goods, see and compare on the one hand, *Polydor*, 2 Feb. 1982, case 270/80, (1982) ECR 329; *Kupferberg*, 26 Oct. 1982, case 104/81, (1982) ECR 3641; *Metalsa*, 1 July 1993, case C-312/91, (1993) ECR 3751; and, on the other hand, *Legros*, 16 July 1992, case C-163/90, (1993) ECR I-4625; *Commission v. Italy*, 25 May 1993, case C-228/91, (1993) ECR I-2701; and *Eurim-Pharm*, 1 July 1993, case C-207/91, (1993) ECR I-3723.

On the agreement establishing the European Economic Area, see *Opel Austria* (above, n. 48).

invocability. The answer probably depends on how effective the United States and the European Community will want the agreements to be. The second is the extent to which the Court of Justice would give a liberal, i.e. a pro-free trade, interpretation of the provisions of transatlantic agreements. Here the answer is probably that the Court of Justice would not go beyond its former case law relating to free trade agreements with EFTA countries (before the EEA). Indeed, it is not the intention of the Community to fully share the internal market *acquis* with the United States, some Member States being strongly opposed to such idea.

E. The consistency of agreements between Member States and third countries with Community law

External agreements which Member States conclude with third countries have to be in conformity with the EC Treaty and EC secondary legislation. For instance, in 1999, the Commission brought infringement proceedings against some Member States on the ground that they had entered into bilateral agreements with the United States in the field of air transport which were not in conformity with Community law.[58] Assuming the Court of Justice were to rule in favour of the Commission, the agreements would have to be renegotiated and, if this were to prove unfeasible, the Member States would have to denounce the agreements.

V. THE MIXING OF COMMUNITY AND MEMBER STATES COMPETENCE IN THE EXTERNAL FIELD: NATIONAL SOVEREIGNTY, LEGAL LOGIC, AND THE NEED FOR COHERENCE

A. Mixed agreements

Quite often, agreements with third countries are concluded by both the Community and the Member States. Almost all important agreements have been concluded under this mixed procedure, including certain agreements of a purely commercial nature such as commodity agreements, which at first sight would seem to fall within the Community's exclusive domain.[59] Mixed agreements can enter into force only after all the Member States have completed their ratification procedures (except for the commercial part of the agreements which falls within the Community's exclusive competence).

[58] See, in particular, the Article 169 (now Article 226) proceedings initiated by the Commission against eight Member States which have concluded 'open-sky' agreements with the United States, 1999 OJ (C 71/7–13).

[59] See the Proba 20 arrangement concluded between the Commission and the Council following Opinion 1/78.

Technical considerations can be invoked in order to justify the mixed procedure. In some cases, the competence of the Community and that of Member States overlap in relation to all or part of the subject matters covered by the agreement. This will be so in areas of shared competence. In other cases, the participation of Member States is due to the fact that parts of the agreement are not within the Community external competence. This may be the case because certain subject matters are outside the scope of the Treaty, criminal law for example. But this may also be the case because the Community has not yet exercised its internal competence. Thus, it may not yet rely on the doctrine of implied powers, even though the subject matter is potentially within its external competence.

These technical explanations carry some weight. However, the use of other, equally convincing, lines of reasoning could, in some instances, lead to the conclusion that the Community is competent to act alone. Many will agree that the conclusion of international agreements according to the mixed procedure has a political explanation. Most Member States are not ready to leave the international stage, which would be the case if the Community were to conclude alone agreements of high international visibility. A good illustration is provided by the Uruguay Round agreements and the establishment of the WTO. The Uruguay Round agreements obviously concerned trade matters and they had a direct bearing on the European internal market. But a majority of Member States wanted to participate in their conclusion. The Court of Justice in Opinion 1/94[60] ruled in their favour and against the Commission which, for its part, had considered that the Community was exclusively competent to conclude the Uruguay Round agreements. The reasoning followed by the Court of Justice in Opinion 1/94 (and subsequently in Opinion 2/92,[61] concerning the OECD decision on national treatment of foreign direct investments), has disturbing implications for the external coherence of the European Union.

The Court could have declared that the Community was not yet exclusively competent to conclude the Uruguay Round agreements in their entirety and that the Member States were still entitled to intervene since, for some parts of these agreements, the Community and the Member States shared competence. This was indeed the reasoning which the Court seems to have followed in Opinion 2/91 (concerning the conclusion of an ILO agreement).[62] There, it stressed the fact that the Community and the Member States were jointly competent to conclude the agreement.

In Opinion 1/94, however, the Court explicitly stated that the Community had not yet acquired the competence necessary to conclude significant parts of the GATS and TRIPs agreements. In other words, Member States were not simply entitled, but had to take part in the con-

---

[60] Cited above, n. 17.   [61] Cited above, n. 35.   [62] Cited above, n. 30.

clusion of the Uruguay Round agreements in order to compensate for the absence of Community competence in relation to parts of the GATS and TRIPs agreements. Such a reasoning logically implies that parts of the Uruguay Round agreements would not (yet) constitute Community law. This raises difficult questions: how then to secure the unitary representation of the European Union in the WTO, the uniform interpretation of WTO law throughout the Member States, the effective use by the European Union of the WTO cross-retaliation mechanism, or Member States compliance with WTO law?

Article 10 (formerly Article 5), first sentence, of the EC Treaty, of course, requires Member States to 'take all appropriate measures . . . to ensure fulfilment of the obligations arising out of the (EC) Treaty or resulting from action taken by the institutions of the Community', but this plainly refers to obligations resulting from Community law and presupposes Community competence, which, according to the Court of Justice, is precisely lacking. However, the second sentence of Article 10 (formerly Article 5) of the Treaty also commands Member States to 'abstain from any measure which could jeopardize the attainment of the objectives of the Treaty'. On the basis of Article 10, second sentence, an argument might perhaps be built which would run as follows: The external completion of the internal market can be seen as an objective of the Community, which Member States should not jeopardize by intervening alone in those areas where the Community is not yet competent, for lack of internal measures, i.e. where Community competence is not per se excluded, but remains provisionally of a potential nature.

It is interesting to note that, in its *Hermes* judgment,[63] the Court of Justice, when confronted with the risk that the TRIPs agreement would not be uniformly interpreted throughout the Community, managed to sidestep the logical consequences stemming from its Opinion 1/94 reasoning. The negative consequences arising from Opinion 1/94 with regard to the external coherence of the European Union in the WTO framework have also been minimized because, when ratifying the WTO agreements, the Community and the Member States did not indicate their respective competence in relation to these agreements. However, the Community and the Member States have still not succeeded in agreeing on a code of conduct in order to ensure that they speak with one voice in the WTO. A code of conduct[64] is needed since, except in the monetary field,[65] the EC Treaty

[63] 16 June 1998, case C-53/96, (1998) ECR I-3637.

[64] A code of conduct was established to determine the respective role of the Community and the Member States in the FAO, but the Court of Justice was called on to settle a dispute between the Council and the Commission regarding the interpretation of the arrangement, see *Commission v. Council*, European Court of Justice, 19 Mar. 1996, case C-25/94, (1996) ECR I-1469.

[65] See Article 111, para. 4.

does not provide a mechanism for that purpose, Article 116 of the EEC Treaty having been abrogated as a result of the Maastricht Treaty.[66]

The preceding discussion has obvious implications for the Transatlantic Economic Partnership to the extent its implementation were to be pursued through the WTO framework or through bilateral agreements between the United States and the Community to which Member States would be party. Things would change, however, if the Council were to decide to negotiate and conclude future agreements dealing with services or intellectual property rights on the sole basis of the new Article 133.[67]

B. The 'mixing' of intergovernmental cooperation and Community measures

In addition to mixed agreements, there is another form of 'mixity'. In certain sectors, measures are taken on the basis of the EC Treaty only after the Council, acting unanimously, has adopted a decision based on the second pillar (CESP) of the TEU. Economic sanctions and the regime applicable to the exportation of dual-use goods offer good examples. In these cases, the policy decision is taken in an intergovernmental framework. It is then implemented through an instrument provided by the EC Treaty, respectively Article 301 (formerly Article 228a) in the case of sanctions and Article 133 (formerly Article 113) in the case of dual-use goods.

In the transatlantic context, the dispute between the European Union and the United States concerning the Helms–Burton legislation provides another illustration of this kind of 'mixity'. The European Union first adopted countermeasures, some based on the EC Treaty, others on the second pillar.[68] It then negotiated with the United States through a delegation comprising representatives of the Community and of all the Member States.

VI. CONCLUSION

The editors of this volume have asked the contributors to focus their attention on the institutional implications arising from the Transatlantic Economic Partnership for the United States and for the European Union. However, I would like to emphasize that probably the most important

---

[66] Article 116 of the EC Treaty which could have served to ensure the external coherence of the common market (even outside the 'commercial field' in the sense of Article 133), was seldom used. Even though its potential usefulness had in no way been exhausted with the passing of time, Article 116 was deleted from the Treaty. This is a rare instance of European economic integration moving backwards.

[67] See above, text accompanying n. 25.

[68] See Council Regulation of 22 Nov. 1996, 1996 OJ (L 309/1), and Common Action of 22 Nov. 1996, ibid., L 309/7.

implications arising from transatlantic regulatory cooperation are for the WTO and the multilateral trade system. The development of transatlantic regulatory cooperation will not immediately and directly affect the structure of the European Union or what one might call the Community constitution. Most Member States would not accept that nor would the European Court of Justice.

This is not to say that transatlantic cooperation will have no influence on the European Union. If transatlantic cooperation does develop, this will compel the European Union to behave more coherently in external matters and, in particular, to complete the external dimension of the Single European market. However, this is not likely to happen overnight. Some Member States do not favour a global approach of the kind exemplified by the failed New Transatlantic Marketplace Initiative. They think that to proceed on the basis of too general a framework might give the United States undue influence on the future development of the internal market.

Most particularly in external affairs, the majority of Member States are not ready, at present, to accept broad transfers of sovereignty made on a permanent basis to the Community. They are, however, quite willing to use the European Community as an instrument to get better access to markets of third countries or to act as a shield when they are the target of US complaints before the WTO or of US unilateral action as in the case of the Helms–Burton legislation.

The development of the external dimension of the Single European market will likely continue to proceed in a piecemeal manner. Community external powers will grow in parallel with the widening and deepening of the internal *acquis communautaire*, as they have done over the years. To a more limited extent, they may also grow as a result of the building up of what one could call a few years from now the *acquis transatlantique*. Indeed, efficient transatlantic regulatory cooperation will require the European Union to act more and more through the European Community.

The implementation of transatlantic regulatory initiatives in Europe

Reimer von Borries

I. IMPLEMENTATION OF INTERNATIONAL AGREEMENTS IN THE EUROPEAN UNION

A. Preliminary remark

This contribution deals with various aspects of the implementation of international agreements within the European Community, as opposed to problems concerning the conclusion of such agreements by the European Community. It is concerned with interface in the sense of the impact and the consequences of international agreements in the internal legal order of the European Union (EU), in particular those to be concluded within the framework of the Transatlantic Economic Partnership (TEP). My purpose is not to offer new visions of European unity or of transatlantic cooperation but to describe procedures and problems as they may arise with regard to the implementation of the TEP programme and action plan.

Obviously it is important to know which are the rules governing the implementation of TEP agreements, and such knowledge should be taken into account in the process of concluding such agreements. Implementation within the European Community means implementation by the European Community and by the Member States, not by the *European Union*, because the European Union—unlike the European Community—is not an international organization endowed with legal personality. The European Union is only a legal framework comprising the three Communities and the cooperation of the Member States in foreign and security policy as well as in police and criminal matters. The European Union is, in other words, only a common legal order, created by the EU Treaty. This is at least the prevailing view in Germany and, in particular, the view of the German Federal Government, even after the entry into force of the Treaty of Amsterdam on 1 May 1999.[1]

---

[1] Matthias Pechstein and Christian Koenig, *Die Europäische Union: Die Verträge von Maastricht und Amsterdam*, 2nd edn. (Tuebingen: I. C. B. Mohr, 1998), 55; Stefan Kadelbach, 'Einheit der Rechtsordnung als Verfassungsprinzip der Europäischen Union?', in Armin von Bogdandy and Claus-Dieter Ehlermann (eds), *Konsolidierung und Kohärenz des Primärrechts nach Amsterdam*, Europarecht Beiheft, nr. 2 (1998), 51.

B. Delimitation of EC and Member States' competences with regard to international agreements

The distribution of competences between the European Community and its Member States is of considerable importance not only for the conclusion, but also for the implementation, of international agreements to which the European Community is a party. Unlike states which (at least potentially) have all-encompassing competences, the European Community has only limited competences (Article 5, sect. 1 EC Treaty).[2] This is equally true for international agreements and internal legislation. It is a fundamental rule of EC law that the EC's range of competences with regard to international agreements does not extend beyond its internal competences.[3]

It follows from this system of distribution of competences among the European Community and the Member States that, if the content of an envisaged international agreement extends beyond the limits of Community competence, the agreement cannot be concluded exclusively by the European Community. Rather the Member States also have to become party to the argument for those provisions which exceed the EC competences.[4] From the point of view of EC law, the agreement then comprises two parts: an EC part and a 'national' part. In the EC terminology, this situation is characterized by the term 'mixed agreements'.[5] Such agreements could also be termed 'EU agreements' (as opposed to pure EC agreements) but this would perhaps lead to confusion since in a non-legal context the term European Union is often used as a substitute for the term European Community. The negotiation, conclusion, and implementation of mixed agreements is obviously much more complicated as compared to pure EC agreements.[6]

C. Specific problems of the implementation of 'mixed agreements'

It is safe to assume that the agreements which will be concluded in the framework of TEP will to a considerable extent be 'mixed agreements'.

---

[2] Hans-Peter Krausser, *Das Prinzip begrenzter Ermächtigung im Gemeinschaftsrecht als Strukturprinzip des EWG-Vertrages*, 1991; Hans D. Jarass, *Die Kompetenzverteilung zwischen der Europäischen Gemeinschaft und den Mitgliedstaaten*, AöR 121 (1996), 173.

[3] Thomas Oppermann, *Europarecht*, 2nd edn (Munich: Verlag C. H. Beck 1999), 723.

[4] Ibid. 723.

[5] Ibid.; Albert Bleckmann, *Europarecht. Das Recht der Europäischen Union und der Europäischen Gemeinschaften*, 6th edn (Cologne, Berlin, Bonn, and Munich: Carl Heymanns Verlag, 1997), 513; Christian Tomuschat in Hans von der Groeben, Jochen Thiesing, and Claus-Dieter Ehlermann (eds), *Kommentar zum EU-/EG-Vertrag* 5th edn (Baden-Baden: Nomos-Verlag, 1997), Commentary to Article 228, no. 24, 48, 55, and 77 (GTE); Christoph Vedder in Eberhard Grabitz and Meinhard Hilf (eds), *Kommentar zur Europaeischen Union*, 3rd edn, Article 228, nos. 18 and 55 (Grabitz/Hilf). As of 1 January 1999 the EC had concluded about 600 bilateral agreements 100 of which were mixed agreements, and 135 multilateral agreements 122 of which were mixed agreements.

[6] Oppermann, *Europarecht* (above , n. 3), 738.

With respect to their implementation, a distinction is therefore necessary between the area of competence of the EC on the one hand ('EC part', subsection 1 below), and of the Member States on the other ('national part', subsection 2 below).

1. Implementation of the EC part

According to Article 300(7) (ex 228(7)) of the EC Treaty, international agreements concluded by the European Community within the scope of its competences are binding not only on the institutions of the European Community themselves but also on the Member States. They are an 'integral part of Community Law'[7] and have priority over secondary Community law.[8] Secondary law has therefore to be interpreted in conformity with international agreements if possible. Since international agreements become 'the law of the land' by their adoption, a 'transformation' by a specific legislative act of the European Community (other than that necessary for their adoption or ratification) is not necessary for their validity.[9] The impact of international agreements is therefore governed by the principle of monism whereas several Member States such as the Federal Republic of Germany adhere to the principle of dualism.[10] A consequence of the 'monistic' approach of Article 300(7) is that the provisions of an international agreement concluded by the European Community do not necessarily require implementing legislation. Furthermore, whenever provisions of such an agreement are clear, unequivocal, and unconditional they are 'self-executing' both at the level of the Member States and the European Community, or, in terms of EC law, ' directly applicable'.[11] However, if the provisions of an agreement are not clear and unequivocal or subject to conditions or if they require further action by the Community in order to be applicable, additional internal provisions must be adopted by the EC for their implementation and application.[12]

These additional provisions may either take the form of a regulation which is 'binding in its entirety and directly applicable in all Member States' (EC Treaty Article 249, ex 189) or of a directive which is 'binding,

---

[7] Case 181/73, *Haegeman*, 1974 ECR 449, 460; Case 87/75, *Bresciani*, 1976 ECR 129, 140; Vedder in Grabitz and Hilf (eds), (above, n. 5), Article 228, no. 45; Tomuschat in GTE (above, n. 5), Article 228, no. 74.

[8] Case C-61/94, *Commission v. Germany*, 1996 ECR I-3989.

[9] Oppermann, *Europarecht* (above, n. 3), 741; Tomuschat in GTE (above, n. 5), Artice 228, no. 59.

[10] Rudolf Geiger, *Grundgesetz und Völkerrecht*, 2nd edn (Munich: C. H. Beck-Verlag, 1994), 195; for a different view see Vedder in Grabitz and Hilf (eds), (above, n. 5), Art. 228, no. 45 and Tomuschat in GTE (above, n. 5), Art. 228, no. 59/60: Article 228 follows neither a pure monistic nor a pure dualistic approach.

[11] Oppermann, *Europarecht*, (above, n. 3), 742; *Geiger* (above, n. 9), 197; for the internal Community law already in the Case 26/62, *Van Gend and Loos*, 1963 ECR 1, 25; for international agreements Case 21–24/72, *International Fruit*, 1972 ECR 1219, 1228; Case 104/81, *Kupferberg*, ECR 1982 3641, 3664.

[12] Tomuschat in GTE (above, n. 5), Art. 228, no. 72.

as to the result to be achieved, upon each Member State to which it is addressed, but . . . leaves to the national authorities the choice of form and methods' (Article 249, ex 189). In the case of directives, implementation therefore requires the transformation of the agreement into the internal law of the Member States, normally by way of a legislative act of the national parliaments.[13] In practice, the Member States adopt the contents of the directive into a new statute or adapt an existing law. Whenever rights and duties or legal interests of individuals are at stake, a formal legislative *act* is necessary in the interest of legal certainty. An administrative decree would not be sufficient.[14]

As a practical example the case of the WTO Agreement on Public Procurement may be cited, which falls under EC competence. In order to implement this agreement, the form of a directive has been chosen by the European Community because the agreement concerned the substance of administrative decisions within the competence of Member State authorities. Their procurement laws hence had to be adapted to the WTO rules.[15] The Mutual Recognition Agreement (MRA) on conformity assessment between the European Community and the United States does not require additional measures by the European Community in order to ensure its implementation. However, it seems to necessitate certain administrative measures by the Member States which they must take in accordance with their obligation 'to take all appropriate measures . . . to ensure fulfilment of the obligations arising out of this Treaty or resulting from action taken by the institutions of the Community' (EC Treaty Article 10(ex 5)).

It has to be emphasized in this context that, as a rule, EC law is carried out by the Member States and only exceptionally by the European Community itself (see the important Declaration no. 43 to the final act of the Intergovernmental Conference of Amsterdam of 17 June 1997 on the administrative execution of Community law). This is true both for international agreements and for internal Community legislation. Even in the area of customs, which falls within the exclusive competence of the European Community, levying the customs duties is the task of the national customs authorities. This is a point in which the European Community differs from the United States where at all levels, national and local, the Federal Government has its own administrative apparatus alongside those of the individual states. This contribution proceeds, therefore, on the assumption that the Member States are principally responsible for the implementation of international agreements of the European Community.

---

[13] Bleckmann, *Europarecht. Das Recht der Europäischen Union* (above, n. 5), 171.

[14] See, for example, Case 29/84, *Commission v. Germany*, 1985 ECR 1667; Case C-433/93, *Commission v. Germany*, 1995 ECR I-2303.

[15] Directive 80/767/EEC, 1980 OJ (L 215/1), revised by Directive 88/295/EEC, 1988 OJ (L 127/1).

2. *Implementation of the 'national part'*

If the contents of an international agreement exceed the EC competences and the Member States are therefore party to the agreement, this implies their direct obligation to implement the respective part of the agreement. This obligation arises out of international law. However, they are equally obliged by EC law to implement the agreement because without the implementation of the national part the agreement as a whole would not be effectively implemented. The EC would be held liable for violation of its international obligations as well, since mixed agreements bind the European Community and the Member States indistinctly vis-à-vis third countries.

If no particular difficulties exist, the Member States will implement the agreement autonomously and separately. If, however, a problem of interpretation or application of the respective provisions arises, the Member States are obliged under EC law to discuss the matter at the EC level with the European Commission and the other Member States in order to ensure a coherent application of the agreement throughout the whole area of the European Community ('obligation to ensure coherence').[16] The interpretation of a 'mixed' agreement may also be important in the context of legal proceedings before national courts. In such cases, the courts may apply to the European Court of Justice for a preliminary ruling on this issue (EC Treaty Article 234, ex 177). The question arises then as to whether or not the European Court of Justice's jurisdiction extends to the interpretation of those provisions of an international agreement which fall into the competence of the Member States (see below).

D. Direct effect of international agreements within the European Union

As mentioned above, international agreements of the EC can be self-executing or directly applicable. This means that individuals may refer to these provisions before national courts and even before administrative authorities of the Member States. According to the European Court of Justice, a provision can be applied directly if it is sufficiently clear and unequivocal and not subject to any conditions.[17]

The Court has applied this principle many times to international agreements, for example with respect to certain free trade and cooperation agreements[18] and also with respect to decisions of institutions created by

---

[16] Opinion 1/94 of the ECJ, 1994 ECR I-5267 *WTO*.

[17] Case 12/86, *Demirel i*, 1987 ECR 3747.

[18] Case 104/81, *Kupferberg*, 1982 ECE 3641/3665; Case C-18/90, *Kziber*, 1991 ECR I-221/226; Case C-113/97, *Babahenini*, 1998 ECR I-183; Gerhard Bebr, *Agreements concluded by the Community and their possible direct effect: From International Fruit Company to Kupferberg*, 1983 CMLR 35; Antonio Caeiros, *L'effet direct des accords internationaux conclus par la CEE*, Revue du Marché Commun 1984, 526.

association agreements, such as those taken by the Association Council set up by the agreement between the European Community and Turkey.[19] On the other hand, the Court has denied direct applicability to the provisions of the GATT 1947, not as a matter of principle (because it is regarded as a 'political question'), but because in its view the specific terms of the relevant provisions are not sufficiently clear and unequivocal and are therefore not suitable for direct applicability.[20] This is also the view of the German Federal Government,[21] which seems convincing if one reads the provisions of the GATT 1947 carefully and without preconceived ideas. However, this issue is still a matter of controversy among academics in Europe, especially in Germany.[22] It remains to be seen how the Court will assess the (identical) provisions of the GATT 1997 in this respect, especially in cases in which the rights and obligations of the parties have been clarified by decisions of the appellate body.

The recognition of a direct effect of an international agreement by the European Court of Justice does not depend on reciprocity.[23] The situation is more complicated in the case of a 'mixed agreement' when the Member States are competent both for the conclusion and for the implementation of a given part of the agreement. In this case, one could assume that the Member States are also competent for the recognition and the refusal of direct applicability of the respective provisions, and it is conceivable that their courts may take different attitudes. This may become relevant with respect to certain provisions of the TRIPs agreement although the Council of the EU, in the preamble to the decision by which it adopted the WTO agreement, has expressly excluded direct applicability for all parts of the WTO agreement.[24]

A further complication results from the fact that the European Court of Justice seems to claim competence for the interpretation of international agreements not only with respect to the provisions falling under EC competence but also to those for which competence rests with the Member States. This is the impression which one could gain from reading the decision of the Court in the *Demirel* case which concerned the provisions of the Association Agreement between the European Community and Turkey

---

[19] Case C-192/89, *Sevince*, 1990 ECR I-3497/3502; Case C-237/91, *Kus*, 1992 ECR I-6807/6811; Case C-277/94, *Taflan-Met*, 1996 ECR I-4085.

[20] Case 21-24/72, *International Fruit*, 1972 ECR 1219; Case C-280/93, 1994 ECR I-5039, 5072 *Germany v. Council*; for a critical view see (among others) Tomuschat in GTE (above, n. 5), Art. 228, nos. 64–8; Meinhard Hilf, 'The Role of National Courts in International Trade Relations', *Michigan Journal of International Law* (1997), 321.

[21] Answer of the Federal Government to a written parliamentary question of MP Kurt Neumann of 30 Mar. 1998.

[22] See, for example, Tomuschat in GTE (above, n. 5), Article 228, no. 68.

[23] Ibid., Article 228, no. 67; Vedder in Grabitz and Hilf (eds), (above, n. 5), Article 228, no. 48.

[24] See the last indent of the preamble of the Decision of the Council of 21 Dec. 1994, 1994 OJ (L 336).

on free movement of workers, which are within the competence of the Member States.[25]

It should be added that the Court consistently, and rightly, takes the view that the direct effect of a provision of Community law does not relieve the European Community and the Member States from their obligation to take action for the implementation of the respective legal act. This jurisprudence, motivated by the principle of legal certainty, also applies to international agreements concluded by the European Community.

E. Application of fundamental principles of Community law

Just as any state can act on the international level only in conformity with its constitution, the European Community is obliged to take its own fundamental principles of law into consideration not only in adopting internal legal acts ('secondary law') but also in concluding international agreements. This means that at the international level the European Community may act only within the limits provided by the principles laid down in the EC Treaty. Part of this 'primary law' of the European Community are the general principles of Community law developed by the European Court of Justice, and especially the fundamental rights of individuals.[26] Furthermore, the European Community is obliged to take into account the so-called 'Four Freedoms' of the European internal market which comprise of the freedom of movement of goods, of persons, of services, and of capital within the European Community. If the European Community fails to respect these principles in concluding an international agreement there will be a gap between its international obligations and its internal legal order. By disregarding the provisions of an international agreement which contradicts primary law at the implementation stage the European Community would of course violate the EC's international obligations vis-à-vis the other contracting parties. This would in turn create difficulties for the internal market. In order to avoid such a dilemma, the European Community must take its internal law into consideration when concluding an international agreement and must refrain from concluding agreements which are not compatible with these principles.

In this context, the question arises whether the subsidiarity principle, which is a part of the Community's primary law, may be relevant for international agreements.[27] Certainly, the subsidiarity principle plays an important role at the stage of the conclusion of international agreements

---

[25] Case 12/86, *Demirel*, 1987 ECR 3747; however, the ECJ may interpret the Community part of a mixed agreement in the context of the whole agreement. Tomuschat in GTE (above, n. 5), Article 228, no. 88.

[26] Case 4/73, *Nold*, 1974 ECR 491; Case 44/79, *Hauer*, 1979 ECR 3927.

[27] Reimer von Borries, 'Das Subsidiaritätsprinzip im Recht der Europäischen Union', *Europarecht* (1994), 263, 281–2.

where there is no exclusive competence of the European Community. In most cases, however, the European Community engages in the conclusion of international agreements only in fields where it has exclusive competence, either on the basis of the EC Treaty itself or on the basis of secondary law.[28] In any case, the subsidiarity principle is not applicable with respect to the implementation of international agreements which the Community has concluded within the limits of its competences. Besides, there is no need to apply this principle because Community law as a rule is administered by the Member States, and not by the Community itself. This does not only apply to the execution of Community powers but constitutes a general principle of the distribution of competences among the European Community and its Member States.

F. Implementation procedures at Community and national level

1. Community level

Whereas the EC Treaty contains special provisions for the conclusion of international agreements by the Community (especially Article 300), it lacks rules concerning their implementation. Therefore, the general rules for the implementation of Community legal acts apply: If the implementation of an international agreement requires further action at the Community level and either a directive or a regulation must therefore be enacted, it is adopted in conformity with the normal rules of internal Community legislation.

(a) The European Community may adopt a directive for the purpose of adapting national law to the provisions of an international agreement on the basis of the provisions of the EC Treaty regarding the approximation of laws (Article 94, ex 100), as it did in the case of the GATT agreement on government procurement. Directives under Article 94 are subject to the so-called co-decision procedure provided for in Article 251 (ex 189b) of the EC Treaty. This procedure requires the proposal of the European Commission to be accepted both by the Council of the European Union and the European Parliament with the majorities provided for in the EC Treaty. The Member States are then obliged to adapt their national laws to the provisions of the directive within a certain time limit.

(b) Alternatively, the Community may enact a regulation on the basis of Article 94. However, whenever a legal act in this area would result in

---

[28] The EC Treaty grants the Community exclusive competence only over a very limited number of areas, primarily trade policy (Article 133), see Opinion 1/75, 1975 ECR 1355, 1364 *local costs*. According to the jurisprudence of the ECJ, the European Community has exclusive competence also in areas where it has legislated. Opinion 1/94, 1994 ECR I-5276 *WTO*; Case 22/70, 1971 E.C.R. 263, 275 *AETR*.

changing existing national law, the Commission will, as a general rule, propose a directive rather than a regulation.[29]

2. National level

The implementation procedures in the Member States for those parts of a mixed agreement which fall within their own competence are the same as those applicable in the case of international agreements which the Member States conclude independently from the Community. In most Member States an international agreement requires specific implementation measures since the ratification of the agreement by Parliament is not sufficient to create individual rights and obligations for the citizens. In the Federal Republic of Germany, which follows the dualistic approach to international agreements, a statute is normally necessary for the implementation of such agreements.

G. Impact of the internal structure of Member States

If the Member States are obliged to pass legislation, in order either to adapt their laws to a Community directive implementing an international agreement or to give effect to an international agreement falling within the scope of their own competence, differences between the internal structures of the Member States may, in certain cases, become relevant in the implementation process. In a Member State which has a centralized structure such as France, the implementation process may be easier than in Member States with a federal structure such as the Federal Republic of Germany or Belgium. This is particularly true if competences of the lower levels such as the individual states in Germany (*Länder*) are concerned. In the case of Germany, even if the implementation is only a matter of the central level (the federation), the second chamber (*Bundesrat*), the representation of the *Länder* at the federal level, may be involved in the legislative process. This is especially the case whenever a statute concerns administrative procedures because, under the German constitution (the *Grundgesetz*), the *Länder* are competent for the administration of federal laws.[30]

---

[29] Angela Bardenhewer and Joern Pipkorn, in GTE (above, n. 5), Article 100, nos. 37 and 38, 68 and 69 with reference to the declaration of the Commission, at the occasion of the signature of the Single European Act of 1986.

[30] Article 83 GG.

II. SPECIFIC PROBLEMS OF INTERNATIONAL AGREEMENTS ON NON-TARIFF BARRIERS FOR PRODUCTS

A. Methods of regulation within the TEP framework

The relevance of the preceding analysis for the implementation of possible future TEP agreements depends essentially on their contents. Most probably they will primarily deal with non-tariff barriers to trade in certain specific areas following a case-by-case approach. Therefore there will not be a 'horizontal' and comprehensive overall agreement. Theoretically the following types of agreements may be concluded:

1. Agreements on consultation procedures

The first type of agreement may contain obligations for consultation, early-warning arrangements, and procedures establishing a permanent dialogue, both at the political and administrative level, as well as among experts, standardization bodies, and industry representatives. They may concern planned legislation in certain critical areas, implementation problems, or enforcement deficits. It is obvious that this type of agreement does not imply specific legal difficulties as long as only consultation procedures and no legal consequences are provided. Notification procedures for new legislative acts which include a temporary standstill, as embodied in the EC Information Directive[31] for technical provisions, are difficult to conceive in an international framework like a TEP agreement. This type of obligation is typical of advanced economic integration, as in the internal market of the European Community. It also requires supervision of its correct application by common institutions, as they exist in the EC context in the form of the European Commission and, in the last instance, the European Court of Justice.

2. Agreements on mutual recognition of procedures

Mutual recognition agreements (MRAs) which concern certification procedures (especially testing certification and certification of production processes which may be found in the existing MRA between the European Community and the United States on conformity assessment[32]), are currently favoured by many politicians and experts.[33] This method is certainly of considerable significance for market access and is relatively easy to implement because it does not concern the substance of regulation.

---

[31] Directive 98/34/EC, 1998 OJ (L 204/37), formerly Directive 83/189/EC, 1983 OJ (L 109/8).

[32] Reimer von Borries, 'Abkommen EG-USA über die gegenseitige Anerkennung', *DAJV-Newsletter* 1/99, 21; see also the Declaration of the Council concerning agreements on the mutual recognition of conformity assessments of June 1999.

[33] See contribution of Sir Leon Brittan, this volume.

3. Agreements on mutual recognition of standards and legal provisions

MRAs concerning substantive law are much more difficult to conceive because they in principle presuppose an equivalent level of protection in the respective areas of law of the parties to the agreement. They are therefore conceivable only on a case-by-case basis following a comprehensive examination of the relevant provisions. Substantive MRAs require a formal treaty. Mutual recognition may not be 'automatic' solely on the basis of certain abstract criteria. It is interesting to note that such an 'automatic' method of 'formal mutual recognition' has been attempted in vain within the European Community. It failed because of considerable differences of opinion among the Member States as to the equivalence of protection.[34] The 'automatic' mutual recognition practised within the European Community on the basis of the Four Freedoms, especially in the area of trade in goods and services, does not fit an international framework. It presupposes an essential similarity of national regulation and a common legal basis which is provided by notions such as the internal market and the proportionality principle in the European Community.

4. Agreements on common standards

Although close cooperation in the field of standardization seems possible within the TEP and would facilitate mutual recognition, it is advisable to pursue these efforts in a broader, multinational framework because otherwise new barriers to trade vis-à-vis third countries would be created. The existing international standardization organizations, in particular ISO, should not be weakened by a purely bilateral approach.

5. Agreements on the harmonization of laws

The most ambitious method is, of course, approximation of laws, i.e. legal harmonization. As the experience of the European Community shows, this goal has to be pursued on a case-by-case basis (although at times within the framework of comprehensive political programmes such as the famous White Paper on the internal market of 1987). This process has in certain cases proved to be extremely cumbersome, at least as long as unanimity was required.[35] In addition, harmonization must fit into a general economic concept such as the European internal market. Therefore, legal harmonization within the TEP framework is even more difficult to

---

[34] Volkmar Goetz, 'Der Grundsatz der gegenseitigen Anerkennung im europäischen Binnenmarkt', in Volkmar Goetz, Peter Selmer, and Ruediger Wolfrum (eds), *Liber amicorum Guenther Jaenicke—Zum 85. Geburtstag* (Berlin etc., 1998) 763, 767.

[35] For example in the case of the Directive 85/384/EEC, 1985 OJ L 223/15 which took over 20 years, and the 13th Directive on takeover bids the Common Position for which has only recently been adopted after ten years of discussion by the Council.

imagine than the mutual recognition of standards and legal provisions.[36] A specific difficulty of transatlantic harmonization for the European Community consists in its impact on the so-called 'acquis communautaire' which would require a revision of existing Community law.

To a certain extent, the method of approximation of laws could perhaps be applied in areas where the 'new approach' is provided for in Community directives, such as in the area of technical safety.[37] However, the 'new approach' presupposes common standards to which reference could be made, and therefore does not become effective if there are no such standards. This is the case even within the European Community. Reference could be made, for example, to ISO standards, because they are often similar to EC standards. ISO standards, however, are much less recognized in the United States and would first have to be introduced there.

B. Problems of legislative implementation

In choosing the adequate method for transatlantic regulatory cooperation, the parties to an agreement have to keep in mind the limited goals of the TEP, which is actually not intended to be a comprehensive free trade area or even a Transatlantic Common Market, but is restricted to the goal of abolishing trade barriers in critical areas.

1. Choice of subjects for TEP agreements

The first problem concerns the selection of appropriate subjects for TEP agreements. Possible areas for regulatory cooperation in the TEP framework may be:

- technical safety;
- protection of health;
- consumer protection;
- environmental protection;
- cosmetic products;
- safety of motor vehicles;
- safety of vessels;
- calibration.

However, one has to keep in mind that not all methods of regulatory cooperation are appropriate for all of these areas. The choice of the method rather depends to a large extent on the characteristics of the subject matter of regulation. The method chosen has, in turn, certain implications for the implementation of the TEP agreements on the EC side.

[36] However, in the framework of the Economic Commission for Europe of the United Nations (ECE), such harmonization was achieved with respect to certain national regulations for cars and aircraft.
[37] Resolution of the Council of 7 May 1985, 1985 OJ (C 136/1).

2. Consultation procedures

An appropriate goal in the process of implementing the TEP would be the creation of effective consultation procedures. Here a number of questions arise: Consultation *ex ante* or *ex post*? Consultation between whom and with which consequences? Should there be special consultation bodies of the TEP parties? These questions have to be dealt with carefully in order to make consultation work effectively. The least that can be said is that these consultation procedures should not interfere with existing legislative procedures of the European Community and its Member States but should serve only to enhance mutual information. A notification procedure as provided for by the EC Information Directive is not conceivable within the TEP because it is very unlikely that the preconditions for an effective implementation of such a procedure can be created by an international agreement, namely the automatic temporary standstill (with direct effect), the examination of national legislation by a special committee, and the harmonization of critical provisions on the Community level.

3. Mutual recognition

MRAs on *procedures* would be easier to conceive than MRAs on the *substance* of regulation.

(*a*) MRAs on substance mean mutual recognition of technical regulations. They could concern machines, toys, construction products, media products, telecommunication equipment, automobile safety, measuring instruments, chemical products, and others. However, it is obvious that MRAs on substance would require a common or at least an equivalent level of protection. It is doubtful whether such an equivalent level of protection exists in all the above-mentioned areas. Both sides would then have to negotiate over the appropriate level of protection, and results could only be achieved (if at all) through technical agreements on a case-by-case basis. Agreements of this type would probably require the participation of the Member States and lead to complicated implementation measures by the European Community and the Member States. Therefore, the prospects of the conclusion of such agreements are less favourable.

(*b*) On the other hand, MRAs on procedures beyond conformity assessment could be conceived of for many of the above-mentioned areas. They could in particular concern test data as well as test results and certificates in order to avoid double testing, which entails a competitive disadvantage.

4. Importance of the level of protection

At this point, the importance of the level of protection for any progress in mutual recognition needs to be emphasized again.[38] It is, indeed, an

---

[38] This, for example, became evident in the case of the application of the EC Directive for the Protection of Data to international data transmissions.

essential precondition not only for the conclusion but also for the effective implementation of such agreements. It is difficult to imagine agreements harmonizing the level of protection on a broader scale, because the respective provisions are often deeply rooted in public opinion and national traditions. They could also result in difficult changes of the secondary law of the European Community, the 'acquis communautaire', and therefore of the implementing legislation of the Member States. Nevertheless, in certain carefully selected areas, this could perhaps be achieved if it promises considerable economic advantages for both the European Union and the United States.

C. Problems of administrative implementation

The method of mutual recognition has certain implications for the administration of all sorts of regulations. It especially concerns the administrative authorities at the regional and the local level, because these authorities will have to apply mutual recognition procedures by examining in each individual case whether the preconditions for the recognition of a product (and thereby the foreign law) are given. In an international framework such as the TEP, there could be no automatic 'presumption' of equivalence, as is the case within the European Community according to the jurisprudence of the European Court of Justice (*Cassis de Dijon*). This means that whenever products are traded between the United States and the European Union which are regulated for safety, health, or other reasons, the responsibility for examining their equivalence falls on the administrative authorities of the Member States. They would accordingly have to be equipped and trained for this task.

D. Remedies

In the majority of the Member States remedies under administrative law permit individuals to go to court if their rights are violated by administrative authorities. However, in some Member States it is more difficult, at least in practice, than in others to apply to the courts because an internal administrative procedure must first be exhausted. Effective TEP agreements would require that individuals have access to the courts to a comparable degree within all Member States.

III. SPECIFIC 'PROBLEM' SECTORS

This contribution deals primarily with trade in goods; however, the TEP will also concern trade in services, and possibly also public procurement, professional qualifications, and transportation. In principle, the same or similar considerations apply in these areas. The principle of mutual recognition of procedures could therefore be considered on a case-by-case basis with respect to certain requirements such as licences, admission procedures, and proof of qualifications. However, it is difficult to conceive of mutual recognition of procedures as a general method for all sorts of problems, or as the solution for whole subject matter areas. Mutual recognition with regard to substantive law will almost certainly be feasible only on a very limited scale.

IV. CONCLUSIONS

This contribution leads to the following conclusions:

1. Agreements concerning the implementation of the TEP will probably to a large extent be 'mixed agreements'.

2. 'Mixed agreements' pose specific problems on the EU side not only as to their conclusion, but also as to implementation.

3. The implementation of TEP agreements may require supplementary legislation on the Community and national level which may bring national parliaments into play.

4. Even if certain provisions of the Community part of mixed agreements have direct effect within the European Community, this does not relieve the Community and the Member States from having to adopt the necessary implementation measures.

Part VII

Transatlantic regulatory cooperation, democracy, and accountability

Transatlantic regulatory cooperation and the problem of democracy

Robert Howse

I. INTRODUCTION

As Susan Marks observes in a wonderfully insightful recent essay, democracy risks 'being fertile material for cant', meaning different things to different people and employed rhetorically to justify all manner or regimes, from juntas relying on fraudulent elections to the worst kind of nationalistic excesses in the name of the 'people'.[1] As in many other contexts, debates about democracy, and democratic deficits in regulatory cooperation, suffer from lack of clarity, to say nothing of lack of agreement between the interlocutors about what democracy means. The first step towards such clarity is to distinguish the main kinds (or models or concepts) of democracy at play, and to consider—both separately and in relation—their possible implications for transatlantic regulatory cooperation. This is the sole object of this brief and modest essay. The models of democracy thus distinguished and discussed are: representative democracy; republicanism or democratic self-determination; consociational or corporatist democracy; decentralization and governmental competition; and deliberative democracy.

II. KINDS OF DEMOCRACY[2]

1. Representative democracy

In modern liberal democracies, the main formal vehicle for democratic legitimation of laws, policies, and regulations is that of representation. The people do not decide each issue directly, through voting in the assembly,

---

[1] Susan Marks, 'Democracy and Global Governance', unpublished manuscript, Cambridge University, 1999, on file with the author, 2.

[2] In defining and distinguishing the various models or kinds of democracy discussed below, I have learned from David Held, 'Stories of Democracy, Old and New', ch. 1 of *Democracy and the Global Order: From the Modern State to Cosmopolitan Governance* (Stanford: Stanford University Press, 1995), and Jürgen Habermas, 'Three Normative Models of Democracy', in *The Inclusion of the Other: Studies in Political Theory* (Cambridge: MIT Press, 1999). In the end, I have had to develop my own categories and distinctions to illuminate the problem.

or even by plebiscite or referendum. Instead, on the basis of more or less universal suffrage,[3] the people elect representatives for fixed terms, who consent to laws and create the legal framework for rule-making and administration. The choice of representation as a means of realizing the democratic ideal reflects awareness by the founders of the modern democratic state of the evils of direct democracy, as exhibited in the self-destruction of the ancient democratic city—demagoguery, instability, mob rule, and factionalism.[4] It also, of course, reflects the practical demands of governance in large, complex commercial states.[5] Representative democracy is a compromise with the principle of technocracy, or specialized competence, and its institutions exhibit as many devices for checking or blunting the crude expression of mass opinion, as for reflecting it.[6] At the same time, the experience of elected dictatorship illustrates that mass mobilization of the populace by demagogues, and the various related evils identified with direct democracy in antiquity, are not necessarily avoided by the representative form of democracy, but could actually be exacerbated by it.

The prevalence and putative legitimacy of representative forms and institutions of democracy,[7] however criticized (voter apathy, machine politics, etc.) and occasionally modified (plebiscites, referenda on some issues), has often led the practitioners of representative governance to be perplexed or irritated by claims that regulatory cooperation contains a democratic deficit. Unlike action by a world government or empire, regulatory cooperation occurs only on the basis of an authorization of cooperative regulatory activity—either *ex post* or *ex ante*—by the constitutional representative institutions of which the national regulators are agents. As Anne-Marie Slaughter has suggested, transnational regulatory cooperation leaves 'the control of government institutions in the hands of national citizens, who must hold their governments as accountable for their transnational activities as for their domestic duties'.[8]

---

[3] We must not forget that in a range of liberal democracies suffrage for women, and even for some racial or religious groups is recent; and of course in most such democracies even today, 'non-citizens' are excluded, even if they work, live, study in and are thus pervasively affected by the policies of the country in question.

[4] James Madison, 'Federalist #10, in Alexander Hamilton, James Madison, and John Jay, *The Federalist Papers* (New York: Times-Mirror, 1961), 77–84.

[5] John Stuart Mill, *On Liberty and Other Essays* (Oxford: Oxford University Press, 1991), 205–470.

[6] See above n. 4, 82.

[7] Indeed, in much competent social science literature one defines (in positive, if not normative) terms democracy as representative democracy. '*Modern political democracy is a system of governance in which rulers are held accountable for their actions in the public realm by citizens acting indirectly through the competition and cooperation of their elected representatives.*' Philippe C. Schmitter and Terry Lynn Karl, 'What Democracy Is . . . and Is Not', *Journal of Democracy*, vol. 2 (1991), 76, italics in original.

[8] Anne-Marie Slaughter, 'The Real New World Order', *Foreign Affairs*, vol. 76 (1997), 186.

What Slaughter recognizes, but inadequately appreciates, is that regulatory cooperation creates—to use the language of principal-agent theory—agency costs that are quantitatively, if not qualitatively, different than those entailed in the purely domestic arena.[9] Agency costs exist whenever agents themselves have interests that diverge from those of the principals on whose behalf they are acting. The specific agency costs problem presented by regulatory cooperation is well-expressed by Eyal Benvenisti in the context of international environmental negotiations, where there is typically *ex post* democratic control through ratification of treaty documents. Even this kind of formal and explicit process of democratic control 'permits very little scrutiny of the negotiators' acts and omissions, because ratification does not allow for amendments and lets alternatives remain unexplored. And even parliamentary debate on ratification often remains clouded. The access of the public to information concerning the international negotiations is invariably very limited. Little is known of which options were offered and discussed, as negotiators have little incentive to provide accurate information to the general public on their performance.'[10]

Information asymmetries as between the direct participants in regulatory cooperation and their democratic principals (including first-order democratic agents such as parliamentarians) make it very difficult to control agency costs through the standard mechanisms of accountability. How does one assess, or second-guess, regulatory officials' claims to have driven the best bargain for their principals. Were it not for the officials' interest in cooperation itself, or in the preservation of friendly working relations with their homologues, might they not have driven a harder bargain, given what they know about their principals? Perhaps they share with homologues a common economic or technocratic outlook or ideology, at variance with the revealed preferences and values of their principals. How do we, the people, assess the extent to which the outcome proposed is a reflection of an official's commitment to this outlook, or even a commitment by the negotiators in common, as opposed to the principals being represented on the other side of the table?

One obvious answer is to make regulatory cooperation more transparent, removing some of the asymmetry in information, through opening the door or at least the window to the negotiating room. But there is a price in having every move an official and/or negotiator makes subject to public scrutiny. It is often thought that precisely what makes regulatory

---

[9] The application of agency theory to the problem of the democratic deficit which follows draws on recent work by Cary Coglianese and Kalypso Nicolaïdis. See also Peter Evans, Harold Jakobson, and Robert Putnam (eds), *Double-Edged Diplomacy: International Bargaining and Domestic Politics* (Berkeley: University of California, 1993).

[10] Eyal Benvenisti, 'Exit and Voice in the Age of Globalization', *Michigan Law Review*, vol. 98 (1999), 200.

cooperation effective is the possibility of informal give-and-take in a climate of trust based on expectations of confidentiality. Thus, when Slaughter praises regulatory cooperation for its effectiveness in relation to other institutional forms of transnational action, she may by implication be praising some of the very qualities of such cooperation that raise particular issues for domestic democratic control.

In Europe, one response to the problem of democratic control of transnational regulatory activity has been to give added power to the European Parliament to control the outcomes of intergovernmental cooperation or negotiation. This is a solution that remains, formally, within the domain of representative democracy. However, it cannot be seriously proposed as an answer within the context of transatlantic regulatory cooperation—although formalizing exchanges and interaction between European and American parliamentarians might reduce one set of information asymmetries.[11] The problem is that the parliamentarians on one side of the Atlantic do not really share a common political vocabulary with those on the other side, and one is unlikely to develop spontaneously on the basis of occasional meetings and encounters. Thus, these dialogues and exchanges between parliamentarians are very likely to have to rely on the intermediation of 'experts'—bureaucrats, diplomats, regulators—with the attendant agency cost problems. But, even strictly as a solution to the intra-European democratic deficit, agency theory suggests that greater empowerment of the European Parliament will not necessarily reduce agency costs. It really depends not only on the degree of formal democratic control already achieved through accountability to national parliaments, but also on the comparative advantage of a European representative institution in lowering the agency costs of intergovernmentalism. It is fair to ask whether, without appropriate means of dealing with information asymmetries, the European Parliament will do a better job of ensuring that agents engaged in intergovernmentalism reflect the interests of their principals.[12]

2. Democracy as republicanism or collective self-determination

While the existing formal institutions of democracy in America and Europe remain overwhelmingly representative in character, the practice and rhetoric of democracy have remained profoundly influenced by a different tradition, critical of the elitism and distance of representative demo-

---

[11] In January 1999 a proposal was adopted by American and EU delegations of legislators to establish a Transatlantic Legislative Dialogue. See Horst Krenzler and Gunnar Wiegand, 'US–EU Relations: More than Trade Disputes', *European Foreign Affairs Review*, vol. 4 (1999), 170.

[12] See Juliet Lodge, 'Transparency and Democratic Legitimacy', *Journal of Common Market Studies*, vol. 32 (1994), 343.

cracy. This is the tradition of republicanism, founded in Europe by Jean-Jacques Rousseau and in America by Jefferson and the anti-Federalists. This tradition understands democracy as the collective self-determination of a community held together by bonds of language, religion, ancestry, or other elements of common identity. Widespread participation is crucial to this conception, and the ills of modern representative democracy (such as citizen apathy, low voter turnout, etc.), are a reflection of the inadequacy of representative forms to the ideal of participation that they themselves appear to honour. Here, democracy is a good in itself, not simply a means of ensuring that people are ruled by laws and policies which reflect their individual interests and values.[13] If there is indeed a current crisis of democracy within the nation-state, as many have claimed, it is in no small measure because, while remaining organizationally representative, liberal democracies have long appealed in their rhetoric to the ideal of collective self-determination—by opposing tyranny elsewhere, whether fascist or communist, and by justifying the nation-state in democratic terms.[14] Measured against such an ideal, both the formal institutions of (representative) democracy, and the way they function, must seem very wanting indeed.

What are the implications for regulatory cooperation of the republican conception of democracy? To the extent that the republican conception places its emphasis on collective self-determination through direct participation, it implies radical decentralization—in other words, the transfer of the greatest power to the lowest level of governance (which was in fact the solution articulated by Rousseau and Jefferson). Yet if one examines the traditional instruments of direct participation idealized by republicans, it is hard to imagine that any autonomous community of the size required by modern demands of economic and technological organization would be small enough to allow their extensive use.[15] On the other hand, if one thinks of the new means of participation (such as the Internet, as powerfully argued by Peter Strauss in this volume[16]), these seem deployable even at levels above those of the nation-state.

But can there be a community of fate, a demos, beyond the level of the nation-state? Behind most of the republican views of democratic

---

[13] See, for instance, Benjamin Barber, *Strong Democracy: Participatory Politics for a New Age* (Berkeley: University of California Press, 1985); Michael J. Sandel, *Democracy's Discontent: America in Search of a Public Philosophy* (Cambridge: Belknap/Harvard, 1996).

[14] On this last point, see Lord Acton, 'On Nationality', in Gopal Balakrishnan (ed.), *Mapping the Nation* (London: Verso, 1996), 17–38.

[15] For a critique of the 'democratic' value of decentralization, see Robert Howse, 'Federalism, Democracy, and Regulatory Reform: A Skeptical View of the Case for Decentralization', in Karen Knop, Sylvia Ostry, Richard Simeon, and Katherine Swinton (eds), *Rethinking Federalism* (Vancouver: University of British Columbia Press, 1995).

[16] See also Joseph H. H. Weiler, 'To Be a European Citizen: Eros and Civilization', in Joseph H. H. Weiler, *The Constitution of Europe: 'Do the New Clothes Have an Emperor' and Other Essays on European Integration* (Cambridge: Cambridge University Press, 1999), 351–3.

self-determination lie not only an emphasis on the special value of the experience of participation in a process of collective decision-making, but also the value of participating with people with whom one shares certain characteristics of identity (language, ethnicity, etc.). Accepting, at least for the sake of argument, the centrality of the affective experience of sharing with one's own, Joseph Weiler has challenged the notion that the bonds in question need to be established through pre-sub-political (purported) identity characteristics such as language or ethnicity. Yet is there any necessary reason why the bonds that create a people or a demos cannot themselves be based on the experience of civic association between individuals who need not belong to any homogeneous pre- or sub-political community of identity—whether through social or economic intercourse, or by acting together to advance shared values or common projects (environmental protection, reduction of poverty, etc.)? In this respect, Weiler argues, there is no reason why Europe itself could not become a demos.[17] Why, then, could we not go further, and attempt to build a transatlantic demos?

One reason why it might be wrong to do so is that a further melding of American and European values would risk creating a monolith of the 'West', threatening Europe's traditional place between East and West, and increasing the isolation of Russia and everything to its east.

Further, the continuing awareness of different collective *ethoi* and different civilizational possibilities *within* the liberal democratic West helps prevent the danger that Tocqueville identified in American democracy and warned Europe against, namely of conformism or the tyranny of opinion.[18]

3. Democracy as decentralization and competitive federalism

A further conception of democracy is that of radical decentralization to the lowest possible level of political authority, to where government is supposedly closest to the people. This conception, which is closely linked to

---

[17] Weiler, *The Constitution of Europe*, (above, n. 16).

[18] Of course, some argue that the transatlantic divide can no longer play this mind-opening role. Saul Bellow suggests that, unlike early generations of Americans, 'We do not look beyond America. It absorbs us completely. No one is stirred to the bowels of Europe of the ancient parapets. A huge force has lost its power over the imagination. Young M.B.A.s, management school graduates, gene-splicers and computerists, their careers well started, will fly to Paris with their wives to shop on the rue de Rivoli and dine at the Tour d'Argent. Not greatly different are the behavioral scientists and members of the learned professions who are well satisfied with what they learned of the Old World, while they were getting their B.A.s.' Saul Bellow, 'My Paris (1983)', in *It All Adds Up: From the Dim Past to the Uncertain Future* (New York: Viking, 1994). But the recent transatlantic disputes over hormone-fed beef and over genetically modified organisms and their regulation, neither of which has been resolved by the technocrats, suggest that Americans can still be provoked, if not charmed, by European difference.

the republican version of democracy as collective self-determination, suggests that it is easier in small communities to accommodate more directly or more fully the voices of all. However, small political communities may well not reflect, much less live up to this ideal. As John Stuart Mill observed: 'what pretends to be local self-government is, too often, selfish mismanagement of local interests by a jobbing and *borné* local oligarchy.'[19] Recent studies of decentralization of governmental functions in developing countries have similarly noted that more local government does not necessarily mean more democracy.[20]

How does this view of democracy play out in terms of transatlantic regulatory cooperation? One view of regulatory cooperation emphasizes and indeed embraces the diffusion of governance across a wide range of actors as a challenge of decentralized coordination. An example is Scott Jacobs' notion of multi-layered regulation—'an intricate network of vertical and horizontal links between all levels of government, often stretching from the lowest to the highest levels'.[21] However, the complexity that inheres in decentralized coordination presents its own risks for democracy. Jean Marensin, writing in the context of decentralization in France, notes: 'the proliferation in our country of concurrent local powers, and each one concerned to maintain its own clientele, the multiplication of committees, associations, professional organisms of all sorts, the complex procedures established between these different levels . . . could well, in time, signify a retreat of democracy to the extent that democracy . . . needs clarity [about lines of accountability].'[22]

Where, however, regulatory cooperation is seen as a negotiation between sovereigns, as in the case of the EU–US MRA, asymmetrical diffusion of regulatory authority within each sovereign power may make agreement more difficult; in order to match the more centralized sovereign's capacity to 'deliver' recognition by all relevant regulatory authorities in its entire market, as it were, the less centralized sovereign may have to centralize regulatory authority within its domain or engage in transaction-cost-intensive coordination arrangements with diffuse authorities.[23]

Vogel has suggested that the centralization of regulatory authority within the European Union may have exacerbated trade tensions with the United States, thereby creating new challenges for regulatory cooperation:

[19] John Stuart Mill, *Autobiography* (London: Penguin, 1989), 151.

[20] See Robert Howse, 'Federalism, Democracy and Regulatory Reform: A Skeptical View of the Case for Decentralization' (above, n. 15), 276.

[21] Scott H. Jacobs, 'Regulatory Co-operation in an Interdependent World: Issues for Government', in OECD (public management service), *Regulatory Cooperation in an Interdependent World* (Paris: OECD, 1995), 17.

[22] Jean Marensin, 'Liberalisme et centralisme en France et Angleterre', *Commentaire*, vol. 56 (1991–2), 735. My translation.

[23] Kalypso Nicolaïdis, 'Mutual Recognition of Regulatory Regimes: Some Lessons and Prospects', in OECD, *Regulatory Reform and International Market Openness* (Paris: OECD, 1996), 185–6.

Commitment to the single market led the EU to harmonize regulations for hormones, animal furs, and eco-labeling. Having been driven to establish a common standard to avoid undermining the single market for goods that were widely traded in Europe, it had to decide which standards to enact. Given the political strength of environmental and consumer groups in the EU's most powerful member states, it was more politically expedient to require that others raise their standards, than it was to force the EU's greener member states to lower them. And once having imposed the standards on domestic producers, it sought to impose them on foreign ones as well. Thus, the creation of the single market has exacerbated trade tensions with the United States, . . . For example had the decisions on hormone use been left to each member state, American beef producers would have been able to export their products to some European nations. The same holds true for American exports of furs, since some countries in Europe are indifferent to the issue of animal protection. The citizens of the various member states are not equally anxious about the consumption of bioengineered food. Likewise, were the enactment of eco-labeling standards left to each member state, some would choose not to develop them.[24]

Here, Vogel seems to suggest that decentralized regulation within the European Union would have better served the interests both of democracy (by allowing citizen preferences for lower standards to count where they are widespread) and transatlantic regulatory cooperation. Yet this need not be the case. For instance, weaker regulation in some European countries might be attributable to disproportionate influence of producer interests relative to that of consumers or environmentalists, rather than to different underlying preferences about health, the environment, or consumer protection. Relatively dispersed interests, like those of consumers, may have greater influence at a higher level of regulatory authority, the collective action problems of organizing such dispersed interests into effective political pressure being mitigated by economies of scale.[25]

The competition model articulates a related, but rather different set of democratic gains from decentralization. One version of this model, based on Tiebout's noted theory of local government,[26] emphasizes that, under decentralized regulation, citizens and businesses can move to the jurisdiction whose regulatory regime best reflects their preferences. Because people are generally much less internationally mobile than capital, this theory has fateful consequences for democratic equality: regulation will most likely reflect the interests of those who can 'threaten' to exit, less

[24] David Vogel, *Barriers or Benefits? Regulation in Transatlantic Trade* (Washington, DC: Brookings Institution, 1997), 59–60.

[25] On the importance of economies of scale to effective environmental activism, see Anthony Scott, 'Piecemeal Decentralization: The Environment', in Robin Boadway, Thomas Courchene, and David Purvis (eds), *Economic Dimensions of Constitutional Change* (Kingston, Canada: John Deutsch Institute for the Study of Economic Policy 1991), 292–3 (writing in the context of the Canadian federation).

[26] Charles Mills Tiebout, 'A Pure Theory of Local Expenditure', *Journal of Political Economy*, vol. 64 (1957), 416.

likely those who are trapped by immobility, and least likely of all those who one might want to leave, for example recipients of social welfare benefits.

More recently, a different model of governmental competition has been proposed, which does not depend on the problematic assumption of mobility.[27] This model builds on Salmon's basic theorem that 'citizens assess their government's performance by comparing [it] to that of governments in other jurisdictions'.[28] The implications of this model for regulatory cooperation are complex. On the one hand, if such cooperation is envisaged as harmonization, it would seem to deprive citizens of the advantages of competition. However, it may be that such competition nevertheless plays itself out as regulators from different countries compete to have 'their' regulatory approach adopted as the common one. This, of course, requires one to believe that the 'best' approach—not necessarily the approach that is similar to that of the most powerful jurisdiction(s)—will eventually win out.

Short of harmonization, however, regulatory cooperation may make it easier for citizens to judge their own government's performance against that of governments in other jurisdictions. Regulatory cooperation entails the flow of information about how things are done in different jurisdictions. It requires reflection on why differences exist. This would especially be true if regulatory cooperation were to become more transparent and participatory, as suggested in the discussion above of the agency costs of representative democracy. The attempt by American agrifood interests to get European regulation of genetically modified food on the WTO negotiating table could well backfire, as it has helped alert American consumer and environmental interests to the particular kinds of risks entailed in this sort of genetic engineering. Ultimately, instead of a trade dispute, the result could be a more cautious regulatory approach on the American side of the Atlantic.

4. Consociational or corporatist democracy

This conception of democracy makes agreement or consensus among organizations or associations representing different groups (for example, business, labour, organized religion, etc.) the, or at least a, central criterion for democratic legitimacy. Because this conception depends on representativity, it raises the agency costs issues discussed above in connection with systems of elected representation. It also raises difficult problems

---

[27] See, most importantly, Albert Breton, *Competitive Governments: An Economic Theory of Politics and Public Finance* (Cambridge: Cambridge University Press, 1996).

[28] As summarized in Albert Breton, Alberto Cassone, and Angela Fraschini, 'Decentralization and Subsidiarity: Toward a Theoretical Reconciliation', *University of Pennsylvania Journal of International Economic Law*, vol. 19 (1998), 45.

about which groups have to be included in order for the agreement among groups to qualify as a democratically legitimate social contract or consensus. Provided such concerns can be addressed, this model of democracy clearly offers some promise for giving transatlantic regulatory cooperation a meaningful democratic pedigree. What, for instance, if trade unions or environmentalist and consumers' groups were to organize themselves transatlantically, along the lines of what business did in the Transatlantic Business Dialogue?[29] Indeed, transatlantic dialogues parallel to the business dialogue were envisaged in the 1995 New Transatlantic Agenda, in the labour, environmental, and consumer areas. Yet these groupings do not seem to have a strong impact on democratic legitimacy, as witnessed by the failure to heed the call of the environmental grouping to halt implementation of the Transatlantic Economic Partnership until its impact on sustainable development could be assessed.[30] Some might say that a tripartite model of transatlantic regulatory cooperation is already visible in the participation in the work of the OECD of the Trade Unions Advisory Council (TUAC) and the Business and Industry Advisory Council (BIAC). Yet the presence of these groups failed to push the Multilateral Agreement on Investment (MAI) negotiations to an outcome that enjoyed broad transnational social legitimacy, thereby pointing up both the representativity and inclusiveness difficulties with the consociational/corporatist model.

5. Deliberative democracy

The deliberative model understands democracy not simply in terms of popular will and decision, but as a legitimation of power that depends on a conception of public justification and deliberative reason. Such an understanding of democracy is to be found in several important accounts of democratic legitimacy in political and legal philosophy, notably those of Jürgen Habermas[31] and of Amy Gutmann and Dennis Thompson.[32] Gutmann and Thompson provide four reasons why deliberation is a cen-

---

[29] See Paula Stern, 'The Trans-Atlantic Business Dialogue: A New Paradigm for Standards and Regulatory Reform', in *OECD, Regulatory Reform and International Market Openness* (Paris: OECD, 1996), 155–64.

[30] See Krenzler and Wiegand, 'EU–US Relations: More than Trade Disputes?' (above, n. 11), 169–70. Krenzler and Wiegand (the former a senior European Commission official at the time of writing) see transatlantic consumer and environmental groupings as a threat to technocratic management of disputes like the beef hormone dispute through regulatory cooperation. What they do not seem to see is that without democratic legitimacy, such technocratic management is unlikely to succeed on its own terms to manage conflict.

[31] Jürgen Habermas, *Between Facts and Norms: Contributions to a Discourse Theory of Law and Democracy*, William Rehg trans. (Cambridge, Mass.: MIT Press, 1996), especially ch. 7, 'Deliberative Politics: A Procedural Concept of Democracy', 287–328.

[32] Amy Gutmann and Dennis Thompson, *Democracy and Disagreement* (Cambridge, Mass.: Harvard/Belknap, 1996).

tral element in democratic legitimacy. First, deliberation contributes to decisions made under conditions of scarcity by displaying to those who lose that 'everyone's claims have been considered on their merits rather than on the basis of wealth, status, or power'. Second, deliberation may lead citizens to take seriously the claims of others, thus enhancing democratic equality. Third, deliberation permits clarification of what is really at stake in disagreements between citizens, allowing, for instance, identification of those conflicts that result from misunderstanding and misinformation, and that could in fact be solved without need for trade-offs between divergent fundamental values. Fourth, deliberation holds out the prospect of learning from one another: 'Through the give-and-take of argument, citizens and their accountable representatives can learn from one another, come to recognize their individual and collective mistakes, and develop new views and policies that are more widely justifiable.'[33]

Gutmann and Thompson's version of the deliberative model of democracy is not, however, uncontroversial. One issue arises from Gutmann and Thompson's[34] employment of certain moral principles that they regard as fundamental to modelling ideal deliberation on a range of public policy issues, thereby reaching substantive policy conclusions which they seem to believe have legitimacy regardless of whether they are, or could be, adopted by citizens in a *real* deliberative process. Thus, Peter Berkowitz suggests:

What remains curious . . . is just how much of their own deliberation—the refinement of commonly held opinions, the intricate reasoning from distilled moral principles, the sifting and weighing of the latest social science research— takes place without the actual involvement of fellow citizens, in the comfort of the study and congenial climate of the seminar room; and to what an extent the legitimacy of the substantive conclusions Gutmann and Thompson reach is, from the perspective of their own principles, independent of whether their fellow citizens can be persuaded to endorse them.[35]

A version of deliberative democracy that responds to this criticism would respect citizens' *real* choices even if these seem irrational as measured against what citizens might be expected to decide in a perfectly rational deliberative process, while at the same time seeking to make the process as perfectly deliberative as possible.

How might deliberative democracy play a role in legitimizing transatlantic regulatory cooperation? From a perspective that emphasizes the importance of rational argument and accurate information for deliberative democracy, requirements such as those in the WTO Sanitary and Phytosanitary Agreements or the Technical Barriers Agreement, that

---

[33] Ibid. 43.
[34] It should be emphasized that Habermas's version of deliberative democracy is not vulnerable to the particular criticism that follows.
[35] Peter Berkowitz, 'The Debating Society', *New Republic* (25 Nov. 1996), 36–42.

oblige governments to undertake explicit, rigorous analyses of risks as well as alternative instruments to address those risks, can enhance democracy within each polity and at the same time form the basis of a democratic dialogue among the polities. Such a dialogue might result in regulatory cooperation, or it might simply end up with each polity accepting differences in regulatory approach as legitimate, i.e. as not premised on or motivated by protectionism, misinformation or prejudice, but simply different values and cultural dispositions. Building on the strong emphasis on trust between regulators in Nicolaïdis' work on Mutual Recognition Agreements,[36] one might go a step further and suggest that such trust about differences in some areas of regulation may enhance the prospects for democratically legitimate regulatory cooperation in areas where there is greater commonality.

Deliberative democracy also offers the promise of using to advantage NGOs, or what is sometimes called transnational civil society, as deliberative intermediaries. The involvement of such groups in deliberative processes is consistent with decision-making authority ultimately remaining with the representative institutions of each polity. Objections to a greater presence of NGOs in the processes of regulatory cooperation, based upon their lack of representativeness or purported lack of internal democracy, would be weighty if not fatal, if this entailed conflating the *mere fact* of their participation or assent with enhanced democratic legitimacy (this being the problem with the consociational or corporatist understanding discussed above). But if we think of NGO involvement as expanding and deepening deliberation through argument and information, there is little reason to worry. In fact, legislators will only listen to an NGO to the extent that it can *persuade* constituents by argument and information—its legitimating power cannot really exceed its argumentative power.

Regulatory cooperation is, of course, not an end in itself. Thus, in those cases where more democracy may mean less regulatory cooperation, we need not think that there is always a tragic choice to be made. On the other hand, where regulatory cooperation is desirable for reasons such as enhancing gains from trade, the prospect that it can be made more democratically legitimate is of course an attractive one. Perhaps the one robust conclusion that may be drawn from this brief examination of the different models of democracy is that the processes of regulatory cooperation should be made more transparent, more inclusive, and more participatory. The conclusion is robust because it turns out that such an evolution would enhance democracy as understood by most of the models (representative, consociational/corporatist, decentralization/competition, and deliberative), while not detracting from democracy as understood by any of them.

---

[36] Kalypso Nicolaïdis, 'Mutual Recognition of Regulatory Regimes' (above, n. 23).

Globalization, transatlantic regulatory cooperation, and democratic values

Ludger Kühnhardt

I. SOME QUESTIONS DERIVED FROM DEMOCRATIC THEORY

'Globalization and democracy', or perhaps 'the democratization of global-ization'—no matter how the issue is phrased, it is driven and nurtured by stereotypes. On the one hand, we have regulatory-obsessed Europeans, and on the other free-trade-minded Americans; the hierarchical and oli-garchic Europeans here, the participatory-minded Americans there. Such headlines are good enough for op-ed comments in newspapers, but not substantial enough to meet the standards of a democratic theory which seeks to deal with the relationships between democratic values and regu-latory mechanisms that are a reaction to globalization. Therefore, the first and foremost requirement from a political science point of view is to out-line some of the parameters and priorities of democratic theory which can serve as a framework to assess the practical questions implied in regula-tory cooperation of any kind, including transatlantic economic regulatory cooperation. By the same token, some dilemmas of democracy must be addressed as well.

Democracy has always been based on rules and regulations. There has never been freedom without limits, or rights without duties, just as there has never been a playground without fences. The consequence for demo-cratic procedures is the following: it is crucial to reflect upon the mecha-nisms which generate, stabilize, and deepen legitimacy. Any democracy is challenged by changing expectations. For the most part, expectations have the tendency to broaden the existing framework in order to explain social relations. The more people talk about democracy, the more of it they want. It is often neglected to ask how 'more' becomes 'better' and will be justified in the long run, when 'more' is no longer 'enough'. From Alexis de Tocqueville and other political theorists we can learn to take note of the fact that egalitarian democracy is insaturable.[1] This is why there is no alternative to representative democracy as the tamed but workable variant of the purist abstraction of the notion of absolute democracy.

---

[1] For a Tocquevillian interpretation, see Ludger Kühnhardt, *Zukunftsdenker. Bewährte Ideen politischer Ordnung für das dritte Jahrtausend* (Baden-Baden: Nomos, 1999), 85–122.

Nevertheless, the question of democratic legitimacy will remain an integral part of the discourse in democratic societies. To ask what is legitimate is to ask what is right and what is good. Democracy, after all, is not only a superficial exercise in populism and tabloid politics. Legitimacy of, or a technocratic struggle over, the most effective regulatory mechanisms, democratic procedures, and democratic institutions, derives from convincing answers to two questions: who does what, and who controls whom? There must be a coherent answer to questions of competence and mandate as the very core of democratic legitimacy.[2] This is also true in the context of transatlantic regulatory cooperation. In contrast to the democratic *optimum*, the democratic *bonum* remains second-best even in this context, but it still is the best possible of all worlds (as Karl Popper has taught us). There is no such thing as a purist democratic answer to the issues that regulatory cooperation poses.

Delegated regulatory power is the reality in any representative democracy. Some dilemmas, however, remain fundamental and probably irresolvable. One is the potentially antagonistic character between transparency and efficiency. Can decisions quickly made be democratic? Can democratic decisions be both efficient and timely? A second problem relates to the realm of issues: Who defines the issues that require democratic participation and transparency? Who has the competence to take up the mandate for decision? A third problem hints at the relationship between law and democratic politics. All democratic politics is based on the principle of majoritarian voting; legal decisions are not. This difference between law and politics, between legal and political decisions might explain the legal authority and the charisma of the rule of law. But is it democratic? In turn, can democratic decisions opposing the law be acceptable even if they are legitimized by the participatory decision of a majority? Negotiated and codified legal consent and the majoritarian principle in democratic theory are, at least to a certain extent, contradictory if not incompatible.

What does this mean for the relationship between transatlantic regulatory cooperation and democratic values? Is transatlantic regulatory cooperation truly reflective of democracy or does it pre-empt democratic aspirations in and of itself?

II. 'GLOBALIZATION' IN THE LIGHT OF DEMOCRATIC THEORY

The market economy can either be understood as the embodiment of the public good or its potential adversary. While some do consider the market as good in itself, others perceive it as the enemy of the public good. At the

---

[2] See Frank Ronge, *Legitimität durch Subsidiarität. Der Beitrag des Subsidiaritätsprinzips zur Legitimation einer überstaatlichen politischen Ordnung in Europa* (Baden-Baden: Nomos, 1998).

end of the twentieth century, most theories have found some middle ground, but the basic issue has yet to be resolved satisfactorily. Who defines the 'public good', and who can legitimately claim to control the markets? The age of globalization has added new elements to these debates.[3] The world has become a marketplace, a global village, and whatever other rhetorical expressions there are. The answers are legal, if not legislative: WTO arbitration rules, transatlantic regulatory mechanisms, and so on. Networking NGO's and Transatlantic Business Dialogues cannot provide for democratically legitimized and accountable answers. Is there any place left in the world of globalization for politics, for democratic politics, for majoritarian voting, and for its inherent principles and consequences?

First of all of course, 'globalization' has to be properly defined. The word is as much of a slogan as is the term 'democracy'. Since everybody seems to apply a different definition, everybody seems to be comfortable in using the terms. Both terms are neither specifically nor exclusively defined, and the more imprecise the definition, the higher its support and identification value. Social science literature on globalization is in full swing, but the enormous output belies the poor content. At the heart of the debate, there are three assumptions:[4]

First, globalization refers to a whole set of trans-societal relations, which have enormously increased in the past years: twenty-thousand non-governmental organizations (NGOs), global financial transactions of up to US$2,000 billion per day, CNN, UN Conferences on Global Warming, or Global Development, global this and global that. The widespread assumption is that globalization has fundamental consequences on States' capacity to act autonomously. The notion of statehood, as it has been shaped in the aftermath of the Treaty of Westphalia, is based on territorial integrity and autonomous capacity for action. The principle of 'territorial integrity' was obsessively pursued during the Cold War era, when the conceptual barrier of 'non-interference into domestic affairs' constituted one of the main shields of totalitarian control in communist countries.

Second, the principle of 'autonomous state capacity' is an issue for today's welfare states which gain legitimacy in the eyes of their citizens as long as they are capable of delivering social goods. Globalization has a decisive impact on this aspiration. It will produce frequent and far-reaching

---

[3] See Dirk Messner (ed.), *Die Zukunft des Staates und der Politik. Möglichkeiten und Grenzen politisscher Steuerung in der Weltgesellschaft* (Bonn: Dietz, 1998); Stephan Gill (ed.), *Globalization, Democratization and Multilateralism* (Tokyo: United Nations University Press, 1997); Anthony G. MacGrew (ed.), *The Transformation of Democracy? Globalization and Territorial Democracy* (Cambridge: Polity Press, 1997); Beate Kohler-Koch (ed.), *Regieren in entgrenzten Räumen* (Opladen: Westdeutscher Verlag, 1998); Anthony Giddens, *Runaway World: How Globalisation is Reshaping Our Lives* (London: Profile Books, 1999).

[4] See Karl Kaiser, 'Globalisierung als Problem der Demokratie', *Internationale Politik*, vol. 53, no. 4 (1998), 3ff.

structural crises in sectors or regions that are exposed to global competition. Furthermore, globalization will give rise to de-democratization by way of domination of global market rules. These favour mobility, local cost advantages, and efficient economic conditions over local competition rules and regulations, which are the result of the local political decision-making process, and they tend to be protective, if not protectionist.

Third, because governments are unable to meet the challenges and pressures of 'economic globalization', there seems to be a growing 'democratic deficit'. Since states are the only framework in which democratic mechanisms, values, and norms have been able to take root, develop, and flourish, globalization is often perceived as equivalent to de-democratization. This development contrasts with the cry for freedom which was heard around the world during the late 1980s and early 1990s. It also contrasts with the means of new technologies which have led to unprecedented global communication and the rapid exchange of ideas and views. Some analysts conclude by dreaming about a cyberspace democracy, which will defeat the de-democratizing curse of globalization with the visionary hope of Internet-democracy, of global town hall meetings challenging Daimler Chrysler and the world financial markets.

Indeed, it seems necessary to structure the debate, pre-empt its jargon, and reflect upon the substance of it. Thus, three issues are relevant regarding democratic theory:

(*a*) democracy and regulatory competition;
(*b*) democracy and new global communication technologies;
(*c*) democracy and the search for global regimes.

III. DEMOCRACY AND REGULATORY COMPETITION

There is a problem of accountability and democratic control with transnational regulatory cooperation in any form, if and in so far as its underlying reason is globalization, defined as market competition without national barriers and regulatory mechanisms. On the one hand, due to globalization, prices will be reduced as a consequence of economies of scale and international competition between firms across the globe. On the other hand, however, investment decisions or tax laws can redirect fiscal resources and undermine predictable employment patterns in an unprecedented way. The protective side of nation-states, regions, and cities has become as permeable, as the sky did for air-based warfare after the Montgolfier balloon first cruised over Europe in 1783. Neo-liberal responses to globalization appear to be necessary. Yet, they are often perceived as contradictory and incompatible with democratic principles. Principles of the market and principles of democracy seem to be contradictory indeed—as long as democracy is defined as welfare-state-democracy, the state as protector of egalitarian norms of justice, democracy as equivalent to social justice, and distribution as equivalent to majoritarian rule. If the state is perceived as part of the solution and not as part of the problem, the market will certainly clash with democratic values. And if state capacity is understood as the capacity to generate social justice and welfare, global competition and its effects must indeed be seen as a challenge to state capacity.

In terms of democratic theory, one must recall the fact that in such a line of thinking 'democracy' is redefined from being a norm to long having become an instrument. If the goal is welfare state and social justice through state capacity on the basis of a consensual social contract, external effects on the parameters of the social contract must indeed be viewed as undermining its root, which is democracy. However, if democracy is considered to be a normative base for competitive action and freedom of choice, then external effects in the context of economic globalization can hardly do harm to the pursuit of democratic parameters. Democratic rule has always had to cope with a mentality of greed. In the past, democratic greed was organized around the social conflict between labour and capital. The new conflict of greed which has already become visible, can be described as one between those who benefit from economic globalization, hence referring to opportunities and new freedoms, and those who are eager to control globalization in the name of national democracy and welfare-state justice by referring to global threats to democracy and welfare state capacities. Instrumentalized national definitions of welfare-state democracy must always, inevitably, fall victim to 'globalization forces'.

IV. DEMOCRACY AND NEW GLOBAL TELECOMMUNICATIONS TECHNOLOGIES

Some see the Internet as a new heaven in a world of globalization. New information technologies generate, in their eyes, more intensive citizen participation, and thus the Internet will reinvent democracy and counterbalance economic globalization with the force of its global outreach. Internet surfing versus corporate decision-making, the lonely Internet freak versus the Wall Street broker? Is this the short version of a new political romanticism? The Internet and other means of new information technologies will certainly foster new elements of citizen participation, spontaneous movements of commitment, and organized interests. There is no clear answer to the following two fundamental preconditions and advantages of structured democracy and the rule of law: accountability and consistency.[5] The Internet cannot compete with the egalitarian basis

---

[5] See Ludger Kühnhardt, 'Wieviel Bytes verträgt der Staat,' in *MUT. Forum für Kultur, Politik und Geschichte*, no. 357 (May 1997), 34–41; Andreas Beierwaltes, *Demokratie und Medien* (Baden-Baden: Nomos, 2000).

of democracy. As long as two-thirds of mankind neither possess a telephone nor a PC with Internet access, popular sovereignty cannot be grounded on anything other than the good old ballot box. India, for example, proves that illiteracy can be overcome by giving parties symbols that people can understand. But who can use the Internet town hall meeting without a PC in his or her hut or castle?

The globalization of technology might gradually deconstruct the notion of the 'public sphere'. It creates new decentralized, in fact individualized, networks. But it cannot provide for a legitimate centre with organizational power, recognizing the egalitarian basis of all democratic values. All Internet surfers may be equal, but how about the rest of mankind? Decision-making mechanisms on the Net will always remain technologically based equivalents of opinion polls and voluntary referenda. The issue of accountability cannot be dealt with in a satisfactory manner. Both democratic principles and norms of the rule of law will be undermined if Internet democracy comes to be regarded as the democratizing control mechanism of economic globalization.

Globalized technologies are themselves an element of the so-called globalization. An old German proverb says that 'it is impossible to drive out the devil with Beelzebub'. Technologies can only and will always be just instruments. In order to transform them into norms and goals, and to give them the credibility of democratic instruments, it would be necessary to completely change the parameters of any decent democratic theory. Accountability can only be maintained when mandates and competencies are transparent and related to responsible personal actors. Technological globalization cannot reinvent democracy. It can broaden the scope of human judgement, but, as all empirical research indicates, it could also produce the opposite. The future of democracy in the age of globalization has to be addressed politically, and not instrumentally.

V.   DEMOCRACY AND THE SEARCH FOR GLOBAL REGIMES

Wherever global regimes of interest aggregation and conflict resolution are being contemplated, a political and legal solution to the problem of democracy is necessary. In the modern history of democracy, the rule of law evolved prior to democracy itself. It thus makes sense to begin the process of global institution-building by legal means and mechanisms, without expecting too much too fast from the potential inherent in democratic participation. Viewed as an evolutionary process, the democratization of global regimes cannot be excluded once and for all. But, it is probably incorrect to assume that it would be possible to begin with democracy as long as even the rule of law is not in sight on a global scale. From global environmental protection regimes to world trade arbitration mechanisms to international courts of justice—at the end of the twentieth century we are witnessing the embryonic stages of a legalization of international relations. NGOs might be the germs of global lobbyists. Yet, they cannot replace accountable national parliaments and cannot even speed up the democratization of international law as long as the law itself remains subject to the political will of its creators, the nation-states.

Democracy depends upon the recognition of its norms and procedures in a given space by a given population. Commitment can grow in the course of time, but no evolutionary optimism can do away with the fact that democracy needs a framework that is viable in both space and time. Only a global state could provide such a framework. According to some optimistic scholars, the world will have reached this stage of global government around 2750, maybe on a Monday morning in early summer.

The only possible way to overcome the current state of global political disorder and to move in the direction of anything even resembling a global state is dependent upon the states that form today's world. The United Nations is driven by such a vision, but, in fact, the United Nations is a United States, sometimes as disunited as it is united. Yet, a truly united world body might become the nucleus of a democratized global regime. So goes the hope, but since the days of Kant one finds theoretical reflections which are much stronger in the field of law than in that of politics. In other words, the universalization of a rule of law seems to be more plausible and conceivable than the universalization of democracy. Is globalization a no-win game for democrats? Or should they aspire to evolve from confederation to rule of law and then from federation to global democracy?

Hope is always useful, although it can become dangerous if it leads to too many unrealistic expectations. In the search for corresponding democratic parameters to economic globalization the State returns to the centre of the analysis. The State may have lost its monopoly capacity in the field of welfare, but whenever it comes to law-making and law enforcement, the State is without parallel, except for the European Union as the most developed transnational legal system. He who aspires to a world government must reckon with today's nation-states or emerging regional units! Depending on temper and mood, this analytical remark can be interpreted as a sign of hope or a sign of pessimism. In any case, whoever wants to create a global regime has to get States involved.

The confederative character of today's world order encourages us also to reflect upon the relationship between democracy and federalism. There are conceptual contradictions between the two notions, stemming from different social realities represented by the two concepts. The point of reference for reflecting about both concepts and their relationship is 'legitimacy'. Democracies are legitimated through egalitarian majority voting. Federal or confederal systems are legitimated either through consent or through qualified majority voting and decision-making patterns. If the principle of consent is applied, all governments are fully responsible for their decisions, and any one of them can block the other. If the principle of qualified or absolute majority voting is applied, the collective will of all individuals represented in the caucus will normally be distorted. For example, Wyoming's population is represented by the same number of senators as is California's. If the European Parliament implemented the principle of absolute proportionality, Luxembourg would be represented by 0.8 Members of Parliament in order to balance the ninety-nine Germans; or, if Luxembourg were to retain its six Members of Parliament, Germany would be eligible for almost 1,000 parliamentarians in the same house. Within the Federal Republic of Germany, one vote from Bremen in the Bundesrat, the Federal Council, is equivalent to thirteen voters from North-Rhine-Westphalia. Federal concepts are limited in their ability to apply egalitarian democratic principles. How can any federation compensate for the 'de-democratizing' effects of globalization? There is simply no panacea for correlating democracy and federalism, either on any regional level or on the global level.

VI. LESSONS OF THE EUROPEAN EXPERIENCE

How does the European Union cope with the dilemmas which this contribution has described? The current state of EU integration is not without problems of democracy and legitimacy, colloquially referred to as the 'democratic deficit' or 'legitimacy deficit'. The debate is as broad as the definitions of both issues, and the practical use of the debate is quite another story. For the sake of a self-critical reflection about the current dilemmas and contradictions of the European integration pattern, four theoretical options can be identified which are dominating the academic debate in Europe on the problems of multilevel governance in the light of democratic values.[6]

Model One: Government by the People. The cosmopolitan approach is focusing on input-oriented factors which will impact and strengthen the legitimacy of the European Union. The key terms used in this context: participation and democratic control; political accountability and separation of powers; individualized representation on the European level. The

---

[6] See Fritz W. Scharpf, 'Community and Autonomy: Multi-level Policy-Making in the European Union', *Journal of European Public Policy*, no. 1 (1994), 219–42; Beate Kohler-Koch, 'Catching Up with Change: The Transformation of Governance in the European Union', *Journal of European Public Policy*, no. 3 (1996), 359–80; Thomas Risse-Kappen, 'Exploring the Nature of the Beast: International Relations Theory and Comparative Political Analysis Meet the European Union', *Journal of Common Market Studies*, vol. 34, no. 1 (1996), 53–80; Marcus Höreth, 'The Trilemma of Legitimacy—Multilevel Governance in the EU and the Problem of Democracy', ZEI Discussion Paper C11/1998 (Bonn: Centre for European Integration Studies, 1998).

practical reform options include: overcoming the democratic deficit by developing democratized supranationality on the basis of a two-system chamber and the European Commission as a 'true' and responsible government. The objective is a federative European Union.

Model Two: Government by Organizations. The post-parliamentarian approach is also input-oriented: all interests of those affected by EU decisions shall be included by way of the broadest possible participation; representation on the EU level shall be rather functional. Reform options according to this model are: overcoming the democratic deficit by intensified participation of semi-public functional organizations; learning and institutionalizing deliberative modes of behaviour. The objective is a European Union defined as a deliberative network of decision-making processes.

Model Three: Government for the People. The technocratic-expertocratic model is output-oriented in its search for stronger legitimacy of the European Union: capacity for problem resolution and Pareto-efficiency matter most; representation on the EU level should primarily be functional. Reform options include: overcoming the democratic deficit by depoliticized means of problem resolution; burden-sharing through independent regulatory agencies; institutionalization of expertise. The objective is a regulatory state, a technocracy.

Model Four: Government of the People. This model is defining legitimacy socially: emphasis is on structural and socio-cultural conditions of legitimate rule; the nation-state is perceived as the only possible frame for democracy; representation on the EU level is predominantly executive. Reform options include the preservation of the principle of unanimity and the reduction of supranational institutions. The objective is a European confederation.

All four models mentioned imply advantages and disadvantages, both on the level of theory and with regard to their ability to be implemented consistently.

This leaves the European Union with almost no alternative but to gradually, incrementally pursue a policy which is primarily based on Model One with a little dose of Model Four, no matter how inadequate some of its paradigms might prove to be in the light of any search for logical consistentency and political cohesion. The European Union remains a regional political union in the making, evolutive as it were so far, with frustrations, deviations, and slow, but gradual steps forward rather than any quantum leap forward or backward.

The conclusion for the evolution of global governance in the light of the challenges and opportunities of 'globality' is that global rule of law and democratic governance can only grow incrementally on the basis of established and consistent regional systems of law and governance. Transatlantic regulatory cooperation is certainly so far the most advanced element of such a rule of law binding the governance systems on both sides of the Atlantic. Based on another logic, NATO is both a legal and a strategic dimension of the same nature, which tends to evolve into the sphere of politics while getting increasingly involved in the export of stability. A true political dimension of transatlantic governance is still missing. It could begin with councils on trade or foreign affairs or agriculture or science and education, in which the ministers and commissioners of the corresponding portfolios of the United States and the European Union meet on a regular basis, supported by meetings of the equivalent parliamentary committees of Congress and European Parliament. But can any transatlantic political cooperation ever be as legitimate and democratic as the emerging political union of the EU?

Model One is based on the idea that legitimacy can only be broadened if the citizens of the European Union will intensify their participation in the European decision-making system, thus effectively controlling political power. The political actors have to receive their mandate as directly as possible from the EU citizens in order to apply the principle of accountability. Separation of power is a must, participation through parliament the perspective.[7] In practical terms this option favours a stronger European Parliament with competences clearly beyond those granted by the Amsterdam Treaty. The European Parliament would have the right of initiative and would completely control the Commission which is gradually developing into a full-fledged European government.

The parliamentary paradigm compares the European constitution-building process with the national experiences of parliamentarized democracy and tries to apply the same model on the EU level. The vision is of a quasi-federalism which will overcome problems of legitimacy and the democratic deficit by way of a full parliamentary system topped with a European Constitution that clearly defines the competences and mandates of the vertical and the horizontal actors. In the logic of this model, a mighty European Parliament alone could realize the principle of political accountability.

The main counter-argument against a stronger parliamentarization of the EU governance system refers to the lack of a 'European people', a European demos, as a basis for any democratic community with consistent identity, traditions, and experiences. Beyond this argument of identity, critics question the efficiency of a parliamentarized system of EU multi-level governance. The more the European Union might gain democratic quality, the more it might lose in decision-making efficiency. Both counter-arguments are, of course, speculative. The multi-linguistic Switzerland demonstrates the ability to form a federation without a lin-

---

[7] See Simon Bulmer, 'The Governance of the European Union: A New Institutionalist Approach', *Journal of Public Policy*, no. 4 (1994), 351–80; Brigid Laffan (ed.), *Constitution-Building in the European Union* (Dublin: Institute of European Affairs, 1996).

guistically defined and forged demos. The argument of limited efficiency is self-serving as long as there can be no empirical evidence for supporting this thesis. More important seems to be the concern about a lack of democratic infrastructure, which is rooted in a lack of a collective identity.

The answer to this could well be pragmatic: nobody has ever tried all the possible means to strengthen and even create all the intermediary structures that could be contemplated in this context. Both political parties and the media have only begun to Europeanize and thus create something equivalent to a 'European public'. Important is the concern that a parliamentarized European Union would weaken the Member States of the EU as legitimizing resources of the European integration process. This is, however, more of a practical argument, relevant in the context of power struggle and resource claims rather than an argument of pure logic. The fear that a European federation would weaken the legitimacy of Member State parliaments is only true if the relationship between the EU Parliament and Member State parliaments is to be defined as a zero-sum game.

A second set of arguments in the context of Model One is putting emphasis on the democratization of the territorial representation.[8] Territorial representation, according to this model, no longer follows the principle of executive representation, i.e. representation through the Member State governments in the European Council. It rather favours the idea of senatorial representation, i.e. representation through directly elected senators. The US model is close at hand as a role model for this approach. Critics worry that the EU Commission might grow in relevance without control since it would no longer be forced to cope with the rather professional and competent national executives of the Member States.

A third set of arguments in the context of Model One is favouring European referenda and plebiscites as a way to broaden the legitimacy and the democracy of the European integration process. Strengths and weaknesses of all possible arguments (pro and con) are well known from the debate on plebiscitarian democracy. The lack of socio-cultural identity within the European Union tends to support the sceptics in this debate. Other proposals in line with Model One support the direct election of a European head of state.

Model Two advances functional representation as a means of realizing democratically legitimized rule in the European Union. Experts should rule instead of parliaments—such is the formula of those who consider parliamentary democracy no longer appropriate, but want to preserve alternatives in line with the principle of democracy.[9] The set of arguments

---

[8] See Philippe Schmitter, 'Representation and the Future Euro-Polity', in *Staatswissenschaften und Staatspraxis*, no. 3 (1992), 379–405.

[9] See Tanja Börzel, 'Policy Networks: A New Paradigma for European Governance', Working Paper No. 97/19, European University Institute: Florence 1997.

in favour of the formation of multiple, semi-autonomous centres of decision-making with shifting sets of members and different areas of functional competence reformulates Lincoln's Gettysburg address in the name of 'Government of organizations, by organizations and for organizations'. Along the line of civil society paradigms, economic actors, interest groups, and social movements are considered to be the adequate subjects of modern (better: postmodern, deconstructivist) democracy. To govern through, as it is called in some of the literature, 'epistemic communities'[10] is a somewhat naive if not ideological answer to the problems of modern complexity and democratic politics. In the name of 'justice' and 'concern', the principle of democratic equality would be undermined and pre-empted if functional representation were to replace democratically legitimized parliamentary representation.

Plato's 'rule of the wise' seems to be the role model of theories of functional representation as well as of any technocratic utilitarian justification of alternatives to the current parameters of European integration. Model Three is based on the assumption that efficiency will be of more importance to the citizens of the European Union than democratic representation and control. Legitimacy will grow with the ability to prove the capacity for action. Practical proposals include the change of the modalities of decision-making processes, including the enlargement of the majoritarian principle. Practical suggestions are meant to limit the majoritarian principle in order to prevent Member States from being forced to accept majoritarian decisions against their own will if vital interests are involved. Effective implementation of EU decisions, a strengthened role of the European Court of Justice and the increased inclusion of experts in the decision-making processes flow from Model Three.

The inspiration of Model Three seems to be the 'regulatory state' which has been defined as the 'fourth branch of government'. To correct market failures by way of social regulation has become a classical paradigm of certain theoretical and practical games.[11] It remains, however, somewhat naive to believe that such a regulatory state would ever be purely based on efficiency criteria without redistributive effects. Concepts based on Pareto-efficiency arguments assume that no one has to control the agency, while the agency itself is under control. Professional self-control would generate deliberative, i.e. criteria-based, arguments instead of an interest-ridden and daunting search for compromises and decision. The plea for independent, professionally legitimized regulatory agencies is light-years

---

[10] See Peter M. Haas, 'Epistemic Communities and International Policy Coordination', *International Organization*, vol. 46 (1992), 1–35.

[11] See Giandomenico Majone, 'The Rise of the Regulatory State in Europe', *Western European Politics*, no. 17 (1994), 77–101; Ian Begg, 'Regulation in the European Union', *Journal of European Public Policy*, no. 3 (1996), 525–35; James Carporaso, 'The European Union and Forms of State: Westphalian, Regulatory or Post-modern?', *Journal of Common Market Studies*, vol. 34 (1996), 29–52.

away from political realities. It is simply inconceivable to assume that policy-making could be depoliticized in a multinational setting as long as the national parameters of policy-making continue to exist. Either regulatory agencies are independent or they remain accountable to parliaments. While the first assumption is almost impossible to conceive, the second one relativizes the whole model by making regulatory agencies what indeed they ought to be in a parliamentary democracy: subject to parliamentary decision-making processes. No matter how far removed they might be from deliberative purity, they are based on the idea of popular sovereignty (input-legitimacy), which has survived for more centuries than probably any contemporary theory of deliberative theory will.[12]

This is also evident with regard to the premises of Model Four. To reorient the legitimacy of European integration would mean to underestimate the proven experiences with a historically singular structure of supranational integration that has taken on the status of a confederation over a long period of time. Sceptics like to talk about the difficulties in forming a common European identity, whatever this 'collective singular' might mean. On the basis of the argument that such a European identity is both far from being a reality and difficult to achieve at all, they favour confederative models of intergovernmental cooperation and integration.

Concrete suggestions support a stronger role for the national parliaments in the processes of European policy-formulation. Although practically all European parliaments, including the associate members of the European Union, have installed 'European Committees' by now, this alone does not strengthen the confederative ambitions. European Committees of national parliaments seem rather to consider themselves as lobbyists for a deepened integration process and thus in favour of the EU decisions being properly implemented into the national context rather than controlling too much of a European 'centralization'. While a return to a European state system of intergovernmental and confederative cooperation seems unlikely, it would in any case mean a step backwards in the resolution of the problems of democracy and legitimacy in a system of multi-level governance as it has developed over more than four decades.[13]

---

[12] See Paul P. Craig, 'Democracy and Rule-Making within the EC: An Empirical and Normative Assessment', *European Law Journal*, vol. 3 (1997), 105–30; Martin Shapiro, 'The Problems of Independent Agencies in the United States and the European Union', *Journal of European Public Policy*, no. 4 (1997), 276–91.

[13] See Neil Nugent, *The Government and Politics of the European Union* (London: Macmillan, 1995); Markus Jachtenfuchs and Beate Kohler-Koch (eds), *Europäische Integration* (Opladen: Westdeutscher Verlag, 1996); Jeremy Richardson (ed.), *European Union: Power and Policy-Making* (London: Routledge, 1996); Wolfgang Eltrich (ed.), *Europäische Integration und die Globalisierung* (München: Hanns Seidel Stiftung, 1998).

VII. WHAT IS TO BE DONE?

I would like to put forth three provocative proposals:

First, get realistic about democracy; shift the focus from 'democracy' to 'legitimacy' and redefine it in a realistic way with a sense of setting priorities in a 'legal-political' and not in a socio-economic sense. Maintain the definition of democracy as a set of norms and procedures, rather than as an instrument to meet the socio-economic realities of the twenty-first century world. Keep accountability and a clear structure of mandates and competences in highest esteem in order to keep the legitimacy of democracies alive in the face of all the scepticism emanating from neo-authoritarian or any purist, day-dreaming positions.

Second, try to tame the tiger of 'globalization' by socio-economic means, without politicizing it in the wrong way. Stop overburdening the concept of democracy by trying to suggest that global democratization could be possible in order to respond to the challenges of globalization with seemingly 'modernized', 'updated' instruments of democracy which pretend to square the circle between welfare-orientated definitions of 'political capacity' and romanticism about 'international' democracy.

Third, support the development of regional regimes along the lines of the European Union, or the United States for that matter. Regional political regimes can broaden the scope of nation-states by pooling sovereignty beyond the nation-states without overdoing it by dreaming about a global state.[14] In order to avoid falling into the trap of cultural relativism, regional parochialism, or possessive inclinations against other regions and their respective experiences, the global community of the twenty-first century has to be organized in concentric circles starting at the grassroots level of life and gradually broadening the horizon: first home and family, then city and region, then state and culture, finally open regionalism and global coordination.

This might not be an ambitious programme, neither sparkling with jargon nor with scientific model-formation. But realism has always proved to be the best basis for both reason and vision. Both reason and vision are needed in the twenty-first century, in which 'globalization' will be replaced by the general recognition of 'globality' as the central point of reference for any local, national, or regional action.

---

[14] See Thomas Jäger and Melanie Piepenschneider (eds), *Europa 2020. Szenarien politischer Entwicklung* (Opladen: Westdeutscher Verlag, 1997); Markus Jachtenfuchs, Thomas Dietz, and Sabine Jung, 'Which Europe? Conflicting Models of a Legitimate European Political Order', *European Journal of International Relations*, vol. 4 (1998), 409–45; Martin Westlake (ed.), *The European Union Beyond Amsterdam* (London: Routledge, 1998).

North Atlantic cooperation and democratizing globalism

Sol Picciotto

I. A CONSTITUTION FOR THE WORLD ECONOMY?

A. Globalization as a political project

Since the mid-1990s, a number of factors and events have focused public concern on the effects and implications of the current phase of globalization. The series of financial crises which reversed the rapid growth of many Asian countries, devastated Russia, and hit Brazil, gave a menacing reminder of the fragility of an open and under-regulated world economy. Although leaders and decision-makers have generally remained convinced of the need to continue to pursue the neo-liberal mission of removal of all national barriers to market access for goods, services, and capital, there has been a greater emphasis on the phasing of liberalization, and the need for it to be accompanied by improvements both in national state regulation and global governance.[1] The World Trade Organization (WTO), the main institutional embodiment of the neo-liberal vision of the world economy, became the focus of controversy and criticism, as the decisions of its panels continued to prioritize global free trade over local concerns as diverse as those of Caribbean smallholder banana producers, European beef consumers, American environmentalists, and Canadian magazine readers. Following the failure of his attempt to secure fast-track negotiating approval from the Congress in November 1997, President Clinton attempted to appease some of the domestic critics in his speech to the GATT 50th anniversary meeting in May 1998, by speaking of the need for the WTO to listen to ordinary citizens, consult representatives of the broad public, and bring openness and accountability to its operations. The point was driven home when the OECD states were forced first to suspend and then abandon the proposed Multilateral Agreement on Investment

---

[1] As to the former, see the World Bank's *World Development Report. The State in a Changing World* of 1997; and for the latter, the report of the Commission on Global Governance, *Our Global Neighbourhood* (Oxford: Oxford University Press, 1995). See also Joseph Stiglitz, 'More Instruments and Broader Goals: Moving Towards the Post-Washington Consensus', 1998 WIDER Lecture (UN University–World Institute for Development Economics Research, Helsinki).

(MAI), after 4 years of preparation and 3 years of intensive negotiations. This was attributed, at least partly, to the failure of the negotiators to 'gain wider popular legitimacy for their actions by explaining and defending them in public', thus leaving themselves open to ambush by a coalition of 'network guerillas'.[2]

In the midst of these events, a number of news sources quoted Renato Ruggiero, then the WTO's Director-General, as saying 'We are writing the constitution of the new global economy'. This quote was taken up and cited by critics of the MAI negotiations, who argued that an excessively pro-business structure was being constructed, largely in secret. Interestingly, the WTO felt the need to issue a press release correcting the story, pointing out that the MAI was being negotiated at the OECD, an entirely different organization consisting of twenty-nine advanced economies, while 80 per cent of the WTO's 132 members are developing countries and economies in transition.[3] Apparently, the report had originated in a speech given by Mr Ruggiero on 16 January 1998 at Chatham House in London, in which he quoted Professor John Jackson as having described the multilateral trading system as a 'constitution' for the world economy.

Mr Ruggiero's primary concern was no doubt to make it clear that the WTO was not responsible for the MAI. However, this was not what those citing the remark were suggesting, since one of the main criticisms of the MAI was precisely that it should not be negotiated at the OECD but in a more inclusive forum such as the WTO. The thrust of the criticism was rather at the lack of openness and accountability of both the negotiations and the structures envisaged for such important international economic institutions.

Indeed, it could be said that a 'constitution for the world economy' is precisely what we should be thinking about. This does not mean that there is either a unified world economy or an emerging global government. However, it does seem clear that the patterns of global socio-economic

---

[2] Guy De Jonquières, 'Network Guerillas', *Financial Times*, 30 Mar. 1998; see also Nick Mabey, 'Defending the Legacy of Rio: the Civil Society Campaign against the MAI', in Sol Picciotto and Ruth Mayne (eds), *Regulating International Business: Beyond Liberalization* (Basingstoke: Macmillan, 1999).

[3] WTO, PRESS/91, 17 Feb. 1998. It added that 'There is no negotiation currently underway in the WTO which focuses on investment'. While this was strictly correct, it was well known that many OECD States had pressed for such a negotiation at the WTO; their intention was to persuade developing countries to join the MAI, which was billed as a 'free-standing' treaty, and several non-OECD Members were admitted to the MAI negotiations. Indeed, following the collapse of the MAI negotiations several of the main participants, notably the European Commission and Japan, quickly began to press for the inclusion of investment in the next WTO negotiating round, based on a slightly modified version of the MAI, and building on the 'educative' work of the WTO's Working Group on Trade and Investment. Despite the WTO press release, the *Christian Science Monitor* of 25 Feb. 1998 was still citing Ruggiero as saying that the MAI would be 'the constitution for a single global economy'.

integration which have developed in the past quarter-century have also entailed major changes in the role and interactions of political structures and processes of accountability and legitimation, both within and between states. These changes have been inadequately considered in the debates around the misleading concept of 'globalization', which create an unhelpful polarity between views that the nation-state is dead or still very much alive. A different approach would consider the implications of these changes for the form and functions of statehood, or more generally for the institutions and structures of the public sphere. In this chapter I will sketch out what I consider these changes to have been, in order to put forward some suggestions which could help to remedy the 'democratic deficit' of the new global public sphere.

B. The special responsibilities of the United States and the European Union

Clearly, the United States and the European Union can and must make a crucial contribution to the process of constitution-building for the world economy. As other contributions in this book spell out in detail, North Atlantic business and trading interests play a preponderant role in the world economy. Their political weight is perhaps even more significant, as was dramatically shown by the NATO action on Kosovo. Yet, as that action also demonstrated, it is crucial that their leadership should be exercised in a way that is sensitive to the concerns of the whole of the world community. While disagreements between these two powerful entities can greatly hinder the work of international organizations, their unity can pose an even greater threat if it disregards or overrides the views of others in the South and East.

Both also have much to contribute from their own history and experience to the design of democratic political institutions for the regulation of corporate capitalism: the United States as a complex federal system with powerful public regulatory agencies and underpinned by a strong rule of law; and the European Union as the pioneer of a new form of still-evolutionary confederation. Yet both must also beware of seeking to impose their own model or perspectives inappropriately on others. Even more importantly, both need to find new ways of accommodating internal demands for accountability in relation to increasingly complex international institutional involvements. Devices such as Fast Track negotiating authority, and the EU's 'Article 113 Committee' no longer respond adequately to the need for public consultations on the wide range of international negotiations and procedures involving public bodies, which have often extensive internal repercussions.[4] At the same time, internal political

---

[4] Under the US Constitution, treaties require the 'advice and consent' of the Senate, by a two-thirds majority. However, it has become accepted that some international agreements

demands can put great strain on international relationships, as evidenced, for example, by the difficulties faced by the European Union in devising a banana import regime which could satisfy its various internal political constituencies while remaining compatible with its international obligations and pressures.

C. Liberalization and democratization

The past quarter-century has seen an increasing process of economic liberalization—the removal of barriers both between and within states to the flows of goods, capital, and labour. Economic liberalization has also been commonly assumed to be linked to political democratization. However, the nature of the interaction is not obvious. While political studies have found that domestic factors have had the strongest influence in democratic transitions, it is also clear that the international context plays an important part through processes of emulation and influence, in which both the European Union and the United States have played major roles.[5] Nevertheless, as Philippe Schmitter has pointed out, the transmission-belt for democratization has been the international communication outside government controls of images and ideas, rather than a simple causal link of economic freedom stimulating political democratization.[6] Indeed, external interests in opening markets and exploiting economic opportuni-

---

may be treated as 'executive agreements' and exempt from the need for this approval (the United States signed the original GATT on this basis). Nevertheless, any agreement which requires changes to domestic law will need to be acceptable to both Houses of the Congress. Under 'fast track', the Congress enables the Executive to enter into complex negotiations (in particular multilateral trade deals) by specifying the topics which may be covered and a deadline, and undertaking that the resulting agreement will be voted upon by both Houses on a take-it-or-leave-it basis. The EU's objective of a common commercial policy, expressed in Article 113 of the Treaty of Rome, includes the negotiation of tariff and trade agreements, which the Article provides should be conducted by the Commission under the authority of the Council and in consultation with a special committee appointed by the Council for this task. This is now Article 133 of the Treaty of the European Community, with the addition of a new paragraph allowing the Council (acting unanimously and after consulting the Parliament) to extend such negotiations to services and intellectual property. While the commercial-policy powers may be exercised by a qualified majority, the Council's residual powers to take action to achieve the objectives of the common market (Article 235, now 308) require unanimous agreement. See Alan Dashwood, 'External Relations Provisions of the Amsterdam Treaty', *Common Market Law Review*, vol. 35 (1998), 1019–45.

[5] Laurence Whitehead (ed.), *The International Dimensions of Democratization: Europe and the Americas* (Oxford: Oxford University Press, 1996).

[6] Philippe Schmitter, 'The Influence of the International Context upon the Choice of National Institutions and Policies in Neo-Democracies', in Whitehead, *International Dimensions* (Oxford: Oxford University Press, 1996), 26–54. He points out that the hypothesis that economic freedom leads to political democracy is an inversion of Kant's assumption that republics would be more likely to engage in international commerce and renounce war (Immanuel Kant, *Toward Perpetual Peace* (1795), in M. J. Gregor, trans. (ed.), *Practical Philosophy* (Cambridge: Cambridge University Press, 1966), 311–51).

ties may entail repression of autochthonous democratic forces or their channelling towards 'western values'.[7]

In fact, far-reaching social changes underly the recent phase of globalization, and the transformations of the character and the interrelationship of the political and economic, the public and private spheres. Autocratic power has been rapidly losing its ability to command automatic deference in both the family and the factory, the classroom and the boardroom. This results from widespread revolts against authoritarian domination and the power to control truth embodied in tradition, involving demands for increased personal freedom and dignity, equality (notably, between women and men), and the ending of coercion.[8] While undermining patriarchy and hierarchy, these anti-authoritarian movements have also paved the way to post-industrial capitalism, with its emphasis on information-management, flexible working, and a global outlook.

They have also stimulated the rethinking of democratic principles and significant constitutional remodelling that have been taking place in what are thought of as the 'mature' democracies. In Britain, for example, the 'Mother of Parliaments' has devolved powers to regional assemblies in Scotland and Wales, incorporated the European Convention on Human Rights into national law, and is finally to democratize its hereditary upper House and introduce freedom of information legislation. Yet even while the UK Government was taking the lead in NATO military action to impose solutions to ethnic problems in the Balkans, the deep-rooted conflicts in Northern Ireland remain apparently intractable. Indeed, some political philosophers argue for a new approach to constitutionalism that can take account of the claims to recognition of multiple, overlapping, and diverse cultural identities, as opposed to the liberal assumption of an undifferentiated and homogenous citizenry.[9] These dilemmas, debates, and changes in the forms of democracy are often ignored in the talk of 'transitions to democracy', which tends to assume a clear distinction between authoritarian states and those with multi-party representative democracy.

However, the overarching challenge is to find new democratic forms matching the new, globally integrated patterns of production and consumption. While there is much talk of the 'democratic deficit' of regional and international institutions, debate about how it might be remedied is at best half-hearted, or even sceptical.[10] This can be readily understood if we

---

[7] Adam Burgess, *Divided Europe: The New Domination of the East* (London: Pluto Press, 1997).

[8] Anthony Giddens, *Runaway World. The Reith Lectures 1999* (from bbc.co.uk accessed 8 May 1999).

[9] James Tully, *Strange Multiplicity: Constitutionalism in an Age of Diversity* (Cambridge: Cambridge University Press, 1995).

[10] Thus, Robert A. Dahl argues that international organizations (including the European Union) are, and can only be, bureaucratic bargaining systems among elites; this conclusion

continue to think in terms of a simple electoral representative model of democracy. No one seriously envisages the possibility of a global government on this pattern, and indeed the greater awareness of the importance of locality and diversity resulting from economic globalization renders it even less believable. Consequently, those who seek a foundation of legitimacy for global economic liberalization tend to resort to prescriptions for universal rights and principles of justice. However, if national governments remain the fulcrum between national and international political structures, a radical liberal vision of cosmopolitan citizenship and universal individual rights lacks any substantial democratic content.

This dilemma can be seen in much of the discussion of the prospects and proposals for 'cosmopolitan democracy'. This debate recognizes that globalization, based on the neo-liberal vision of the removal of barriers and the unleashing of the forces of economic self-interest, is at best unstable if it cannot deliver social justice, and that global social-justice issues must be debated and resolved within a global public sphere.[11] However, there is too little understanding or analysis of the nature of this global public sphere. It is frequently said to entail the emergence of some sort of global or international 'civil society'. Yet, there is considerable vagueness about who are the members of such a global civil society; and in the perspective of international relations they are seen in an undifferentiated way as 'non-state actors', as opposed to states (meaning governments) which are the 'traditional' members of international society. Certainly, the more sophisticated theorists concede that 'the spatial reach of the modern nation-state did not fix impermeable borders for other networks', and that 'political communities have rarely—if ever—existed in isolation as bounded geographical totalities, and they are better thought of as overlapping networks of interaction'.[12] Indeed, one can go further and point out that territorially-defined states have themselves always formed overlapping and interlocking spheres, as the exercise of State powers was mediated through the flexible concept of jurisdiction. Thus, the classical liberal international State system of Kant and Smith was already composed of interdependent states, and the growth of corporate industrial capitalism has since the second half of the nineteenth century depended on international

flows from his view that the problem of delegation, already great for national representative systems, becomes insuperable for international politics: 'Can International Organizations be Democratic? A Skeptic's View', in Ian Shapiro and Casiano Hacker-Cordón, *Democracy's Edges* (Cambridge: Cambridge University Press, 1999), 19–36. See also Peter L. Lindseth, 'Democratic Legitimacy and the Administrative Character of Supranationalism: the Example of the European Community', *Columbia Law Review*, vol. 99 (1999), 628.

[11] Richard Devetak and Richard Higgott, 'Justice Unbound? Globalization, States and the Transformation of the Social Bond', *International Affairs*, vol. 75 (1999), 483–98.

[12] David Held, *Democracy and the Global Order: From the Modern State to Cosmopolitan Governance* (Cambridge, UK: Polity Press, 1995), 225.

arrangements, many of which (such as the system of intellectual property) resulted from debates and pressures of 'international civil society'.[13]

Hence, the problem of globalization does not simply result from 'disjunctures' between nationally organized political systems and increasingly globally oriented economic activity, or even power structures. It stems from changes in the form and functions of the State itself, as well as its international structures, resulting from the dynamic of socio-economic relations. What globalization means, and the shape it might take, are as much political as economic questions. A new global public sphere has been under construction for some time, but it has come from the policies and decisions of international elites. The question now is whether and how it can be democratized.

II. GLOBAL GOVERNANCE NETWORKS

A. The fragmentation of the public sphere

Consideration of appropriate democratic principles and institutions for the global public sphere should be based on analysis of its particular character, rather than an extrapolation of inappropriate and in many ways dated national models of majoritarian representative democracy. A good starting-point is provided by the buzzword 'global governance'. This seems to have been introduced into the parlance of the so-called Washington consensus by World Bank officials, constrained by its constitution from intervening in the domestic political affairs of states, who found 'governance' a useful euphemism in raising issues such as corruption.[14] However, it also reflected a technicist view of social management which had a wider resonance. Thus, among some theorists of political science and public administration it has been used to analyse changing patterns of state–market coordination, resulting from failures of government or political control and responding to social complexity, which can be more decentralized and interactive.[15] In this sense it paralleled the concept

---

[13] For a more detailed analysis, see Sol Picciotto, 'The Regulatory Criss-Cross: Interaction between Jurisdictions and the Construction of Global Regulatory Networks', in W. Bratton, J. McCahery, S. Picciotto, and C. Scott (eds), *International Regulatory Competition and Coordination* (Oxford: Clarendon Press, 1996), 89; and C. N. Murphy, *International Organization and Industrial Change. Global Governance since 1850* (Cambridge, UK: Polity Press, 1994).

[14] Yves Dezalay and Bryant Garth, *The Internationalization of Palace Wars* (Chicago: Chicago University Press, forthcoming), ch. 11. The World Bank was also influenced to take greater account of the role of the state by the success of the East Asian 'developmental states': R. Wade, 'Japan, The World Bank, and the Art of Paradigm Maintenance: *The East Asian Miracle* in Political Perspective', *New Left Review*, no. 217 (1996), 3–36.

[15] See Jan Kooiman, *Modern Governance: New Government-Society Interactions* (London: Sage Publications, 1993). Renate Mayntz, from a systems-theory perspective, traces the term back to German debates on 'soziale Steuerung', used as an equivalent for the Parsonian concept of control (as in control hierarchy); however, this obscured the distinction between

of 'regulation', which has also come to be used either in a general sense of the capacity of the social system to adapt and stabilize in response to politico-economic dynamics (as in the French 'regulation school'), or more particularly to refer to explicit, legally formalized mechanisms for directing or supervising market-based activities.

The use of these terms is both descriptive and normative. They reflect real historical developments, with the transformation of large-scale industrial production and of centralized planning systems (both State and corporate), leading to the emergence of more flexible and interactive modes of production and distribution based on electronic technologies, as well as the major changes in money and finance involving new forms of market intermediation of savings and investment. At the same time these concepts are often used to legitimize the increasingly important role of a variety of professionals operating in the increasingly large interface between the State, which has been substantially 'privatized,' and the market, which is dominated by corporate networks. Not surprisingly, each group tends to give its own ideological spin to the terms: policy-makers and lawyers advocate deliberately-designed governing mechanisms and formalized regulation, while economists emphasize the self-governing capacities of market-based systems.

Thus, an important aspect of globalization has been a process of fragmentation of the public sphere, reflecting shifts in the character and relationships of private and public institutions, and resulting in systems of layered governance based on regulation.[16] A number of writers have described this in terms of the emergence of regulatory webs or networks, although their analyses of the phenomenon and its implications differ in various ways. Notably, Anne-Marie Slaughter[17] refers to the 'disaggregation' of the State, and the development of international regulatory cooperation through intergovernmental networks. John Braithwaite and Peter Drahos have conducted an impressive survey and analysis of the role of global regulatory webs in the globalization of business.[18] Giandomenico Majone also points to the growing phenomenon of delegation of public functions or powers to specialist and often technical bodies, and sees EU

governing (the intentional application of measures to achieve goals) and governance (which recognizes that social subsystems have autonomous capacities to develop and will react and adapt to governing measures): Renate Mayntz, 'Governing Failures and the Problem of Governability: Some Comments on a Theoretical Paradigm', in Kooiman, *Modern Governance*, 9 (translated and revised from an article published in German in 1987).

[16] Organization for Economic Cooperation and Development, *Regulatory Cooperation for an Interdependent World* (Paris: OECD, 1994). See also Sol Picciotto, 'Networks in International Economic Integration: Fragmented States and the Dilemmas of Neo-Liberalism', *Northwestern Journal of International Economic Law*, vol. 17 (1996/7), 1014.

[17] Anne-Marie Slaughter, 'The Real New World Order', *Foreign Affairs*, vol. 76 (1997), 183–97, and see also her contribution in this volume.

[18] John Braithwaite and Peter Drahos, *Global Business Regulation* (Cambridge: Cambridge University Press, 2000).

agencies in practice as transnational regulatory networks.[19] More fundamentally, Manuel Castells in his monumental three-volume account of what he describes as *The Information Age* considers that networks are the prime characteristic of the emerging social structures, and also describes the European Union as the Network State.[20]

Despite some differences in their analyses, each of these writers also recognizes that this process entails a rethinking of accountability or legitimacy. In the remainder of this contribution I will explore some of the proposed legitimation or democratization arrangements, grouped around two models.

B. The Kantian model and epistemic communities

Some see no need to revise the dominant existing model of representative democracy based on the nation-state, but would seek to ensure its adoption in all states, which should be bound together within a strong framework of international law and institutions embodying individual human rights. In this perspective 'equal rights of the citizens may offer the most effective strategy for compensating the "democratic deficit" of international organizations'.[21] This would actualize Kant's vision of 'Perpetual Peace', based on a confederation or League of republican states which would renounce war and pursue reciprocal economic benefits through trade, under an umbrella of principles embodying individual cosmopolitan rights.[22]

This ultra-liberal view assumes that the pursuit of individual self-interest, especially through economic exchange, is ultimately beneficial to all, so that the development of principles embodying individual rights, and the adjudication of conflicting rights-claims, would be sufficient to ensure universal consent and legitimacy. This would therefore justify even the entrenchment of internationally agreed principles so as to override national parliamentary supremacy, to secure the 'effective judicial protection of the transnational exercise of individual rights'.[23] Many, even

---

[19] Giandomenico Majone (ed.), *Regulating Europe: European Public Policy* (London: Routledge, 1996). Equally, US lawyers such as Alfred Aman, have pointed out how domestic regulatory reforms have facilitated the globalization of markets, but that they require a new approach 'that enables citizens in individual jurisdictions to transcend the idea that their "place" is limited by national boundaries or their own particular geography'. See Alfred Aman, 'A Global Perspective on Current Regulatory Reform: Rejection, Relocation, or Reinvention?', *Indiana Journal of Global Legal Studies*, vol. 2 (1995), 464.

[20] For his discussion of networks, see especially the Conclusion to volume 1, *The Rise of the Network Society* (Oxford: Blackwell Publishers, 1996), and on Europe, ch. 5 of his 3rd vol., *End of Millennium* (Oxford: Blackwell Publishers, 1998).

[21] Ernst-Ulrich Petersmann, 'How to Constitutionalize International Law and Foreign Policy for the Benefit of Civil Society?', *Michigan Journal of International Law*, vol. 20 (1998), 28.

[22] Kant, *Toward Perpetual Peace* (1795).

[23] Petersmann, 'How to Constitutionalize International Law' (above, n. 21), 26.

lawyers, will be sceptical of the faith this places in general liberal principles of law: democracy is far more than the rule of law. Law can at best provide a framework for adjudicating competing claims of right: political processes must decide who should have what rights. This was seen, for example, in the debates around the MAI, which was criticized on the grounds that it would grant strongly enforceable rights for corporations and investors without any concomitant responsibilities, and impose 'disciplines' on states without strengthening state regulatory capacity.[24]

Others have put forward somewhat modified, neo-Kantian models, which accept the need for a strengthening of the international institutional framework to provide an underpinning for 'cosmopolitan democratic public law'; but what seems to be envisaged does not appear very different from what I have described as the ultra-liberal model, somewhat reinforced by improving the representativeness of regional and international organizations.[25] There are clear contradictions and limits to the neo-Kantian models,[26] and a new approach should begin by more adequately taking into account the ways in which the changed nature of the State and the fragmentation of the public sphere entail new modes of accountability and hence new democratic forms at all levels.

A different, but in many ways complementary, approach is taken by some of those who do accept that the new modes of governance raise new issues of accountability. These are the political and international relations theorists who have identified the important role of regulatory networks in the regional and international spheres, but regard them as an essentially technocratic infrastructure, or a delegation of administrative powers.[27]

[24] See Picciotto and Mayne (eds), *Regulating International Business* (above, n. 2).

[25] This appears to be the argument of Held, *Democracy and the Global Order* (above, n. 12); see also David Held, 'Cosmopolitan Democracy and the Global Order: A New Agenda', in James Bohman and Mathias Lutz-Bachman (eds), *Perpetual Peace* (Cambridge, Mass.: MIT Press, 1997), 235–51.

[26] These are explored by the contributors to James Bohman and Mathias Lutz-Bachman's edited collection *Perpetual Peace* (Cambridge, Mass., MIT Press 1997), although they are generally concerned for various reasons to rescue what can be salvaged rather than look for a new approach. As the Editors of the collection point out in their Introduction, 'Escaping the dilemmas of despotism and fragmentation remains the most difficult institutional challenge of a cosmopolitan order; showing how the public use of reason permits both unity and difference is a task that the Kantian conception of reason has yet to solve.' Ibid. 18.

[27] In international relations, this is essentially a variant of regime theory: see e.g. Volker Rittberger (ed.), *Régime Theory and International Relations* (Oxford: Clarendon Press, 1993); J. Rosenau and E.-O. Czempiel (eds), *Governance without Government* (Cambridge: Cambridge University Press, 1992). For a thorough treatment of supranationalism as delegated administrative or normative power, with an incisive analysis of the legitimacy problems it poses, see Lindseth, 'Democratic Legitimacy' (above, n. 10). Lindseth suggests that the entire ensemble of the supranational institutions of the European Community should be characterized as 'a kind of administrative agency of the several Member States', since 'its institutional legitimacy does not flow from an en masse political mobilization, globally transferring sovereignty in a constitutional sense' (ibid. 659). This is perhaps somewhat circular and static: another view is that the construction of transnational institutions has also been a response to legitimation crises at the national level, a view compatible with the broader perspective with

From this perspective, specialists or experts can be regarded as facilitating the normal channels of government and international relations, by dealing with detailed and essentially technical tasks, thus making it easier for the traditional democratic government structures to resolve the more general and important political issues. This approach has been theorized by Emanuel Adler and Peter Haas, who argue that the 'epistemic communities' of experts sharing a common set of values can facilitate the resolution of global policy issues by 'narrowing the range within which political bargains could be struck'. As an example, they cite the way in which the core of the Bretton Woods monetary system, fixed rates and the dollar-gold standard, was agreed by expert consensus, leaving a narrower range of issues such as the extent of balance-of-payments support to be 'resolved through purely political muscle'.[28] However, the insider memoirs of Raymond Mikesell give a very different and more plausible flavour of those negotiations, showing that the 'experts' of 1943–5 were highly political individuals such as Harry White, and that key matters, such as the proposed IMF quotas, were calculated on the basis of political acceptability, although put forward as objective and scientific in order to facilitate acceptance.[29]

This suggests that the growth of international regulatory or governance networks does not constitute a reduction of the scope of interstate politics, but its pursuit by other means.[30] Certainly, this may entail an attempt to 'depoliticize' issues, by deploying scientific, managerial, or professional techniques and basing their solution on universalizing discourses. However, such techniques are neither neutral in themselves, nor in the processes of their development and application. To operate effectively, they must interact with intersecting epistemologies, within a process that can also reflect wider public concerns, in order to produce generally acceptable value judgements. For example, while it is clearly desirable to ask scientists to evaluate the health risks of particular food-production techniques (such as hormones to enhance the beef or milk production from cattle), the acceptability of these techniques depends also on a variety of other social and economic factors, which affect for example the likelihood of high dosages being administered on farms. In the end, it entails a social

which Lindseth opens his article, that 'supranational delegation [could be viewed] as the next stage in a process of diffusion and fragmentation of normative power that has dramatically altered the balance of power at national level over the course of the twentieth century' (ibid. 632).

[28] Emanuel Adler and Peter M. Haas, 'Conclusion: Epistemic Communities, World Order, and the Creation of a Reflective Research Programme', *International Organization*, vol. 46 (Special Issue on Knowledge, Power and International Policy Coordination) (1992), 378.

[29] Raymond F. Mikesell, *The Bretton Woods Debates: A Memoir* (Princeton: Princeton University Press, 1994).

[30] Yves Dezalay, 'Between the State, Law and the Market: The Social and Professional Stakes in the Construction and Definition of a Regulatory Arena', in Bratton *et al.* (eds), *International Regulatory Competition* (above, n. 13), 59.

value judgement, balancing potential health risks against productivity improvements. That specific technical issues cannot easily be isolated from wider cultural, social, and political factors is also borne out by the frequent experience of wide divergence of views and disagreements on decisions between experts or specialists from different national and cultural backgrounds.[31]

Thus, while there is an important role for specialist expertise in regulatory decision-making, it is important that it should be exercised within a framework that is accountable and responsive. This includes direct democratic accountability, since the powers of regulators have important social effects, even if they are narrow in scope (for example, central bankers' powers to set short-term interest rates, utility regulators' powers over pricing or service obligations, or the role of scientists in setting the allowable catch from a fishery). Much of the discussion of regulation starts from the mistaken assumptions that it is an external 'imposition' on markets, only justified in cases of 'market failure', and limited to market-facilitation rather than redistribution. These assumptions underpin the view that market-facilitative regulation can and should be guided purely by 'efficiency' considerations, and can therefore be done technocratically, since only decisions involving 'redistribution' or the allocation of scarce resources entail social value judgements and thus require political legitimation. In fact, a market economy cannot exist without norms of many kinds, from technical standards to semi-formal regulation as well as formal legal rules, and it is these norms that create and define property rights, the institutions and structures of production and distribution, and the conditions of competition.[32] They therefore have a major impact on livelihoods, health and living standards, and their legitimacy depends on wide social acceptability. The importance and complexity of such forms of regulation has increased in post-industrial, globalized capitalism. As Peter Strauss points out (in this volume), this has led to pressure for new forms of democratization of the accountability of formal regulatory rule-making even at national level, which accept that it is not a merely technical matter, but must be done as a process of open interaction with a wide public, and subject to checks on the exercise of private influence.

We may take as an example at this point the provisions of the EU–US Mutual Recognition Agreement, which is perhaps the centre-piece so far of transatlantic regulatory cooperation within the TEP.[33] The basic prin-

---

[31] Studies show that officials in bureaucracies that are represented as technocratic (such as the European Commission) understand their role as political, and are concerned that their policies should be acceptable to the public: see e.g. C. Landfried, 'Beyond Technocratic Governance: The Case of Biotechnology', European Law Journal, vol. 3 (1997), 255–72.

[32] David Campbell and Sol Picciotto, 'Exploring the Interaction between Law and Economics: the Limits of Formalism', Legal Studies, vol. 18 (1998), 249–78.

[33] Agreement on mutual recognition between the European Community and the United States of America—Joint Declaration, London, 18 May 1998; Official Journal L 031, 04/02/1999, 3–80.

ciples laid down in the Framework agreement require each state to accept that compliance with its technical standards or requirements will be certified by conformity assessment bodies of the other state, once they have been duly designated and in relation to agreed sectors and regulations. Thus, in principle, neither state gives up its 'sovereign' rights to decide its desired levels of regulatory protection, but merely delegates to administrative agencies of the other the technical task of verifying conformity.[34] There are various procedures for consultation, information exchange, and even the possibility by agreement of joint audit/inspection in order to maintain confidence in the conformity assessment process, but they are purely on an inter-agency basis. These arrangements may prove functional for uncontroversial standards, although the lengthy period taken to establish them indicates they have not been unproblematic. However, it is unlikely that they would carry adequate legitimacy in relation to standards, however technical, which have raised significant concerns among the importing country's consumers, such as ensuring that the hormone dosage administered to cattle on farms ensures a negligible level of potentially cancer-causing residues.

C. Deliberative or direct democracy

The discussion of the limits of neo-Kantian models for democratizing globalism points to the need for new concepts and forms of democratic accountability, responding to the fragmentation of the public sphere, and the more dispersed, decentralized, and multi-layered forms of regulating the exercise of social power. Indeed, this process of fragmentation both results from the limits and contradictions of previous, state-centralized forms, and also stimulates new forms of legitimation. The very decentralization of decision-making itself entails and provides opportunities for accountability, since power is less concentrated. To that extent it is accurate to see a connection between liberalization and increased liberty and even accountability. The dispersal of decision-makers provides automatic checks and balances, since a decision by one committee or regulator is rarely definitive. The much greater opportunities for strategic behaviour and regulatory arbitrage generates regulatory competition, which has the potential for ratcheting standards up as well as down. Although this tends to favour those with greater opportunities for mobility, and to destabilize and thus downgrade existing, socially-embedded regulatory arrangements and

---

[34] Joan Claybrook, of Public Citizen, in a statement to the Transatlantic Consumers Dialogue on 23 April 1999 that was generally critical of the inadequacy of public consultation on international trade issues, expressed strong reservations over the harmonization of consumer-protection standards, but accepted harmonization of industrial standards and especially of testing procedures, although she did not address the issue of mutual recognition. (Statement of Joan Claybrook, www.harmonizationalert.org/joan.htm, accessed 16 June 1999.)

capacities, it also opens up prospects for strategic actions by new types of citizen groups and social organization.[35] This helps to explain the mushrooming growth of issue-oriented social movements broadly described as Non-Governmental Organizations (NGOs).

However, the constitution of democracy requires the formulation of principles, adapted to the emerging forms of the new public sphere, but which explicitly aim to structure it to ensure the most effective forms of popular participation. The dangers of liberalization and globalization are that they unleash socially destructive behaviour based on the competitive pursuit of self-interest, as existing normative and institutional restraints are undermined or dismantled. Who can be genuinely surprised when full-blooded liberalization results in widespread corruption and the rapid growth of organized crime, as has occurred for example in Russia?

Thus, new democratic constitutional principles should foster active deliberation by citizens, based on the articulation and evaluation of generally applicable values in a variety of public fora and institutions. The most helpful and relevant approaches, in my view, emerge from the work of political theorists arguing for new forms of direct democracy based on deliberative principles, and aiming to contain or counterbalance instrumental rationality by fostering public debate and decision-making through communicative interaction and reasoning.[36] They attempt to respond to the challenge posed to both liberal and republican (or communitarian) democracy by social fragmentation, which generates a politics of identity and views that differences are unassimilable.[37]

These proposals do not reject representative government, but in fact respond to the ways in which it has been transformed. Bernard Manin has comprehensively and convincingly analysed these transformations, with the progressive breakdown of party-democracy, in which parliaments became a register of the relative force of clashing interests which governments aimed to resolve by compromises. He charts the rise of a new form of representation, in a context of greater complexity and unpredictability, in which politicians offer to an electorate which now 'appears, above all, as a *public* which responds to the terms that have been presented on the political *stage*' a choice among images which are 'highly simplified and

[35] For detailed analysis with many examples and practical suggestions, see Braithwaite and Drahos, *Global Business Regulation* (above, n. 18).

[36] John S. Dryzek, *Discursive Democracy* (Cambridge: Cambridge University Press, 1990). Although this approach owes much to Jürgen Habermas, I think it can avoid his unhelpful separation between the 'lifeworld' and that of technical and instrumental rationality, and the need to establish ideal, uncoerced, communicative contexts. The social structures of power, including communication, should be seen in a more dialectical way, and the changes in the structure of the public sphere open up possibilities, many of which Habermas himself recognizes, for reconstituting a more effective democracy, which in turn can counteract inequalities of power.

[37] Seyla Benhabib (ed.), *Democracy and Difference: Contesting the Boundaries of the Political* (Princeton: Princeton University Press, 1996).

schematic political representations'.[38] Opinions on specific issues are no longer pre-formed or defined by group political identities, and hence must be formulated and developed through debate in various public forums, although such debate is dominated by communications media that are perhaps less partisan, but more prone to drama and sensationalism. This again indicates the importance of ensuring that government takes place within a broader framework of debate and decision-making which is open to the active involvement of issue groups and concerned citizens. In the final section of this contribution, I suggest in outline the basic principles for constituting the public sphere in the spirit of active, deliberative, democratic participation, combined with some practical suggestions indicating their particular relevance to globalization.

III. CONSTITUTIVE PRINCIPLES FOR A GLOBAL PUBLIC SPHERE

New forms of active citizenship and political action have been developing, often around the local and national impact of regional or global policies. The recognition that the public sphere has become fragmented into multiple intersecting networks and overlapping jurisdictional spheres emphasises the importance of building democratic participation through new political principles, institutions, and practices. These should recognize the diversity of political sites in which public policies are developed and implemented, also involving processes of interaction between these sites.

Such principles must attempt to transcend the two main traditional constitutional models, which are increasingly proving inadequate for the contemporary phase of globalization. On the one hand, liberal conceptions, based on a view of society as composed of individuals pursuing their self-interest, see the role of the polity as complementing the market, and as aiming to identify the optimal collective interest either by authoritarian means (Hobbes), or via majoritarian representative democracy (Locke). Post-industrial capitalism, with its integrated global production and marketing networks, raises a wide range of social, environmental, and moral issues, which cannot adequately be resolved by aggregating private interests, using either authoritarian or democratic methods. The alternative model of civic republicanism rejects the narrow view of citizenship based on weighing and balancing competing individual interests. However, its stress on an ethical politics based on visions of the common good implies a communitarianism requiring shared values, which in today's culturally fractured world takes reactionary forms, and may generate conflict rather than consensus.

[38] Bernard Manin, 'The Metamorphoses of Representative Government', *Economy & Society*, vol. 23 (1994), 160, 163.

As Jürgen Habermas has suggested, whereas both these views tend to see the state as the centre, deliberative politics can be adapted to a decentred society: 'This concept of democracy no longer needs to operate with the notion of a social whole centered in the state and imagined as a goal-oriented subject writ large. Just as little does it represent the whole in a system of constitutional norms mechanically regulating the interplay of powers and interests in accordance with the market model.'[39] Others also have stressed the attractiveness of a direct, deliberative form of participatory democracy for solving problems in ways unavailable to representative systems: 'collective decisions are made through public deliberation in arenas open to citizens who use public services, or who are otherwise regulated by public decisions. But in deciding, those citizens must examine their own choices in the light of the relevant deliberations and experiences of others facing similar problems in comparable jurisdictions or subdivisions of government.'[40] In this perspective, decision-making, especially by public bodies, should result as far as possible from active democratic participation based on discursive or deliberative rather than instrumental reasoning. Instead of the pursuit of individual interests based on the assumption of fixed preferences, the aim is to go beyond an objectivist rationality (in which choices are considered to be made by ref-

[39] Jürgen Habermas, 'Three Normative Models of Democracy', in Benhabib, (ed.), *Democracy and Difference* (above, n. 37), 27. Habermas nevertheless argues that his own concept of a 'politically socialising communicative context' can be translated from the nation-state to the European sphere, which entails building 'a European-wide, integrated public sphere . . . in the ambit of a common political culture' (Habermas, 'Remarks on Dieter Grimm's "Does Europe Need a Constitution?"' *European Law Journal*, vol. 1 (1995), 306). Others have put forward neo-republican models for a 'multi-level' European citizenship (usefully summarized in R. Bellamy and A. Warleigh, 'From an Ethics of Integration to an Ethics of Participation: Citizenship and the Future of the European Union', *Millennium*, vol. 27 (1998), 447–70), which imply that the republican version of participatory democracy can be translated to the European level (although this is contested by Habermas). However, it seems to me important to accept that even Europe, which has a strong institutional base and some elements of a common political culture, does not form an integrated political unit, and hence that democratic forms need significant adaptation. It is clear, for example, that the European Parliament must play a different role from that of national parliaments, and hence it must be differently organized, just as national parliaments must adapt to deal with the Europeanization of the legislative process. This is perhaps the practical political response to the debate about the 'European demos', usefully summarized and evaluated by Lindseth, 'Democratic Legitimacy' (above, n. 10), 675–83.

[40] J. Cohen and C. Sabel, 'Directly-Deliberative Polyarchy', *European Law Journal*, vol. 3(4), (1997), 313–14. Oliver Gerstenberg introduces the work of Cohen and Sabel into the debate on democracy in the European Union by pointing out how this vision opens up the argument that supranationalism can itself be the focus of this type of radical democracy, since it goes beyond existing forms of constitutional democracy bounded by market-state-civil society, and showing that new forms of governance based on deliberative coordination are not conventionally public or private, pointing to a new division of labour between political agencies and directly deliberative problem-solving units: Gerstenberg, 'Law's Polyarchy: A Comment on Cohen and Sabel', *European Law Journal*, vol. 3 (1997), 343–58. See also Christian Joerges and Jürgen Neyer, 'From Intergovernmental Bargaining to Deliberative Political Processes: the Constitutionalisation of Comitology', ibid. 273–99.

erence to absolute and objective standards), without falling into the trap of relativism.[41] Thus, while accepting that there is no single objective standard of truth, since perspectives are always subjective (and hence epistemology is to that extent relativist), truth can be said to be an emergent property of the deliberative interaction between perspectives (and hence its ontology is objective).

Deliberative democracy accepts the existence of a diversity of perspectives, and aims to facilitate interactive deliberation about values through which preferences may change, or may be accommodated to each other. An emphasis on process may help to overcome the weaknesses of this model if conceived as a political ideal, or as relying on the generation of consensus purely through the public use of reason. Account must also be taken of inequalities of power, which generate conflicting interests as well as imbalances in the capacity to participate in a politics based on reasoning.

To this end, constitutional principles should aim as far as possible to protect the public sphere from the instrumental pursuit of private interests. Clearly, subjectivity resulting from each person's experiences, background and aspirations is inevitable, but this should be reflexively acknowledged so that individuals and groups maintain openness to the arguments of others. Above all, public arenas should be insulated from undue influence from private interests, and debate should be conducted in terms of explicitly articulated values and aims. This objective is fundamental to the four general principles which I would put forward as constitutive of a direct-democratic, deliberative public sphere: transparency, accountability, responsibility, and empowerment. I will briefly discuss each of these in turn, although in practice they are interdependent.

A. Transparency

Economic liberalization and globalization have led to the increasing articulation of the requirement of transparency, but it has until recently generally been directed at national governments, aiming to reduce bureaucratic obstacles to market transactions. Thus, many provisions in the WTO agreements require transparency of national regulatory and administrative procedures. This is because it is considered that regulatory measures, policies, and proposals adopted by one State may, in the context of increased global economic integration, act as obstacles to market access by firms in other States. Thus, the WTO agreements include obligations not only for accessible publication of national regulations, but also for the establishment of national contact points to provide information (including translations of relevant texts), and even for prior notification of proposals

---

[41] John S. Dryzek, *Discursive Democracy* (Cambridge: Cambridge University Press, 1990).

for non-standard regulations with an opportunity to make comments.[42] In the context of EU–US relations, it has now been recognized that transparency is the 'bedrock' for preventing conflicts and facilitating problem resolution, for both economic and political issues.[43]

However, there are virtually no formal provisions regarding transparency of international bodies and arenas. Indeed, intergovernmental negotiations and activities are especially opaque, and both politicians and officials generally stress the importance of confidentiality in this realm, which is often excluded from national freedom of information requirements. In the European Union, it was only as a result of the legitimacy crisis which began to be recognized in the negotiation of the Maastricht Treaty that principles of transparency have begun to be adopted for EU institutions.[44] This was finally formally recognized in the Treaty of Amsterdam signed in June 1997, and Article 255 of the consolidated Treaty establishing the European Community now gives any EU citizen or resident a right of access to documents of the Council, Commission, and

[42] Notably, Article 7 and Annexe B of the Agreement on Sanitary and Phytosanitary Measures (SPS) require States to notify in advance any proposals for regulations which are not based on an international standard, to 'allow reasonable time for other Members to make comments in writing, discuss these comments upon request, and take the comments and the results of the discussions into account'; developed countries must provide translations of documents in English, French, or Spanish. The agreement on Technical Barriers to Trade (TBT), which requires States to base their technical regulations on international standards where they exist except where they would be 'an ineffective or inappropriate means for the fulfilment of the legitimate objectives pursued', focuses on transparency of conformity-assessment procedures (Article 10), including the requirement for enquiry points which can provide documents at reasonable cost (and for developed countries, in English, French, or Spanish). The TRIPs agreement (Article 63) also includes obligations to publish and notify laws, regulations, final judicial rulings, and administrative rulings of general application.

[43] *EU–US Early Warning and Problem Prevention: Principles and Mechanisms*, adopted at Bonn, 21 June 1999.

[44] The Final Act of the Treaty on European Union signed at Maastricht on 7 February 1992 included Declaration No. 17, stating that 'transparency of the decision-making process strengthens the democratic nature of the institutions and the public's confidence in the administration', and recommending that the Commission submit a report to the Council by 1993 on measures to improve public access to information. This resulted in the approval by the Council and Commission on 6 December 1993 of a Code of Conduct, which stated the general principle that 'the public will have the widest possible access to documents held by the Commission and the Council', but which also required the institutions to refuse access to any document whose disclosure would undermine 'the protection of the public interest (public security, international relations, monetary stability, court proceedings and investigations)', and permitted them to refuse access 'in order to protect the institution's interest in the confidentiality of its proceedings'. Journalists, MEPs, and activists have waged several battles to try to ensure these exclusions are interpreted strictly, with some support from the ECJ: see Tony Bunyan, *Secrecy, Democracy and the Third Pillar* (London: Kogan Page, 1999), and *Heidi Hautala v. Council of the EU*, Case T-14/98, Judgment of Court of First Instance, 19 July 1999. Typically, this case concerned the Council's refusal to supply a report on the criteria for arms exports, on the grounds that disclosure could be harmful for the EU's relations with third countries, and although the Court annulled the decision it did so only because the Council had not considered whether the report could be published with sensitive parts removed.

Parliament, subject to 'general principles and limits on grounds of public or private interest', to be drawn up by the Council.

This is an exceptional, perhaps even unique, provision in an international treaty, but should be regarded as a constitutive principle for all international bodies, and indeed any serious international regulatory activity. Nevertheless, such a principle will inevitably remain ineffective if subject to broad exceptions, and if both the general rules and individual decisions on what can be revealed are left to each body to decide for itself.[45] Effectiveness could perhaps be improved by the establishment of Ombudsmen, as has also been done in the European Union,[46] to monitor the transparency of international bodies, and to investigate or adjudicate claims of confidentiality. The principle of transparency is just as important for apparently technical bodies, as has been pointed out by Willem Buiter in a trenchant critique of the traditionalist approach adopted by the European Central Bank, which he describes as 'typical of a central banking tradition that was, until recently, dominant across the world, which views central banking as a sacred, quasi-mystical vocation, a cult whose priests perform the holy sacraments far from the prying eyes of the non-initiates'.[47]

Transparency has now been greatly facilitated by the opportunities opened up by the Internet. Indeed, some international bodies have begun to make extensive use of this medium to make their documentation available. It is obviously very advantageous for an organization such as the WTO to be able to give such instant online access to its large and growing documents archive to all those in its 132 member countries who require it. The Internet also offers possibilities for much more interactive consultation of relevant communities and the public, discussed by Peter Strauss in this volume, and some organizations are beginning to make use of this. In practice, however, there are very great inequalities in the capacity to access the Internet;[48] so that to realize the opportunities it offers also

[45] Thus, the initial proposals emerging from discussions of officials of EU institutions for implementation of Article 255 (ex Article 191a) (discussion paper on public access to Commission documents, 23 Apr. 1999, SG.C2/VJ/CDD(99)83) apparently suggested that only documents concerning legislative measures would be regarded as 'accessible', while internal 'working documents' would be 'non-accessible', and even the former might be embargoed until after the formal adoption of the decision: see *Statewatch*, vol. 9, no. 2 (Mar.–Apr. 1999). Such a proposal is hardly likely to gain approval, but that it was made at all is revealing of the official perspective.

[46] C. Grønbeck-Jensen provides an interesting evaluation from a Scandinavian perspective, particularly apposite since these countries have been influential in the moves towards transparency in the European Union; but he points out that the EU Ombudsman has no real teeth, having no better access to documents than the citizen: 'The Scandinavian tradition of open government and the European Union: problems of compatibility?', *Journal of European Public Policy*, vol. 5 (1998), 185–99.

[47] W. H. Buiter, 'Alice in Euroland', *Journal of Common Market Studies*, vol. 37 (1999), 181–209.

[48] Saskia Sassen, 'Digital Networks and Power', in Mike Featherstone and Scott Lash, *Spaces of Culture* (London: Sage Publications, 1999), 49–63; 'Access to the Network Society—

requires active programmes to broaden effective participation by all affected and concerned citizens.

Finally, perhaps the key requirement is to develop and sustain information media which can help to provide the kind of forum that active public participation in deliberative debate requires. That everywhere the public's distrust of politicians is equalled only by its cynicism about journalists is a serious indictment of our political systems. There are certainly some media organizations in some countries, as well as many able and committed individuals, dedicated to providing a rich context of information and facilitating debate. However, the media overall, in some countries more than others, are subservient to government agendas and commercial imperatives,[49] and hence tend to reflect received or elite opinion. Thus, a key requirement for transparency in the public sphere is to ensure guarantees of media independence from both government and private dominance.

B. Accountability

The past few years have seen increasing concern and debate about the accountability of all kinds of participants in public-policy debates. Even in countries with apparently well-established systems of representative democracy, politicians have been subjected to new scrutiny over their acceptance of bribes, political donations, or campaign financing, as well as debates about the relationship of their personal lives and morality to their public functions. Such issues have been very widespread, not confined to countries undergoing identifiable political transitions (such as Italy, with its 'tangentopoli' scandals linked to the collapse of the Christian Democracy–Communist duopoly). This shows that they are symptomatic of generalized changes in the role of elected politicians, indicated in Bernard Manin's analysis of the changing nature of representative democracy discussed above. The increased diversity and complexity of policy issues, and the decline of mass-party politics, places new responsibilities on politicians to develop specialist expertise and resources, and to manage their information sources scrupulously. They themselves are also increasingly concerned with their responsiveness to public opinion, whether expressed in their postbags (and e-mails), opinion polls, or focus groups. However, the increased importance of personal charisma or 'name recognition' for the standing of politicians, as opposed to policy or principles, has undermined their legitimacy as political representatives.

Who is in the Loop and on the Map?', in United Nations, *Human Development Report* (New York: UN, 1999), 61–6.

[49] See, e.g., the papers in the special issue of *Journal of International Affairs,* vol. 47, no. 1 (1993), 'The Power of the Media in the Global System'.

For a variety of reasons it has become increasingly plain that democratic accountability of public bodies cannot rest only on their accountability via parliaments and elected politicians. Indeed, some kinds of decisions (such as control over interest rates) have been insulated from the political domain to protect them from 'short-run' electoral considerations. An increasingly wide range of matters have been delegated to specialist bodies operating under defined mandates, with powers either of recommendation or of actual decision. Where there is a governmental input, it is generally made by non-elected officials, who are subject to only superficial supervision by a succession of partially briefed elected politicians. Often, issues are not resolved by a decision from one particular body, but subject to interacting decision-making powers of various bodies, even at national level, and even more so globally. Thus, the development and use of biotechnology depends on decisions by patent offices, scientific and ethical committees, food and drug regulators, national governments, and perhaps ultimately WTO dispute-settlement procedures. It is important not only that all such public bodies operate under explicit and specific accountability mandates, but also that their decisions are taken in a context of well-informed debate involving as broad a range of the public as possible. The channels of accountability are now less vertical, leading into central government, and more horizontal, entailing interaction between various local, national, regional, and international public arenas.

Thus, while elected politicians certainly should play an important and perhaps determinant part, ensuring accountability within the public sphere entails the involvement of a wide range of entities and groups, all of which have their own constituencies and accountability mechanisms. This is perhaps the reason for the increased use in recent years of the somewhat amorphous term 'civil society'. The point here is that there is no single accountability mechanism to the broad public. Participants in public debate can make different contributions, but it is incumbent on each of them to clarify to whom and how they are accountable. Indeed, there have been increasing pressures for all kinds of organizations to improve their accountability, not only to their direct members but to a wider constituency of stakeholders.

Corporations have come under pressure to be responsive to the needs and demands of their customers, suppliers, workers, and contractors, as well as local communities and the wider society in respect of some of their activities. Their traditional focus on the 'bottom line' of direct costs and revenues to generate shareholder value has now been overtaken by the need for a more continuous two-way dialogue with this wider constituency, and concern for the 'triple bottom line' and long-term values such as reputation. No doubt many business managers need to be convinced that this entails more than just improved communication of decisions made in their boardrooms; but it is no coincidence that the lead is being taken by companies that have been hit by unexpected public reactions to policies which they believed had the legitimacy of approval by all relevant regulatory bodies. This has been shown, for example, by Shell's experiences over the Brent Spar oil platform disposal and the impact of its oilfields on local communities in eastern Nigeria, and those of biotechnology companies in relation to genetically modified organisms. The damage to investor confidence in the biotechnology sector should bring home to all concerned the importance of improving public confidence in regulatory decisions.

In reply, many have challenged the various campaigning organizations or NGOs to justify their claims to represent public opinion. Such organizations cover a wide gamut, and clearly do have a responsibility to clarify for whom they speak, as well as to maintain an active dialogue with their members and stakeholders. They are vulnerable to 'bottom-line' pressures from their sources of funding, which may lead them to adopt high-profile campaigns or maintain positions for their attractiveness to the media rather than their intrinsic validity. There may be differences of perspective between different elements of their constituencies, for example subscribers and contributors in developed countries and those in less-developed countries who are the intended beneficiaries of development organizations. Interest-group institutions, such as business and trade associations and trade union organizations, in principle represent their members, and can claim accountability ultimately via election; but, certainly at the international level, this may be a distant link. There is much they could do to improve the active involvement of their grass-roots memberships.

In summary, the roles of various kinds of participants should be defined according to the contribution they can make to public debate based on generally applicable values. Procedures for consultation and involvement in decision-making should reflect their particular roles, as well as accommodating and safeguarding against possible distortions resulting from advancement of private interests.

C. Responsibility

Participants in public deliberation may also be said to have obligations of responsibility, which are distinct from their accountability to their particular constituencies.[50] These include principles for maintaining a separation between involvement with private interests and the conduct of public

[50] This of course depends on who is included in that constituency: for example, it is argued that potential conflicts between corporations' duties to their shareholders and to their stakeholders should be avoided by limiting their accountability to shareholders, while accepting that they have broader social responsibilities. I prefer here to use the term 'responsibility' in relation to how debate should be conducted.

duties and activities, as well as norms and practices of responsible behaviour developed by and for particular groups and professions. The acceptability and effectiveness of public-policy decisions increasingly depend on the quality of the reasons supporting them, which in turn requires all those involved in debates to uphold high standards of probity. This is evidenced by the increased attention being given to ethical standards by and for a wide range of groups and professions, many of which have been formally articulated in codes or even in law.

An important aspect of this is to define and police the line between professional or public responsibilities and obligations to a commercial client or employer. Thus, banks and financial intermediaries are now obliged to report suspicious transactions under money-laundering legislation, enacted nationally but stimulated and monitored by the international regulatory network centred on the Financial Action Task Force.[51] External auditors may have specific responsibilities to report to regulatory authorities, for example to banking supervisors, if they uncover breaches of regulatory requirements. Officials or civil servants may be protected from disciplinary or even legal proceedings for breaches of confidence if they can show that they acted in the public interest. However, too often the formal rules on these matters are not designed to encourage or protect disclosures in the public interest, but rather to protect public or private bureaucracies from undesirable obligations or revelations. Their strengthening should be regarded as a significant contribution towards the democratization of global governance.

More broadly, all those involved as information gatekeepers or knowledge producers, now more than ever, need to operate reflexively, and with an awareness of how their professional or scientific practices and contributions impact on the quality of public debate. These matters are not uncontroversial, as can be seen for example in the debates in the United Kingdom about the scientific evaluation of the potential dangers from genetically modified organisms.

D. Empowerment

My final principle should be regarded as an overriding one, for without it the other proposals for strengthening the public sphere as a deliberative arena would do little more than provide an alibi for the maintenance and extension of the system of elite decision-making. It is all too easy for those with decision-making power to pay lip-service to the need for public consultation or participation, although one can still be surprised at the frequency with which they neglect even this bare minimum. It is often only

---

[51] A typical informal global regulatory body, set up by a decision of the Group of Seven, but located at the OECD in Paris: see http://www.oecd.org/fatf/.

as a result of a policy setback, such as the breakdown of the MAI negotiations or the failure to obtain 'fast-track' authority, that those in power resort to a 'charm offensive' to try to win support from potential critics. Frequently, also, they prefer to distinguish carefully between procedures for consultation with public interest or activist groups, and their discussions with business or corporate interests. Indeed, this type of separation has been institutionalized in the TEP, which began life largely as an attempt to respond more directly to the needs of big business, and only subsequently added a Transatlantic Consumer Dialogue to the Transatlantic Business Dialogue.[52] This inevitably raises suspicions that decision-makers are more open to influence from private interest groups, and that they regard consultation with public interest groups and concerned citizens (or even legislators) as an irritating time-waster, perhaps necessary to forestall subsequent criticism. It is all too rare to find an acknowledgement that the quality of public decisions can be improved if they take place in a context of full participation by all concerned and affected groups.

The challenge, therefore, is to find ways to ensure effective participation in debate and decision-making especially of disadvantaged citizens and groups. Much of the political opposition to and disaffection with globalization and liberalization results from the unleashing of forces which exacerbate inequalities within and between States. This is often portrayed as a battle between the global market and the national State, a view which tends to neglect the ways in which the transformation of the world market is being brought about by complex processes of international re-regulation. To take a key example, the restructuring of global telecommunications, in which giant firms battle for market shares, entails struggles over technical standards, sectoral regulation (notably governing interconnection rights and charges) and competition rules, through interactions between a variety of national and international bodies. A key issue, which has for several years been preoccupying the International Telecommunications Union (ITU), is the system of settlements in respect of international calls, which entails revenue-sharing resulting in transfers mainly from developed to developing countries estimated at US$7–10 billion per year.[53] There is considerable pressure to reform this system, to end discrimination in charges between international and national calls, in line with the liberalization of telecommunications services negotiated bilater-

---

[52] Maria Green Cowles, 'The Transatlantic Business Dialogue: The Private Face of Transatlantic Relations', in Eric Philippart and Pascaline Winand (eds), *Policy-Making in US–EU Relations: the New Transatlantic Agenda Revisited* (Manchester: Manchester University Press, forthcoming).

[53] Dr Henry Chasia, ITU Deputy Secretary-General, Opening Remarks to the Annual Council of the Commonwealth Telecommunication Organization, Trinidad & Tobago, 29 Sept. 1998; this and much other documentation on the issue is available in the special area of the ITU website, www.itu.int.

ally, regionally (especially in the European Union) and through the WTO. Yet it is also widely recognized that a truly global telecommunications system is unattainable unless equivalent (or better) means are found to finance the expansion and upgrading of telecommunications networks in developing countries.[54]

This clearly shows that global battles over regulation also concern revenue distribution and redistribution, not just 'neutral' rules allowing markets to operate 'freely'. Many other debates and battles over international regulatory arrangements also have (re)distributional consequences or implications, running often to many millions or billions of dollars, such as competition laws and policies, environmental protection schemes, intellectual property rights, food-safety requirements, agricultural support and rural development measures, prudential rules for financial institutions, and international tax arrangements. Too often the talk of 'market friendly' regulation implies rules that favour the economically powerful, whereas balanced and sustainable long-term economic growth may require measures to protect, encourage, and stimulate less-developed or disadvantaged groups, regions, and countries.

An important function of direct democracy is to open up the received wisdom of closed bureaucratic or technocratic decision-makers to critical and destabilizing ideas. This perhaps cannot be institutionalized without blunting the critical edge of political protest, although sometimes well-considered and substantiated arguments take second place to spectacular actions designed to attract media attention. Responsive and confident political systems can find ways to make themselves more open to external critical input. This can include, for example, public forums or commissions with powers to conduct inquisitions into policies or issues, or citizen juries to which specific decisions could be delegated, based on systematic presentation and examination of evidence.

It is hard not to close a contribution of this kind without some stirring rhetoric about the importance of this matter for the future of the planet in the new millennium. Major issues are certainly at stake, but their scope and complexity are hard to grasp in the round. Globalization seems to produce scandals, panics, and crashes, which we can hope will remain episodic events. However, not only systemic stability is at stake in the construction of global governance, but our ability to establish the conditions for economic activity finally to respond to the needs of the world's poor and disposessed for dignity and social justice.

---

[54] See the comprehensive Briefing Report by Michael Tyler, *Transforming Economic Relationships in International Telecommunications* (1998) of the ITU Regulatory Colloquium No. 7, on The Changing Role of Government in an Era of Telecommunications Deregulation of 3–5 Dec. 1997, published in Mar. 1998 (Geneva: ITU) and available on www.itu.int (accessed 27 Jan. 2000).

Agencies on the loose? Holding government networks accountable

Anne-Marie Slaughter

In his speech to the conference that was the genesis of this volume, Sir Leon Brittan commented that he had observed, in the MRA negotiations, 'greater eagerness between governments than between agencies', a reluctance that he hoped would be overcome.[1] This distinction between 'government' and 'agency' may seem unremarkable, certainly if viewed through the lens of bureaucratic politics. But it is striking and indeed theoretically unintelligible when viewed from the perspective of traditional scholarship in international law and international relations. Both disciplines start from the fundamental premise that states are the principal actors in the international system and that they are unitary actors— 'billiard balls', in Arnold Wolfers' memorable phrase.[2] The state is represented by a designated government institution—typically the Foreign Office, or perhaps the head of state or an agency such as the Treasury or the Central Bank for specified purposes. But how then could a distinction emerge between the 'government' and the 'agencies'?

The answer expresses a fundamental truth about transatlantic regulatory cooperation: it is often motivated and virtually always implemented by government institutions—in this case regulatory agencies or departments—acting and interacting quasi-autonomously from the rest of the government. Interacting intensively with one another, these agencies form regulatory networks that become increasingly institutionalized.[3] Various authors have various names for these networks; in my terminology they are a subset of the larger and growing phenomenon of 'government networks'.[4]

---

[1] See contribution of Sir Leon Brittan, this volume.

[2] Arnold Wolfers, *Discord and Collaboration: Essays on International Politics* (Baltimore: John Hopkins Press, 1962), 19.

[3] Sol Picciotto, 'Networks in International Economic Integration: Fragmented States and the Dilemmas of Neo-Liberalism', *Northwestern Journal of International Law and Business*, vol. 17 (1996–7); see also Scott H. Jacobs, 'Regulatory Co-operation for an Interdependent World: Issues for Government', in *Organisation for Economic Co-operation and Development, Regulatory Co-operation for an Interdependent World* (1994) 15–16 ('[A] web of formal and informal intergovernmental regulatory relationships is emerging in the OECD area (and beyond) that simultaneously empowers and constrains governments with respect to their ability to solve problems through regulation').

[4] Anne-Marie Slaughter, 'The Real New World Order', *Foreign Affairs*, vol. 76 (1997); Anne-Marie Slaughter, 'Governing the Global Economy through Government Networks', in

The growth of government networks is an exciting and fruitful phenomenon that lies at the core of transatlantic regulatory cooperation. As an organizational form, networks have the advantages of speed, flexibility, and decentralization. These attributes allow them to function particularly well in a rapidly changing environment that thrives on the exchange of information and the ability to use it in different ways according to local context. Further, as both corporations and civic organizations such as NGOs have quickly discovered, networks are the fastest way to attain genuine global reach.

Yet networks also portend new problems. Above all, they summon suspicion—of secrecy, technocracy, exclusion, conspiracy. These various concerns typically cluster under the umbrella label of 'accountability'. How to hold the agencies participating in transgovernmental networks accountable to the democratic constituencies they serve domestically? How to ensure abroad at least the degree of democracy we enjoy at home?

This contribution focuses on that problem, seeking to canvass and distinguish the various types of objections raised as 'accountability' concerns and to offer some possible solutions. It identifies three distinct although interrelated critiques of transnational regulatory networks: their invisibility/lack of access, the inferior quality of decisions taken, and their illegitimacy. Each of these objections can be addressed on its own terms. Beyond these specifics, however, it is important to begin thinking of networks of government officials as an increasing and increasingly important form of global governance. In that context, we need to begin formulating 'constitutional' principles that can structure and regulate transgovernmental relations. The final section of the chapter sketches three such principles, as the first round of a larger debate.

I. THE ACCOUNTABILITY CRITIQUE(S)

The best place to start is to examine the actual charges laid against government networks under the general label of lack of accountability. These charges tend to lump together several different concerns, each of which must be unpacked and addressed on its own terms in the context of an overall definition of accountability and the purposes it is meant to serve. Only then can we begin to craft responses.

Michael Byers (ed.), *The Role of Law in International Politics* (Oxford: Oxford University Press, 2000).

A. Defining accountability

In its broadest sense, accountability means responsiveness.[5] Accountability in a democratic society means responsiveness to the people—the responsiveness of the governors to the governed. Mature democracies have developed a number of mechanisms to assure such responsiveness. First is the specific creation of exact rules designed to regulate the behaviour of government institutions. These rules can be substantive, setting forth principles, directives, and limits that define the mandate and the operational space of a particular set of government officials. Alternatively, these rules can be procedural, requiring a particular mode of decision-making that gives individuals and groups affected by the decisions taken meaningful input into them.

A second principal mode of assuring accountability is a set of *ex post* mechanisms to allow the governed to respond to and/or reject decisions already taken. For elected officials and many of the bureaucratic officials they appoint and control, the mechanism is typically elections themselves. For non-elected officials, such as judges, the mechanism may be requirements that they provide a public rationale and justification for their decisions, often referred to as 'giving reasons requirements'.[6] These requirements permit regular response and critique by those who are subject to decisions along with sustained efforts to change them. For still other non-elected officials who are insulated from the election cycle, such as central bankers, the principal mechanism is the quality of their performance, as measured by their ability to achieve the goals that are written into their mandate.

Both the *ex ante* and the *ex post* procedural requirements are typically what is meant by 'transparency'. The premise is that government actions must be visible and accessible to the governed in a way that allows a meaningful response. Transparency is too often merely a mantra, however, invoked with little analysis of the precise purposes it is meant to achieve. Claims of a 'lack of transparency' may not actually address the underlying problem. Conversely, the standard response of enhancing transparency to address charges of unaccountability may privilege form over substance. As Joseph Weiler observes with regard to charges of a democracy deficit within the European Union: 'Transparency and access to documents are often invoked as a possible remedy to this issue. But if you do not know what is going on, which documents will you ask to see?'[7]

[5] My definition and discussion of accountability are informed by discussions at a workshop on accountability of international institutions hosted by Professor Robert O. Keohane, Duke University, 7–8 May 1999.

[6] Martin Shapiro, 'The Giving Reasons Requirement', *The University of Chicago Legal Forum*, (1992), 179–220.

[7] Joseph H. H. Weiler, 'To Be a European Citizen: Eros and Civilization', in *The Constitution of Europe* (Cambridge: Cambridge University Press, 1999), 349.

In sum, 'accountability' can have multiple specific meanings, reflecting an array of devices to assure responsive government. When critics claim that government networks are not accountable, they are actually concerned with a number of specific and distinct problems, each of which can be addressed through one or more of the mechanisms identified above. The next section unpacks these problems and seeks to translate the general charge of lack of accountability into a bill of particulars.

B. Accountability critiques of government networks

The accountability critique of government networks is widespread. According to Philip Alston, if my analysis of the existence and growth of these networks 'is correct . . ., [i]t implies the marginalization of governments as such and their replacement by special interest groups . . .'.[8] More precisely, 'It suggests a move away from arenas of relative transparency into the back rooms . . . and the bypassing of the national political arenas to which the United States and other proponents of the importance of healthy democratic institutions attach so much importance.'[9] Antonio Perez, identifying a related argument about networks among national and international bureaucrats in Abram and Antonia Chayes' *The New Sovereignty*, accuses them of adopting 'Platonic Guardianship as a mode of transnational governance', an open 'move toward technocratic elitism'.[10] And Sol Picciotto, who also chronicles the rise of government networks but from a more explicitly critical perspective, argues: 'A chronic lack of legitimacy plagues direct international contacts at the sub-state level among national officials and administrators.'[11] He attributes this lack of legitimacy to their informality and confidentiality, precisely the attributes that make them so attractive to the participants.[12]

These various criticisms can be distilled into three broad claims. First, is the charge of invisibility and hence lack of access for groups affected by decisions and policies emanating from regulatory networks. Alston insists that regulatory cooperation through networks of rational government officials 'suggests a move away from areas of relative transparency into the back rooms'—back rooms to which interested parties are denied access. On any level, this critique is a process objection, a claim that decision-making in a democracy entitles those affected by the decision to participate in the process. Perez's reference to 'technocratic elitism' captures

---

[8] Philip Alston, 'The Myopia of the Handmaidens: International Lawyers and Globalization', *European Journal of International Law*, vol. 8 (1997), 435, 441.

[9] Ibid.

[10] Antonio F. Perez, 'Who Killed Sovereignty? Or: Changing Norms Concerning Sovereignty In International Law', *Wisconsin International Law Journal*, vol. 14 (1996), 463, 476.

[11] See Picciotto, 'Networks in International Economic Integration', (above, n. 3), 1014, 1047.

[12] Ibid. 1049.

the same sentiment; government by bureaucrats without popular input threatens to replace democracy with technocracy. From this perspective, the very notion of a 'network' as the vehicle for policy coordination and collaboration is suspect because it has no tangible existence beyond personal contacts and conversations. It generalizes no process visible enough to permit input.

Second is the substantive charge of bad government decisions. Process claims can be justified on their own terms as the tangible expression of democratic values. But they can also be advanced more instrumentally, on the premise that decisions made by bureaucrats without popular input are likely to be bad decisions—narrowly focused, less deliberative, less responsive to the full range of affected constituencies, and even less creative. This is the other face of technocratic elitism: the claim that removal of decision-making from national political arenas deprives decision-makers of input that is valuable not only to ensure a healthy process but also to improve the results of that process. 'Platonic guardianship' in this view is likely to be not only paternalistic but short-sighted.

The third charge is closely related to the first two: illegitimacy. Even assuming that transgovernmental networks are producing 'good' substantive decisions and policies, the networks themselves are suspect. Legitimacy here is a matter of perception as much as reality, perception that is fuelled not only by exclusion of affected groups from decision-making processes but also by the very existence of a 'network' rather than a formal governmental institution. The essence of a network is a *process* rather than an *entity*; thus it cannot be captured or controlled in the ways that typically structure formal legitimacy in a democratic polity. To see the point in a more vivid context, consider the feminist fear of 'old-boy networks'. Developing countries are often equally suspicious of developed-country networks. Hence the fear of 'technocratic elitism' concerns not only the legitimacy of a network of technocrats, but also policy-making by network generally.

II. TOWARDS ENHANCED ACCOUNTABILITY: SKETCHING SOME SOLUTIONS

These three critiques—invisibility/lack of access, inferior decisions, and legitimacy—are interrelated but distinct problems. The next part of this contribution sketches some possible responses to each of these critiques while simultaneously locating the critiques in the larger context of multiple mechanisms of global governance. The larger effect is not to identify problems and outline definitive solutions, but to offer ideas towards possible solutions that will help move beyond critique towards a more productive debate.

A. The critiques in context

Before turning to some possible solutions, it is important to take note of several more general responses. Critics charging government networks with lack of accountability all too often ignore comparisons between networks and other mechanisms and institutions of global governance. They may also hold transgovernmental networks to an impossibly high standard of accountability without supporting evidence of the problems they purport to identify.

To begin with, the asserted need for access to transgovernmental decision-making processes assumes that regulatory networks are developing and implementing substantive policies in ways that differ significantly from outcomes that would be reached as the result of purely national processes or of negotiations within traditional international institutions. Although reasons exist to accept this premise with regard to policy initiatives such as the 1988 Capital Accord adopted by the Basle Committee,[13] it is less clear regarding other networks, even within the financial arena. Network initiatives are theoretically subject to the normal political constraints on domestic policy-making processes once they are introduced at the domestic level. Arguments that they circumvent these constraints rest on the presumed ability of national officials in the same issue area to collude with one another in ways that strengthen their respective positions vis-à-vis bureaucratic rivals or legislative overseers back home. This presumption is often contested by experts in the different fields of financial regulation and requires further research on a case-by-case basis.

More generally, many government networks remain primarily talking shops, dedicated to the sharing of information, the cross-fertilization of new ideas, and the development of common principles based on the respective experiences of participating members. Informational power is soft power, persuasive rather than coercive.[14] It is 'the ability to get desired outcomes because others want what you want'.[15] Specific government institutions may still enjoy a substantial advantage over others due to the quality, quantity, and credibility of the information they have to exchange.[16] But in giving and receiving this information, even in ways that may significantly affect their thinking, government officials are not exercising power in the traditional ways for which polities find it necessary to hold them accountable. We may need to develop new metrics or even new conceptions of accountability geared to the distinctive features of power in the Information Age.

---

[13] Ethan B. Kapstein, 'Supervising International Banks: Origins and Implications of the Basle Accords' (Essays in International Finance Series No. 185, 1991), 185.

[14] Robert O. Keohane and Joseph S. Nye, Jr., 'Power and Interdependence in the Information Age', *Foreign Affairs*, vol. 77 (1998), 81, 86.

[15] Ibid.   [16] See ibid. 89–92 (discussing 'the politics of credibility').

A second and related response raises the question whether and when direct accountability is necessary for legitimate government. Some domestic institutions, such as courts and central banks, are deemed to act legitimately without direct accountability. Legitimacy may be conferred or attained independent of mechanisms of direct accountability; performance may be measured by outcomes as much as process. Insulated institutions are designed to counter the voters' changing will and whim, to garner the benefits of expertise and stability and to protect minorities. Many of the policy arenas in which government networks are likely to be most active are those in which domestic polities have agreed that a degree of insulation and expertise are desirable. Why then should the transgovernmental extension of these activities assure interested parties more access to decision-making than they have at home?

A third response is: 'accountable compared to what?' The presumed accountability or lack thereof of government networks must be contrasted with the accountability of international organizations on the one hand, and NGOs on the other. International organizations are hardly known for their accountability to anyone other than diplomats and international lawyers, which helps explain their relative disrepute in many countries. And accountable to whom? The UN suffers from the perennial perception that it is responsive primarily to its own bureaucracy; the IMF and to a lesser extent the World Bank are widely seen as fronts for the United States; EU institutions have been in crisis over a purported 'democracy deficit' for much of this decade; the WTO draws populist fire for privileging free trade, and hence the interests of large corporate interests best positioned to benefit from free trade, above employment, welfare, environmental, human rights, and cultural concerns of interest to large numbers of voters.[17]

NGOs hardly fare better. Although they must routinely sing for their supper and thus depend on their ability to persuade individual and institutional contributors of the worth of their activities, many if not most are single-issue groups who target a particular demographic and political segment of society and may well wield power quite disproportionate to the number of their supporters. Further, their contributors rarely have any direct control over policy decisions once the contribution is made, or,

---

[17] Consider the following passage from political scientist Henry Nau, which sounds virtually the same themes as Alston's critique of government networks: 'Whose political interests [are] being served by international institutions? Realists said state interests, but the major states today are democracies and consist of many societal and special interests that do not reflect a single government, let alone national interest. Critics of international institutions suspect that these special interests, especially corporate and bureaucratic elites with stakes in globalization, now dominate international organizations and use them to circumvent democratic accountability.' Henry Nau, 'Institutional Skepticism', Letter to the Editor, *Foreign Policy*, vol. 111 (Summer 1998), 168.

equally important, any means of ensuring how their contribution was spent.[18]

In this context, government networks have a major advantage. They are composed of the same officials who make and implement regulations domestically. To the extent that these networks do actually make policy, and to the extent that the policies made and subsequently adopted at the national level differ significantly from the outcome of a purely domestic regulatory process, it is reasonable to expect that other domestic political institutions—legislators, courts, or other branches of the bureaucracy—will extend their normal oversight functions to transgovernmental as well as domestic activities. Public-interest watchdogs are also likely to become more aware of transgovernmental activity and more insistent on participating in it. As Kal Raustiala has documented, provisions have been made for NGOs to participate in international environmental law regimes following the procedures developed for the expansion of the regulatory state in the United States following the New Deal.[19] It is not unreasonable to expect similar developments involving government networks.

B. Three modest proposals

Each of the specific charges distilled above can and should be addressed on its own terms. The responses below are not intended to be definitive, but at least to suggest ways of taking the accountability critique seriously and beginning to adapt the technology of governance to create or maintain the same degree of accountability as obtains for administrative agencies domestically.

1. Virtual visibility

Information technology may hold the key to responding to the challenge of invisibility—rendering the network itself and its decision-making processes visible. By making networks 'virtual', we can make them real. Web sites have many advantages for participants in government networks—offering a central site for the dissemination of information and the coordination of activities. At the same time, a Web site creates a public face for a network—the first step towards developing a more human face.

Many of the more institutionalized networks, such as the Basle Committee and IOSCO already have Web sites—for their members as well as the general public. Their Web sites give them permanence, much like headquarters and stationery for a more traditional organization. The tan-

---

[18] Peter J. Spiro, 'New Global Potentates: NGO's and the Unregulated Marketplace', *Cardozo Law Review*, vol. 18 (1996), 957–69; P. J. Simmons, 'Learning to Live with NGO's', *Foreign Policy*, no. 112 (1998), 82–96.

[19] Kal Raustiala, Note, 'The "Participatory Revolution" in International Environmental Law', *Harvard Environmental Law Review*, vol. 21 (1997), 537, 579–84.

gible (or rather virtual) instantiation of a network via a Web site also makes it possible to draw in a wide range of other actors in organized initiatives. Consider the creation of the Joint Year 2000 Council by the Basle Committee, the BIS Committee on Payment and Settlement Systems (CPSS), IOSCO, and IAIS. The formation of the Council was welcomed by the G-7 Finance Ministers; its Secretariat is provided by the BIS. Its mission was to encourage the development of coordinated national strategies to address the Year 2000 problem, including the development of a global databank of contacts in individual countries covering a wide range of actors in both the private and public sectors; the issuance of policy papers on specific Year 2000 issues; the provision of supervisory guidance on assessing Year 2000 preparations by financial institutions. It acknowledged and welcomed efforts by the World Bank and other international institutions to help address the Year 2000 problem, but has been focusing its attention directly on both private and public actors in the global financial supervisory community.[20] If public opinion and government power so required, similar energies could be devoted to networking with private and public actors devoted to enhancing global democracy in various ways.

The Internet is the ultimate network, enabling but also requiring those who would organize themselves in the Information Age to follow its form. As virtual visibility increasingly becomes actual reality for individual citizens, Web sites will become the focus of a range of regulatory efforts. First is likely to be a variety of transparency requirements, such as a record of meetings held and issues discussed and decided, as well as a calendar of upcoming meetings and projects. To the extent that participants in a government network are engaged in actual policy-making or implementation activities, they can be required to adopt notice and comment procedures along the lines developed in US administrative law. Such procedures are already being advanced to enhance the accountability of EU regulatory networks.[21] Less formally, they can also sponsor on-line discussions of various kinds with those subject to their regulations.

In many ways the Internet might appear antithetical to expanding accountability. Thomas Friedman argues that the defining characteristic of the Internet is that 'we are all connected but no one is in charge'.[22] The concern with the accountability of government networks is precisely that 'no one's in charge'. But creating a virtual incarnation of a government network through a Web site allows those who would be in charge—voters,

---

[20] Joint Year 2000 Council, Press Release (6 July 1998) <http://www.bis.org/press/p980706.htm>.

[21] Francesca E. Bignami, 'The Democratic Deficit in European Community Rulemaking: A Call for Notice and Comment in Comitology', Harvard International Law Review, vol. 40 (1999), 451.

[22] Thomas L. Friedman, Editorial, 'Judgment Not Included', New York Times, 27 Apr. 1999, A23.

congressional committees, regulated entities—to begin to assert control or impose constraints in a number of ways. They need not be silent observers or passive consumers of information; rather, they can themselves be increasingly active participants in the network.

2. Improving the quality of network decisions

To address the 'bad-decisions' problem, assuming it can be more precisely identified, the most promising possibility is the growth of legislative networks. Legislative oversight is the standard response to administrative delegation in both parliamentary and presidential systems. Where administrative officials are increasingly making decisions in conjunction with their foreign counterparts, it might well behove legislative oversight committees to coordinate with their counterparts as well. Regular meetings between directly elected representatives from different countries on issues of common concern will help broaden the horizons of individual legislators in ways that are likely to feed back to their constituents. Coordinating legislation through direct legislator interaction rather than through treaty implementation may also result in faster and more effective responses to transnational problems, although the ability to generate legislation independent of the executive obviously varies in different national political systems.

In some areas, national legislation has been used to facilitate the growth of government networks.[23] In others, such as human rights and the environment, national legislators are increasingly recognizing that they have common interests. In the European Union, governments are increasingly having to submit their European policies to special parliamentary committees, who are themselves networking.[24] The result, according to German international relations scholar Karl Kaiser, is the 'reparliamentarization' of national policy.[25] In addition, legislative networks can be used to strengthen national legislative institutions. For instance, the Association of African Election Authorities was founded in 1997. It is composed both of government officials and leaders of NGOs directly involved in monitoring and assisting elections.

Other examples include legislative networks nested within international organizations, as discussed further below. These networks, by

[23] MOUs between the US SEC and its foreign counterparts, for instance, have been directly encouraged and facilitated by several US statutes passed expressly for the purpose. Faith T. Teo, 'Memoranda of Understanding among Securities Regulators: Frameworks for Cooperation, Implications for Governance' (manuscript on file with author, Harvard Law School, 1998), 29–43.

[24] Shirley Williams, 'Sovereignty and Accountability in the European Union', in Robert O. Keohane and Stanley Hoffmann (eds), *The New European Community: Decisionmaking and Institutional Change* (Boulder, Colorado: Westview Press, 1991).

[25] Karl Kaiser, 'Globalisierung als Problem der Demokratic', *Internationale Politik* (Apr. 1998), 3.

allowing the regulators or parliaments of weak states to participate in global governance, serve the function both of setting a good example for fragile institutions as well as lending their strength and status to the organization in question. The OSCE parliamentary assembly, for example, has played an important role in legitimizing Eastern European parliaments by monitoring elections and including them in all OSCE deliberations. The controversy surrounding the OSCE's rejection of the Belarussian delegation for membership demonstrates that membership in the OSCE Assembly has become a symbol of its government's legitimacy for Belarussia.[26]

In encouraging the growth of legislative networks, however, it is important to recognize the distinctive features of much transgovernmental regulatory rule-making. Transgovernmental networks typically do not adopt binding rules or agreements; they are far more likely to formulate model codes or compilations of 'best practices'. The message is that 'well-governed countries or well-regulated economies have the following features', with some recommendations about how to achieve them. Enforcement of these principles is left to the enormous number of foreign investors that Friedman calls the 'electronic herd'.[27] It is not clear what 'accountability' even means in this context; the problem is much more likely to be that the distributional consequences of adopting particular models of regulation are neither factored into the decision-making process nor made clear as a consequence. Legislators seeking to influence those decisions must thus focus on insisting that regulators take account of the wider social and political context in determining 'best practices' or regulatory prototypes.

3. Enhancing legitimacy

Improving the visibility, accessibility, and monitoring of government networks in all the ways suggested above should simultaneously help redress their legitimacy problems. Publicizing process will reassure some and engage others; creating legislative networks will help normalize the entire concept of transgovernmental regulatory governance. Publicizing the results of transgovernmental cooperation, even if only through routine legislative hearings on the provision of requested information, may also clarify precisely when and how the distinctions between recommended practices, agreed principles, and joint understandings have an actual impact on domestic policy.

Even if fully successful, however, such measures could at best address legitimacy problems at a domestic level. At the global level, critics will

---

[26] Aleksandr Potemkin, 'Session of OSCE Parliamentary Assembly Ends in Moscow', *ITAR-TASS News Agency*, 9 July 1997.

[27] Thomas L. Friedman, *The Lexus and the Olive Tree* (New York: Farrar, Straus & Giroux, 1999), 90–119.

likely continue to find a ready audience for claims ranging from techno-cratic conspiracy to neo-imperialism. Most trenchant will be accusations of regulation 'cloning', the deliberate replication of developed-country regulatory institutions and structures on developing countries and the cre-ation of a global technocratic elite who are socialized to ignore the distrib-utive effects and political trade-offs implicit in their regulatory choices. These charges may seem silly in the transatlantic regulatory context when 'transatlantic' means United States–European Union, but they will re-emerge sharply when transatlantic is expanded to involve interactions with Africa and Latin America.

To address legitimacy concerns in global context, I propose two initial strategies. First is to develop a framework that acknowledges that the 'soft power' of persuasion is still power. Just as it may be successfully wielded by those who possess it, it may also be resented by those subject to it. The remainder of this section sketches some of the issues raised by the exercise of soft power. The second strategy is to offer several general principles of transgovernmental governance, principles formulated from the perspec-tive of a hypothetical global community. That is the subject of the final sec-tion.

Soft power, as defined by Joseph Nye, is the power flowing from an abil-ity to convince others that they want what you want rather than an ability to compel them to forgo their preferences by using either threats or rewards.[28] Soft power rests much more on persuasive than coercive authority, a base that may in turn require a capacity for genuine engage-ment and dialogue with others. The power exercised through government networks is much more likely to be soft power than hard power; indeed, one of the distinguishing characteristics of such networks, as of bilateral regulatory relations, is that agreements reached are likely to be explicitly non-binding. Persuasion is the dominant currency.

For many, the absence of coercion might seem to end all accountability concerns. But soft power is still power. To determine whether and how those who exercise it should be held accountable requires a closer look at its nature and impact in specific contexts. It is helpful to construct a styl-ized spectrum with pure informational exchanges at one end and appar-ent persuasion efforts conducted against a backdrop of very unequal bargaining power and ready leverage for actual coercion at the other. The question to be asked at each point along the spectrum is whether power is being exercised by government officials in a way that should trouble their constituents, and if so, how can accountability be enhanced. I will sketch several possible scenarios here.

Consider first the case of pure dialogue and exchange of information among government officials and their foreign counterparts. If judges, or

[28] Keohane and Nye, 'Power and Interdependence in the Information Age' (above, n. 14), 81, 86.

regulators, or even legislators, learn about alternative approaches to a problem facing them in the process of disseminating their own nation's solution, and views that solution more critically thereafter, is there an accountability problem? The answer is likely to be that accountable government does not seek to constrain the sources of knowledge brought to bear on a particular governance problem, but rather the ways in which that knowledge is acted on.

Fair enough, but many government officials will think and act differently as a result of their participation in transgovernmental networks in ways that we cannot and arguably should not control. Judges, for instance, who meet with their foreign counterparts, report a subtle but undeniable change in their perspectives and attitudes towards their domestic cases simply as a result of conversations with judges who face the same issues in other countries and other legal systems and resolve them differently. Perhaps they will actually decide a case differently, as Judge Calabresi apparently did as a result of his awareness of a European precedent in a recent Second Circuit decision.[29] This broadening of intellectual horizons is the essence of comparative perspective, as Justice Ruth Bader Ginsburg notes in an article discussing not only US but also EU and Indian approaches to affirmative action. She calls for an 'international human rights dialogue' on this issue, but notes that the majority of the Supreme Court still thinks that comparative constitutional analysis is 'inappropriate'.[30] Justice O'Connor has similarly stumped the country urging lawyers to cite more comparative and international law.[31]

Justice Ginsburg paints her brethren's position as provincial and anti-intellectual; Justice Scalia would argue that hers is anti-democratic. In his characteristically pungent phrase: 'We must never forget that it is a Constitution for the United States of America that we are expounding.'[32] Yet if other countries come up with promising approaches to hard issues bedevilling US courts or other government officials, does democratic duty condemn them to deliberate ignorance? Surely not, as long as a judge makes the extent of reliance on foreign sources clear, just as he or she would with domestic sources, and the basis for that reliance is the creativity of the foreign approach or the power of its logic rather than any independent desire to emulate a particular foreign system or fall into step with global public opinion.

[29] *United States v. Then*, 56 F.3d 464, 468–9 (2nd Cir. 1995).
[30] Ruth Bader Ginsburg and Deborah Jones Merritt, 'Affirmative Action: An International Human Rights Dialogue', *Rutgers Race and the Law Review*, vol. 1 (1999), 193, 228.
[31] See, e.g., Sandra Day O'Connor, 'Broadening our Horizons: Why American Judges and Lawyers Must Learn about Foreign Law', *International Judicial Observer* (International Judicial Academy/ASIL), June 1997 (article adapted from speech given by Justice O'Connor at the 1997 spring meeting of the American College of Trial Lawyers), 2.
[32] *Thompson v. Oklahoma*, 487 US 815, 869 n. 4 (1988) (Scalia, J., dissenting).

A similar but more subtle problem arises with government regulators who participate in a wide variety of exchanges with their foreign counterparts. Elementary psychology teaches that those who would persuade others of their views are likely to be most effective when they appear equally willing to be persuaded of their listeners' positions. Such a psychological posture, however, may well result in genuine dialogue and a degree of persuasion on both sides. In short, the power of persuasion is likely to flow both ways. For scholars such as Lani Guinier, the potential for such a two-way exchange is the essence of 'power with' rather than 'power over'; a model of power that holds enormous potential for creative synergies and growth.[33] But from the perspective of voters seeking to hold officials accountable to a particular constituency and set of preferences, at least the decision to enter into such a dialogue, with partly unforeseen consequences, must be either authorized *ex ante* or monitored *ex post*.

Even the exercise of pure soft power may thus be more problematic than it first appears. Much more troubling, however, are situations in which soft power appears to mask hard power. Consider the following examples. The US Securities and Exchange Commission has succeeded in replicating itself in many developing countries. It provides technical assistance with various strings attached, such as the requirement that the recipient country pass legislation giving its securities regulators the same margin of independence from legislators that the SEC possesses in the United States.[34] The environmental agencies of the United States, Canada, and Mexico are linked in an 'environmental enforcement network' under NAFTA auspices, a development that the US Environmental Protection Agency trumpets but its Mexican counterpart regards as a thinly veiled apparatus for imposing US-style regulation and enforcement on Mexico. Finally, organizations like IOSCO and the Basle Committee are all busily adopting codes of 'best practices' in securities or central-bank regulation, codes for 'voluntary adoption' by any nation that so desires. The designers of these codes, who are overwhelmingly from industrialized countries with highly developed regulatory systems, see them as 'technical' or 'nonpolitical'; their promulgation simply offers less-developed states the opportunity to help themselves by adopting and adapting state-of-the-art regulatory technology. Yet for many states on the receiving end, choice is an illusion. These codes are increasingly likely to be 'enforced' by private investors and increasingly by international institutions such as the IMF and the World Bank.[35] In such cases persuasion translates directly into coercion.

---

[33] Lani Guinier, 'Rethinking Power', *Tanner Lectures on Human Values*, 4–5 Nov. 1998 (lectures given by Professor Guinier at Sanders Theater, Harvard University).

[34] Teo, 'Memoranda of Understanding' (above, n. 23).

[35] Michael G. Froman, 'The Global Economy, the International Financial Crisis and their Impact on Sovereignty and International Law' (manuscript on file with author, Harvard Law School, 23 Apr. 1999).

Systematic thinking about the accountability of government networks requires recognizing that soft power is still power. Its exercise is on the whole preferable to hard power; even a small dose of direct coercion is the fastest way to bring out paeans to the virtues of persuasion. Nevertheless, soft power raises a distinct set of concerns both for its wielders and its subjects. To the extent that global dialogue among regulators or judges or legislators changes minds and practices in unexpected ways, the best solution does seem to be transparency, in the form of full disclosure of sources. Foreign ideas should not be emulated solely because they are foreign, but neither should they be rejected solely because they are not homegrown. To the extent that soft power serves as a mask for hard power, the links between the two mechanisms should be exposed and addressed up front. In other words, if a model code promulgated by a 'technical committee' of a transgovernmental organization is likely to become a template for financiers both private and public, then the representation of countries on that committee should be correspondingly broadened. Still a further step would be to require approval of or at least comment on any kind of model code by non-technocrats in developing countries, with a particular focus on distributional consequences. Developed-country regulators could be required to engage in the same kind of analysis before proceeding to negotiate bilateral agreements with their developing-country counterparts, analysis that would be fed into prior legislative approval of such initiatives.

It is impossible to develop a one-size-fits-all approach to accountability. Even the very tentative and general suggestions advanced here would need to be carefully contextualized. But the exercise of asking questions about the accountability of soft power and seeking to distinguish when it is problematic and when not as the predicate for developing specific solutions is both legitimate and necessary. Moreover, these solutions can be developed in the broader context of a few general principles of transgovernmental governance that can be applied to all government officials interacting with one another in virtually any context.

III. TOWARDS CONSTITUTIONAL PRINCIPLES OF TRANSGOVERNMENTALISM

A more fundamental response to enhancing the legitimacy of government networks from the perspective of the global community is a constitutional response: an effort to develop general principles that express the deeper values that government networks should serve. Specific mechanisms of control and constraint could then be developed to ensure that these principles are realized in specific cases. Three such principles are the principle of legitimate difference, the principle of positive comity, and the principle of positive conflict. These principles have already been developed, although not always explicitly, in US–EU regulatory relations, as well as within the European Union. Thus it seems particularly appropriate to advance them here as candidates for wider adoption.

A. Legitimate difference

The first principle of transnational governance should be the principle of legitimate difference. As Justice Cardozo put it while on the Second Circuit:

> We are not so provincial as to say that every solution of a problem is wrong because we deal with it otherwise at home . . . The courts are not free to enforce a foreign right at the pleasure of the judges, to suit the individual notion of expediency or fairness. They do not close their doors unless help would violate some fundamental principle of justice, some prevalent conception of good morals, some deep-rooted tradition of the common weal.[36]

In conflicts of law, the principle of legitimate difference is limited by the public policy exception, whereby a court will not apply a foreign law that would be otherwise applicable if it violates a fundamental principle of public policy. The principle of legitimate difference assumes that the public policy exception would be applied only rarely, in cases involving the violation of truly fundamental values. In the US context, fundamental equates with constitutional, in the sense that state courts cannot invoke the public policy exception to bar enforcement of another state's act unless that act arguably violates the Constitution itself.[37]

Transposed from the judicial to the regulatory context and from the United States to the global context, the principle of legitimate difference should be adopted as a foundational premise of transgovernmental cooperation. All regulators participating in cooperative ventures of various kinds with their foreign counterparts should begin from the premise that 'difference' per se reflects a desirable diversity of ideas about how to order an economy or society. 'That we deal with it otherwise at home' is not a reason for rejecting a foreign law or regulation or regulatory practice unless it can be shown to violate the rejecting country's constitutional rules and values.

The principle of legitimate difference applies most precisely to foreign laws and regulations. But a corollary of the principle is a presumption that foreign government officials should be accorded the same respect due to national officials unless a specific reason exists to suspect that they will chauvinistically privilege their own citizens. Several examples from the

---

[36] *Loucks v. Standard Oil Co.*, 120 N.E. 198, 201 (N.Y. 1918).

[37] The full faith and credit clause of the Constitution requires each state to recognize the acts of another. US Const. art. 4, §1, cl. 1. It is a basic instrument of federalism, knitting the states into one larger polity.

judicial context illustrate the point. In the Laker antitrust litigation, US federal district judge Harold Green decided not to restrain the British parties from petitioning the British Government for help. Judge Green was presuming the same good faith on the part of the British executive as he would on the part of the US executive in a parallel circumstance and assuming that the British executive would not automatically ally with its own citizen in a case involving a foreign citizen in a foreign court.[38] The Seventh Circuit Court of Appeals has also made this premise explicit in several cases. In the *Amoco Cadiz* case, it chose to defer to a ruling by the French executive branch under the *Chevron* doctrine requiring deference to US agencies.[39] And more recently, in a case arising under federal trademark legislation, Judge Easterbrook argued that foreign courts could interpret such statutes as well as US courts, noting that the entire *Mitsubishi* line of Supreme Court precedents 'depend on the belief that foreign tribunals will interpret US law honestly, just as the federal courts of the United States routinely interpret the laws of the states and other nations'.[40]

Note that thus formulated, the principle of legitimate difference lies midway on the spectrum from comity to mutual recognition. Traditional comity prescribes deference to a foreign law or regulation unless a nation's balance of interests tips against deference. Legitimate difference raises the bar for rejecting a foreign law by requiring the balance of interests to include values of constitutional magnitude. 'Mutual recognition', on the other hand, has become an organizing principle in regimes of regulatory cooperation, as an alternative to either national treatment or harmonization.[41] As practised between Member States of the European Union, mutual recognition requires two countries to recognize and accept all of each other's laws and regulations in a specific issue area.[42] This state

[38] *Laker Airways Ltd. v. Sabena, Belgian World Airlines*, 731 F.2d 909 (D.C. Cir. 1984).

[39] *In re* Matter of Oil Spill by the Amoco Cadiz Off the Coast of France on March 16, 1978, 954 F.2d 1279, 1312–13 (7th Cir. 1992) (per curiam). The Chevron doctrine was set forth in *Chevron USA. Inc. v. Natural Resources Defense Council, Inc.*, 467 US 837, 844 (1984) (holding that 'a court may not substitute its own construction of a statutory provision for a reasonable interpretation made by the administrator of an agency. We have long recognized that considerable weight should be accorded to an executive department's construction of a statutory scheme it is entrusted to administer . . .').

[40] *Omron Healthcare, Inc. v. Maclaren Exports Ltd.*, 28 F.3d 600, 604 (7th Cir. 1994).

[41] Kalypso Nicolaïdis, 'Mutual Recognition of Regulatory Regimes: Some Lessons and Prospects', Jean Monnet Working Paper No. 97/7 <http://www.law.harvard.edu/programs/JeanMonnet/papers/97/97-07.html>.

[42] After the Cassis de Dijon decision of 1979, in which German authorities were forced to respect French liquor standards, the European Commission announced the 'mutual trust' principle: if one state's rules allow a product to be marketed, all other states should have confidence in the first State's judgment and likewise allow the product to be marketed. Case 120/78, *Rewe-Zentral AG v. Bundesmonopolverwaltung fur Branntwein*, ECR 649 (1979). This concept has contributed significantly to creating an integrated internal market. It has been read to require mutual recognition of educational diplomas, so that professionals from one EU country are now largely free to practise in another without repeating their education. Council

represents a step towards closer and enduring cooperation by effectively assuming that the constitutional test has been met and passed for an entire corpus of foreign laws and regulations. Thus legitimate difference offers an intermediate position: it reflects the intent of regulatory officials who seek further cooperation with one another to move beyond mere comity but does not require them to establish or even to work towards mutual recognition.

In sum, legitimate difference is a principle that preserves diversity within a framework of a specified degree of convergence. It enshrines pluralism as a basis for, rather than a bar to, regulatory cooperation, leaving open the possibility of further convergence between legal systems in the form of mutual recognition or even harmonization, but not requiring it. At the same time, however, it does not try to stitch together or cover over differences concerning fundamental values, values involving basic human rights and liberties or the organizing principles for a social, political, or economic system. At a more practical level, the principle of legitimate difference would encourage the development of model codes or compilations of 'best practices' in particular regulatory issue areas, letting the regulators in different countries figure out for themselves how best to adapt them to local circumstance.

It is also important to be clear, however, on what a principle of legitimate difference will *not* do. It does not help individuals or government institutions figure out which nation should be the primary regulator in a particular issue area or with regard to a set of entities or transactions subject to regulation. Thus it cannot answer the question of which nation should be in the position of deciding whether to recognize which other nation's laws, regulations, or decisions are based on legitimate difference. But it can nevertheless serve as a *grundnorm* of global governance for regulators exploring a wide variety of relationships with their transnational counterparts. If regulators are not prepared to go even this far, then they are unlikely to be able to push beyond paper cooperation.

B. Positive comity

Comity is a long-standing principle of relations between nations. The classic definition for American lawyers is the formulation in *Hilton v. Guyot*: 'neither a matter of obligation on the one hand, nor of mere courtesy and good will on the other . . . comity is the recognition which one nation allows within its territory to the legislative, executive, or judicial acts of

Directive 75/362, 1975 OJ (L 167/1); Council Directive 89/48, 1989 OJ (L 19/16). Additionally, it has been applied to banking regulation, where branches of foreign banks are now supervised not by the host state, but by the authorities of the state of the head office, or home state. This approach reflects that each EU state accords a high degree of 'mutual trust' to the banking supervisory capabilities of the others. See Second Council Directive 89/646 on credit institutions, 1989 OJ (L 386/1).

another nation.'[43] 'Recognition' is essentially a passive affair, signalling deference to another nation's action. Positive comity, on the other hand, mandates a move from deference to dialogue. It is a principle of affirmative cooperation between government agencies of different nations. As a principle of governance for transnational regulatory cooperation, it requires regulatory agencies to substitute consultation and active assistance for unilateral action and non-interference.

Positive comity has developed largely in the antitrust community, as an outgrowth of ongoing efforts of EU and US antitrust officials to put their often very rocky relationship on a firmer footing. For long decades the US policy of extraterritorial enforcement of US antitrust laws based on the 'direct-effect' doctrine, even in various modified forms, was met by diplomatic protests, administrative refusals, and a growing number of foreign blocking statutes that restricted access to important evidence located abroad or sought to reverse US judgments.[44] The US Government gradually began to change course, espousing principles of comity and restraint in congressional testimony and in its international antitrust guidelines.[45]

In addition, US regulators began relying less on unilateral state action and more on agency cooperation. In the early 1980s the United States entered into separate cooperation agreements with the Governments of Australia (June 1982) and Canada (March 1984). In both agreements, the parties consented to cooperate in investigations and litigation by the others even when this enforcement affected its nationals or sought information within its territory. In return, the parties agreed to exercise 'negative comity'—to refrain from enforcing competition laws where such enforcement would unduly interfere with the sovereign interests of the other

---

[43]   159 US 113, 163–4 (1895).

[44]   Beginning with *United States v. Aluminum Co. of America (Alcoa)*, the Sherman Act was held applicable to foreign conduct that had a direct, substantial, and foreseeable effect on US trade and commerce. 148 F.2d 416, 440–5 (2d Cir. 1945). This 'direct-effect' jurisdiction quickly became a source of tension with other states that argued that the United States had no right to assert jurisdiction over persons that were neither present nor acting within US territory. Governments whose nationals and interests were affected by US antitrust law filed diplomatic protests and amicus briefs, refused requests for assistance, invoked national secrecy laws, and eventually began passing blocking laws specifically aimed at the frustration of US antitrust enforcement. Spencer Weber Waller, 'National Laws and International Markets: Strategies of Cooperation and Harmonization in the Enforcement of Competition Law', *Cardozo Law Review*, vol. 18 (1999), 1111, 1113–14; see also Joel R. Paul, 'Comity in International Law', *Harvard International Law Journal*, vol. 32 (1991), 1, 32; Joseph P. Griffin, 'EC and US Extraterritoriality: Activism and Cooperation', *Fordham International Law Journal*, vol. 17 (1994), 353, 377.

[45]   Spencer Weber Waller, 'The Internationalization of Antitrust Enforcement', *Boston University Law Review*, vol. 77 (1997), 343, 375. By 1988 the Department of Justice stated that it would only challenge foreign anticompetitive conduct that directly harmed US consumers. Robert D. Shank, 'The Justice Department's Recent Antitrust Enforcement Policy: Toward A "Positive Comity" Solution to International Competition Problems?', *Vanderbilt Journal of Transnational Law*, vol. 29 (1996), 155, 165.

party.[46] These agreements have led not only to greater cooperation between states,[47] but also to more effective enforcement of the antitrust statutes of both parties.[48] Several other countries, such as Germany and France (1984) as well as Australia and New Zealand (1990), have adopted similar bilateral arrangements addressing mutual assistance, including notification of activities, enforcement cooperation, and information exchange.[49]

In 1991 the United States executed an extensive antitrust cooperation agreement with the European Community.[50] The Agreement contained provisions on notification of enforcement activities, as well as information sharing and biannual meetings.[51] Most notably, the Agreement was the first to include the principle of positive comity. Article V of the Agreement provides that if Party A believes that its 'important interests' are being adversely affected by anticompetitive activities that violate Party A's competition laws but occur within the territory of Party B, Party A may request that Party B initiate enforcement activities.[52] Thus, Government B, in deference to Government A, is expected to consider enforcement steps that it might not otherwise have taken.[53]

[46] Charles F. Rule, 'European Communities–United States Agreement on the Application of their Competition Laws Introductory Note', *International Legal Materials*, vol. 30 (1991), 1487, 1488. The United States signed a comparable agreement with Germany in 1976. See Steven L. Snell, 'Controlling Restrictive Business Practices in Global Markets: Reflections on the Concepts of Sovereignty, Fairness, and Comity', *Stanford Journal of International Law*, vol. 33 (1997), 215, 234.

[47] No use of the Canadian federal blocking statute has been reported since the signing of the 1984 Agreement. See Waller, 'The Internationalization of Antitrust Enforcement' (above, n. 45), 368.

[48] In the past five years, cooperation between United States and Canadian antitrust agencies has led to prosecutions in the fax paper and plastic dinnerware industries. See Charles S. Stark, 'International Antitrust Cooperation in NAFTA: The International Antitrust Assistance Act of 1994', *US–Mexico Law Journal*, vol. 4 (1996), 169, 171–2.

[49] Nina Hachigian, 'Essential Mutual Assistance in International Antitrust Enforcement', *International Lawyer*, vol. 29 (1995), 117, 138. Antitrust cooperation has also been developing on a multilateral scale. The Organization for Economic Cooperation and Development (OECD) has established regular consultation conferences among national competition officials and has drafted a recommendation on antitrust cooperation, which encourages 'notification, exchange of information, coordination of action, consultation and conciliation on a voluntary basis'. See Waller, 'The Internationalization of Antitrust Enforcement' (above, n. 45), 362–3 (quoting 'Revised Recommendation of the Council Concerning Co-operation Between Member Countries on Anticompetitive Practices Affecting International Trade', *International Legal Materials*, vol. 35 (1996), 1314, 1315–17). More recently, a group of twelve experts called the International Antitrust Code Working Group proposed an International Antitrust Code to be adopted as a plurilateral trade agreement under the General Agreement on Tariffs and Trade (GATT). Under the Code, an International Antitrust Authority would be established, consisting of a president and an International Antitrust Council to ensure observance of the Code by contracting parties. See Shank, 'The Justice Department's Recent Antitrust Enforcement Policy' (above, n. 45), 186.

[50] See 'Agreement Regarding the Application of their Competition Laws, 23 September 1991, EC–US', *International Legal Materials*, vol. 30 (1991), 1491.

[51] Ibid. 1056–9.   [52] See Griffin, 'EC/US Extraterritoriality' (above, n. 44), 376.

[53] James R. Atwood, 'Positive Comity—Is It a Positive Step?', in Barry Hawk (ed.), *International Antitrust Law & Policy: Annual Proceedings of the Fordham Corporate Law Institute* (Fordham Corporate Law Institute, 1993), 79, 84.

This notion of positive comity is the converse of the traditional idea of deference, or 'negative comity'. Unlike the earlier agreements concluded by the United States with Australia and Canada, the EC Agreement focuses less on protecting the sovereign interests of one jurisdiction against the antitrust activities of the other and more on facilitating cooperative and even coordinated enforcement by antitrust authorities.[54] Where deference would tend towards less affirmative enforcement action, positive comity was designed to produce more affirmative enforcement.[55] While the EC–US Agreement reflects the increasing trend towards transnational cooperation in antitrust enforcement, the extent of enforcement coordination and information sharing contemplated by the agreement was unprecedented.[56] In practice, the Agreement has spurred an increase in the flow of information between the parties.[57] In addition, there has been increased enforcement of antitrust objectives, both quantitatively and qualitatively.[58] In coordinating their activities, the Parties under the Agreement work together to minimize the disruption to international trade that multiple uncoordinated investigations might otherwise cause.[59]

Can positive comity be translated from the antitrust context into a more general principle of governance? Two potential objections arise. First is the concern of many within the antitrust community that positive comity is a label with little content. In the words of one critic, 'It is not realistic to expect one government to prosecute its citizens solely for the benefit of another.'[60] The point here is that positive comity could only work where both governments involved already have a direct interest in prosecuting because the behaviour in question directly affects them, in which case cooperation is likely to occur anyway.[61] Further, any desire to undertake an investigation on behalf of a foreign government risks a domestic backlash.[62]

The second objection is a converse concern that to the extent positive comity works, it assumes enormous trust and close continuing relations

[54] See Rule, 'European Communities–United States Agreement on the Application of their Competition Laws' (above, n. 46), 1488.

[55] See Atwood, 'Positive Comity—Is It a Positive Step?' (above, n. 53), 84.

[56] See Rule, 'European Communities–United States Agreement on the Application of their Competition Laws' (above, n. 46), 1487.

[57] Joseph P. Griffin, 'EC/US Antitrust Cooperation Agreement: Impact on Transnational Business', *Law and Policy in International Business*, vol. 24 (1993), 1051, 1063.

[58] See generally Joel Klein and Preeta Bansal, 'International Antitrust Enforcement in the Computer Industry', *Villanova Law Review*, vol. 41 (1996), 173, 179.

[59] See Rule, 'European Communities–United States Agreement on the Application of their Competition Laws' (above, n. 46), 1490. This increased efficiency has also proved attractive to businesses themselves. In *United States v. Microsoft Corp.*, after learning that both the Department of Justice and the European Commission were investigating their licensing practices, Microsoft agreed to waive its confidentiality rights under US antitrust law to permit the two authorities to exchange confidential information. See Shank, 'The Justice Department's Recent Antitrust Enforcement Policy' (above, n. 45), 179.

[60] See Atwood, 'Positive Comity—Is It a Positive Step?' (above, n. 53), 87.

[61] Ibid.   [62] Ibid. 88.

between particular national regulatory agencies—factors that cannot be generalized. Spencer Waller points out that cooperation among agencies responsible for antitrust policy creates a community of competition officials who have been trained and socialized to speak, write, and think about competition issues in a similar way.[63] Thus if positive comity works anywhere, it should work here, but how can we adopt positive comity as a global principle of transnational regulatory cooperation before a relatively high level of cooperation has already been established?

The response to both these objections is a simplified and less stringent version of positive comity. As a general principle it need mean no more than an obligation to act rather than merely to respond. In any case in which Nation A is contemplating regulatory action and in which Nation B has a significant interest in the activity under scrutiny, either through the involvement of its nationals or through the commission of significant events within its territorial jurisdiction, the regulatory agency of Nation A has a duty at the very least to notify and consult with the regulatory agency of Nation B. Nation A's agency must further wait for a response from Nation B before deciding what action to take, and must notify Nation B's agency of any decision taken. Even the critics of positive comity acknowledge that to the extent a commitment to positive comity facilitates increased communication and exchange of information between governments, it may have an impact at the margin.[64] This communication and exchange of information in turn lays the foundation for more enduring relationships that ultimately ripen into trust. Thus at a global level, a principle of positive comity, combined with the principle of legitimate difference, creates the basis for a pluralist community of regulators who are actively seeking coordination at least and collaboration at best.

C. Positive conflict

The third and final norm of transnational governance should be one of positive conflict. To many the very notion may seem an oxymoron. But conflict in many domestic societies is seen as the motor of positive change, as the engine of economic growth in the form of competition, and as the lifeblood of politics. Conflict in the international arena, by contrast, is worrisome because of the possibility, however distant, that it could escalate into military conflict. Conflict between states is thus a problem to be solved and an eventuality to be avoided.

However, among liberal democracies the possibility of military conflict is so small as to be almost completely discounted in ordinary transgov-

---

[63] See Waller, 'National Laws and International Markets' (above, n. 44), 1125.
[64] See Atwood, 'Positive Comity—Is It a Positive Step?' (above, n. 53), 88.

ernmental relations.[65] This presumed absence of military conflict leads to a new view of non-military conflict. In US–EU regulatory relations, at least, conflict should be understood and addressed the same way as in domestic politics. Indeed, routine conflicts may well be more heated than in relations between liberal and non-liberal states, both because relations are less dense and thus generate fewer conflicts and because when conflicts do arise they are quickly dampened through high-level diplomacy.[66] Intra-family relations are often sharper than relations among friends, precisely because the depth of the relationship and thus the diminished likelihood of serious consequences flowing from a quarrel are taken for granted.

These conflicts should not, however, simply be endured. They should be accepted and perhaps even welcomed as a dynamic force that will ultimately deepen and improve the relationship. Writing about 'social conflicts as pillars of democratic market societies', Albert Hirschman underlines a point made by the German sociologist Helmut Dubiel: 'social conflicts themselves produce the valuable ties that hold modern democratic societies together and lend them the strength and cohesion they need.'[67] Hirschman reviews the long intellectual history of this idea, arguing that, due to its paradoxical power, it is 'reinvented with considerable regularity' in literatures ranging from political philosophy to development studies.[68]

No one suggests, however, that conflict cannot also be powerfully destructive of social relations. Thus the task, as Hirschman presents it, is to move beyond identification of the phenomenon of positive conflict to an understanding of the conditions under which conflict is more likely to act as a 'glue [than] a solvent'.[69] He develops the claim that conflicts in 'pluralist market societies', or more accurately the process of learning to 'muddle through' a 'steady diet' of such conflicts, are more likely to be productive.[70] The conflicts typical of these societies, in his view, have three basic characteristics:

1. They occur with considerable frequency and take on a great variety of shapes.

---

[65] The argument here does not simply flow from the democratic peace literature. As Robert Keohane and Joseph Nye pointed out in the 1970s, transgovernmental interaction is itself a measure of complex interdependence, which they argued was also characterized by a very low likelihood of military conflict. Anne-Marie Slaughter, 'International Law in a World of Liberal States', *European Journal of International Law*, vol. 6 (1995), 503, 512–13.

[66] By routine conflicts I exclude long-running and highly charged conflicts such as that between Libya and the United States over the Lockerbie bombing or between North Korea and the United States. These types of conflict generate an immediate international response, even if they then stalemate for long periods.

[67] Albert O. Hirschman, *A Propensity to Self-Subversion* (Cambridge: Harvard University Press, 1995), 235.

[68] Ibid. 237 (emphasis omitted).   [69] Ibid. 239.

[70] Ibid. 242–3, 244 (emphasis omitted).

2. They are predominantly of the divisible type and therefore lend themselves to compromise and to the art of bargaining.

3. As a result of these two features, the compromises reached never give rise to the idea or the illusion that they represent definitive solutions.[71]

Conflicts of the 'divisible type' refers to conflicts that are essentially distributive, 'conflicts over getting more or less' of something, as opposed to non-divisible 'either–or' conflicts 'that are characteristic of societies split among rival ethnic, linguistic, or religious lines'.[72] The conflicts that arise in US–EU regulatory relations are most likely to fit this 'divisible type' description, even though many have strong cultural overtones. They are thus likely to contribute to the construction of a strong transnational society. In particular, moving beyond Hirschman, they are likely to give rise to what Robert Cover called a 'jurisgenerative process'.[73] The procedures and substantive principles developed over the course of repeated conflicts among the same or successive actors take on precedential weight, through both learning processes and the pragmatic necessity of building on experience. As they become increasingly refined, these procedures and principles are increasingly likely to be codified in informal and increasingly formal ways.

This jurisgenerative process is the flip side of the legal-process insight that law is a tool more for managing conflict than resolving it.[74] Projecting some of the precepts of this school onto the international arena, Abram and Antonia Chayes depict compliance with international regulatory agreements as a process of 'managing' the problems that face countries seeking to comply with their obligations but often unable to do so for a variety of reasons.[75] They do not draw the further link between conflict

---

[71] Hirschman, A Propensity to Self-Subversion (above, n. 67), 246.   [72] Ibid. 244.

[73] Robert M. Cover, 'The Supreme Court, 1982 Term—Forward: Nomos and Narrative', Harvard Law Review, vol. 97 (1983), 4, 15, cited for a similar proposition in Harold Hongju Koh, 'The 1994 Roscoe Pound Lecture: Transnational Legal Process', 75 Nebraska Law Review (1996).

[74] Henry M. Hart, Jr. and Albert M. Sacks, The Legal Process: Basic Problems in the Making and Application of Law (prepared for publication from the 1958 tentative edition by William N. Eskridge, Jr. and Philip P. Frickey) (New York: Foundation Press, 1994), lxxi–lxxii.

[75] Abram Chayes and Antonia Handler Chayes, The New Sovereignty: Compliance with International Regulatory Agreements (Cambridge: Harvard University Press, 1995), 22–8. Other authors have similarly applied the legal-process insight in the context of international law. See, e.g., Note, 'Taking Reichs Seriously: German Unification and the Law of State Succession', Harvard Law Review, vol. 104 (1990), 588, 598 (noting that '[r]ules reflect underlying conflicts between competing values. They do not resolve, but rather manage, these conflicts by balancing irreconcilable policies.'). Another counter-intuitive relationship between law and conflict emerges from recent writings on international criminal trials. Jose Alvarez draws on Mark Osiel's work depicting international criminal trials as a way of managing 'civil dissensus', preventing closure over bloody and long-running social conflicts but channelling competing versions of the story and ensuring that as many voices as possible are heard. Jose E. Alvarez, 'Crimes of States/Crimes of Hate: Lessons from Rwanda', Yale Journal of International Law, vol. 24 (1999), 365, 469–83. The idea of 'civil dissensus' is an interesting further elaboration of 'positive conflict'; however, it is unlikely that the kinds of conflicts arising from transnational regulatory relations will generate the same deep passions and wounds as the commission of mass atrocities.

itself and a strong social order, but it is not a far step from their conception of compliance to a vision of a symbiotic relationship in which law manages conflict and repeated conflict helps build strong transnational relationships and generates the principles that ripen into law.[76]

Given these various rationales for understanding conflict as a positive phenomenon, what would a norm of 'positive conflict' actually mean as a governance principle? First, it dictates an attitude shift, requiring all parties to see conflict as a process to be managed rather than as an evil to be avoided or suppressed. Second, it is a process that can be managed largely by the regulators themselves, without the necessary intervention of diplomats, although courts and legislators are also likely to be involved. Third, all participants must understand that any conflict is inevitably part of a series of conflicts; they are players in a repeated game. This awareness not only dictates moderation in the hope of reciprocal treatment from the other side in the future, but also encourages all sides to crystallize and build on their past experience.

A final consideration regarding the principle of positive conflict involves transgovernmental regulatory cooperation beyond US–EU relations. Although transgovernmental regulatory networks are most concentrated among OECD countries, they extend to regulatory agencies in many different kinds of countries. In some cases, such as contact between environmental regulators in the United States and China, these ties are a way of creating some cooperative relations between countries that are otherwise often opposed to one another. Conflict of any kind between such countries still has the possibility of escalating into military conflict, and must be handled accordingly. Thus to adopt positive conflict as a global governance norm for regulatory networks would require an ongoing awareness of the distinction between positive and negative conflicts.

These three principles—legitimate difference, positive comity, and positive conflict—each build on the other. Together they frame a regime of pluralism, active cooperation, and productive if often messy conflict. Even if all regulators around the world were to adopt these principles in a charter governing relations with their foreign counterparts, however, it would not solve all the potential accountability problems that have been raised and discussed in this contribution. The perception of 'regulators on the loose', particularly when coupled with more general suspicion of the seemingly inexorable forces of globalization, is easy to manipulate and hard to address satisfactorily. But in addition to adapting domestic

---

[76] Chayes and Chayes developed their analytical framework with regard to international regulatory treaties; it applies equally well to transnational regulatory relations. In earlier work Abram Chayes elaborated the link between regulatory law and public policy, arguing that the resolution of regulatory issues necessarily involves broad debates over public policy and public values. Abram Chayes, 'The Role of the Judge in Public Law Litigation', *Harvard Law Review*, vol. 89 (1976), 1281, 1302.

governance structures in various ways and creating various Internet-based processes of decision-making that will enhance transparency and access, developing explicit principles of transnational governance will help establish regulatory networks as a legitimate form of governance, complementary to international and supranational institutions and national governments.

IV. CONCLUSION

Transnational regulatory cooperation is not only an important dimension of US–EU relations, but an increasingly important mechanism of global governance. Networks of government officials engaged in the same general endeavour and facing similar problems in the domestic context can work with one another to remove obstacles posed by national differences, exchange information about promising solutions, and develop common approaches to regulatory problems. At the same time, as this volume makes clear, transgovernmental regulatory relations are often a site for sharp conflict—often all the sharper for arising among friends.

For many observers of government networks, however, questions of conflict versus cooperation are less important than questions of accountability. The transnational nature of these activities suggests the slipping free of domestic constraints. Shadowy legions of technocrats appear to be forging consensus with one another at the expense of wider domestic constituencies. Whether true or not, the perception of the secretive and illegitimate nature of much of this activity is troubling and potentially damaging to the long-term effectiveness of transgovernmental governance. Yet adapting both the concept and the mechanisms of accountability to this new form of governance requires identifying and addressing the problem directly. This contribution is a first step along that road. The destination may someday be a transgovernmental constitution.[77]

---

[77] Brian T. Fitzgerald, 'Software as Discourse: The Power of Intellectual Property in Digital Architecture', *Cardozo Journal of Arts and Entertainment Law*, forthcoming 2000 (manuscript on file with author).

The challenges of globally accessible process

Peter L. Strauss

A note for the reader: In the conference the present volume reflects, this contribution was as much a visual as an auditory experience. Its principal aim was to open to view the possible implications of wider government and citizen use of the Internet for policy formation in the transatlantic regulatory community. Using the projected image of an Internet connection and moving through various examples of Internet use made it possible to engage the participants demonstrably in ways the print medium simply does not permit. The site illustrations that the publisher has kindly agreed to reproduce below may give an idea, but they too lack precisely the ingredients of immediacy and interactivity the Internet affords. The reader wishing to test or explore the ideas presented here is invited to read this contribution beside an open Internet connection, so as to respond to what is on the screen as well as on the printed page.

A domestic American administrative lawyer invited to contribute to a conference on transatlantic regulatory cooperation approaches the task with some trepidation, fearing his subject may be as obscure to the participants as theirs may be unknown to him. In addressing the subject of transatlantic regulatory cooperation and democratic values, however, I am hopeful about the possibilities of interchange. I start from the supposition that transatlantic regulatory cooperation will entail significant coordination of regulation. To win acceptance for their results, the partners would need at least to understand the growing American conviction that even technological regulation is the product of political action as well as expertise. The procedures the American Administrative Procedure Act prescribes for rule-making were distinctive even when it was adopted. In the fifty-three years since its enactment they have been increasingly adapted to accommodate public engagement and political influence. This ineluctable process of democratization carries its own implications for the formation of regulatory policy on an international scale. More strikingly, the explosive growth in use of the Internet by both politicians and governmental organizations over the past few years has created an intimacy of engagement between citizen and government that could not have been imagined even a decade ago.

The occasions for transatlantic regulatory cooperation lie not simply in the economic globalization reflected in so many of the papers in this volume, but also in the demands of what might be described as the obverse of subsidiarity.[1] By the end of the last century, the industrial age had created a national market in the United States, necessitating an ever-widening national control of issues previously dealt with by the individual states. Today, in much the same way, global markets are generating tasks to which national governments, even governments as large as the United States, are no longer capable of responding. Indeed, the problems of the global commons or the regulation of child labour transcend the geography suggested by our transatlantic focus. These are not disputes between the United States and Europe—however much one might believe that a concerted transatlantic effort would, at least initially, produce some headway on them. But the immediate issues of trade and capital volatility within the transatlantic community are large enough to make clear the practical need for, and not simply the advantages of, coordinated regulatory effort.

The American papers on the question of interface between international regulatory initiatives and domestic legal and institutional environments call attention to some of the salient eccentricities of the American political process. A focus on 'democratic values' suggests the value of considering our domestic regulatory environment in a political sense. The special nature of our political arrangements is of course a well-established element of dealing with the United States at the level of treaties; when one finishes with the President and the Secretary of State, it remains necessary to deal with the Senate. It may be possible to negotiate with a single, more or less unitary, authority; but the results must be satisfying to a multitude—who need share no political allegiance with the negotiator and, in any event, are not under his political control. Similar phenomena may be confidently, and increasingly, expected at the level of regulation. Even as we move towards globalization, the changes that have named our time the 'information age' are moving politics and decision ever nearer to the citizen.

Before turning to information-age developments, I sketch some widely understood ways in which expectations about democratic participation and accountability have already transformed American regulatory practice. If, as it seems, the European contributions to this volume embody the premise that regulatory judgement is *expert* judgement—the judgement of a professional elite—then these transformations in themselves could complicate transatlantic regulatory cooperation. In the United States, the idea that regulators are, or can be, simply experts has been dead for at least twenty years and one cannot expect it easily to revive. While expertise is an undoubted element of regulation, politics also has a role to play.

American-style rule-making is the great invention of the American Administrative Procedure Act (APA). As formulated more than a half century ago, rule-making was a very simple procedure. Even in that simple form, rule-making was rather more open and directly participatory—and

---

[1] See especially the contribution of Eleanor Fox, this volume.

in that sense democratic—than the ways in which, even today, subsidiary legislation is generated on the Continent. The Act required a federal agency wishing to adopt subsidiary legislation to give to the public notice of what it proposed to do, to afford anyone who wished the opportunity to respond to that notice with views, comments, suggestions, and the like, and then subsequently to publish with its regulation an explanation of what it had done and in particular a response to the comments that it had received. One might suppose that these procedures, in and of themselves, significantly democratized how the federal government would deal with the problems presented by subsidiary legislation.

The past half century's developments illustrate America's bias against making laws—many think these developments have led to an 'ossification' of the rule-making process—and some profound changes in the direction of democratization. One element is transparency. Starting with enactment of the Freedom of Information Act (FOIA) in the late 1960s[2] (reinforced, for multi-member commissions, by the Government in the Sunshine Act[3]), virtually every aspect of rule-making has been brought into public view and made the possible subject of commentary. Particularly is this so for the scientific data on which agencies propose to rely in technological settings. Today, no agency could expect to complete rule-making successfully unless its data had been made open and exposed to public view and comment, essentially from the beginning. No statute specifically requires such openness towards scientific data; the APA says nothing about data in its very limited description of the notice with which rule-making must commence,[4] and the FOIA is in terms an independent statute lacking any relationship to other procedures. But technologically based rule-making moved to centre stage at about the same time as FOIA was enacted. Courts soon appreciated how data-dependent technological rule-making was and how important were its consequences. Courts recognized that *anyone* could use FOIA to demand 'all information the agency regards as significant to its pending rulemaking on [subject]'—with only a very limited possibility that one of the Act's exemptions would free the agency from having to disclose that data. There quickly followed the proposition that 'it is not consonant with the purpose of a rulemaking proceeding to promulgate rules on the basis of . . . data that [in] critical degree is known only to the agency'.[5] By analogy to the necessary conditions of

---

[2] The Act is codified at 5 USC. §552. The description in the text draws on Peter L. Strauss, 'From Expertise to Politics: The Transformation of American Rulemaking', *Wake Forest Law Review*, vol. 31 (1996), 745 and Peter L. Strauss, 'Changing Times: The APA at Fifty', *University of Chicago Law Review*, vol. 63 (1996), 1389.

[3] The Act is codified at 5 USC. §552b.

[4] 5 USC. §553(b): '. . . The notice shall include . . . (3) either the terms *or* substance of the proposed rule *or* a description of the subjects and issues involved' [emphasis added].

[5] *Portland Cement Ass'n v. Ruckleshaus*, 486 F.2d 375, 393 (D.C. Cir. 1973), further developed in *United States v. Nova Scotia Food Prod. Corp.*, 568 F.2d 240 (2d Cir. 1977).

scientific debate and truth-testing, our courts have made it clear that such data must be exposed in the course of rule-making if a rule reliant on it is to be sustained.

Alongside heightened requirements of transparency, the last quarter-century has also seen a steady increase in the extent of rationalized political control of rule-making, reflected in a trend towards coordinating and rationalizing the rule-making process from the centre of our government. This development may also have been catalysed by a statute, the National Environmental Policy Act of 1969,[6] which imposed on agencies an obligation of broadscale analysis for possible environmental impacts, reaching well beyond the conventional limits of their particular mandates. On this model, Presidents beginning with Nixon invented, and then delegated to their Vice-Presidents for enforcement, requirements for rule-making analysis and coordination. These initially took the form of an obligation on agencies to engage in a form of economic impact analysis before proposing any regulation likely to have an important effect on the national economy; they then matured into an obligation, as well, that agencies share the development of their regulatory agenda with the White House. These requirements have been echoed, although not yet precisely confirmed, in statutes addressing particular problems, such as agency demands for information from the public[7] or agency action that might have a particular impact upon small businesses. As a result, federal rule-makers may have to produce differential rules for what might ordinarily seem to be unitary technical problems, for example accommodating the particular problems of small business or of states and localities. They may also be obliged to follow different and rather more elaborate procedures when dealing with important rules, or information-demanding rules, than in dealing with others.

One could point to other developments, as well, that reflect this quite political view of rule-making. Congress has moved from a failed effort to establish the right of either chamber to 'veto' undesired rules, to a requirement that all adopted rules be laid before it for possible statutory disapproval. It has enacted procedures for negotiated rule-making that frankly recognize, and build on, the perception of rules as an accommodation of competing interests. In this trend towards rejection of a technocratic view of rule-making, one finds both a forthright recognition that rule-making is in part the product of a process of essentially political interest representation, and a struggle to articulate appropriate controls over the rawest forms of political influence. Thus, the formalized procedures for negotiating proposals for rule-making are careful to ensure catholicity of representation in the private as well as public interests that will participate in

---

[6] Pub. L. No. 91–190, 83 Stat. 852 (1970) (codified as amended at 42 USC §§4321–47 (1994)).
[7] Paperwork Reduction Act, 44 USC. §§3501–20 (1994).

the formulation of the proposals. One finds requirements—more informal than legal, but in some particular contexts explicit—that any contacts between rule-makers and interested members of the public should be noted and made available to public view. A variety of institutional arrangements do what they can to keep politics—particularly partisan presidential politics—separate from the governmental processes of regulatory coordination that are recognized as being an essential part of the presidential role. We are, indeed, still in the midst of a constitutional struggle that one might expect to have been resolved after two hundred years, about where the power or duty to develop subsidiary legislation lies— whether it lies in the President himself, whether he can command what happens at the agency level, or rather whether it is for the agency to enact, subject to some level of presidential supervision.

Both our increased recognition of the political character of rule-making and our provision for rule-making's greater transparency present major challenges for transatlantic regulatory cooperation. To the extent that Europeans maintain the view that the formulation of subordinate legislation is essentially technocratic in concept and private in practice, it will not be easy to develop an effective interface with American rule-making as it has evolved. These difficulties will only be compounded, in my judgement, by the emerging influence of the Internet on the practice of government, the subject to which the remainder of this contribution is addressed.

At the outset, it is proper to concede that the Internet phenomenon, and thus its impact on the shape of governance, has been a dramatic presence for only a few years even in the United States, where Internet use has had perhaps its most widespread and explosive impact. In the developing world, computers have hardly penetrated—although even there one may be talking only about the passage of years. Europe is rather more like, if not completely in, the American style. What the Internet promises to do— demonstrably in recent American experience—is not merely to expand access to information about government, but also to move government closer to the citizen, by providing a framework that facilitates the active participation of citizen groups.[8]

If, in the bureaucratic adage, 'knowledge is power', then the breadth, depth, and searchability of information that can be brought to each citizen's home by the Internet is itself transformative. Of course the decision must first be made to place information where it can be found, but in my judgement the incentives to do so will be profound, even apart from the contributions of democracy. The legitimacy values of notice, and the contribution it can make to informed self-regulation, are simply too important; 'secret law' is not only an abomination in democratic terms, but also profoundly inefficient. We can therefore confidently expect ever-widening

---

[8] See contribution of Sol Picciotto, this volume.

pools of information about government activity to become available in electronic form. This is a course on which Europe has already embarked, as the European Community already maintains a rich site of official documents.[9] What was previously found on a few library shelves is now in everyone's home; the limited and constructed index of a print document has now been replaced by the infinitely plastic capacities of the search engine.

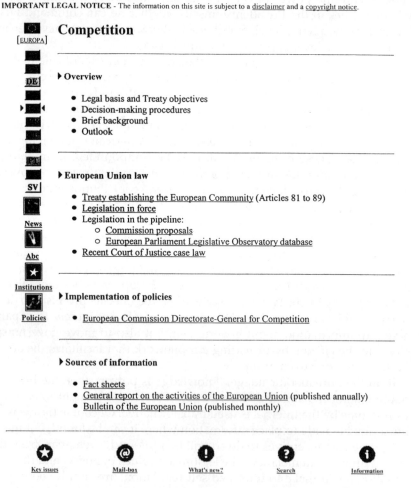

IMPORTANT LEGAL NOTICE - The information on this site is subject to a <u>disclaimer</u> and a <u>copyright notice</u>.

Competition

[EUROPA]

DE

▸**Overview**

- Legal basis and Treaty objectives
- Decision-making procedures
- Brief background
- Outlook

SV

News

Abc

▸**European Union law**

- <u>Treaty establishing the European Community</u> (Articles 81 to 89)
- <u>Legislation in force</u>
- Legislation in the pipeline:
  - ○ <u>Commission proposals</u>
  - ○ <u>European Parliament Legislative Observatory database</u>
- <u>Recent Court of Justice case law</u>

Institutions

Policies

▸**Implementation of policies**

- <u>European Commission Directorate-General for Competition</u>

▸**Sources of information**

- <u>Fact sheets</u>
- <u>General report on the activities of the European Union</u> (published annually)
- <u>Bulletin of the European Union</u> (published monthly)

★ **Key issues**   @ **Mail-box**   ❗ **What's new?**   ❓ **Search**   ❶ **Information**

Item 1. Document resource page from the European site

[9] http://europa.eu.int

American developments in this regard are suggestive of just how extensive this body of information might become, and how its availability may transform current regulatory practice. Up to now, the documents collected by an agency in the course of a rule-making constituted a single set of papers—perhaps dispersed across agency desks, but even if collected in one place still a resource of quite limited availability. Similarly, in the usual course, informal documents such as opinions of counsel on interpretive matters would find very limited official circulation, even though they were public in a formal sense. Unless a private publisher identified a market willing to pay for the expenses of collection and printing—and this did happen often enough to indicate the value that access to such documents can have to the private community[10]—they would be available only in one or a few government offices, arranged perhaps in simple subject matter or even chronological order. If, for example, an automobile manufacturer wanted to know what interpretations had already been given to a rule promulgated by the Department of Transportation's National Highway Traffic Safety Administration (NHTSA) requiring certain safety appliances to be installed on automobiles, it could hire a lawyer to go to the Administration's offices. There, the lawyer would be permitted to spend however many hours it would take to review the Administration's files of prior interpretations and attempt through personal effort to identify the relevant interpretations of the applicable standard. Inevitably, the cost of such searches limited the occasions on which they were made. That cost also limited both the influence of any particular interpretation and the incentive the agency's office of counsel might feel to achieve consistency in its work. Even with high incentives to consistency, the limits of paper indexing made it possible that earlier work bearing on a present problem simply would not be found.

Today the Department of Transportation maintains every document it receives in an electronic docket, available through the Internet. The incentive to do so is internal and economic. This practice means that many in the Department can be working with the same material simultaneously, and it is dramatically lower in cost than maintaining paper copies and document rooms. But of course the impact is also that participants in any Department proceeding now have ready access, wherever they are, to all the documents the Department chooses to associate with any given docket. The result seems likely to be much better informed and possibly iterative commentary in rule-makings and similar proceedings, where participants previously could not readily discover the contributions of others interested in the matter.

The Department of Transportation docket files are graphics files. Like the documents some agencies make available in a graphics (PDF) format,

---

[10] CCH Tax services; GM and AIAM collections of NHTSA letters at http://www.nhtsa.dot.gov/cars/rules/interps/welcome.html#aiam

DMS Web

search	reports	help/info	DOT
submit	feedback	support	TASC

♦ <u>United States Department of Transportation Privacy and Disclaimer Notice</u>

♦ <u>We want your feedback!!</u>
Please take a moment to tell us how you like the new DMS Web. We also encourage you to submit your ideas on how to make DMS Web even better.

♦ <u>New support system</u>
If you encounter any problems, such as a forgotten User ID and Password or any errors in the system, please use the new DMS Web support form for fastest response.

♦ <u>DMS Web introduction</u>
For those of you who are new to our site please take a few moments to read our "<u>Introduction to DMS Web</u>" page. This will give you valuable information and will answer many of the common questions users have asked. It is especially valuable for learning how to view the documents and how to use the various search criteria.

♦ <u>Services we provide to Government agencies</u>
Please take a moment to read about the services available for those of you in Government agencies. This will give you valuable information about how we can serve you in meeting your information management needs.

♦ <u>Search</u>
　　Search the Dockets and Documents on the DMS Web.

♦ <u>Reports</u>
　　Up-to-date Filing information

♦ <u>Submit</u>
　　On-Line Comment and Filing Submission to the Docket Management System

♦ <u>Help & Information</u>
　　How-to's, DMS Web News, contacts and information.

search	submit	reports	help/info	support	feedback

U.S. Department of Transportation
Dockets
400 7th Street, SW Plaza 401
Washington, DC 20590
1-800-647-5527
Version: 13-OCT-99

Item 2. Picture of http://dms.dot.gov/

they are hard to search for text content. No such problem exists, however, with files maintained in text formats, whether as simple text or in the more complex word-processing formats in which they may have been produced. When the General Counsel of NHTSA decided to make his opinions interpreting the Administration's rules available and searchable on the Web, he transformed an expensive professional's work requiring

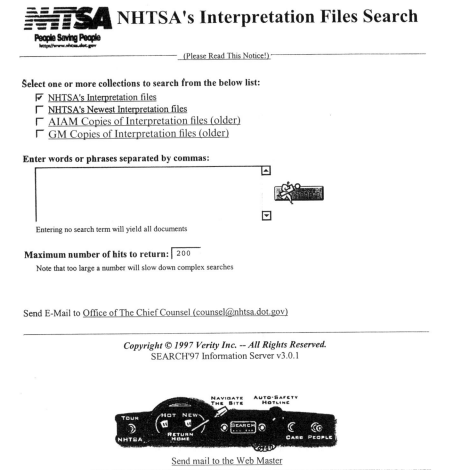

Item 3. Picture of http://www.nhtsa.dot.gov/cars/rules/interps/

hours of time in distant Washington into a 10-second search routine performable wherever an Internet connection can be made. The value of this action is suggested by donations made by General Motors and the American Institute of Automobile Manufacturers (AIAM) once this step had been taken. NHTSA's General Counsel was able to post only opinions generated after 1988, when his office began universal word-processing of its work; GM and AIAM had been keeping their own electronic records from an earlier date, for the reason suggested by the cost of occasional search. Perhaps as an encouragement to the General Counsel to continue his practice once begun, they provided copies of those earlier records for posting on the site.

Note the line near the top of the NHTSA search page that reads 'Please read this notice'. A person following this link is brought to a page that invites reliance on the opinions found on the site, albeit with a warning that they can be superseded, and that they are the product of the particular facts and the circumstances under which the opinion was sought. Evidently this makes searching all the more valuable.

At the moment, few American agencies are as forthcoming about their interpretations as NHTSA. Quite a number do not yet post them or, if they do, post them in ways that are not as conveniently searchable as NHTSA's are. Moreover, perhaps under the impact of Court of Appeals decisions that threaten to require observance of full rule-making procedures for interpretations that courts find were seriously meant,[11] several agencies that *do* make their opinions available also warn the reader that their advice is *not* reliable. The warning is perhaps a necessary formality under lawyers' advice; one wonders why any governmental actor, hoping to induce self-regulation and efficient planning, would wish to appear perverse. The judicial opinions I refer to seem largely to undervalue the utility of agencies' announcing how they intend to exercise their undoubted discretion; perhaps those announcements will be challenged infrequently and, when not thus put in doubt, prove reliable in fact. The immediate point is to see how the Internet shortens the distance between agency and citizen, even when seen simply as a means by which information can be provided.

The implications for transatlantic regulatory cooperation are noteworthy. American partners are likely to come to the table with their own expectations formed about the kinds of information that should be available. If we imagine the cooperation as inter-agency, and suppose that the European partners might—simply from their prior experience—prove more reluctant to emerge into the electronic 'sunlight', the American side may well find it difficult to compromise in the direction of privacy; its clientele will resist giving up access to information they already have, and will expect the same level of transparency in an expanded realm of regulation. If, as seems likely, regulation becomes increasingly a matter of publicizing norms which regulated interests are then invited to meet in whatever ways maximize their own benefit—rather than by rigorous control from the centre—effective provision of information about expectations, and the means by which they can be met, will become all the more essential.

The electronic connection offers, in this regard, a relatively costless means of subscribing in advance for desired notifications from government authority. Government currently notifies the public of regulatory initiatives through the bulky and undifferentiated medium of a daily gazette, through press releases that may or may not be effectively filtered

---

[11] *Community Nutrition Institute v. Young*, 818 F.2d 943 (D.C. Cir 1987) (per curiam).

Office of Solid Waste and Emergency Response

Subscribe to the Brownfields Update Notification System

Brownfields has recently implemented a list server capability. A list server is an electronic mailing list that makes it possible to reach all individuals in a specified group with a single e-mail message sent over the Internet. By adding your name to the Brownfields List Server, you will receive periodic announcements and press releases related to the Brownfields Initiative.

To **subscribe** to the Brownfields List Server:

1. Send an e-mail to Listserver@unixmail.rtpnc.epa.gov
2. Put nothing in the subject of the e-mail.
3. In the body of the e-mail type the following line, where "FIRSTNAME" and "LASTNAME" equals your name: subscribe Brownfields FIRSTNAME LASTNAME

Example:
subscribe Brownfields John Public

To **unsubscribe** to the Brownfields List Server:

1. Send an e-mail to Listserver@unixmail.rtpnc.epa.gov
2. Put nothing in the subject of the e-mail.
3. In the body of the e-mail type the following line: unsubscribe Brownfields

Example:
unsubscribe Brownfields

Note: To subscribe or unsubscribe to the Brownfields List Server you must send your e-mail message from the location at which you normally send or receive mail.

[Environmental Justice Homepage | OSPS Home]
[EPA Home | Search | Browse | What's New]

[Brownfields Updates | Using this Site | Site Statistics]

URL: http://www.epa.gov/swerosps/bf/listserv.htm
Last Updated September 30, 1997
Please E-mail comments on these Web pages to:
Jim Maas, Data Manager at: Maas.James@epamail.epa.gov

Item 4. Picture of http://www.epa.gov/swerosps/bf/listserv.htm

by intermediate information providers such as newsletters, or by individual notifications by mail that may be expensive, delayed, and complicated to handle. The electronic posting of data need occur only once, and immediately becomes available to anyone who has trained a search engine to engage in a periodic sweep for it. Beyond this, agencies can create e-mail machines (list-servers) at minimal expense that automatically post notices bearing on pre-identified subjects to all who have asked for them. Instead of the whole of the Federal Register, which must be mechanically searched for matters of possible relevance, one receives pointed notice of those matters in which one has identified an interest. Again, this pre-filtering dramatically enhances the information connection between agency and interested citizen.

In the context of transatlantic regulatory cooperation, the international mails would be avoided, as would be the need for foreign counsel. Once such a utility were in place, the time required for effective notice would be shortened by days if not weeks.

Thus far, we have been assuming a certain passivity on the part of the receivers of information, i.e. the citizens subject to the possibility of regulation (or regulatory protection); it has been a matter of enhancing the availability of information to them about government and its demands (or protections). Yet, in my judgement, the more remarkable changes occurring (and likely to continue to occur) are those that promise a growing interactivity, that open the possibilities of dialogue and response, and that thus increase the engagement of the citizen in government. Here, the place of democratic values is indeed of central importance.

That the Internet easily permits the creation of a virtual negotiation room for the formulation of policy is widely appreciated. In her contribution,[12] Anne-Marie Slaughter remarked on the Asian Pacific Economic Cooperation (APEC) site organized through the University of Washington as a policy-maker's Internet tool. This particular facility, which is organized for limited groups rather than the general public, has evident utility for transatlantic regulatory cooperation. Persons wishing to use it—e.g. regulatory bodies separated by the Atlantic or any other persons they may invite to join them—may establish a conference. Doing so permits the instantaneous exchange of drafts and ideas within the constituted group, full sharing of data resources, and the like. All matters within the conference are encrypted for maximum security. Persons with even a casual Internet knowledge can begin using it in a matter of minutes. APEC's limitation of participants to invited guests, moreover, is simply a matter of its choice, not of technological necessity, and any such limitation would be inconsistent with American rule-making procedures. In my judgement, adding open access to the interactivity offered by such a site is precisely the step that will join 'democratic values' with regulatory cooperation. Both American procedural commitments, and recent developments in use of the Internet in the United States make such a joinder virtually irresistible.

The emergence of the Internet as a potentially transformative political force was signalled in November 1998 by the election of Jesse Ventura to

---

[12] See contribution of Anne-Marie Slaughter, this volume.

Official Site Of The Jesse Ventura Volunteer Committee

Join The Jesse Net!
The Online Network Of Ventura/Schunk Supporters

Visit The JesseStore Online
Your Source For Official Jesse Ventura Merchandise

**Governor
Jesse Ventura**

**Lt. Governor
Mae Schunk**

Governor Ventura's Message
Regarding Light Rail

April 11, 1999
To: All JesseNet Members
From: Jesse Ventura
RE: Light Rail Transit

First, thank you for being part of the JesseNet. Your JesseNet participation on this list of Ventura/Schunk supporters increases the influence Lt. Governor Mae Schunk and I have in the state legislature. You are helping us do the job we were elected to do. We appreciate your support.

Today I am mobilizing the JesseNet for the first time. I need your help moving an important light rail transpiration bill through the legislature. I am asking you to send an e-mail to two key legislators urging them to pass the Ventura/Schunk light rail initiative. And I am asking you to tell your friends to do the same.

Here's the story In a nutshell. Twin Cities traffic is getting more and more congested. It will only get worse as the population grows. Light rail transit will help relieve congestion and provide economic development benefits as well. Minnesota has never been as well positioned to begin light rail development as it is now. The Governor and Lt. Governor support it. The MN Department of Transportation commissioner supports it. The head of the Metropolitan Council supports it. The Minnesota Senate supports it.

The problem is, certain Minnesota House Republicans are not supporting it.

It's time to do something. We've wasted years and years on planning. If we act now, Minnesota has a chance to compete and win $250 million in federal funds to support the construction of Light Rail transit on the Hiawatha Corridor. This will be the beginning of an expanded light-rail system in the future. It takes an appropriation of $60 million in state funds to leverage these dollars. If we don't act now, there won't be another opportunity until at least the year 2004. All those funds will find their way to other cities in other states.

The names, telephone numbers and e-mail links of the key legislators are below. Be respectful with your e-mail messages and phone calls. We don't have to storm their offices with torches and pitchforks just yet. Simply advise these legislative leaders that you support the Ventura/Schunk light rail initiative, and urge them to do

Item 5. Picture of http://www.jesseventura.org/issues/literail/jnetrail.htm

be the Governor of Minnesota. It is fairly widely known that he is a former professional wrestler who, seeking election as an independent, defeated candidates of both major political parties. Less well known, perhaps, is that he did so on a limited budget, without access to the volume of television advertising that his opponents were able to employ with budgets

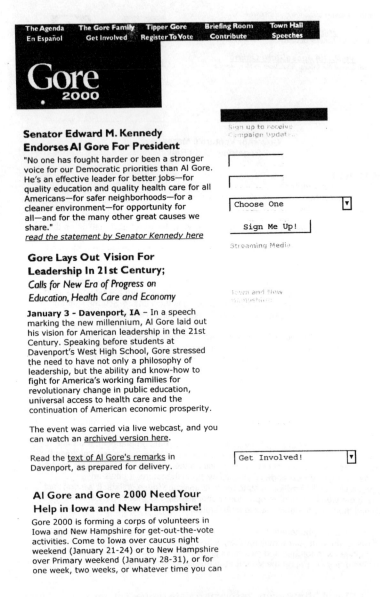

Item 6. Picture of http://www.algore2000.com/

twenty or so times as large. Instead, he spent the bulk of his funds in developing an Internet site that sought actively to engage those who came to it—seeking out their opinions, enlisting their assistance in organizing, distributing campaign materials through a list-server to all who enrolled for that. Following his election, Ventura maintained the site, using it to enlist

page contents
Overall View
Abstract
Disclaimer
Contacts
Go On

This website is a
large reference
manual to
describe a
spiralling series of
decision process
steps—and
accompanying
concepts.

Decision Process Guidebook
How To Get Things Done
In Government

Reclamation's / Guide's / Help
home page (Front door)

Site map / Take / Index
and contents (a tour)

New!

Examples: <u>Create a vision for your office</u>
<u>Make sense out of complex situations</u>
<u>Make decisions in your own life</u>

<u>Index</u> to guide topics

Updated material on <u>consent/consensus</u>, <u>NEPA</u>, and <u>indicators</u>.

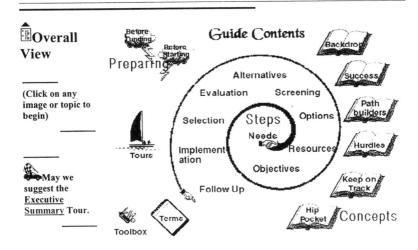

**Overall
View**

(Click on any
image or topic to
begin)

**May we
suggest the
Executive
Summary** Tour.

Item 7. Picture of http://www.usbr.gov/guide/

public support for initiatives that members of the state legislature—with
whom he does not share party allegiances—might otherwise find unat-
tractive. For example, when two influential Republican members of the
legislature threatened to block construction of light rail transportation for
the state's largest city, he broadcast a call to his supporters to contact them;
the fact that the legislators had Internet addresses made responding to that
call extremely simple. Whether or not the governor succeeds in securing
the authorization that he wants, the effort itself is striking, as is the citizen-
empowerment that it represents.

You will not be surprised to learn that all those seeking presidential nominations have created similar sites, where the visitor is invited to register opinions, to enrol in a list-server for the delivery of campaign materials, and the like. If the candidates themselves are not reading the responses they get, their political apparatus is surely doing so. One could characterize the development negatively, as providing only an illusion of contact; yet if instead one considers the experience of the perhaps somewhat unsophisticated citizen—previously lacking any such immediate-seeming contact with a candidate, sitting at home, choosing whether or not to respond, and registering what seems personally important—one can perhaps picture a significant moment of change in the political dynamic. Without purporting to analyse what is going to come of this, one can foresee that something *might* come of this, that our political lives may be about to change in quite remarkable ways.

Agencies as well as politicians may be interested in enlisting the understanding and participation of their publics, and as some of them establish such connections one easily imagines general expectations for the behaviour of all agencies growing. We have already seen one aspect of this, in the provision of readily searchable information about agency regulations and policy. Information about organization and processes is a simple next step. The Bureau of Reclamation is a widely dispersed bureaucracy responsible for the collection and distribution of much of the water in the arid western part of the United States. Perhaps for the enlightenment of its own bureaucracy, but also in a gesture freely available to the public, the Bureau established a site explaining how its decisions (and those of similar bureaucracies) are made. The site is rather detailed and, if one believes that the fuller engagement of 'hands-on' activity stimulates learning, can be expected to generate its own expectations about participation and its values. Anyone who is interested in how the Bureau of Reclamation works, or by extension how other parts of the government work—in short, how to get things done in government—now has this available to them. Procedures whose discovery might previously have required a lawyer's advice are now plainly stated in open view.

The use of the Internet to provide assistance to people who become involved with the complexities of government—another kind of venture that might seem to promote 'democratic values'—is also growing. Two sites warrant mention here. The American Small Business Administration maintains a Web site for the proprietors of small businesses, associated with its Ombudsman and Regulatory Fairness Councils. A small business finding that it has a problem dealing with government finds here access to those who may be able to map the electronic route through the government and thus assist in securing fair treatment.[13] Similarly, the Vice

---

[13] http://www.sba.gov/regfair/

Text Version

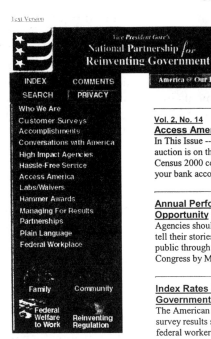

Vice President Gore's
National Partnership *for*
Reinventing Government

AWARDS   NEWS   CALENDAR
FAQs   SPEECHES TOOLS
INITIATIVES LINKS   LIBRARY

INDEX   COMMENTS
SEARCH   PRIVACY
Who We Are
Customer Surveys
Accomplishments
Conversations with America
High Impact Agencies
Hassle-Free Service
Access America
Labs/Waivers
Hammer Awards
Managing For Results
Partnerships
Plain Language
Federal Workplace

Family   Community

Federal
Welfare   Reinventing
to Work   Regulation

Select a Federal One Stop:

Acquisitions
Asset Sales
BudgetNet
Business Advisor
Communicators
Computers
Consumer Gateway   Go!

America @ Our Best   *In time for the 21st Century...*

Updates: January 3, 2000

Vol. 2, No. 14
Access America Online Magazine
In This Issue -- Plan ahead. Wild horse
auction is on the Internet on January 12. Can
Census 2000 count on you? Help find missing children. Are
your bank accounts safely insured?

Annual Performance Report Is Strategic
Opportunity
Agencies should take advantage of a strategic opportunity to
tell their stories to Congress, other policy-makers, and the
public through their first annual performance reports due to
Congress by March 31, 2000.

Index Rates Satisfaction With
Government Services
The American Customer Satisfaction Index
survey results show that, in many cases,
federal workers do a very good job in servicing citizens and,
in some cases, perform as well or better than their private
sector counterparts.

GovExec.com Story

Morley Winograd Opens Media Seminar
"Today's conference is about connecting the public with their
government,"NPR Director Morley Winograd told
communicators and program staff from 140 government
agencies over the country, professors and students from
seven D.C. area universities, and representatives from 30
private sector organizations and media.

GovExec.com
Reporters to Agencies: Tell Us Your Stories
A key to public affairs success is putting a human face on
government operations, journalists and federal officials said
Wednesday.

Item 8. Picture of http://www.npr.gov

President's office has built a site to assist state and local officials find their
way around the federal government—often enough a complicated, con-
fusing proposition. This site, like the Bureau of Reclamation's, has been
posted in a completely public way, so that citizens having no connection
with state and local government have equal access to it.[14] This site is part

[14] http://www.statelocal.gov/

of a more sweeping initiative under the Vice President's direction, styled the National Performance Review, that has undertaken, in its words, the reinvention of government—a reinvention that is heavily dependent on the Internet and at the same time acts as a kind of cheerleader for the Internet's potential. Here one finds an electronic magazine, *America Online*, celebrating Internet developments in government, giving news of awards and notable 'success stories' and offering other unmistakable encouragements to the further development of Internet government.

Perhaps the most dramatic developments in the federal government's use of the Internet, with the corresponding advancement of 'democratic values', have been experienced in the context of rule-making. While most rule-making remains a paper procedure, it is finding its way with increasing frequency into the electronic forum—with notices given, comments received, and data (including comments) made available for inspection and response. The result is to transform the process into one considerably more transparent and interactive than its paper equivalent. Conducted for the moment as experiments, or in settings in which public participation may be thought particularly likely, this process will inevitably spread. Two notable examples may suggest the future.

The Agricultural Marketing Service (AMS) of the Department of Agriculture has authority to define the conditions of cultivation that permit farmers of produce for sale in interstate commerce to call it 'organic'. The AMS proposed a new rule that would have redefined 'organic' produce in ways that would permit the use of some fertilizers, such as treated municipal waste, that were not currently in favour with organic farmers and their customers. The rule-making was posted to the AMS Web site, with electronic comments encouraged, and at the same time access given to comments, as filed, as well as to the transcripts of public meetings that the Service held in various parts of the country. Over 200,000 persons responded, mostly negatively. The Department withdrew its proposal for further revision, and undertook a number of studies of technical questions that had been raised in the comment process. The documents produced in response to these studies were themselves also posted, and comments invited, as the rule-making process continued. At this point, the entire affected community—consumers as well as producers—is engaged in a manner that simply would not have been possible in a paper-oriented process. Any individual may search the data and existing body of comments, and send his or her own input, independent of any other, and without significant cost to the government beyond the trivial costs of maintaining the site and the 'democratic' costs of attending to the input that has been catalysed in this way.[15]

The Federal Deposit Insurance Corporation (FDIC) recently had a similar experience with its proposed 'Know Your Customer' rule—a rule with

---

[15] See generally http://www.ams.usda.gov/nop/

significant privacy as well as other implications. Like the AMS, the FDIC proposed the rule in an electronic format, where citizens and others could find it and make responsive comments. The agency collected well over 200,000 comments, and publicly tabulated them to show their provenance and, in a summary way, their concerns. The summary table is reproduced on the next page, and from it one can see that privacy issues have excited the largest, but by no means the only, concerns expressed, and that citizens were the largest, but hardly the only, participants in the process. Issues of agency authority, cost burden, and competitive disadvantage also figure. Banks and their commercial customers also appear. On 29 March 1999 the agency announced that it had been dissuaded from issuing the proposed rule, and withdrew it from consideration. This is not democracy in the standard sense; no votes occurred, and the agency that, in the end, did not adopt the rule in light of the comments it received was not elected and could not be diselected. As agencies go, the FDIC (a banking agency) is rather more remote from the politically responsible President and Vice President than most. Nonetheless, it is difficult to ignore 353,000 comments—or the expectations that the capacity to register one's views in this way will inevitably carry with it.

As these processes become better established on this side of the Atlantic, the pressures to use them as well in matters of transatlantic regulatory cooperation will surely increase. In that cooperation, moreover, the coordinative, immediate, and interactive capacities of the Internet will prove seductive, wholly apart from these democratic pressures. Thus, the question will be the extent to which that process is opened up to the vision and even the participation of the concerned public, beyond a responsible bureaucratic elite. Certainly compared to the state of affairs in which *only* that elite uses these mechanisms, such a development would have to be considered as constituting an expression of democratic values. One might of course object, as occurred in our discussions, that the Internet-using community is itself an elite one relative to the general population. If at the margins that is so, the breadth of participation in the two rule-makings for which we have broad experience suggests that—in comparison to paper-only rule-makings—the eliteness of this form of participation is open to doubt. Today in the United States, and tomorrow in Europe, the proper contrast is not between this community and those who do not have computer access, but between this community and the far more limited population that would participate in rule-making in the absence of Internet access. In this respect, the Internet appears to be a mechanism for the emergence, not of bureaucratic turf protection, as some have feared,[16] but of the very public concerns and pressures so often and eloquently evoked here in relation to hormone-treated beef and genetically altered produce.

---

[16] See, e.g., contribution of Sir Leon Brittan, this volume.

KNOW YOUR CUSTOMER ISSUES

ISSUE	ASSOCIATION	BANK	BANK HOLDING CO	INDIVIDUAL
Customer Definitions	36	483	12	894
Cost Burden	48	1543	22	9982
Competitive Disadvantage	43	1236	16	2474
Privacy	108	2045	29	217468
Account Size Threshold	4	98	5	2290
Authority	37	464	8	71091
Y2K	20	351	3	625
Significant Adverse Impact	25	615	13	1402
Electronic Banking Compliance	5	15	1	77
Scope of Regulation	11	219	3	1372
Redundant	31	821	11	4402
Effective Date	9	114	4	51
Establish Plan within 6 months	3	23	1	14
Program Contents	8	169	5	269
Internal Controls/Training	4	59	1	104
Documentation Availability	2	364	8	11048
Ineffective Crime Measure	21	33	0	34
Opposed in General (no reason)	6	70	0	9339
Other**	37	413	13	9417
TOTAL	458	9135	155	342353

* Numbers do not match for technical reasons, information requests marked initially as comments, duplicates, etc.
** Examples of substantive comments in OTHER
– Abuse of Power
– Criminalizes citizens
– paper work burden

Item 9

Today in the United States, and tomorrow in the international regulatory community, the Internet will have important impacts on regulatory processes and, in particular, their democratic values.

Part VIII

The future of regulatory cooperation: strategic directions and institutional implications

Regulatory cooperation and managed mutual recognition: elements of a strategic model

Kalypso Nicolaïdis

Regulatory cooperation deserves analytical attention both in its own right and as a forerunner for the effect of interdependence on other policy areas and international governance in general.[1] While there have long been instances of regulatory cooperation, the web of complex multi-layered linkages across local, national, and regional borders that we now see emerging constitutes a new kind of *transnational regulatory governance*. I use the term 'governance' here to indicate that, increasingly, regulatory cooperation involves not only the sharing of information and ideas and the coordination of policy design, but also joint adoption of rules and shared enforcement authority managed through transnational regulatory networks. To be sure, like other forms of international cooperation, transnational regulatory arrangements simultaneously empower and constrain governments in their policy-making. But to a greater extent than with other types of international cooperation, the pooling of sovereignty—in this case regulatory sovereignty—influences the form of government itself and not only its environment. The core analytical issue here is to understand how regulatory governance can reach out across borders without involving radically new degrees of centralization such as the nineteenth century model of nation-state formation. The normative issue is to assess these developments in terms of accountability and ask what citizens have to gain.

In order to address these questions, this contribution presents a strategic model of international regulatory cooperation and does so with an ulterior motive. A strategic model combines the functions both of a

---

[1] For earlier work on regulatory cooperation, see for instance, *Regulatory Cooperation for an Interdependent World* (Paris: OECD Publications, 1994); George Bermann, 'Regulatory Cooperation Between the European Commission and US Administrative Agencies', *The Administrative Law Journal of the American University*, vol. 9, no. 4 (Winter 1998); Adrienne Heritier Windhoff, *Ringing the Changes in Europe: Regulatory Competition and the Transformation of the State* (1996); Jane C. Kang, 'International Regulatory Cooperation: Where We've Been and Where We're Going', *Futures Derivative Law Report* (1997); William Bratton et al. (eds), *International Regulatory Competition and Coordination: Perspectives on Economic Regulation in Europe and the United States* (1996); *The Limits of Liberalization, Regulatory Cooperation and the New Transatlantic Agenda* (Washington, DC, American Institute for Contemporary German Studies, Conference Report, 1997); Giandomenico Majone, *Regulating Europe* (London: Routledge, 1996).

typology—addressing the question 'what is meant by regulatory cooperation?'—and of an action plan—asking 'under what conditions are alternative paths to regulatory cooperation most effective or appropriate?' Its
main usefulness, I believe, is to help relate alternative strategies for regulatory cooperation to one another, distinguishing between building blocks
that represent complementary features of such strategies and those that
are straightforward alternatives. Having set up the landscape in broad
brushstrokes, I will then present the ulterior motive. I argue that not all
regulatory strategies are created equal and that, as regulatory cooperation
becomes subservient to trade imperatives, 'managed mutual recognition'
will become the dominant form of regulatory cooperation in the decades
to come. Managed recognition involves a new form of transnational
governance that combines horizontal and vertical delegation of regulatory
authority but eschews supranationalism both in organizational terms
(through regulatory networks) and in normative terms (through institutionalized extraterritoriality).[2]

While aimed at developing a general framework for analysis, the
account provided gives special attention to regulatory cooperation
between the United States and the European Union. International regulatory cooperation can occur at a bilateral, regional, or multilateral level.
Transatlantic cooperation is particularly interesting in this regard as it is
essentially a bilateral form of cooperation, while at the same time each side
represents a complex form of regional (or, in the US case, 'federal') regulatory cooperation. In theory, such bilateral cooperation is embedded
within and authorized by multilateral forms of cooperation. In practice,
this link is certainly contested.[3] Whatever the case, the negotiations
between the United States and the European Union on mutual recognition
agreements (MRAs), both those already completed on a number of products and the current negotiations over services, provide a vivid illustration
of the multiple motives and dimensions characterizing such negotiations.

This contribution is organized as follows. In Part I, I present in succinct
form the building blocks of the strategic model, asking why, about what,
and how international cooperation takes place. In Part II, I provide a
dynamic analysis of the model, identifying the dominant instances of
international regulatory cooperation and assessing them in terms of centralization and accountability. Finally, in Part III, I focus on the particular

---

[2] I believe it would be excessive to describe this kind of work as full-fledged theory. A theory ought to provide testable and falsifiable hypotheses about alternative cause-and-effect
relationships as a basis for interpreting and relating observable phenomena. Here, I suggest
plausible hypotheses regarding dominant forms and dynamics of regulatory cooperation.

[3] For a discussion of such embeddedness in the WTO multilateral context see Kalypso
Nicolaïdis, 'Non-Discriminatory Mutual Recognition: An Oxymoron in the New WTO
Lexicon?', in Petros Mavroidis and Patrick Blatter (eds), *Non Discrimination in the WTO: Past
and Present* (Ann Arbor: University of Michigan Press, The World Trade Forum series, 2000).

dynamics of managed mutual recognition, analysing under what conditions we are likely to see it emerge as the dominant form of cooperation.

I. BUILDING BLOCKS FOR A MODEL OF REGULATORY COOPERATION

There are many alternative 'paths' to regulatory cooperation. Regulators may be led to talk and work with each other for different reasons and about different dimensions of their activities. Their regulatory cooperation may also take different forms. A strategic model of regulatory cooperation must address three questions: why?, about what?, and how? Alternative 'paths' to cooperation correspond to different combinations of these levels of analysis. Figure 1 summarizes the different levels.

A. Why? Actors' strategic and institutional motivations

Traditionally, political scientists build their theories on the identification and testing of independent variables, that is, factors which explain why certain developments happen and not others. In building a strategic model, I propose a typology of actors' motivations primarily as a descriptive/analytical tool. In this context, I make my explanatory assumptions explicit, but I nevertheless present them as assumptions rather than focus on justifying them.

One can categorize reasons for regulatory cooperation in various ways—for instance according to the values that are addressed (such as economic, political, cultural, and democratic[4]), or according to the kind of problems they seek to remedy (such as externalities, loss in economies of scale, aspirations for universality). As other authors in this volume suggest, different theories will privilege different explanatory factors. Public-choice theorists emphasize the contrast between situations where capture is present and situations where it is not, whereas neo-institutionalists ask whether cooperation takes place in an institutionally dense environment or not.[5] If one adopts instead a game theoretical framework, types of regulatory cooperation will be distinguished according to the type of game or dilemma in which actors find themselves, e.g. coordination games or prisoners' dilemmas.[6] The factors chosen for distinction are meant to highlight the most significant differences for the purpose of analysis.

---

[4] Scott Jacobs, 'Regulatory cooperation for an interdependent world: issues for government', in *Regulatory Cooperation for an Interdependent World* (Paris: OECD Publications, 1994), 15–48.

[5] See contribution by Giandomenico Majone in this volume.

[6] See, for instance, Walter Mattli (ed.), *The Political Economy of Standardization* (Cambridge: Cambridge University Press, 2000).

Figure 1 International Regulatory Cooperation: A Strategic Model

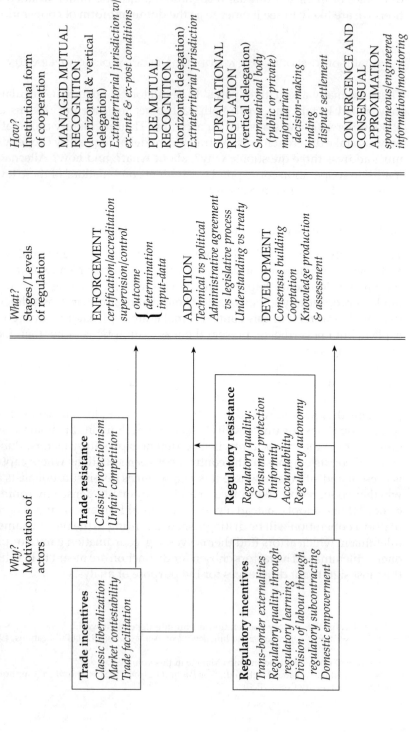

Why?
Motivations of actors

Trade incentives
Classic liberalization
Market contestability
Trade facilitation

Trade resistance
Classic protectionism
Unfair competition

Regulatory incentives
Trans-border externalities
Regulatory quality through regulatory learning
Division of labour through regulatory subcontracting
Domestic empowerment

Regulatory resistance
Regulatory quality:
Consumer protection
Uniformity
Accountability
Regulatory autonomy

What?
Stages/Levels of regulation

ENFORCEMENT
certification/accreditation
supervision/control
{ *outcome*
  determination
  input-data

ADOPTION
Technical vs political
Administrative agreement vs legislative process
Understanding vs treaty

DEVELOPMENT
Consensus building
Cooptation
Knowledge production & assessment

How?
Institutional form of cooperation

MANAGED MUTUAL RECOGNITION
(horizontal & vertical delegation)
Extraterritorial jurisdiction w/ ex-ante & ex-post conditions

PURE MUTUAL RECOGNITION
(horizontal delegation)
Extraterritorial jurisdiction

SUPRANATIONAL REGULATION
(vertical delegation)
Supranational body (public or private)
majoritarian
decision-making
binding
dispute settlement

CONVERGENCE AND CONSENSUAL APPROXIMATION
spontaneous/engineered
information/monitoring

I believe that the most fundamental distinction among types of regulatory cooperation stems from whether the actors driving the process belong to one or the other of two worlds: the trade world or the regulatory world. These worlds obviously correspond to different institutional cultures and loyalties, norms of behaviour, and procedural habits. They hold different beliefs about the desirable goals and priorities of policies and belong to separate transnational 'epistemic communities'.[7] Most importantly, whether regulatory motives per se are primary or ancillary to the process arguably provides the most important clue to the strategy of the actors involved and thus to the ultimate form of cooperation. Finally, distinguishing between these two sides of regulatory cooperation leads to highlighting the motivation to resist as well as to promote such cooperation, the other key to understanding the ultimate form that cooperation takes.

1. *Regulatory imperatives*

The first, most straightforward and compelling reason for cooperation among regulators is to deal with regulatory problems that cannot be tackled effectively within the confines of national boundaries because they relate to one or another kind of *trans-border externality*. This is often the case in environment or finance. In this regard, it is important to note the role of what has been referred to as 'global drama', that is spectacular events which highlight or dramatize a threat which might be systemic and thereby appear to call for a regulatory response across borders.[8]

The second type of regulatory imperative has to do with improving the efficiency and quality of regulation through regulatory learning. Regulators have come to discover that they can do their job better and gain administrative advantage by exploiting the commonality of issues that they face with other regulators and therefore the economies of scale to be gained from joint action. The goal is to rationalize decision-making in order 'not to reinvent the regulatory wheel' in the words of George Bermann[9]—this both to save regulatory resources through the pooling of know-how and to optimize the design of regulation through learning about best practices. More proactively, 'peer' pressure to modernize and upgrade regulatory systems leads to publicly justified rules that are thus likely to be of higher quality.[10] Such cooperation is all the more attractive

---

[7] See Peter Haas (ed.), *Knowledge, Power and International Policy Coordination* (University of South Carolina Press, 1997).

[8] Sol Picciotto, 'The Regulatory Criss-Cross : Interaction between Jurisdictions and the Construction of Global Regulatory Networks', in McCaherty, Bratton, Picciotto, and Scott, *International Regulatory Competition and Cooperation* (Oxford: Oxford University Press, 1996), 117–18.

[9] See George Bermann, 'Managing regulatory rapprochement: institutional and procedural approaches', in *Regulatory Cooperation for an Interdependent World* (Paris: OECD Publications, 1994).

[10] OECD, *Regulatory Cooperation* (above n. 1), 23.

the greater the technical or scientific component of the problem at hand. This does not mean that rule-making is simplified through cooperation; on the contrary, regulatory cooperation increases rather than decreases the complexity of regulation. But complexity in turn usually improves the regulatory fit.

A third reason for transnational cooperation lies in the gains to be had from a better international division of labour among regulators, or what might be termed *regulatory subcontracting*. Given budgetary and human constraints, regulatory bodies have a lot to gain in subcontracting tasks to each other in the day-to-day business of implementing and enforcing regulations, whether through inspections, testing, certification, or licensing. Gains to be had through allocating analytical and testing responsibilities to foreign counterparts and the reciprocal borrowing of administrative capacity usually depend on gains to be had from regulators' functional and territorial specialization. A laboratory may be especially equipped to test the safety of tropical products or a certain type of drug. Testing equipment, facilities, or personnel can be very expensive (think of the famous simulation of an aircraft landing crash), and it may be worthwhile to avoid duplication. Clearly, when it comes to flying inspectors to factories or workplaces around the world, one has to wonder why the local guy would not do. In addition to avoiding duplication costs, there may be positive reasons for relying on local knowledge of potentially unsafe or fraudulent practices where the familiarity of the regulator with the regulatee may be key—notwithstanding, of course, concerns about corruption or capture. This type of cooperation has to be predicated on the mutual confidence of regulators in each other's standards of enforcement, though, as we will see below, it need not be based on similarity of the standards enforced.

Finally, regulators may want to cooperate across borders for domestic strategic reasons, as such cooperation may result in their *empowerment* on the domestic scene vis-à-vis other actors. Regulators may be concerned about influence and thus prefer to expand the scope of their jurisdiction by creating new fora in which they play a part. This may at the same time increase their margin of manoeuvre vis-à-vis an executive or legislative branch that is the original source of their authority.[11] Autonomy is arguably the most highly valued feature of the environment for regulatory bodies that find that their goals, values, and operating procedures are hampered by outside intervention, especially of a political nature. By cooperating with their counterparts from other countries, they acquire extra-national credibility that empowers them on the domestic front.

[11] See Thomas C. Singher, 'Regulatory Derivatives: Does Transnational Regulatory Cooperation Offer a Viable Alternative to Congressional Action', *Fordham International law Journal* (1995); Giandomenico Majone, 'Regulatory Legitimacy in the United States and the European Union: The Organizational Dimension', in Kalypso Nicolaïdis and Robert Howse, *The Federal Vision: Legitimacy and Levels of Governance in the US and the EU* (Oxford: Oxford University Press, 2001).

2. Trade imperatives

While these are all strong rationales for cooperation, it is often the case that regulators are led to cooperate among themselves indirectly, that is, as a result of the trade imperative. The trade-related costs of lack of transnational regulatory cooperation are well known.[12] Differences between standards and regulations across borders may simply lead to duplication costs, representing the sum of all the adaptation costs incurred by firms or individuals striving to comply with domestic rules as they operate across borders. More drastically, regulatory difference can simply constitute the functional equivalent of a total ban on a given export if the importing country's insistence that economic actors fall under its prescriptive jurisdiction simply renders impossible certain types of interactions. This is especially the case in the world of e-commerce. Regulatory barriers to trade first came to be addressed by GATT in the late 1970s under the label of non-tariff barriers, meaning that they constitute one of a range of trade barriers beyond tariffs and quotas. Since then, the international trade community has expanded its definition of the kinds of domestic regulation (or lack thereof) that could constitute a trade impediment, broadly defining the goal as one of market openness and contestability rather than simply non-discrimination. Because social regulation and consumer protection have become increasingly prevalent, the mission that trade diplomats pass on to regulators under this logic is titanic. Free-trade advocates have come to argue that concerted trade-friendly regulatory reform at the domestic level ought to become the core instrument of trade liberalization.[13]

There has developed more recently a second, trade-driven incentive for regulatory cooperation, namely the concern for 'fair trade' or 'fair competition' in contexts where regulatory differences among countries are regarded as providing one side with an unfair advantage in the competition for markets. In this case, regulators are asked by their trade colleagues worried about protectionist pressures to reduce the differences between the regulations that pertain to the conditions of production of the goods and services as distinct from their actual characteristics. More broadly, regulatory and trade imperatives can converge in the desire to curb the risk of regulatory competition by adopting common binding standards or regulations. In this case, the concern goes beyond that of unfair competition viewed from a static perspective. Regulatory competition occurs when, in the face of regulatory differences across borders, regulators become subject to pressures from governments or private actors to change their regulation to favour the competitiveness of their industry. In this

---

[12] See Jagdish Bagwati and Robert Hudec (eds), *Fair Trade and Harmonization: Prerequisites for Free Trade?* (Cambridge, Mass: The MIT Press, 1996).

[13] For a summary of OECD studies, see *The OECD Report on Regulatory Reform* (Paris: OECD Publication, 1997).

instance, regulatory cooperation constitutes a recourse to maintain regulatory quality while re-establishing a level playing field for international trade.

At the same time, however, regulatory cooperation can also be justified as a means of creating some degree of regulatory competition and consumer choice in the first place. While some regulatory competition occurs under the non-cooperative status quo, to the extent that home rules affect competitiveness, there needs to be some sort of international agreement involving regulatory transfer in order for different rules to be directly applicable on the same territory. Regulatory cooperation creates the framework within which regulatory competition is allowed to take place. Advocates of regulatory competition will argue that it introduces 'consumer sovereignty' and enhances the potential for consumers to compare the value of different regulatory systems. It is seldom the case, however, that regulatory competition constitutes the primary rationale for cooperation. Rather, arguments in its favour contribute in shaping the extent and form of regulatory cooperation.

In short, liberal trading rules and policies call into question domestic regulations either by framing them as 'non-tariff barriers' (product regulations) or by exposing them to regulatory competition (process regulations). Regulators may choose to cooperate in order to compensate for both sets of effects or may be pressured into doing so in order to allow for the expansion of this liberal trading agenda.

3. Trade and regulatory resistance

In their drive to bring about trade liberalization through regulatory cooperation, free traders may encounter two broad types of resistance. First, of course, is the resistance on the trade side coming from the potential losers from any market-opening deal. Protectionism in the face of potential competition is nothing new, except for the fact that in a regulatory context protectionist resistance may emanate not only from the firms or individuals whose markets are threatened by the removal of trade barriers on their home turf, but also by those who want to avoid the unnecessary costs involved in meeting higher or different standards as a result of regulatory cooperation. Resistance may also emanate from the 'regulatory industry' as a market player in its own right which stands to lose a captive market at home, as foreign laboratories, agencies, professional associations, or universities become accredited to issue stamps of approval to those targeting their domestic market. Nevertheless, protectionist interests in sectors that are highly regulated and warrant this type of regulatory cooperation appear to be more disparate and less well-organized than their counterpart interests in traditional agricultural or industrial sectors.

The most vocal and effective resistance to the demand for regulatory cooperation on the part of the trade community comes from the regulatory side. The first reason that regulators themselves invoke in their resistance to regulatory cooperation is their very *raison d'être*, namely the need to protect the public interest. Consumer protection, they argue, is likely to be jeopardized under schemes of international division of labour. There are often good reasons to suppose that the market failure that gave rise to the regulation in the first place will likely be magnified internationally (e.g. due to the incapacity of the consumer to assess the soundness of the product). Underlying attitudes to risk and standards of protection may vary too widely across countries to be amenable to cooperation.[14] Such differences may be simply unbridgeable. Regulators are often supported in this stance by domestic consumer groups who question the trustworthiness of foreign regulators or their own ability to monitor them. There is no doubt that regulators have in many cases sound reasons to feel that the 'public interest' may not be defended as well by their counterparts, especially since the notion is bound to be defined differently elsewhere. This rationale is often bolstered by two more general arguments appealing to broader political considerations. One is that regulatory cooperation may lead to international uniformity which would negate the diversity of tastes and customs of individuals around the world. The other is that such cooperation decreases the accountability of regulators by diffusing responsibility and rendering decision-making processes more opaque to consumer scrutiny.

Notwithstanding the strength of these arguments, resistance is likely to be waged at least as much on institutional grounds as on normative grounds. If regulators value their autonomy vis-à-vis other domestic actors as stated above, they have no more reason to want to let foreign counterparts constrain it than they would their own ministers or representatives. In the end, regulatory cooperation may appear as a slippery slope leading to sacrifices in autonomy that are bound to become increasingly unacceptable.

4. *Scenarios for regulatory cooperation in the transatlantic context*

Where do these four sets of rationales leave us? They obviously may be combined in many different ways. I would argue, however, that there are three dominant scenarios for regulatory cooperation. First is what I would call the 'expert show': regulators cooperate for their own reasons, but, faced with the likely consequences of their action on the competitive environment, protectionist groups mobilize against them. This has been the case, I would argue, for professional services in the European Union and elsewhere. Generally, however, regulator-led cooperation is low-key and the main impediment to this kind of cooperation is simply the complexity

---

[14] See, for instance, Alan O. Sykes (ed.), *Products Standards for Internationally Integrated Goods Markets* (Washington, DC: Brookings Institute, 1995).

of the issues involved and the difficulty in bridging the gap between different regulatory systems. Second, it may be the case that this type of regulator-driven cooperation gets upgraded to a 'political show' in which politicians from different countries agree on a general mandate aimed at their respective regulators in order to appear to be addressing issues that are highly visible to citizens, such as drug trafficking or money laundering. An example would be the Transatlantic Declaration and the ensuing regulatory cooperation. These constitute high-stake mandates with low trade or expert motivation, which are likely to linger until politicians start to demand results to show for their summits.

Finally, there is the 'trade show' where regulatory cooperation is traded-led and regulators resist the demand for cooperation or seek to circumscribe it in ways that address their concerns about the level of standards or institutional autonomy. When involved in such 'trade shows' regulators and trade diplomats from one side are more often than not at odds with one other and thus sometimes enter into trans-border strategic alliances with their foreign counterparts. The international game pitting the trade and regulatory epistemic communities against one another may even in some cases prevail over the traditional conflict between national positions. There is an important asymmetry, however, between the United States and the European Union in this respect. In the European Union, it has long been the case that regulators have seen their modus operandi subordinated to the trade culture prevalent in the European Union. Internal developments have in turn shaped their attitudes externally. When the European Union began negotiating MRAs with the United States in the mid-1990s, its position was to a great extent shaped by its market-opportunity prospects, for example in the pharmaceutical sector. Concerns about the US regulatory system had less to do with evaluation of standards of consumer protection and more to do with the fragmentary character of the system, which constitutes in itself a major regulatory barrier. In the United States, on the other hand, the great regulatory agencies like the FDA and the FCC had never seen their activities subordinated to trade imperatives. They said so vehemently and the FCC was even allowed to bail out of the trade talks altogether. In this case, the regulators' concern for autonomy became a defining feature of the negotiations.

B. About what? stages of regulations

The next question that the model addresses is 'international cooperation about what?' There are three fundamental levels of regulation, corresponding to the three stages of regulation-making. Regulatory cooperation concerned with each of these stages relies on different instruments and carries different consequences. The OECD has labelled these stages as 'pre-regulatory arrangements', 'regulatory arrangements', and 'post-regulatory arrangements'.[15] But such categories are somewhat misleading, since each of these stages ought to be considered as an integral part of the regulatory process. They are:

- *Development of regulation.* At this level, regulators cooperate by exchanging data, information, and knowledge that constitute input relevant to policy design. Data can be scientific, regarding, for instance, a forecast of environment effects or an assessment of the health or safety risks of certain types of products. Or it can be socio-economic, regarding, for instance, mean attitudes to risk and economic impact. Regulators can also engage in ongoing consultation, notification, and debates regarding adequate criteria for regulation and seek eventually to reach a consensus over them. Mutual participation in rule-making is also a mechanism of cooperation at the development stage. Coordination at this stage may also serve to establish the 'equivalence' of standards in order to facilitate the implementation of agreements over the enforcement of such standards, as in the case of the first generation of US–EU MRAs.[16] What matters chiefly at this stage, however, is the process of consensus-building and the progressive convergence in regulatory culture that may accompany it, rather than the end result in itself. There is no legally binding consequence to cooperation at this stage but its function is to attempt to coordinate regulatory action so as to increase regulatory effectiveness when addressing cross-border problems.

- *Adoption of regulations.* Regulatory authorities can further cooperate over the adoption of regulations by linking their respective processes of rule-making in order to reach joint or congruent decisions on the content of these regulations. Reaching a joint decision simply means that the parties agree on a common regulation, which can range in specificity from a common and specific standard to a general rule of behaviour. These decisions may be legally binding to different degrees. They can take the form of treaties enforceable through international law or they may be inter-agency agreements which bind governments but do not require the same kind of ratification and scrutiny that treaty-type regulations require. Within the European Union, they generally take the form of directives that have supremacy over national law. In other words, the joint adoption of regulations can be achieved at a political or technical level, through legislative or administrative instruments. On the other hand, regulators may simply aim to reach congruent decisions, that is agree on a common approach or even an actual standard at the development stage, and then

---

[15] OECD, *Regulatory Cooperation* (above, n. 1), 40. See also, for instance, Christopher D. Olive, 'The Ongoing Process of International Bank Regulatory and Supervisory Convergence: A New Regulatory—Market Partnership', *Annual Review of Banking Law* (1997).

[16] See *The Limits of Liberalization* (above, n. 1), 35–8. For a more detailed description of the 'Policy Coordination Scale' see Les Metcalfe, 'The weakest link: building organisational networks for multi-level regulation', in OECD, *Regulatory Cooperation* (above, n. 1), 60 and 69–70. See also George Bermann (above, n. 9), 75–7.

undergo separate, albeit parallel, processes of adoption at the domestic level. In all cases, regulatory authorities seek the approximation of their regulation so as to address a common problem, be it of a regulatory or trade nature. It is especially in the latter case that regulatory cooperation limited to the development stage is not sufficient to attain the result needed.

• *Enforcement of regulation.* In some instances, the key challenge is not agreement on the adoption of rules or regulation themselves, but rather on the way these rules are to be applied or enforced by enforcement authorities in the countries themselves. The term 'enforcement' is used here not only in the narrow legal sense of intervention by regulatory or judicial authorities in case of breach of law, but in the more general sense of the range of activities necessary to ensure that a given rule is interpreted, applied, and enforced adequately by the parties concerned. Certification, licensing, or approval all refer to this last stage of rule-making. Cooperation in enforcement can consist of pooling resources to create enforcement agencies at the supranational level or agreeing on mutual recognition between enforcement authorities. It can be aimed at the *input* level of enforcement (data gathering and analysis), at the *determination* level of enforcement (establishing whether the product or the service is to be considered lawful), or at the final *outcome* stage (issuing stamps of approval or certificates of conformity, thus having a direct effect on market access). Cooperation in enforcement can remain at the level of certification of the goods and services or can include recognition or joint conduct of the accreditation process itself, that is the giving of official approval to the bodies in charge of licensing or certification (laboratories, universities, professional associations, regulatory agencies, and ministries). To the extent that these certification bodies hold a monopoly on market access, only cooperation at the latter level will result in free cross-border trade.

C. How? institutional form of cooperation

1. Organizational and substantive dimensions

The third element of a strategic model of regulatory cooperation addresses the question: How is such cooperation conducted? Institutional forms of cooperation can vary a great deal. By institutional form, I mean both the organizational and the legal or normative form under which such cooperation comes to be articulated. Cooperation between various tiers of government or actors with public authority may take place through a variety of formal or informal agreements, protocols or treaties, and it may be embedded in different kinds of norms and operational procedures. There are many important features that may help us distinguish between institutional forms of cooperation. Are they formal or informal? Do they involve only discussion and exchange or also negotiations over specific outcomes? Do national governments retain a veto over such results? Do these results have a binding effect? Is the organizational underpinning of cooperation purely intergovernmental or does it involve a body with supranational powers? While these are all valid questions, I believe that they can be fruitfully subsumed under a single criterion, that of delegation.

2. Streamlining the OECD typology: vertical v. horizontal delegation

As stated earlier, it is crucial to choose criteria for distinguishing clearly among ideal *alternative* forms of regulatory cooperation. This is where, I believe, existing typologies are weakest. The OECD, for instance,[17] provides a fourfold typology of regulatory relationships: 1, negotiated regulation, such as treaties, developed through 'a formal and legally-binding process of decision making in which the details of regulatory requirements, legal obligations or responsibilities are agreed by each participating government'; 2, cooperative regulation based 'not on formal legal instruments but on more flexible agreements', and ranging from casual contacts to high-level accords relating to all three stages of cooperation described in the preceding section; 3, delegated regulation consisting of the granting of competence by one level of government to another (as in supranational delegation, decentralization at the sub-state level and nationalization from subnational authorities upwards); and 4, semigovernmental regulation developed by private bodies.

This typology provides a useful starting point, but does not always describe mutually exclusive alternatives (category 3, for instance, can be combined with either category 1 or 2). It thus needs to be amended so as to specify criteria that define genuine alternatives. In order to do this, I focus on what I believe to be the core institutional question, namely, does the cooperation involve some kind of delegation of competence and, if so, what kind? Delegation is not necessarily used here in a formal legal sense, but simply to denote the transfer of competence away from an original regulatory authority to a new one. Delegation can be vertical (to a supranational level of authority, public or private) or horizontal (to another authority at the same jurisdictional level, whether another government or a private organization with public authority). Such delegation is usually 'negotiated', whether under consensual rules or not. What matters is that, in the end, the regulatory regime escapes the total control of national regulators, partially or entirely. On the other hand, cooperation that is

---

[17] In its report published in 1994, the OECD provided a comprehensive view of what it called 'regulatory diversification' as an intricate network of vertical and horizontal links between all levels of government often stretching from the lowest to the highest level of government with tasks shared and scattered throughout regulatory networks. See *Regulatory Cooperation* (above, n. 1).

informal (the OECD's cooperative regulation) or consensual decision-making that does not lead to a delegation of authority (some of the 'negotiated cooperation' in the OECD typology) both fall in the same category of 'non-delegation'. To be sure, delegation may be a matter of degree, with competence transferred and control lost only partially. Nevertheless, as we consider ideal-types, we need to assess on the basis of existing evidence whether a significant degree of delegation has taken place or not. A cooperative relationship may involve one or several of three elements of delegation, each of which is itself a matter of degree:

• *Decision-making: loss of veto by individual governments.* Even when decisions are made or collective action is taken, there is not necessarily delegation if each party holds a veto over outcomes. Under majoritarian rule-making, however, a party may have to bow to a decision or accept actions undertaken by other parties of which it does not approve. This is true not only at the stage of rule-making itself, but also at the enforcement stage where regulators from one country may have to accept a majority decision over standards of enforcement.

• *Management and monitoring: extranational bodies with some degree of autonomy.* Either supranational bodies (vertical delegation) or national-level bodies from other jurisdictions (horizontal delegation) may be involved in the development and, above all, in the implementation of regulations, or indeed in the monitoring of such implementation. In the supranational case, if such bodies are more than a 'secretariat' (with competence entirely circumscribed by the will of national regulating authorities), then some delegation has taken place. The European Commission, for instance, holds delegated legislative and executive power, and thus regulatory power. The WTO or ITU secretariats do not. In some cases, however, intergovernmental committees set up under the latter may acquire a degree of autonomy warranting the label of delegation. In the transnational case, where there has been horizontal delegation, rules may be developed, implemented, or enforced by public or private bodies with regulatory authority in another jurisdiction over which host state authorities have no or only partial control.

• *Binding character and dispute settlement: conflict resolution as rule-making.* More often than not, regulatory cooperation is founded on informal relationships rather than formal agreements, protocols, or treaties. Nevertheless, agreements with no formal status may be regarded as binding, at least in honour, as in the case of the capital adequacy provisions of the Basle Committee or the coordination of antitrust enforcement between the European Union and the United States.[18] In some cases, however, the outcome expected from regulatory cooperation may indeed be formally binding, leading to new entitlements regarding market access. If an agree-

[18] Sol Picciotto, 'The Regulatory Criss-Cross' (above, n. 8), 113–15.

ment is binding, this may lead to the need for some kind of dispute-settlement mechanism, which in turn may allow panels or courts to interpret rules agreed upon by governments in a way that may differ from what was originally foreseen. The more general the rules (e.g. general standards rather than specific rules) and the faster the rate of obsolescence of regulations, the greater the potential for delegation to a supranational judiciary.[19] Of course, real delegation only occurs if parties do not have an implicit or explicit veto over the adoption of court or panel rulings. Arguably, only post-WTO adjudication over the GATT truly involves delegation. Horizontal delegation occurs when one allows other countries' judicial bodies to pass judgment on matters relevant to one's jurisdiction.

On the bases of these criteria, we can define four institutional forms of regulatory cooperation (see Table 1):

Table 1: Forms of regulatory cooperation according to types of delegation

Vertical delegation:	No	Yes
Horizontal delegation:		
No	Convergence and consensual harmonization	Supranational regulation
Yes	Mutual recognition	Managed mutual recognition and supranational enforcement

1. Convergence and consensual harmonization (no delegation). This form of regulatory cooperation relies simply on direct collaboration between regulators of different countries, acting through a range of methods ranging from simple exchange of information, to exchange of scientific data relevant to regulatory decision-making, to the actual adoption of similar regulations. Such adoption could even occur through a formalized process of negotiation, but this would have to be by consensus and without binding effects justifying supranational dispute settlement. Similarly, governments may collaborate in enforcing certain regulations (say in dealing with financial fraud), but in doing so they stop short of transferring any competence to the other side.

---

[19] For a discussion of the difference between rules and standards in domestic and international contexts and their respective impact on jurisdictional leeway, see for instance, Frederick Schauer, *Playing by the Rules* (Clarendon Law Series, 1991); Cass Sunstein, 'Problems with Rules', *California Law Review*, 83 (July 1995), 953–1023; Louis Kaplow, 'Rules vs Standards: An Economic Analysis', *Duke Law Journal*, 42 (1992), 557–629. For an application to the international context, see Kalypso Nicolaïdis and Joel P. Trachtman, 'From Policed Regulation to Managed Recognition: Mapping the Boundary in GATS', in Pierre Sauve and Robert M. Stern (eds), *Services 2000: New Directions in Services Trade Liberalization* (Washington, DC: Brookings Institution Press, 2000).

2. Supranational regulation (vertical delegation). This form of regulatory cooperation involves not only harmonization of regulations and enforcement procedures, but also some degree of transfer of competence above the nation-state to entities that, while usually constituted by nation-states, are not entirely controlled by them. This category includes not only intergovernmental organizations, but also private international organizations that have been granted the authority to develop standards or enforce them.

3. Mutual recognition (horizontal delegation). This form of regulatory cooperation is based on the transfer of competence to other regulatory entities at the same level of governance. Regulators can recognize other countries' regulation as equivalent, or at least recognize the enforcement capacity of other countries as equivalent, and delegate this function to them. Private professional bodies can agree to register professionals whose rights of practice have been recognized in another country. Accreditation bodies can accept the stamps of approval granted to laboratories or universities by their peers in other countries. Horizontal delegation, like vertical delegation, usually involves a degree of sharing of tasks and responsibilities, but only qualifies as such if some degree of competence falls completely outside the purview of national regulators. It can be argued that mutual recognition is a mere waiver of regulatory requirements on the part of the host country, rather than a delegation of authority.[20] This view, however, does not sufficiently allow for the conditional character of mutual recognition. The condition is indeed that regulators from one side deem regulation in the other as appropriate, equivalent, or compatible. The calculation is indeed that there shall be a jurisdictional transfer, rather than an acceptance that a product or a service will escape any jurisdiction. I have argued elsewhere that it is precisely because mutual recognition is more appropriately thought of as horizontal delegation that its imposition by *judicial fiat* is problematic in terms of legitimacy.[21] In other words, it is precisely this dimension of delegation that distinguishes mutual recognition from an extreme version of national treatment.[22]

4. Managed mutual recognition (horizontal and vertical delegation). If horizontal delegation is combined with vertical delegation, we are in the presence of one form or another of managed mutual recognition. Managed mutual recognition is a form of regulatory cooperation in which regulatory competence is transferred from one jurisdictional authority to

[20] Robert Howse, 'Comments', in Pierre Sauve and Robert M. Stern (eds), *Services 2000: New Directions in Services Trade Liberalization* (Washington, DC: Brookings Institution Press, 2000).

[21] Kalypso Nicolaïdis, *Mutual Recognition Among Nations: The European Community and Trade in Services*, PhD Dissertation (Cambridge, Mass.: Harvard University, 1993) ; Kalypso Nicolaïdis, 'Mutual Recognition of Regulatory Regimes: Some Lessons and Prospects, in *Regulatory Reform and International Market Openness* (Paris: OECD Publications, Nov. 1996).

[22] Kalypso Nicolaïdis and Joel Trachtman, 'From Policed Regulation' (above, n. 19).

another, subject to provisions and mechanisms aimed at curbing the potential effects of such a transfer in terms of regulatory competition. In this context, vertical delegation is a necessary complement to horizontal delegation if and when the latter calls for the creation of common minimal rules and a dispute-settlement mechanism to manage potential disagreements over the residual conditions and scope of market access. I will come back to these characteristics of managed mutual recognition in the last section.

II. DYNAMIC ANALYSIS: ALTERNATIVE PATHS TO REGULATORY COOPERATION

On the basis of these building blocks, we can now ask how these three dimensions—motivations for, stages of and forms of cooperation—relate to one another and thus analyse alternative paths to regulatory cooperation.

A. Relationship between actors' motivation and selected stage of regulation

To start with, regulators will focus on different stages or levels of the regulatory process, depending on why they engage in regulatory cooperation in the first place.

If the initial motivation is regulatory in nature, regulators are more likely to focus on the first level (viz. development of regulation) where they can learn from each other while at the same time retaining control over the outcome in the adoption and enforcement stages. Given that resources are expanded mostly at the development stage, the only reason from a regulator's viewpoint to formally move to cooperation at the adoption stage is if convergence through cooperation at that first stage was simply not sufficient to bring about desired results: the joint imposition of higher standards to address a common problem or negative externalities due to differences in local standards. Gains in terms of regulatory resources from international division of labour between regulators are likely to be slightly greater at the level of enforcement, given the highly decentralized nature of the process. But here again, while regulators might have an interest in subcontracting the gathering of input to others in order to reach their own determination, there is little reason to subcontract the approval/enforcement process per se.[23] Regulators do, however, have an interest in minimizing conflict-generating extraterritorial enforcement of

---

[23] George Bermann, for instance, argues that 'governments that are seriously interested in international regulatory cooperation will support the creation of a regime that directly fosters the joint development of regulatory policy, but still disfavor giving up their ultimate regulatory authority'. George Bermann (above, n. 9), 77.

national regulations by taking into account the concerns of other regulators in setting their own enforcement capacity.[24]

Conversely, from a trade perspective the need for regulatory cooperation is a functional need connected to the outcome of regulation, e.g. the end result for the firm, individual, or product being regulated: a single passport or a single stamp granting access to foreign markets. Cooperation at the adoption and enforcement stages is what matters. One subsequent key question is whether, from a trade perspective, greater gains are to be had through cooperation at the adoption or the enforcement stage. The common view is that cooperation gains are greater at the adoption stage since the highest costs for the industry stem from the inability to produce homogeneous products subject to a single standard or regulation. In short, harmonization or mutual recognition of standards is the real thing. Yet, I would argue, there are industries where the higher cost stems from the duplication of approval processes per se, whether because the standards themselves are vague and general, albeit very stringent ('thou shalt do no harm') or because approval is a very costly process. As a matter of fact, the two often go together. In such cases (e.g. pharmaceuticals, toys), the number, length, and characteristics of tests is what matters. In still other cases (e.g. e-commerce), it is the requirement of presence abroad for enforcement purposes (establishment for firms or professionals, registration for Web sites), rather than only the application of foreign standards, that constitutes the real barrier to movement across borders.

Is there any functional requirement for a specific ordering principle between stages of regulation-making when it comes to international cooperation? The answer to this question lies both in assumptions about relative gains on the trade side, as discussed above, and in assumptions about feasibility—in other words, about relative resistance on the regulatory side. As a baseline, it would seem logical that regulatory cooperation in a given area should start with the development stage—thus inducing mutual familiarity and trust—and then move on to the next two stages. In most cases, however, the prevailing logic has been the reverse. To the extent that regulatory cooperation has been trade-driven, efforts have initially been concentrated on the adoption and enforcement stages. In the European Union, regulatory cooperation accompanying the single market first addressed adoption of regulations (the new approach) and then enforcement (the global approach). This preference seems to have been based on the assumption that the real gains to be had from regulatory cooperation lie at the adoption stage.

In other contexts (for example, EFTA), however, the enforcement stage has been apparently tackled first, in part on the assumption that conces-

---

[24] Scott Jacobs, 'Regulatory cooperation in an interdependent world', in OECD, *Regulatory Cooperation* (above, n. 4), 27.

sions in terms of regulatory control at the enforcement stage are less sensitive than those at the adoption stage. It is easier for regulators, this assumption goes, to approximate their approach to testing products or to subcontract this task to each other than to seek to harmonize or mutually recognize regulations that reflect deep-seated historical, institutional, and cultural differences among countries. Nevertheless, experience with the conduct of these negotiations has shown that regulatory cooperation over enforcement or approval is much more sensitive than trade negotiators initially assumed.[25] This is in part because enforcement requirements and procedures also reflect deep-seated differences among countries in attitudes towards risk and in part because the institutional incentives determining the 'capacity to deliver' trade liberalization through regulatory cooperation vary enormously across countries.[26] Regulatory agencies in the United States (like the FDA or FCC), for instance, have proved much more resistant to cooperation with their foreign counterparts for the purpose of trade liberalization through the mutual recognition of certification than was initially foreseen at the start of the MRA negotiations. This, even though the negotiations did not involve the recognition of actual standards. The same agencies that would willingly engage in exchanges of information regarding the development stage balked at a shift in the aim and level of their cooperation to serve trade purposes.[27] Even in the European Union, delegation for the purpose of enforcement has apparently proved much more difficult and controversial than the new approach to standardization itself.[28]

[25] See Americo Beviglia Zampetti, 'Market Access through Mutual Recognition: The Promise and Limits of GATTS Article VII', in Pierre Sauve and Robert M. Stern (eds), *Services 2000: New Directions in Services Trade Liberalization* (Washington, DC: Brookings Institution Press, 2000); Kalypso Nicolaïdis, 'Mutual Recognition of Regulatory Regimes' (above, n. 21); and Kalypso Nicolaïdis and Joelle Schmidt, 'Exploring a New Paradigm for Trade Diplomacy: Managed Mutual recognition between the United States and the European Union', in *Proceedings of the European Union Community Association World Conference* (Brussels: Office of Publications of the European Community, 1997).

[26] A significant source of difference in risk-aversion relates to whether regulators are more concerned with avoiding type 1 or type 2 errors, that is the risk associated with authorizing a product that may harm vs the opportunity cost of withholding a beneficial product. On the institutional side, core determinants of the 'capacity to deliver' are public regulatory autonomy and private regulatory accountability. For a discussion, see Kalypso Nicolaïdis, 'Mutual Recognition Regimes: Towards a Comparative Analysis', *Working Paper 8* (Cambridge, MA: Center For International Affairs, Harvard University, 1998). On why US and EU agencies have different capacities to commit see also George Bermann, 'Regulatory Cooperation' (above, n. 1), 958–60 and 980.

[27] The US Federal Aviation Administration is a good example since it backed out of the MRA negotiations altogether. For a discussion of its prior cooperation efforts, see George Bermann, 'Regulatory Cooperation with Counterpart Agencies Abroad: The FAA Aircraft Certification Experience', *Law and Policy in International Business*, vol. 24 (1993), 669.

[28] See Kalypso Nicolaïdis and Michelle Egan, 'Regulatory Cooperation and Market Governance: Alternative Patterns of Standardization and Mutual Recognition', in Walter Mattli (ed.), *The Political Economy of Standardization* (Cambridge: Cambridge University Press, 2000).

In the end, the relationship between cooperation at these three levels is a dynamic one and varies across contexts and countries. Cooperation at the level of development might prepare the ground for the next two levels. But conversely, engaging in a process of cooperation over the last two levels might ultimately lead to cooperation at the level of development under the guise of 'confidence-building measures'. And cooperation at the third level of enforcement might ultimately lead to cooperation at the level of adoption as regulators from each side become more familiar with the foreign standards and rules that they are contributing to enforce.

B. Relationship between stage of regulation and form of cooperation

The other side of the dynamic of this model has to do with how stages or levels of rule-making may in turn be more or less amenable to international cooperation depending on the form that such cooperation takes. Conversely, we may ask what cooperative form best accommodates each of these levels of cooperation.

Cooperation at the development stage usually implies neither vertical nor horizontal delegation. At this level, consensus is the rule and there are no binding outcomes over which dispute settlement would be necessary. There may be some degree of regulatory subcontracting in the gathering of data as the input of regulation, but since the way in which these data are to be taken into account is optional, this does not amount to delegation per se. This lack of delegation usually makes the development stage the preferred level of cooperation on the part of regulators.

When regulators cooperate with regard to the adoption stage, they may simply engage in a joint process of decision-making with a view to adopting similar or at least compatible rules in all jurisdictions (i.e. approximation of regulations). In order to achieve this result, parties may or may not adopt some overriding rule at the supranational level (e.g. directives in the EU context, WTO agreements, international conventions), which in turn may or may not involve delegation, e.g. non-unanimous decision-making, autonomous extranational bodies, and some binding process of dispute resolution. Thus delegation becomes necessary to the extent that pure cooperation without delegation fails to deliver sufficiently reliably on the result sought. The key question at this stage is whether the delegation is vertical or horizontal. The experience of the European Union seems to have shown that at the adoption stage, horizontal delegation alone (e.g. pure mutual recognition) is generally not feasible without prior convergence-based cooperation. More to the point, we usually observe some level of vertical delegation alongside horizontal delegation, to the extent that the binding character of the recognition needs to be enforced by dispute-settlement bodies.

On the other hand, cooperation at the enforcement stage often starts without delegation at all, as when regulatory subcontracting only concerns the input to the enforcement stage. Regulators may take the data provided by their counterparts into account as input in their decision.[29] But if cooperation is trade-driven, and therefore chiefly concerned with outcomes, then it is much more likely to involve horizontal than vertical delegation. In other words, we very seldom see the creation of supranational enforcement agencies as such charged with authorizing certain types of actions (competition agencies), accrediting licence-issuing institutions, or issuing licences themselves ('supranational laboratories'). Such missions are much more resource-intensive and sensitive than the creation of international standards per se and carrying them through most often involves a physical control and presence rendering delegation much more tangible. To be sure, to the extent that the agreement is binding, some level of vertical delegation is once again involved, but only with regard to the development of 'common enforcement procedures' and dispute mechanisms for enforcing them.

The institutional form of cooperation varies not only with the stage of rule-making per se, but also with the extent to which, given the initial motivation for regulatory cooperation, the choice of levels is made by regulators or government officials and trade diplomats. Traditionally, any interstate cooperation (regulatory cooperation included) was centralized through the government and coordination of national regulation would come about through diplomatic means including intergovernmental agreements. This would be true even in cases where regulatory cooperation was driven by regulatory motives. Increasingly, however, this model is replaced by direct contact between regulators. Horizontal cross-border contacts, bypassing the central government and the foreign office, are established on the basis of functional needs and responsibilities. This kind of contact is less likely than contact driven by central governments to turn into delegation. To the extent that regulators themselves enjoy delegated authority (from the legislative branch or the government), such authority is not theirs to delegate again.[30] In any case, they are less inclined to do so than others who more easily bargain away an authority they do not personally hold. In the end, functionally based horizontal contacts are likely to lead to delegation under two conditions: if regulators themselves see an advantage in binding their counterparts, and if such contacts are captured by a trade agenda. I will come back to the latter case below.

It is becoming increasingly clear that such delegation is more likely to be horizontal or horizontal and vertical than simply vertical. In part because adapting existing institutions often seems preferable to creating new ones, 'multi-layered regulatory systems'—as the OECD describes them—are

---

[29] For a discussion, see, for instance, OECD Secretariat, 'Lessons for regulatory cooperation: the case of the OECD test guidelines programme', in OECD, *Regulatory Cooperation*, 141–54.

[30] See George Bermann, 'Regulatory Cooperation' (above, n. 1).

more likely to develop as decentralized systems in which many national and sub-national centres continue to act more or less as peers.[31]

It is important to note that the emergence of regulatory networks alongside delegation of regulatory authority has a different function depending on the stage of regulation. From a substantive viewpoint, regulatory networks constitute a functional response to three kinds of developments: the international scope of the regulatory issue, the complexity of the problem which the regulation seeks to address, and the resource intensity of the regulatory remedy.[32] If networks expand to address the development stage, they are mainly information networks meant to share resources so as to optimize the design of regulations and deal with complex problems more efficiently. If these networks accompany vertical delegation, they are meant to serve as mechanisms not only for consensus-building in order to support the adoption of supranational regulation, but also for the exchange of information across borders regarding the enforcement of regulation, responsibility for which is usually delegated back to domestic authorities working in concert.

Finally, if regulatory networks accompany horizontal delegation, they primarily constitute mechanisms for mutual monitoring to the extent that regulators seek continued reassurance that their counterparts are applying their standards appropriately, and that if this is not observed to be the case such delegation might be reversible. This is especially the case where horizontal delegation applies to the enforcement stage. Furthermore, several analysts have stressed that such networks are mechanisms to build trust between regulators across borders.[33] I would argue, however, that while trust-building may be a beneficial secondary effect of such networks in the long run, it usually does not constitute their primary aim: regulators seek to continue spying on each other to the extent that regulatory externalities prevail. If trust were the name of the game, regulatory networks would become looser over time. We actually observe the reverse.

From an organizational standpoint, networks are usually not congruent with existing institutions except, sometimes, as points of attachment. They are links that grow between power nodes according to functional needs rather than formal organizational membership; their members are therefore not easily identifiable and their output not easily attributable. Analysts have rightly pointed out that a challenge of legitimacy arises from the evolution of regulatory networks outside the established institutional structure of the state, including prevailing values, norms, and

---

[31] Scott Jacobs, 'Regulatory cooperation in an interdependent world' in OECD, *Regulatory Cooperation* (above, n. 4), 24.

[32] *Regulatory Cooperation* (above, n. 1).

[33] See, for instance, Giandomenico Majone, 'The Rise of the Regulatory State in Europe', *West European Politics* 17/3 (1994), 77–101; Les Metcalfe, 'The weakest link: building organisational networks for multi-level regulation', in OECD, *Regulatory Cooperation* (above, n. 1), 57–8; and Kalypso Nicolaïdis, 'Mutual Recognition of Regulatory Regimes' (above, n. 21).

expectations and the broader framework of accountability that the state supplies.[34] Even at the national level, regulatory networks are not accountable to voters, citizens or consumers, except perhaps in times of extreme crisis. Even then, accountability tends to be shifted upwards to the political level. When it comes to networks across borders, supporting a degree of delegation to counterparts in other polities, the accountability link becomes even more tenuous. Because it is hard to see how regulatory networks and systems of international regulatory delegation can ever benefit from input legitimacy—defined in terms of processes of democratic participation—they ultimately will need to be assessed in terms of output legitimacy.[35] Delegation through networks will need to deliver.

III. THE DOMINANT PARADIGM: MANAGED MUTUAL RECOGNITION

As I have argued elsewhere, I believe that managed mutual recognition will become the core paradigm for international cooperation in the next decade.[36] Lying at the nexus of regulatory and trade cooperation, it can serve the goals of both communities, although the regulatory cooperation that emerges does so more often than not in spite of the institutional cultures and goals of domestic regulators. As I will argue below, however, there are good reasons to suppose that regulators will adopt this paradigm in the face of new constraints. To start with, we need to describe more specifically what managed mutual recognition actually entails.

A. Motivation: the primacy of trade imperatives

As stated at the outset of this contribution, managed mutual recognition is a form of regulatory cooperation motivated primarily by trade-liberalization concerns. Some analysts refer to it as 'trade facilitation' to the extent that it does not address classical trade barriers, that is, regulations introduced with a protectionist intent. Given the well-known difficulty of distinguishing between trade barriers on the basis of intent, the notion is necessarily misleading. In any case, we need to think of the rise to prominence of managed mutual recognition in two stages. First, mutual recognition as a form of horizontal delegation of regulatory authority represents an

[34] Sol Picciotto, 'The Regulatory Criss-Cross', in *Regulatory Cooperation* (above, n. 8), 118; Peterson and O'Toole, 'Federal Governance in the US and the EU: A Policy Network Perspective', in Kalypso Nicolaïdis and Robert Howse (eds), *The Federal Vision* (above, n. 11); Anne-Marie Slaughter, in this volume.

[35] Fritz Sharpf, *Governing Europe: Effective and Democratic?* (Oxford: Oxford University Press, 1999).

[36] Kalypso Nicolaïdis, *Mutual Recognition Among Nations* (above, n. 21); Kalypso Nicolaïdis, 'Mutual Recognition of Regulatory Regimes' (above, n. 21); Kalypso Nicolaïdis, 'Non Discriminatory Mutual Recognition' (above, n. 3).

alternative both to regulatory autonomy—the principle of 'national treatment' strictly interpreted and its corollary trade-impeding effects—and to vertical delegation as a mechanism of trade liberalization. Both vertical and horizontal delegation are means of creating single rules and standards across jurisdictions from the perspective of the actors being regulated (simple consensual approximation cannot achieve this result to the extent that it does not entail mutual guarantees concerning the application of compatible regulations). But horizontal delegation comes to be preferred over vertical delegation because the latter tends to be a more drawn-out process in that it implies reaching agreement over the content of regulation and/or creating common enforcement bodies—a process that may be neither possible nor desirable.[37]

At the same time, however, we need to account for the 'managed' character of mutual recognition, which entails the reintroduction of regulatory imperatives through the backdoor, as it were. Analysts have widely observed that pure mutual recognition in the form of a straightforward reallocation of authority from host to home country may, under certain conditions, lead to regulatory competition between national regulatory systems as national authorities try to privilege their respective nationals in the international competitive game while attracting foreign investment into their jurisdiction. If such incentives are sufficient to counteract the disincentives in terms of regulatory goals, a race to the bottom is likely to result. But in fact we rarely observe 'pure' mutual recognition. Instead, the management of recognition is the trick that regulators have found to satisfy their political masters and trade colleagues while at the same time minimizing the effects of recognition in terms of regulatory competition. The conditions and caveats attached to horizontal delegation are meant to insure against such competition by transforming mutual recognition into a sophisticated form of regulatory cooperation.[38] In short, the 'management' of recognition may be thought of as the contribution of regulators to the process of recognition. What then are the specific ways in which they manage such recognition?

---

[37] For a defence of this argument see, for instance, Jane C. Kang, 'The Regulation of Global Futures Markets: Is Harmonization Possible or Even Desirable?', *Northwestern Journal of International Law and Business*, vol. 17 (1996).

[38] Other analysts have pointed out this characteristic of mutual recognition as 'decentralization plus'. Les Metcalfe concludes his discussion on the EU's 'new approach' to regulatory cooperation by stating: '[I]t would be wrong to conclude that this process of regulatory management is totally decentralised. In fact, in some areas there are important back-up arrangements and emergency procedures that do operate through central points in the regulatory network.' See Les Metcalfe, 'The weakest links', in OECD, *Regulatory Cooperation*, (above, n. 33), 53.

B. Institutional form: the attributes of managed mutual recognition

I have introduced managed mutual recognition as a complex institutional form of cooperation involving both horizontal and vertical forms of delegation. Whereas pure mutual recognition would consist only of horizontal delegation, the managed character of recognition implies, among other things, that extraterritorial jurisdiction can be accompanied by *ex ante* and *ex post* conditions and other safeguards involving some degree of vertical delegation and is only made possible through the existence and development of regulatory networks. Table 2 summarizes the attributes of mutual recognition that give it a 'managed' character for products, professional services, and financial services.

• *Prior conditions for equivalence between national systems.* The most widely noted attribute of mutual recognition is the prior establishment by the parties involved of some sort of equivalence between their national regulatory systems, both at the level of underlying standards and at the level of licensing or accreditation procedures. 'Equivalence' here simply means that the parties have agreed on what would constitute acceptable differences (a kind of mutual recognition threshold) and that they deem their respective systems to have reached such equivalence either through convergence, through some kind of harmonization process, or by agreement to respect supranational regulations. Prior conditions can thus be sought through cooperation at any of the three stages/levels of cooperation.

• *Automaticity and regulatory scope.* Another means of restricting the impact of mutual recognition is to ensure that it is not immediately applied to the whole scope of regulation but only to relevant parts. The corollary to this caveat is that recognition will not usually be automatic for its beneficiaries. At a minimum, parties will have to provide proof of licensing in their home country. Usually, some residual regulatory jurisdiction will be left to the host country, either because some residual functions are deemed to be crucial to the 'public interest' in that country or because they are simply easier to carry out there (e.g. tests of knowledge of national law for lawyers or random conformity checks for banks). In the transatlantic context, the regulatory scope of MRAs was the subject of intense negotiations, with regulators, especially on the US side, seeking to narrow their scope as much as possible. Obviously the more that automaticity is reduced, the less we can really speak of horizontal delegation and the more we are back to the status quo ante. As a result, this is where contestation is most likely to occur and the need for dispute resolution in the application of mutual recognition most likely to arise.

• *Scope of market access.* Thirdly, we need to ask what kind of market access is granted, and on what terms, through mutual recognition. There are several ways in which the scope of market access can be narrowed

Table 2: The main attributes of 'managed mutual recognition'

Examples:	Products	Professional services	Financial services
Variation in:			
Prior conditions: Requirements for equivalence between national systems	a. Equivalence of health, safety and other technical standards b. Equivalence of standards of enforcement, including of testing and certification procedures c. Mutual recognition of accreditation bodies d. *Ex-ante* confidence building measures	a. Equivalence of professional standards b. Equivalence of accreditation and licensing procedures c. Inter-recognition between competent bodies	a. Equivalence of prudential standards b. Equivalence of authorization and licensing procedures
Automaticity: Regulatory scope of recognition and residual entry requirements from entrant's point of view	a. Test data & inspection report vs final approval b. Additional tests and approval procedures	a. Eligibility: recognition of professional training and competence b. Compensatory requirements	a. Notification by home state b. Proof of licensing c. Additional spot checks
Scope of access: Limitations on scope of access to importing country market	Usually full scope of access except for consumer type (limitations on market access stem from other market characteristics, e.g. distribution channels, fragmented domestic jurisdiction)	a. Right to practise vs title b. Scope of permissible activity c. Rules of conduct and enforcement d. Cross-border supply vs establishment e. Temporary vs permanent right of access	a. Initial entry vs ongoing supervision b. Scope of permissible activities/products c. Rules of conduct and enforcement d. Cross-border supply vs establishment e. n.a. f. Consumer type
Ex-post guarantees: Alternatives to host country control	a. Mutual monitoring b. Collaboration and accountability c. Competition law and dispute resolution mechanisms d. Case-by-case safeguards and overall reversibility		

through the conditions attached to access. For instance, the scope of permissible activities or products can be restricted. Alternatively, mutual recognition can apply only to cross-border supply and not to establishment-based activities, or vice versa. It can even apply to some consumer types and not others as in the case of insurance regulation in the EU single market. It is usually harder to circumscribe the scope of market access for products once they have been let in, except for obligations to use specified distribution channels and for the effect of jurisdictional fragmentation as is the case between the states in the US.

• *Ex-post guarantees*. Finally, mutual recognition may be managed after adoption through a host of *ex-post* guarantees. For one, regulatory networks may be set in place to carry out mutual monitoring so as to ensure the continued compatibility between regulatory systems over time. These networks also serve to carry out joint tasks involved in the management of mutual recognition, including joint upgrading and enforcement of regulations. Most importantly, mutual recognition agreements such as the US–EU MRAs include reversibility clauses and mechanisms to determine whether such reversibility is warranted.

As I have pointed out elsewhere, managed mutual recognition can be viewed in a static or a dynamic manner.[39] At a given point in time, variations along each of these four dimensions can be seen as indicating how far parties have travelled down the road to full recognition. Dynamically, the adoption of managed mutual recognition should be viewed as a process rather than an outcome, involving trade-offs between these dimensions that may change over time. It is a process that sets in motion parallel mechanisms of horizontal delegation of regulatory authority and ongoing regulatory collaboration. As regulatory collaboration bears its fruits, the scope and automaticity of recognition can progressively expand. Moreover, regulators can contribute to the liberalization process even if they do not feel comfortable with one or another regulatory aspect of it simply by establishing trade-offs between the different attributes described above. How confident the parties are about the degree of equivalence between their systems will determine how automatically they are ready to grant recognition. Scope for access might be inversely related to automaticity. If prior conditions do not seem entirely right but the political agenda dictates liberalization, the scope of recognition can be narrowed down or *ex-post* guarantees strengthened. Alternatively, the need to spell out prior conditions of equivalence may be reduced if reversibility is a plausible option of last resort. Thus, while managed mutual recognition is a highly demanding form of regulatory cooperation, it is more amenable

---

[39] For a more detailed discussion, see Kalypso Nicolaïdis, 'Promising Approaches and Principal Obstacles to Mutual Recognition', in *International Trade in Professional Services: Advancing Liberalization through Regulatory Reform* (Paris: OECD Publications, 1997) and Nicolaïdis, 'Non Discriminatory Mutual Recognition' (above, n. 3).

to trial and error than most other forms of cross-border collaboration. This adaptation process in turn is greatly facilitated by the existence and development of regulatory networks.

C. Stages of rule-making: the regulators' agenda

In the end, the institutional form of managed mutual recognition is linked to the stage of regulation that it addresses. As discussed earlier, each stage corresponds to a different set of incentives and constraints. And for each stage, we can ask to what extent the design of managed mutual recognition can help recapture the regulator's agenda. For instance, horizontal functional contacts between regulators may have existed before, but then become captive to the trade agenda (e.g. pharmaceuticals in the transatlantic case). In such cases, regulators can rely on some degree of preexisting mutual understanding, but may also be forced into greatly accelerating the pace of the initial 'courting'. If mutual recognition covers only the enforcement stage, regulators have greater margin initially to reduce the regulatory scope and plan for its progressive expansion. In this case, the functional networks built to induce regulatory convergence through delegation can turn into the means for confidence-building measures capable of supporting MRAs, e.g. some degree of horizontal and vertical delegation. Mutual recognition at the enforcement stage may in turn lead to mutual recognition of the content of regulation in a partially circumscribed segment of the market, to the extent that regulators can learn about and trust their counterpart's regulations in the intervening period. This is the expectation that is often put forth as one of the prospects for transatlantic cooperation.

Ultimately, regulators may become 'converted' to the benefits of managed mutual recognition if they come to observe that the drawbacks feared do not materialize and if they come to experience unforeseen benefits. Chief among the latter are the benefits of regulatory division of labour in a time when institutional resources are scarce and when regulatory agencies need to defend their practices to the taxpayers. It is this realization that finally turned the FDA around in the context of the transatlantic MRAs. A similar push led the EU Commission, in the case of European competition law, to advocate the mutual recognition of enforcement by the Member States themselves.

In the end, however, the true test of the viability of managed mutual recognition will be the legitimacy that it commands among the wider public. The great advantage of managed mutual recognition is that it is a highly effective form of international cooperation that seeks to minimize vertical delegation and the corollary fears of centralization and 'world government' that have become increasingly widespread among the popular critics of globalization. If, as discussed above, it is true that networks facilitate non-institutionalized participation, then mutual recognition as a form of horizontal delegation may be a potentially more inclusive procedure than classical vertical delegation.[40] At the same time, however, this form of cooperation involves a greater loss of control on the part of regulators that needs to be counterbalanced by greater *ex-post* accountability. Thus, for instance, the foreign counterpart may decide to delegate public authority to private bodies or associations, for tasks that are considered part of the public domain in the country doing the recognizing. In this context, ensuring transparency and transborder liability becomes key.[41] Parties need to think of both private and public transnational accountability not only as means of attributing blame and punishing abuse but also as a mean of increasing the effectiveness of regulatory cooperation.[42]

Finally, it is worth stressing that problems of horizontal accountability are bound to become even more accute in the Internet era. As services and products are not only ordered but also consumed directly on the Web, horizontal delegation of authority may become a de facto obligation, simply codifying existing extraterritorial practices and circumscribing them only to the extent technologically possible.[43]

IV. CONCLUSION

This contribution sought to present a simplified model of regulatory cooperation that can account for a broad range of regulatory relationships. It provides a typology of such regulatory relationships by crossing three relevant dimensions: 1, the initial motivation for regulatory cooperation; 2, the level at which such cooperation is conducted, corresponding to the three stages of rule-making, namely rule development, rule adoption, and rule enforcement; and 3, the institutional form of cooperation, defined by whether or not some sort of delegation is being negotiated and, if so, whether it is vertical or horizontal.

The typology in turn is meant to serve as a basis for developing a universal model of regulatory cooperation, by which I mean an analysis

---

[40] Kal Raustiala, 'The Participatory Revolution in International Environmental Law', *Harvard Environmental Law Review*, vol. 31 (1997).

[41] See Pinelopi Makrodimitris, 'Transparency, Accountability and Private Actors', 90 *American Society of International Law Proceedings* (1996); George Bermann (above, n. 9), 85–90.

[42] See OECD, *Regulatory Cooperation* (above, n. 1), 65.

[43] See, for instance, David G. Post, 'The "Unsettled Paradox": The Internet, the State and the Consent of the Governed', *Indiana Journal of Global Legal Studies*, vol. 5 (1998); Phillip R. Trimble, 'Globalization, International Institutions, and the Erosion of National Sovereignty and Democracy', *Michigan Law Review*, vol. 95 (1997); William Drake and Kalypso Nicolaïdis 'Global Electronic Commerce and the General Agreement on Trade in Services: The "Millennium Round" and Beyond', in Pierre Sauve and Robert M. Stern (eds), *Services 2000: New Directions in Services Trade Liberalization* (Washington, DC: Brookings Institution Press, 2000).

outlining the dynamics of such cooperation, the paths it is likely to follow, and the main connections among motives, levels, and forms of cooperation. This contribution only provides some preliminary comments in this regard and calls for further elaboration of the model. I have discussed what I believe is the most fundamental distinction in the world of regulatory cooperation, namely the distinction between trade-driven and regulatory-driven cooperation. This in turn affects the degree of resistance associated with such cooperation and therefore ultimately the extent to which cooperation will be focused on development, adoption, or enforcement of rules across borders as well as the ultimate form of regulatory cooperation. Regulatory motives will favour the former, while trade motives will favour the latter two.

Increasingly, however, the development and strengthening of regulatory networks is allowing these two strands of regulatory cooperation to converge. Managed mutual recognition may be thought of as the expression of such convergence. While governments may have initially encouraged their regulatory authorities or agencies to engage in mutual recognition across borders for trade-liberalization purposes, such regulatory cooperation may take on a life of its own. Regulators seek ways to manage mutual recognition so as to ensure the pursuit of their regulatory objectives while reluctantly bowing to trade pressures, and in the process discover the benefits of regulatory learning and subcontracting. At the same time, cooperation led by regulatory objectives encourages acceptance of differences in regulatory systems and standards by constituting a test of compatibility. As globalization increasingly leads to calls for protectionism, the publicized development of regulatory cooperation may come to serve the free-trade agenda just as the trade-liberalization objective has come to be appropriated by regulators in the European and transatlantic contexts.

Building the 'Transatlantic Economic Partnership': are new general institutions needed?

Wulf-Henning Roth

I. THE QUESTION

The question of whether new, general institutions are needed for the development of the 'Transatlantic Economic Partnership' (TEP) arises from the insight that a fruitful and effective development of the transatlantic economic relations will have to be accompanied by an efficient institutional structure. An answer to the question can be given in a satisfactory manner only if we have a conception of what the TEP really signifies and what the partners of the TEP are seeking to achieve.

If the partners of the TEP—the United States and the European Union—are striving for a far-reaching Free Trade Agreement (Transatlantic Free Trade Agreement; Transatlantic Economic Space; North Atlantic Economic Community),[1] the answers to our question may be different from those for a TEP that is restricted to the mere harmonization of social and environmental policies, the mutual recognition of standards, and some sort of regulatory cooperation on the basis of sectoral agreements. Moreover, a convincing answer to our question must draw on an analysis of the existing and evolving institutional structure of the Transatlantic Economic Partnership, as set forth in the Action Plan,[2] adopted on 18 December 1998: whether the institutional set-up provided in the Action Plan is functioning in an effective manner and to what extent there are actual or potential shortcomings in the present state of affairs.[3] The time span since the adoption of the Action Plan has certainly been too short to permit a reliable judgement on the workability and effectiveness of the

---

[1] A discussion of these conceptions may be found in Ellen Frost, *Transatlantic Trade: A Strategic Agenda* (Washington: Institute for International Economics, 1997), 65; see also Wolfgang Reinicke, *Die Transatlantische Wirtschaftsgemeinschaft—Motor für eine neue Partnerschaft?* (Gütersloh: Verlag Bertelsmann Stiftung, 1997); Christoph Bail, Wolfgang Reinicke, and Reinhardt Rummel, *EU–US Relations: Balancing the Partnership—Taking a Medium-Term Perspective* (Baden-Baden: Nomos Verlagsgesellschaft, 1997).

[2] Transatlantische Wirtschaftspartnerschaft—Aktionsplan, Brüssel, 4. Nov. 1998—126777/98.

[3] Bail *et al.*, *EU–US Partnership* (above, n. 1), 36, argue that the vast range of tasks described in the TEP Action Plan will overburden the existing infrastructure.

existing institutional structure. Accordingly, I will not discuss the question of whether new institutions are needed in the light of (not yet existing) experience with the present institutional structure, but rather on the basis of the goals that are—quite ambitiously—described in the New Transatlantic Agenda (NTA), the Joint US–EU Action Plan, both of 3 December 1995,[4] and the Action Plan of the Transatlantic Economic Partnership of December 1998. Secondly, I will consider the question in the light of the precedents which have been set by each partner by having respectively concluded the North American Free Trade Agreement (NAFTA) and the Agreement on the European Economic Area (EEA).

I would like to develop my contribution in the following steps:

First, I will summarize the basic goals which TEP is meant to pursue and the institutional framework that it envisions.

Second, I will turn to existing precedents as a potential blueprint for the development of the institutional structure of TEP: the European Economic Area and the NAFTA. Both agreements may be taken as a valuable indication as to how far the TEP partners might be willing to go in setting up new institutions with legislative and adjudicative power.

Third, I will argue that what is feasible, and what is probably most urgently needed, is a mechanism devoted to the prevention and settlement of any emergent (trade) disputes between the two TEP partners in an efficient and effective manner.

II. THE TRANSATLANTIC ECONOMIC PARTNERSHIP

A. Its goals

The goals of the TEP may be summarized as follows:

1. In addition to initiating a dialogue with regard to future negotiations on a multilateral level—the WTO—(Action Plan No. 2), it strives for a far-reaching development of bilateral relations towards progressively reducing or eliminating barriers that burden or hinder the free flow of goods, services, and capital (Action Plan No. 3).

2. As tariffs are no longer a major burden for trade in the transatlantic area (except in the sector of agriculture),[5] any further development of trade will have to tackle the very same problems which the European Union has attempted to solve in the last twenty or thirty years in its endeavour to create a single market.[6] Allowing trade between the United States and the

---

[4] Both texts are published in US Information and Texts, No. 089, 7 Dec. 1995, Washington, DC, US Information Service; reprinted e.g. in Bail et al., EU–US Partnership (above, n. 1), 191, 198.

[5] For a survey of existing tariffs, see Frost, Transatlantic Trade (above, n. 1), 13. US tariffs on European goods are considerably lower than European tariffs on US goods.

[6] James Mathis, 'Mutual Recognition Agreements', Journal of World Trade, vol. 32 (1998), 8.

European Union to flow unimpeded by diverging regulations, standards, regulatory systems, and agencies will need action in three directions:

(i) To a certain extent, the relevant regulations will have to be harmonized with the aim of creating equivalent standards of protection for consumers, the environment, etc. (Action Plan No. 3.1.3.).

(ii) As far as standards are not identical, but equivalent, mutual recognition of standards is a feasible way to remove barriers to trade (Action Plan No. 3.1.2.).

(iii) Regulatory cooperation shall be strengthened in two ways:
- first, by way of mutual recognition of regulatory procedures and certifications;
- and secondly, by actively cooperating in matters of common interest.

3. Two more points deserve being mentioned:

(i) The TEP Action Plan calls for more intense efforts to settle the bilateral trade disputes (Action Plan No. 1), and

(ii) it proposes an 'early warning system' with regard to those issues which may in the future give rise to trade disputes (Action Plan No. 3.5.1. and 4).

B. Institutional structure

The institutional structure set forth in the TEP Action Plan (under No. 4) consists of essentially four components:

1. A half-year US–EC summit (somewhat reminiscent of the European Council in its early days in the 1970s).

2. Regular meetings on the level of ministers.

3. The Steering Group (TEP-SG), which has the function to supervise the functioning and development of the TEP and of the agreements which have been and shall be concluded. The Steering Group is, moreover, meant to serve as a kind of consultation body preventing and settling trade disputes.

4. Within the framework of the agreements to be concluded, joint committees and subcommittees shall be established, with the Mutual Recognition Agreement on certification procedures of 22 June 1998[7] being considered as a model.

It is apparent that the institutional structure as provided for by the TEP is strictly intergovernmental in nature. The TEP has not established an executive institution with an organizational infrastructure of its own. Whether such an institution is needed will depend on the performance of the TEP Steering Group and the effective work of the joint committees and subcommittees to be installed. What is noticeable is that there are no (even intergovernmental) institutions entrusted with legislative or adjudicative

---

[7] OJ 1999 L 31/1.

power whatsoever. In the following I will address the question whether a case for such institutions can be made.

III. A NEW INSTITUTION WITH LEGISLATIVE POWER?

The establishment of a new institution with legislative power could be advanced with some vigour if the TEP were meant to develop towards some kind of a Transatlantic Free Trade Area (TAFTA) in the not-too-distant future. A proposal for a TAFTA had, indeed, been made years ago,[8] but has not been pushed ahead for a number of reasons that shall not be discussed here.[9]

What is of particular interest with regard to our subject, however, is that both the United States and the European Union have been most reluctant to establish institutions with legislative power in the framework of the free trade agreements to which they are partners.

1. The Agreement on the European Economic Area of 1992 (EEA), concluded between the European Community (and the Member States) and the countries of the European Free Trade Association (EFTA) other than Switzerland has installed a number of EEA institutions.[10] Here we encounter the EEA Council (Article 89 et seq.) which is responsible for giving the 'political impetus' in the implementation of the EEA Agreement, Article 89, para. 1, and the EEA Joint Committee (Article 92 et seq.) which is given the task of ensuring the effective implementation and operation of the Agreement. The Joint Committee is the competent forum for the exchange of views and information (much like the TEP Steering Group) and for the settlement of disputes (Article 111). Moreover, it decides on the transformation of Community legislation into EEA law (Article 102) and may therefore be considered as an institution which is entrusted with legislative power. What is decisive at this point is that the whole and very complicated procedure set up in this regard only serves one purpose: to

[8] Cf. Christoph Bail, Wolfgang Reinicke, and Reinhardt Rummel, 'The New Transatlantic Agenda and the Joint EU–US Action Plan: An Assessment', in Bail *et al.* (eds), *EU–US Partnership* (above, n. 1), 6; Bart Kerremans, 'Transatlantic Trade Policy Relations: Bilateral and Multilateral Implications of the Emerging Transatlantic Marketplace in Goods', in TEPSA (ed.), *Implementation of the New Transatlantic Agenda and Future Prospects—Final Report* (1998), 8.

[9] Cf. Stephen Woolcock, 'US–EC Commercial Relations', in Bail *et al.* (eds), *EU–US Partnership* (above, n. 1), 144.

[10] For an overview, see the contributions in Thérèse Blanchet, Risto Piiponen, and Maria Westman-Clément, *The Agreement on the European Economic Area (EEA)* (Oxford: Oxford University Press, 1994), 27; Jacot-Guillarmod (ed.), *EEA Agreement* (Zürich: Schulthess, 1992), 549; Waldemar Hummer, in Manfred Dauses (ed.), *Handbuch des EU-Wirtschaftsrechts*, (München: Becksche Verlagsbuchhandlung, 1998 edn.), K.III, paras. 171–234; Andrew Evans, *The Integration of the European Community and Third States* (Oxford: Clarendon Press, 1996), 331; Friedl Weiss, 'The Oporto Agreement on the European Economic Area—A Legal Still Life', *Yearbook of European Law*, vol. 12 (1992), 419.

transpose newly created Community legislation to the European Economic Area, and thereby to the Member States of the EEA in order to create legal homogeneity[11] to the utmost extent.[12] The Joint Committee has no authority whatsoever to either initiate or enact legislation which is binding on the European Communities or its Member States. The legislative procedure in the EEA is restricted to the adoption of Community law on the level of the EEA.[13] The explanation for this rather one-sided solution is, of course, that the concept of the EEA is based on the expectation that in the end all EEA Member States will accede to the European Union.[14]

2. In the NAFTA the United States has not gone any further. On the one hand, Article 2001 provides for the Free Trade Commission, comprising cabinet-level representatives of the parties, whose function is to supervise the implementation of the Agreement, and to oversee the work of all committees and working groups[15] to be established under the Agreement. The Free Trade Commission is assisted by a permanent Secretariat (Article 2002). On the other hand, the Free Trade Commission does not have authority to bind the Parties by legislative or regulatory measures.[16] Nor has the NAFTA created any other (supranational or intergovernmental) institution with legislative powers that transcend those of the NAFTA partners.[17] Legislative powers still rest with the NAFTA partners. All relevant regulations have to be established by way of international agreements.

3. Both free trade agreements—EEA and NAFTA—may be taken as a signal that chances are low that the United States or the European Union will be prepared to give up some of their legislative powers in favour of an intergovernmental or supranational institution in the framework of the TEP or some future TAFTA. Viewed from the perspective of the European Union, any transfer of legislative powers to another institution will by necessity reduce the influence of the governments of the Member States, and their electorates. It is suggested that the mounting concern with regard to the ongoing shift of legislative powers from the Member States

[11] As to this notion, see Marise Cremona, 'The "Dynamic and Homogeneous" EEA: Byzantine Structures and Variable Geometry', *European Law Review*, vol. 19 (1994), 518.

[12] Armando Toledano Laredo, 'The EEA Agreement: An Overall View', *Common Market Law Review*, vol. 29 (1992), 1204.

[13] See Hummer in Dauses (ed.), *EU-Wirtschaftsrecht* (above, n. 10), K.III. paras. 188–9.

[14] Wolfgang Burtscher, 'Der Europäische Wirtschaftsraum (EWR) und die Beziehungen der EG zu den EFTA-Staaten', in Röttinger and Weyringer, *Handbuch der europäischen Integration* (Wien: Manzsche Verlags- und Universitätsbuchhandlung, 1991), 501; Frost, *Transatlantic Trade* (above, n. 1), 72.

[15] See Frederick Abbott, *Law and Policy of Regional Integration* (Cambridge, Mass.: Kluwer Law and Taxation Publishers, 1995), 97.

[16] Ibid. 28.

[17] Jon Johnson, *The North American Free Trade Agreement* (Aurora, Ontario: Canada Law Book Inc., 1994), 484.

to the Union should be taken seriously. The electorates in the Member States would probably deeply resent a supranational legislative body that is even more removed from their influence than the decision-making process on the European level.

IV. A NEW INSTITUTION WITH ADJUDICATORY POWER?

A. The case for a court-like institution

If one conceives of the TEP as the first step on the way to TAFTA, the idea of installing an institution with adjudicative power might have some appeal. An even stronger case could be made if the TEP were on its way to a Free Trade Union with some basic principles comparable to the market freedoms of the EC Treaty—free movement of goods, services, persons, and capital—which need to be given a concrete interpretation in relevant cases. It is indisputable that the success story of the European Community is to a considerable extent due to the adjudication of the European Court of Justice at Luxembourg.[18] The Court has eventually successfully settled trade conflicts between the Member States (such as the 'lamb war' between the United Kingdom and France[19] or the 'wine war' between Italy and France[20]). It was the institution of the Court and its—sometimes neglected[21]—authority which in the end had an obviously restraining effect on the actions of the Member States. Therefore, it does not seem to be too far-fetched to speculate about a court-like body in the institutional framework of the TEP—some kind of US-EU Trade Court which will authoritatively settle disputes arising between the partners. Whether such an institution with adjudicative power should be seriously proposed depends, however, on the willingness of both partners to develop the TEP towards some kind of TAFTA and to submit to a procedure of conflict resolution on legal terms and under binding legal standards.

B. European Union

1. The EEA-Court precedent

As for the European Union, we may refer to the experience with the European Economic Area.[22] In its original version, the Agreement on the

---

[18] For a critical account of the Court's role, see Haltje Rasmussen, *On Law and Policy in the European Court of Justice* (Dordrecht: Martinus Nijhoff Publishers, 1986), ch. 6; Hjalte Rasmussen, *The European Court of Justice* (Copenhagen: Gadjura, 1998), ch. 11.

[19] ECJ 25. 9. 1979, Case 266/78 (*Commission v. French Republic*), ECR 1979, 2729.

[20] ECJ 4. 3. 1982, Case 42/82 R (*Commission v. French Republic*), ECR 1982, 841—interlocutory decision; ECJ 22. 3. 1983, Case 42/82 (*Commission v. French Republic*), ECR 1983, 1013.

[21] ECJ, 28. 3. 1980, Case 24 and 97/80 R (*Commission v. French Republic*), ECR 1980, 1319.

[22] For an account of the evolution, e.g., Evans, *Integration* (above, n. 10), 353.

EEA did indeed provide for a supranational court with the competence to definitively interpret the EEA Agreement and the EEA secondary law that was to be transposed from Community law. The Court was to be partly composed of members of the European Court of Justice and of members of the EFTA Court.

In its Opinion 1/91, the European Court of Justice blocked the installation of the EEA Court, but for reasons that are irrelevant for our discussion. The ECJ argued that the structure of the EEA Agreement was meant to put the EEA Court in a position to interpret Community law, and that the EEA Court could therefore prejudice the interpretation of Community law by the Court of Justice. In the words of the Court: The 'agreement . . . takes over an essential part of the rules—including the rules of secondary legislation—which govern economic and trading relations within the Community and which constitute, for the most part, fundamental provisions of the Community legal order. Consequently, the agreement has the effect of introducing into the Community legal order a large body of legal rules which is juxtaposed to a corpus of identically-worded Community rules.'[23] The Court goes on to argue that, given the EEA Agreement's objective of ensuring homogeneity of the law throughout the EEA, there will be repercussions of the construction of the EEA agreement by the EEA Court on the construction of the corresponding rules of Community law. Accordingly, the court system set up by the EEA agreement would condition the future construction of Community law and thereby conflict with the responsibility of the Court of Justice under Article 220 EC (ex Article 164).[24]

2. Opinion 1/91 and its consequences

At the same time, Opinion 1/91 is unequivocal about the compatibility of an international agreement which sets up its own court system with Community law. Though the Court of Justice has—on the basis of Article 234 EC (ex Article 177)—jurisdiction over the interpretation of international agreements to which the Community is a partner, the Court expressly stated that 'where . . . an international agreement provides for its own system of courts, including a court with jurisdiction to settle disputes between the Contracting Parties to the agreement, and, as a result, to interpret its provisions, the decisions of that court will be binding on the

---

[23] ECJ 4. 12. 1991, Opinion 1/91, ECR 1991, I-6079, 6106 cons. 41–2.

[24] Ibid., cons. 46–7. Moreover, the EEA Agreement provided that the EEA Court had jurisdiction with regard to the settlement of disputes, brought before the Court by a 'Contracting Party'. Thereby, the EEA Court was given the competence to rule on the respective competences of the Community and the Member States as regards the matters governed by the provisions of the agreement. This would amount to an infringement of the autonomy of the Community legal order and the exclusive jurisdiction given to the Court of Justice in these matters; see ECJ (above, n. 23) I-6105 cons. 34–5. The present system has found the approval of the Court in ECJ 10. 4. 1992, Opinion 1/92, ECR 1992 I-2821.

Community institutions, including the Court of Justice'.[25] The Court of Justice would therefore be under a duty to follow the interpretation of the international agreement given by the other (international) court. In very clear words the Court of Justice states:

An international agreement providing for such a system of courts is in principle compatible with Community law. The Community's competence in the field of international relations and its capacity to conclude international agreements necessarily entails the power to submit to the decisions of a court which is created or designated by such an agreement as regards the interpretation and application of its provisions.[26]

3. United States

The experience in setting up an institution with adjudicatory powers in an international agreement are probably less encouraging in the United States. NAFTA, the most ambitious free trade agreement concluded by the United States so far, contains provisions on dispute settlement, but it does not install a court or court-like institution for the construction of the Agreement and the resolution of disputes. This reflects a clear policy choice: the United States does not seem ready to opt for an adjudicatory institution that would issue judgments binding not only upon the Contracting Partners, but also upon the national courts. In NAFTA the United States has deliberately adopted a looser and less-intrusive arrangement.[27] My estimate is that—absent some compelling reasons for installing a court-like institution—the United States will not be prepared in the foreseeable future to consent to such an institution.

4. Should a court-like institution be advocated at all?

Given these positions at the outset, one may wonder whether a court-like institution should be advocated at all. The answer will depend on whether such an institution may be regarded as appropriate (as compared to some other settlement mechanism) to resolve the most important trade disputes between the TEP partners that are likely to arise. Ongoing and future disputes between the United States and the Community concern a quite diverse set of issues.

Disputes may, first of all, relate to the construction of agreements concluded between the TEP partners, such as the Agreement on the Mutual Recognition of Certification Procedures of 22 June 1998,[28] or the Agreement on Measures for the Protection of Health Concerning Trade with Animals and Animal Products of 16 March 1998.[29] The Agreement on mutual recognition, in its Article 14, provides for a Joint Committee which shall be responsible for all issues concerning the functioning of the

---

[25] ECJ (above, n. 23) I-6106 cons. 39.   [26] ECJ (above, n. 23) I-6106 cons. 40.
[27] Johnson (above, n. 17), 488.   [28] OJ 1991 L 31/1.
[29] OJ 1998 L 118/1.

Agreement. The Committee may therefore serve as a discussion forum for the exchange of views on the construction of the Agreement (cf. Article 14, §4 sect. d), though with no competence to take a binding decision.[30] A court-like institution could be given such an interpretative competence with binding force for the TEP partners. A less intrusive arrangement for the TEP partners might consist of a mechanism to reach agreement either in the Joint Committee or—on the proposal of the Joint Committee—in the TEP Steering Group.

Second, the Agreement on Mutual Recognition also deals with the power of the TEP partners to establish, by regulations or other measures, a level of protection deemed appropriate for the protection of safety and life of human beings, plants, and animals, for the protection of health, environment, and consumers (Article 15, §2). At this point the Agreement deals with one of the most sensitive issues: the protection of the relevant public interest of one TEP partner vis-à-vis goods imported from the Partner State. It is notable that Article 15, §2 leaves it expressly to the Partners of the Agreement to define the relevant level of protection which they deem appropriate for themselves. If the TEP were to be developed towards a Free Trade Agreement, encompassing some basic freedoms (free movement of goods and services) as general principles, a court-like institution would be confronted with the problem of solving the conflict between free trade on the one hand and public-policy considerations on the other.

As the recent disputes concerning the use of hormones and gene-treated plants indicate, American and European notions as to the relevant public interest may turn out to differ sharply. The definition and the understanding of the public interest on both sides of the Atlantic seem to reflect deep-rooted attitudes that relate to history and cultural traditions, based on prevailing value choices and ethical considerations.[31] It is submitted that a court-like institution would not be an appropriate instrument to cope with this problem.

It is true that in the European Union the Court of Justice has—in its adjudication concerning the basic freedoms—dealt exactly with this issue. By the famous *Cassis de Dijon* jurisprudence,[32] the Court has restricted the leeway for the Member States to define and pursue their public interest.

---

[30] Disputes on the interpretation of the Agreement will probably be resolved by an informal consultation process in the Steering Group. If the dispute cannot be resolved, a partner may suspend its obligations with regard to a specific sectoral annexe (Article 16) or even terminate the Agreement as a whole (Article 21, §3).

[31] Bail *et al.*, in Bail *et al.* (eds), *EU–US Partnership* (above, n. 1), 26–7; Reinicke, *Transatlantische Wirtschaftsgemeinschaft* (above, n. 1), 65. It is suggested that the mutual recognition principle ('What is okay for the US consumer should also be okay for the European consumer') does not work in those situations either.

[32] ECJ 20. 2. 1979, Case 120/79 (Cassis de Dijon), ECR 1979, 649.

However, we should not overlook the preconditions for such a jurisprudence:

- The European Court of Justice was in a position to base its adjudication on a widely-shared 'European' ideology. Criticism with regard to its adjudication was for a long time subdued, being easily misconceived as anti-European.
- The active role of the Court in shaping the European Single Market was widely accepted as part of the European enterprise, overcoming institutional deficiencies of other institutions like the Council (requirement of unanimity in Article 94 [ex Art. 100] of the EC Treaty).
- The Court acted as a European institution, as an umpire of a quasi-federal system. Its adjudication was not perceived as dispute-settling between partners of a free-trade-union (though it sometimes was), but rather as a means of building a European constitution by vesting the freedoms with some bite. Winners and losers among the states were—at least in the middle or long run—not clearly identifiable.

A court-like institution to be set up in the framework of the TEP or TAFTA would act in a totally different social, economic, ideological, and legal environment:

- There is no common ideological basis to back up such an institution.
- The judgments would always concern a bipartisan relationship with winner and loser clearly discernible.
- The economic and social implications of any ruling would be immediately felt.
- The readiness for and the degree of acceptance of a ruling of a TEP/TAFTA court by the partners and their population may be much lower as compared to the European Court of Justice.

If this analysis is correct, divergences as to the conception of what can be described as 'public interest' should be dealt with by political instruments rather than by an adjudicatory procedure based on general rules.[33] Such divergences should be attempted to be overcome or at least reduced by harmonizing the relevant standards with the instrument of international agreements. Moreover, the partners to the TEP should develop mechanisms whereby public policy considerations of the other partner are taken care of in the process of drafting legislation, setting regulatory standards, or developing procedures and standards for risk management.[34]

---

[33] Reinicke, *Transatlantische Wirtschaftsgemeinschaft* (above, n. 1), 70: supranational decision-making could be counterproductive.

[34] See TEP Action Plan No. 3.1.1. (under b.), 3.5.1. (under f.); cf. Reinicke, *Transatlantische Wirtschaftsgemeinschaft* (above, n. 1), 71: taking a transatlantic perspective when formulating new product or environmental standards.

Such a mechanism could encompass an obligation to consult the other partner, and to take notice of the relevant public interest involved. Such an *ex-ante*-conflict-avoidance approach would have a considerable potential to reduce the conflict between regulations of the TEP/TAFTA partners.

Finally, a third type of controversy that has vexed the trade relations between the United States and the Community relates to such issues as anti-dumping and subsidy control. Such controversies will arise as long as the TEP falls short of a Free Trade Union with its own competition and subsidy-control regime. Given the strong economic implications and the extreme difficulty of evolving clear-cut legal rules in this area, it is submitted that these issues do not seem particularly appropriate for an adjudicative procedure.[35]

V. DISPUTE SETTLEMENT

If a court-like institution cannot be advocated as appropriate, it is submitted that some kind of effective dispute-settlement procedure is needed in the framework of the TEP. Given the relevant provisions in NAFTA and the EEA agreements as precedents, there is a chance that the TEP partners will opt for such a procedure in the not too distant future.[36]

A. EEA

To start with the EEA Agreement, we encounter a two-stage dispute-settlement procedure. The parties to the EEA Agreement (i.e. the EC—not its Member States—and the EFTA Member States) may call on the EEA Joint Committee to deal with questions of construction and application of the EEA Agreement (Articles 111, §1, 105). The Joint Committee (consisting of the representatives of the Contracting Parties) may take a decision by unanimous vote that is binding on the Parties. If an agreement is not reached in the Joint Committee, the dispute may be taken to the EEA Arbitration Tribunal if the case concerns a dispute over the scope or duration of safeguard measures or the proportionality of rebalancing measures.[37] For questions of construction of the EEA Agreement the

---

[35] Cf. Michael Trebilcock and Robert Howse, *The Regulation of International Trade* (London: Routledge, 1995), 407.

[36] An overview of dispute settlement with regard to international organizations: Henry Schermers and Niels Blokker, *International Institutional Law* (The Hague and London: Martinus Nijhoff, 1995), §§648–69; with regard to dispute settlement in international economic law and alternative methods, see the contributions by Peter Behrens and Karl-Heinz Böckstiegel in Ernst-Ulrich Petersmann and Günther Jaenicke (eds), *Adjudication of International Trade Disputes in International and National Economic Law* (Fribourg: University Press Fribourg, 1992), 59.

[37] As distinct from a question concerning the interpretation of the EEA Agreement; Article 111, §4.

Contracting Parties may, under certain conditions, agree to request the European Court of Justice to give a ruling on the construction of the relevant provisions.

B. Europe Agreements

A somewhat comparable two-stage approach has been introduced into the so-called Europe Agreements, concluded between the European Union and the Central European states, like Poland, Hungary, and, most recently, Slovenia.[38] The Contracting Parties may call on the Association Council (which is composed of the Contracting Parties) concerning a dispute over the interpretation or application of the Agreement.[39] Decisions are taken unanimously. In the case that a dispute cannot be solved by a decision, a Contracting Partner may initiate an Arbitral Proceeding before a Tribunal of three members. The Tribunal will decide by a majority vote, the decision being binding for the Contracting Partners obliging them to take the necessary and appropriate measures.[40]

C. NAFTA

The NAFTA has—all details left aside[41]—established a similar two-stage procedure.[42] At stage one, the Free Trade Commission is attributed the power to 'resolve disputes that may arise regarding the interpretation or application of the Agreement' (Article 2001, §2 sect. c). Stage two provides for a dispute-settlement procedure (Articles 2005 et seq.), concerning not only the interpretation and application of NAFTA, but also disputes arising under GATT/WTO (Article 2005 §1).[43] Following a consultation and conciliation period, an arbitral panel will be established at the request of one party. The Arbitral Final Report, though binding on the Parties, cannot be enforced by them against each other. Non-implementation of the

---

[38] OJ 1999 L 51/1.

[39] Article 113 Europe Agreement with Slovenia.

[40] For an analysis of the dispute-settlement procedures contained in other Agreements concluded by the European Union, see Koen Lenaerts and Eddy de Smijter, 'The European Community's Treaty-Making Competence', Yearbook of European Law, vol. 16 (1996), 54.

[41] A special mechanism to be considered in this context is the Binational Panel System for Antidumping and Countervailing Duty Matters under Chapter 19 of NAFTA. See Eric Pan, 'Assessing the NAFTA Chapter 19 Binational Panel System: An Experiment in International Adjudication', Harvard International Law Journal, vol. 40 (1999), 379.

[42] An overview is given by Abbott, Regional Integration (above, n. 15), 100; Jeffrey Bialas and Deborah Siegel, 'Dispute Resolution under the NAFTA: The Newer and Improved Model', in Judith Bello, Alan Holmer, and Joseph Norton (eds), The North American Trade Agreement: A New Frontier in International Trade and Investment in the Americas (Washington: American Bar Association (Section of International Law and Practice), 1994), 315.

[43] For a discussion of the relationship to the WTO Dispute Settlement Understanding: Abbott, Regional Integration (above, n. 15), 102.

Arbitral Final Report gives the complaining Party the right to suspend benefits of equivalent effect (Article 2019, §1).

D. A proposal

Both the EEA Agreement and the NAFTA dispute settlement system may serve as a model for TEP. An agreement to be concluded between the TEP partners could provide for a two-stage procedure:

- Stage One would call on the Partners to first submit their dispute to the TEP Steering Group that could in the near future be given a somewhat more institutional structure as a Free Trade Commission, following the NAFTA model. Such an institutional upgrading of the Steering Group might have a lasting influence on its self-understanding, on its ability to develop solutions acceptable to both Partners, and on its willingness to oversee and enforce the process of economic cooperation.
- Stage Two should provide for arbitral proceedings, comparable to those in the NAFTA.

It is submitted that such a dispute settlement mechanism should cover as broad a range of issues as possible: interpretation and application of the Agreements concluded and still to be concluded by the TEP partners; disputes arising under the WTO agreements; other trade-related issues, such as the extraterritorial effect of laws, and the like.

The TEP dispute settlement mechanism should be given priority over the WTO dispute settlement mechanism.

VI. CONCLUSIONS

A realistic perception of what the partners of the TEP are prepared to develop as an institutional framework in a TEP/TAFTA context should take the NAFTA and EEA Agreement as precedent. Taking this as the basis of my conclusions, I would like to summarize my contribution in two points:

1. New, general institutions with legislative and/or adjudicative powers should not be advocated for the foreseeable future.

2. What is needed are mechanisms that effectively prevent and settle trade disputes between the Partners of the TEP.

- With regard to trade disputes (concerning Agreements, issues relating to WTO, and other issues) a two-step settlement procedure should be installed (first stage: Steering Group; second stage: Arbitral Tribunal) by an international agreement.
- The partners should submit to an obligation to take notice of and to take into account the public interest of the other partner in all relevant matters, especially with regard to evolving legislation.

Globalization and transatlantic regulatory cooperation: proposals for EU-US initiatives to further constitutionalize international law

Ernst-Ulrich Petersmann

I. GLOBALIZATION AS A CONSTITUTIONAL CHALLENGE

Transnational corporations and foreign investments from North America and Europe are driving a globalization of production and markets—a process already favoured by worldwide trade liberalization, deregulation, a movement to market economies, and the growth of global communication networks. The economic dominance of American and European business also entails a legal dominance of American and European business laws and practices. The resulting globalization of Western legal standards is reflected in the regulation of financial and capital markets, securities law, accounting standards, credit-rating practices, forms of private commercial transactions, commercial arbitration, and international cooperation among competition agencies. Not only do capital markets and transnational networks of financial and business centres influence national laws and government policies, but export industries also strongly influence the new intergovernmental trade and investment agreements, such as the General Agreement on Trade in Services (GATS), the Agreement on Trade-Related Intellectual Property Rights (TRIPS), the 1997 Agreement on Trade in Information Technology, the 1998 GATS Protocol on Telecommunications Services, and the 1999 GATS Protocol on Trade in Financial Services.

A. Competition as a governance mechanism requires constitutional rules

Despite these developments, the globalization fuelled by microeconomic actors will not ensure a global market economy unless markets are kept open by competition rules. The global restructuring of private business strategies has transformed about 70 per cent of world trade into intra-industry and intra-firm trade. Almost 60 per cent of foreign direct investments are now carried out by means of international mergers and acquisitions of foreign enterprises which may lead to abuses of dominant market positions. At the same time, the recent abandonment of the OECD negotiations on the Draft Multilateral Agreement on Investment (MAI) has shown the political limits of producer-driven, non-transparent functional international 'net-working' among business and governments. The short-sighted opposition by US antitrust authorities to the EU's proposals for negotiating international competition rules in the World Trade Organization (WTO) is yet further evidence that industry interests and bureaucratic self-interests (e.g. in protecting the autonomy of US antitrust agencies and their preference for 'unilateralism' and 'bilateralism' rather than 'trade multilateralism') may not coincide with the general citizen interests in maximizing consumer welfare and human rights.

What is called for is a parallel restructuring of intergovernmental cooperation and international law. The 'Americanization' of private and public international economic law described by Saskia Sassen[1] needs to be accompanied by a 'constitutionalization' of foreign policies so as to prevent private self-regulation and 'export-driven' intergovernmental regulation from leading to 'market failures' and 'government failures'. The increasing private capacity for transnational rule-making welcomed by Sassen can claim democratic legitimacy only to the extent that it contributes to the individual utility, equal rights, and social welfare of all people.

B. Need for 'constitutionalizing' international law

The state-centred Westphalian system of classical international law rests on authoritarian interpretations of state sovereignty which favour power politics but do not effectively protect human rights, rule of law, and 'democratic peace' across frontiers. The modern worldwide recognition of human rights as part of general international law, together with the increasingly transnational exercise of economic freedoms and other individual rights of 'civil society', creates a need for constitutionalizing foreign policies and global economic integration. Human rights law and theory postulate that citizens confer on governments only limited powers that must be exercised in a way that maximizes the equal civil, political, economic, and social constitutional rights of citizens. In contrast to corporatist concepts of private self-regulation based on economic, technological, and legal dominance of American and European industries, the transatlantic dialogue needs to be guided by the American and European historical experience of constitutionalism as the most effective means of protecting individual freedom and other citizen rights against abuses of private and public power. The globalization of economic markets requires a globalization of legal guarantees of freedom, non-discrimination, rule of law and democratic governance in order to enable

---

[1] See the contribution of Saskia Sassen, this volume.

consumers to voice their individual preferences, to induce producers to satisfy consumer preferences efficiently, and to prevent governments from unduly restricting and distorting transnational cooperation among citizens. Europe and North America have the longest political experience with constitutionalism and should use their transatlantic dialogue for joint political initiatives designed to strengthen the 'constitutional foundations' of global competition as governance mechanism that can function efficiently only in a constitutional framework for 'democratic peace' at home and abroad.

C. Rule of law and democracy must begin at home

The Uruguay Round negotiations leading to the 1994 WTO Agreement demonstrate that joint American–European leadership can prompt other states to accept new worldwide institutions based on multilateral legal guarantees of freedom, non-discrimination, and rule of law across frontiers. At the same time, the growing incidence of trade disputes between the European Union and the United States (e.g. over the EU's import restrictions on bananas, hormone-treated beef, and genetically modified food) bears witness to the constitutional insight that the rule of law must begin at home: even though the EC Treaty clearly prescribes that the EC's international agreements 'shall be binding on the institutions of the Community and on Member States' (EC Treaty Article 300(7), ex 228 (7)), and notwithstanding a dozen GATT and WTO dispute-settlement findings confirming the illegality of the EU's import restrictions on bananas since 1993,[2] the EU institutions (including the Court of Justice) have continued openly to ignore GATT and WTO rules for over six years and thus restrict the freedom and welfare of EU citizens without any legal and democratic legitimacy. Obviously, the WTO legal and dispute-settlement system cannot remain effective if the domestic constitutional systems of WTO Members do not protect the rule of law in transnational relations.

My argument is that the United States and Europe should use their economic and political weight to promote new constitutional rules not only to build increasingly global economic markets, but also to protect the international rule of law and international 'democratic peace'. While the dominance of the United States and the European Union has prompted many third countries to deregulate their national laws voluntarily so as to attract more foreign investments, can we also expect third countries to react positively to EU–US pressures to strengthen human rights and democracy? Just as US post-war initiatives for the Bretton Woods Agreements and for GATT could produce an unprecedented period of worldwide peaceful

---

[2] Cf. Ernst-Ulrich Petersmann, 'The WTO Panel and Arbitration Reports on the EC Banana Regime', *Bridges between Trade and Sustainable Development* (Apr. 1999), 3–4.

cooperation and prosperity because they were accompanied by the US initiative for the UN Charter and US support for European integration law, so modern global integration requires bold EU–US initiatives to further constitutionalize international law and international organizations and thereby protect freedom, rule of law, and democratic peace beyond Europe and North America.

II. GLOBAL COMPETITION REQUIRES GLOBAL COMPETITION RULES: PROPOSALS FOR INCLUDING COMPETITION RULES INTO THE WTO SYSTEM

According to the US Supreme Court, 'antitrust laws . . . are the Magna Carta of free enterprise. They are as important to the preservation of economic freedom and our free enterprise system as the Bill of Rights is to the protection of our fundamental freedoms.'[3] Even though US antitrust economists today chiefly focus on maximizing economic efficiency, US antitrust law has also been concerned for many decades with dispersion of power, the freedom of independent producers and traders lacking market power, and effective competition in open markets with many rivals.[4] When the German and EC competition laws were adopted in 1957, the declared objectives were likewise not only the promotion of economic efficiency and consumer welfare, but also the limitation and decentralization of public and private power, pluralism, democracy and market integration across Europe.[5] Due also to their incorporation into the association and cooperation agreements that the European Union has concluded with almost all other states in Europe, EC competition law principles have promoted economic freedom, competition, consumer welfare, and judicial protection of individual rights throughout Europe, with far-reaching repercussions beyond economics. These include the protection of personal and political freedom, establishment of independent competition authorities, and judicial control of governmental and private anticompetitive practices. Similarly, the national competition laws introduced by almost thirty less-developed countries during the 1990s aimed not only to maximize economic efficiency but also to protect economic freedom, limit abuses of power, deregulate protected markets, and promote effective competition as a dynamic process of rivalry and discovery.

---

[3] *United States v. Topco*, 405 US 596, 610.

[4] Cf. Eleanor M. Fox, 'The Modernization of Antitrust', *Cornell Law Review*, vol. 66 (1981), 1140–92.

[5] On the 'constitutional functions' of competition rules see Ernst-Ulrich Petersmann, 'Legal, Economic and Political Objectives of National and International Competition Policies,' *New England Law Review*, vol. 34 (1999), 145–62.

The initiative by the European Union to negotiate international competition rules in the WTO[6] led to the establishment of a WTO Working Group on the Interaction between Trade and Competition Policy at the WTO Ministerial Conference in 1996. By mid-1999, three major approaches and policy recommendations had emerged from the more than 100 submissions by WTO members and from discussions within this Group. They follow:

A. Proposals for unilateralism and bilateralism

A few submissions (notably those made by the United States) suggest that national competition laws and bilateral cooperation are optimal policy instruments. Yet, trade-policy experience with unilateralism and bilateralism shows the high cost of this approach. Thousands of bilateral trade and investment agreements, coupled with countless international conflicts flowing from the unilateral application of trade and competition laws to producers and traders in foreign jurisdictions, have produced high economic costs, mercantilist exemptions from national competition laws for export cartels and regulated sectors, legal insecurity, and conflicting decisions by competition authorities on international mergers and other business practices. Bilateral cooperation among competition authorities in applying their existing competition laws to transnational restraints of competition is no substitute for multilateral competition rules that would help the more than 100 countries lacking competition laws to introduce such rules over the opposition of domestic industries. As in trade policy, multilateralism is also more rule-oriented and efficient than bilateralism and unilateralism in competition policy. Furthermore, multilateralism is consistent with what has been recommended as a 'common law approach' to antitrust cooperation—namely, a prudent evolution of rules and case-specific bilateral cooperation that starts with a few multilateral substantive and procedural minimum standards (as, for example, in the GATS Protocol on Telecommunications and in the TRIPS Agreement) which do not prejudice either the higher standards and judicial enforcement systems in industrialized countries or their case-specific cooperation with competition authorities abroad. Such multilateral minimum standards would pose a risk neither to the autonomy of US antitrust agencies nor to the highly developed US antitrust laws and judicial enforcement remedies, especially if it were made clear that the WTO dispute-settlement procedures could not be used for challenging decisions in individual cases.

---

[6] Cf. Ernst-Ulrich Petersmann, 'The Need for Integrating Trade and Competition Rules in the WTO World Trade and Legal System', in G. Parry and H. Steiner (eds), *Freedom and Trade*, vol. 3 (London: Routledge, 1998), 97–118; Ernst-Ulrich Petersmann, 'The International Competition Policy of the EC and the Need for an EC Initiative for a "Plurilateral Agreement on Competition and Trade" in the WTO', in Francis Snyder (ed.), *Constitutional Dimensions of European Economic Integration* (The Hague: Kluwer, 1996), 289–336.

B. Proposals for worldwide competition rules in the WTO

The European Union has advanced the idea of adopting new WTO rules which would in turn require the adoption of a comprehensive competition law applicable to specific anti-competitive practices of both private and public undertakings, supported by provisions for a domestic competition enforcement authority with sufficient powers of investigation and procedures through which private parties would have access to both competition authorities and domestic courts. Much like the protection of intellectual property rights in the TRIPS Agreement, multilateral competition rules in the WTO would offer many advantages:

(*a*) They would render the WTO rules on market access and market distortions more effective by preventing their undermining or circumvention by private market access-barriers and market distortions.

(*b*) An integrated framework for controlling public and private restraints on competition would help to limit progressively the effect of anti-competitive exceptions found both in trade laws (notably for anti-dumping and other safeguard measures designed to protect import-competing producers rather than undistorted competition) and in competition laws (such as exemptions for export cartels and regulated industries).

(*c*) By promoting cooperation among domestic competition authorities (via both 'positive comity' and 'negative comity'), international minimum standards would contribute to avoiding conflicts in the extraterritorial application of domestic competition laws to international mergers and to transnational restraints of competition.

(*d*) International competition rules would also protect the general citizen interest in liberal trade and competition by helping governments in the more than 100 countries currently lacking national competition laws to overcome domestic protectionist resistance to the introduction of such laws.

(*e*) The traditional focus of competition policy on general consumer welfare, individual rights, and judicial protection would enhance the democratic legitimacy of WTO law and its political acceptance by 'civil society'.

C. Proposals for additional WTO market-access guarantees

A different 'WTO approach' recommended notably by less-developed countries (e.g. by Hong Kong) focuses more on the complementary 'market-freeing functions' of liberal trade and competition rules than on the 'regulatory functions' of competition laws (e.g. merger control rules, market dominance rules, establishment of independent competition authorities). Under this view, strengthening existing GATT and GATS market access commitments (e.g. their extension to exclusionary anticompetitive practices of private and public undertakings) and liberalizing still pervasive governmental and private market access barriers are politically more important than the longer-term goal of adopting competition laws in all WTO members.

D. Constitutional functions of competition rules

Like human rights and liberal trade rules, competition rules are legal pre-conditions for the proper functioning of markets. The concerns voiced by US competition authorities—that US antitrust law and practice cannot be improved, that WTO negotiations tend to be 'producer-biased', and that international competition rules may adversely affect US antitrust laws and the discretion of US competition agencies—all miss the point. They over-look the fact that additional WTO guarantees for open markets and undis-torted competition would offer important benefits to the United States, without adversely affecting the much higher standards of US competition law and policy; they also ignore the need for 'international constitution-building' in transnational relations.

Contrary to the unique US experience of over 200 years of constitutional democracy and over 100 years of effective antitrust enforcement, most WTO members have no competition laws or have introduced them only recently. While the unilateral application of national antitrust law to for-eign enterprises and bilateral cooperation with foreign competition authorities may be effective policy tools for US antitrust authorities, this is simply not true for most other countries which have no competition laws and/or no national competition authorities capable of effectively review-ing the business practices of foreign enterprises. Like international human rights and liberal trade guarantees, international competition safeguards of open markets and undistorted competition are of constitutional impor-tance in protecting freedom and competition at home and abroad. Also, most European countries introduced *national* competition laws only after having accepted *international* competition rules embodied in EC law or in the free-trade agreements concluded with the European Union. Past expe-rience with coordination of competition policies within the OECD confirms that the political support necessary for introducing multilateral competition rules can only be generated in 'comprehensive package nego-tiations' (such as those that established the WTO, EC, and NAFTA) which offer clear benefits to export industries in major trading countries and therefore receive their political support.

From a human rights and citizen perspective—as well as from the WTO perspective of promoting non-discriminatory conditions of competition worldwide—competition policy should be defined broadly: all government policies should aim at maximizing equal freedom, non-discriminatory conditions of competition, and consumer welfare. As long as trade authorities restrict and distort import and export competition, and competition authorities exempt export cartels and 'regulated industries', governments cannot claim to have a consistent and non-discriminatory competition policy that maximizes consumer welfare. Because it is impossible to calculate 'social welfare' in a comprehensive sense (i.e. as the sum of the utility of all domestic citizens), we need simplifying assumptions. In the field of competition policy, for example, we might focus on 'consumer surplus' (i.e. the excess of social valuation of a product over the price actually paid), or on the absence of output and price limitations as a means of preventing illegitimate wealth transfers from consumers to producers. Yet, government campaigns to maximize economic efficiency are not credible as long as the government restricts and distorts import and export competition and reduces consumer welfare for the benefit of a few domestic producers. Competition-oriented reforms of the world trade and legal system including the WTO are necessary for rendering both trade and competition policies more coherent and for thereby enhancing economic freedom, non-discrimination, effective opportunities for competition, and consumer welfare across frontiers.

III.   WTO LAW AS A MODEL FOR FURTHER EU–US INITIATIVES FOR REFORMING THE LAW OF INTERNATIONAL ORGANIZATIONS?

Thanks to EU and US leadership, the WTO Agreement has become a model for promoting freedom, non-discrimination, rule of law, deregulation, compulsory dispute settlement, and appellate review throughout the world. The WTO Agreements (including TRIPS, the telecommunications agreement, and WTO work programmes on electronic commerce, competition policy, and investments) are of constitutional significance in promoting individual freedom and peaceful international cooperation also outside the economic area. The TRIPS Agreement, for instance, emphasizes 'that intellectual property rights are private rights' (preamble) and must be protected through national laws and national and international judicial protection. Should the GATS and TRIMS Agreements include similar guarantees for trade-related investment rights in view of the fact that future liberalization of international services supplied by 'commercial presence' will require additional WTO legal guarantees for foreign investments? Should future investment disputes in the WTO be depoliticized and 'decentralized', for example by permitting direct access of foreign investors to international arbitration or court proceedings, as under the ICSID Convention, EC law, and NAFTA? Has the time come for mainstreaming human rights into the WTO legal system, thus following the model of integrating human rights protection in European law?

National and international human rights law recognizes that, as stated in the preamble to the 1966 UN Covenant on Economic, Social and Cultural Rights, 'the ideal of free human beings enjoying freedom from fear and want can only be achieved if conditions are created whereby everyone may enjoy his economic, social and cultural rights, as well as his civil and political rights'. Yet, even though practically everyone's personal development depends on his 'investment activities' (e.g. investing time and money in acquiring professional qualifications) and 'trade activities' (e.g. trading the fruits of labour in exchange for goods and services necessary for human survival and personal development), UN human rights covenants protect neither freedom of investment, nor private property rights, nor freedom of trade. In contrast to the 'judicial double standard' in US constitutional law which accords a higher level of scrutiny to the protection of civil and political rights than economic and social rights,[7] the European Court of Justice has construed the EC Treaty guarantees of free movement of goods, services, persons, and capital as giving rise to individual rights to be protected by national and EC courts. The EC focus on economic rights illustrates that human rights, and their legal basis in social contract theory and constitutional law, must be conceived of in a dynamic perspective maximizing the moral, civil, political, economic, and social rights of citizens vis-à-vis the dynamically evolving restraints imposed by governments and political circumstances. Both UN and EU human rights law rightly emphasize the 'indivisibility' of civil, political, and economic rights. Guarantees of economic freedom and property rights are no less important for consumer welfare and for the professional and personal development of most people than their civil and political rights. In this regard, the regional integration law of the European Union and NAFTA offers important lessons for the future design of the worldwide law of the WTO and other international organizations.

For instance, the political failure of the OECD negotiations on the Multilateral Agreement on Investment (MAI), as well as the one-sided focus of those negotiations on the treatment and legal protection of foreign investors, confirm that international negotiations on investment rules (like those on competition rules) tend to be politically more acceptable and legitimate in the framework of international agreements (such as the WTO, EC, and NAFTA Agreements) which broadly integrate diverse societal interests in a more balanced manner. In order to increase democratic legitimacy and accountability, the WTO should more systematically integrate non-governmental organizations (NGOs) into WTO work, possibly on the model of the EC's advisory Economic and Social Committee which consists of 'representatives of the various categories of economic and

---

[7] Cf. Henry J. Abraham, *Freedom and the Court*, 5th edn (Oxford: Oxford University Press, 1988), 1 et seq.

social activity, in particular, representatives of producers, farmers, carriers, workers, dealers, craftsmen, professional occupations and representatives of the general public' (EC Treaty Article 257, ex 193). Granting NGOs institutionalized direct access to the WTO, and requiring them to submit joint and therefore more balanced advisory opinions on WTO matters, could enhance the transparency, quality, and democratic acceptability of WTO negotiations and rule-making. Article 295 (ex 222) of the EC Treaty, according to which 'this Treaty shall in no way prejudice the rules in Member States governing the system of property ownership', offers another important lesson for future WTO negotiations and WTO law: international liberalization and legal protection of investments were achieved in the European Union through international market-access guarantees, even though such politically controversial issues as nationalization, expropriation, and compensation of enterprises were left to national laws, human rights law, and to judicial clarification of the relevant international law rules.

As the first new worldwide institution of the post-Cold War era, the WTO can serve as a model for the legal and constitutional reforms that are necessary in other worldwide organizations. Thomas Jefferson's insight—that 'institutions must advance and keep pace with the time'—calls for the adaptation of the International Monetary Fund and other UN agencies to the modern 'international economic law revolution' and 'human rights revolution'. More specifically:

- The express WTO provisions on membership of the European Union could serve as a model for membership in the IMF of monetary unions (like the European Union) as well as membership in the UN of political unions.
- The compulsory WTO dispute settlement and appellate review systems should serve as a model for strengthening the rule of international law in other worldwide organizations.
- The express WTO requirements of compliance with the UN Charter, the IMF Agreement, environmental agreements, WIPO provisions, and relevant international product and production standards should prompt other international organizations similarly to promote the mutual consistency of international agreements.
- Proposals for helping the majority of UN Member States lacking national competition laws and lacking democratic constitutional systems to introduce such law and systems should lead to a joint integrated development programme of all worldwide organizations and to the mainstreaming of human rights into the law of all international organizations.

IV. THE EU–US 'ALLIED FORCE' INITIATIVE FOR PROTECTING HUMAN
RIGHTS IN KOSOVO: A PRECEDENT FOR CONSTITUTIONALIZING UN LAW?

Constitutional democracies and European integration are similarly 'founded
on the principles of liberty, democracy, respect for human rights and fundamental freedoms, and the rule of law' (Article 6, ex F, EU Treaty).
Governments have only limited powers and must reckon with harsh sanctions (under Article 7 (ex Article F.1) of the EU Treaty and Article 309 (ex 236)
of the EC Treaty) if they breach these constitutional obligations.

Apart from this constitutional primacy of human rights over government
discretion, European integration law also bears witness to the Kantian
insight that 'democracies don't fight each other'. There will soon have been
50 years of 'democratic peace' among the fifteen EC Member countries, and
the new initiatives of the Amsterdam Treaty and of the EU Summit Meeting
of June 1999 for strengthening the common foreign and security policy of
the European Union as well as the EU's focus on human rights and democracy (EU Treaty Article 11 (ex J.1)) hold out the promise of further progress.
These developments are no less important to European integration than the
economic achievements of the common market and monetary union, and
they actually support the latter. By linking market integration to judicial
and political protection of fundamental rights and rule of law, economic
integration law can win further democratic legitimacy and become a powerful instrument for promoting 'Kantian peace'.

In a sense, the political and military interventions by the EU–US 'Allied
Force' to protect human and minority rights in Kosovo reflect these constitutional concerns for the primacy of human rights protection and
'democratic peace'. At the same time, these interventions clash with the
power-oriented premises of the UN Charter, under which prior authorization for the threat and use of military force by NATO may be blocked
by UN Security Council members having less than fully democratic traditions. Similar conflicts between democracies and non-democracies are
likely to recur in future restructuring and democratization processes in
countries formerly governed by non-democratic regimes. Should the
EU–US 'Allied Force' intervention serve as a model for future threats to
'democratic peace' in Europe? Can it serve as a model for pragmatic
reforms of the power-oriented UN legal and security system which as it
now stands—lacking guarantees of compulsory jurisdiction and judicial
protection of human rights at the national and international levels—cannot effectively protect human rights, rule of law, and democratic peace?

As explained already in Kant's draft treaty for 'Perpetual Peace' (1795),
'democratic peace' depends on national and international constitutional
guarantees of fundamental rights and rule of law, of the sort that might be
expected of NATO, the Council of Europe, and EC law. The UN Charter

cannot be 'constitutionalized' by amendments pursuant to Articles 108 or 109 against the will of the many non-democratic UN Member States, nor by 'constitutional jurisprudence' of the International Court of Justice. Just as the GATT 1947 had to be replaced by the WTO in order to prompt all countries to accept the WTO legal guarantees of freedom and the compulsory WTO dispute-settlement system, the 1945 UN Charter would have to be replaced by a democratic collective security system.[8] Joint EU–US initiatives for pragmatic constitutional reforms of the UN legal system will be increasingly necessary for rendering human rights, rule of law, and democratic peace more effective in Europe and beyond.

In maintaining the political consensus for such joint constitutional reforms in favour of effective protection of human rights, it is useful to recall the common European and American tradition of constitutionalism as a source of legitimacy of constitutional reforms and as the historically most important 'political invention' for limiting abuses of government powers. Although constitutional experiences and traditions differ from country to country, constitutional democracies in Europe and North America are based on a limited number of established 'constitutional principles'.[9] These principles include:

- Plato's idea of a government of laws, rather than a government of individuals who risk abusing their government powers;
- Aristotle's idea of protecting the long-term interests of citizens by means of constitutional rules of a higher legal rank so as to limit abuses of post-constitutional policy-making;
- Montesquieu's and Madison's ideas of the separation of legislative, executive, and judicial government powers, coupled with other institutional 'checks and balances' (such as the ancient Greek and Roman proposals, for example, by Polybius and Cicero, for a 'mixed constitution' with monocratic, aristocratic, and democratic elements balancing one another);
- Locke's social-contract theory based upon the ideas of inalienable human rights, limited government powers, and a right of citizens to resist abuses of such powers (embodied in various modern constitutions, e.g. Article 1 of the German Basic Law of 1949);
- Rawlsian 'principles of justice' and of fairness 'that free and rational persons concerned to further their own interests would accept in an initial position of equality as defining the fundamental terms of their association'.[10]

[8] Cf. Ernst-Ulrich Petersmann, 'How to Constitutionalize the United Nations?' in V. Götz, P. Selmer, and R. Wolfrum (eds), *Liber amicorum G. Jaenicke*, (Berlin: Springer, 1998), 313–52; Ernst-Ulrich Petersmann, 'How to Constitutionalize International Law and Foreign Policy for the Benefit of Civil Society?', *Michigan Journal of International Law*, vol. 20 (1999), 1–30.

[9] For details see Petersmann, 'How to Constitutionalize International Law?' (above, n. 8).

[10] John Rawls, *A Theory of Justice* (Oxford: Oxford University Press, 1973), 11.

The English Revolution during the seventeenth century, the American and French human rights revolutions during the eighteenth century, and the recent human rights movements leading to the political overthrow of communist regimes in Eastern Europe all have in common that citizens had to fight for the primacy of human rights vis-à-vis authoritarian abuses of government powers. Foreign policy powers and international law must be no less governed than domestic policy powers and national laws by the premise of liberal constitutionalism—namely, that values can be derived only from the individual human being, and that 'the ideal of free human beings enjoying freedom from fear and want can only be achieved if conditions are created whereby everyone may enjoy his economic, social and cultural rights, as well as his civil and political rights' (as proclaimed in the Preamble to the 1966 UN Covenant on Economic, Social and Cultural Rights). The frequent violations of UN law—like the frequent violations of GATT and WTO law, even by the European Union and United States—demonstrate that foreign-policy powers and respect for international law require much more effective constitutional control by parliaments, courts, and the citizens. The 'international rule of law' would in turn benefit from a more pronounced democratic legitimacy of international rules, coupled with greater respect for human rights by international institutions (such as the UN Security Council) and their Member States. Crucial in this regard is effective access to national and international courts, and judicial protection not only of the rights of governments but, much more importantly, also the rights of citizens who must no longer be treated merely as the subservient objects of foreign policies.

Neither national nor international rules enforce themselves. The common political experience in constitutional democracies suggests that reliance on the good intentions of benevolent governments is a much less-effective safeguard than 'democratic enforceability' of the rules by citizens themselves acting through national courts. The time has come for additional EU–US initiatives for constitutionalizing UN law and for 'anchoring' human rights and international guarantees of economic freedom more firmly in domestic constitutional systems. One such possibility would be to ensure that certain WTO rules may be invoked and enforced through domestic courts. Constitutional reforms of this sort would also contribute to strengthening the domestic constitutional systems within the United States and the European Union, for at present judicial protection of the transnational exercise of citizens' rights within both polities is still less effectively protected than the exercise of comparable economic rights within the domestic market.

Index